INSTRUCTOR'S MANUAL

ENTRADAS

EL ESPAÑOL POR ETAPAS

SECOND EDITION

Includes Instructor and Student Tapescripts

Theodore V. Higgs
San Diego State University

Judith E. Liskin-Gasparro
Middlebury College

Frank W. Medley, Jr.
University of South Carolina

Heinle & Heinle Publishers
A Division of Wadsworth, Inc.
Boston, Massachusetts 02116 USA

INSTRUCTOR'S MANUAL

INTRODUCTION

This segment of the *Instructor's Annotated Edition* of *Entradas* is intended particularly for those who are teaching a beginning-level foreign language for the first time. It includes suggestions on teaching strategies, explanations of various activity types, and tips for integrating components of the text and taking full advantage of the book's focus on receptive skills development. The chapter notes provided in this section are supplementary to the annotations found in the *Instructor's Annotated Edition* of the text.

Entradas is a fully integrated program designed to provide beginning-level college students with immediately useful language skills in Spanish. The authors' proficiency-oriented, integrative approach to teaching assumes that the four skills and the cultural references reinforce one another, that adequate time must be allowed for assimilation of material, that teaching techniques should be student-centered and, most importantly, that the goal of teaching must be to make students independent users of Spanish. The degree to which this program is successful will, of course, depend largely on the ways in which the materials are used.

The goals of the program are expressed in terms of student performance. As students accomplish linguistic tasks successfully in the classroom, they will gain self-confidence, learn to rely on themselves and each other, and expand their risk-taking in real-life communicative situations.

The goals of this program are to

1. expose students to natural language so that they can draw upon this input when they begin to produce the language themselves
2. prepare students to communicate in survival situations by emphasizing language tasks rather than structures: ordering a meal, making travel arrangements, making purchases, and the like
3. emphasize the act of communicating rather than the grammatical structures and vocabulary

By focusing on language tasks rather than on language structures, students can begin to express themselves communicatively at an earlier stage. In the *Entradas* program, students are given frequent opportunities for personalized expression in conjunction with an ample selection of authentic listening and reading materials. As they begin to sort out which language elements they need for the task at hand, their productive skills improve.

Because it is based on communication, and because the authors believe that creative use of the language is possible from the outset, *Entradas* encourages maximum interaction from the beginning. Frequent exposure to authentic printed and spoken materials prepares students to communicate simply but effectively in Spanish and encourages rapid development of listening and reading comprehension skills. The activities emphasize strategies for communication: how to initiate, maintain, and close conversations; how to communicate and respond to needs, problems, feelings, plans, and opinions; how to act and react appropriately in a variety of face-to-face situations.

The Spanish that students practice in class is meant to be realistic—what they would hear and speak in a Spanish-speaking environment. It is assumed that the instructor will conduct the class largely in Spanish, even though significant portions of the text are written in English. Based on teacher feedback from the first edition of *Entradas*, the authors have decided to use English in the grammatical and cultural commentaries and in many of the direction lines in Chapters 1 through 4, and to increase the use of Spanish in these areas as the students progress. Beginning with Chapter 5 the cultural segments are in Spanish, and beginning with Chapter 9 almost all direction lines are in Spanish. Because the textbook is designed to serve primarily as an out-of-class resource for students, the authors must assure that the explanations and direction lines are comprehensible without the assistance of the teacher.

Teachers are encouraged to make the presentation of new material in Spanish whenever possible. It is expected that the Spanish used by the instructors will not be a contrived language (i.e., highly controlled vocabulary and structures), but that it will be closer to the natural and spontaneous language that is used among individuals who are proficient in Spanish. Grammar is not presented for its own sake, but as a means of transmitting a spoken or written message as accurately as possible. Each chapter and *etapa* contains the necessary grammar and vocabulary related to the central theme, giving students the freedom to express their own ideas as creatively as possible.

The *Entradas* program is realistic and positive in its expectations, allowing instructors the flexibility necessary for effective teaching in programs that meet three days per week for two semesters, or the equivalent amount of time in a quarter system. In those programs in which beginning-level classes meet more frequently or over a longer period of time, provision is made to include all of the ancillaries as instructional components. Optimum use of the textbook with the Workbook/Laboratory Manual requires approximately eight to ten hours of contact time per chapter, depending on the amount of outside preparation expected of the students. A detailed sequence of instruction is included in this section on page IM8.

The authors believe that the essential goal of language teaching is to inspire in the students the confidence and willingness to use whatever elements of language they have at their disposal in order to communicate. *Entradas* aims at dispelling the notion that students must wait until they enter advanced Spanish courses for real communication to take place.

ON DEVELOPING FUNCTIONAL ABILITY IN SPANISH

Conceptual, partial and full control. Most college-level students begin the study of Spanish with a certain intuitive awareness of the concepts underlying language as a system of communication. For the most part this awareness is restricted to characteristics of their native language. English speakers, for example, have no difficulty with the idea that things have names, or that there are singulars and plurals, and that there is past, present, and future time. On the other hand, they find it difficult to conceptualize gender as it relates to nouns in Spanish or to grasp the differences between "state" and "trait" (*estar/ser*) or indicative and subjunctive moods.

The learner's first task is to develop conceptual control of a new idea or structure. As the concept becomes increasingly clear, a student begins to develop partial control of the linguistic and communicative elements involved. Eventually, students achieve mastery of the concept through continual recycling of concepts and vocabulary, and their performance begins to reflect full control through consistently accurate usage.

Listening and reading comprehension. During the initial stages of language learning, students tend to process the target language in terms of native language equivalents, often expecting to find a word-for-word correlation between the two languages. To encourage them to begin communicating orally as they would in a Spanish-speaking environment, *Entradas* begins each chapter with prelistening activities that focus attention on listening for general meaning. The postlistening activities sensitize the students to the ways in which the meanings have been conveyed linguistically.

In order to produce more efficient readers, the authors have elected to begin almost immediately with connected texts, since students need to be able to derive meaning from units larger than unconnected sentences. By working with paragraphs, whole texts, advertisements, and other samples of authentic language, students will learn that it is not necessary to understand every word of the text in order to comprehend what they are reading. Instead, they will come to realize that it is the **purpose** for which they are reading that dictates the information they should glean from the passage. As the students progress, the activities that accompany the readings require more detailed understanding of the content of the passages, as well as more productive language use in order to carry out the tasks.

Speaking and writing. *Entradas* encourages students to develop facility in generating language—speaking and writing Spanish—as well as in the *receptive* skills of listening and reading. It is assumed that they will be able to understand more than they can say, and to read more than they are able to write. A consistent effort, however, is made to encourage self-expression, both oral and written. Ample opportunity exists for the instructor to follow up reading and listening comprehension tasks with spontaneous speaking and writing activities.

Authentic language samples. The authors have consciously refrained from simplifying the language of

Entradas with unnatural structural and lexical constraints. The content of the passages incorporates the redundancy, repetition, discourse indicators, and cognates necessary to render the text globally comprehensible. The prescribed tasks take into account both real-life uses of language and the linguistic and communicative capabilities of the learners, using authentic samples of the language wherever possible and including some activities based on specially scripted passages to provide more highly focused practice in areas that tend to be problematic for non-native speakers.

TEACHING WITH THE ENTRADAS PROGRAM

The student textbook consists of an introductory chapter followed by twelve full-length chapters.

Each chapter begins with Communicative Objectives that summarize the communicative functions and content areas to be presented in the chapter. From these emerge the spoken and (to a lesser extent) written texts that are the core of each chapter. The selection and sequencing of grammar topics in the second edition reflect recommendations from users of the first edition, and are based on a consideration of how well the grammatical point enables the learner to carry out the communicative objectives of the lesson. The objectives generally move from the concrete and personal to the more abstract and outwardly focused.

Chapters are subdivided into three *etapas*, each related to the chapter theme and following a set organizational scheme. In most chapters, the first *etapa* focuses on listening comprehension, the second *etapa* on reading comprehension, and the third *etapa* on the development of writing skills. Development of oral expression skills is common to all *etapas*.

The *Entradas* program provides an unprecedented amount of audio input:

The Instructor's Tape. Play in class twice: once at the beginning of the *etapa* in the section called *Entrada*, then at the end of the *etapa* in the section called *Otra vuelta*.

The Student Tape. Assign for homework before students begin each *etapa*. The tapes provide a systematic introduction to vocabulary by native speakers. Activities in the textbook (*Empezar a escuchar*) provide guided practice. Students will then hear dialogues using the vocabulary and functions of the chapter in context (*Escuchar*). Again, activities in the textbook provide guidance and comprehension checks.

The Laboratory Tape Program. Students listen to these tapes in the lab. Accompanying activities are in the *Escuchar* section of the Workbook/Laboratory Manual.

***Beginning the first* etapa.** Before students attempt to practice the chapter functions themselves, they are given several kinds of listening practice to identify the functions in an everyday context. The first of these is called an *Entrada*. The *Entrada* listening segment that begins each *etapa* can be found on the instructor's tape and is to be played in class. It is also on the laboratory tape program. Because it is important to foster students' ability to listen to spoken language without visual support, the script for this segment is found only in this Instructor's Manual.

It is important to prepare students for what they are going to hear by first establishing the context through a prelistening activity, such as brainstorming about what one would expect to hear in a conversation on the topic mentioned. After hearing the selection once or twice, the instructor can ask the comprehension questions that follow.

The next two listening sections of the first *etapa* are designed for students to do outside the classroom. The *Empezar a escuchar* section, with listening segments on the student tape, consists of five parts: *Leer, Repetir, Identificar, Escribir,* and *Reconocer*. This section prepares students for the listening material that follows in the *Escuchar* section. The vocabulary that students practice in *Empezar a escuchar* appears in the student text; this is the first task in which they are expected to produce the new language of the chapter. Students first read, then repeat, these words and phrases as they listen to the student tape outside of class. Next, students practice identifying the words in the context of a sentence through listening and writing. Finally, they are asked to check their own work and make any necessary corrections in the sentences they have written. One variation is to go over the *Leer* section in class, eliciting students' ideas about the vocabulary. The rest of the *Empezar a escuchar* section can then be assigned as homework and collected.

Next, students proceed to the *Escuchar* sections, that also should be done outside of class. Here, as listening preparation, students perform two sets of tasks—the *Enfoque comunicativo* and the *Enfoque lingüístico*—during and after listening to the two conversations, the *Episodios*. In the *Enfoque comunicativo*, students are directed toward identifying content information from the *Episodio* dialogue they hear (this part could be played in class). In the *Enfoque lingüístico*, students are asked to focus on the language that was used in order to accomplish a specific task. Once they have completed these listening tasks, students can check their comprehension by completing the *Verificar* section (true/false questions) that is found immediately after the second *Enfoque lingüístico*. Students should spend approximately one hour on these two listening sections.

Instructors might like to have students act out the *Episodios*, or comment on the strategies they used to derive meaning from what they heard. Occasionally, students might be asked to write out their answers as a homework assignment. Students must be made aware that content and form are equally important features of language.

The second and third etapas. The second *etapa* of each chapter has a slightly different organizational scheme. Following the *Entrada*, a reading component is included, comprised of *Antes de leer,* prereading activities with a Reading Strategy and vocabulary lists (headed *Preparación* and *Estudiar y practicar*), guidance activities entitled *Leer,* and follow-up activities headed *Después de leer.*

The third *etapa* of each chapter addresses writing, again corresponding to the underlying organizational format. Following the *Entrada*, there is a preparatory section (*Antes de escribir*) that includes Writing Strategy, *Preparación*, and *Estudiar y practicar* components, then one or more reading, speaking, and/or writing tasks presented in the follow-up section. As with the *Leer* activities, the exercises provide an opportunity for students to apply and practice the strategies introduced. In addition, the activities included in this portion of the third *etapa* usually combine skills (i.e., reading and writing, speaking and writing) into more integrative tasks.

Aumentar el vocabulario. *Aumentar el vocabulario* is the central vocabulary presentation of the *etapa*. Organized by semantic groupings, it both recycles vocabulary from other sections of the text and introduces new words and expressions. Additionally, one section of high-frequency vocabulary is presented visually in order to bind meaning more closely with language (a corresponding transparency master is included in the ancillary materials).

Because of the emphasis on receptive skills, there is some vocabulary that is geared to comprehension rather than production. When presenting the vocabulary to students, try to help them focus on the most useful words and phrases; they can add these to the special section called *Vocabulario personalizado* at the end of each chapter.

The vocabulary should first be presented by the instructor in the classroom, with a focus on the more commonly used words and expressions contained in the *Aumentar el vocabulario* and in the brief informative notes called *Uso práctico del español*. Some teachers make flash cards and others develop a picture file or additional transparencies and handouts to make their presentations of the vocabulary as visual as possible. A clear distinction should be made by the instructor between what should be mastered for productive purposes, what should be controlled receptively, and what might be excluded from the assignment.

It is important to present the vocabulary in clusters, and then to practice it with exercises from the *Ponerlo a prueba* section directly following. Regardless of the manner in which instructors plan to present new vocabulary with **Entradas**, it is important to try to spend a minimum of one class period in presentation, practice, and review. A complete list (*Vocabulario*) for all three *etapas* is provided at the end of each chapter.

Investigar la gramática. *Investigar la gramática* presents elements of Spanish structure from the perspective of their communicative value. The extensive exercises and activities that follow in *Ponerlo a prueba* are designed to help the students move from controlled practice to more open-ended communication. The grammar explanations emphasize how a specific point is used within the larger framework of communication. They are short and functional and do not cover every rule and exception.

The grammatical explanations can be read outside of class and then quickly reviewed in class to answer any questions that may arise. Where possible, the classroom presentation by the instructor should begin with something already familiar to, and understood by, the students, and then move into more open-ended practice, where students are encouraged to expand on their answers and personalize their responses. As a follow-up to classroom activities, additional communicative practice of the grammatical structures is included in the *Escribir* section of the Workbook/Laboratory Manual.

Ending an etapa. The exercises found in the *¡Tienes la palabra!* section are role-plays and interviews, mostly survival-oriented situations that allow students to use the previously presented material creatively with minimal intervention from the instructor. Either the instructor or one or more students can model the role-play for the rest of the class. Next, students break into pairs or small groups and simultaneously enact the situation while the instructor circulates about the room, correcting errors and giving information as needed to facilitate the activity.

A variation is to have a third student in each group act as a reporter or secretary, taking notes during the role-plays. After all groups have finished, each reporter informs the entire class of what happened. The instructor's role is, again, to monitor the groups' conversations and supply vocabulary words on request. The reporting phase provides a source of motivation for carrying out the task and is a real-life use of language. During these communicative activities, error correction should only be undertaken when an error interferes with understanding.

Recycling is an important feature of *Entradas*. Informal recycling occurs through inclusion of material in subsequent exercises, activities, and situations. In addition, the *Entrada* on the instructor's cassette is recycled formally once each *etapa*, in the *Otra vuelta* section. Here, the instructor replays the same *Entrada* segment that students heard at the beginning of the *etapa*. Students are now required to extract more information from the taped segment than they did the first time.

Prior to the *Otra Vuelta*, it is suggested that the instructor prepare students for listening by seeing how much they remember of the segment and then giving them some idea of the new information they will be asked to identify. This second playing of the *Entrada* segment gives students a better sense of the progress they have made since the beginning of the *etapa*. The instructor may elect to ask the questions in Spanish, in order to maintain the target language as the medium of instruction.

Cultural content. Culture is integrated directly into many parts of the *Entradas* program. Students listen to authentic materials and read authentic texts in the Workbook/Laboratory Manual. In addition, there are two sections that focus specifically on culture. The *Ventanilla al mundo hispánico* is a short, specific explanation of some cultural insight into Hispanic life and language (either oral or written) that is related to the *Episodios*. The *Comentario cultural* is a longer, more detailed explanation, usually accompanied by an in-class exercise that allows students to apply this cultural information to real-life situations. Beginning in Chapter 5, both the *Ventanillas* and the *Comentarios* are presented in Spanish. Many of the *Comentarios culturales* can be followed by an investigative writing or speaking activity in which students research information related to the *Comentario* and prepare a short oral or written report in Spanish.

Actividades de integración. At the end of each chapter there are open-ended written and oral activities called *Actividades de integración*. Their purpose is to tie together the vocabulary and structures of the three *etapas* and rework them in relation to the chapter's communicative objectives. Often these activities can be expanded into multi-task exercises. Instructors should plan to spend as much time as possible on these activities, since they represent the culmination of the language functions that have been presented throughout the chapter. If desired, these can be supplemented with activities from the Workbook/Laboratory Manual or other components of the complete *Entradas* program.

Integration of the ancillary materials. In addition to the student textbook and tapes, there are a variety of ancillary materials that can be used to expand upon or supplement the text activities. The components include:

- Workbook/Laboratory Manual
- Laboratory tape program
- Testing program
- Tapescripts for student and instructor tapes (included in the Instructor's Manual)
- Laboratory tapescript
- *Atajo:* Writing Assistant for Spanish (software)
- *Mosaico cultural* video

Both Heinle & Heinle and the authors feel strongly that a good program is continually evolving and that the best evaluations of materials come from the instructors and students who use them on a daily basis. Please send any comments or questions about the *Entradas* program to the authors, care of Heinle & Heinle Publishers, 20 Park Plaza, Boston, MA 02116, (800) 237-0053.

INSTRUCTIONAL OVERVIEW

As a result of the interrelationship between the *Entradas* text and its ancillaries, the program is compatible with most instructional configurations. The textbook with the Workbook/Laboratory Manual, but without any other ancillaries can be taught effectively in approximately ninety hours (i.e., in a course that meets three hours per week over a period of thirty weeks), excluding testing. In those courses meeting four hours per week for thirty weeks, the *Atajo:* Writing Assistant software program, which is keyed to many activities in the workbook, can be included as an instructional component. The *Mosaico cultural* video and its accompanying Video Guide can be utilized in courses meeting five hours per week.

In courses that meet three times per week, the entire *Entradas* program with all ancillaries can be implemented by extending the instruction over three semesters. The following chart illustrates how the sequence of instruction might be spread over the various times frames.

Configuration A: Semester 1 of two-semester sequence

Week	3 hrs./week Workbook/Lab Man.	4 hrs./week *Atajo:* Writing Asst., Workbook/Lab Man.	5 hrs./week *Atajo:* Writing Asst., Workbook/Lab Man., Video & Video Guide
1	Introduction Prelim. chap.	Introduction Prelim. chap.	Introduction Prelim. chap.
2	Prelim. chap. Chapter 1	Prelim. chap. Chapter 1	Prelim. chap. Chapter 1
3	Chapter 1	Chapter 1	Chapter 1
4	Chapter 1 Chapter 2	Chapter 1 Chapter 2	Chapter 1 Chapter 2
5	Chapter 2	Chapter 2	Chapter 2
6	Chapter 2 Chapter 3	Chapter 2 Chapter 3	Chapter 2 Chapter 3
7	Chapter 3	Chapter 3	Chapter 3
8	Chapter 3 Chapter 4	Chapter 3 Chapter 4	Chapter 3 Chapter 4
9	Chapter 4	Chapter 4	Chapter 4
10	Chapter 4 Chapter 5	Chapter 4 Chapter 5	Chapter 4 Chapter 5
11	Chapter 5	Chapter 5	Chapter 5
12	Chapter 5 Chapter 6	Chapter 5 Chapter 6	Chapter 5 Chapter 6
13	Chapter 6	Chapter 6	Chapter 6
14	Chapter 6 Review	Chapter 6 Review	Chapter 6 Review
15		Semester Examination	

Configuration A: Semester 2 of two-semester sequence

Week	3 hrs./week Workbook/Lab Man.	4 hrs./week *Atajo:* Writing Asst., Workbook/Lab Man.	5 hrs./week *Atajo:* Writing Asst., Workbook/Lab Man., Video & Video Guide
1 (16)	Introduction Review	Introduction Review	Introduction Review
2 (17)	Review Chapter 7	Review Chapter 7	Review Chapter 7
3 (18)	Chapter 7	Chapter 7	Chapter 7
4 (19)	Chapter 7 Chapter 8	Chapter 7 Chapter 8	Chapter 7 Chapter 8
5 (20)	Chapter 8	Chapter 8	Chapter 8
6 (21)	Chapter 8 Chapter 9	Chapter 8 Chapter 9	Chapter 8 Chapter 9
7 (22)	Chapter 9	Chapter 9	Chapter 9
8 (23)	Chapter 9 Chapter 10	Chapter 9 Chapter 10	Chapter 9 Chapter 10
9 (24)	Chapter 10	Chapter 10	Chapter 10
10 (25)	Chapter 10 Chapter 11	Chapter 10 Chapter 11	Chapter 10 Chapter 11
11 (26)	Chapter 11	Chapter 11	Chapter 11
12 (27)	Chapter 11 Chapter 12	Chapter 11 Chapter 12	Chapter 11 Chapter 12
13 (28)	Chapter 12	Chapter 12	Chapter 12
14 (29)	Chapter 12 Review	Chapter 12 Review	Chapter 12 Review
15 (30)	Semester Examination		

Configuration B: Semester 1 of three-semester sequence

Week	Chapter and related ancillaries, including Workbook/Lab Man., *Atajo:* Writing Asst., *Mosaico cultural* Video, and Video Guide
1	Introduction and Preliminary Chapter
2	Chapter 1
3	Chapter 1
4	Chapter 1
5	Chapter 2
6	Chapter 2
7	Chapter 2
8	Chapter 3
9	Chapter 3
10	Chapter 3
11	Chapter 4
12	Chapter 4
13	Chapter 4
14	Review
15	Semester Examination

Configuration B: Semester 2 of three-semester sequence

Week	Chapter and related ancillaries, including Workbook/Lab Man., *Atajo:* Writing Asst., *Mosaico cultural* Video, and Video Guide
1 (16)	Review
2 (17)	Chapter 5
3 (18)	Chapter 5
4 (19)	Chapter 5
5 (20)	Chapter 6
6 (21)	Chapter 6
7 (22)	Chapter 6
8 (23)	Chapter 7
9 (24)	Chapter 7
10 (25)	Chapter 7
11 (26)	Chapter 8
12 (27)	Chapter 8
13 (28)	Chapter 8
14 (29)	Review
15 (30)	Semester Examination

Configuration B: Semester 3 of three-semester sequence

Week	Chapter and related ancillaries, including Workbook/Lab Man., *Atajo:* Writing Asst., *Mosaico cultural* Video, and Video Guide
1 (31)	Review
2 (32)	Chapter 9
3 (33)	Chapter 9
4 (34)	Chapter 9
5 (35)	Chapter 10
6 (36)	Chapter 10
7 (37)	Chapter 10
8 (38)	Chapter 11
9 (39)	Chapter 11
10 (40)	Chapter 11
11 (41)	Chapter 12
12 (42)	Chapter 12
13 (43)	Chapter 12
14 (44)	Review
15 (45)	Semester Examination

CHAPTER NOTES

Before beginning each chapter, read through the annotations included in the *Instructor's Annotated Edition* of the text, as well as the notes on the individual chapter.

Capítulo preliminar

1. The primary purpose of the *Capítulo preliminar* is to introduce the students to the organization of the chapters in *Entradas* and to give them some basic classroom vocabulary so that Spanish can be used as the primary medium of communication.

2. Point out to students that the listening activities requiring the use of a tape will be so indicated in the left margin and that the approximate length of each segment is indicated as well.

3. Students may need guidance at first regarding the use of the Student Tapes. For the preliminary chapter we recommend that you play the Student Tape in class and show them how to do the *Empezar a escuchar* and *Escuchar* sections.

Section	Time needed
Entrada	5 min.
Empezar a escuchar*	15 min.
Escuchar*	10 min.
Verificar*	2 min.
Ventanilla al mundo hispánico	3 min.
Aumentar el vocabulario	10 min.
Uso práctico del español	5 min.
Ponerlo a prueba†	20 min.
Investigar la gramática	5 min.
Ponerlo a prueba†	20 min.
¡Tienes la palabra!	15 min.
Otra vuelta	5 min.
Comentario cultural	5 min.
Total class time per *etapa**	120 min.
× 3 etapas	360 min.
Actividades de integración	
(1 per chapter)	30 min.
Total class time per chapter†	390 min.

* The amount of time will vary, depending upon whether the materials are assigned as out-of-class homework.

† This section is not included in the *Capítulo preliminar*.

4. Use the preceding chart as a timing guide until you become accustomed to the sections of the *etapa*.

5. Many of the activities in *Entradas* call for students to work in small groups. You may want students to pair up with someone of the opposite sex, or of the same sex, or with someone with the same color of hair, eyes, and so on. The basis for the formation of the groups should be determined by the task to be carried out.

Capítulo 1

1. **Page 14:** It is important to use Spanish in the classroom from the beginning. Reassure the students by emphasizing that you do not expect them to understand everything you say, and that if they have questions at the end of the class hour you will respond to them in English. You will probably find that, within a short time, they will understand most of what you say.

2. **Page 14:** Have students try to determine what the *Entrada* is going to be about before they listen to it. Point out to them that just reading the instructions and questions will give them some clues.

3. **Page 16:** Go over students' responses to the *Verificar* section in class to check comprehension of the two *Episodios* in the *Escuchar* section on the student tape.

4. **Page 18:** Each *etapa* contains a section of vocabulary that is presented visually. In Chapter 1, when presenting *La familia de César*, explain the meaning of *los abuelos, los padres, los tíos, los primos*. You may also want to explain the custom of naming children after their parents: *Rafaelito, Carlitos*.

5. **Page 21:** Although the *vosotros* form is included in verb charts and conjugations throughout *Entradas*, it is not used actively. You may elect to use it, however, in the drills, exercises, and other material.

6. **Page 28:** The *Preparación* activity prepares students for the selection that is to be presented by developing expectations about the content. In each instance, the students' prior knowledge of the type of text or the topic is activated by the preliminary questions.

7. **Page 33:** The numbers 1–100 are introduced in conjunction with addresses so that students can practice

them within a real-life context. From this point on, page numbers, item numbers, dates, time, etc., can be referred to completely in Spanish.

8. **Page 41:** The *Antes de hablar* section prepares students for the role plays that follow in the *Hablar* section. You may want to have students write out the phrases in addition to saying them, but make sure that the conversations they invent in *Hablar* are spoken, rather than read or memorized from a script.

Capítulo 2

1. **Page 64:** The term *ocho días* is used to refer to a week because when one enumerates the days of the week in Spanish one begins and ends with *el lunes*. *De hoy en ocho días* expresses the idea of "a week from today."

2. **Page 67:** In exercises and activities that call for a creative response, keep in mind that there may be a number of appropriate answers. Students should be encouraged to play with the language, since trial and error is a valuable aspect of language learning. During these creative activities, you will want to make only corrections that are necessary to maintain the flow of information. In other words, if a student says something that is meaningless, you might respond with *¿Perdón? No te entendí*.

3. **Page 68:** In the more communicative activities, insist that responses have as much truth value as possible.

4. **Page 88:** As a follow-up to the *Actividad* following the writing strategy, read several descriptions without using names and see if students can guess which of their classmates are the authors. At the same time, you can make the necessary corrections.

5. **Page 99:** Many of the photographs, especially those of signs or ads, offer an opportunity for class discussion. Have students guess at the meanings of some of the words, such as *zarzaparrilla* (sarsaparilla, a sweet soft drink flavored with the dried roots of any of several tropical American plants) in the photo on page 99.

Capítulo 3

1. **Page 105:** In Chapter 3 the reading strategy is in the first *etapa*, and the listening comprehension segments are in the second *etapa*.

2. **Page 110:** A variety of visuals can be used to teach weather expressions, such as pictures, photos, and videos.

3. **Page 120:** When introducing terms related to requesting silence or other matters of behavior, emphasize the situational contexts within which these terms would (and would not) be appropriately used.

4. **Page 120:** You may wish to share with students the phrase *¡Cállate la boca!,* which is quite insulting. *¡Cierra el hocico!* is even more insulting because it attributes the physical characteristics of an animal to a human being. It compares with the English phrase "Shut your trap!"

5. **Page 121:** Point out to students that *desvestirse* means the same thing as *quitarse la ropa*.

6. **Page 123:** You can introduce the third-person singular reflexive forms by having another student answer the question *¿A qué hora se despierta...?*

7. **Page 123:** Additional questions that can be used to practice the tener expressions are 4. *¿Qué hacen tú y tus amigos si tienen hambre a las 12:00 de la noche?* 5. *Si tienes mucho sueño pero también tienes que estudiar, ¿qué haces?* 6. *¿De qué tienes miedo?* 7. *¿Tienes interés en la política internacional? ¿Y en el gobierno estudiantil?* 8. *Entre tus amigos, ¿quién tiene fama de llegar siempre tarde?*

8. **Page 134:** Advise students that to express that something doesn't matter, they could say *No importa* or *No es importante*. They should be cautioned to use each one accurately since the two are frequently confused, resulting in grossly incorrect Spanish. (**No es importa.* or **No importante.*)

9. **Page 140:** Many drawings and photographs lend themselves well to comparative descriptions. Look through your picture file or have students bring in pictures about which they can make a statement of comparison.

10. **Page 143:** With the *Actividades de integración*, encourage students to expand beyond the questions and responses suggested in the activities.

Capítulo 4

1. **Page 149:** As a follow-up to the *Enfoques lingüísticos,* students can talk about their own wishes regarding vacations.

2. **Page 150:** When students find statements in the *Verificar* section that are false, have them make the necessary changes so that the statements become accurate.

3. **Page 165:** Following the *Ventanilla al mundo hispánico,* reassure students that the Spanish they are learning will be understood throughout the Hispanic world. Should they happen to be in one region for an extended period of time, they will soon pick up any specialized regional vocabulary and structures necessary to communicate effectively.

Capítulo 5

1. **Page 196:** A wall map could be used for an in-depth discussion of the various countries mentioned in this and other chapters and could be incorporated into some of the activities as a point of reference.

2. **Page 196:** Notice that in Chapter 5 some of the more familiar direction lines, the *Ventanillas,* and the *Comentarios culturales* change to Spanish.

3. **Page 199:** Point out to students that *el patio* is sometimes used in combination with another word to designate "front yard," *el patio delantero,* and "backyard," *el traspatio* or *el patio trasero.*

4. **Page 203:** If you choose to have students use a dictionary, or even the *Entradas* glossaries, with exercise CH on page 203, allow some additional time in class to familiarize students with the ways in which this resource can best be used. They need to learn to verify the meaning of a word by checking both English-to-Spanish and Spanish-to-English. They also need to be familiarized with the parts of speech so that they don't attempt to use nouns for verbs (e.g., *mosca* for *volar*) and the like.

5. As the students become more creative in the role-plays, you may find that you need to allow more time for these activities.

6. Other items that might be mentioned with respect to the *Comentario cultural* [*El pan*] on page 231 follow.

   ■ The potato, the tomato, chocolate, and many fruits were unknown in Europe until they were brought from the Americas.

   ■ A tortilla in Mexico is a thin pancake made of either corn meal (*tortilla de maíz*) or wheat flour (*tortilla de harina*). It is often rolled around a filling of meat, beans, or cheese, or served flat as a type of bread. Sometimes, flour tortillas are fried in hot oil, which causes them to puff up, and are served with honey. This is called a *sopapilla.* At other times, the tortilla will be torn into smaller pieces and used as an edible spoon. In Spain, a tortilla is a dish similar to a quiche or an omelet, prepared in a skillet on top of the stove. The ingredients are primarily eggs, potatoes, and onions.

   ■ Chocolate is made from *cacao* beans. The Maya and Aztec Indians of Mexico had cultivated *cacao* beans long before the arrival of Columbus in the New World. The Aztecs believed that the first *cacao* beans came from a garden in paradise and that they bestowed wisdom and knowledge on those who consumed them. The beans were ground and used to prepare a rich drink. They were also used for money. The word chocolate comes from two Mayan words, meaning "sour water."

Capítulo 6

1. **Page 253:** The title of the *Entrada* to the *Segunda etapa* is taken from a popular Colombian song about the city of Cartagena, which is further described in the reading selection.

2. **Page 259:** When presenting the progressive forms, emphasize that they are used much less frequently in Spanish than in English.

3. **Page 268:** In order for students to carry out the tasks in the *Hablar y escuchar* section of the *Tercera etapa,* they will need to be familiar with the *Entrada* to the *etapa* (see the instructor annotations for suggestions on how to sequence the materials in class).

Capítulo 7

1. **Page 290:** The subjunctive mood is introduced for the first time in this chapter. Initially, students will use the subjunctive for impersonal expressions, and to express emotions, wishes, and volition. As they move through the succeeding chapters, each of these uses is treated more fully, and more practice is provided. At this point students are not asked to decide whether or not to use the subjunctive. Instead, the activities are designed to familiarize the students with situations in which the mood is used and to give them a context within which to practice the various forms.

2. **Page 293:** The *Ventanilla* entitled *Está en su casa* presents several phrases used to welcome a guest into one's home. For students who might ask, a common *despedida* that conveys the same state of welcomeness is *vuelva cuando quiera*.

3. **Page 294:** By this time, students should be producing some connected discourse, rather than isolated sentences. Encourage them to use more connectives and to link their sentences when they write so that there is more cohesiveness in their language.

4. **Page 307:** As new vocabulary is introduced, students can be asked to prepare definitions in Spanish. Similarly, they can practice circumlocuting, or talking their way around words they don't yet know.

5. **Page 309:** Because a number of diminutives have negative connotations or suggest a considerable degree of informality, students should be cautioned about generating diminutive forms that are new to them.

6. **Page 316:** The *Entrada* to the *Tercera etapa* may have to be played several times for the students to sequence the events.

7. **Page 329:** The end vocabulary of this chapter includes additional sports terms. A number of sports were previously included in Chapter 2.

Capítulo 8

1. **Page 332:** You might begin this chapter with a discussion of such topics as storytelling, the oral tradition in literature, family history, and the like. Have students speculate about why some cultures place more of an emphasis on these activities than other cultures. Ask them to think more specifically about the kinds of things we mention when we talk about members of our own families, then play the *Entrada* to see what doña Consuelo says.

2. **Page 335:** Celebration of a child's First Communion (*la Primera Comunión*) is particularly significant in the predominantly Roman Catholic Hispanic cultures. It signifies that a person has reached the age where he or she has the ability to distinguish between right and wrong. It also means that the person understands the teachings and beliefs of the Church. Thus the First Communion carries great importance among the faithful and is cause for both thanksgiving and celebration. It is often referred to as *el día más feliz de la vida*.

3. **Page 337:** The word *quinceañera* refers to the girl celebrating her fifteenth birthday. *La fiesta de los quince*, or often just *los quince*, is used to refer to the celebration itself.

4. **Page 347:** Although many of the words in the story by Gabriel García Márquez will be new to the students, they should be able to derive general meaning from the passage. In addition, the excerpt provides an opportunity for them to practice guessing the meaning of some words based on the context in which they are used.

5. **Page 362:** Additional vocabulary is mentioned in the annotation.

la caja de cambios	transmission
el embrague	clutch
los faroles	headlights
el guardafango	fender

    In Mexico and some other parts of Latin America, the word for "fender" is *la defensa*.

el parachoques	bumper

Capítulo 9

1. As students move into more complex role-plays, encourage them to talk around words they cannot recall or that they have not yet learned.

2. As a prelistening activity for the *Entrada* of the *Tercera etapa* you might ask students to recall a public service announcement they have heard regarding a health hazard. Ask them what information is usually included in these types of announcements.

3. Additional vocabulary items that might be included with the *Aumentar el vocabulario* of the third *etapa* in Chapter 9 are *la quimioterapia* (chemotherapy), and *la radiación* (radiation).

Capítulo 10

1. As a follow-up to the *Comentario cultural* [*La puntualidad*] on page 435, have students mention other potential misunderstandings that could result from a lack of awareness of the cultural perceptions of punctuality.

2. The *Comentario cultural* [*Las fiestas*] on page 452 mentions national holidays of several countries. The region that is now Bolivia, Colombia, Ecuador, Panamá, Perú, and Venezuela was called *la Gran Colombia* upon its liberation from Spain in 1819. Simón Bolívar was the first president.

3. Both *mami* and *mamita* are very familiar forms of the word *mamá*, and are usually associated with the speech of very young children. However, as terms of endearment, children may continue to use these forms of address for a number of years. The masculine form, *papi*, is used to address the father. The use of diminutives has already been discussed on page 309.

Capítulo 11

1. Guadalajara, the capital of the state of Jalisco, is the second largest city in Mexico. It is located about 300 miles northwest of Mexico City and is an important manufacturing and international trade center. In particular, Guadalajara is noted for its fine pottery and hand-blown glass. The city was founded about 1530, and several of the buildings in the *zócalo* date from the 1600s. In town, there are numerous small parks as well as *Agua Azul*, a beautifully maintained public park surrounding a small lake where visitors can rent boats or picnic along the shoreline. The *Mercado de la Libertad* is one of the larger and better known marketplaces in Mexico. There is no better music to be found anywhere than in the quaint *Plazuela de los Mariachis*, where one can sit in outdoor cafés and listen to strolling mariachi bands.

2. Students might enjoy hearing a synopsis of *Fuenteovejuna*, the play by Lope de Vega mentioned in the *Ventanilla al mundo hispánico* on page 472. If you are not familiar with the play, perhaps a colleague who teaches literature would agree to speak to your class.

3. As a prelistening activity for the *Entrada* of the *Segunda etapa*, have students talk about the advantages and disadvantages of taking correspondence courses. See how closely their opinions fit the comments made by the people in the *Entrada*.

4. Have students find the abbreviations on the business cards on page 495 for the following words and expressions:

Avenida	Av.
Colonia	Col.
Distrito Federal	D.F.
Licenciado	Lic.
María	Ma.
Morelos	Mor.
Número	N^{o}.
Sociedad Anónima	S.A.
Teléfono	Tel.

5. Students would probably enjoy seeing actual samples of advice columns from Spanish-language publications, if you have access to any.

Capítulo 12

1. Call students' attention to the way Roberto ends his letter on page 516 by using the third person. Point out that this is very common in Spanish.

2. Most of the *profesiones y oficios* will have both masculine and feminine forms. Have students provide the forms for those genders not listed.

TAPESCRIPTS

Capítulo preliminar [Instructor Tape]

ENTRADA "Buenos días, clase"

Locutor: Buenos días, clase. Mi nombre es Roberto Ochoa. Yo soy el profesor. Nuestro libro de texto es *Entradas*. Vamos a usar también un cuaderno de ejercicios. En la clase, vamos a hablar mucho español y vamos a escribir todos los días. Es importante tener siempre una pluma o un lápiz. Ahora, vamos a conocernos.

[Student Tape]

EMPEZAR A ESCUCHAR

Repetir

Vamos a...
escribir
el cuaderno de ejercicios
el profesor
tener
(No) Tengo...
la pluma
el lápiz
Es muy importante...
todos los días

Identificar

1. Tengo el cuaderno de ejercicios.
   Tengo el cuaderno de ejercicios.
2. Es muy importante tener un lápiz.
   Es muy importante tener un lápiz.
3. Vamos a escribir todos los días.
   Vamos a escribir todos los días.

ESCUCHAR

EPISODIO: En la clase de español

Profesor: Buenos días, Carlos.
Estudiante: Buenos días, profesor Ochoa.
Profesor: Ahora, vamos a escribir un ejercicio en el cuaderno de ejercicios.
Estudiante: ¡Ay, profesor! No tengo lápiz.
Profesor: Carlos, es muy importante tener un lápiz o una pluma en la clase de español. Vamos a escribir todos los días.

Capítulo 1 [Instructor Tape]

PRIMERA ETAPA

ENTRADA "Hola, ¿qué tal?"

Gustavo: Hola, ¿qué tal?
Luisa: Hola.
Gustavo: ¿Cómo te llamas?
Luisa: Me llamo Luisa.
Gustavo: ¿Estudias en la universidad aquí?
Luisa: Sí, estudio literatura. Y tú, ¿cómo te llamas?
Gustavo: Me llamo Gustavo.
Luisa: ¿De dónde eres, Gustavo?
Gustavo: Yo soy de México. ¿Y tú?
Luisa: Yo soy de Los Ángeles.
Gustavo: ¿Quieres bailar?
Luisa: Lo siento mucho, Gustavo, pero tengo que ir a la biblioteca. Voy a estudiar esta noche.
Gustavo: Oye, entonces, ah... ¿quizás el próximo domingo nos podemos ver para bailar?
Luisa: Sí. Mientras tanto, adiós. Hasta luego.
Gustavo: Adiós.

SEGUNDA ETAPA

ENTRADA "Por favor..."

Hombre: Buenas tardes.
Mujer: Buenas tardes.
Hombre: Por favor, busco la calle Robles, número 1728.
Mujer: Ah, no. Está usted en el número 1722. ¿Cómo se llama la familia que usted busca?

Hombre:	Es la familia Méndez... eh, Francisco y Ana María Méndez.
Mujer:	Ah, sí, los conozco. Son mis vecinos. El 1728 es la pequeña casa blanca. La segunda a la derecha.
Hombre:	Ah, muy bien. Muchas gracias, señora.
Mujer:	A la orden.

TERCERA ETAPA

ENTRADA El primer día de clases

Alicia:	Esta clase va a ser interesante, ¿verdad?
Roberto:	Sí. El profesor es muy simpático. ¿Cómo te llamas?
Alicia:	Me llamo Alicia San Martín. ¿Y tú?
Roberto:	Yo me llamo Roberto Hernández.
Alicia:	¿De dónde eres, Roberto?
Roberto:	Soy de San Antonio, Texas. ¿Y tú, Alicia?
Alicia:	Soy de Santiago de Chile.
Roberto:	¿Ah, sí? ¡Qué interesante!
Alicia:	Oye, Roberto, quiero presentarte a mi compañera de cuarto, Elena Rodríguez.
Roberto:	Hola, Elena, mucho gusto. ¿Tú también eres de Chile?
Elena:	No, soy de México, de Guadalajara, estado de Jalisco. Tú estás en mi clase de biología también, ¿verdad?
Roberto:	Sí, estoy tomando biología.
Elena:	¡Qué bueno!
Roberto:	Pues bien, tengo que irme. Tengo que ir a la biblioteca, tengo mucho que estudiar. Adiós.
Alicia:	Adiós, hasta luego.
Elena:	Adiós.

Student Tape

PRIMERA ETAPA

EMPEZAR A ESCUCHAR

Repetir
Buenos días.
¿Cómo está usted?
Muy bien, gracias.
Buenas tardes.
¿Qué tal?
Buenas noches.
¿Cómo estás?
Con permiso.
estudiar

Identificar

1. Buenos días, doctora Suárez.
   Buenos días, doctora Suárez.
2. ¿Cómo está usted?
   ¿Cómo está usted?
3. Hola, César. ¿Cómo estás?
   Hola, César. ¿Cómo estás?
4. ¿Qué tal?
   ¿Qué tal?
5. Bueno, hasta luego.
   Bueno, hasta luego.

Escribir

1. Buenos días, César.
   Buenos días, César.
2. Hola, Patricia. ¿Cómo estás?
   Hola, Patricia. ¿Cómo estás?
3. Buenas tardes, doctora.
   Buenas tardes, doctora.
4. ¿Cómo está usted?
   ¿Cómo está usted?

ESCUCHAR

EPISODIO 1: "Buenos días"

Sr. Martínez:	Buenos días, doctora Suárez.
Dra. Suárez:	Buenos días, señor Martínez. ¿Cómo está usted?
Sr. Martínez:	Muy bien, gracias, profesora. ¿Y usted?
Dra. Suárez:	Muy bien.
Patricia:	Buenas tardes, César.
César:	Hola, Patricia. ¿Qué tal?
Patricia:	Bien, ¿y tú?
César:	Bien, gracias.

ESCUCHAR

EPISODIO 2: "Buenas noches, señora"

Roberto:	Buenas noches, señora. ¿Cómo está usted?

Señora:	Estoy bien, gracias, Roberto. ¿Y tú?	Raquel:	Hola, David.
Roberto:	Muy bien, gracias. ¿Está César?	David:	¿Qué tal, Raquel?
Señora:	Sí, está en su cuarto, estudiando.	Raquel:	Muy bien. Oye, qué día más lindo hoy, ¿verdad?
Roberto:	Bueno. Con permiso, señora. Voy a estudiar con él.	David:	Sí. ¡Es hermosísimo! A propósito, ¿qué cursos sigues este semestre?

SEGUNDA ETAPA

ANTES DE LEER

Estudiar y practicar

la amistad
el año
el apartado postal
la comida
cortés
los deportes
ir al cine
el joven
los pasatiempos
el pelo (negro)

TERCERA ETAPA

ANTES DE HABLAR

Leer en voz alta:

¿Cómo te llamas?
Me llamo...
Mucho gusto.
Encantado.
Igualmente.
¿De dónde eres?
Soy de (California).
¡Qué interesante!
¡Qué bueno!
¿Conoces (California)?
(No) Conozco (California).
Quiero presentarte a (mi compañero de cuarto).
Tengo que irme.

Capítulo 2

[Instructor Tape]

PRIMERA ETAPA

ENTRADA David y Raquel hablan de sus cursos

Raquel:	Pues, tengo filosofía, historia de los Estados Unidos, francés y biología.
David:	¡Ah! yo estoy en el curso de biología también.
Raquel:	¡Ah! ¡qué bueno! ¿Y qué cursos sigues tú?
David:	Además de biología, tengo español, inglés e historia del arte. Y, ¿a qué hora es tu curso de biología?
Raquel:	A las ocho y cuarto.
David:	¡Ah! ¡qué bien, yo también!
Raquel:	Oye, ¿por qué no tomamos un café?
David:	Bien. Vamos a la cafetería.

SEGUNDA ETAPA

ENTRADA Una conversación con Elena Rodríguez

Ramón:	Buenas tardes, Elena María. Soy Ramón Peña Ruiz y escribo para el periódico de la universidad. Oye, sabes, te agradezco mucho esta entrevista.
Elena:	De nada.
Ramón:	Dime, Elena María, ¿cuál es tu nombre completo?
Elena:	Mi nombre completo es Elena María Rodríguez Olivares.
Ramón:	Y, ¿de dónde eres?
Elena:	Soy de Guadalajara, estado de Jalisco, México.
Ramón:	¿En qué vas a especializarte?
Elena:	Um... Quizás biología o química.
Ramón:	Bien. ¿Es la primera vez que vienes a los Estados Unidos?
Elena:	Sí, es mi primera vez.
Ramón:	Oye, te entrevisto porque he oído que corres para competencia.

Elena:	Sí, he dedicado mucho tiempo de mi vida a ello.
Ramón:	Y, ¿qué distancia corres?
Elena:	Corro maratones.
Ramón:	¡Qué bien! ¿Cuándo empezaste a correr?
Elena:	Hace muchos años, durante la escuela primaria.
Ramón:	¿Qué planes futuros tienes para continuar corriendo?
Elena:	Practicar mucho para las siguientes olimpiadas.
Ramón:	¡Magnífico, Elena María! Oye, gracias por darme esta entrevista, ¿eh?
Elena:	A tu servicio.

TERCERA ETAPA

ENTRADA "¿Quieres tomar un café?"

Marcos:	Déjame ver tu horario de clases.
Elena:	Aquí lo tienes. ¿Qué cursos tienes este semestre?
Marcos:	Los lunes, miércoles y viernes tengo historia, francés... ¡Ah! mira. Estoy en tus clases de historia y de biología. ¡Qué suerte! ¿Me ayudas con la biología? Odio el trabajo de laboratorio.
Elena:	De acuerdo. Me encantan las ciencias. Pienso hacer investigación científica en el futuro. Mira, yo te ayudo con la biología si tú me ayudas con la historia.
Marcos:	Menos mal. A mí me encanta la historia. ¿Y a ti no te gusta?
Elena:	Nada. Soy fatal para la historia. Las fechas me matan. Y además, no sé casi nada de la historia norteamericana.
Marcos:	No te preocupes. Ya verás que vas a aprender muy rápido. Ya que vives aquí en los Estados Unidos, va a ser muy fácil. Pero no tenemos clase ahora. ¿Querrías tomar un café?
Elena:	Gracias, sí, me gustaría. Vamos ya, que a la una tengo otra clase.

> Student Tape

PRIMERA ETAPA

EMPEZAR A ESCUCHAR

Repetir

¡Oye!
¿Qué hora es?
primero
nervioso
Tengo ganas de (comenzar).
Cálmate.
No es para tanto.
No te preocupes.
fácil
Ya verás.

Identificar

1. Alicia y Elena hablan en la cafetería.
   Alicia y Elena hablan en la cafetería.
2. Tengo mi primera clase, y estoy nerviosa.
   Tengo mi primera clase, y estoy nerviosa.
3. Yo también, pero tengo ganas de comenzar.
   Yo también, pero tengo ganas de comenzar.
4. ¿Qué hora es? ¿Ya son las nueve?
   ¿Qué hora es? ¿Ya son las nueve?
5. No te preocupes. La clase va a ser muy fácil.
   No te preocupes. La clase va a ser muy fácil.
6. Hombre, ya verás.
   Hombre, ya verás.

Escribir

1. Alicia y Elena hablan en la cafetería.
   Alicia y Elena hablan en la cafetería.
2. Tengo mi primera clase, y estoy nerviosa.
   Tengo mi primera clase, y estoy nerviosa.
3. ¿Qué hora es?
   ¿Qué hora es?
4. No te preocupes.
   No te preocupes.
5. La clase es muy fácil.
   La clase es muy fácil.

ESCUCHAR

Episodio 1: "Oye, Alicia, ¿qué hora es?"

Elena: Oye, Alicia, ¿qué hora es?
Alicia: Son las ocho y media.
Elena: Tenemos la sesión de orientación a las nueve, ¿verdad, Alicia?
Alicia: Sí, en Adams Humanities, número 2112.
Elena: Va a ser mi primera clase en los Estados Unidos. Estoy nerviosa.
Alicia: Yo también, Elena, pero tengo ganas de comenzar.

ESCUCHAR

Episodio 2: "¡Cálmate, Marcos!"

Paco: Cálmate, Marcos. No es para tanto.
Marcos: Para ti, no. Tú eres norteamericano, Paco, y ya conoces el sistema. Pero yo acabo de llegar de Bogotá. La sesión de orientación va a ser mi primera clase en los Estados Unidos.
Paco: No te preocupes, Marcos, todo va a ser muy fácil. Comienza a las nueve, ¿verdad?
Marcos: Sí, en 30 minutos. Oye, Paco, tú vas a estar con nosotros, ¿no?
Paco: Claro. Hombre, ya verás. Te va a gustar.

SEGUNDA ETAPA

ANTES DE LEER

Estudiar y practicar

cocinar
correr
el fin de semana
Me gusta (leer).
nadar
Pienso (ser maestro).
el tiempo libre

TERCERA ETAPA

ANTES DE HABLAR

Leer en voz alta:
Déjame ver (tu horario de clases).

¡Qué casualidad!
Me encanta(n) (los idiomas).
Odio (la economía).
Soy fatal para (la historia).
(Las fechas) me mata(n).
¿Quieres (tomar un café)?
Me gustaría mucho.

Capítulo 3

Instructor Tape

PRIMERA ETAPA

ENTRADA Una emisión de radio

Locutor: Buenos días. Son las siete en punto de la mañana. Hoy es lunes, quince de septiembre. Y ahora les presentamos el resumen meteorológico para el día de hoy. Hace muy buen tiempo, y seguirá haciendo muy buen tiempo todo el día. Realmente va a ser un día maravilloso. En estos momentos, hace fresco, cincuenta y cinco grados Fahrenheit, trece grados centígrados. Va a subir la temperatura luego a setenta y cinco grados, veinticuatro grados centígrados. Va a ser un día de mucho sol, con un cielo azul, y brisas suaves. Un día ideal para salir y disfrutar de la naturaleza.

SEGUNDA ETAPA

ENTRADA "Vamos a salir esta noche"

Raquel: Vamos al cine esta noche. ¿Qué te parece?
David: ¿Qué ponen?
Raquel: Bueno, ¿te interesa una película norteamericana? En el Teatro Madrid Uno ponen *El imperio del sol*. Es de ese director tan famoso, Steven Spielberg. Dicen que la película es buenísima.
David: ¡Ah! no sé. ¿Qué más hay?
Raquel: Pues en el Cine Rex ponen *La familia*, una película italiana. Aquí dicen que es simplemente maravillosa.
David: ¡Ah! está bien eso. ¿A qué hora es?

Raquel: Ponen *La familia* a las cinco y a las siete y media de la tarde, y a las diez y cuarto de la noche.

David: ¿Y *El imperio del sol*? Solamente para comparar.

Raquel: Es a las cuatro y a las siete y cuarto de la tarde y a las diez y cuarto de la noche. Casi igual.

David: Entonces, ¿qué te parece si vamos a ver la película de Mastroianni, *La familia*?

Raquel: Muy buena idea. Como la ponen a las siete y media, podemos ir a cenar después.

TERCERA ETAPA

ENTRADA Un anuncio de radio

Locutor: ¡No se la pierdan! ¡Una oportunidad única, única y fabulosa! ¡La venta anual de Mueblería Sánchez! Una venta como ninguna otra. ¡Una oportunidad inigualable! Ofrecemos muebles para toda la casa. ¿Por qué tienen que pasar vergüenza con sus muebles viejos y feos? Con poquísimo dinero puede hacer que la casa luzca nueva con muebles de última moda en todos los estilos. No estamos vendiendo muebles, ¡estamos regalándolos! Para el dormitorio: tocadores, camas, mesitas. Para la sala: sofás, sillones, mesas, lámparas, sillas. ¡Mueblería Sánchez! Precios bajísimos. En el número veinte de la calle Argentina. ¡Mueblería Sánchez! Aparcamiento gratis, y para su mayor comodidad, estamos a sus órdenes siete días a la semana, de nueve a nueve. ¡Mueblería Sánchez! Número veinte, calle Argentina. ¡Donde los muebles se regalan! No se demore. ¡Váya en seguida a Mueblería Sánchez! En el número veinte, calle Argentina.

Student Tape

PRIMERA ETAPA

ANTES DE LEER

Estudiar y practicar
la actuación
el conjunto
limpiar
llamar

la misa
pasar

SEGUNDA ETAPA

EMPEZAR A ESCUCHAR

Repetir
tarde
madrugar
me despierto
temprano
estar de vuelta
calladito
¡Dormilona!
desayunar
¿Me esperas?
tener prisa

Identificar

1. A mí me gusta madrugar.
   A mí me gusta madrugar.

2. Elena se viste calladita.
   Elena se viste calladita.

3. No tengo prisa. Mi primera clase comienza a las nueve.
   No tengo prisa. Mi primera clase comienza a las nueve.

4. ¡Dormilona! ¿Por qué no corres conmigo?
   ¡Dormilona! ¿Por qué no corres conmigo?

5. Puedo estar de vuelta antes de las seis y media.
   Puedo estar de vuelta antes de las seis y media.

6. ¿Me esperas para desayunar?
   ¿Me esperas para desayunar?

Escribir

1. A mí me gusta madrugar.
   A mí me gusta madrugar.

2. No tengo prisa.
   No tengo prisa.

3. ¡Dormilona!
   ¡Dormilona!

4. Puedo estar de vuelta temprano.
   Puedo estar de vuelta temprano.

5. ¿Me esperas para desayunar?
   ¿Me esperas para desayunar?

ESCUCHAR

Episodio 1: La rutina diaria de Elena

Elena: Pues, Alicia, ¿a qué hora sueles levantarte?

Alicia: ¿Yo? Lo más tarde posible. Por lo general, me levanto a las siete y cuarto o a las siete y media.

Elena: A mí me gusta madrugar. Siempre me despierto temprano, y me levanto antes de las seis para correr cuando hace fresco.

Alicia: ¡Ay, Elena, qué energía tienes! ¿Cómo hacemos entonces?

Elena: A ver. Corro solamente cinco kilómetros los días de clase. Si me levanto a las cinco y media, puedo estar de vuelta antes de las seis y media.

Alicia: ¡Qué horror! ¿Las cinco y media? ¿Las seis y media? ¡Dios mío!

ESCUCHAR

Episodio 2: La rutina de Alicia

Alicia: Pues, Elena, tú puedes correr si quieres, pero a mí me gusta dormir. Si te bañas y te vistes calladita, puedo dormir hasta las...

Elena: ¡Dormilona! ¿Por qué no te levantas para correr conmigo?

Alicia: ¡Qué horror! No me gusta el ejercicio, y mucho menos a las cinco y media. Si me levanto a las siete y media y me baño rápido, ¿me esperas para desayunar?

Elena: Sí, cómo no. No tengo prisa. Mi primera clase comienza a las nueve.

TERCERA ETAPA

ANTES DE ESCRIBIR

Estudiar y practicar

El físico
alto
bajo
delgado
de mediana estatura
flaco
gordo
guapo
pelirrojo
el pelo castaño
el pelo negro
rubio

La personalidad/otros rasgos
abierto
agradable
antipático
celoso
cómico
generoso
reservado
serio
tacaño

Capítulo 4

[Instructor Tape]

PRIMERA ETAPA

ENTRADA "¿Tiene Ud. un espejo, por favor?"

Mujer: Buenas tardes. Vengo a sacarme una foto para el pasaporte. ¿Dónde tiene usted un espejo? Quiero arreglarme el pelo un poco antes de que me saque la foto.

Fotógrafo: Naturalmente. Aquí tengo un espejo. Está encima de la mesa.

Mujer: ¡Uy! Estas fotos siempre salen muy mal. La gente se parece a encarcelados. ¿Qué sé yo?

Fotógrafo: ¡Ah, no, no, no, no, no! Usted no tiene por qué preocuparse. Yo soy el mejor fotógrafo del mundo. A ver... ¿adónde va... adónde va usted de viaje?

Mujer: Bueno, pienso pasar las vacaciones de Navidad en el Perú. Tengo familia en Lima, y además, es verano, ¿eh?

Fotógrafo: ¿Quiere mirar a la derecha?... ¿Y qué ciudades va... va a visitar?

Mujer: Ah, pues pienso visitar Cuzco, las ruinas de Machu Picchu, con mis primos.

Fotógrafo: ¡Ummm!... Un poco más abajo, un poco más abajo... Ya. Ahora un minuto para que se revelen. ¿Cuánto tiempo va a estar allí?

Mujer:	Ah pues, tres semanas más o menos. ¡Estoy muy emocionada con la idea del viaje!
Fotógrafo:	Me alegra mucho. ¡Perfecto! Aquí están sus fotos.
Mujer:	¡Ay! ¡Qué bien salieron! Muchas gracias.
Fotógrafo:	Pues, ya se lo había dicho. Muy bien. ¡Qué tenga usted buen viaje!
Mujer:	¡Felices Pascuas!
Fotógrafo:	Igualmente.
Mujer:	Adiós.

SEGUNDA ETAPA

ENTRADA Haciendo los arreglos

Oficial:	Buenos días. Consulado del Perú. ¿En qué puedo servirle?
Patricia:	Sí, señor. Por favor, quiero ir a su país en tres semanas y necesito una visa.
Oficial:	Tiene usted que llenar una solicitud de visado, pero podemos hacerlo por teléfono.
Patricia:	Bien, de acuerdo.
Oficial:	¿Cuál es su primer apellido?
Patricia:	Laval.
Oficial:	¿Y su segundo apellido?
Patricia:	No llevo segundo apellido. No estoy casada.
Oficial:	Entiendo. Y ahora si me dice su nombre, por favor.
Patricia:	Patricia Ann.
Oficial:	¿Y cuál es la fecha de nacimiento?
Patricia:	El quince de octubre de mil novecientos sesenta y tres.
Oficial:	Muy bien. ¿Dónde vive usted?
Patricia:	En Manzanita, trescientos dos en Silver Lake, Los Ángeles, California.
Oficial:	¿Cuál es el país de nacimiento?
Patricia:	Los Estados Unidos.
Oficial:	¿Y su nacionalidad legal?
Patricia:	Estadounidense.
Oficial:	¿Y cuál es su profesión?
Patricia:	Estudiante.
Oficial:	Ahora, ¿me puede usted decir el número de su pasaporte?
Patricia:	Ah, perdón, no lo tengo ahora conmigo.
Oficial:	Y, ¿me puede decir cuál es el motivo del viaje?
Patricia:	Para visitar a mis parientes que viven allí. También me gustaría mucho ir a esquiar. Creo que es el mes de más nieve en su país, ¿no?
Oficial:	Sí, efectivamente, así es. Muy bien. Turismo. ¿Y cuánto tiempo piensa quedarse en Perú?
Patricia:	Un mes, aproximadamente.
Oficial:	Le enviaré hoy mismo esta documentación para que la complete, la firme y nos la devuelva.
Patricia:	Señor, por favor, ¿y cuánto tiempo se demora en recibir la visa? Fíjese que yo salgo en tres semanas.
Oficial:	Aproximadamente una semana.
Patricia:	Ah, perfecto. Muchas gracias.
Oficial:	Gracias a usted. Adiós.
Patricia:	Adiós.

TERCERA ETAPA

ENTRADA En la aduana

Oficial:	Buenas tardes, señorita. Bienvenida a Lima, Perú.
Patricia:	Muchas gracias.
Oficial:	¿Tiene usted algo que declarar?
Patricia:	No. Solamente ropa y artículos de uso personal.
Oficial:	¿Trae licores?
Patricia:	No, nada de licores.
Oficial:	Ummm... ¿Comida?
Patricia:	No, tampoco.
Oficial:	¿Plantas?
Patricia:	No, no traigo plantas.
Oficial:	¿Productos animales?
Patricia:	Le he dicho que no, señor.
Oficial:	¿Tiene algo de origen vegetal?
Patricia:	No, no, no. Nada de eso.

Oficial: Abra las maletas por favor.
Patricia: Aquí está.
Oficial: Um... Déjeme ver. ¿Qué tiene en esa caja?
Patricia: Es un regalo para mi sobrina.
Oficial: Ah... ábrala, por favor.
Patricia: Como usted ve, es un vestido. Aquí tiene la factura, veinte dólares. Es el vestido de una niña.
Oficial: ¡Ajá! Ya veo, ya veo. ¿Y qué tiene en esa bolsa de plástico?
Patricia: Pero señor, ¡son fotos de la familia!
Oficial: Muy bien. Muy bien, señorita. Puede cerrar las maletas.
Patricia: Muy bien. Gracias.
Oficial: Y que lo pase usted muy bien en el Perú.
Patricia: Bueno. Hasta luego.

> Student Tape

PRIMERA ETAPA

EMPEZAR A ESCUCHAR

Repetir

la playa
¡Qué envidia!
la molestia
de ninguna manera
estar seguro
el invitado
afortunadamente
la plata
acompañado
divertido

Identificar

1. Vamos a pasar mucho tiempo en la playa.
   Vamos a pasar mucho tiempo en la playa.
2. ¡Qué envidia! Todos ustedes van a lugares interesantes.
   ¡Qué envidia! Todos ustedes van a lugares interesantes.
3. ¿De verdad no es mucha molestia para tu familia?
   ¿De verdad no es mucha molestia para tu familia?
4. ¡De ninguna manera! Puedes estar seguro de una calurosa bienvenida.
   ¡De ninguna manera! Puedes estar seguro de una calurosa bienvenida.
5. Afortunadamente, tengo casi toda la plata de mi trabajo.
   Afortunadamente, tengo casi toda la plata de mi trabajo.
6. Sensacional. Y si quieres, puedes viajar acompañado.
   Sensacional. Y si quieres, puedes viajar acompañado.
7. ¿Acompañado? Claro que sí. Todo es más interesante y divertido así.
   ¿Acompañado? Claro que sí. Todo es más interesante y divertido así.

Escribir

1. Vamos a pasar mucho tiempo en la playa.
   Vamos a pasar mucho tiempo en la playa.
2. Todos ustedes van a lugares divertidos.
   Todos ustedes van a lugares divertidos.
3. No es ninguna molestia para mi familia.
   No es ninguna molestia para mi familia.
4. Afortunadamente, tengo casi toda la plata de mi trabajo.
   Afortunadamente, tengo casi toda la plata de mi trabajo.
5. Es más divertido viajar acompañado.
   Es más divertido viajar acompañado.

ESCUCHAR

Episodio 1: "¡Cómo pasa el tiempo!"

Elena: ¡Cómo pasa el tiempo! Ya hace cuatro meses que estamos en la universidad. Tengo tantas ganas de ir a casa, de ver a mis padres, a mi hermanita... Yo sé que Guadalajara está relativamente cerca, pero me siento muy lejos.

Alicia: Yo lo mismo. Pero Santiago está de verdad muy lejos. Voy a pasar todo el mes de vacaciones allá. Mi mamá me escribe que el verano está precioso este año. Vamos a pasar mucho tiempo en la playa.

Paco: Ah... ¡Qué envidia! Todos ustedes van a lugares interesantes, mientras yo... Pues yo me quedo aquí en los Estados Unidos.

Marcos: Pues, hombre, ¿por qué no vienes a Bogotá conmigo? Yo te invito. Puedes quedarte en mi casa y conocer a mi familia.

ESCUCHAR

EPISODIO 2: "¡Es una idea magnífica!"

Paco: ¿Visitarte en Bogotá, Marcos? ¡Me parece una magnífica idea! ¿De verdad que no es mucha molestia para tu familia?

Marcos: De ninguna manera. Puedes estar seguro de una calurosa bienvenida. En efecto, Roberto dice que va a pasar casi todas las vacaciones en Colombia. Piensa pasar por Cali y Cartagena, y después ir a Bogotá a quedarse con nosotros allí. No hay ninguna diferencia entre un invitado o dos en la casa, ¿verdad?

Paco: Sensacional. Y afortunadamente, tengo casi toda la plata de mi trabajo con la profesora Suárez. Tengo que pasar los primeros días de las vacaciones en El Paso, porque vamos a tener una reunión de toda la familia allí. Pero puedo salir para Colombia después del Año Nuevo. ¿Qué te parece?

Marcos: Perfecto. Puedes viajar con Roberto. Yo sé que a él le gustaría viajar acompañado. Todo es mucho más interesante y divertido así, ¿no?

Paco: Claro que sí. Tengo que comenzar a hacer los preparativos ahora mismo. Necesito sacar un pasaporte y pedir una visa. Tenemos muy poco tiempo.

Marcos: Bueno, manos a la obra. Parece que todos vamos a pasar las vacaciones estupendamente.

SEGUNDA ETAPA

ANTES DE LEER

Estudiar y practicar
comprobar
el equipaje
la etiqueta
el extranjero
la maleta
el viajero

Capítulo 5

[Instructor Tape]

PRIMERA ETAPA

ENTRADA En busca de alojamiento

Roberto: Paco, ¿quieres otro café?

Paco: Sí, cómo no. ¿Y tú?

Roberto: Sí, yo también. Mira, recogí este folleto. Tiene toda una lista de pensiones y hoteles. A ver... quizás hay algo interesante para nosotros aquí.

Paco: Ah, muy bien. ¿Queremos una habitación con baño, eh?

Roberto: Con baño. Y con dos camas sencillas.

Paco: Claro. Y, este... a ver qué más. Tiene que ser barata, ¿eh?

Roberto: ¡Barata porque de dinero tenemos muy poco! ¿Y qué te parece ubicación? ¿Dónde debe estar?

Paco: Pues, preferiblemente cerca del centro.

Roberto: Creo que sí. Y... ¡ah! Y con el almuerzo incluido.

Paco: Claro que sí.

Roberto: A ver si hay algo en esta lista... pensión, Pensión Gómez, Pensión Restrepo.

Paco: Ah, mira sí. Restrepo.

Roberto: Restrepo. ¡Um! Vamos a ver... Espera un momento. Voy aquí al teléfono y voy a llamar.

Paco: Muy bien.

Roberto: Vuelvo en seguida.

Paco: Muy bien.

Paco: Roberto, ¿qué pasa?

Roberto: Pues, acabo de llamar a esa pensión, la Pensión Restrepo. Y me parece que hemos encontrado lo que necesitamos.

Paco: Ah, muy bien.

Roberto: Hablé con la señora Restrepo que es la dueña, la señora... y es muy simpática. Y tiene exactamente lo que necesitamos.

Paco:	Ah, ¿sí?		Mesero:	El plato especial del día es langosta al vapor.
Roberto:	Una habitación con baño y dos camas sencillas.		Elena:	Ah, muy bien. Yo quiero langosta al vapor, arroz, ensalada de lechuga y tomate.
Paco:	Perfecto.		Mesero:	¿Desean entremeses?
Roberto:	Y la ubicación también es perfecta. Está en el pleno centro del pueblo.		Elena:	No, gracias.
			César:	Yo sí. Quiero la sopa de ajo. De plato principal, el bistec medio cocido… no me gusta la carne tan cocida que esté negra.
Paco:	¡Qué bueno!			
Roberto:	Y de precio… Bien… No… La habitación no es muy cara.		Mesero:	Muy bien.
Paco:	Vamos, entonces. Vamos a ver si nos gusta.		César:	Además, papas fritas, brócoli y ensalada de aguacate.
Roberto:	Sí. Y… también… y de comida nos van a dar el almuerzo incluido en el precio de la habitación. ¿Qué te parece?		Mesero:	¿Qué desean para beber?
			Elena:	César, querido, escoge tú el vino.
			César:	Bien, mi amor. ¿Qué te parece un Rioja del ochenta y dos?
Paco:	Mejor, entonces.			
Roberto:	Vamos a ir, entonces.		Elena:	Muy bien.
Paco:	Vamos.		Mesero:	¿Algo más?
Roberto:	¿Quieres?		Elena:	No, más tarde pedimos el postre.
Paco:	Um.		César:	Sí, sí. Ahora no.
Roberto:	Bien.		Mesero:	Muchas gracias.
			César:	Muchas gracias.

SEGUNDA ETAPA

ENTRADA En el restaurante

César:	Oye, ¡qué bueno que nos dieron una mesa íntima al lado de la ventana, Elena!
Elena:	Sí, éste es uno de mis restaurantes favoritos.
César:	Hacía tiempo que no salíamos juntos a cenar.
Elena:	Ay, mi amor, es que trabajas demasiado. Tenemos que hacer esto más a menudo.
César:	Sí, tienes razón. Pero ésta es una ocasión especial, y escogiste el lugar ideal para celebrar el fin del semestre.
Elena:	Me gusta este restaurante porque está decorado con muy buen gusto. Y la comida es excelente.
César:	Y lo han puesto más íntimo, ¿no? Tiene un ambiente muy romántico que va con el color de tus ojos.
Elena:	Ah… aquí está el mesero.
Mesero:	Buenas noches. ¿Están listos para pedir?
César:	Sí, sí. ¿Qué recomienda usted, por favor?

TERCERA ETAPA

ENTRADA En el restaurante Casa María

Roberto:	Bueno, aquí estamos. Así que conoces este restaurante, ¿verdad? ¿Qué me recomiendas?
Carmencita:	Todo lo que sirven aquí es buenísimo…
Mesero:	Buenas tardes. ¿Están listos para pedir?
Roberto:	Creo que sí, gracias. ¿Cuáles son los platos del día?
Mesero:	Pues hoy tenemos camarones con salsa verde, chuletas de cerdo con salsa de fruta, y las legumbres del día son zanahorias y arvejas. De postre tenemos una torta de chocolate riquísima. Y también nuestro flan María, que es una especialidad de la casa.
Roberto:	Carmencita, ¿qué deseas? ¿Has decidido?
Carmencita:	Sí, Roberto, gracias. ¿Me puede traer los camarones, por favor, con arroz y arvejas?

Mesero: Sí, señorita, cómo no. ¿Y usted, señor?

Roberto: Tengo más hambre que la señorita. ¿Cuál es la sopa del día?

Mesero: Tenemos una sopa de ajo que es la especialidad de la casa. Se la recomiendo, señor.

Roberto: Entonces, tráigame la sopa, por favor, y de segundo plato quiero el pollo asado con papas fritas y zanahorias. ¿Me puede traer también una ensalada de lechuga y tomate?

Mesero: Cómo no, señor. ¿Y para beber?

Roberto: Media botella de vino blanco, por favor.

Mesero: ¿Y han decidido ya lo que quieren de postre, o prefieren esperar?

Carmencita: Ya sé que voy a tomar el flan. Lo he comido aquí antes, y siempre está riquísimo.

Roberto: Y, creo que voy a probar la torta de chocolate, ya que usted nos la recomienda.

Mesero: Muy bien. Ahora les traigo el pan y el vino.

Student Tape

PRIMERA ETAPA

EMPEZAR A ESCUCHAR

Repetir

al lado de
el cirujano
el contador
el gerente
el huésped
jubilado
la modista
mudarse
el periodista
el vecino

Identificar

1. En este momento, hay cuatro huéspedes más en la pensión.
   En este momento, hay cuatro huéspedes más en la pensión.

2. El señor Pedroza es periodista, y el señor Lima es un profesor jubilado.
   El señor Pedroza es periodista, y el señor Lima es un profesor jubilado.

3. Entre los vecinos, conozco muy bien a la señora de Valdivia, que es modista.
   Entre los vecinos, conozco muy bien a la señora de Valdivia, que es modista.

4. El doctor Meléndez es cirujano, y su esposa trabaja en el centro.
   El doctor Meléndez es cirujano, y su esposa trabaja en el centro.

5. La familia de enfrente acaba de mudarse a Cali.
   La familia de enfrente acaba de mudarse a Cali.

6. El señor Gaitán es gerente del Banco de la República, y su esposa es contadora.
   El señor Gaitán es gerente del Banco de la República, y su esposa es contadora.

Escribir

1. Hay cuatro huéspedes más en la pensión.
   Hay cuatro huéspedes más en la pensión.

2. El señor Pedroza es periodista.
   El señor Pedroza es periodista.

3. El doctor Meléndez es cirujano.
   El doctor Meléndez es cirujano.

4. La familia de enfrente acaba de mudarse a Cali.
   La familia de enfrente acaba de mudarse a Cali.

5. La señora de Gaitán es contadora.
   La señora de Gaitán es contadora.

ESCUCHAR

EPISODIO 1: En la pensión

Doña Josefina: Bienvenidos, señores, la casa es suya. Durante el almuerzo van a conocer a los otros huéspedes de la pensión. Fernando y José son estudiantes en la Universidad del Valle. El señor Pedroza es periodista y el señor Lima es un profesor jubilado.

Paco: Sí, tenemos ganas de conocerlos a todos. También es muy bonita la vecindad, y esperamos dar un paseo antes de comer.

Doña Josefina: ¡Cómo no! Y también van a descubrir que son muy amables los vecinos. Pues en la casa que está al lado del parque vive la señora Valdivia del Castillo, que es modista. Al otro lado, viven los Meléndez. El doctor Meléndez tiene mucha fama en la región porque es un cirujano excelente.

ESCUCHAR

Episodio 2: Más vecinos de doña Josefina

Roberto: El doctor Meléndez tiene una hija, ¿no es verdad? Creo que la vi esta tarde.

Doña Josefina: Sí, se llama María del Carmen, pero todos le dicen Carmencita. Estudia en el Colegio del Sagrado Corazón.

Roberto: Es hermosísima... ¿Simpática también?

Doña Josefina: Desde luego. Son gente muy fina. Como les dije, el doctor es un cirujano muy conocido, y doña Julia, su esposa, trabaja en el consulado de los Estados Unidos en el centro, cerca de la Plaza de Caicedo. Además, tenemos unos vecinos nuevos, la familia de enfrente, que acaba de mudarse a Cali desde Popayán. Creo que su apellido es Gaitán. Todavía no los conozco bien, pero sé que los dos van a trabajar en el Banco de la República; él de gerente y ella de contadora. Tienen cuatro hijos.

SEGUNDA ETAPA

ANTES DE LEER

Estudiar y practicar

el arreglo
la jardinería
la marca
el pastel
la relojería
la sucursal
el surtido

TERCERA ETAPA

ANTES DE LEER Y ESCRIBIR

Estudiar y practicar

el ave
la carne
la ensalada
la entrada
la legumbre
el postre
la sopa

Capítulo 6

[Instructor Tape]

PRIMERA ETAPA

ENTRADA Veraneo mexicano

Locutor: César y Elena hablan por teléfono.

César: ¡Hola, Elena! Habla César.

Elena: ¡Hola! César. ¿Qué hay de nuevo?

César: Pues nada de particular. Quería decirte que acabo de hablar con un tío mío que vivió en México durante unos años, y me describía algunas de sus experiencias.

Elena: ¿De veras? No sabía que tenías parientes en México.

César: Yo tampoco lo sabía. Pero parece que cuando vivía allí, visitó varias ciudades.

Elena: ¿Oh? ¿Cuáles?

César: Pues me dijo que en aquél entonces frecuentaba los museos y los teatros de la ciudad de México, y que hacía compras en los famosos mercados de Taxco. También, siempre que tenía la oportunidad, visitaba Acapulco y descansaba allí en las playas exquisitas.

Elena: Pero... ¿no mencionó nada de Guadalajara?

César: ¡Claro que sí! Dijo que la ciudad es una de las más bonitas de toda la República.

Elena: ¡Menos mal! Veo que sí conoce bien mi patria.

SEGUNDA ETAPA

ENTRADA Cartagena de Indias, Cartagena del mar...

Locutor: Este es el momento de conocer Colombia y disfrutar de unas vacaciones inolvidables, por las siguientes razones. La primera es de orden económico. Hoy día en Colombia, cualquier hotel, restaurante, o discoteca cuesta aproximadamente la mitad del servicio equivalente en España. La segunda es Cartagena de Indias. Sin lugar a dudas, es la ciudad más bella del Caribe. Su rico pasado histórico y colonial se respira por sus calles, mezclado al aroma de la brisa del mar que baña sus costas. Y finalmente, para los aficionados al sol, sus playas. Son inmensas y blanquísimas. Salpicadas del verde tropical de sus palmeras. Y llegan hasta el agua azul turquesa, de un mar siempre caliente y acogedor en cualquier época del año. Cartagena de Indias es colorido y belleza. Un sedante para el espíritu.

TERCERA ETAPA

ENTRADA En la recepción del Hotel Bahía

Empleado: Buenas tardes, señores. A sus órdenes.

Roberto: Gracias, señor. Yo soy Roberto Hernández, y este señor es mi amigo, Francisco Méndez. Tenemos reservaciones para seis noches.

Empleado: Un momento, por favor. Voy a ver si tengo sus reservaciones aquí. A ver... A ver... Sí, señores. Aquí las tengo: dos personas, una habitación, seis noches, a partir de hoy, ¿verdad?

Roberto: Sí, señor. Muchas gracias. ¿Podemos ver el mar desde la habitación?

Empleado: No pueden verlo, pero sí pueden oírlo. Y además, tienen una linda vista de la piscina.

Roberto: ¿Hay baño completo en la habitación?

Empleado: Cómo no, señor. Hay lavamanos, tina y ducha. Y tenemos servicio de restaurante las veinticuatro horas del día.

Roberto: Genial. Éste sí es un hotel de lujo.

Empleado: Gracias, señor. Ud. es muy amable. Su habitación está en el primer piso.

Paco: ¿Señor, no podemos tener una habitación en el sexto o séptimo piso? Es que nos molesta el ruido de la calle y de la piscina.

Empleado: Lo siento mucho, señores. Es la única habitación que tenemos esta semana. Hay un congreso de ingenieros aquí toda la semana y el hotel está completamente lleno. Además, las habitaciones en los pisos más altos son mucho más caras.

Paco: Ah, bueno. Entiendo. Entonces, Roberto, vamos a aprender a vivir con un poco de ruido, ¿no?

Roberto: Parece que sí. Ahora no me importa. Yo sólo quiero descansar un par de horas.

Empleado: A propósito, señores, ¿conocen ustedes Cartagena?

Paco: No, es la primera vez que estamos aquí.

Empleado: Bueno, ustedes verán que hay una guía en la habitación. Todo lo que quieren saber de nuestra bella ciudad, allí está la información. Que disfruten mucho su estancia aquí.

Roberto: Gracias, muy amable.

Student Tape

PRIMERA ETAPA

EMPEZAR A ESCUCHAR

Repetir

¿En qué puedo servirles?
hacer los arreglos
por tierra
por avión
a dos cuadras de
los precios bajos
alquilar
el cheque de viajero
firmar

Identificar

1. Buenos días, señores. ¿En qué puedo servirles?
   Buenos días, señores. ¿En qué puedo servirles?
2. Queremos hacer los arreglos para ir a Cartagena.
   Queremos hacer los arreglos para ir a Cartagena.

3. ¿Cómo prefieren viajar? ¿Por tierra o por avión?
   ¿Cómo prefieren viajar? ¿Por tierra o por avión?
4. El hotel está a dos cuadras de la playa y tiene precios muy bajos.
   El hotel está a dos cuadras de la playa y tiene precios muy bajos.
5. Entonces no nos cuesta mucho alquilar una sola habitación.
   Entonces no nos cuesta mucho alquilar una sola habitación.
6. ¿Cómo prefieren pagar, en efectivo, con cheques de viajero, o con tarjeta de crédito?
   ¿Cómo prefieren pagar, en efectivo, con cheques de viajero, o con tarjeta de crédito?

Escribir

1. Paco y Roberto hacen los arreglos para su viaje a Cartagena.
   Paco y Roberto hacen los arreglos para su viaje a Cartagena.
2. Prefieren viajar por avión.
   Prefieren viajar por avión.
3. El hotel está a dos cuadras de la playa.
   El hotel está a dos cuadras de la playa.
4. Los precios son bajos, pero van a alquilar una sola habitación.
   Los precios son bajos, pero van a alquilar una sola habitación.
5. Deciden pagar con cheques de viajero.
   Deciden pagar con cheques de viajero.

ESCUCHAR

Episodio 1: ¿Por tierra o por avión?

Agente: Buenos días, señores. ¿En qué puedo servirles?

Roberto: ¿Señor González? Acabo de hablar con usted por teléfono. Soy Roberto Hernández. Queremos hacer los arreglos para ir a Cartagena. ¿Se acuerda Ud?

Agente: Sí, cómo no. ¿Cómo quieren viajar? ¿Por tierra o por avión?

Roberto: ¿Te acuerdas, Paco, que el otro día cuando hablábamos del viaje a Cartagena pensábamos viajar en autobús, pero después decidimos que no teníamos suficiente tiempo? Por favor, ¿cuánto cuesta el viaje en avión?

Agente: Pues, en clase turista cuesta $20.000 pesos. Esto es moneda nacional, por supuesto. Serán $110,00 dólares norteamericanos. En primera clase es más caro.

Roberto: ¡Huy! No podemos. Necesitamos dos boletos de clase turista.

Agente: Y ¿cuándo quieren viajar?

Paco: Pensábamos ir mañana. ¿Hay vuelo?

Agente: Claro que sí. Hay vuelos todos los días. ¿Quieren que les prepare los boletos ahora?

Paco: Sí, por favor.

ESCUCHAR

Episodio 2: "¿Dónde quieren alojarse?"

Roberto: ¿Aquí también podemos hacer reservaciones para un hotel en Cartagena?

Agente: Cómo no, señor Hernández. ¿Dónde quieren alojarse?

Roberto: Pues, no conocemos Cartagena. ¿Hay algo cerca de la playa?

Agente: Sí. Esa área se llama Boca Grande y hay de todo. El Hotel Bahía está a dos cuadras de la playa y es muy barato. ¿Van a compartir una habitación?

Roberto: Sí. No tenemos dinero para alquilar dos habitaciones.

Agente: Entonces, voy a hacerles reservaciones para mañana, el día 19, en el Hotel Bahía. ¿Cuántas noches van a estar en Cartagena?

Roberto: Bueno, pensamos pasar seis noches allí.

Agente: ...Hasta el día 25. Bueno. Volviendo a los boletos de avión, ¿van a pagar en efectivo, con cheque o con tarjeta de crédito?

Paco: ¿Podemos pagar con cheques de viajero?

Agente: Cómo no, señor Méndez.

Paco: Entonces, si nos puede hacer las reservaciones, por favor. Roberto, ¿tienes los cheques de viajero?

Roberto: Sí. Aquí los tengo. ¿Los firmo ya?

Paco: Sí. Fírmalos y nos vamos, que ya me está dando hambre.

SEGUNDA ETAPA

ANTES DE LEER

Estudiar y practicar

al nivel del mar
el balneario
el castillo
la derrota
en exposición
fundar
llegar a ser
la madera
las mercancías
la mazcla
el museo
el paraíso
el puerto
la temperatura promedio
el ultramar

TERCERA ETAPA

ANTES DE HABLAR

Estudiar y practicar

a sus órdenes
el baño
la ducha
el lavamanos
lo siento mucho
lleno
la piscina
el piso
la tina

Capítulo 7

[Instructor Tape]

PRIMERA ETAPA

ENTRADA "¿Qué precio lleva...?"

Locutor: Paco y Roberto van de compras antes de salir para Bogotá.

Roberto: Oye Paco, necesito comprar un regalito para mi sobrina, Anita.

Paco: Buena idea. ¿Qué buscas?

Roberto: Pues, no sé exactamente. Busco algo que no cueste mucho, pero que sea bonito, y que represente el país.

Paco: Entonces, ¿por qué no nos pasamos por este mercado de artesanía para ver si tienen algún recuerdo que sea bonito y barato?

Vendedora: Buenos días, señores. ¿En qué puedo servirles?

Roberto: Buenos días. Andamos en busca de algún regalito para mi sobrina, que tiene ocho años.

Vendedora: Muy bien. Prefiere alguna curiosidad, una cinta de música tradicional, joyería, ropa...

Roberto: ¡Joyería! ¿Tiene Ud. aretes o pulseras que no cuesten demasiado?

Vendedora: ¡Claro que sí, señor! Tenemos un surtido completo, desde el oro y esmeraldas hasta plata con piedras semipreciosas como ópalo, turquesa...

Roberto: Pero señorita, no puedo gastar tanto. Además, es una niña de ocho años. Tal vez otra cosa.

Paco: Mira, Roberto. Aquí tienen reproducciones de estatuas precolombinas.

Roberto: ¡Excelente! ¿Tienen una que tenga la apariencia de un búho? Anita tiene una colección de pájaros, y esto sería perfecto.

Paco: Sí. Aquí hay una, y está bien hecha, hasta con la firma del escultor. ¿Qué te parece?

Roberto: Es exactamente lo que buscaba. Señorita, ¿qué precio lleva?

Vendedora: ¿A Ud. le gusta? Pues, es una de nuestras esculturas más populares, y a ustedes les doy un precio especial, como, a ver... ¿Qué les parece $8.500 pesos?

Roberto: ¡Uf! Sí que es bonito, pero no puedo pagar tanto. ¿Aceptaría Ud. 4.000?

Vendedora: No, señor, no puedo. Mire como el escultor ha incorporado los detalles. Se lo doy por 7.000.

Roberto: ¿5.000?

Vendedora: 6.000.

Roberto:	Por 5.500 me la llevo.
Vendedora:	Pues señor, el precio más bajo que puedo aceptar es 5.550.
Roberto:	Entiendo, señorita, pero mi oferta más alta es 5.500. No puedo pagar más.
Vendedora:	Muy bien. ¿Desea Ud. que la envuelva?
Roberto:	No, gracias. La llevo así. Voy a ponerla en mi maleta.
Vendedora:	Como Ud. diga. Muchas gracias, señores. Que disfruten de su estancia en Cartagena.
Roberto:	Gracias, señorita.

SEGUNDA ETAPA

ENTRADA Una cena en casa

Luisa:	¡Hola, David! ¡Bienvenidos! Pasen, pasen. Están en su casa.
David:	Hola, Luisa, gracias. Te presento a mi amiga Raquel Heidt. Raquel, mi amiga Luisa Salazar.
Raquel:	Encantada, Luisa, David me ha hablado mucho de ti. Te especializas en literatura comparada, ¿no?
Luisa:	Sí. Me encanta leer. ¿Qué más te ha dicho David de mí? Nada malo, espero.
Raquel:	¡Qué va! Todo lo contrario.
Luisa:	Pues, antes que nada, quisiera presentarles a Gustavo García, de México. Gustavo, Raquel y David también son estudiantes.
Raquel:	Encantada, Gustavo.
David:	Mucho gusto, Gustavo. ¿Hace cuánto tiempo que estás aquí?
Gustavo:	Pues, no mucho. Acabo de empezar mis estudios aquí. Pero es la segunda vez que visito el país. Así que lo conozco un poco.
Luisa:	Adelante, adelante. Pasen ustedes. ¡No tenemos que hablar en el portal! Están en su casa.
Raquel:	¡Ah, muchas gracias! Uy... ¡Qué casa más linda tienes! Ah... Oye... Y este cuadro, ¿de quién es?
Luisa:	¿Te gusta? Es un retrato de mi bisabuelo. La propiedad en donde estamos actualmente fue concedida a mi familia por el rey de España en 1780, de acuerdo con el sistema de repartimiento de aquel entonces.
Raquel:	Sí. Ya me lo dijo David. ¡Qué interesante! Hemos estado discutiendo las encomiendas en la clase de historia, pero la verdad es que no lo entiendo muy bien hasta ahora.
Luisa:	Ni yo tampoco. Sólo sé que el patriarca era un encomendero y que mi familia ha vivido en esta región desde el siglo XVIII. Bueno, pues, ¿pasamos al jardín?

TERCERA ETAPA

ENTRADA "Aquí tienen su casa"

Marcos:	Mamá, te presento a Paco y a Roberto, mis amigos de la universidad.
Consuelo:	Encantada de conocerlos. Aquí tienen su casa.
Roberto:	Muchas gracias, y mucho gusto en conocerla, doña Consuelo. Yo soy Roberto Hernández.
Paco:	Y yo soy Francisco Méndez, señora. Todos me dicen Paco.
Consuelo:	Pues, muy bienvenidos a Bogotá. ¿Por qué no se sientan aquí en la sala y descansan un ratico? ¿Se les ofrece algo de la cocina?
Marcos:	Gracias, mamá. Quizás un chocolatico con pan. Quiero que Paco y Roberto nos cuenten todas sus experiencias en Cali y en Cartagena.
Consuelo:	Yo también. Un momento, que voy a preparar el chocolate.

Student Tape

PRIMERA ETAPA

EMPEZAR A ESCUCHAR

Repetir

meter la pata
tener fama de

mal educado
unos consejos
el cariño
descalzo

Identificar

1. No quiero meter la pata.
   No quiero meter la pata.
2. Nosotros los norteamericanos tenemos fama de ser muy maleducados.
   Nosotros los norteamericanos tenemos fama de ser muy maleducados.
3. ¿Puedes darme unos consejos muy generales?
   ¿Puedes darme unos consejos muy generales?
4. Sí. Nunca andes descalzo en la casa.
   Sí. Nunca andes descalzo en la casa.
5. Con paciencia y con cariño se vence todo.
   Con paciencia y con cariño se vence todo.

Escribir

1. Paco no quiere meter la pata.
   Paco no quiere meter la pata.
2. Dice que los norteamericanos tienen fama de ser muy maleducados.
   Dice que los norteamericanos tienen fama de ser muy maleducados.
3. Marcos le da unos consejos muy generales.
   Marcos le da unos consejos muy generales.
4. Dice que no deben andar descalzos en la casa.
   Dice que no deben andar descalzos en la casa.

ESCUCHAR

Episodio 1: Las preocupaciones de Paco

Marcos: Bueno, amigos. Aquí está su casa. Por ahora vamos a dejar el equipaje en el coche porque mi mamá tiene muchas ganas de conocerlos. Ya tengo todo planeado; más tarde buscamos una discoteca en donde puedan llegar a conocer la vida nocturna de nuestra bella ciudad.

Roberto: Buena idea, Marcos. Ya nos conoces bien, ¿eh?

Paco: Pues, por mi parte estoy muy nervioso. Esta va a ser la primera vez que estoy en la casa de una familia colombiana.

Marcos: No te preocupes, Paco. Aquí todos somos familia. Todo es muy informal.

Paco: Yo sé, pero no quiero meter la pata, y los norteamericanos tenemos fama de ser muy mal educados. ¿Qué hago para ser un buen invitado?

ESCUCHAR

Episodio 2: "¿Puedes darme unos consejos?"

Paco: ¿Puedes darme unos consejos muy generales, sólo para comenzar?

Marcos: Claro que sí. Primero, no le digas ni mamá ni Consuelo a mi mamá. Dile señora de Colón o doña Consuelo. Segundo, nunca andes descalzo en la casa. Tercero, no dejes tus cosas en el baño; después de bañarte o lavarte los dientes, por ejemplo, saca tu toalla y tus otras cosas y déjalas en tu pieza. Con esos tres consejos ya tienes todo lo que necesitas, por lo menos para comenzar.

Paco: Gracias. Me siento mucho mejor, pero todavía tengo un poco de miedo de conocer a tu mamá.

Marcos: Pues, ya le dije a ella que las costumbres son muy diferentes en los Estados Unidos. De nuevo, te digo que no estés tan nervioso. Con paciencia y con cariño se vence todo.

SEGUNDA ETAPA

ANTES DE LEER

Estudiar y practicar

los alrededores
colmado
contar con
la convivencia
disfrutar de
la fogata
el paisaje
el paseo
principiar

TERCERA ETAPA

ANTES DE ESCUCHAR Y ESCRIBIR

Estudiar y repetir

bueno...
el club campestre
el club de pesca
jugar al golf
el pase
pues...
regatear

Las actividades turísticas

Consuelo: Bueno, amigos. Cuéntenos todo.

Roberto: Bueno, señora. Primero que nada tengo que decirle que nos ha gustado muchísimo todo lo que hemos visto de su país. Estuvimos en Cali por un rato, y allí no hicimos más que conocer. Fuimos a la Universidad del Valle y les hicimos una presentación a los estudiantes de inglés. Allí conocimos a un ex-gobernador del estado, y él nos dio un pase al club campestre. Pudimos jugar al golf todas las tardes y después nadar, sin tener que pagar nada. Fue sensacional.

Paco: Pero creo que por mucho que nos gustó Cali, más nos gustó Cartagena, ¿verdad, Roberto?

Roberto: Creo que sí. Nos quedamos en el Hotel Bahía, en Boca Chica, y desde allí pudimos hacer todo. Fuimos una noche al Castillo de San Felipe y vimos el espectáculo de luz y sonido. Otra noche invitamos a dos muchachas y comimos en el Club de Pesca. Yo pedí langosta a la termidor, pero Paco pidió lomo, como siempre.

Paco: Pues, no molestes, Roberto. Ya sabes que odio los mariscos.

Consuelo: ¿Y visitaron el mercado cuando estaban en Cartagena?

Roberto: Sí, señora. A Paco le encanta ir de compras. Fuimos dos veces al mercado y aprendimos a regatear bastante bien. ¡Y menos mal! Porque Paco tiene una lista increíble de regalos que tiene que comprar.

Paco: Pues, sí, pero tú siempre insistes en acompañarme, porque a ti te gusta hablar con los vendedores.

Capítulo

[Instructor Tape]

PRIMERA ETAPA

ENTRADA "Tenemos una familia pequeña"

Doña Consuelo: Buenos días y bienvenidos.

Roberto y Paco: Gracias doña Consuelo. Es usted muy amable.

Paco: Es un placer. ¡Qué cuadro más interesante, señora!

Doña Consuelo: Sí, Paco, tienes razón. Estamos muy orgullosos de él. Un amigo de la familia nos lo pintó cuando mis hermanos y yo éramos muy jóvenes. Llegó a ser después un pintor muy conocido en Colombia. ¿Quieren saber un poco más de mi familia, ya que conocen a Marcos?

Roberto: Cómo no...

Paco: Claro que sí.

Roberto: Por supuesto.

Doña Consuelo: Nací en Bogotá y soy de una familia relativamente pequeña. Estos son mis padres que están jubilados y que, gracias a Dios, gozan de buena salud. Somos solamente cuatro hermanos, tres mujeres y un varón. Yo soy la menor. Mi hermano, Jorge, es el mayor. Es presidente de una compañía de importación aquí en Bogotá, pero viaja por todo el mundo. Es soltero. Nunca se casó. Y por eso, siempre invita a los sobrinos, a Marcos y a sus primos, a visitarlo. Marcos estuvo con él en París el año pasado. Qué suerte, ¿verdad?

Paco: Sí...

Roberto: Eso sí, ¡qué bueno!

Doña Consuelo:	Mi hermana mayor, Luz María, decidió ser monja y dedicar su vida a Dios y a la religión. Entró al convento cuando tenía dieciocho años. Ahora es enfermera y trabaja en una misión en las montañas del Perú. Mi otra hermana, Graciela, está casada y vive con su esposo y sus tres hijos en Cali. Los vemos muy a menudo. Graciela trabaja con niños. Es maestra de kinder.	Paco:	Pues, sí, pero a pesar de eso, subíamos por una escalera vieja e insegura para llegar al segundo piso. En el centro había un poste. El que se quedaba contaba hasta cien contra el poste, mientras los demás se escondían. Me tocó a mí contar. Cuando terminé de contar, comencé a buscarlos, retrocediendo lentamente y sin quitar los ojos del poste. Sin darme cuenta me caí por la escalera hasta el primer piso. Se me partieron el brazo izquierdo y también la clavícula. Perdí el conocimiento y mis hermanos tuvieron que llamar al médico, que afortunadamente, vivía en la casa vecina.

SEGUNDA ETAPA

ENTRADA   Un juego peligroso

Locutor: Escucha mientras Paco cuenta la historia de un accidente que ocurrió cuando era niño, y pon los acontecimientos en órden cronológico.

Doña Consuelo:	Bueno, Paco, me imagino que tu vida también ha tenido sus momentos. Cuéntame.
Paco:	Tiene usted razón, doña Consuelo. Cuando yo era niño, vivíamos en San Diego, en California. Yo siempre tenía dificultades en el colegio. Era muy travieso, y buscaba cualquier forma de molestar a mis hermanos y a mis padres. En ese entonces, San Diego era una ciudad más bien pequeña y no había mucho que hacer.
Roberto:	Cuéntales de la vez que jugabas a las escondidas con tus hermanos.
Paco:	¡Ah, sí! me acuerdo. Pues, es que nuestra casa era muy vieja, estilo victoriano. Detrás de la casa había un edificio que antes servía de establo y para guardar carruajes. En la parte de arriba había espacio para almacenar heno para los caballos. A menudo, los muchachos de la vecindad jugábamos a las escondidas allí en el segundo piso. Sólo se podía subir al segundo piso por una escalera, que estaba en un rincón.
Roberto:	Era peligroso para los niños, ¿no?

Doña Consuelo:	¡Qué mala suerte! ¿Qué pasó después?
Paco:	Pues, estuve con el brazo enyesado unas semanas. El día que me quitaron el yeso jugaba en el jardín con unos amiguitos y una niña me pegó con un palo, justo en el brazo izquierdo, que se me partió de nuevo.
Doña Consuelo:	¡Qué desgracia!

TERCERA ETAPA

ENTRADA   "Nunca me pasó nada por el estilo…"

Locutor: Escucha mientras Paco y Roberto hablan de la juventud de Roberto. Mientras escuchas, identifica dónde vivía Roberto y qué hacía para pasar el tiempo. Además, apunta dos actividades mencionadas por los jóvenes.

Roberto:	Pues, no puedo agregar nada muy interesante a esta conversación. A mí nunca me pasó nada por el estilo, Paco.
Paco:	Vaya… eso no lo creo. ¿Dónde vivías?
Roberto:	Vivía con mi familia en San Antonio, Texas, en un barrio que se llamaba Edgewood. Mi casa estaba cerca de una base de la Fuerza Aérea de los Estados Unidos. En mi barrio casi todos éramos mexicanoamericanos, y siempre jugábamos (al) fútbol y (al) béisbol

Paco: en un lote cerca del colegio. Yo era el único que tenía un bate para jugar (al) béisbol, así que mis amigos tenían que portarse bien conmigo o no los dejaba usarlo.

Paco: ¿Y eso es todo lo que hacías?

Roberto: Pues no. También había un río cerca de la casa en donde mis hermanos, mis amigos y yo pescábamos y a veces nadábamos. Yo creo que mi niñez fue muy tranquila.

Paco: Bueno dime, Roberto, ¿nunca tuviste problemas en el colegio?

Roberto: No. Yo siempre me llevaba bien con mis amigos, y mis padres me hacían estudiar mucho. Me gustaban todos mis profesores. Después de mudarnos a San Diego todo siguió igual.

Paco: Y, ¿seguiste jugando al fútbol?

Roberto: Pues, no. Fíjate que en la secundaria aprendí a bailar, y lo que más me divertía era ir a fiestas todos los fines de semana con mis amigos. Siempre hacíamos lo mismo, con el mismo grupo de amigos.

Paco: Parece que tu vida era más bien aburrida que tranquila. Tú y tus amigos, ¿no robaban los tapacubos de los autos? ¿No molestaban a sus profesores ni rompían ventanas en las casas abandonadas? Así nos divertíamos mucho mis amigos y yo.

Roberto: No, éramos todos muy conformistas. Nos parecía más fácil ser así.

Student Tape

PRIMERA ETAPA

EMPEZAR A ESCUCHAR

Repetir

los gemelos
mientras
junto
casi
lindo
orgulloso
el apagón
el susto
aprovechar
besar
prender
enojarse

Identificar

1. Aquí están los gemelos el día que nacieron.
   Aquí están los gemelos el día que nacieron.
2. Cuando eran niños, hacían todo juntos.
   Cuando eran niños, hacían todo juntos.
3. Tenían casi dos años cuando saqué esta foto.
   Tenían casi dos años cuando saqué esta foto.
4. ¡Qué lindos se ven aquí!
   ¡Qué lindos se ven aquí!
5. Marcos está muy orgulloso de sus hermanitos.
   Marcos está muy orgulloso de sus hermanitos.
6. Hubo un apagón. ¡Qué susto!
   Hubo un apagón. ¡Qué susto!

Escribir

1. Marcos está muy orgulloso de los gemelos.
   Marcos está muy orgulloso de los gemelos.
2. ¡Qué lindos están en esta foto!
   ¡Qué lindos están en esta foto!
3. El apagón duró solamente unos segundos.
   El apagón duró solamente unos segundos.
4. Marcos aprovechó la oscuridad para besar a Marina.
   Marcos aprovechó la oscuridad para besar a Marina.
5. El hermano de Marina se enojó.
   El hermano de Marina se enojó.

ESCUCHAR

Episodio 1: "Aquí están los gemelos"

Doña Consuelo: Déjenme presentarles a mis otros hijos mientras toman el chocolate. Aquí están los gemelos el día que nacieron. En aquel entonces, Marcos tenía sólo seis años.

Roberto: Usted tiene muchas fotos de ellos, ¿no?

Doña Consuelo: Claro, Roberto. Todas las fotos en este álbum son de ellos.

Paco: ¿Ah, sí? ¿Cómo se llaman?

Doña Consuelo: El varón se llama David y la niña se llama Isabel. Nacieron el 5 de noviembre de 1972. Ya van a ver que cuando eran niños hacían todo juntos.

Paco: Y, ¿cuántos años tenían cuando sacaron esta foto?

Doña Consuelo: Tenían casi dos añitos. Todos estábamos en Chía ese día, comiendo fresas con crema.

Roberto: ¡Qué lindos están! Pero Marcos, yo no sabía que tus hermanos eran gemelos. Tú sólo nos dijiste que tenías un hermano y una hermana.

Marcos: Imposible. Yo estoy muy orgulloso de mis hermanitos, y a todos les digo siempre que son gemelos. No pusiste atención cuando te lo dije.

Paco: Bueno, no peleen. Yo quiero ver más fotos.

ESCUCHAR

Episodio 2: El apagón

Paco: Yo quisiera ver más fotos.

Doña Consuelo: Pues, hay miles. Aquí estábamos preparándolos para la primera comunión. Y aquí estamos en la fiesta de los quince años de Isabelita.

Paco: Un día inolvidable, ¿no?

Doña Consuelo: Sí, por muchas razones. Y me acuerdo muy bien de ese día. La fiesta iba a comenzar a las nueve de la noche. Hacía frío y llovía mucho. Nadie quería salir de casa porque la noche estaba tan fea. Pero por fin dejó de llover, y todos llegaron al Hotel Tequendama. Todo iba muy bien, todos bailaban, tomaban y se reían cuando de pronto se fue la luz. ¡Qué susto! Pero afortunadamente el apagón duró sólo unos segundos, y pudimos seguir. ¿Te acuerdas, Marcos?

Marcos: Sí, mamá. Me acuerdo muy bien. Cuando ocurrió el apagón yo estaba bailando con Marina. Aproveché la oscuridad y la besé. Pronto se prendieron otra vez las luces. ¡Qué vergüenza! Nos vio su hermano y casi me mata.

SEGUNDA ETAPA

ANTES DE LEER

Estudiar y practicar

agitado
atardecer
el cordón
lograr
el recuerdo
sin embargo
soñar
las tinieblas

Capítulo 9

[Instructor Tape]

PRIMERA ETAPA

ENTRADA Se abre la Clínica Buena Vista

Locutor: Tenemos el gusto de informar al público sobre la apertura de la Clínica Buena Vista. La Clínica Buena Vista está ubicada en la calle Sol, número veinticinco, frente al Banco Nacional. Allí les ofrecemos los más importantes servicios médicos para usted y su familia. Servicios obstétricos y pediátricos, fisioterapia, un laboratorio clínico con el más moderno y eficaz equipo técnico, incluso servicio de radiografía. A la disposición también de nuestros pacientes ofrecemos un banco de sangre. Y en caso de emergencia, tiene usted la seguridad de nuestra atención permanente, las veinticuatro horas del día. La Clínica Buena Vista, en el número veinticinco de la Calle Sol. Para más información, llámenos al dos, setenta y seis, cuarenta y tres, ochenta y uno. Otra vez, nuestro número de teléfono es el dos, setenta y seis, cuarenta y tres, ochenta y uno.

SEGUNDA ETAPA

ENTRADA Tres nuevos médicos en la Clínica Buena Vista

Locutor: La Clínica Buena Vista tiene el gusto de informar a nuestro estimado público sobre los tres renombrados profesionales que colaborarán con nosotros. Y sobre los campos de especialización y las horas de consulta de los mismos. El doctor Mauricio Garcés, oftalmólogo, enfermedades y cirugía de los ojos, lentes de contacto. Consulta: lunes, miércoles, viernes, de las tres hasta las seis de la tarde, previa cita. La doctora Marta Martínez de Velasco, pediatra, enfermedades de niños. Consultas: todos los días, de las diez de la mañana a la una de la tarde. La doctora Ana María León, dermatóloga, enfermedades de la piel, alergia, tumores cutáneos. Consulta: los lunes y jueves de las dos hasta las cinco de la tarde. La Clínica Buena Vista, en el número veinticinco de la Calle Sol. Para más información o para hacer una cita, llámenos al dos, setenta y seis, cuarenta y tres, ochenta y uno. Dos, setenta y seis, cuarenta y tres, ochenta y uno.

TERCERA ETAPA

ENTRADA "¡Peligro!"

Locutor: Acabamos de recibir el siguiente informe del Ministerio de Salud. "Rogamos al público que preste especial atención a este anuncio porque se trata de un asunto de suma gravedad. Bajo ninguna condición deben consumirse ni ostras ni mejillones que vengan de las aguas del Golfo de Morrosquillo, ya que éstos tienen altos niveles de petróleo que resultan ser tóxicos a la persona que los ingiera. Se ha impuesto una prohibición contra la cosecha y venta de estos mariscos por un período de seis meses. Los síntomas de toxicidad incluyen mareo, fiebre, diarrea y dolores del estómago. Para evitar problemas asociados con estos productos contaminados, no se debe comprar ningún marisco que venga de la región mencionada, ni se deben pedir en los restaurantes los platos que contengan estos ingredientes. Si tiene cualquier síntoma de toxicidad, si está mareado, si tiene fiebre, si sufre dolores de estómago o diarrea, váyase inmediatamente al hospital. Gracias por su atención."

Student Tape

PRIMERA ETAPA

EMPEZAR A ESCUCHAR

Repetir

la fiebre
¡Esto es el colmo!
tomar el pelo
recetar
aliviar
el síntoma
la pastilla

Identificar

1. ¡Y para colmo, tengo una fiebre altísima!
   ¡Y para colmo, tengo una fiebre altísima!
2. No tenía ningún síntoma antes de acostarme.
   No tenía ningún síntoma antes de acostarme.
3. ¡Qué desgracia!
   ¡Qué desgracia!
4. Pensaba que mis amigos me estaban tomando el pelo.
   Pensaba que mis amigos me estaban tomando el pelo.
5. El médico me va a recetar unas pastillas.
   El médico me va a recetar unas pastillas.

Escribir

1. ¿Qué síntomas tienes?
   ¿Qué síntomas tienes?
2. ¡Tengo una fiebre altísima!
   ¡Tengo una fiebre altísima!
3. El médico me va a recetar algo.
   El médico me va a recetar algo.
4. ¡Qué desgracia!
   ¡Qué desgracia!

ESCUCHAR

Episodio 1: "¿Qué te pasa, Susana?"

Elena: Despiértate, Susana, que ya vamos a correr.
Susana: ¡Ay! No puedo. No dormí nada.

Elena: ¿Qué te pasa? ¿Te sientes mal?

Susana: Sí. ¡Me duele mucho el estómago! Tengo unos dolores horribles, una fiebre altísima y, para colmo, desde las cinco y treinta de la mañana estoy en el baño vomitando y con diarrea. En casa mis amigos me dijeron que no tomara el agua cuando estuviera aquí en los Estados Unidos, y yo pensaba que me estaban tomando el pelo. Pero ahora...

Elena: ¡Vaya! Tu condición no tiene nada que ver con el agua. ¿Cuál será la causa de esta enfermedad? ¿Algo que comiste anoche?

Susana: Fíjate que no. ¿No te acuerdas de que anoche llegué tan cansada del viaje, que sólo tomé un vaso de agua mineral antes de acostarme?

ESCUCHAR

EPISODIO 2: "¿Y si me muero antes de las 9:00?"

Susana: Ay, Elena, no sé qué hacer. ¡Me siento tan mal!

Elena: Pues, ahora tan pronto como sean las nueve voy a llamar al médico. Es posible que te pueda recetar algo que te alivie el dolor y los otros síntomas que tienes.

Susana: ¿Y si me muero antes de las nueve?

Elena: No te preocupes. Por ahora tómate dos pastillas de Mejoral y hasta que te vea el médico no tomes nada más que té, agua mineral o refrescos.

Susana: Está bien. ¿Me llamas tú al médico, por favor? ¡Ay qué desgracia!

SEGUNDA ETAPA

ANTES DE LEER

Estudiar y practicar

la alberca
apenas
el clavado
deslizarse
empaparse
nocivo
nutrir

TERCERA ETAPA

ANTES DE LEER Y ESCRIBIR

Estudiar y practicar

el agradecimiento
el aparato
la barrera
el cupón
la intervención quirúrgica
merecer
poner al corriente
el tumor cerebral

Capítulo 10

PRIMERA ETAPA

ENTRADA Invitación a una recepción

Lorenzo: Diga...

Teresa: Hola, Lorenzo. Te habla Teresa.

Lorenzo: Hola, Teresa, ¿cómo estás?

Teresa: Muy bien, ¿y tú? Te llamo porque voy a dar una fiesta el viernes, dieciséis de septiembre. ¿Quieres venir?

Lorenzo: ¡Magnífico! Claro que sí. ¿Cuál es el motivo de la fiesta?

Teresa: Vamos a celebrar la independencia de México.

Lorenzo: ¡Ah, qué bien! ¿Dónde es la fiesta?

Teresa: La fiesta es en el salón de mi residencia. ¿Puedes traer vino?

Lorenzo: ¡Claro! Con mucho gusto. Ah, Teresa, ¿A qué hora es la fiesta?

Teresa: A las nueve, ¿te parece?

Lorenzo: ¡Magnífico! Hasta el viernes, Teresa.

Teresa: Bueno, nos vemos...

Profesora: Diga...

Teresa: Buenas tardes, Profesora Jiménez, habla Teresa.

Profesora: ¡Hola, Teresa! Me alegro de oírte. ¿Cómo estás?

Teresa: Muy bien, gracias. Me gustaría invitarla para celebrar la independencia de México, el dieciséis de septiembre. La fiesta es en el salón de mi residencia. ¿Puede traer cintas de música bailable?

Profesora: El dieciséis, ¿qué día es?

Teresa: Es viernes.

Profesora: ¡Ay! cuánto lo siento, Teresa. Pero el viernes no voy a estar aquí. Tengo que dar una conferencia en Nueva York y voy a estar fuera todo el fin de semana.

Teresa: ¡Qué lástima, profesora! La vamos a extrañar.

Profesora: ¡Gracias por invitarme!

Teresa: Bueno, hasta luego.

Profesora: Adiós.

SEGUNDA ETAPA

ENTRADA "¡Qué fiesta más divertida!"

María Luisa: ¡Hola, Carlos! ¿Cómo te va?

Carlos: ¡Hola, María Luisa! ¿Cómo estás? ¿Dónde has estado todo este tiempo?

María Luisa: Ah... Pues, déjame que te cuente lo de la fiesta este fin de semana. Fue la fiesta de despedida para un grupo de estudiantes internacionales.

Carlos: Ah, sí. Los que se iban a graduar dentro de unas semanas.

María Luisa: Sí, esa misma.

Carlos: Yo quería ir, pero no pude.

María Luisa: Ah...

Carlos: ¿Quiénes fueron? ¿Fue alguien quien yo conozco?

María Luisa: Sí. Fue en el club internacional y todos los invitados eran socios.

Carlos: ¿Es verdad que todos tenían que llevar un traje regional de su país?

María Luisa: Sí, la anfitriona, que es de la Argentina, estaba vestida de gaucho.

Carlos: ¡Qué interesante! ¿Y lo pasaron bien?

María Luisa: Uy... La fiesta empezó por la tarde y nadamos en la alberca. Luego cantamos unas sevillanas y hasta se bailó el tango. Ya de noche, se contaron unos chistes...

Carlos: ¡Qué lástima no haber ido!

TERCERA ETAPA

ENTRADA "Hola, mami..."

Mamá: Dígame...

Hijo: ¡Hola, mami! ¿Cómo estás? ¿Me oyes bien?

Mamá: Sí, hijo, suenas como si estuvieras aquí. ¡Qué alegría! ¿Cómo estás?

Hijo: Estoy bien. Estoy bien, mami.

Mamá: ¿Pero estás resfriado?

Hijo: Bueno, sí... Tuve un resfriado hace dos días. No te preocupes, ¿eh?

Mamá: ¿Qué hace mucho frío todavía?

Hijo: Sí, todavía hace mucho frío y llueve mucho, mucho.

Mamá: Dime, ¿has conocido a mucha gente?

Hijo: Sí, he conocido sobre todo a amigos de Jorge. Son todos muy simpáticos.

Mamá: ¿Qué tal Jack?

Hijo: Ah, ¡Jack es comiquísimo! Y su hermano gemelo es alegre, alegre.

Mamá: Y chicas, ¿has conocido a algunas chicas?

Hijo: Eh... Sí, especialmente Susan. Es la amiga de Jack. Es muy viva y me lleva a conocer a muchos lugares.

Mamá: Susan es norteamericana, claro.

Hijo: Sí, sí, sí. Pero me llevo... Nos caemos muy bien. Me llevo muy bien con ella. No es como el estereotipo que tenía de las mujeres de los Estados Unidos. Tú sabes, ¿no?

Mamá: Sí, sí, es verdad eso del estereotipo. Y, ¿qué tal la comida?

Hijo: ¿La comida? Uu... Bueno, creo que no es mala pero la carne no se compara con la de la Argentina. Echo de menos los grandes bifes que me hacías cuando estaba en casa.

Mamá:	Bueno, hijo, pero come. Aunque no te guste, debes alimentarte...
Hijo:	Pero es difícil, mamá. La gente come aquí muy rápidamente. Se van en seguida a trabajar o a ver la televisión. No se sientan a la mesa a conversar como nosotros.
Mamá:	Sí, sí, sí... Y, ¿cómo te va con el inglés?
Hijo:	Sí... Si supieras, me defiendo bastante bien. Pero hablan muy rápido y no comprendo muchas veces.
Mamá:	¿Y tu hermano te ayuda?
Hijo:	Sí, de vez en cuando. Pero sabes, ya aquí en este país, se habla mucho español. Susan lo habla bastante bien.
Mamá:	¿Sabes ya cuando vuelves a Buenos Aires?
Hijo:	Para finales de mes. Vuelvo el día veinticinco. ¿Está bien?
Mamá:	Bueno, cuando quieras. Nos darás una gran alegría.
Hijo:	Bueno, sí... Adiós, mamá... Hasta pronto, ¿eh?
Mamá:	Bueno, ¡cuídate!
Hijo:	¡Los extraño!
Mamá:	Adiós...

> Student Tape

PRIMERA ETAPA

EMPEZAR A ESCUCHAR

Repetir

tener el gusto de...
se llevará a cabo...
debido a
el compromiso
previo
si me hiciera el favor de...
saludar

Identificar

1. Los señores Suárez tienen el gusto de invitarlos a una fiesta.
   Los señores Suárez tienen el gusto de invitarlos a una fiesta.
2. La fiesta se llevará a cabo el doce de este mes.
   La fiesta se llevará a cabo el doce de este mes.
3. Debido a un compromiso previo, Paco no puede asistir.
   Debido a un compromiso previo, Paco no puede asistir.
4. Si me hiciera el favor de saludar a los estudiantes de mi parte.
   Si me hiciera el favor de saludar a los estudiantes de mi parte.
5. Se lo agradecería mucho.
   Se lo agradecería mucho.

Escribir

1. Tenemos el gusto de invitarlos a una fiesta.
   Tenemos el gusto de invitarlos a una fiesta.
2. La fiesta se llevará a cabo el doce de este mes.
   La fiesta se llevará a cabo el doce de este mes.
3. Debido a un compromiso previo, Paco no puede asistir.
   Debido a un compromiso previo, Paco no puede asistir.
4. Si me hiciera el favor de saludarlos de mi parte.
   Si me hiciera el favor de saludarlos de mi parte.
5. Se lo agradecería mucho.
   Se lo agradecería mucho.

ESCUCHAR

Episodio 1: "¿Qué invitación? ¿A qué?"

Roberto:	¿Sí? Habla Roberto Hernández.
Paco:	Oye, Roberto, ¿qué tal? Soy Paco. Acabamos de recibir una invitación...
Roberto:	¿Una invitación? ¿De quién? ¿A qué?
Paco:	Pues, no sé exactamente... Es de la profesora Suárez, y dice que es para una fiesta norteña. ¿Qué es eso?
Roberto:	Mira, dime exactamente lo que dice.
Paco:	Te la leo. Dice "Fiesta norteña. Con motivo del fin del año escolar, la Profesora Filomena Suárez y su esposo, el profesor Antonio Suárez, tienen el gusto de invitarlos a una fiesta norteña, que se llevará a cabo el doce de este mes, a las ocho de la noche, en el Salón de Profesores."

Roberto: Pues, tampoco entiendo qué significa "fiesta norteña", pero parece que sólo es una fiestecita para celebrar la llegada del fin del semestre.

Paco: Así parece. Pues, mira, tenemos que responder diciéndoles que sí o que no.

Roberto: Bueno. Pienso volver dentro de poco, y luego lo hacemos.

SEGUNDA ETAPA

ANTES DE LEER

Estudiar y practicar

denotar
estar al tanto de
evitar
la pareja
el rato
tener en cuenta

TERCERA ETAPA

ANTES DE LEER Y ESCRIBIR

Estudiar y practicar

el aguafiestas
darle las gracias a alguien
defenderse
en cuanto a
extrañar
impedir
Le ruego que...

Capítulo 11

Instructor Tape

PRIMERA ETAPA

ENTRADA "Dime lo que debo hacer..."

María Cristina: Diga...

Rita: ¿Aló? ¿María Cristina?

María Cristina: Sí, soy yo.

Rita: Habla Rita. Te llamo para pedirte un consejo. ¿Te acuerdas de aquellos dos chicos que conocimos en la fiesta de Marta, Enrique y Mariano?

María Cristina: Sí, claro... Aunque vagamente.

Rita: Pues, después de la fiesta, me han llamado los dos para invitarme a salir y no sé qué hacer.

María Cristina: ¿Enrique es el joven que estudia en la universidad...?

Rita: No, Enrique tiene veintiocho años y es ingeniero.

María Cristina: Y ¿a qué te ha invitado Enrique?

Rita: Me ha invitado a ver una película. Mariano me ha invitado a comer en un restaurante y a bailar. Ay, no sé... Es que son muy diferentes.

María Cristina: Diferentes... ¿Cómo?

Rita: Bueno, Enrique es extrovertido. Tiene un gran sentido del humor y es un chico muy interesante.

María Cristina: Y Mariano, ¿cómo es Mariano?

Rita: Bueno, Mariano tiene veinte años. Es más bien introvertido. A veces un poco aburrido, pero le gusta mucho bailar, y le encantan las películas norteamericanas.

María Cristina: Bueno, conociéndote como te conozco, creo que lo pasarás mejor con Enrique.

Rita: ¡Ay... sí! Gracias, María Cristina, por sacarme de la duda. Adiós.

María Cristina: ¡Ánimo, eh! Diviértete mucho con Enrique.

SEGUNDA ETAPA

ENTRADA ¡Aprenda por correo!

Julio: Buenas tardes, profesora. Soy Julio Ramos Arias. ¿Recuerda? Tengo una cita con usted. ¿Puedo interrumpirla?

Profesora: Sí, sí, cómo no. Buenas. Pase usted. ¿En qué puedo servirle? Y, ¿cómo van estos primeros días en la universidad?

Julio: ¡Ah! bastante bien. Bastante bien. Un poco nervioso todavía, ¿sabe? Pero, tengo

	problemas con el inglés. Por eso vine. ¿Qué me aconseja usted para mejorar?
Profesora:	Um… Fíjese, hay dos posibilidades. Primero, existe un curso intensivo. Y luego, hay uno por correspondencia. ¿Cuál le conviene mejor?
Julio:	¿Un curso intensivo? Tengo… Tengo… cuatro cursos ya. Yo creo que no. Quizás el de… el curso por correspondencia. Dígame, ¿qué ventajas tiene ese curso?
Profesora:	Bueno, la ventaja del curso por correspondencia es que incluye cassettes de pronunciación y se puede estudiar en casa.
Julio:	¿Y se aprende escuchando solamente?
Profesora:	Sí, sí… porque hay un enfoque en el uso práctico del idioma oído y leído.
Julio:	Ah, pero a mí me aburre sólo escuchar.
Profesora:	Bueno, mire, es que incluye también vocabularios ilustrados y cassettes de video.
Julio:	¡Ah, sí, sí! Eso es mejor. ¿Y hay alguna desventaja?
Profesora:	Éste… Que yo vea, no hay oportunidad de practicar con otros estudiantes. No se conoce al profesor y no pone énfasis en hablar espontáneamente.
Julio:	Y, ¿a quién le entrego las lecciones?
Profesora:	Ah, pues… Tiene que entregar todas las lecciones por correo.
Julio:	Y, ¿cómo se determina la nota?
Profesora:	La nota está determinada por el examen final, ¿eh?
Julio:	¡Ah! bien. Eso me parece bueno. Entonces, creo que voy a considerar esta posibilidad. Le aviso mañana para que me dé la dirección a dónde escribir, ¿bien?
Profesora:	Muy bien. Yo estaré aquí por la tarde.
Julio:	Bueno. Muchas gracias, profesora. Hasta mañana.
Profesora:	Muy bien, hasta luego.
Julio:	Adiós.

TERCERA ETAPA

ENTRADA "¡Qué vida más cruel!"

Roberto:	¡Ay! ¡Qué vida más cruel!
Paco:	¿Qué pasa, hombre?
Roberto:	Hombre, no sé lo que voy a hacer. Me siento tan solo, sin mi Carmencita.
Paco:	¡Ay! Carmencita. Mira, tenemos que pagar la cuenta de teléfono, ¿sí?
Roberto:	¡Ay! Paco, eso también…
Paco:	Sí, por todas las llamadas a Colombia.
Roberto:	Pero, no sé lo que voy a hacer, Paco. Es que no tengo dinero. No tengo ni un centavo, hombre.
Paco:	Y, ¿para tus libros?
Roberto:	Para mis libros… No tengo para los libros, no tengo para los cursos. ¡Qué no tengo dinero! ¡No tengo ni un centavo! No sé lo que voy a hacer. Estoy desesperado.
Paco:	Pues, mira… Tenemos que pagar la cuenta. Si no, nos van a desconectar. Y además, el alquiler, lo tenemos que pagar la semana próxima.
Roberto:	Pues, mira… No sé lo que voy a hacer. Déjame en paz, Paco. Me voy a encerrar en el cuarto y no voy a salir de allí por toda una semana.
Paco:	Hombre, qué mal andas, ¿eh?
Roberto:	¡Ay! ¡Qué desesperado estoy! ¡Qué solo me encuentro!

Student Tape

PRIMERA ETAPA

EMPEZAR A ESCUCHAR

Repetir
el asunto
hacer bromas

matricularse
copiar
hacer trampa
fracasar
echar
la culpa
la incertidumbre
la mentira piadosa

Identificar

1. Necesito un consejo sobre un asunto bastante serio.
   Necesito un consejo sobre un asunto bastante serio.
2. No hagas bromas. Hablo muy en serio.
   No hagas bromas. Hablo muy en serio.
3. Un estudiante nuevo acaba de matricularse en la clase.
   Un estudiante nuevo acaba de matricularse en la clase.
4. Entró el profesor y nos dijo que entregáramos las tareas.
   Entró el profesor y nos dijo que entregáramos las tareas.
5. Temo que el profesor vaya a creer que hacía trampa.
   Temo que el profesor vaya a creer que hacía trampa.
6. No quiero que el profesor lo eche de la clase.
   No quiero que el profesor lo eche de la clase.
7. Pero si digo la verdad, tendré la culpa de su fracaso.
   Pero si digo la verdad, tendré la culpa de su fracaso.

Escribir

1. Roberto necesita un consejo sobre un asunto bastante serio.
   Roberto necesita un consejo sobre un asunto bastante serio.
2. Hablo muy en serio.
   Hablo muy en serio.
3. Un estudiante nuevo acaba de matricularse en la clase.
   Un estudiante nuevo acaba de matricularse en la clase.
4. Roberto no hacía trampa.
   Roberto no hacía trampa.
5. Si el otro fracasa, tendrá que irse de la universidad.
   Si el otro fracasa, tendrá que irse de la universidad.

ESCUCHAR

Episodio 1: Un asunto bastante serio

Marcos: Oye, César. Necesito un consejo sobre un asunto bastante serio.

César: Pues claro, Marcos. Estoy a tus órdenes. ¿En qué puedo servirte?

Marcos: No hagas bromas. Hablo muy en serio. Tiene que ver con decir mentiras o decir la verdad.

César: Pues, ¿cuál es el problema? Claro que siempre debes decir la verdad.

Marcos: Generalmente, estoy de acuerdo, pero en este caso no estoy tan seguro.

César: Bueno. Cuéntame más y después hablamos.

ESCUCHAR

Episodio 2: El dilema de Marcos

Marcos: Todo empezó ayer cuando entré en la clase de matemáticas y me senté al lado de un estudiante que acababa de matricularse en la clase. Me pidió la tarea, y pensé que él solamente quería saber qué problemas habíamos tenido que preparar. Unos minutos después, me di cuenta de que los estaba copiando, y en ese momento entró el profesor y nos dijo que entregáramos las tareas. Así que él y yo le entregamos trabajos idénticos, y me temo que el profesor crea que yo hacía trampa, cuando en realidad jamás intenté hacerlo.

César: Pues, ¿no puedes decírselo al profesor?

Marcos: Sí, pero más tarde el nuevo estudiante me confesó que si no salía bien en ese curso, iba a fracasar y tendría que irse de la universidad. Si ahora yo hablo con el profesor y le digo que el otro copió mi trabajo, sé que lo va a echar de la clase, y tendré yo la culpa de su fracaso.

César: Pues entonces, sí que estás en un dilema. Por un lado, no quieres que el profesor crea que hiciste trampa. Pero por el otro, no quieres que sufra el otro estudiante. Me alegro de que hayas consultado conmigo, pero no sé qué decirte, de verdad.

SEGUNDA ETAPA

ANTES DE LEER

Estudiar y practicar
alimentar
burlón
crecer
chismear
destacarse
detener
enterarse (de)
el novio
parar

TERCERA ETAPA

ANTES DE LEER Y ESCRIBIR

Estudiar y practicar
la angustia
caleño
el comportamiento
encaprichado
espantoso
lo antes posible
medio muerto
la ojeras
resultar
últimamente

Capítulo

| Instructor Tape |

PRIMERA ETAPA

ENTRADA "¡Ay de mí!"

Ernestina: ¿Aló?
Graciela: Hola, Ernestina. Soy Graciela. ¿Cómo te va?
Ernestina: Bien, bien. Pero tengo mucho trabajo. Y tú, ¿qué tal?
Graciela: Pues, más o menos bien. Te llamé porque necesito consejos, eh? Salí con Jorge anoche y... no sé...
Ernestina: Ah, sí ¿con Jorge?
Graciela: Sí. Pasó a buscarme con Elena y Mario.
Ernestina: ¡Ah! ¿Adónde fueron?
Graciela: Dimos una vuelta y después a un restaurante. Luego, ellos se fueron y Jorge y yo fuimos al cine y a tomar una copa.
Ernestina: ¿Y después de la copa?
Graciela: Charlamos bastante rato y llegamos a casa tardísimo.
Ernestina: Bueno, todo parece muy bien. ¿Cuál es el problema entonces?
Graciela: Ay... Resulta que Jorge se va a los Estados Unidos a continuar sus estudios. Y quiere que yo vaya con él.
Ernestina: Estupendo, ¿no?
Graciela: No... No cuando se lo conté a mis padres. Se opusieron rotundamente.
Ernestina: ¡Qué horror!
Graciela: Dicen que para irme con él, tenemos que casarnos.
Ernestina: ¡Qué problema! ¿Y por qué no te casas? Jorge es un buen partido.
Graciela: Ah, sí, ¡claro! Pero yo no estoy segura de que me quiero casar todavía.
Ernestina: ¡Qué lástima! Algún día te arrepentirás.
Graciela: ¡Qué desgracia! ¿Qué voy a hacer?

SEGUNDA ETAPA

ENTRADA Un encuentro feliz

Julia: Dígame. ¿Con quién quiere hablar?
Pilar: Con Julia, por favor.
Julia: Soy yo.
Pilar: Ah, Julia. Habla Pilar. Te llamé anoche y no estabas en casa. ¿Adónde fuiste?
Julia: Es que anoche tenía una cita con Javier Vargas.
Pilar: ¿Javier Vargas? ¿El colombiano guapísimo?
Julia: Sí, el mismo. Fíjate que ahora vive en Miami.
Pilar: Y, ¿por qué está en Miami?
Julia: Porque como es abogado, consiguió un buen empleo en una firma norteamericana.
Pilar: Cuéntame. ¿Te divertiste mucho?

Julia: Ay, sí... Vino a buscarme a las ocho. Y me trajo un precioso ramillete de flores. Fuimos a comer a un restaurante colombiano.

Pilar: ¿El Chibcha?

Julia: Precisamente... Comimos muy bien. Y después fuimos a ver un espectáculo y a bailar. ¡Volvimos a casa a las tres de la mañana!

Pilar: Oye, chica... ¡Qué suerte tienes! Todas quisiéramos salir con él. Ya sé que es muy guapo pero no sé nada más de él. Dime, ¿cómo es?

Julia: Pues, es un poquito tímido, pero muy simpático. Y baila muy bien.

Pilar: Mira, ¿por qué no almorzamos juntas mañana y me cuentas más detalles?

Julia: ¡Estupenda idea! Nos vemos en la cafetería a la hora de siempre. Hasta mañana.

Pilar: Hasta mañana.

TERCERA ETAPA

ENTRADA "¡Que te vaya bien!"

M1: Lucía, ¿qué te parece esta fiesta que nos han dado?

Lucía: ¡Estupenda, chico!

M1: Yo la estoy gozando, pero mucho. Es curioso. Aquí, a nosotros, a los estudiantes extranjeros, nos han tratado como si estuviéramos en casa.

Lucía: La verdad es que yo siempre me he sentido en casa. La he pasado muy bien aquí.

M1: Sí, el trato siempre ha sido, pero muy amable. Y esta fiesta ya es el colmo. ¡Esto es lo mejorcito!

Lucía: La vamos a pasar muy, muy bien.

M1: Estoy de acuerdo. Creo que sí.

M2: Hola, ¿qué tal, Arturo?

Arturo: Hola.

M2: ¿Qué piensas hacer este verano, hombre?

Arturo: Ah, pues, me voy a Buenos Aires, ¿sabes? Tengo una hermana que vive allí.

M2: ¿Y qué hace en Buenos Aires ella?

Arturo: Está casada con un argentino. ¿Sabes que viví con una familia encantadora? Estaban tan preocupados con mi viaje que me pidieron que los llamara tan pronto llegara a Buenos Aires.

M2: Ah... Tuviste suerte, eh. Qué bien.

Beatriz: Y tú, Rodrigo... ¿Qué piensas hacer?

Rodrigo: Me voy a esquiar a Chile. Me encanta esquiar. Y pienso invitar a Celso y a Esteban que son aficionados al esquí.

Beatriz: Oye, ¿y dónde aprendiste a esquiar?

Rodrigo: Oh... Pues todo mi vida.

Beatriz: Ah... ¡Qué barbaridad!

Lucía: Beatriz, ¿qué planes tienes para el verano?

Beatriz: Yo voy a pasar las vacaciones en San Andrés y Providencia. Voy a la playa a broncearme y leer dos o tres fotonovelas.

Rodrigo: Oye, pero Beatriz... Hace frío, ¿no?

Beatriz: Oye, pero San Andrés y Providencia están en el Caribe...

Rodrigo: Ah... Ah... Sí. Está bien. Sí, sí, te entiendo ahora.

Student Tape

PRIMERA ETAPA

EMPEZAR A ESCUCHAR

Repetir

a pesar de
cargar
contar con
estar enamorado
mover palancas
el salario

Identificar

1. Cuenta con que te quiero más que nunca.
   Cuenta con que te quiero más que nunca.
2. A pesar de mis esfuerzos, sólo pude sacar una C.
   A pesar de mis esfuerzos, sólo pude sacar una C.
3. Mi papá tiene palanca en la compañía.
   Mi papá tiene palanca en la compañía.
4. Voy a cargar y descargar camiones de carga.
   Voy a cargar y descargar camiones de carga.

5. Es un trabajo pesado, pero el salario es excelente.
   Es un trabajo pesado, pero el salario es excelente.
6. Mis padres no creen que estemos de verdad enamorados.
   Mis padres no creen que estemos de verdad enamorados.

Escribir

1. Roberto quiere más que nunca a Carmencita.
   Roberto quiere más que nunca a Carmencita.
2. A pesar de mis esfuerzos, sólo saqué una C.
   A pesar de mis esfuerzos, sólo saqué una C.
3. Es un trabajo pesado, pero el salario es excelente.
   Es un trabajo pesado, pero el salario es excelente.
4. Va a cargar y descargar camiones de carga.
   Va a cargar y descargar camiones de carga.
5. Mis padres no creen que estemos de verdad enamorados.
   Mis padres no creen que estemos de verdad enamorados.

SEGUNDA ETAPA

ANTES DE LEER

Estudiar y practicar

el apoyo
atraer
insoportable
madurar
padecer
superar

TERCERA ETAPA

ANTES DE LEER Y ESCRIBIR

Estudiar y practicar

la acciones
estorbar
el familiar
justo
las mercaderías
perjudicar
el presupuesto
el principio
provechoso

ENTRADAS

EL ESPAÑOL POR ETAPAS

INSTRUCTOR'S ANNOTATED EDITION

ENTRADAS

EL ESPAÑOL POR ETAPAS

SECOND EDITION

Theodore V. Higgs
San Diego State University

Judith E. Liskin-Gasparro
Middlebury College

Frank W. Medley, Jr.
University of South Carolina

Heinle & Heinle Publishers
A Division of Wadsworth, Inc.
Boston, Massachusetts 02116 USA

The publication of the second edition of *Entradas* was directed by the members of the Heinle & Heinle College Spanish and Italian Publishing Team:

Carlos Davis, *Editorial Director*
Patrice Titterington, *Production Editor*
Cheryl Carlson, *Marketing Manager*

Also participating in the publication of this program were:

Publisher: Stanley J. Galek
Assistant Editor: Kimberly Etheridge
Editorial Production Manager: Elizabeth Holthaus
Manufacturing Coordinator: Jerry Christopher
Project Manager: Phyllis Larimore
Text Design and Layout: Carol H. Rose
Cover Art: Susan Johnson
Cover Design: Jean Hammond
Illustrator: Diane Bigda
Maps: Deborah Perugi

Copyright © 1993 by Heinle & Heinle Publishers, Inc.
All rights reserved. No part of this publication may be reproduced or transmitted in any form or by any means, electronic, or mechanical, including photocopy, recording, or any information storage and retrieval system, without permission in writing from the publisher.

Manufactured in the United States of America

ISBN 0-8384-2535-6 (Instructor's Annotated Edition)

10 9 8 7 6 5 4 3 2 1

Heinle & Heinle Publishers is a division of Wadsworth, Inc.

INTRODUCTION

Entradas, second edition, is a completely redesigned program intended to develop functional ability in oral and written Spanish during the first year of college-level language study. These materials are designed to help students communicate simply but effectively in Spanish. The program helps students develop basic speaking, listening, reading, and writing skills through high-frequency language activities.

Entradas, second edition, represents a milestone in Spanish instruction at the introductory level. Among the benefits the program offers students are

- extensive amounts of comprehensible input, both listening and reading

- a complete listening program for use at home that guides students through structured prelistening activities, listening, and postlistening exercises

- extensive authentic reading selections and related activities for in- and out-of-class use located in the textbook, the workbook, and the teacher's resource materials

- a systematic program for developing reading and writing strategies that proceeds throughout the textbook

- emphasis on everyday, high-frequency situations paired with realistic linguistic tasks for beginning language learners

- division of chapters into manageable lessons called *etapas;* each *etapa* represents a complete cycle of skill-getting practice evolving into meaningful, practical skill-using exercises and activities

- functional vocabulary that emphasizes the use of high-frequency phrases (expressions such as *me gusta* and *no te preocupes*) to enable students to begin speaking right away

- frequent recycling of vocabulary, expressions, and grammar for a built-in review across chapters

- a clear distinction between what students should do at home and what they do in the classroom for best use of valuable class time

- grammar sequencing driven by the communicative functions that serve as the organizing principles of the text; structures are immediately usable when performing chapter tasks

PHILOSOPHY AND APPROACH

The *Entradas* program was inspired by the authors' experience in assessing functional use of language and in designing programs that develop the ability to use language in meaningful contexts. In addition, extensive documents and suggestions made over the years by users of the first edition of *Entradas* have been systematically incorporated into the second edition.

Several principles underlie the content and organization of the new edition of *Entradas*. First, students acquire skills that they practice, whether receptive or productive. For students to be able to use Spanish successfully, they must have opportunities to practice the language in the classroom and at home. Receptive skills can and should progress at a more rapid pace than productive skills. Each *etapa* of each chapter begins with listening segments, interspersed with prelistening and postlistening activities. This focus on receptive skills exposes students to useful language without pressuring them to respond at the same level. It also provides them with an expanded vocabulary when they are still expressing themselves at a simpler level in speaking and writing.

The use of authentic texts for reading activities goes hand-in-hand with the emphasis on receptive skills. Two types of texts are used in the second edition of *Entradas:*

- written and spoken materials produced by native speakers for native speakers, not aimed at an audience of language learners
- written and spoken materials produced for language learners, but with a minimum of unnatural grammatical and lexical constraints, so that they are natural-sounding to native speakers of Spanish

Spoken passages were created by native speakers and were chosen for their appropriateness and appeal to university undergraduates. The passages contain redundancy, repetition, discourse indicators, cognates, and other features that facilitate global comprehension. The tasks the authors have designed take into account real-life users of Spanish and also the linguistic and communicative capabilities of learners.

In order for students' productive skills to develop, they must express their own meanings as early as possible and have ample opportunity to practice language creatively. Knowledge of grammar allows students to move from controlled practice of language forms to open-ended activities. A variety of activities call for work in pairs or small groups to complete communicative tasks, sharpening the focus on using language for communication and giving students the tools they need to become successful communicators.

Setting realistic goals for students is an essential component of language instruction. According to the descriptions of proficiency levels in the 1986 ACTFL Proficiency Guidelines, it is reasonable to expect that many students who use the *Entradas,* second edition, program will reach the Intermediate Low or Intermediate Mid Level of proficiency in speaking and writing, and Intermediate High or Advanced Level in listening comprehension by the end of the full-year course. Students are not expected to achieve full control of structures beyond the Intermediate Level. Advanced structures are presented for receptive and partial productive control, providing a basis for further study of Spanish.

COMPONENTS

The *Entradas,* second edition, package has two types of materials: those for the student and those for the instructor. In addition to the student text and the Instructor's Annotated Edition, this mutually supporting network of learning components includes the following.

Student Tape One 60-minute tape packaged with the student textbook. The tape contains a complete listening program for student use outside of the classroom. (For more information, see Chapter Organization.)

Instructor Tape This is intended for optional in-class use and contains a short semi-scripted listening selection that introduces the theme of each *etapa*. Corresponding comprehension exercises are in the text. The *Entradas* on the instructor tape are also found in the laboratory tape program for student reference.

Student Workbook/Laboratory Manual The manual is divided into twelve chapters, each reflecting the functions, contexts, and language of the student text. Each workbook chapter has three sections. The reading section contains authentic materials. Students can complete this section at any time while they are working on the corresponding chapter in the textbook. The writing section is composed of grammar exercises and writing tasks that students are likely to encounter in real life. This section is organized by *etapa* so that assignments can be made as students progress through the corresponding *etapas* of the textbook. The listening section is based on the Laboratory Tape Program that integrates materials from all three *etapas*. Students are expected to work on the listening section of the Workbook/Laboratory Manual as they approach the end of a chapter, because these tasks are the most challenging of the three contained in the workbook.

Laboratory Tape Program This program accompanies the Workbook/Laboratory Manual, and contains the listening segments of the manual. It also contains preliminary practice in pronunciation and intonation. The Laboratory Tapescript also includes the workbook answer key.

Testing Program This program includes the following components: two quizzes and one cumulative test per chapter; answer keys with auditory comprehension scripts; guidelines on oral testing.

***Mosaico cultural* Video Program and Video Guide** A 120-minute program, this video was filmed in five different Spanish-speaking countries, as well as in Hispanic cities in the United States. It consists of twelve ten-minute programs. Each program presents a different cultural theme that promotes cross-cultural comparisons. Each recycles and practices the vocabulary and language functions presented in the text. The video guide contains complete tapescripts and pre- and postviewing student activities for each program.

Atajo: **Writing Assistant for Spanish**   This is a software package that provides students with special tools to help them through the beginning stages of writing in Spanish. It includes a bilingual dictionary, a verb conjugator, an on-line grammar reference feature, an index to functional phrases, a thematic dictionary, an on-line word processor, and a tracking program that helps instructors see how an individual student approaches the writing process. It is available for networks, individual workstations, and for purchase by students.

CHAPTER ORGANIZATION

The student textbook, *Entradas,* second edition, consists of an introductory chapter and twelve full-length chapters. The preliminary chapter, *¡Bienvenidos!,* introduces students to the Spanish language, the excitement and rewards of learning another language, and the book's organization and content. In order to reduce anxiety, the preliminary chapter teaches learning strategies that students can use in the classroom and at home. The entire chapter should be done in class, although the listening material is on the student tape.

The remaining twelve chapters are each divided into three *etapas* that focus on different language skills. The *etapas* contain both skill-acquiring and skill-using activities. The twelve full-length chapters are organized as follows.

Chapter title and communicative objectives   Summarize chapter context and content. In general, the chapters progress from concrete and personal subjects to the more abstract or outwardly focused. Grammar topics are introduced as useful in carrying out the communicative objectives.

Primera etapa   Emphasis on listening and speaking

Entrada   A short listening selection (on the Instructor Tape) introduces the theme of the *etapa*. The text contains prelistening information and broad comprehension exercises.

Empezar a escuchar   This section, which consists of a segment on the student tape and exercises in the text, prepares students for listening to the main dialogue by teaching key words and expressions. Students should do this section at home in approximately one hour. It is divided into five parts:

Leer   *Escribir*
Repetir   *Reconocer*
Identificar

Escuchar The dialogue is contained in *Episodios* on the student tape. Pre- and postlistening activities, *Enfoques,* are in the text. The *Escuchar* section is best done as homework, and should take approximately one hour.

Verificar This is a general comprehension check to be done in class.

Ventanilla al mundo hispanico This section provides insights into Hispanic life and language. These segments are in English through Chapter 3 and in Spanish thereafter.

Aumentar el vocabulario Presentation of vocabulary is organized by semantic groupings. This section introduces new vocabulary and recycles old vocabulary. Students are not expected to memorize the entire list, but to familiarize themselves with the various groupings and choose words and expressions that best meet their needs.

Uso práctico del espanol This section occurs in most *etapas* and contains brief notes on structures or vocabulary relevant to that particular *etapa*'s functions.

Investigar la grámatica This section provides elements of Spanish structure according to their usefulness.

Ponerlo a prueba These are exercises that follow *Uso práctico* and *Investigar* sections and are used to encourage students to develop a broader and more personal range of linguistic expression.

¡Tienes la palabra! These open-ended activities, such as role-plays and interviews, provide students with opportunities to use language creatively and with minimal intervention from the instructor.

Otra vuelta This section is an optional relistening to the *Entrada* segment (in class or language lab) and exercises that delve more deeply into the passage.

Comentario cultural Lengthier than the *Ventanilla al mundo hispánico,* this section explores Hispanic values, attitudes, and behavior from an intercultural perspective. Accompanying exercises in some chapters invite students to apply this cultural information to real-life situations. These are in Spanish after Chapter 3.

The sections *Ventanilla al mundo hispánico* through *Comentario cultural* as listed in *Primera etapa* occur in the *Segunda* and *Tercera etapas* as well.

Segunda etapa Emphasis on reading

> ***Entrada***
>
>> ***Antes de Leer*** Thematic and vocabulary preparation for the reading selection
>>
>>> Reading strategy
>>> *Preparación*
>>> *Estudiar y practicar*

> *Leer* An authentic reading passage
>
> *Después de leer* Comprehension and personal questions based on the reading

Tercera etapa Emphasis on writing

> *Entrada*
>
> *Antes de hablar (escuchar, leer) y escribir* Preparation for speaking (listening, reading) and then writing
>
>> *Preparación*
>> *Estudiar y practicar*
>> Writing strategy
>
> *Hablar (Escuchar, Leer)* Using new vocabulary
>
> *Escribir* Writing activities
>
> *Actividades de integración* Additional open-ended speaking and writing practice for everything learned in the chapter
>
> *Vocabulario* A complete list with topical divisions and sections called *sustantivos, verbos y expresiones verbales, otras palabras,* and *otras expresiones;* included is *vocabulario personalizado,* a space for students to record additional words and expressions

ACKNOWLEDGMENTS

The authors wish to express their appreciation to the many individuals who have contributed to the second edition of *Entradas.* We thank the users of the first edition, whose thoughtful and insightful observations—both oral and written—prompted us to make changes that have undoubtedly strengthened the program. Similarly, the comments of the native readers who perused the manuscript have been most helpful as we strive to maintain both authentic and culturally appropriate language samples throughout the text.

To Carolyn L. Hansen and Gillian D. Paul, colleagues at the University of South Carolina, go a special accolade. Their willingness to assist in the revision of the Workbook/Laboratory Manual, and to serve as critical readers of the text throughout the production process—often on very short notice—was of inestimable value.

The authors wish to thank other colleagues who have participated in the revision process by responding to questionnaires, attending focus sessions, evaluating sample chapters, offering suggestions, and otherwise contributing selflessly of their expertise in the realization of this second edition.

Cathy Anderson, The Pennsylvania State University
Concha Barba, College of Charleston
Jorge Cubillos, University of Delaware
Ken Fleak, University of South Carolina
Carmen Garcia, Miami University-Ohio
Rita Goldberg, St. Lawrence University
Lynn Carbón Gorell, The Pennsylvania State University
Pam Hernández, Texas Lutheran College
Crista Johnson, University of Delaware
Judy Langston, University of Southern Carolina
Ana Martínez, The Pennsylvania State College
Keith Mason, University of Virginia
Harry Rosser, Boston College
Nancy Schnurr, Washington University
Elvira Swender, Syracuse University
Carolyn Tamburo, University of California

Many thanks to EMC, who directed the audio program. We extend our appreciation to the following people who participated in the recording: Ludmilla Amundson, Carlina Barría, Juanita Garcia-Godoy, Francisco Gonzalez, Galo Gonzalez, Laura Richardson, David Sunderland, and Jorge Walkup.

As authors, we recognize the crucial importance of a highly competent and professional editorial and production staff to successful materials development project. Thus we express our most sincere appreciation to the development staff of Heinle & Heinle: to Marisa French for initiating the revision process; to Erika Skantz for seeing us through preparation of the manuscript; to Patrice Titterington and Phyllis Larimore for tolerating our tirades and inconsistencies as we worked our way through copyedit, galleys, and page proofs; and to Carlos Davis for bringing order out of chaos. We are also grateful to the many freelancers who were instrumental to the project: Tracy Barrett, Anne Cantú, Danielle C. Havens, Margaret Hines, Lois Poulin, Janet de Prosse, Ana María Rodino, Ernst Schrader, Carl Spector, Laura Westlund, and Christine Wilson.

Finally, we acknowledge our gratitude to Charlie Heinle and Stan Galek, who have maintained their commitment to the publication of foreign language materials that fulfill the needs of classroom teachers and who first encouraged us to undertake this project. Their belief in the importance of these materials and their unwavering confidence in us as authors have influenced our attitudes and efforts throughout the process.

CHAPTER ORGANIZATION

Section Title	Function	In/Out of Class
Title and Communicative Objectives	Summary	
PRIMERA ETAPA	Listening and speaking	
Entrada	Thematic intro	Either

Empezar a escuchar
    Leer
    Repetir
    Identificar
    Escribir
    Reconocer
	Preparation	Out

Escuchar
    Enfoques
    Episodios
	Listening	Out

Verificar	Comprehension check	In
Ventanilla al mundo hispánico	Cultural notes	Either
Aumentar el vocabulario	Vocabulary building	Either
Uso práctico del español (most *etapas*) *Ponerlo a prueba*	Vocabulary and grammar notes	Either
Investigar la gramática *Ponerlo a prueba*	Presentation of grammar and practice	In
¡Tienes la palabra!	Role-playing	In
Otra vuelta	Reprise of *Entrada*	Either
Comentario cultural	Longer cultural notes	Either
SEGUNDA ETAPA	Reading	
Entrada	Thematic intro	Either

Antes de leer
    Reading strategy
    Preparación
    Estudiar y practicar
	Preparation	Out

Leer	Reading	Out
Después de leer	Comprehension check	In
Ventanilla to *Comentario:* as above		
TERCERA ETAPA	Writing	
Entrada	Thematic intro	Either

Antes de hablar (*escuchar, leer*) *y escribir*
    Preparación
    Estudiar y practicar
    Writing strategy
	Preparation	Out

Hablar (escuchar, leer)	Reading (etc.)	In
Escribir	Writing	Out
Ventanilla to *Comentario:* as above		
Actividades de integración	Review	Both
Vocabulario	Vocabulary lists	

CONTENTS

Chapter/Etapa	Objectives	Activities
Capítulo preliminar *¡Bienvenidos!* p. 1	Strategies for understanding Spanish Greet someone Classroom expressions Common courtesy Express ownership	*Escuchar:* *En la clase de español*
Capítulo 1 *¡A conocernos!* p. 13		
PRIMERA ETAPA *Los saludos* p. 14	Greet people	*Escuchar:* "Buenos días" / "Buenas noches, señora"
SEGUNDA ETAPA *Mucho gusto en conocerte* p. 27	Introduce yourself Give and receive autobiographical information	*Leer:* Personal ads
TERCERA ETAPA *En la residencia estudiantil* p. 40	Talk about future activities Express interest and surprise Bid farewell	*Hablar:* "Mucho gusto en conocerte" VIDEO PROGRAM 1

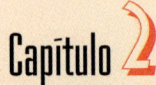

Capítulo 2 *¡A conocernos más!* p. 59

PRIMERA ETAPA *Antes de la primera clase* p. 60	Give, request, and understand information Tell time	*Escuchar:* "Oye, Alicia, ¿qué hora es?" / "¡Cálmate, Marcos!"

Strategies	Grammar	Culture	Vocabulary
	Gender and nouns	Regional varieties of Spanish Origins of Spanish	*El salón de clase* *Expresiones de cortesía*
	Irregular verbs: *estar, ser, tener, ir*	Addressing people *La tarde y la noche*	*La ciudad y la casa* *Los colores* *Los puntos cardinales* *La familia y los amigos*
Use background knowledge	Nouns and adjectives	*Las direcciones* *Presentaciones y saludos*	*Los meses del año* *Los números* *Países y nacionalidades* *Saludos y despedidas*
Organize information	Regular *-ar* verbs	*Los Estados Unidos de México* *Hay muchos Santiagos* VIDEO PROGRAM 1: *A caballo* The horse and the expansion of the Spanish empire	*La universidad* *Pronombres personales*
	Regular *-er* and *-ir* verbs	*Los sistemas de educación* *El reloj de 24 horas*	*Bebidas y refrescos* *La universidad* *Palabras interrogativas* *La comida*

Chapter/Etapa	Objectives	Activities
SEGUNDA ETAPA *En la sesión de orientación* **p. 73**	Express likes and dislikes	*Leer:* Descriptions of the professor and students
TERCERA ETAPA *Déjame ver tu horario de clases* **p. 84**	Give and understand simple directions Talk about future activities	*Hablar:* "Déjame ver tu horario de clases" / "¿Quieres tomar...?" *Escribir:* Self-description VIDEO PROGRAM 2

Capítulo 3
Día tras día p. 103

PRIMERA ETAPA *A mí me gusta madrugar...* **p. 104**	Recount a sequence of events Talk about the weather Express preferences Make a phone call	*Leer:* Planes para el fin de semana
SEGUNDA ETAPA *"¿Tienes planes para el fin de semana?"* **p. 118**	Discuss daily activities	*Escuchar:* La rutina diaria
TERCERA ETAPA *¡A arreglar el cuarto!* **p. 131**	Tell where things are located Describe people and objects Make comparisons	*Escribir:* La descripción de un amigo (una amiga) VIDEO PROGRAM 3

Capítulo 4
Haciendo planes p. 147

PRIMERA ETAPA *"¿Qué planes tienes para las vacaciones?"* **p. 148**	Recount a sequence of events or recent experiences	*Escuchar:* "¡Como pasa el tiempo!" / "¡Es una idea magnífica!"

Strategies	Grammar	Culture	Vocabulary
Use knowledge of context	Verbs with irregular *yo* forms	*La educación bilingüe* *Los apellidos hispanos*	*Deportes y actividades* *El tiempo y la hora* *El trabajo* *Palabras descriptivas*
Link sentences with connecting words	Talking about the future Stem-changing *-ar* and *-er* verbs in present tense	*En otros países se estudia inglés* Use of *tú* and *usted*, *vosotros* and *ustedes* VIDEO PROGRAM 2: *Latinos en los Estados Unidos* The growing presence of Latinos in the United States	*Palabras enumerativas* *Planes y deseos* *Expresiones de tiempo, lugar, modo y cantidad*
Read for specific information	Stem-changing *-ir* verbs in the present tense	Answering the telephone	*Llamar por teléfono* *El tiempo* *La rutina diaria* *Expresiones con* **tener** *Preposiciones*
	Expressions with *tener* Reflexive verbs	Metric system and Celsius scale *Actividades y pasatiempos en el mundo hispánico*	*La personalidad* *El físico* *El cuarto de la residencia y los muebles*
Organize your descriptions	*Las comparaciones*	*Las telenovelas* *La casa* VIDEO PROGRAM 3: *Sones y ritmos* The diversity of regional music	
	Changing adjectives into adverbs The preterite tense	*Las estaciones del año* *El dinero*	*Fiestas* *Dinero y compras* *Problemas* *Estaciones del año* *Los viajes* *Actividades*

Chapter/Etapa	Objectives	Activities
SEGUNDA ETAPA *"Vamos a Colombia"* **p. 161**	Make travel plans	*Leer:* Travel brochure on Colombia
TERCERA ETAPA *"Vamos a hacer las maletas"* **p. 173**	Express negation	*Escribir:* Tarjeta de entrada a Colombia VIDEO PROGRAM 4

Capítulo 5

A conocer la vecindad p. 195

PRIMERA ETAPA *La pensión de doña Josefina* **p. 196**	Give and seek information Talk about the past	*Escuchar:* En la pensión / Más vecinos de doña Josefina
SEGUNDA ETAPA *Conociendo la vecindad* **p. 209**	Order food in a restaurant	*Leer:* Advertisements
TERCERA ETAPA *La cita con Carmencita* **p. 221**	Make generalizations and recommendations Express preferences and dislikes	*Escribir:* Restaurant review VIDEO PROGRAM 5

Capítulo 6

Para orientarnos p. 237

PRIMERA ETAPA *Viajeros y huéspedes* **p. 238**	Seek information Make travel arrangements	*Escuchar:* ¿Por tierra o por avión? / "¿Dónde quieren alojarse?"
SEGUNDA ETAPA *Conozca Cartagena* **p. 253**	Give directions	*Leer:* Cartagena brochure

Strategies	Grammar	Culture	Vocabulary
Read for general information	*Por* and *para* The preterite tense	*Variantes léxicas en el mundo hispánico* *Los chicanos*	*La ropa* *El correo* *Negación y afirmación*
Learn to paraphrase	Affirmative and negative expressions More about the preterite tense	*Hacer aduana* *¿Es más formal la vida en los países hispanos?* VIDEO PROGRAM 4: *Personajes inolvidables* Mini-portraits of famous people	

	The present perfect Another visit with the preterite tense	*Los nombres de pila* *El alojamiento*	*Las tiendas y sus productos* *Las legumbres* *Los condimentos* *Las profesiones* *La vecindad / El vecindario*
Use visual clues	Direct complements	*Comiendo en casa o en la calle* *Tiendas y vendedores* *La vida escolar*	
Work on writing and rewriting	More about the verb *gustar* Indirect complements	*La comida del mundo hispánico* *El pan* VIDEO PROGRAM 5: *Ricos sabores* Regional foods and dishes	

	Saber and *conocer* The imperfect tense	*El cambio* *Medios de transporte público*	*¡A viajar!* *Alojamiento* *El baño* *La cuenta y los precios* *La historia* *Las direcciones* *Materias y minerales* *La frequencia* *Palabras para indicar posición*
Anticipate and predict content	The present progressive Another look at *por* and *para*	*Conservando el pasado* *Las ferias*	

Chapter/Etapa	Objectives	Activities
TERCERA ETAPA *Servicios y amenidades* **p. 268**	Tell anecdotes and stories	*Hablar:* Problemas en la recepción *Escribir:* A letter of complaint VIDEO PROGRAM 6

Capítulo 7
¡Aqui tienen su casa! p. 289

PRIMERA ETAPA *"¿Qué debo hacer?"* **p. 290**	Talk about what might (or might not) occur Make purchases To ask for and give advice	*Escuchar:* Las preocupaciones de Paco / "¿Puedes darme unos consejos?"
SEGUNDA ETAPA *"Bienvenidos a Bogotá"* **p. 304**		*Leer:* San Antonio
TERCERA ETAPA *Un poco de todo* **p. 316**	Express desires and influence others	*Escribir:* Travel story VIDEO PROGRAM 7

Capítulo 8
"Juventud, divino tesoro..." p. 331

PRIMERA ETAPA *Cuentos de niños* **p. 332**	Make polite requests and give commands Make general statements about what other people say and do Tell anecdotes and stories	*Escuchar:* "Aquí están los gemelos" / El apagón
SEGUNDA ETAPA *Un niño travieso* **p. 345**	Express how you feel about situations and events	*Leer:* "Los suyos", por Gabriel García Márquez

Strategies	Grammar	Culture	Vocabulary
Communicate forcefully	The preterite and imperfect used together	*El agua corriente* *Las leyendas religiosas* VIDEO PROGRAM 6: *Pasajeros a bordo* Regional and urban transportation	
	Introduction to the subjunctive	*"Está en su casa"* *Ir de compras* *La informalidad formal*	*Los lugares de actividad social* *Los deportes* *La casa* *Los espacios*
Preview the internal organization	Two complementary pronouns with the same verb	*Las formas diminutivas de los nombres* *El diminutivo*	*Los muebles y los trastos* *La mesa* *Los números ordinales*
Tell a story	Expressing desires and influencing others	*La geografía de Colombia* *El regateo* VIDEO PROGRAM 7: *Detalles y colores* Detail and color in artistic expression	
	Polite requests and formal commands Expressing generalizations	*La quinceañera* *La familia*	*El automóvil* *El cuerpo humano* *Día y noche* *Expresiones de emoción* *La nueva tecnología* *Generalizaciones*
Identify sentence segments	Familiar commands The subjunctive with expressions and verbs of emotion	*Expresiones de emoción* *Juegos y actividades de los niños*	*Palabras relacionadas con los deportes*

Chapter/Etapa	Objectives	Activities
TERCERA ETAPA *Roberta, el hijo modelo* **p. 359**	Understand descriptions of experiences others have had Express doubts, denial, and disbelief regarding situations and events	*Hablar y escribir:* *Una anécdota acerca de los automóviles* VIDEO PROGRAM 8

Capítulo

¡Dios mío! ¿qué te pasa? p. 375

PRIMERA ETAPA *"¿Te sientes mal?"* **p. 376**	Understand short public announcements related to personal health and health care Talk about illness and injury Make simple hypothetical statements	*Escuchar:* *"¿Qué te pasa, Susana?" / "¿Y si me muero antes de las 9:00?"*
SEGUNDA ETAPA *"¡Me duele todo el cuerpo!"* **p. 388**	Talk about past experiences Ask for and give advice	*Leer:* The benefits of swimming
TERCERA ETAPA *Enfermedades y hospitales* **p. 403**	Deal with situations related to medical treatment and services	*Leer:* *Carta-testimonio de una madre americana* *Escribir:* *Una historia médica* VIDEO PROGRAM 9

Capítulo

¡A divertirnos! p. 421

PRIMERA ETAPA *Una fiesta norteña* **p. 422**	Extend, accept, and decline invitations Ask for and give advice Narrate and describe events Talk about what might (or might not) exist or occur	*Escuchar:* *"¿Qué invitación? ¿A qué?"* *Leer:* *"Es usted muy amable..."*

Strategies	Grammar	Culture	Vocabulary
Give your story a point	Making impersonal statements Expressing certainty versus uncertainty, doubt, denial, and disbelief	*El fútbol* *Criar a los niños* VIDEO PROGRAM 8: *Juegos y diversiones* Traditional games and pastimes	
	Emphasizing ownership or possession More on stem-changing verbs	*¡No tomes el agua!* *Los curanderos*	*Accidentes y los estados físicos* *Enfermedades y condiciones médicas* *Medicinas y remedios* *Los órganos del cuerpo humano* *La sala de emergencia*
Note key points in each paragraph	Keeping track of previous information The imperfect subjunctive	*La farmacia* *El hospital y la clínica*	
Transfer thought to language	The verb *doler* More on the "wish-list" subjunctive	*Cuando alguien estornuda...* *Más sobre las medidas métricas* VIDEO PROGRAM 9: *Remedios tradicionales y modernos* Traditional and modern health care	
	Ojalá + subjunctive More on the imperfect and subjunctive	*"Te invito..."* *La puntualidad*	*Despedidas* *Expresiones llamativas* *Saludos*

xxiii

Chapter/Etapa	Objectives	Activities
SEGUNDA ETAPA "¿Qué me pongo?" **p. 437**	Make explanations Talk about the future	*Leer:* "Los 'sí' y los 'no' de la etiqueta…"
TERCERA ETAPA La correspondencia personal **p. 453**		*Leer y escribir:* Una carta de agradecimiento; una carta personal VIDEO PROGRAM 10

Capítulo 11

¿Qué me aconsejas? p. 467

PRIMERA ETAPA Las mentiras piadosas **p. 468**	Ask for and give advice Speculate about the future Make simple hypothetical statements	*Escuchar:* Un asunto bastante serio / El dilema de Marcos
SEGUNDA ETAPA El chisme y la realidad **p. 480**	Talk about unplanned occurrences	*Leer:* "¡Chisme!"
TERCERA ETAPA Querida Tía Lilia **p. 495**		*Leer y escribir:* "Preocupado y desesperado" VIDEO PROGRAM 11

Capítulo 12

¡Hasta pronto! p. 513

PRIMERA ETAPA "Te quiero más que nunca…" **p. 514**	Talk about activities in progress Express emotions	*Leer:* "Te quiero más que nunca" / "¡Cómo son los padres!"
SEGUNDA ETAPA "Y yo te quiero a ti…" **p. 527**		*Leer:* "¿Padeces de solofobia?"

Strategies	Grammar	Culture	Vocabulary
Recognize relationships between words and phrases	The future The conditional	*Hispanohablantes esta-dounidenses* *Las fiestas*	
Write thank-you notes	*Más que* and *más de* Verbs that have prepositions	*El día del santo* *Expresiones de cortesía* VIDEO PROGRAM 10: *Creencias y celebraciones* Religious holidays and celebrations	
	Use of the infinitive as a noun Stating conditions and hypotheses	*El individuo frente al grupo* *La solidaridad*	*Notas escolares* *La justicia* *Bromas y chismes* *La cara y los cosméticos*
Read between the lines	Talking about unplanned occurrences The subjunctive with certain conjunctions	*Las mujeres y el trabajo* *Títulos y tarjetas de presentación*	
Explain a situation	More about reflexive verbs Anticipating events and actions	*Asuntos del corazón* *"¿Qué dirá la gente?"* VIDEO PROGRAM 11: *Pueblos indígenas* Pre-Columbian communities in Mexico and Bolivia	
	Review of the verb *estar* with the gerund and past participle Review of the subjunctive	*Los términos cariñosos* *Más sobre enchufes y palancas*	*El amor y las relaciones románticas* *Los continentes* *El trabajo y los negocios*
Look for cohesive elements	Reviewing the Reading Strategies	*Salir en grupos* *Cuando los jóvenes quieren salir en pareja*	

Chapter/Etapa	Objectives	Activities
TERCERA ETAPA *El gran crisol del mundo* **p. 537**	Anticipate future events Make plans for staying in touch	***Leer:*** *"Ética y cortesia en los negocios"* ***Escribir:*** *Un articulo sobre los negocios* VIDEO PROGRAM 12

Strategies	Grammar	Culture	Vocabulary
Have an overall plan	The comparatives *mayor* and *menor* Reviewing the Writing Strategies	*Proverbios y refranes* *Ciudadanos del mundo* VIDEO PROGRAM 12: *Profesiones y oficios* Traditional and non-traditional professions	

¡Bienvenidos!

Capítulo preliminar

COMMUNICATIVE OBJECTIVES

In this chapter, you will learn

- some strategies for understanding Spanish
- how to greet someone
- some classroom expressions and vocabulary
- some common courtesy expressions
- how to express ownership

Strategies for Beginning Your Study of Spanish

The word *entrada* means "entry." This textbook and its accompanying materials will provide you with an entry into the world of Spanish, not only the language but also the culture of its speakers. As you begin your study of Spanish you will find much that will be new and perhaps even strange. You will also discover much that is surprisingly familiar to you.

Many of the new Spanish words you will learn are called cognates. These are words that are very similar in form and meaning in both English and Spanish. Here are some common health-related words in Spanish taken from Chapter 9 of *Entradas*. See if you can guess what they mean:

la aspirina, la inyección, la medicina, el síntoma

Not all cognates are as easy as the ones you've just seen. Sometimes Spanish words are merely similar to their English equivalents: *escuela* means "school"; *gobernador* means "governor."

Sometimes whole classes of words can be guessed, not only from Spanish to English but also from English to Spanish. What do you think the following Spanish words mean?

la civilización, la administración, la colección, la porción

How do you think the English word "institution" is written in Spanish? If you said *la institución,* you have successfully deduced a strategy that already makes hundreds of Spanish words part of your available vocabulary: many nouns that end in "-tion" in English end in *-ción* in Spanish.

Whenever you read or listen to Spanish, try to find out beforehand what the passage you read or hear will be about and what kind of information you will need to identify. Many times the context of a passage will itself provide important clues to its content. As you proceed, try to pick out the cognates and other familiar material. Relax as much as possible, and focus on whatever portion of the material you can understand. This may seem to be very little at first, but the more you learn, the better you will be able to use what you already know to guess about what is new. Also, throughout *Entradas* you will be asked questions that cover only the most important points of the Spanish you have read or heard, not every detail of the material.

People You Will Meet During the Year

In *Entradas* you will get to know several characters in a variety of settings. These characters and their experiences make up the storyline of the twelve chapters of the text. Some of the more important people are:

Marcos Colón: a native of Bogotá, Colombia. Marcos is an undergraduate student at the university, majoring in French literature. He lives with his aunt and uncle in a small house at 1621 Robles Street.

Francisco Méndez: a young Mexican-American college student whom everyone calls "Paco." Paco speaks both English and Spanish and plans to become a teacher in a bilingual program. Paco, who is from San Diego, lives with his roommate, Roberto Hernández, in an apartment at 1728 Robles Street, near Marcos. Paco helps Professor Suárez in her English class.

Roberto Hernández: another Mexican-American student, from San Antonio, Texas. Roberto is majoring in business and plans to travel in South America. He and Paco are roommates.

Alicia de San Martín: a student from Santiago, the capital of Chile. Alicia is a business major, and hopes to work for a multinational company in Santiago upon graduation. She likes to study and to watch television.

Elena María Rodríguez Olivares: a student from Guadalajara, Mexico, who is a marathon runner. Elena began running when she was in elementary school, and hopes to compete in the Olympics. Elena and Alicia are roommates in the college dormitory. She plans to major in either biology or chemistry.

Susana Rodríguez: Elena's younger sister. Susana visits Elena at the university.

La profesora Filomena Suárez: a professor of English and Spanish who works closely with the Spanish-speaking students at the university. She is from Mexico City and has lived in the United States for 15 years. She likes to read and to cook.

Getting to Know Your Textbook

Each of the twelve chapters of *Entradas* is divided into three major sections called *etapas* ("stages" or "phases"). The *etapas* consist of a variety of sections intended to introduce you to new material, help you practice it, and then learn to apply it to express your own meanings in Spanish. The material at the beginning of each *etapa*, which is called the *Entrada,* is found on audiocassette rather than in the textbook. Your instructor will have a tape of the *Entradas* for classroom use, although you can find the same material at the end of the laboratory tape for each chapter. The first *etapa* of each chapter also has an extensive listening comprehension section. The listening material for this section is on your own student tape, which you will probably use outside of class. Your instructor will also assign listening comprehension practice outside of class in the *Workbook/Laboratory Manual.*

The second and third *etapas* of each chapter focus on the development of reading comprehension and writing or speaking skills, respectively.

There are marginal notes labeled **OJO** ("caution") throughout the text. These tips, strategies, and reminders are a special feature of *Entradas.* They will point out features of the language you might have forgotten, refer you to explanations you might need, and remind you of rules and special cases.

The remainder of this introductory chapter gives you an abbreviated look at the structure of the listening comprehension *etapas* while providing you with some Spanish to get you started. Good luck! *¡Buena suerte!*

The *Entrada* segment of each *etapa* is recorded on the instructor tape for classroom use and on the laboratory tape program for practice outside the classroom. It is not on the student tape.

Focus student attention on the listening task before you play the tape.

The *Otra vuelta* activity at the end of each *etapa* is a somewhat more difficult comprehension activity based on the *Entrada*. Use it now if your students find the *Entrada* easy to understand.

ENTRADA

Play instructor tape, 1 min.

OJO: Don't worry if you don't understand every word of the *Entrada.* Just focus on the three pieces of information that you need to understand.

"Buenos días, clase"

You are going to hear a short passage in Spanish. Listen carefully and try to guess

- the name of the person who is talking
- what the person's job is
- the name of a book that is mentioned

1. The person is
   a. Ramón Otero   b. Raúl Ortega   c. Roberto Ochoa
2. The person's job is
   a. profesor   b. señor   c. policía
3. The book is
   a. *De nada*   b. *Entradas*   c. *Empanadas*

¡OJO! The *Entrada* is found at the end of each chapter of the laboratory tapes. Refer to it for extra practice.

EMPEZAR A ESCUCHAR

> Play student tape, 1 min.

Explain that this material is on the student tape and will usually be assigned as homework. It is being done in class this time for practice. Use your copy of the student tape and go through the steps of the *Empezar a escuchar* section carefully, making sure that students understand the purpose of each one.

Words are presented in the order in which they appear in the *Entrada*.

Have students first read the words and then repeat them for reinforcement using both visual and aural/oral channels.

These sentences are paraphrased or lifted verbatim from the *Episodio*. Remind students to focus on the words and phrases they have already practiced, and not to be distracted by what they may not yet understand.

Sentences are for dictation.

Stress to students the importance of developing good habits of proofreading and analysis.

Leer

Vamos a...	We're going to . . . / Let's . . .
escribir	to write
el cuaderno de ejercicios	workbook
el (la) profesor(a)	teacher, professor
tener	to have
(No) Tengo...	I (don't) have . . .
la pluma	pen
el lápiz	pencil
Es muy importante...	It's very important . . .
todos los días	every day

Repetir

Listen to your student tape and repeat the words and phrases you hear.

Words are listed in the order in which they appear in the *Episodios* ("Episodes") that follow. Repeat the words and phrases, rewinding the tape as many times as necessary until you feel comfortable with the pronunciation.

Identificar

On a separate sheet of paper, write in a column the words and phrases in Spanish from the list in the preceding *Leer* section. You will hear some sentences on the tape. Whenever you hear one of these words or phrases, write next to it the number of the sentence in which it appears. Each sentence will be read twice. You may stop and start the tape as often as you wish to listen to the sentences.

Don't worry if you don't understand everything. Just focus on picking out the familiar words and phrases.

Escribir

You will hear some sentences in Spanish. Each one will be read twice. Write them down as you listen, starting and stopping your tape as needed. Refer to the *Leer* section for help.

Reconocer

This is your chance to check carefully what you have written. Have you spelled the words correctly? Are the accent marks over the right letter? Do you have the gender (*el, la*) right? Refer to the *Leer* section or the glossary for help as needed.

Each of the sentences you have just written contains one or more of the words and phrases from the *Leer* list. Read the sentences carefully, and underline as many of the words and expressions from the list as you can find. As you read, make any necessary corrections in your sentences. Pay particular attention to the written accent marks because the conventions of Spanish may be new to you.

EPISODIO: En la clase de español

ESCUCHAR

| Play student tape, 1 min. |

The *Escuchar* section is on the student tape. It usually has two *Episodios*.

This activity focuses on meaning.

There are usually two *Episodios* in each listening *etapa*. You have already heard much of it in the *Empezar a escuchar* section.

Enfoque comunicativo

Focus just on the comprehension activity here. Don't worry about what you can't understand.

You will hear an instructor speaking with a student. As you listen, see if you can

- identify the student by name
- figure out the instructor's intended classroom activity
- understand what the student is missing

1. The student's name is:
2. The planned activity is:
3. The student is missing:

Enfoque lingüístico

This activity focuses on specific functions and phrases. Follow up by asking students questions that elicit the same or similar phrases: *¿Tienes cuaderno / pluma / lápiz?*

This activity asks you to focus on how certain phrases or ideas are expressed in Spanish.

Listen to the *Episodio* section again and identify the words the student uses to explain his problem to the instructor. Write down the sentence in which he explains his problem.

VENTANILLA AL MUNDO HISPÁNICO   Regional Varieties of Spanish

Beginning with Chapter 5, all of the *Ventanillas al mundo hispánico* are in Spanish.

Like English and many other languages, Spanish is not identical in all Hispanic countries. However, these variations in Spanish are not critical to understanding. Spanish is a much more uniform language than English, for instance.

Perhaps you have heard the expression "Castilian Spanish." This refers to the Spanish that is spoken in the central region of Spain, particularly around

Madrid, the capital. Although the language of virtually every Spanish-speaking country has features that distinguish it from other varieties, the core of the language is essentially the same wherever it is spoken. As you use your Spanish in conversation with Spanish speakers from different regions, you will see how easily regional differences are overcome.

AUMENTAR EL VOCABULARIO

OJO: You can combine this expression with verbs: *Es muy importante escribir; Es muy importante hablar.*

Study new vocabulary by reading it aloud, writing it on flash cards, and by going back to words and expressions that are harder to remember.

Buenos días.	*Hello. / Good morning.*
Es muy importante...	*It is very important . . .*
todos los días	*every day*

Some common classroom vocabulary:

ahora	*now*
bueno/-a	*good*
la clase	*class*
el cuaderno	*notebook*
el cuaderno de ejercicios	*workbook*
escribir	*to write*
hablar	*to speak*
el lápiz	*pencil*
leer	*to read*
el libro	*book*
malo/-a	*bad*
mucho/-a	*a lot*
la palabra	*word*
el papel	*paper*
la pluma	*pen*
el (la) profesor(a)	*teacher, professor*

Common classroom expressions used by students:

¿Cómo se dice *page* **en español?**	*How do you say "page" in Spanish?*
¿Qué quiere decir "página"?	*What does* página *mean?*
Más despacio, por favor.	*More slowly, please.*
Tengo una pregunta.	*I have a question.*
(No) Entiendo.	*I (don't) understand.*

Common classroom expressions used by teachers:

Abre el libro a la página...	*Open the book to page . . .*
¿Hay preguntas?	*Are there any questions?*

Contesta en español, por favor.   *Please answer in Spanish.*
Escucha.   *Listen.*
Lee (en voz alta).   *Read (out loud).*
Repite, por favor.   *Please repeat.*

USO PRÁCTICO DEL ESPAÑOL   Some Expressions of Courtesy

OJO: *¿Cómo te llamas?* and *Me llamo…* are examples of idiomatic expressions, which cannot be translated directly into English. Learn them as fixed expressions without worrying about what each word means.

Por favor.   *Please.*
(Muchas) Gracias.   *Thanks (a lot).*
De nada.   *You're welcome.*
Hola.   *Hello.*
¿Cómo te llamas?   *What is your name?*
Me llamo…   *My name is . . .*
Mucho gusto.   *I'm pleased to meet you.*
¡Perdón!   *I'm sorry!*

Ponerlo a prueba

In the full-length *etapas*, one vocabulary activity after the *Aumentar el vocabulario* section usually deals only with one part of the vocabulary list. The first activity in *Ponerlo a prueba* practices the *Uso práctico del español* section.

A. ¡Perdón! One of your classmates has just introduced himself or herself to you, but you didn't catch his or her name.

- Tell the person you're sorry.
- Ask the person politely to speak more slowly and to repeat his or her name.
- Thank the person, and say you're pleased to meet him or her.

Only two vocabulary activities are provided here. There are several in each of the full-length *etapas* in the book.

B. ¿Cómo se dice? Provide an appropriate response to each situation.

1. You would like the speaker to slow down.
2. You want to hear something one more time.
3. You want to know the Spanish word for "car."
4. You are confused and need clarification.
5. You want to indicate that you do not understand what has just been said.

INVESTIGAR LA GRAMÁTICA   Gender and Nouns

All nouns in Spanish are either "masculine" or feminine," and the gender of a noun is as much a part of its use as its meaning is. In the *Leer* and *Aumentar el vocabulario* sections throughout the book, masculine nouns are usually preceded by the word *el,* which is referred to as the masculine article (*el artículo masculino*). The plural of *el* is *los*. Feminine nouns are preceded by the feminine article *la*. The plural of *la* is *las*. The words *el, la, los* and *las* all mean "the."

La clase de español es buena.
Las plumas son malas.
Abre **el** libro, por favor.
Los profesores hablan (*speak*) español.

Notice the articles in the words and expressions in the preceding *Aumentar el vocabulario* section. Is the word *día* masculine or feminine? How can you tell? What word refers to a male teacher? A female teacher?

Masculine nouns may also be preceded by the word *un* and feminine nouns by the word *una*. Both *un* and *una* mean "a" or "an." In some contexts they mean "one."

Tengo (*I have*) **un** cuaderno de español.
Tengo **una** pregunta.

The plural of *un* is *unos*. The plural of *una* is *unas*. Both *unos* and *unas* mean "some."

Tengo **unas** clases interesantes.
Tengo **unos** libros.

Ponerlo a prueba

A. **Tiene** (*He has / She has*) **uno.** The following people have one of each of the nouns that follow. Express this according to the cues. Use the verb form *tiene* in each sentence.

Modelo: Elena / libro
Elena tiene un libro.

1. Guillermo / cuaderno
2. Patricia / pluma
3. El profesor / clase de español
4. Roberto / pregunta
5. Luisa / lápiz

B. **¿De quién son?** (*Whose are they?*) For each of the following items, say to whom it belongs, according to the cues. Follow the models. **¡OJO!** Possession is indicated in Spanish by the phrase *de* + (*persona*). In Spanish an apostrophe is never used to show possession.

Modelos: libro / Susana   *el libro de Susana*
libros / Carlos   *los libros de Carlos*

1. cuaderno / Anita
2. clases / Pedro
3. papel / Tomás

4. plumas / Sara
5. preguntas / Mario
6. lápiz / Carolina

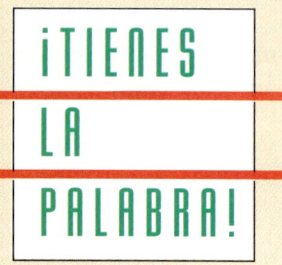

¡TIENES LA PALABRA!

Do the following activities with a partner.

A. ¡Hola! Working with another student, make up a short conversation in which

- you greet your partner
- your partner greets you
- you tell each other your names
- you respond to each other's introduction

B. En mi mochila (*In my backpack*). Take out of your *mochila* all of the following items that you may have: pens, pencils, notebooks, books, and loose papers. Now tell your partner that you have **one** or **some** of each item.

Other items you may have in your *mochila*: *la grabadora* (personal tape player); *la carpeta* (folder); *la calculadora* (calculator).

OTRA VUELTA

Play instructor tape, 1 min.

Listen again to the tape of the *Entrada*. Write down the sentence that the instructor uses to greet the class.

COMENTARIO CULTURAL

All of the *Comentarios culturales,* beginning with Chapter 5, are in Spanish.

The Origins of Spanish

The most direct linguistic ancestor of Spanish is a variety of classical Latin spoken around the fourth century A.D. that gave rise to the Romance languages—a whole family of languages that includes, among others, Italian, French, Portuguese, and Spanish.

Roughly sixty percent of contemporary Spanish vocabulary can be traced directly to Latin. The remainder comes from a variety of other languages, including Basque, Arabic, Greek, and, since the arrival of Spaniards in the Americas in the late fifteenth century, from indigenous languages such as Nahuatl (Mexico), Mayan (Mexico and Guatemala), and Quechua (the southern Andean region stretching roughly from Quito, Ecuador to Tucumán, Argentina).

English has also borrowed many words from Latin. You may be surprised to discover that many infrequently used words that sound "elegant" in English, such as "culpable," turn out to be very commonly used in Spanish; *culpable* means "guilty" in Spanish and is frequently used.

Can you guess what these Spanish words mean: *introvertido, inteligible, microcosmos, matriculación?*

Actividad. Read the following advertisement from a newspaper in Bogotá, Colombia. By looking for similar words (cognates) between English and Spanish, see if you can determine

1. the name of the advertiser
2. what type of clientele the restaurant is trying to attract
3. where to call for reservations
4. what the address of the establishment is

> Students are asked to focus first on the information that they are to look for in the text. This procedure is used throughout the book with both listening and reading comprehension tasks.

VOCABULARIO

El salón de clase
Classroom

clase (f)   class
cuaderno (m)   notebook, workbook
ejercicio (m)   exercise
español (m)   Spanish
lápiz (m)   pencil
libro (m)   book
palabra (f)   word
papel (m)   paper
pluma (f)   pen
pregunta (f)   question
profesor(a) (m/f)   professor

Verbos y expresiones verbales (*Verbs and verbal expressions*) del salón de clase

Abre el libro a la página...   *Open your book to page . . .*
¿Cómo se dice...?   *How do you say . . . ?*
Contesta en español, por favor.   *Answer in Spanish, please.*
Es muy importante...   *It's very important . . .*
escribir   to write
Escucha.   Listen.
hablar   to speak
¿Hay preguntas?   *Are there any questions?*
Lee (en voz alta).   *Read (out loud).*
leer   to read
Más despacio, por favor.   *More slowly, please.*
(No) Entiendo.   *I (don't) understand.*
(No) Tengo...   *I (don't) have . . .*
¿Qué quiere decir...?   *What does . . . mean?*
Repite.   Repeat.
Tengo una pregunta.   *I have a question.*

Otras palabras
Other words

ahora   now
bueno/-a   good
malo/-a   bad
mucho/-a   a lot
un(a)   a(n), one
unos/-as   some

Otras expresiones
Other expressions

Buenos días.   *Hello. / Good morning.*
¿Cómo te llamas?   *What is your name?*
De nada.   You're welcome.
Hola.   Hello.
Me llamo...   *My name is . . .*
(Muchas) Gracias.   *Thanks (a lot).*
Mucho gusto.   *I'm pleased to meet you.*
¡Perdón!   I'm sorry!
por favor   please
todos los días   every day
Vamos a...   *We're going to . . . / Let's . . .*

VOCABULARIO PERSONALIZADO

¡A conocernos!

Capítulo 1

COMMUNICATIVE OBJECTIVES
In this chapter, you will learn several ways to
- greet people
- introduce yourself
- give and receive basic autobiographical information
- talk about future activities
- express interest
- express surprise
- bid farewell

PRIMERA ETAPA

Los saludos

ENTRADA

Play instructor tape, 1 min.

Encourage students to develop hypotheses about the *Entrada*.

There are three ways to use this preliminary listening material.
   1. Begin with *Aumentar el vocabulario* and assign the *Entrada* (on lab tapes), *Empezar a escuchar,* and *Escuchar* sections as homework.
   2. Play the *Entrada* in class and then skip to *Aumentar el vocabulario.* Assign *Empezar a escuchar* and *Escuchar* as homework.
   3. Assign *Empezar a escuchar* and *Escuchar* as homework prior to the class period in which you play the *Entrada.* Play the *Entrada,* review homework, and proceed to *Aumentar el vocabulario.* Encourage students to use the *Entrada* form as a model and to write answers on a separate sheet of paper.

"Hola, ¿qué tal?"

You are going to hear a short conversation. Because you are just starting to study Spanish, you will not understand everything that is said. But listen carefully and try to figure out

- how many people are talking
- where they are
- in a very general way, what they are talking about

1. How many people are talking?
2. Where do you think they are?
   a. at a party
   b. on the street
   c. in the library
3. How can you tell? List the clues that helped you figure it out.
   a.
   b.
4. Do the people in the conversation know each other, or are they meeting for the first time?
5. How can you tell? List the clues that helped you figure it out.
   a.
   b.

EMPEZAR A ESCUCHAR

Play student tape, 2 min.

The words included in the *Leer* section are needed to understand the *Episodios.* All of these words are also included in *Aumentar el vocabulario.*

Leer

Buenos días.	*Good morning.*
¿Cómo está usted?	*How are you?* (*formal*)
Muy bien, gracias.	*Very well, thank you.*
Buenas tardes.	*Good afternoon.*
¿Qué tal?	*How's it going?*
Buenas noches.	*Good evening. Good night.*
¿Cómo estás?	*How are you?* (*familiar*)

Con permiso.	*Excuse me. (to leave a group)*
estudiar	*to study*

Repetir

Listen to your student tape and repeat the words and phrases you hear.

Identificar

On a separate sheet of paper, write in a column the words and phrases in Spanish from the preceding *Leer* list. You will hear some sentences on your tape. Whenever you hear one of these words or phrases, write next to it the number of the sentence in which it appears. Each sentence will be read twice. You may stop and start the tape as often as you wish while listening.

Escribir

You will hear some sentences in Spanish. Each one will be read twice. Write them down as you listen, starting and stopping your tape as needed.

Reconocer

Each of the sentences you have just written contains one or more of the words and phrases from the preceding *Leer* list. Read the sentences carefully, and underline as many of the words and expressions from the list as you can find. As you read, make any necessary corrections in your sentences. Pay particular attention to punctuation and accent marks because the conventions of Spanish may be new to you.

EPISODIO 1: "Buenos días"

Enfoque comunicativo

You are about to hear some people greet each other in the first *Episodio* on your student tape. As you listen, see if you can identify

- the different phrases that people use to greet each other
- two different titles of address

Saludos (*Greetings*)	Forms of address
1.	_____ Suárez
2.	
3.	_____ Martínez

OJO: These words are presented in the order in which they appear in the *Episodios*. Watch especially for accent marks.

The *Leer* and *Estudiar y practicar* lists are held to a maximum of ten key words in order to make it easier for students to handle the listening, reading, or speaking activity that follows.

Follow-up: Because the *Leer* words are given in the order in which they appear in the *Episodios,* they are not in logical order. Have students group them by greeting, response, formal, and informal.

The *Empezar a escuchar* and *Escuchar* sections are recorded on the student tape. All subsections—*Leer, Repetir, Identificar, Escribir, Reconocer,* the *Episodios,* and the *Enfoques*—should be done outside of class, either before or after the *Entrada* listening segment. (See the annotation next to *Entrada.*)

ESCUCHAR

Play student tape, 1 min.

Although students may not have had all the necessary vocabulary to understand every word of the *Empezar a escuchar* and *Escuchar* sections, they should understand that they are making educated guesses from context and that the sequence of activities in the *Empezar a escuchar* section will help them to understand the conversations in the *Empezar* section. Go over selected exercises from both sections in class to check that students are doing the listening homework with care.

Enfoque lingüístico

You may have noticed that in some instances the people you heard addressed each other as *tú*, and in other instances as *usted*. *Tú* and *usted* are subject pronouns that mean "you." Their use is determined by the relationship between the two speakers. Listen to *Episodio 1* on your student tape again and write down who used *tú* and who used *usted*.

ESCUCHAR

Play student tape, 1 min.

Encourage students to focus their thoughts by writing answers to the *Enfoque comunicativo* and the *Enfoque lingüístico*. Have them check their responses with a partner as a warm-up activity in class.

EPISODIO 2: "Buenas noches, señora"

Enfoque comunicativo

In the next *Episodio* on your student tape, you will hear a short conversation between two people. As you listen, see if you can determine

- where the conversation takes place
- who the *señora* might be

1. This conversation takes place in
   a. César's house
   b. Roberto's house
2. The *señora* is probably
   a. Roberto's mother
   b. César's mother
   c. César's sister

Go over *Verificar* exercises in class to check comprehension of the two *Episodios* in the *Escuchar* section on the student tape.

OJO: See the section *Ventanilla al mundo hispánico* that follows for the answer.

Enfoque lingüístico

Why do you think Roberto addressed the *señora* with the *usted* form? Why do you think the *señora* used the *tú* form with Roberto?

VERIFICAR

Have students check answers to *Verificar* with a partner. Review those where there is significant discrepancy. Even at this early stage, encourage students to correct the statements that are false, such as item 4.

¿Sí o no?

Listen once again to the two *Episodio* conversations on the student tape and verify the following statements.

1. La doctora Suárez es profesora.   Sí   No
2. La doctora Suárez y el señor
   Martínez son buenos amigos.   Sí   No
3. César y Patricia son buenos amigos.   Sí   No

4. César estudia en casa con Patricia.   Sí   No
5. Roberto visita a César por la mañana.   Sí   No

VENTANILLA AL MUNDO HISPÁNICO   Addressing People in Spanish

Ventanilla al mundo hispánico is a specific section that relates to a cultural aspect of the *Episodios*.

Follow-up questions: 1. How should you greet your teacher when you arrive in class? 2. A friend you see on campus? 3. The receptionist in the doctor's office when you arrive for an appointment?

In Spanish, when people are not on a first-name basis, it is more common to address someone using just a title (*señor, doctora*) than to use the title plus the last name. Notice in the first conversation that the two people first greet each other as *señor Martínez* and *doctora Suárez*, but then call each other by just the title, *señor* and *doctora*. In the last conversation, Roberto addresses his friend's grandmother as *señora*. Notice, also, that when these titles are written in Spanish, only the abbreviation is capitalized: *doctora Suárez* but *Dra. Suárez*; *señor Martínez* but *Sr. Martínez*. Two formal forms of address in Spanish are *don* + first name and *doña* + first name: *don Roberto* (*D. Roberto*) and *doña Filomena* (*Dª. Filomena*). Even though *don* and *doña* are used with first names, they are reserved for very formal usage.

AUMENTAR EL VOCABULARIO

Aumentar el vocabulario organizes new words and phrases in broad categories partially based on the *Leer* vocabulary. Have students focus on high-frequency words and phrases. Feel free to ignore words that seem unnecessarily low-frequency to you.

OJO: *Simpático/-a* and *amable* are synonyms. Note that *simpático/-a* does **not** mean "sympathetic."

OJO: Notice that all of the indented words in this list are related to the preceding boldface word (or words).

OJO: Learn together pairs of words that have a relationship to each other: the opposites *abrir* and *cerrar, la entrada* and *la salida,* or the related words *la puerta* and *la ventana.*

el (la) amigo/-a — friend
   amable — friendly, kind
   simpático/-a — nice
abrir — to open
   cerrar — to close
   entrar — to enter
   pasar — to pass, go in
   Pase usted. — Come in. / Go ahead.
la casa — house
   en casa — at home
   el cuarto — room
   la entrada — entrance
   la puerta — door
   la salida — exit
   la ventana — window
Con permiso. — Excuse me.
las despedidas — farewells
   Adiós. — Good-bye.
   Buenas noches. — Good night.
   Hasta luego. — See you later.
   ¡Nos vemos! — See you!

OJO: Say *Pase usted* when you want to be polite or formal, or when you don't know who is at the door. If you are speaking to a friend or a family member, say *Pasa*.

OJO: Use *Con permiso* when you are going to reach over or pass in front of another person. Remember to use ¡*Perdón!* when you have done something that requires forgiveness, such as bumping into someone.

OJO: Remember that you learned *mucho/-a* in the Preliminary Chapter. *Muchas* is a plural form.

OJO: Notice that *Buenas noches* is both a *saludo* and a *despedida*.

el día	day
la mañana	morning
la tarde	afternoon
la noche	night
estar	to be
Gracias.	Thank you.
Muchas gracias.	Thank you very much. / Many thanks.
ir	to go
Vámonos.	Let's leave. / Let's get going.
¿Quién?	Who?
los saludos	greetings
Buenos días.	Good morning.
Buenas tardes.	Good afternoon.
Buenas noches.	Good evening.
Hola.	Hi.
¿Cómo estás?	How are you? (*familiar*)
¿Cómo está usted?	How are you? (*formal*)
¿Qué tal?	How's it going?
también	also
tener	to have
la universidad	university
la biblioteca	library
el (la) estudiante	student
estudiar	to study
el (la) profesor(a)	professor

LA FAMILIA DE CÉSAR

Each *etapa* contains a section of vocabulary that is presented visually.

OJO: You may need some of these words to talk about your family: *la madrastra* (stepmother), *el padrastro* (stepfather), *el hermanastro* (stepbrother), *la hermanastra* (stepsister), *el sobrino* (nephew), *la sobrina* (niece), *el cuñado* (brother-in-law), *la cuñada* (sister-in-law).

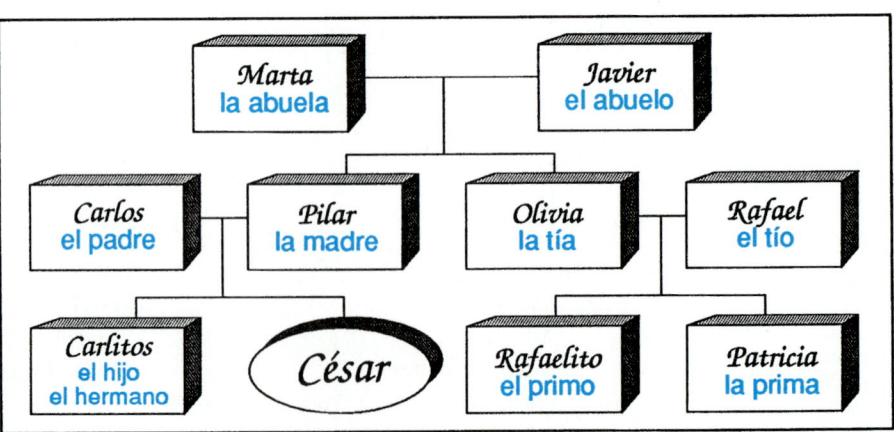

Preguntas (*Questions*)

1. ¿Quién es la madre de César?
2. ¿Quién es la madre de Rafaelito y Patricia?
3. ¿Quién es el hermano de César?
4. ¿Quién es la hermana de Pilar?
5. ¿Quién es el tío de Patricia?
6. ¿Quiénes son los padres (*parents*) de Olivia y Pilar?
7. ¿Quién es la tía de Carlitos y César?
8. ¿Quién es la prima de Carlitos?

OJO: You can use the same form for each answer: 1. ¿Quién es la madre de César? _____ es la madre de César.

1. Students can respond with just a name. Model sentences for longer responses: *Pilar es la madre de César.* 2. Have students think of additional questions about César's family.

USO PRÁCTICO DEL ESPAÑOL   Los saludos

The *Uso práctico del español* section teaches a specific functional aspect of language—whether it is lexical, structural, or cultural—by focusing on its use instead of on the rules surrounding it.

Subject pronouns are discussed in greater detail in the upcoming *Investigar la gramática* section.

The expressions that people use to greet each other in Spanish are determined both by the relationship between the individuals and by the time of day they meet. People who are professional acquaintances but not personal friends tend to speak in a more formal way, while young people who are classmates and friends are far more casual. Spanish has several ways of expressing degrees of formality and informality, as well as personal closeness and distance. Sometimes it is a question of the expressions that are used. For example, you would use *Buenos días* or *Buenas tardes* in a more formal situation than one in which you would use *Hola.* Sometimes it is a question of whether you address the other person by his or her first name or last name.

Speakers of Spanish also distinguish between formal and casual language by choosing between two different words for the pronoun "you." *Usted* (often abbreviated *Ud.*) is used by adults to address people whom they do not know or whom they know only in a professional or business context. Young people use *usted* (*Ud.*) with adults, especially those who are not family friends. The familiar form of address (*tú*) is used between family members and friends and with children. Although usage varies from country to country, in general, the *usted* form is more frequently used in Latin America than in Spain. The plural form of *usted* is *ustedes.*

The *Ponerlo a prueba* exercises practice the vocabulary—both from the list and from what is visually presented—as well as the *Uso práctico del español.*

Ponerlo a prueba

A. Los saludos. Give an appropriate greeting for the person at the time of day mentioned. Give the person a name if necessary.

Modelo: El profesor de español a las 8:00 de la mañana
Buenos días, profesor.

OJO: A formal greeting (*buenos días*) is used with an instructor instead of the more casual *hola.* The time of day determines that it is *buenos días* rather than another greeting.

1. La profesora de español a las 8:00 de la mañana
2. Un amigo a las 11:00 de la mañana
3. La abuela de una amiga a las 4:00 de la tarde
4. La madre de un amigo a las 9:00 de la noche
5. Tu hermana a las 6:00 de la tarde
6. El profesor de historia a las 2:00 de la tarde

B. **¿Qué dices y qué haces?** (*What do you say and what do you do?*) Give the best response for each situation.

Modelo: (You want to study quietly in your room.) ¿Qué haces?
a. abrir la puerta   b. cerrar la puerta   c. estudiar en la biblioteca
b. cerrar la puerta

1. (You are leaving the library.) ¿Qué haces?
   a. abrir la puerta   b. cerrar la puerta   c. estudiar en la biblioteca
2. (You see a friend.) ¿Qué dices?
   a. Hola. ¿Cómo estás?   b. Muchas gracias.   c. Pase usted.
3. (You see your aunt.) ¿Qué dices?
   a. Buenas tardes, prima.   b. Buenos días, abuelo.
   c. Buenas noches, tía.
4. (your father's nephew) ¿Quién es?
   a. mi tío   b. mi primo   c. mi abuelo
5. (You leave the house of your friend, César.) ¿Qué dices?
   a. Buenos días, César.   b. Vámonos, César.   c. Hasta luego, César.
6. (your grandmother's daughter) ¿Quién es?
   a. mi prima   b. mi madre   c. mi hermana

C. **Situaciones.** Give the appropriate expression for each of the following situations.

1. You open the door for your teacher.
2. Somebody has just given you something you asked for.
3. It is time for you and a friend to leave for the movies.
4. You need to walk in front of someone to get to your seat in the movie theater.
5. You are leaving a party at 11:30 P.M. (address the host or hostess).
6. You leave a friend's house but will see her later that day.

CH. **Definiciones.** Choose the word from the *Aumentar el vocabulario* section that matches each of the definitions. **¡OJO!** Use your guessing skills, since you will not understand every word.

1. El lugar en que se recibe una educación. Hay clases, profesores y estudiantes.

2. Los padres, los hermanos, los tíos, etc.
3. El hermano de mi padre
4. Una característica de un buen amigo (una buena amiga)
5. La entrada a un cuarto
6. El lugar en la universidad donde se encuentran los libros
7. La actividad principal de los estudiantes

D. **Mini-diálogos.** With a partner, make greetings and responses appropriate to the time and relationships indicated.

1. 7:30 A.M., your younger brother or sister
2. 10:00 A.M., your professor
3. 12:30 P.M., a friend
4. 2:00 P.M., a police officer who stops you for speeding
5. 8:00 P.M., the parents of your boyfriend or girlfriend
6. 8:05 P.M., your boyfriend or girlfriend

INVESTIGAR LA GRAMÁTICA   Los verbos irregulares **estar, ser, tener, ir**

Investigar la gramática focuses on high-frequency grammatical structures as they relate to the chapter functions. For example, estoy and tengo are essential to the functions of greeting and talking about oneself.

Point out to students that the format used here to introduce the subject pronouns corresponds to the paradigm used to present verbs in their conjugated form.

In English, you know that it is usually necessary to include the subject with a verb. For example, the phrase "speak Spanish" would be ambiguous, since there is no indication as to **who** speaks Spanish. In English, to clarify the meaning, we must add either a pronoun (I, you, he, she, it, we, they) or a noun (Carlos, my friends, Peruvians). In Spanish, the subject pronouns are:

yo	I	nosotros/-as	we
tú	you (*familiar*)	vosotros/-as	you (*familiar, pl*)
él	he	ellos	they (*m*)
ella	she	ellas	they (*f*)
usted	you (*formal*)	ustedes	you (*formal/familiar, pl*)

Verb forms are often displayed in a special format called a conjugation. The forms of the verbs are always given in the same order, whether you use the subject pronouns or not. In Spanish, the subject pronouns are usually used only for emphasis or clarity.

As you learn how to form and use verbs in Spanish, you will become aware of the fact that by changing the ending of the verb you can indicate what the subject of the verb is (such as "I," "you," or "they") regardless of whether the subject is specifically stated. You will also learn that verbs in Spanish are considered regular or irregular. You will soon learn how to create the forms of regular verbs, but in this *etapa* we begin with four irregular verbs that are very frequently used: *estar, ser, tener,* and *ir.*

Ser and estar

Two of the verbs, *estar* and *ser,* are both expressed in English by the verb "to be." *Ser* and *estar,* however, are not synonyms. In fact, their meanings are very different.

Here is the verb *estar* in the present tense.

yo	estoy	nosotros/-as	estamos
tú	estás	vosotros/-as	estáis
él/ella	está	ellos/-as	están
usted	está	ustedes	están

I am	*we are*
you (familiar) are	*you (familiar, pl) are*
he/she is	*they are*
you (formal) are	*you (formal/familiar, pl) are*

OJO: Notice that you use the same form, *está,* with *él, ella,* and *usted.*

Explain the use of the *vosotros* form in Spain. Students should be aware of the form, because it will be included in verb charts and conjugations, although not practiced actively.

OJO: Your instructor will explain the way the pronoun "you" is expressed in different parts of the Spanish-speaking world. Refer also to the explanation in the *Comentario cultural* in Chapter 2, third *etapa.*

Estar has several meanings, some of which you will learn later. Here are two very common uses of *estar* that you have already seen in this *etapa.*

a. to talk about how someone feels

¿Cómo **estás**?	*How are you?*
Estoy bien, gracias.	*I'm fine, thanks.*

b. to tell where something or someone is located

¿**Está** César?	*Is César at home?*
Sí, **está** en su cuarto.	*Yes, he's in his room.*

OJO: 1. ¿*Está César?* means the same thing as ¿*Está en casa César?* (Is César at home?). 2. Notice that no subject pronouns are used. When the subject is obvious from context or from the ending of the verb, it is not usually stated.

Ser also is expressed by the verb "to be" in English, but it has different meanings from *estar.* Here is the conjugation of *ser* in the present tense.

yo	soy	nosotros/-as	somos
tú	eres	vosotros/-as	sois
él/ella	es	ellos/-as	son
usted	es	ustedes	son

I am	*we are*
you (familiar) are	*you (familiar, pl) are*
he/she is	*they are*
you (formal) are	*you (formal/familiar, pl) are*

Ser is used:

a. to identify a person, place, or object

¿Cuál **es** tu libro?
Es el libro de español.

Which one is your book?
It's the Spanish book.

b. to give a definition

¿Qué **es** una biblioteca?
Es un edificio (*building*) que tiene muchos libros.
¿Qué **es** un estudiante?
Es una persona que estudia.

What is a library?
It's a building that has a lot of books.
What is a student?
It is a person who studies.

c. to classify or categorize people, places, or objects by their characteristics

¿**Es** usted estudiante?
No, no **soy** estudiante, **soy** profesor.
Patricia **es** muy simpática.

Are you a student?
No, I'm not a student; I'm a teacher.
Patricia is very nice.

OJO: You can classify people, places, or objects by many criteria: national origin, height, age, personality characteristics. *Ser* is used in all such cases.

Tener and *ir*

Two other common irregular verbs are *tener* (to have) and *ir* (to go). Here are their conjugations in the present tense.

tener		ir	
tengo	tenemos	voy	vamos
tienes	tenéis	vas	vais
tiene	tienen	va	van

Tener is used:

a. to talk about what someone has

Tengo muchos amigos en la universidad.
La biblioteca **tiene** una entrada.
Tenemos una buena clase de español.

I have a lot of friends at the university.
The library has one entrance.
We have a good Spanish class.

b. with *que*, followed by an infinitive, to express what one **has to do**

Tengo que estudiar.
Roberto **tiene que** hablar con César.
Los estudiantes **tienen que** hablar español en la clase.

I have to study.
Roberto has to talk to César.
The students have to speak Spanish in class.

OJO: Pronouns are not included in these conjugations so you can get accustomed to using pronouns only to add emphasis or specify the subject if it is not clear.

OJO: Many verb constructions in Spanish include a particular preposition that follows the verb, like *voy a* + infinitive. Practice saying sentences to yourself that use the preposition, so that the whole expression, such as *voy a estudiar* or *voy a leer*, becomes second nature to you.

Ir is used:

a. with the word *a* to express the concept of movement toward something

Voy a casa.
Los estudiantes **van a** la biblioteca.
Vamos a clase todos los días.

I am going home.
The students are going to the library.
We go to class every day.

OJO: *Ir + a + infinitivo* is a common way to talk about the future in Spanish.

b. followed by *a + infinitivo* to express an intent to do something in the future

¿**Vas a** estudiar en tu cuarto? *Are you going to study in your room?*
Voy a leer un libro. *I am going to read a book.*
Vamos a escribir todos los días. *We are going to write every day.*

Ponerlo a prueba

Expand this exercise by including definitions taken from the vocabulary activities in this *etapa*.

A. Definiciones. Give a definition for each of the following words using the cues indicated. Then ask the question that would lead naturally to your definition. Follow the model.

Modelo: el cuarto / una parte de la casa
El cuarto es una parte de la casa. ¿Qué es un cuarto?

OJO: Try to think up additional definitions for *estudiantes*.

1. los estudiantes / personas que van a clases
2. "Buenos días" / un saludo
3. la biblioteca / un edificio (*building*) que tiene muchos libros
4. la abuela / la madre de mi (*my*) madre
5. "Hasta luego" / una despedida
6. abrir / el contrario (*opposite*) de cerrar

OJO: Remember to use *estar* to express location.

B. ¿Dónde está todo el mundo? (*Where is everyone?*) David is somewhat distracted; he is not sure where his friends are. Provide him with the information he needs by creating sentences out of the elements given.

Modelo: Miguel / biblioteca *Miguel está en la biblioteca.*

These structured exercises can be made more communicative by asking students the follow-up question *¿Por qué?* (Why?) and having them answer: *¿Por qué está Miguel en la biblioteca? Miguel está en la biblioteca porque tiene que estudiar.* Try to have students work with the meaning of the sentence while they practice using the language forms.

1. César / cafetería
2. Patricia / su cuarto
3. Carlos y Julia / la entrada de la universidad
4. la profesora Suárez / la entrada de la universidad también
5. Laura y yo / biblioteca
6. ustedes / la clase de español
7. tú y Carmen / en casa

C. Las obligaciones. Patricia and César are talking about what their friends have to do. Using one element from each column, create sentences with the appropriate forms of *tener que*.

OJO: Form as many sentences as possible.

Yo		estar en clase por la tarde
Roberto		hablar español en la clase
Martín y yo	tener que	escribir todos los días
Los estudiantes		estudiar mucho
Usted		cerrar las ventanas
Tú		ir a la cafetería

Use the follow-up question *¿Por qué?* to make this activity more open-ended.

CH. **¿Adónde va?**   Say where each person listed is going.

   Modelo: Marcos / la universidad
   Marcos va a la universidad.

1. Paco / la biblioteca
2. tú / la biblioteca también
3. Linda y Flora / la clase de español
4. yo / la clase de español también
5. Patricia y tú / la casa de Roberto
6. nosotros / la casa de Roberto también

D. **¿Qué va a hacer (*to do*)?**   Now say what the same people are going to do.

   Modelo: Marcos / estudiar en la biblioteca
   Marcos va a estudiar en la biblioteca.

1. Paco / entrar en la biblioteca
2. tú / entrar en la biblioteca también
3. Linda y Flora / hablar español en la clase de español
4. yo / hablar español en la clase de español también
5. Patricia y tú / conversar en la casa de Roberto
6. nosotros / conversar en la casa de Roberto también

OJO: First think about the meanings of *ser* and *estar* that you have learned. For each sentence, decide whether you want to use *estar* to express health or location or whether you want to use *ser* to express identification, definition, or classification. Then complete the sentence with the appropriate form.

E. **¿Ser o estar?**   Complete the sentences.

1. Paco _____ en la biblioteca.
2. Paco _____ un estudiante excelente.
3. La biblioteca _____ en el centro (*middle*) de la universidad.
4. Paco y yo _____ en una clase de español.
5. La clase _____ muy buena.
6. Los estudiantes _____ simpáticos.
7. El profesor de español _____ simpático también.

Actividad F is open-ended. To guide students, model the questions they will ask and the answers they will give: *¿Tienes una familia grande? ¿Tienes una familia pequeña? Tengo una familia grande/pequeña.* Divide the class into groups of five people. Then have one person per group report on the results.

F. **Encuesta.**   ¿Tienes una familia grande (*large*) o pequeña (*small*)? Go to five people in the class and ask whether they have large or small families. Then report your results so they can be tabulated on the board.

OJO: Remember to use the verb *estar* to express location.

G. **¿Dónde está?**   Working with a partner, tell (or guess) where the following people are at this moment.

1. el presidente de los Estados Unidos
2. el profesor (la profesora) de español
3. un miembro (*member*) de tu familia (*specify the person*)

A. Una conversación con un amigo (una amiga). Working with a partner, do the following:

1. Greet your partner.
2. Inquire how your partner is.
3. Find out whether your partner has to study this afternoon and, if so, where (*¿dónde?*) he or she is going to study.

¡Tienes la palabra! is always one or more role plays that are based on the *etapa* or chapter functions. Encourage students to embellish their dialogue lines if they wish.

B. Una visita (*visit*) en casa. You arrive at the home of a friend. With a partner, act out the following situation.

Estudiante A (visitor)

1. You knock on the door. (Your friend opens it.) Greet your friend.
2. Inquire how your friend is.
3. Accept the invitation to enter, and say that you are going to close the door.

Estudiante B (host)

1. (You hear a knock.) Open the door. Greet your friend.
2. Inquire how your friend is.
3. Invite your friend in, and thank your friend for closing the door.

OTRA VUELTA

Play instructor tape, 1 min.

Play the *Entrada* section from the first *etapa* in class or have students listen in the laboratory.

Now listen again to the conversation that you heard at the beginning of this *etapa* and do the following.

1. The man asks the woman a lot of questions. Write down in Spanish two of his questions.
2. Do the two speakers part company at the end of the conversation, or do they dance? How can you tell?

COMENTARIO CULTURAL

The *Comentarios culturales* for Chapters 1–4 are in English.

Point out that people generally go to bed very late in Spain and in some parts of Latin America, and that the evening meal is often eaten at 9:00 or 10:00 P.M.

La tarde y la noche

The range of hours that is understood as afternoon (*la tarde*) or evening (*la noche*) is different in Spanish-speaking countries from the United States. In the United States, afternoon is generally thought of as the hours between noon and about 5:00 or 6:00 P.M., that is, the end of the working day. Evening begins at that point and extends until the individual retires for the night.

In most Spanish-speaking countries, afternoon (*la tarde*) extends later than in the United States. In most parts of Latin America, it would be quite common for two people to agree to meet at 7:00 in the afternoon, *a las siete de la tarde*. In Spain, the notion of afternoon extends even later, so you might arrange to meet a friend *a las 8:00 (ocho) de la tarde,* but probably *a las 9:00 (nueve) de la noche*.

Actividad. Indicate whether the following times of day belong to *la mañana, la tarde,* or *la noche* in Spanish-speaking countries.

Modelo: 1:00 P.M.   *Es la tarde.*

1. 8:00 A.M.
2. 4:00 P.M.
3. 9:30 A.M.
4. 7:30 P.M.
5. 10:00 P.M.
6. 6:30 P.M.
7. 5:30 P.M.
8. 1:30 A.M.

SEGUNDA ETAPA

Mucho gusto en conocerte

ENTRADA

Play instructor tape, 1 min.

OJO: Before you listen to the tape, read the introduction to the *Entrada* and study the questions. Take a guess at the answers, and then check yourself as you listen.

"Por favor..."

You are now going to hear a short conversation. Don't worry if you do not understand everything that is said, but listen carefully and see if you can determine

- how many people are talking
- where they are
- in a general way, what they are talking about

The second *etapa* of each chapter will contain a reading component instead of the oral *episodios* included in the first *etapa*. The purpose of these selections is to help students develop processing skills for dealing with written texts.

1. How many people are talking?
2. Where are they?
   a. at a party
   b. at the university
   c. at the entrance to a house
3. How can you tell? List the clues (words and expressions) that helped you figure it out.
   a.
   b.

ANTES DE LEER

READING STRATEGY 1

Use your background knowledge of the subject

As you begin to read Spanish, you may not recognize all of the words you encounter in the text, even though the situation or topic may be quite familiar to you. Use what you already know about the type of text and the subject to help you anticipate the content, and to provide clues to the meaning of new words. For example, if you are reading a job advertisement, your background knowledge of what such ads typically contain (qualifications, responsibilities, benefits, salary, and so on) can help you guess at the meaning of words you do not know. For this reason, once you have identified the type or topic of the reading in question, it is a good idea to reflect on what you know about the material as you read and try to understand the text.

OJO: The *Preparación* activity helps you comprehend the selections that follow by having you use your background knowledge about similar kinds of materials you may have read many times in English.

Preparación

Many newspapers and magazines have a section or a column in which readers write letters or advertisements in order to meet new friends or find pen pals. As you think about these kinds of advertisements, answer the following questions.

- What kind of information would you expect to find in these short advertisements?
- How might a personal ad placed by a person looking for a pen pal (*correspondencia*) differ from one placed by a person interested in establishing a more personal relationship (*amistad*)?

Segunda etapa

	Correspondencia	*Amistad*
1.		
2.		
3.		

■ List three things that you would expect a person to say about himself or herself in these two kinds of advertisements.

> *Información autobiográfica* (Autobiographical information)
> 1.
> 2.
> 3.

Margin notes:

Once students have prepared their lists (either in class or as homework), have them volunteer their responses and write a comprehensive list on the board.

OJO: Write here any additional information you would expect to find in a personal ad looking for a friend or a pen pal.

In the early chapters, in order to use selections that ⟦Play student tape, 1 min.⟧ are not contrived, it is necessary to treat some verb forms as vocabulary items. Words that students need know only receptively at this point are glossed as **OJO** notes in the student text.

Items are listed in alphabetical order in the reading selections. This procedure will be followed throughout the text.

Estudiar y practicar

la amistad	friendship
el año	year
el apartado postal	post office box
la comida (china)	(Chinese) food, meal
cortés	courteous, polite
los deportes	sports
ir al cine	to go to the movies
el (la) joven	young person
los pasatiempos	hobbies
el pelo (negro)	(black) hair

▲▲▲▲

LEER

OJO: The terms *hispano/-a* and *latino/-a* are used in the United States to refer both to a native of a Spanish-speaking country and to a U.S. citizen whose family is originally from a Spanish-speaking country.

OJO: The term *americano/-a* is used to refer to people from North, Central, and South America. As a result, it does not serve well to indicate national origin.

As you read the advertisements, look for the following information.

■ the sex of the person writing the ad
■ the age of the person writing the ad
■ the purpose of the ad

1 JOVEN LATINO, 31 años, desea corresponder con latina de 23–35 años. Responderé a todas las cartas que reciba. Fotografía y teléfono por favor. Carlos L., Alameda 3482, El Paso, TX 79924.

2 SEÑORA HISPANA SERIA, de 50 años, desearía conocer señor (americano, preferible) de 50 a 60 años, con fines de amistad únicamente. Me gusta la ópera, el ballet, ir al cine y leer, y me encanta la TV. Desearía conocer a alguien con gustos parecidos, que sea inteligente, cortés y de buenos principios. Responde C-1001, *Mundo Hispánico*.

Capítulo uno   ¡A conocernos!

OJO: 1. *Conocer* means "to meet a person." You will learn in the third *etapa* that it also means "to be acquainted with a place." 2. *Me gusta / Me encanta* means "I like." You will learn more about this structure in Chapter 2.

3 **JOVEN LATINA,** 5', estudiante, pelo negro, amable, desea conocer o corresponder con estudiante responsable y simpático. Pasatiempos: practicar deportes, me encanta comida china. María Luisa, Apartado Postal 2714, Miami, FL 33133.

DESPUÉS DE LEER

Datos generales.   Provide the missing information, based on the ads.

	1	2	3
sexo	____	____	____
edad (*age*)	____ años	____ años	____ años
fin (*purpose*): (¿amistad o correspondencia?)	____	____	____

Some instructors have students select pen pals from another class or another institution for ongoing writing projects. Others arrange pen pal exchanges with students in other countries. Lists of pen pals are often available through *Hispania,* the journal of the American Association of Teachers of Spanish and Portuguese (AATSP).

¿Cómo son? (*What are they like?*)   All of the writers have given some information about themselves and have described the person they are looking for (*buscan*). Make a list of the information they have provided.

	1	2	3
descripción:	_____ _____	descripción: _____ _____	descripción: _____ _____
busca:	_____ _____	busca: _____ _____	busca: _____ _____

Así soy yo (*That's the way I am*).   Imagine that you or a friend wants to place a personals ad. Prepare a short entry about yourself or your friend.

AUMENTAR EL VOCABULARIO

OJO: You have already learned the related words *el amigo* (*la amiga*) and *amable.*

la amistad   *friendship*
el año   *year*
   ¿Cuántos años tienes?   *How old are you?*
   Tengo ____ años.   *I am ____ (years old).*

OJO: Some useful phrases: *Soy rubio/-a* (I am blond); *Tengo el pelo castaño* (I have brown hair); *Soy pelirrojo/-a* (I am red-headed); *Tengo el pelo negro* (I have black hair); *Tengo el pelo gris/blanco* (I have gray/white hair).

OJO: Because the title *señorita* connotes both marital status and youth, the term *señora* is also used to refer to a more mature single woman. Remember that you learned in the first *etapa* that the word *doña* with a first name is also used to address or refer to mature women, for example, *doña Consuelo*.

la comida	food, meal
cortés	courteous, polite
aburrido/-a	boring, bored
inteligente	intelligent
interesante	interesting
la correspondencia	correspondence
la carta	letter
grande	big, large
pequeño/-a	small, little
el pasatiempo	hobby, interest
ir al cine	to go to the movies
practicar los deportes	to play sports
el pelo	hair
castaño	brown (for hair color)
rubio/-a	blond
el señor	man, gentleman
la señora	lady, woman (married or widowed), wife
la señorita	young, unmarried woman
el (la) chico/-a	boy; girl
el hombre	man
el (la) joven	young person
el (la) muchacho/-a	boy; girl
la mujer	woman
vivir	to live
el apartado postal	post office box
el apartamento	apartment
la calle	street
la dirección	address

OJO: Public restrooms are labeled *damas* and *caballeros,* which are more formal and courteous terms than *hombre* and *mujer*. *El chico* (*La chica*), used principally in Spain, and *el muchacho* (*la muchacha*), more common in Latin America, are two of the many terms that refer to children and young people. *El* (*La*) *joven* refers specifically to a teenager or young adult, rather than to a child.

Ventanilla al mundo hispánico — Las direcciones en español

OJO: As you read explanations like this one, think up examples to practice with, such as your address and telephone number, as well as those of your friends.

OJO: When a zero is at the beginning of a group of two numbers, you say the two digits one at a time. For example, if your telephone number is 321-0502, you would say in Spanish, *Mi teléfono es el tres veintiuno, cero cinco, cero dos.*

Addresses in Spanish are given with the name of the street first, and then the number of the house. If Carlos lives at 3482 Alameda Street, this would be expressed in Spanish as *la calle Alameda, número 3482.*

When you say numbers such as addresses or telephone numbers, you usually group them into sets of two. Carlos would give his address as *Calle Alameda, número treinta y cuatro ochenta y dos.* His friend Marcos would give his as *Calle Robles, número dieciséis veintiuno.* If your phone number is 924-1625, in Spanish you would say *Mi teléfono es el nueve, veinticuatro, dieciséis, veinticinco.*

LOS COLORES

OJO: There are several words for the color brown. Some common ones are *marrón* and *pardo/-a*. Remember that brown hair is expressed as *pelo castaño*. *Moreno/-a* is used to refer to a dark-skinned person.

OJO: Other colors are *rosado/-a* (pink) and *beige*. To express light or dark shades of color, use *claro* and *oscuro*: *verde claro* (light green), *gris oscuro* (dark gray).

Segunda etapa

Encourage students to use *es* to form a complete sentence: *El limón es amarillo.*

Note that this activity does not require control of noun/adjective agreement. Since it is explained and practiced in the *Investigar la gramática* section of this *etapa,* the concept can be introduced at this point.

¿De qué color es...? Match up the items on the left with the colors on the right.

____ 1. el limón
____ 2. el dominó
____ 3. el tomate
____ 4. el elefante
____ 5. el chocolate
____ 6. el océano
____ 7. la planta

a. café
b. azul
c. rojo/-a
ch. amarillo/-a
d. gris
e. verde
f. blanco/-a y negro/-a

USO PRÁCTICO DEL ESPAÑOL   Los números de uno a cien

1 uno	11 once	21 veintiuno
2 dos	12 doce	30 treinta
3 tres	13 trece	31 treinta y uno
4 cuatro	14 catorce	40 cuarenta
5 cinco	15 quince	50 cincuenta
6 seis	16 dieciséis	60 sesenta
7 siete	17 diecisiete	70 setenta
8 ocho	18 dieciocho	80 ochenta
9 nueve	19 diecinueve	90 noventa
10 diez	20 veinte	100 cien

OJO: The word *y* is never used after *cien* or *ciento.* It is used only between the tens digit and the ones digit, as in *noventa y uno* or *ciento noventa y uno.*

The numbers 21 through 29 are usually written as single words: *veintiuno, veintidós, veintitrés, veinticuatro,* and so on. From 31 through 99 the tens number is followed by the separate word *y* and then the units number: *treinta y uno, cuarenta y dos, cincuenta y tres,* and so on. To count even higher, for numbers between 101 and 199, you change *cien* to *ciento* and then add the rest of the number. For example, 101 is *ciento uno;* 156 is *ciento cincuenta y seis,* and 194 is *ciento noventa y cuatro.*

Ponerlo a prueba

A. **Repetir.**   Practice saying the following addresses and phone numbers.

1. Marcos vive en la calle Robles, número 1621.
2. Paco también vive en la calle Robles, número 1728.
3. El teléfono de Paco es el 924-2311.

4. El teléfono de Marcos es el 921-1820.
5. Rosita vive en la calle Olmos, número 8909.
6. El teléfono de Rosita es el 845-0370.

B. Conocer a Rosaura. Imagine that you are meeting Rosaura for the first time. Give an appropriate response to each of her comments and questions.

1. Me llamo Rosaura Martínez.
2. Vivo (*I live*) en un apartamento pequeño en la calle Central. ¿Y tú?
3. ¿Cuál es tu dirección?
4. Bueno, tengo que ir a casa.

C. Preguntas personales

1. ¿Cómo te llamas?
2. ¿Vives en una casa o en un apartamento?
3. ¿Cuál es tu dirección?
4. ¿Tienes vecinos simpáticos?
5. ¿Tienes una familia grande o pequeña?
6. ¿Cuál es tu color favorito?

CH. Definiciones. Match up the definitions with words and expressions from the *Aumentar el vocabulario* section.

1. el color de un taxi
2. el contrario de interesante
3. el color del chocolate
4. por ejemplo, ir al cine, leer un libro, etc.
5. el edificio donde vive la familia
6. el contrario de grande
7. relación entre dos amigos

D. Situaciones. Give an appropriate response to each of the following situations.

1. You meet someone who tells you his or her name.
2. The person asks what you are studying.
3. You ask the person for his or her telephone number.
4. You tell the person where you live.

INVESTIGAR LA GRAMÁTICA Nouns and Adjectives

You have already learned that nouns in Spanish are either masculine or feminine, and that the words *el, la, los,* and *las* are used to indicate the gender and number of nouns.

In Spanish all adjectives have to "agree" with the nouns they describe. Since all nouns are either masculine or feminine **and** are either singular or plural, the adjectives that modify or describe them reflect both their gender and number.

Many adjectives in Spanish have four forms.

OJO: Nouns that end in a consonant, like *la mujer,* form the plural by adding *-es.*

Point out that although most adjectives follow the noun, some, including the definite and indefinite articles, precede it.

	Masculine	*Feminine*
Singular	**un** caballer**o** simpátic**o** **el** amig**o** hispan**o**	**una** mujer simpátic**a** **la** amig**a** hispan**a**
Plural	**unos** caballer**os** simpátic**os** **los** amig**os** hispan**os**	**unas** mujer**es** simpátic**as** **las** amig**as** hispan**as**

You have learned some adjectives that end in consonants or *-e,* like *interesante, cortés, inteligente, grande,* and several colors. These adjectives do not change to show gender and consequently have just one singular form and one plural form.

la mujer interesante   las mujeres interesantes
el joven cortés   los jóvenes corteses
el suéter (*sweater*) azul   los suéteres azules
la casa gris   las casas grises

Adjectives of nationality are an exception. When the masculine singular form ends in a consonant, the adjective still changes to show gender as well as number.

OJO: Notice that the word *estudiante* can be either masculine or feminine. You can tell the gender of a word by its article, the adjectives that modify it, and the context.

	Masculine	*Feminine*
Singular	un estudiante **español** el caballero **francés**	una estudiante **española** la comida **francesa**
Plural	dos estudiantes **españoles** los caballeros **franceses**	dos estudiantes **españolas** las comidas **francesas**

Possessive Adjectives

In the first *etapa* you learned that one way to say that one person is related to another is to use *de* before the person's name.

OJO: Remember that you can **never** use the "-'s" form to show possession in Spanish.

la madre de César   *César's mother*
la abuela de Patricia   *Patricia's grandmother*

You can show that someone possesses an object in the same way.

la carta de Paco Paco's letter
las plumas de los estudiantes the students' pens

If you want to use the words "my," "your," "his," and so on, to show possession, rather than mention the person specifically, you use possessive adjectives.

mi	*my*	nuestro/nuestra	*ours*
tu	*your (familiar)*	vuestro/vuestra	*your (familiar, pl)*
su	*his, her, your (formal)*	su	*your (formal/familiar, pl), their*

Like other adjectives in Spanish, these possessives agree with their nouns in gender and number. Look at the following examples, and you will see that the possessive adjectives agree with the noun that is possessed.

mi libro	*my book*	mis libros	*my books*
tu carta	*your letter*	tus cartas	*your letters*
su clase	*his/her, their/your class*	sus clases	*his/her, their/your classes*

Mis clases son interesantes. **Nuestra** clase es grande. **Nuestros** amigos **chinos** viven (*live*) en una casa **blanca** en la calle Santiago.

OJO: Note this important difference from English: the possessive adjective agrees with the thing **possessed,** not with the **possessor.** "My books" is expressed with *mis* because the thing possessed (*libros*) is plural.

Review of *ser* and *estar*

Remember what you have learned about the verbs *ser* and *estar*. The verb *ser* followed by an adjective is used to define or characterize people or things. To do this, use *ser* with an adjective.

— ¿Cómo **es** tu mejor amiga? *What is your best friend like?*
— **Es** interesante y amable. *She is interesting and nice.*

An adjective with *estar* is used to report perceptions or impressions, how someone or something looks, seems, or feels. *Estar* is never used to define.

— ¿Cómo **está** tu amiga? *How is your friend feeling?*
— **Está** muy aburrida con sus clases. *She is feeling very bored with her classes.*

OJO: How would you say, "She is bored because the professor is boring"? *Está aburrida porque el profesor es aburrido.* To say how she is feeling, use *estar;* to characterize the professor as boring (or interesting or smart), use *ser.*

Ponerlo a prueba

A. **Creo que...** (*I think . . .*) Say the sentences aloud, substituting the underlined words with the following cues.

1. Los amigos españoles son muy simpáticos. (**our, your, my**)
2. La clase de arte es aburrida. (**his, their, your [pl]**)
3. Los tíos viven (*live*) en Santiago de Chile. (**my, David's, your**)
4. El abuelo vive en Santiago de Chile también. (**our, their, Alicia and Samuel's**)
5. Las cartas son muy interesantes. (**your, Linda's, his**)

Segunda etapa

OJO: Remember to use *unos/-as* to express "some."

B. **Tengo unos.** The following people have more than one of the nouns listed. Express this according to the cues.

Modelos: Elena / (libro interesante)   *Elena tiene unos libros interesantes.*
Marcos / (amigo español)   *Marcos tiene unos amigos españoles.*

1. Los señores Romero / (amigo aburrido)
2. Tomás / (pasatiempo interesante)
3. Linda y Jorge / (ventana grande) en su casa
4. Inés / (profesora excelente)
5. Patricia / (amiga china)
6. Enrique / (clase mala)

OJO: In each case figure out which noun the adjective refers to, and then decide whether it is masculine or feminine, singular or plural. Also, note that the verb *ser* is used in these sentences because people are being described in terms of their characteristics.

C. **¿Cómo son?** (*What are they like?*) Complete these brief descriptions of people who are looking for pen pals or new friends, using the correct form of the word in parentheses.

1. Nancy es (simpático) y tiene el pelo (castaño).
2. Daniel y Mario son (inteligente) y (cortés).
3. Anamaría es (hispano). Es (alto: *tall*) y (moreno).
4. Luis es (amable) y le gusta (*he likes*) la comida (chino).
5. Yvette y su hermana Celestina son jóvenes (francés). Son (rubio) y (simpático).
6. Rafael es (colombiano). Busca (*He is looking for*) amigos (norteamericano).

CH. **Combinaciones.** Make as many sentences as possible by using one element from each column.

Mi mejor amigo	estar	interesante
Mis profesores	ser	aburrido
Los amigos nuevos		simpático
Mi familia		grande
Mis clases		cortés
Uno de mis amigos		hispano

D. **¿Quiénes son estas personas?** Is there anyone in your class who fits the following descriptions?

1. Es buen(a) atleta.
2. Es inteligente y simpático/-a.
3. Es pelirrojo/-a.
4. Tiene el pelo negro.
5. Es hispano/-a.

OJO: When another syllable is added to words that have a written accent on the last syllable, like *francés* and *alemán*, the words lose the written accent: *franceses, alemana.*

E. **Lista de pasajeros.** You are the captain of a cruise ship, and like to announce to the passengers on the first night how many people of each nationality are on the cruise. Your steward has gotten the count; you read it aloud.

Modelo: alemanes   *Tenemos catorce alemanes.*

alemán	14	inglés	6
francés	22	colombiano	15
mexicano	17	chino	11
estadounidense	30	japonés	9

F. **Información, por favor.** Form small groups of four or five people and have one person in each group ask the others the following questions.

- ¿Cómo te llamas?
- ¿Cuál es tu número de teléfono?
- ¿Cuál es tu dirección?
- ¿Cuántos años tienes?

Write down the information gathered and prepare a telephone directory with addresses for the group. Use these headings as a guide.

Nombre   Dirección   Teléfono   Edad

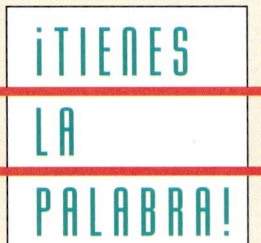

With a partner:

- Introduce yourself.
- Find out whether your partner lives at the university or at home. (*¿Vives en...?*)
- Ask for your partner's address. (*¿Cuál es...?*)
- Ask your partner to give you a phone number to call in an emergency (*en una emergencia*).
- Ask your partner's age.
- Find out your partner's favorite color. (*¿Cuál es tu color favorito?*)
- Give the same information about yourself.
- Thank your partner for the conversation.

OTRA VUELTA

Play instructor tape, 1 min.

Now listen again to the conversation between the man and the woman that you heard at the beginning of this *etapa*. Answer the following questions.

1. What address is the man looking for?
2. Whose house is the man looking for?
3. Why is the woman able to help him?

COMENTARIO CULTURAL

Presentaciones y saludos (*Introductions and greetings*)

Introductions and greetings among Spanish-speaking people are always accompanied by gestures. When two people meet for the first time, they always shake hands (*se dan la mano*) upon being introduced. When people who are already friends greet each other, females will kiss each other on one or both cheeks, males will shake hands, and a male and female will kiss each other on the cheek. Men friends, particularly when they have not seen each other recently, give each other a strong embrace (*un abrazo*), and heartily slap each other on the back.

There is in general more physical contact between friends in Spanish-speaking countries than in the United States. Men tap each other on the arm or shoulder in a friendly fashion to emphasize a point during their conversations. Women friends often walk along the street arm in arm, and frequent physical gestures of affection between parents and children persist as the children become teenagers and adults. Even recent acquaintances stand closer to each other in face-to-face conversation.

En latinoamérica es costumbre dar la mano al encontrarse con amigos.

Greetings and leave-takings are a very important way Spanish-speaking people show their concern and respect for each other. Time and energy are spent making certain that each person feels warmly welcomed and knows how much he or she will be missed upon departure.

Actividad. Practice introducing yourself to other members of the class by saying your name, responding appropriately to the other person's name (*Mucho gusto* or *Un placer*) and giving each other a firm handshake.

Practice greeting a good friend and giving him or her *un abrazo*.

En la residencia estudiantil

ENTRADA

Play instructor tape, 1 min.

El primer día de clases

You are going to hear a short conversation. Don't worry if you do not understand everything you hear. Listen carefully to figure out

- how many people are talking
- where they are
- in a general way, what they are talking about

The *Entrada* of this *etapa* is closely related to the tasks that students have to perform in the *Hablar* section. Suggestions: 1. Assign the *Leer en voz alta* words for homework, and play the *Entrada* in the next class. (You can do this while you are still working on the previous *etapa*.) Then, assign the *Hablar* section for the next class. 2. Play the *Entrada* in class before assigning the *Hablar* section as homework. 3. Have students listen to the *Entrada* in the language lab as homework.

1. How many people are talking?
2. Where do you think they are?
   a. at a party
   b. in the university
   c. on the street
3. List two topics that came up in the conversation
   a.
   b.

ANTES DE HABLAR

Play student tape, 1 min.

Preparación

In this section you will learn what people say in Spanish when they meet, make introductions, and inquire where someone is from. Even though your vocabulary is still quite limited, you will be able to recombine the phrases you know to exchange information with your classmates.

Leer en voz alta:

¿Cómo te llamas?	What's your name?
Me llamo...	My name is . . .
Mucho gusto.	Pleased to meet you.
Encantado/-a.	Pleased to meet you.
Igualmente.	The same here. / Likewise.
¿De dónde eres?	Where are you from?
Soy de (California).	I am from (California).
¡Qué interesante!	How interesting!
¡Qué bueno!	How nice!
¿Conoces (California)?	Have you ever been to California?
(No) Conozco (California).	I have (never) been to (California).
Quiero presentarte a (mi compañero/-a de cuarto).	I'd like you to meet (my roommate).
Tengo que irme.	I have to leave.

OJO: ¿De dónde eres? asks "Where are you from?" in the sense of "Where were you born?"

¡OJO! If you were speaking to someone older or in a formal situation, you would use the *usted* form: ¿De dónde es usted? Practice saying these to someone with sentences using the *usted* form: ¿Conoce usted California? Quiero presentarle a mi compañero/-a de cuarto.

Practicar

Imagine that you are out with a friend, and the friend runs into someone he or she knows. What would your friend say in this situation to

- greet the friend
- inquire about the friend's family
- introduce you to the friend

Now practice what you would say to

- respond to the introduction
- ask where the friend is from
- express interest, since you have never been to that place
- explain that you and your friend have to leave, because you are going to the movies

OJO: Since you are asking about how people feel, use *estar* in this question.

OJO: You learned the expression *ir al cine* in the second *etapa*.

HABLAR

This section consists of two role plays. Students should perform these in pairs without using notes or scripts, in order for them to serve as true speaking activities.

OJO: You have practiced this phrase as *Mucho gusto*. The longer form, *Mucho gusto en conocerte*, is slightly more formal.

OJO: Remember to shake hands as part of the introduction.

Add a third person to some of the pairs from the previous activity, to stay within the same context as much as possible.

"**Mucho gusto en conocerte.**" Act out the following scene with a partner.

> *Estudiante A*
>
> It is the beginning of the school year, so you do not yet know the other students in your classes. You sit down in the cafeteria next to someone you recognize.
>
> 1. Greet the student. Ask if he or she is in your Spanish class.
> 2. Introduce yourself.
> 3. Ask the student where he or she is from.
> 4. Express interest in the place.

> *Estudiante B*
>
> Someone you recognize from your Spanish class but do not yet know sits down next to you in the cafeteria and starts a conversation.
>
> 1. Respond to the greeting and to the student's question.
> 2. Respond to the introduction.
> 3. Tell the student where you are from, and find out the same information.
> 4. Express interest in the place.

"**Quiero presentarte...**" In groups of three, write out the following dialogue with an appropriate sequencing of speakers, as you might expect it to occur. Then, act out the scene for the rest of the class.

> *Estudiante A*
>
> Imagine that you and the person from your Spanish class whom you have just met are finishing your meals in the cafeteria. Your roommate comes over.
>
> 1. Introduce your new friend to your roommate.
> 2. Say that you have to go to the library.
> 3. End the conversation by saying good-bye to the other two people.

Estudiante B

You are being introduced to your new friend's roommate.

1. Acknowledge the introduction.
2. Find out where *Estudiante C* is from, and give that information about yourself.
3. Say that you have to leave because you have a class.
4. End the conversation by saying good-bye to the other two people.

Estudiante C

Your roommate introduces you to someone from his or her Spanish class.

1. Acknowledge the introduction.
2. Find out where *Estudiante B* is from, and give that information about yourself.
3. Say that you are going to have a cup of coffee (*tomar un café*).
4. End the conversation by saying good-bye to the other two people.

The purpose of the *Después de hablar* section is to incorporate a carefully designed writing component that will place emphasis on the process of composition and written expression. Each chapter contains a writing strategy that focuses students' attention on different aspects of communicating information and ideas in written form.

DESPUÉS DE HABLAR

WRITING STRATEGY 1

Organize your information

Learning to express yourself in writing involves much more than being able to join letters to form words, words to form sentences, and sentences to form paragraphs. The first thing you must do is decide **what** you want to communicate, and then arrange that information in the proper sequence. Once you have done that, you are ready to begin writing.

Letter to a new acquaintance. Imagine that you have been asked to write a brief introduction of yourself to your Spanish teacher. What are five pieces of information you might include?

Because Writing Strategy 1 is the first presented, the idea of cohesion is not addressed. However, you may want to mention to the students that more than one piece of information can be included in the same sentence by using linking words.

1.
2.
3.
4.
5.

Now, look at the list and decide on the best order of presentation. For example, you would probably tell the professor your name before anything else.

Once you have sequenced the information, write out the sentences so that they form a short paragraph.

Ventanilla al Mundo Hispánico   Los Estados Unidos de México

A map of Mexico is needed for the following activity.

Like the United States, Mexico is a republic composed of states and a federal district (*el Distrito Federal,* abbreviated D.F.). When Elena introduces herself to Alicia in the *Entrada* at the beginning of the third *etapa,* she says: "*Soy de Guadalajara, estado de Jalisco.*" This is similar to a U.S. resident's saying: "I am from Austin, Texas." Guadalajara is the capital of the state of Jalisco. There are 31 Mexican states, of which six border on the United States.

Actividad.   The following Mexican students are at a conference in the capital and are introducing themselves. How would they give their names and say where they are from?

Modelo: Laura Martínez / Manzanillo / Colima
Me llamo Laura Martínez. Soy de Manzanillo, estado de Colima.

1. Esteban Sánchez / Oaxaca / Oaxaca
2. Mauricio Moreno de Alba / Mérida / Yucatán
3. Isabel Morales / Hermosillo / Sonora
4. Luz María Pérez / Fresnillo / Zacatecas
5. Mario López / León / Guanajuato
6. Carolina Meléndez / La Paz / Baja California del Sur
7. Miguel Ortiz / Guadalajara / Jalisco
8. Ernestina Rodríguez / Jalapa / Vera Cruz
9. Antonio Rivas / Monterrey / Nuevo León

AUMENTAR EL VOCABULARIO

¿Cómo te llamas?   What is your name?
Me llamo...   My name is . . .

Tercera etapa

OJO: The verb *conocer* means "to be acquainted with, to know" when you are talking about knowing a person or a place. Knowing information is expressed with the verb *saber,* which you will learn in Chapter 2.

OJO: This is a partial list. If your nationality or the nationality of your ancestors is not included, use your dictionary to find the words you need to talk about yourself and your family, or ask your instructor for help.

Explain that the entire landmass containing North, Central, and South America is referred to as *América,* and that the United States is *los Estados Unidos de América,* often abbreviated as *EEUU.*

Note that some adjectives of nationality are presented here. Those for Latin American countries are presented in the map that follows this list.

OJO: Adjectives of nationality are written with lowercase letters in Spanish. Names of countries are capitalized.

OJO: Check your dictionary for the names of African countries and their adjectives of nationality such as *Ghana, ghaneano/-a, Egipto, egipcio/-a.*

    Mucho gusto.   *Pleased to meet you.*
    Encantado/-a.   *Pleased to meet you.*
    Igualmente.   *The same here. / Likewise.*
conocer   *to know (a person); to have been to (a place)*
    ¿Conoces...?   *Are you familiar with . . . ?*
    (Yo) Conozco...   *I am familiar with . . .*
irse   *to go away, leave*
    tengo que irme   *I have to leave*
    llegar   *to arrive*
    salir   *to leave, to go out*
    venir   *to come*
la nacionalidad   *nationality*
    alemán/-ana   *German*
    español(a)   *Spanish*
    estadounidense   *person from the United States*
    francés/-esa   *French*
    inglés/-esa   *English*
    italiano/-a   *Italian*
presentar   *to introduce*
    Quiero presentarte a...   *I'd like you to meet . . .*
¡Qué interesante!   *How interesting!*
    ¡Fíjate!   *Imagine that!*
    ¡Menos mal!   *That's a relief.*
    ¡Qué bueno!   *How nice.*
    ¡Qué impresionante!   *How impressive.*
ser de   *to be from*
    ¿De dónde eres?   *Where are you from?*
    África   *Africa*
    Alemania   *Germany*
    Asia   *Asia*
    España   *Spain*
    Estados Unidos   *United States*
    Europa   *Europe*
    Francia   *France*
    Inglaterra   *England*
    Italia   *Italy*
la vida estudiantil   *student life*
    bailar   *to dance*
    el (la) compañero/-a de cuarto   *roommate*
    conversar   *to converse, chat*
    charlar   *to converse, chat*
    descansar   *to rest, relax*
    escuchar música   *to listen to music*
    mirar/ver televisión   *to watch television*

OJO: *El dormitorio* means "bedroom in a house," not "residence hall" or "college dormitory."

el pasillo	hallway, corridor
la residencia	dormitory, residence hall
trabajar	to work

EL MAPA DE LA AMÉRICA CENTRAL Y LA AMÉRICA DEL SUR

Point out the origins of names of some Latin American countries: Argentina from Latin meaning "silver," related to French *argent;* Ecuador is the Spanish word for "equator"; Colombia is named after *Cristóbal Colón;* Bolivia is named for *Simón Bolívar, el Libertador;* Venezuela is a diminutive of Venice; Puerto Rico means "rich port"; Costa Rica means "rich coast."

Look at the map on page 47 and note the following:

Colombia es **un país.** Bogotá es **la capital** de Colombia. Otras dos **ciudades** en el mapa son Caracas y Lima.

¿En qué región está?   Indicate where the following countries are located.

Modelos: Colombia   *Colombia está en el noroeste de la América del Sur.*
              Guatemala   *Guatemala está en el norte de la América Central.*

1. Venezuela
2. Argentina
3. Panamá
4. Nicaragua
5. Chile
6. Brasil
7. Bolivia
8. Uruguay
9. El Salvador

Follow up: 1. Have students say where the university is located and where their states are located. 2. Ask the question *¿Cuál es la capital de...?*

USO PRÁCTICO DEL ESPAÑOL   Los números de 100 a 1.000.000

OJO: 1. Note that *mil* is invariable: *mil, dos mil,* and so on. 2. When talking about large quantities, *un millón* and *dos, tres,* etc. *millones* are followed by *de* when the number is an even multiple of one million: *Hay quince millones (15.000.000) de hispanos en los Estados Unidos.* But when the number is not an even multiple of one million, *de* is not used: *Hay quince millones quinientos mil (15.500.000) hispanos en los Estados Unidos.* 3. In Spanish, periods are often used to separate groups of large numbers, rather than commas.

100 cien	500 quinientos	900 novecientos
101 ciento uno...	600 seiscientos	1.000 mil
200 doscientos	700 setecientos	2.000 dos mil...
300 trescientos	800 ochocientos	1.000.000 un millón
400 cuatrocientos		

Large numbers are useful for talking about the value of expensive items.

Esta casa vale (*is worth*) $125.000 (ciento veinticinco mil dólares).

They are also useful for reporting dates and other statistics.

Hay aproximadamente 15.000.000 (quince millones) de hispanos en los Estados Unidos.

México declaró (*declared*) la independencia en 1810 (mil ochocientos diez).

¡OJO! Large numbers are necessary for expressing yearly dates, but don't forget how to use smaller numbers for expressing days of the month. For example, April 18 is expressed in Spanish as *el dieciocho de abril.* This way of talking about dates works for every day of the month except the first, which is always *el primero.* For example, November 1, 1975, is *el primero de noviembre de mil novecientos setenta y cinco.* Note also the way years are expressed.

OJO: The months are not capitalized in Spanish.

Here are the months of the year in Spanish:

enero	January	julio	July
febrero	February	agosto	August
marzo	March	septiembre	September
abril	April	octubre	October
mayo	May	noviembre	November
junio	June	diciembre	December

Ponerlo a prueba

A. ¡A practicar! Practice saying the following dates in Spanish.

1. March 11, 1957
2. December 25, 1841
3. July 4, 1776
4. August 1, 1690
5. May 31, 1964
6. tu cumpleaños (*birthday*)
7. el cumpleaños de Jorge Wáshington
8. la fecha de hoy (*today's date*)

B. ¿Cuánto vale? Say how much the following items are worth, using the cues in parentheses.

1. Un apartamento en Nueva York ($850.000)
2. Una casa en California ($475.000)
3. Un televisor (*television set*) modesto ($299)
4. Un estéreo excelente ($1.715)
5. Vivir en la residencia estudiantil por un año ($4.600)
6. Un Ferrari ($190.000)

C. Comentarios y respuestas. Match the comments on the left with the most appropriate response on the right.

Comentarios

_____ 1. ¿Conoces Santiago de Chile?
_____ 2. No conozco a Alicia de San Martín.
_____ 3. ¿En qué residencia vives?
_____ 4. Caracas está en el oeste de Venezuela, ¿verdad?
_____ 5. ¿De dónde eres?

Respuestas

a. Soy de Guadalajara.
b. Es de Santiago de Chile.
c. Vivo en Perkins Hall.
ch. No, está en el norte.
d. Sí, es la capital.

CH. Poner en orden lógico. Put the following words in logical order as indicated in parentheses.

1. (*outside to inside*) la calle, la residencia, el pasillo
2. (*smallest to largest*) noventa, cincuenta, ochenta, cuarenta
3. (*east to west*) Inglaterra, Alemania, Francia, Estados Unidos
4. (*arrive to leave*) salir, llegar, charlar, entrar
5. (*least interesting to most interesting*) fascinante, aburrido, interesante

D. Preguntas personales

1. ¿De dónde eres?
2. ¿De dónde es la familia de tu madre? ¿y la de tu padre?
3. ¿Conoces un país hispano? ¿Cuál?
4. ¿Tienes un compañero (una compañera) de cuarto?
5. ¿De dónde es?

E. Indicaciones geográficas. Say where the places in each of the following pairs are located with respect to each other.

Modelo: San Diego / Los Ángeles
San Diego está al sur de Los Ángeles.

1. Francia / España
2. Nueva York / Madrid
3. México / Colombia
4. Los Estados Unidos / Cuba
5. Miami / Chicago
6. Chile / Bolivia

INVESTIGAR LA GRAMÁTICA Regular -ar Verbs

In the first *etapa* of this chapter you learned several very common irregular verbs. They are called irregular because you must learn their forms individually. Fortunately, most verbs in Spanish are regular. That means that once you know the infinitive, you can use them immediately, since all regular verbs share the same endings.

There are three classes of regular verbs: *-ar* verbs, *-er* verbs, and *-ir* verbs. Since the great majority of verbs in Spanish are those that end in *-ar,* you will study them first. You will learn the *-er* and *-ir* verbs in Chapter 2.

Here are two -ar verbs that you already know in the present tense.

hablar

yo hablo	nosotros/-as hablamos
tú hablas	vosotros/-as habláis
él / ella / usted } habla	ellos/-as / ustedes } hablan

bailar

yo bailo	nosotros/-as bailamos
tú bailas	vosotros/-as bailáis
él / ella / usted } baila	ellos/-as / ustedes } bailan

To make any verb negative, place the word "*no*" right in front of it.

Marcos estudia literatura; **no estudia** matemáticas.

Elena y Alicia **no estudian** los sábados por la noche; charlan y bailan con sus amigos.

Ponerlo a prueba

A. Los fines de semana. Paco and Marcos are discussing what they and their friends do during the weekend. Complete their sentences using the elements given.

Modelo: Alicia / mirar televisión / por la noche
Alicia mira televisión por la noche.

OJO: Remember to use subject pronouns only for emphasis or clarity.

1. Elena / estudiar mucho / en la biblioteca
2. Elena y Alicia / charlar con sus amigas / en la residencia
3. Tú y yo / trabajar / los sábados
4. La profesora Suárez / preparar / una cena (*dinner*) especial
5. Uds. / llegar tarde (*late*) / a la fiesta (*party*)
6. Yo / no entrar / en la biblioteca
7. Tú / escuchar / música latina

B. Las quejas (*complaints*). You have gone to the university counseling center. All of your friends are complaining constantly, and you want to tell someone about it. Use one element from each column to make as many sentences as possible.

La persona		La queja
Marcos y Paco		la comida de la cafetería
Elena	odiar (*to hate*)	la clase de historia
Alicia		toda clase de ejercicio
Los estudiantes		estudiar los fines de semana
Todos nosotros		el fútbol americano
Yo		la música clásica

C. Un día típico en la vida de Susana. Complete the story of Susana's typical daily routine.

Susana _____ (**entrar**) en la clase de español. _____ (**Ser**) su clase favorita. El profesor _____ (**ser**) interesante y simpático. Susana _____ (**estudiar**) mucho para (*for*) sus clases. _____ (**Ir**) a la biblioteca por la tarde y _____ (**estudiar**) con mucha concentración. Sus amigos _____ (**conversar**) en la biblioteca, pero (*but*) Susana no _____ (**hablar**) con sus amigos cuando _____ (**estar**) en la biblioteca. Por la noche _____ (**descansar**) en su residencia. Ella y sus amigos _____ (**charlar**) y _____ (**mirar**) televisión. Susana _____ (**practicar**) guitarra y _____ (**llamar**: *to call*) a su familia por teléfono también.

CH. Entrevista. Find out the following information from your partner, and report it to the class.

- si (*whether*) estudia en la biblioteca o en su residencia
- si llega tarde a sus clases
- si tiene un intercambio de correspondencia con alguien (*someone*)
- si trabaja o si solamente (*only*) estudia

D. La vida estudiantil. Use this form to get your partner's opinion on the quality of life in your college or university. Record your partner's responses by putting checks in the appropriate columns.

La calidad de la vida estudiantil: una encuesta (**poll**)

Preguntas	Respuestas
1. ¿Dónde vives?	Residencia / Casa
◾ residencia	
◾ en casa	
2. ¿Es bueno vivir...?	
◾ en la residencia	Sí / No
◾ en casa	Sí / No

3. ¿Tienes compañero/-a de cuarto? Sí / No
4. ¿Es grande o pequeño el cuarto? Grande / Pequeño
5. ¿Te gusta (*Do you like*)...?
   - la comida en la cafetería Sí / No
   - la biblioteca Sí / No
   - el programa de deportes Sí / No

OJO: Remember to make the adjective agree with the noun *clases* in your response.

6. ¿Cómo son tus clases?
   - interesantes
   - aburridas
   - buenas
   - malas

¡TIENES LA PALABRA!

OJO: To talk about what countries your partner has been to, you say *Conoce...*

OJO: Remember to say *tus padres* and *tus abuelos* to your partner when you convert these cues to direct questions.

Do the following activities with a partner.

A. ¿Conoces otro país? With a partner, find out
   - whether he or she has ever been to a Spanish-speaking country
   - whether your partner has friends in another country or region

Report the information to the class. Then, interview your partner to find out
   - de dónde son sus padres
   - de dónde son sus abuelos

B. ¿Cuánto vale una casa? (*How much does a house cost?*) In groups of four, discover what the average cost of a house is in each person's neighborhood or city. Use the following form to record the information.

Región	*Costo de una casa*
1.	
2.	
3.	
4.	

OTRA VUELTA

Play instructor tape, 1 min.

Now listen again to the conversation that you heard at the beginning of the third *etapa* and write down the following information.

1. The names of the three people and where they are from

   | Nombre | Ciudad (City) | País (Country) |

   a.
   b.
   c.

2. The university class that is mentioned by name

COMENTARIO CULTURAL

Hay muchos Santiagos

When someone asks where you are from, there are several ways you can answer the question correctly. The choice you make usually depends on the context in which the question is asked. For example, if you are traveling in Mexico and someone asks you the question, you would most likely respond with *Soy de los Estados Unidos,* or name the country from which you come. On the other hand, in another context you might answer by indicating the region, as in *Soy del Caribe.* Sometimes, the name of the city is sufficient, as in *Soy de Madrid.* In other instances, more information might be included, as in *Soy de Hialeah, cerca de Miami.* Occasionally, it is necessary to add the name of the country, as in *Soy de Santiago de Chile.* It is important to add the *de Chile* for clarification, since there are several cities of the same name in the Hispanic world. Santiago de los Caballeros, for example, is the second largest city in the Dominican Republic, and Santiago de Cuba is an industrial city on the southeast coast of Cuba. Santiago de Compostela is located in the northwestern corner of Spain and has been a center for religious pilgrimages since the Middle Ages.

Here is a list of cities that might be confused if only the name of the city is used.
   Athens, Greece
   Cambridge, England
   Cartagena, Colombia
   Geneva, Switzerland
   Granada, Spain
   Lima, Perú
   London, England
   Paris, France
   San Jose, California
   Valencia, Spain
In addition, the names of countries can be confused with cities or towns of the same name, unless the speaker is specific.

Actividad. Decide how people who live in the following locations would introduce themselves, and indicate what confusion might arise from a less-than-complete response.

Athens, Alabama
Barcelona, Spain
Cambridge, Maryland
Cartagena, Spain
Geneva, New York
Granada, Nicaragua
Lima, Ohio
London, Kentucky
Mexico, Maine

Moscow, Idaho
New Orleans, Louisiana
Paris, Texas
Peru, Indiana
Port-of-Spain, Trinidad
San José, Costa Rica
Trinidad, Colorado
Valencia, Venezuela

ACTIVIDADES DE INTEGRACIÓN

Play video

Program 1 *A caballo*
The horse and the expansion of the Spanish empire

A. **Soy yo.** Write a short autobiographical statement in which you include the following information:

- your name
- the fact that you are a student
- the name of your university or college
- where you live (*Vivo en...*)
- where you are from originally (*Soy de...*)

B. **Imagínate.** Act out the following situations with another student.

1. Interview a student in your class and prepare a short report. Find out

    - where the person lives
    - whether he or she has a large or small family
    - how many brothers and sisters he or she has
    - where his or her family is from

2. You are the subscription manager for a newspaper. A new customer has just told you that he or she wants to subscribe to the newspaper. You ask for the information you need and write it on the form.

Nombre:

Dirección:

Casa / apartamento:

Código postal (*Zip code*):

Teléfono:

C. **En tu opinión...** Ask your partner's opinion about the following topics. Use the form to record your partner's responses.

En tu opinión, ¿es mejor (*better*)...?

- tener una familia grande o una familia pequeña
- vivir en una casa o en un apartamento
- vivir en casa o en una residencia
- tener compañero/-a de cuarto o no

VOCABULARIO

The end-of-chapter vocabulary represents new words that have been introduced in the chapter. You are **not** expected to be able to produce all of these words at this time. The words are presented here in semantic groupings to make it easier for you to find the words you need to communicate about the topics included in the chapter.

La ciudad y la casa
The city and the home

apartado (m) postal   *post office box*
apartamento   *apartment*
calle (f)   *street*
capital (f)   *capital*
casa (f)   *house*
centro (m)   *center*
ciudad (f)   *city*
cuarto (m)   *room, bedroom*
dirección (f)   *address; direction*
entrada (f)   *entrance*
puerta (f)   *door*
salida (f)   *exit*
ventana (f)   *window*

Los colores
Colors

amarillo/-a   *yellow*
anaranjado/-a   *orange*
azul   *blue*
beige   *beige*
blanco/-a   *white*
café   *brown*
castaño   *brown (for hair color)*
gris   *gray*
morado/-a   *purple*
negro/-a   *black*
rojo/-a   *red*
rosado/-a   *pink*
rubio/-a   *blond*
verde   *green*

Los puntos cardinales
Directions (of the compass)

este (m)   *east*
noreste (m)   *northeast*
noroeste (m)   *northwest*
norte (m)   *north*
oeste (m)   *west*
sur (m)   *south*
sureste (m)   *southeast*
suroeste (m)   *southwest*

La familia y los amigos
Family and friends

abuela (f)   *grandmother*
abuelo (m)   *grandfather*
abuelos (m/f pl)   *grandparents*
amiga (f)   *friend (female)*
amigo (m)   *friend (male)*
amistad (f)   *friendship*
chica (f)   *girl*
chico (m)   *boy*
familia (f)   *family*
hermana (f)   *sister*
hermano (m)   *brother*
hermanos (m pl)   *siblings*
hombre (m)   *man*
joven (m/f)   *young person*
madre (f)   *mother*
muchacha (f)   *child (female)*
muchacho (m)   *child (male)*
mujer (f)   *woman*
padre (m)   *father*
padres (m pl)   *parents*
prima (f)   *cousin (female)*
primo (m)   *cousin (male)*
señor (m)   *man, gentleman*
señora (f)   *woman, lady (married or widowed), wife*
señorita (f)   *young, unmarried woman*
tía (f)   *aunt*
tío (m)   *uncle*
tíos (m pl)   *aunt and uncle*

Los meses del año
Months of the year

año   *year*
mes   *month*
enero   *January*
febrero   *February*
marzo   *March*
abril   *April*
mayo   *May*
junio   *June*

julio *July*
agosto *August*
septiembre *September*
octubre *October*
noviembre *November*
diciembre *December*

Los números
Numbers

uno/-a *one*
dos *two*
tres *three*
cuatro *four*
cinco *five*
seis *six*
siete *seven*
ocho *eight*
nueve *nine*
diez *ten*
once *eleven*
doce *twelve*
trece *thirteen*
catorce *fourteen*
quince *fifteen*
veinte *twenty*
treinta *thirty*
cuarenta *forty*
cincuenta *fifty*
sesenta *sixty*
setenta *seventy*
ochenta *eighty*
noventa *ninety*
cien, ciento *one hundred*
doscientos/-as *two hundred*
trescientos/-as *three hundred*
cuatrocientos/-as *four hundred*
quinientos/-as *five hundred*
seiscientos/-as *six hundred*
setecientos/-as *seven hundred*
ochocientos/-as *eight hundred*
novecientos/-as *nine hundred*
mil *one thousand*
un millón *one million*
dos millones *two million*

Países y nacionalidades
Countries and nationalities

África (f) *Africa*
africano/-a (m/f) *African*
Alemania (f) *Germany*
alemán/-ana (m/f) *German*
argentino/-a (m/f) *Argentinian*
Asia *Asia*
boliviano/-a (m/f) *Bolivian*
brasileño/-a (m/f) *Brazilian*
colombiano/-a (m/f) *Colombian*
costarricense (m/f) *Costa Rican*
chileno/-a (m/f) *Chilean*
ecuatoriano/-a (m/f) *Ecuadorian*
España (f) *Spain*
español(a) (m/f) *Spaniard*
Estados Unidos (m pl) *United States*
estadounidense (m/f) *person from the U.S.*
francés/-esa (m/f) *French*
Francia (f) *France*
guatemalteco/-a (m/f) *Guatemalan*
hondureño/-a (m/f) *Honduran*
Inglaterra *England*
inglés/-esa (m/f) *English*
Italia *Italy*
italiano/-a (m/f) *Italian*
mexicano/-a (m/f) *Mexican*
nacionalidad (f) *nationality*
país (m) *country*
panameño/-a (m/f) *Panamanian*
paraguayo/-a (m/f) *Paraguayan*
peruano/-a (m/f) *Peruvian*
salvadoreño/-a (m/f) *Salvadoran*
uruguayo/-a (m/f) *Uruguayan*
venezolano/-a (m/f) *Venezuelan*

Saludos y despedidas
Greetings and farewells

adiós *good-bye*
Buenas noches. *Good evening. / Good night.*
Buenas tardes. *Good afternoon.*
Buenos días. *Good morning.*
¿Cómo está usted? *How are you? (formal)*
¿Cómo estás? *How are you? (familiar)*
Hasta luego. *See you later.*
Hola. *Hi.*
¡Nos vemos! *See you!*
¿Qué tal? *How's it going?*
Vámonos. *Let's leave. / Let's get going.*

La universidad
The university

biblioteca (f) *library*
compañero/-a (m/f) de cuarto *roommate*
estudiante (m/f) *student*
pasatiempo (m) *hobby, interest*
pasillo (m) *hallway, corridor*
profesor(a) (m/f) *professor, teacher*
residencia (f) *residence hall, college dormitory*
universidad (f) *university*
vida (f) estudiantil *student life*

Pronombres personales
Subject pronouns

yo *I*
tú *you (familiar)*
él *he*
ella *she*
usted *you (formal)*
nosotros/-as *we*
vosotros/-as *you (familiar, pl)*
ellos/-as *they*
ustedes *you (formal/familiar, pl)*

Vocabulario

Palabras descriptivas
Descriptive words

aburrido/-a *boring, bored*
amable *friendly, kind*
cortés *courteous, polite*
grande *big, large*
impresionante *impressive*
inteligente *intelligent*
interesante *interesting*
pequeño/-a *small, little*
simpático/-a *nice*

Verbos y expresiones verbales
Verbs and verbal expressions

abrir *to open*
bailar *to dance*
cerrar (ie) *to close*
conocer *to be familiar with, acquainted with (a place); to meet; to know a person*
conversar *to converse*
charlar *to chat*
descansar *to rest, relax*
entrar *to enter*
escuchar música *to listen to music*
estar *to be*
estudiar *to study*
¡Fíjate! *Imagine that!*
ir (al cine) *to go (to the movies)*
irse *to go away*
llegar *to arrive*
mirar (televisión) *to watch (television)*
pasar *to pass, go in*
Pase usted. *Come in. / Go ahead.*
pensar *to think*
practicar deportes *to play sports*
presentar *to introduce*
salir *to leave*
ser de *to be from*
tener *to have*
tener que *to have to (do something)*
trabajar *to work*
venir *to come*
ver *to see*
vivir *to live*

Otras palabras y expresiones útiles
Other useful words and expressions

carta (f) *letter*
comida (f) *food, meal*
Con permiso. *Excuse me (asking for permission).*
¿Conoces...? *Have you ever been to (a place)?*
correspondencia (f) *correspondence*
¿Cómo te llamas? *What's your name?*
¿Cuántos años tienes? *How old are you?*
¿De dónde eres? *Where are you from?*
despedida (f) *farewell*
día (m) *day*
en casa *at home*
en mi opinión *in my opinion*
encantado/-a *pleased to meet you*
Gracias. *Thank you.*
Igualmente. *The same here. / Likewise.*
mañana (f) *morning*
mapa (m) *map*
Me llamo... *My name is . . .*
¡Menos mal! *That's a relief! / It's a good thing!*
Muchas gracias. *Many thanks. / Thank you very much.*
Mucho gusto. *Pleased to meet you.*
Muy bien, gracias. *Very well, thank you.*
noche (f) *night*
pelo (m) *hair*
¡Qué bueno! *How nice.*
¡Qué impresionante! *How impressive.*
¡Qué interesante! *How interesting!*
¿Quién? *Who?*
Quiero presentarte a... *I'd like you (familiar) to meet . . .*
saludo (m) *greeting*
Soy de... *I am from . . .*
también *also*
tarde (f) *afternoon*
Tengo ____ años. *I am ____ years old.*

VOCABULARIO PERSONALIZADO

¡A conocernos más!

Capítulo 2

COMMUNICATIVE OBJECTIVES

In this chapter, you will learn several ways to

- give, request, and understand information
- express likes and dislikes
- tell time
- give and understand simple directions
- talk about future activities

Antes de la primera clase

ENTRADA

Play instructor tape, 1 min.

David y Raquel hablan de sus cursos

Listen to the following conversation between David and Raquel as they talk about their classes. Although you may not understand everything they say, listen especially for the courses they are taking. As you listen, refer to the following list and check the names of the four courses each is taking. Listen carefully because there are some courses on the list that David and Raquel do **not** mention in their conversation.

Asignatura

el alemán	la biología
el español	la física
el francés	la filosofía
el inglés	la historia de los Estados Unidos
el cálculo	la historia de Europa
la historia del arte	

EMPEZAR A ESCUCHAR

Play student tape, 3 min.

Leer

¡Oye!	*Hey!* (*to get someone's attention*)
¿Qué hora es?	*What time is it?*
primero/-a	*first*
nervioso/-a	*nervous*
Tengo ganas de (comenzar).	*I want to (get started).*
Cálmate.	*Settle down.*
No es para tanto.	*It's not so bad as all that.*
No te preocupes.	*Don't worry.*
fácil	*easy*
Ya verás.	*You'll see.*

Repetir

Listen to your student tape and repeat the words and phrases you hear.

Identificar

On a separate sheet of paper, write in a column the words and phrases in Spanish from the list in the preceding *Entrada* section. You will hear some sentences on your tape. Whenever you hear one of these words or phrases, write next to it the number of the sentence in which it appears. Each sentence will be read twice. You may stop and start the tape as often as you wish.

Escribir

You will hear some sentences in Spanish. Each one will be read twice. Write them down as you listen, starting and stopping the tape as needed.

Reconocer

Each of the sentences you have just written contains one or more of the words and phrases from the preceding *Leer* list. Read the sentences carefully, and underline as many of the words and phrases from the list as you can find. As you read, make any necessary corrections in your sentences.

ESCUCHAR

Play student tape, 1 min.

EPISODIO 1: "Oye, Alicia, ¿qué hora es?"

Enfoque comunicativo

Alicia and Elena are talking in the cafeteria about their first university class. As you listen to their conversation on your student tape, try to figure out

- what class it is
- what time it starts

La clase es:	a. español	b. inglés	c. sesión de orientación
La hora:	a. 8:00	b. 8:30	c. 9:00
	(las ocho)	(las ocho y media)	(las nueve)

Enfoque lingüístico

Listen again to the conversation between Elena and Alicia and write down

- what Elena says to get Alicia's attention at the beginning of the conversation
- what Elena says to indicate that she is nervous

ESCUCHAR

Play student tape, 1 min.

Episodio 2: "¡Cálmate, Marcos!"

Enfoque comunicativo

Marcos and Paco are also in the cafeteria and are talking about the *sesión de orientación*. As you listen to their conversation on your student tape, try to figure out

- how Marcos feels
- how Paco feels

> Circle the word *Sí* if the statement is true, and *No* if it is false.
>
> | | | |
> |---|---|---|
> | Marcos está nervioso. | Sí | No |
> | Paco está nervioso. | Sí | No |

Enfoque lingüístico

Listen again to the conversation between Marcos and Paco and write down

- two expressions that Paco uses to calm Marcos down
- the name of the city that Marcos mentions

VERIFICAR

¿Sí o no?

Now listen to the whole conversation again. As you listen, indicate whether the following statements are true (*Sí*) or false (*No*).

1. La sesión de orientación es en *Adams Humanities*.	Sí	No
2. Paco está muy nervioso.	Sí	No
3. Marcos es de Bogotá, Colombia.	Sí	No
4. Marcos y Paco están en la sesión de orientación.	Sí	No
5. Marcos conoce el sistema de educación en los Estados Unidos.	Sí	No

Ventanilla al mundo hispánico — Los sistemas de educación

One of the reasons the international students in the preceding *Episodios* are nervous is that the educational system in the United States is indeed different from that in Europe and Latin America. Universities in those regions are generally very large. Most of the classes, which are also large, are held in auditoriums and follow a lecture format, with no small discussion sections. Students enter a particular *facultad,* or school, such as engineering or law, at what would be the undergraduate level in the United States, and take courses exclusively in their own field.

AUMENTAR EL VOCABULARIO

la cafetería	*cafeteria*
comer	*to eat*
el comedor	*dining room*
la cocina	*kitchen*
el desayuno	*breakfast*
el almuerzo	*lunch*
la cena	*dinner*
comenzar (ie)	*to begin, start*
¿Cuál?	*Which (one)? / What?*
¿Cuándo?	*When?*
¿Cuánto/-a?	*How much?*
¿Dónde?	*Where?*
¿Por qué?	*Why?*
¿Qué?	*What?*
el curso	*course*
las ciencias políticas	*political science*
la psicología	*psychology*
la historia	*history*
la economía	*economics*
las matemáticas	*math*
la biología	*biology*
la informática	*computer science*
la química	*chemistry*
la contabilidad	*accounting*
fácil	*easy*
difícil	*difficult*
imposible	*impossible*
nervioso/-a	*nervous, anxious*
alegre	*glad, happy*
contento/-a	*happy, pleased*
No te preocupes.	***Don't worry.***
Cálmate.	*Settle down.*
¡Manos a la obra!	*Let's get to work!*
Claro.	*Of course.*
¡Oye!	*Hey! (to get someone's attention)*
No es para tanto.	*It's not so bad as all that.*

OJO: *Cuántos/-as* means "how many" and is used for things that can be counted.

OJO: You may also see this word spelled *la sicología*.

OJO: Additional courses that may be useful to know are *la sociología* (sociology), *el periodismo* (journalism), *el arte* (art), *la música* (music), *la filosofía* (philosophy), *la física* (physics), *la ingeniería* (engineering). Use your dictionary or ask your instructor for the names of other courses you may be taking.

Remind students that they learned another reassuring expression, *Menos mal,* in Chapter 1.

primero/-a	first
segundo/-a	second
tercero/-a	third
cuarto/-a	fourth
quinto/-a	fifth
tener ganas de (+ inf.)	to want to, to feel like (*doing something*)
desear	to want, desire
querer (ie)	to want
Ya verás.	You'll see.

LOS DÍAS DE LA SEMANA

SEPTIEMBRE						
lunes	martes	miércoles	jueves	viernes	sábado	domingo
		1	2	3	4	5
6	7	8	9	10	11	12
13	14	15	16	17	18	19

ayer (*yesterday*), **hoy** (*today*), **mañana** (*tomorrow*)

OJO: You can now say the complete date: *Hoy es lunes, el 20 de septiembre de 19...*

The Hispanic calendar normally begins with *lunes* and ends with *domingo*. The phrase "on Monday," meaning "next (or last) Monday," is expressed simply by *el lunes*. To express the plural of the days of the week, you change *el* to *los* and add *-s* to *sábado* and *domingo*. For example, *el sábado* would become *los sábados* if you are speaking about more than one Saturday.

El domingo voy a Chicago.	On Sunday I am going to Chicago.
Los domingos visitamos a los abuelos.	On Sundays we visit our grandparents.
Los lunes estudiamos en la universidad.	On Mondays we study at the university.

OJO: Use your guessing skills.

¿Qué día es? Read the following phrases and identify the day that is being referred to.

1. el día antes del (*before*) viernes
2. un día que no tenemos clases
3. tu día favorito de la semana

4. el día después del (*after*) martes
5. los días que tenemos clase de español

USO PRÁCTICO DEL ESPAÑOL ¿Qué hora es?

OJO: Notice that *ser* is used to tell time. Add this to the uses of *ser* that you have already learned.

In this chapter people talk about what time they do certain things. Here are some of the time expressions you have already heard.

¿Qué hora es? *What time is it?*
Son las ocho y media. *It is 8:30.*
La sesión de orientación comienza *The orientation session starts at 9:00.*
 a las nueve.

OJO: To help you learn how to tell time, the times used as examples in this section have been written out in words. Of course, you would normally use numerals when you write the time in Spanish, as you do in English.

Here are some answers to the question *¿Qué hora es?*

Es la una.   Son las tres.   Son las nueve.

To say what time it is, begin with *Son las...* . *Es la...* is used with *la una* only.

Time before or after the hour is expressed by saying the hour plus or minus the number of minutes. Use *y* for plus, and *menos* for minus.

Point out that the popularity of digital clocks is creating a tendency in Spanish, just as in English, to say the numbers exactly as they are read.

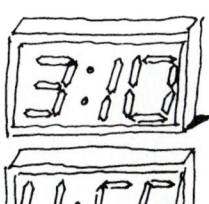 Son las tres y diez.

 Son las cinco menos cinco.
Son las cuatro y cincuenta y cinco.

 Son las once y veintitrés.

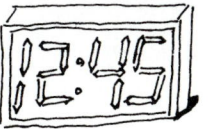 Es la una menos quince.
Son las doce y cuarenta y cinco.

For quarter- and half-hour times, the expressions *y cuarto* and *y media* are often used instead of *y quince* and *y treinta*.

Es la una menos cuarto. 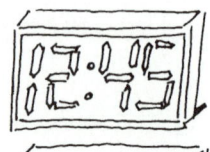 Es la una menos quince.

Son las siete y media. 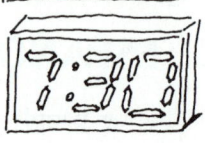 Son las siete y treinta.

Son las doce y cuarto. 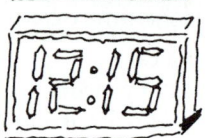 Son las doce y quince.

The answer to the question *¿A qué hora... ?* (At what time does something happen?) always includes the word *a*.

—**¿A qué hora** es tu clase de inglés? —**Es a** la una y veinte.

—**¿A qué hora** es la sesión de orientación? —**Es a** las nueve.

Ponerlo a prueba

A. ¿Qué hora es? Say aloud the times indicated on each of the following clocks.

Modelo: *Son las tres y cuarto de la madrugada.*

1.

4.

2.

5.

3.

6.

Primera etapa

Additional ordinal numbers are introduced in the Uso práctico of Chapter 7, second etapa.

B. Poner en orden. Put the activities listed in the order in which you do them on a typical day. Then report them to the class by starting your sentences with: *Primero... ; Segundo... ; Tercero... ; Cuarto... ; Quinto... .*

Modelo: *Primero, voy a la cafetería para el desayuno a las siete y media. Segundo...*

1. Voy a la clase de español.
2. Estudio en... (la biblioteca, mi cuarto, etc.).
3. Hablo con mis amigos.
4. Voy a la cafetería para el desayuno.
5. Voy a mi clase de...

C. El uso de expresiones tranquilizadoras (*Using reassuring expressions*). For each of the following situations, choose an expression from the *Aumentar el vocabulario* section that you might use in response.

1. You and your friend have taken a break, and now you are eager to start studying again.
2. A friend asks you if you think he is good enough to make the basketball team this year.
3. Your friend is very nervous about the economics exam she is taking later today.
4. Your friend is looking worried just after taking her Spanish exam.

CH. ¿Cómo te sientes? (*How do you feel?*) Using words from *Aumentar el vocabulario* choose the expression that matches how you would feel in each of the following situations.

Modelo: *Vas a un concierto de Los Lobos el sábado.*
¡Estoy contento/-a!

The response to item 2 is Estoy aburrido/-a, introduced in Chapter 1.

1. Es el primer día de clases en la universidad.
2. Tu clase de filosofía no es interesante.
3. Tu hermana tiene un amigo muy amable.
4. Una persona simpática te invita (*invites you*) a una fiesta.

D. Un día en la vida de Carlota Espinosa. Imagine that you are following Carlota around for a day and are making a record of where she is at various times. Use the elements of time and place to recreate Carlota's whereabouts at the hours listed. Report the time and Carlota's location. The first one is answered for you in the *modelo*.

Modelo: *Son las siete de la mañana. Carlota está en su cuarto.*

Hora
7:00 de la mañana

Lugares posibles
en su cuarto

Hora	Lugares posibles
9:00 de la mañana	en la clase de español
1:00 de la tarde	en la cafetería
2:00 de la tarde	en la casa de sus padres
5:00 de la tarde	en el cuarto de una amiga
10:00 de la noche	en la entrada de la residencia
12:00 de la noche	?

OJO: Give as much information as possible in your responses.

E. Información sobre (*about*) los estudios

1. ¿Qué días de la semana tienes clases?
2. ¿Tienes clases por la mañana, por la tarde o por la noche?
3. ¿Estás nervioso/-a en tus clases? ¿Estás aburrido/-a?
4. ¿Tienes una clase muy difícil? ¿Qué clase es?
5. ¿Tienes ganas de estudiar el sábado por la noche?

INVESTIGAR LA GRAMÁTICA   Los verbos regulares que terminan en **-er** e **-ir**

In Chapter 1 you learned several very common irregular verbs, as well as the regular *-ar* verbs. In this *etapa* you will learn the forms of the other two classes of regular verbs, those that end in *-er* and *-ir*. Their endings in the present tense are very similar. Note that they differ only in the *nosotros* and *vosotros* forms.

comer (*to eat*)

yo com**o**	nosotros/-as com**emos**
tú com**es**	vosotros/-as com**éis**
él / ella / usted } com**e**	ellos/-as / ustedes } com**en**

vivir (*to live*)

yo viv**o**	nosotros/-as viv**imos**
tú viv**es**	vosotros/-as viv**ís**
él / ella / usted } viv**e**	ellos/-as / ustedes } viv**en**

Los estudiantes que **viven** en las residencias **comen** en la cafetería.
En julio y agosto **abrimos** las ventanas por la mañana.

The students who live in the residence halls eat in the cafeteria.
In July and August we open the windows in the morning.

Ponerlo a prueba

A. Más actividades durante los fines de semana. Paco and his friends mention more of their weekend activities. Complete their sentences using the elements provided.

Modelo: Alicia / ver televisión por la noche
Alicia ve televisión por la noche.

1. Elena / correr (*to run*) por la mañana
2. Los amigos / comer en la cafetería
3. Tú y yo / salir (*to go out*) con tus primos
4. La profesora Suárez / escribir (*to write*) y leer (*to read*) los sábados y los domingos
5. Nosotros / conocer (*to meet*) a amigos nuevos
6. Tú / nunca (*never*) ver (*to watch*) televisión los domingos
7. Tú y yo / querer salir todas las noches (*every night*)
8. Yo / no leer los sábados; no abrir los libros

B. ¿Qué haces en estos lugares? (*What do you do in these places?*) Use the following verbs listed, as well as others you know, to say what you do in each of the places mentioned.

bailar	descansar	estudiar	practicar
comer	escribir	leer	vivir
charlar	escuchar		

1. en mi cuarto
2. en la residencia
3. en el gimnasio (*gym*)
4. en la cafetería
5. en la biblioteca
6. en el laboratorio de lenguas (*language lab*)
7. en las clases
8. en casa con mi familia
9. en las fiestas
10. en un concierto (*concert*)

Now say what your friends do in these places. Follow the models, according to whether your friends do the same things as you or not. Use your imagination!

Modelo: Yo **estudio** en la biblioteca y mis amigos **estudian** allí también.

or: Yo **estudio** en la bibioteca, pero mis amigos **charlan.**

C. Alicia habla de la vida estudiantil. Alicia is talking about her life at the university. Complete her story.

Alicia habla: Elena y yo ____ (**estar**) muy contentas en la universidad. ____ (**Tener**) muchos amigos y las clases ____ (**ser**) muy interesantes. La residencia donde nosotras _____ (**vivir**) es muy buena también. Elena y yo _____ (**ir**) a las clases por la mañana. La cafetería _____ (**abrir**) a las 11:30, pero nosotras _____ (**tener**) clase hasta (*until*) las 12:00. La comida generalmente _____ (**ser**) buena, pero Elena _____ (**comer**) ensalada (*salad*) solamente (*only*). Dice (*She says*) que no _____ (**tener**) energía si _____ (**comer**) mucho para el almuerzo. Por la tarde yo _____ (**leer**) en nuestro cuarto, pero Elena siempre _____ (**estudiar**) en la biblioteca. A las 5:00 Elena _____ (**practicar**) los deportes en el gimnasio, pero yo _____ (**mirar**) televisión o (*or*) _____ (**descansar**) en el cuarto. Los lunes yo siempre _____ (**escribir**) una carta a mi familia en Chile.

CH. **¿Y tú?**   Answer the following questions.

1. Raúl lee el periódico (*newspaper*) todos los días (*every day*). Y tú, ¿qué lees?
2. Pedro vive en casa con su familia. Y tú, ¿dónde vives?
3. Marta mira televisión por la noche. Y tú, ¿qué miras?
4. Elena lee y estudia en la biblioteca. Y tú, ¿dónde lees y estudias?
5. Alicia escribe cartas todos los lunes. Y tú, ¿cuándo escribes cartas?
6. Tomás no abre sus libros hasta (*until*) noviembre. Y tú, ¿cuándo abres tus libros por primera vez (*for the first time*)?

OJO: Before you and your partner start this activity, practice turning these items into questions.

D. "**Soy nuevo/-a (*new*).**"   Imagine that you are a new student at your university. Talk to your partner to get the following information.

- a qué hora abren la cafetería para el desayuno
- si el programa de deportes es bueno
- si los estudiantes estudian los sábados por la noche o si salen con sus amigos
- si los estudiantes escriben mucho para sus clases
- si hay un buen lugar para escuchar música cerca de (*near*) la universidad

OJO: Plan how you are going to formulate the questions before you begin the activity.

E. **Entrevista.**   Find out the following information from your partner, and report it to the class.

- qué estudia este semestre
- si trabaja, y dónde
- dónde desea vivir en el futuro

If time permits, follow up *Actividad F* by having students ask their interviewees *¿Por qué?* for questions that were simply answered *sí* or *no*. Connectors are treated in the third *etapa* of this chapter.

F. **¿A qué hora?**   Form groups of three. Two of you will interview each other to find out at what time each of you does the following activities. If one of you does not do an activity, use *no* + **verb**. The third person is the recorder who notes the responses and reports them to the class.

Modelo: leer el periódico

   Estudiante A: *¿A qué hora lees el periódico?*

Primera etapa

Introduce pero and y so recorders can compare and contrast interviewees. Encourage third-person plural verb forms when responses coincide.

Estudiante B: *Leo el periódico a las cinco de la tarde. ¿Y tú?*
Estudiante A: *Leo el periódico a las nueve de la noche.*
Estudiante C: *B lee el periódico a las cinco de la tarde, pero A lee el periódico a las nueve de la noche.*

¿A qué hora... ?

- ir a la biblioteca para estudiar
- practicar los deportes
- tener la clase de español
- mirar televisión
- comer

¡TIENES LA PALABRA!

Do the following activities with a partner.

A. ¿Miras televisión? You are an international student who is interested in knowing about the television-watching habits of North Americans, because you have heard that watching television is very popular in the United States. Ask another student

- whether he or she watches television
- when he or she watches—in the morning, afternoon, or evening
- whether the programs are interesting
- what his or her favorite program is

B. Información, por favor. You need to find out the hours at which meals are served in the cafeteria. Ask your classmate, who is taking the role of an employee at the cafeteria,

- at what time breakfast is served
- at what time lunch is served

You are curious, so you also ask

- if the food is good
- which meal is his or her favorite

OTRA VUELTA

Play instructor tape, 1 min.

Now listen again to the *Entrada* at the beginning of this *etapa*. Using the following form, identify which courses David is taking and which ones Raquel is taking. Place **D** or **R** next to the appropriate courses. They have one class together; can you figure out which one it is?

Asignatura

_____ el español   _____ la historia de los Estados Unidos
_____ el francés   _____ la historia de América Latina
_____ el inglés   _____ la historia del arte
_____ la biología   _____ la filosofía

COMENTARIO CULTURAL

El reloj (*clock*) de 24 horas

In Spanish-speaking countries, the 24-hour clock is often used for official purposes, such as transportation schedules (buses, trains, airplanes) and the hours that a business or government office is open to the public. The 12-hour clock is used in conversation. This means, for example, that two people arranging to see a movie would decide to go *a las nueve de la noche,* but the printed schedule for the movie might list the showing as *a las 21h* (*a las veintiuna horas*).

Actividad. Look at the following television schedule and answer the questions.

1. ¿A qué hora comienza el programa "Adderly"? ¿A qué hora corresponde en el reloj de 24 horas?
2. ¿Cuántos programas comienzan a las 9:30 de la noche? ¿A qué hora corresponde en el reloj de 24 horas?

Preguntas: 1. Busca un programa popular norteamericano. ¿A qué hora es? ¿En qué canal? 2. ¿Qué programa empieza a las nueve en el canal 4? 3. ¿Hay una telenovela (soap opera) en el horario? ¿Cómo se llama? ¿A qué hora empieza? 4. ¿Hay un programa de música clásica en el horario? ¿Cuál es?

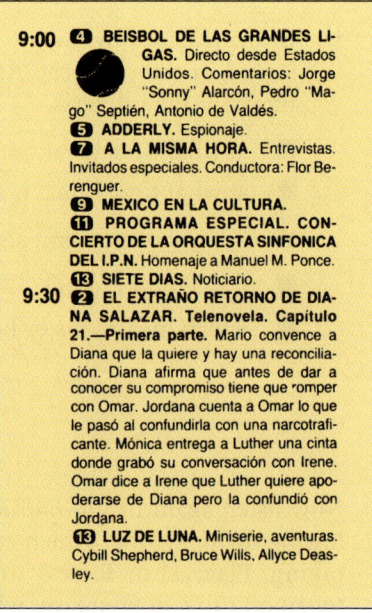

SEGUNDA ETAPA

En la sesión de orientación

ENTRADA

Play instructor tape, 2 min.

Una conversación con Elena Rodríguez

You will hear a conversation between Elena and another person. As you listen, try to figure out

- what kind of conversation it is
- two facts you learn about Elena

Contesta en español:
1. ¿Es una conversación social o es una entrevista (*interview*)?
2. Información acerca de Elena
   a.
   b.

ANTES DE LEER

READING STRATEGY 2

Use your knowledge of context

In the same way that your background knowledge enables you to understand what you read, your knowledge of the context can help you to anticipate the content of a given text. For example, the questions you read in the advice column of the newspaper prepare you to understand and interpret the answers. Thinking about the context of what you read is another way you can facilitate your understanding of the text.

Preparación

When people introduce themselves in a classroom setting, what kinds of information do they usually give? If you were asked to introduce yourself in writing to someone in three or four sentences, what would you say about yourself? *Contesta en español.*

Me llamo _____ .   Estudio _____ .
Soy de _____ .   _____ .

Estudiar y practicar

Study and practice spelling these words and phrases in preparation for the reading and writing activities that follow.

cocinar	*to cook*	nadar	*to swim*
correr	*to run*	Pienso (ser maestro).	*I plan/intend*
el fin de semana	*weekend*		*(to be a teacher).*
Me gusta (leer).	*I like (to read).*	el tiempo libre	*free time*

LEER

Professor Suárez has written a brief note to each of her students introducing herself and asking them to send her a short paragraph about themselves, which she will share with other members of the class prior to the first day of classes.

> Bienvenidos a la universidad. Soy la profesora Filomena Suárez y enseño inglés y español. Soy de la ciudad de México, pero llevo 15 años aquí en los Estados Unidos. En mi tiempo libre me gusta leer y cocinar. ¡Preparo unos platos estupendos!

Now, here are excerpts from the students' responses. As you read the segments from the letters, see if you can determine each person's name, where each is from, what each person's major course of study is, and one item of personal information.

> Me llamo Roberto Hernández y soy de San Antonio, Texas. Paco Méndez y yo somos compañeros de cuarto. En mi tiempo libre me gusta leer y quiero estudiar negocios.

Soy Paco Méndez y ayudo a la profesora Suárez en sus clases de inglés. Soy de San Diego, pero mis abuelos son de México. Estudio inglés y educación primaria, porque pienso ser maestro en un programa bilingüe. Me gusta bailar, nadar y comer. ¡Sobre todo me gustan los platos que prepara la profesora Suárez!

Me llamo Marcos Colón y soy de Bogotá, Colombia. Me gustan las artes y los idiomas. Pienso estudiar la literatura francesa. Vivo con mis tíos aquí en la ciudad. Los fines de semana me gusta escuchar música latina y bailar con mis amigos.

Me llamo Alicia San Martín y soy de Santiago de Chile. Elena Rodríguez y yo somos compañeras de cuarto. Voy a estudiar negocios. Pienso trabajar en una multinacional en Santiago un día. Elena y yo somos muy diferentes. Yo odio toda clase de ejercicio. Los fines de semana me gusta estudiar y ver televisión.

OJO: Una multinacional means una compañía multinacional.

Me llamo Elena Rodríguez y soy de México, de la ciudad de Guadalajara, estado de Jalisco. Llevo solamente una semana en los Estados Unidos. Pienso estudiar biología o química porque me fascinan las ciencias. Me gustan los deportes. Me gusta correr en maratones y practicar el tenis.

DESPUÉS DE LEER

Actividad. Complete the following class information sheet.

OJO: D.F. stands for *Distrito Federal*, and is often used to refer to the capital city of Mexico.

Nombre	Ciudad	Especialización	Nota personal
Filomena Suárez	México, D.F.	profesora	lee y cocina

VERIFICAR

¿Sí o no?

Read all six introductions again, and indicate whether the following statements are true (*Sí*) or false (*No*).

1. Roberto y Paco son compañeros de cuarto. Sí No
2. Paco cree que la profesora cocina muy bien. Sí No
3. Paco Méndez es un estudiante internacional. Sí No
4. A Marcos Colón le interesa la literatura. Sí No
5. Elena Rodríguez va a estudiar negocios. Sí No
6. Alicia San Martín corre en maratones. Sí No

VENTANILLA AL MUNDO HISPÁNICO La educación bilingüe

Paco plans to be a teacher in a bilingual program after he finishes his education. Many countries, including the United States, have laws and public policies concerning bilingualism. For example, Paraguay is officially a bilingual country; Spanish and *guaraní*, the indigenous Indian language, are spoken by about equal numbers of people, and most people speak both languages. As is typical in most bilingual countries, children in Paraguay, especially those in rural areas, speak *guaraní* at home, and learn Spanish when they go to school.

AUMENTAR EL VOCABULARIO

cocinar	*to cook*
preparar	*to prepare*
el plato	*plate, dish; food (course, meal)*
enseñar	*to teach*
aprender	*to learn*
ayudar	*to help*
pensar (ie)	*to plan, intend; to think*
esperar	*to hope, expect*
Me gusta/gustan...	*I like . . .*
No me gusta/gustan...	*I don't like . . .*
odiar	*to hate, detest*
el tiempo libre	*free time*
correr (en maratones)	*to run (in marathons)*
descansar	*to rest*
el fin de semana	*weekend*
nadar	*to swim*
el trabajo	*work, job*
la multinacional	*multinational company*
el programa bilingüe	*bilingual program*

Me gusta/gustan is presented here as a lexical item. Explain as quickly as possible that the verb is singular or plural in accordance with what is liked, and that "I" is expressed by *me*, not *yo*. It is enough at this point to say that *yo* is never used with *gustar*. The use of *gustar* is explained in *Uso práctico del español* of this *etapa*.

LOS DEPORTES Y LAS ACTIVIDADES

OJO: If your favorite sports or activities are missing, use your dictionary. Some additional ones are *la lucha libre* (wrestling), *levantar pesas* (to lift weights), *patinar* (to skate).

jugar al béisbol   jugar al baloncesto   jugar al fútbol

OJO: Use your guessing skills, since you will not know all the words.

Most of the activities incorporate words that are easily identifiable as cognates or through context. Encourage students to guess the meanings of these new words.

Descripciones. Figure out the sport or activity that each phrase refers to.

1. Hay dos jugadores, o hay cuatro; usan raquetas y una pelota.
2. Hay nueve jugadores en cada equipo; usan un bate y una pelota.
3. Es una actividad individual; se hace en el agua.
4. Hay cinco personas en cada equipo; se juega (*it is played*) en un gimnasio.
5. Es un deporte muy popular en Europa.

USO PRÁCTICO DEL ESPAÑOL Likes and Dislikes

In her letter earlier in this *etapa* Alicia says, *¡Yo odio toda clase de ejercicio!* If she had wanted to state her dislike in a milder way, she might have said, *No me gusta el ejercicio* or *No me gustan los deportes* ("I don't like sports").

One of the most common ways in which likes and dislikes are expressed in Spanish is with the phrases *me gusta(n)* and *no me gusta(n)*.

No me gusta el fútbol americano.
Me gustan los deportes.
Me gusta escuchar música latina.
Me gusta bailar, nadar y comer.

OJO: *Gusta* in the singular is used with infinitives, even if there are several.

OJO: Try not to be influenced by English. The *gustar* construction is important in Spanish, and you need to use it correctly.

Notice that the verb *gustar* is used differently from the other verbs you have learned so far. It takes its ending, either the singular *-a* or the plural *-an,* from the number of objects or activities that the speaker enjoys.

You can state your likes and dislikes more strongly if you wish. For example, if you like dancing very much you say *Me gusta mucho bailar.* If you like both skiing and running but you like skiing better, you say *Me gusta correr, pero me gusta más esquiar.* If you really dislike dancing, you can say *No me gusta nada bailar.*

Spanish has other verbs that are used like *gustar.*

| Me encanta(n)... | *I love . . .* |
| Me interesa(n)... | *I am interested in . . .* |

As with *gustar,* the verb is singular or plural in agreement with what the speaker is referring to.

Me encanta la historia. *I love history.*
Me interesan mucho las ciencias. *I am very interested in the sciences.*
No me interesa la literatura francesa. *I'm not interested in French literature.*

Ponerlo a prueba

Encourage students to expand their responses by adding information such as, *No me gusta ver televisión, pero sí me gusta el programa "Murphy Brown";* or *Me gusta escuchar la música latina, pero odio (or me gusta más) la música clásica.*

OJO: Try to add details: *Me gusta _____, pero me gusta más _____; Me gusta mucho _____,* etc.

A. Hablando de los gustos. Using the expressions of likes and dislikes that you know, say how you feel about each of the following activities.

1. el tenis
2. los deportes acuáticos (*water sports*)
3. ver televisión
4. esquiar
5. correr
6. escuchar la música latina

Now say whether or not you are interested in the following academic areas.

1. los negocios
2. la ciencia política

3. los idiomas
4. la economía
5. la biologia
6. las matemáticas

OJO: Use your guessing skills; do not be concerned if you do not understand every word.

B. **Definiciones.** Choose the word or expression from the *Aumentar el vocabulario* section that best matches each of the following definitions.

1. la actividad profesional de tu profesor(a)
2. el sábado y el domingo
3. un programa en que se usan dos idiomas
4. el francés, el italiano, el español, por ejemplo
5. el acto de preparar comidas
6. lo que hacen (*do*) algunos estudiantes, además de (*in addition to*) estudiar

C. **Combinaciones.** Make sentences that apply to you personally by combining one element from each column.

Mi familia y yo	correr	toda clase de ejercicio
Yo	aprender	en (ciudad)
Mi compañero/-a de cuarto	vivir	todos los días
Mis amigos	odiar	el español

CH. **Hablando más de los gustos.** Say whether you like or do not like each of the following. Remember to use (*No*) *Me gusta* with objects in the singular, and to use (*No*) *Me gustan* for objects in the plural.

1. la música latina
2. los maratones
3. la pizza
4. las actividades orales en la clase de español
5. los programas románticos de televisión

D. **Más información sobre los estudios**

1. ¿Cuáles de tus cursos te gustan más?
2. ¿Qué estudia tu compañero/-a de cuarto?
3. ¿Qué estudia tu mejor amigo/-a (*best friend*)?
4. ¿Tienes un curso de inglés? ¿Cuántos días por semana tienes la clase?
5. ¿Trabajas rápido o despacio? En tu opinión, ¿cuál es mejor (*better*)?
6. ¿Cuál te gusta más, estudiar en casa o en la biblioteca?
7. ¿Cuándo y a qué hora estudias? ¿Por qué?

INVESTIGAR LA GRAMÁTICA   Verbs with Irregular *yo* Forms

Some verbs have only one irregular form in the present tense: the *yo* form. Here are some of the more common ones.

ver	*to see*	yo **veo,** tú ves, Ud./él/ella ve, nosotros/-as vemos, vosotros/-as veis, Uds./ellos/ellas ven
dar	*to give*	yo **doy,** tú das...
saber	*to know (a fact)*	yo **sé,** tú sabes...
hacer	*to do, make*	yo **hago,** tú haces...
poner	*to place, put*	yo **pongo,** tú pones...
salir	*to depart, leave*	yo **salgo,** tú sales...
traer	*to bring*	yo **traigo,** tú traes...
conducir	*to drive*	yo **conduzco,** tú conduces...
conocer	*to know or to meet (a person)*	yo **conozco,** tú conoces...

The -ir *stem-changing verbs are presented in Chapter 3, third* etapa.

OJO: Note the difference between *oír,* "to hear," and *escuchar,* "to listen to." "I hear the music" is *Oigo la música,* and "I listen to music every day" is *Escucho música todos los días.*

Other common verbs have irregular forms in addition to the *yo* form.

decir	to say, tell	digo, dices, dice, decimos, decís, dicen
oír	to hear	oigo, oyes, oye, oímos, oís, oyen
venir	to come	vengo, vienes, viene, venimos, venís, vienen

Ponerlo a prueba

A. **La vida ordenada de Alicia.** Alicia has a very orderly life, and she likes to do everything on schedule. Change the following sentences so that they apply to you. Be sure to add *no* to the sentence if it wouldn't be true for you.

Modelo: Sale de su cuarto a las 8:00 de la mañana.
Salgo de mi cuarto a las ocho de la mañana también.
No salgo de mi cuarto a las ocho. Salgo a las siete y media.

1. Desayuna rápido.
2. Tiene su primera clase a las 9:00.
3. Sabe todas las respuestas en las clases.
4. No conoce a muchas personas en sus clases.
5. Pone todos sus libros en orden en su cuarto.
6. Por la noche ve televisión y hace la tarea.

OJO: Note that subject pronouns are not used in the responses because they are not necessary for clarity or emphasis. The exception is item 6, in which the speaker's opinion is contrasted with that of *los profesores* in item 5.

B. **Una carta.** Inés García is writing home to her family to tell them about her life in college. Using the elements given, write part of her letter for her.

Modelo: (Yo) tener / cinco clases   *Tengo cinco clases.*

1. (Yo) conocer / bien a la profesora Suárez
2. (Yo) saber / dónde estar / mis clases y dónde estar / la biblioteca
3. (Mis amigos y yo) salir / los viernes y sábados
4. (Yo) hacer / mucha tarea

5. Los profesores decir / que (nosotros) tener / que trabajar mucho
6. Yo decir / que (nosotros) tener / que descansar también
7. (Yo) ver / a mi primo Francisco todos los días
8. (Yo) salir / con él de vez en cuando (*sometimes*)
9. (Yo) no oír / nada de mi prima Raquel
10. (Ella) venir / a los Estados Unidos en diciembre

C. Información personal sobre tu vida universitaria

1. ¿A qué hora sales de tu cuarto o tu casa por la mañana?
2. ¿Dónde pones tus libros cuando regresas (*return*) a tu cuarto o casa?
3. ¿Dónde haces la tarea?
4. ¿Conoces a todos los estudiantes en tu clase de español?
5. ¿Sabes un poco de español? ¿Te gusta?
6. ¿Cuándo ves a tu familia?
7. ¿Qué dicen tus amigos que asisten a (*attend*) otras universidades? ¿Están contentos con sus clases, la vida social, etc.?

CH. ¿Qué saben? Form groups of four students with one serving as the recorder. Each person in the group should state two facts about the university (*Sé que...*). The recorder makes up the list and reports the two or three most interesting facts to the class.

D. ¿Quién lo dice? Now go back to the same groups and say who is responsible for each fact. The phrases you will need are

Yo digo que...
Tú dices que...
(*Nombre del* [*de la*] *estudiante*) dice que...

Extra activity: *¿Qué traen a clase?* Each person should take out a small item that he or she usually brings to class. Students should make sure that they know how to say the item in Spanish before this activity begins. Have them put the item in a bag that you will supply.
1. You remove an item from the bag and ask, *¿Qué es esto?* The class responds with the name of the item, or you provide it.
2. You then ask, *¿Quién siempre trae esto a clase?* The student whose item it is responds, *Yo siempre traigo ____ a clase.*

¡TIENES LA PALABRA!

A. La tarea. Interview your partner to find out

- if he or she has a lot of homework
- where he or she does homework
- when he or she does homework
- which professors give a lot of work

B. Los deportes: Una encuesta. Form groups of three or four students. One student uses the form provided and interviews the others in the group.

OJO: The question you should ask in each case is *¿Te gusta...?* Encourage the members of your group to give details: *Me gusta ver el fútbol americano, pero no me gusta jugar; Me gusta nadar, pero me gusta más correr.* Write the name of each person in the space that corresponds to that person's response for a particular sport.

¿Te gustan los deportes?

Deporte	Me encanta(n)	Me gusta(n)	No me gusta(n)	Odio
ver el fútbol americano				
jugar al tenis				
nadar				
correr				
los deportes acuáticos				

OTRA VUELTA

Play instructor tape, 2 min.

Listen again to the interview with Elena Rodríguez that you heard at the beginning of this *etapa*. Then complete the following sentences.

1. El nombre completo de Elena es Elena...
2. Es la... vez que Elena está en los Estados Unidos.
3. En el futuro Elena espera correr en...

El fútbol es el deporte más popular del mundo. En esta foto las emociones de los jugadores son muy evidentes.

COMENTARIO CULTURAL

Los apellidos (*last names*) hispanos

Although the people in this chapter have been introduced to you with one last name—Suárez, Colón, Rodríguez, and so on—Hispanics often use two *apellidos,* especially in formal situations. The first *apellido* is the father's last name (*el apellido paterno*), and the second is the mother's last name (*el apellido materno*). Although some married women may prefer to retain their original *apellidos*, other married women drop the *apellido materno* and replace it with the (husband's) *apellido paterno*, preceded by the word *de*. For example, Elena Rodríguez Olivares is the daughter of Jorge Luis Rodríguez Cisneros and María Pilar Olivares de Rodríguez. If she marries a man whose *apellido paterno* is Márquez, her name will then be Elena Rodríguez de Márquez. Their children's *apellidos* will be Márquez Rodríguez. The *apellido materno* is very useful to tell apart the many people who have common names, such as Rodríguez, Sánchez, and González. Remember that the *apellido paterno* is used for putting names in alphabetical order, so Elena would be listed under the R's.

Preguntas

1. If you lived in a Spanish-speaking country, what would your *apellido paterno* and *apellido materno* be?
2. Figure out your mother's and father's *apellidos*.
3. Introduce yourself to at least two other people in the class, using both of your *apellidos*. Remember the phrases you will need:
   —Buenos días, me llamo...
   —Mucho gusto. Yo me llamo...
   —Mucho gusto.
   ¡No se olviden (*Don't forget*) de darse la mano!

TERCERA ETAPA — Déjame ver tu horario de clases

ENTRADA

"¿Quieres tomar un café?"

You will hear a conversation between Elena and Marcos about their courses. As you listen, try to figure out

- what courses they are taking
- what courses they think will be easy or difficult

Tercera etapa

- the words Marcos uses to express his feelings about science courses
- the words Elena uses to express her feelings about history courses
- what Marcos says to invite Elena for coffee
- what Elena says to accept the invitation

1. Cursos de Marcos y Elena, ¿fáciles o difíciles?

	Marcos	Elena
historia		
inglés		
biología		
francés		

2. Las palabras de Marcos: _____ de laboratorio.
3. Las palabras de Elena: _____ la historia.
4. La invitación
   Marcos dice:
   Elena dice:

ANTES DE HABLAR

Preparación

When you invite a friend to do something with you, what do you say? Imagine what you would say in the following situations.

- Invite a friend to go out for a quick snack or a cup of coffee.
- Invite someone you would like to get to know better to an event, such as a lecture or a concert on campus.

Often we issue an invitation in the context of a conversation. A typical topic of conversation for students is how they feel about certain subject areas. How would you express your feelings about a subject area for which you have talent and interest?

1.
2.

What would you say to express your feeling about a subject area for which you feel you have no talent or interest?

1.
2.

| Play student tape, 1 min. |

Leer en voz alta:

Déjame ver (tu horario de clases).	Let me see (your schedule).
¡Qué casualidad!	What a coincidence!
Me encanta(n) (los idiomas).	I love (languages).
Odio (la economía).	I hate (economics).
Soy fatal para (la historia).	I'm terrible at (history).
(Las fechas) me mata(n).	(Dates) kill me.
¿Quieres (tomar un café)?	Would you like (to have a cup of coffee)?
Me gustaría mucho.	I'd like to very much.

OJO: The verb *matar* means "to kill." The verb will be singular if the subject is singular, and plural if the subject is plural: *La química me mata*, but *Las fechas me matan.*

Practicar

Imagine that you have just registered for classes. You see a friend. What would you say to convey the following? *Contesta en español.*

- You want to see what classes your friend is taking.
- You are surprised to discover that you have a class in common.
- You really like one of the subjects you will be studying.
- You are dreading taking another of your classes.

Now imagine that you are the friend. What would you say to convey the following?

- You want to reassure your friend that the course he or she is dreading won't be so bad.
- You would like to invite your friend to do something with you.

OJO: Remember that you already know the expressions *cálmate* and *no te preocupes.*

HABLAR

"Déjame ver tu horario de clases." Act out the following scene with a partner.

This section consists of two role plays. Students should be guided from the beginning to perform them in pairs without using notes or scripts, so they will serve as true speaking activities.

Estudiante A

You have just registered for your classes. You see a friend on the steps of your residence hall.

1. Greet the friend.
2. Ask to see your friend's course schedule.
3. You and your friend will be in a class together. Express your surprise.
4. You are really dreading this particular course. Express the feeling that you are not cut out for that subject.
5. You have to be at work shortly. Excuse yourself and say good-bye.

Tercera etapa

OJO: You aready know the phrase ¡Qué bueno!

Estudiante B

You have just registered for your classes. A friend greets you on the steps of your residence hall.

1. Return the greeting.
2. Your friend wants to see your course schedule. Say that you are pleased with your schedule.
3. Your friend discovers that you will be in one of the same classes. Express your pleasure about this.
4. Express that you really like the course that you will have together. It is your best subject. Say something reassuring to your friend, who is worried about that same course.
5. Your friend needs to leave, and you do too. Say good-bye.

"¿Quieres tomar... ?" Act out the following scene with a partner.

Estudiante A

You are in the library, and have reached a point of frustration with the homework for one of your classes. A friend comes over to where you are studying.

1. Greet the friend. Express your frustration.
2. In spite of your friend's reassurances, you are still frustrated. In addition, it is 11:00 P.M. and you do not want to study anymore.
3. Accept your friend's invitation. Comment that you do **not** want to talk about this class.

Estudiante B

You are studying in the library, and notice that one of your friends who is studying nearby looks very frustrated. You go over to the friend.

1. Greet your friend.
2. Respond to your friend's expression of frustration by asking to see his or her homework (*la tarea*). Tell your friend to calm down, that it is really not difficult.

OJO: You already know the phrase *vámonos,* which means "Let's go."

3. It is late. Invite your friend to go have a cup of coffee.
4. Urge your friend to go now because the snack bar (*el café*) closes (*se cierra*) at midnight.

DESPUÉS DE HABLAR

In addition to comunicating to people by talking to them, we also communicate by writing. This section will help you develop your writing skills in Spanish.

WRITING STRATEGY 2

Link your sentences with connecting words

Paragraphs that are a collection of short, choppy sentences create an impression in the reader of stiffness and childishness. Even though your knowledge of Spanish is quite limited, you can start now to link your sentences by using a few simple conjunctions: *y* (and), *pero* (but), *también* (also), and *además* (besides.) Also, see where you can avoid repetition by using synonyms and antonyms. Sometimes it is even possible to eliminate the repetitious element altogether.

Práctica. How might you revise the following paragraph fragments to make them smoother and less repetitious? There may be more than one right answer.

1. Me gustan mucho los idiomas. No me gustan nada (*at all*) las ciencias.
2. Me gusta el béisbol. Me gusta el tenis.
3. Odio la historia. Las fechas me matan. No me gusta leer tanto (*so much*).

Actividad. Look again at the introductions in the second *etapa* of this chapter. You are going to write one for yourself. Be sure to include the following information.

- your name
- where you are from
- what your interests are

After you have written a final draft, review it carefully, making your sentences flow by using connectors and avoiding repetition.

Ventanilla al mundo hispánico — En otros países se estudia inglés

Although Elena and Marcos will study English in the United States, they have probably already studied English for a number of years. In most of Latin America and Europe, foreign languages are a required part of the curriculum. Students start to learn English by the age of ten and often start a second foreign language when they begin high school. They typically graduate from high school having had seven or eight years of English.

AUMENTAR EL VOCABULARIO

después de	*after*
antes de	*before*
hasta	*until*
el horario	*schedule*
el semestre	*semester*
el laboratorio (de lenguas)	*(language) laboratory*
tomar	*to drink (either alcoholic or nonalcoholic beverages)*
beber	*to drink (usually alcoholic beverages)*
el azúcar	*sugar*
la bebida	*beverage (usually alcoholic)*
la crema	*cream*
el limón	*lemon*
la tarea	*homework*
Déjame ver (tu tarea).	*Let me see (your homework).*
Soy fatal para (la historia).	*I'm terrible at (history).*
la invitación	*invitation*
invitar	*invite*
el baile	*dance*
la conferencia	*lecture*
matar	*to kill*
(El inglés) me mata.	*(English) is killing me.*
rápido	*quickly*
despacio	*slowly*
¡Qué casualidad!	*What a coincidence!*
¡Qué suerte!	*What (good) luck!*

Remind students that when the subject is plural, they will use the plural form of the verb *matar*: *Las ciencias políticas me matan.*

OJO: You already know the related word *bailar,* "to dance."

OJO: *La conferencia* is a false cognate. Also, *la lectura* means "reading," as in a poetry reading.

LAS BEBIDAS Y LOS REFRESCOS

OJO: The word used for "juice" in Spain is *el zumo*.

el té

el café

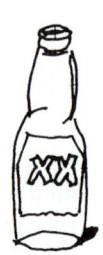
la cerveza

el vino tinto

el vino blanco

el refresco

el vaso de agua

el agua mineral

la taza de chocolate

el jugo de manzana / naranja

la leche

la copa de vino

Encourage students to express their opinions about the beverages: *Me gusta el chocolate, pero odio el café.* Expansion: Have students refer to the time of day without a specific hour: *Tomo café por la mañana, pero no por la tarde.*

OJO: Use the definite article (*el, la,* and so on) when you are talking about an item in general: *Odio el café.* Omit the article when you are referring to only a portion of the world's supply of that item: *Tomo café por la mañana.*

¿A qué hora? Say at what time of day you are most likely to drink the following beverages. If there is a beverage you never drink, you should say *Nunca* (Never) *tomo...* .

Modelo: el té
Tomo té a las cuatro de la tarde.

1. el chocolate
2. la leche
3. los refrescos
4. la cerveza
5. el vino
6. el jugo de naranja
7. el café (con leche y azúcar)
8. el agua mineral

USO PRÁCTICO DEL ESPAÑOL Hablando del futuro

In their introductions in the second *etapa*, Paco, Marcos, Elena, and Alicia wrote about their plans for the future. Spanish has a number of expressions that serve the function of expressing what is **going to** happen, or what you are **planning** or are **hoping** for in the future.

Here are some of the most frequently used expressions. All of them include the infinitive of the verb that states the future activity or event. One that you already know is *ir + a +* infinitive.

Alicia **va a** estudiar negocios.
Alicia is going to major in business.

Here are some other ways to talk about the future.

pensar (ie) + *infinitive*

Paco **piensa** ser maestro en un programa bilingüe.
Paco plans / intends to be a teacher in a bilingual program.

Note that *pensar* is a stem-changing verb. Students need only recognize, not produce, the verb for now.

esperar + *infinitive*

Marcos **espera** estudiar la literatura francesa.
Marcos hopes/expects to study French literature.

desear + *infinitive*

Elena **desea** estudiar las ciencias.
Elena wants to study science.

Ponerlo a prueba

OJO: Look back at the second *etapa* if you need to refresh your memory about the characters in the book.

OJO: The present tense of all verbs can be used to talk about events in the immediate future.

A. Hablando del futuro. Make as many true statements as possible, using one element from each column.

Paco Méndez	va a	estudiar literatura
Alicia San Martín	espera	trabajar en un programa bilingüe
Elena Rodríguez	piensa	estudiar negocios
Marcos Colón	desea	trabajar en una multinacional

B. Hablando de los gustos. Using *Me gusta(n)* or *No me gusta(n)* say whether you like or do not like each of the following food, drinks, and activities.

1. los refrescos
2. la cerveza
3. el café con leche y azúcar
4. las hamburguesas
5. el vino blanco

Questions on the Café Bustelo ad: ¿Conoces el café Bustelo? ¿Te gusta? ¿Te gusta el café en general?

OJO: Remember to use (*No*) *Me gusta* with infinitives and with objects in the singular, and to use (*No*) *Me gustan* for objects in the plural.

OJO: Use your guessing skills; do not be concerned if you do not understand every word.

6. bailar
7. la leche
8. comer
9. el jugo de manzana
10. los idiomas

C. Definiciones. Choose the word or expression from the *Aumentar el vocabulario* section that best matches each of the following definitions.

1. una bebida que tiene cafeína
2. la bebida que dan las vacas (*cows*)
3. una bebida alcohólica de color rojo
4. el lugar donde se hacen (*are done*) experimentos científicos
5. el trabajo que los estudiantes hacen en casa, por ejemplo, leer y escribir
6. una división del calendario académico, de aproximadamente 10 a 15 semanas
7. los granos blancos que las personas ponen en el café
8. el líquido principal de la naturaleza

CH. Combinaciones. Make as many truthful sentences as you can using one element from each column.

Modelo: *Marcos escucha la música latina.*

La profesora Suárez	estudiar	San Diego
Paco	enseñar	inglés y español
Elena	practicar	maratones
Marcos	correr	el ejercicio
Alicia	escuchar	la literatura
Yo	odiar	Santiago de Chile
	ser de	las ciencias
		negocios
		la música latina

D. Preguntas personales

1. ¿Cuáles son tres actividades que te gustan?
2. ¿Te gusta más la literatura o la ciencia?
3. ¿Te gusta practicar los deportes o mirarlos (*watch them*)? ¿Qué deportes te gustan más?
4. ¿Qué te gusta hacer los fines de semana?
5. ¿Te gusta más la música latina o la música norteamericana *rock*?
6. ¿Cuál te gusta más, el café o el té? ¿Con leche? ¿Con azúcar?
7. Si tomas café, ¿cuántas tazas tomas por día?

E. Información personal. Complete the following sentences by giving personal information.

Modelo: La profesora Suárez es de México, pero/y yo soy de...
La profesora Suárez es de México, pero yo soy de Iowa.

1. La profesora Suárez lleva quince años viviendo en los Estados Unidos, pero/y yo llevo... viviendo en...
2. Los abuelos de Paco son de México, pero/y mis abuelos son de...
3. Paco piensa ser maestro, pero/y yo pienso...
4. Alicia espera trabajar en Santiago en el futuro, pero/y yo...
5. La compañera de cuarto de Alicia se llama Elena, pero y mi compañero/-a de cuarto...

Encourage truthful responses by offering the option pero yo no tengo compañero/-a de cuarto.

F. Información, por favor. Complete the following sentences about your schedule.

1. Tengo _____ clases. (número)
2. Mis clases son...
3. Mi curso favorito es...
4. Mi curso más fácil es...
5. Mi curso más difícil es...
6. La noche de más fiestas en la universidad es...

INVESTIGAR LA GRAMÁTICA Stem-Changing -ar and -er Verbs in the Present Tense

Stem-changing verbs are verbs that have a change in the vowel of the stem (the vowel before the *-ar*, *-er*, or *-ir* ending of the infinitive). All the endings, however, remain completely regular.

In this *etapa* we will consider only verbs that end in *-ar* and *-er*. There are only two changes possible for these verbs: *e* → *ie* or *o* → *ue*.

These stem-changing verbs are indicated in vocabulary lists by the notation (*ie*) or (*ue*) after the infinitive form: *pensar* (*ie*) "to think" or *soñar* (*ue*) "to dream." This means that there is a change of *e* → *ie* or *o* → *ue*. The *-ar* and *-er* stem-changing verbs change only in the present tense.

OJO: There is one exception: *jugar* (*ue*) has the change *u* → *ue*.

pensar (ie)		soñar (ue)	
pienso	pensamos	sueño	soñamos
piensas	pensáis	sueñas	soñáis
piensa	piensan	sueña	sueñan

Point out that some of these verbs (*querer, tener, poder*) have irregularities in other tenses, but that they are regular stem-changing verbs in the present tense except for *tengo*. The *-ir* stem-changing verbs are presented in the next chapter.

OJO: Remember that the *yo* form of *tener* is *tengo*.

Here are some other frequently used *-ar* and *-er* stem-changing verbs. Note that you have already seen some of them.

e → ie

cerrar	to close
comenzar	to begin
querer	to want
tener	to have

u → ue

jugar	to play

o → ue

almorzar	to have lunch
colgar	to hang (up) (a picture or a telephone)
encontrar	to find
poder	to be able
volver	to return, go back

Ponerlo a prueba

A. **Captar el momento.** Diego is studying photography and has decided to concentrate on family life. He asks Marcos's aunt if he can visit their home and take pictures of the family as they engage in their everyday activities. Here are some of the scenes he has captured.

1. Los niños _____ en la sala (*living room*). (**jugar**)
2. La tía de Marcos _____ la puerta del cuarto del bebé. (**cerrar**)
3. Marcos y su primo Jorge _____ a casa. (**volver**)
4. Los abuelos _____ ir al cine. (**pensar**)
5. Eva _____ el diploma de Jorge en la sala. (**colgar**)
6. ¡El bebé _____ a caminar (*to walk*)! (**comenzar**)
7. La tía _____ un ratón (*mouse*) en la cocina. (**encontrar**)
8. Los tíos de Marcos _____ en el patio. (**almorzar**)
9. Los niños _____ jugar al béisbol por la tarde. (**poder**)

B. **Los deseos.** Everybody in the *residencia* likes to talk to Marilú about their problems and their plans. But sometimes Marilú needs someone to talk to, so she calls her mother to confide some of the problems she has heard. Complete her sentences using the appropriate form of the verb indicated.

1. Paco _____ salir con Elena. (**querer**)
2. Pero Elena _____ jugar al tenis con Marcos. (**tener ganas de**)
3. Alicia desea ver a su mamá; _____ mucho a su familia. (**querer**)
4. Yolanda _____ salir de la universidad y sus amigos _____ tristes (*sad*). (**pensar, estar**)
5. Todos los estudiantes de la universidad _____ recibir buenas notas, pero no estudian mucho. (**querer**)

OJO: *Soñar con* means "to dream about."

OJO: *CH.* Before you begin, practice formulating the question that you will need to ask the other members of your group.

Extensions for *CH:* 1. Use this same format for other questions, for example, who eats lunch the latest. 2. Guide the groups in giving other rationales for why a different schedule is better than one of no early classes: *Tengo el mejor horario. Tengo todas mis clases por la mañana y puedo estudiar/trabajar por la tarde.* As a follow-up, have the members of each group decide what would be an ideal schedule for their group. They should be asked to give at least one reason why they prefer the schedule they prepare.

For *D.* model the questions and possible responses before students begin the activity. If necessary, write key questions on the board.

OJO: *El maestro (la maestra)* refers to a teacher in the elementary grades. *El profesor (la profesora)* is a teacher in high school or college.

C. Decir la verdad. Finish the following statements by offering some information about yourself. Use the phrases provided in parentheses to make the transition.

Modelo: A Roberto le gusta cenar temprano, (pero/y a mí...)
... *pero a mí me gusta cenar muy tarde.*

or: ... *y a mí también me gusta cenar temprano.*

1. Elena almuerza a la 1:00, (pero/y yo...)
2. Elena corre todos los días, (pero/y yo...)
3. Elena sueña con ganar más maratones, (pero/y yo...)
4. Marcos odia hablar por teléfono, (pero/y yo...)
5. Marcos cuelga el teléfono después de cinco minutos, (pero/y yo...)
6. Alicia comienza a estudiar a las 10:00 de la mañana y termina a las 11:30 de la noche, (pero/y yo...)
7. Alicia puede estudiar constantemente, (pero/y yo...)
8. Roberto siempre vuelve a su casa en Texas para las vacaciones, (pero/y yo...)
9. Marcos y Paco juegan al fútbol todos los fines de semana, (pero/y yo...)
10. Marcos encuentra su felicidad (*his happiness*) en la literatura y los idiomas, (pero/y yo...)

CH. ¿Quién puede dormir más? (*Who can sleep longer?*) Divide into groups of four. Each person asks the next what time his or her first class starts. Compare your group's results with the other groups' to find out *quién tiene el mejor horario.* Assume that the best schedule is the one that allows you to get up as late as possible in the morning.

D. Firmas. Find one person in the class who falls into each of the following categories and get a signature from each. Be sure to get a different signature for each line.

Categoría	*Persona*
1. almorzar con los mismos amigos todos los días	_____
2. jugar al fútbol americano	_____
3. jugar al tenis o al ráquetbol	_____
4. soñar todas las noches	_____
5. pensar cenar en casa	_____
6. no volver a casa para las vacaciones de diciembre	_____
7. pensar ser maestro/-a o profesor(a) en el futuro	_____

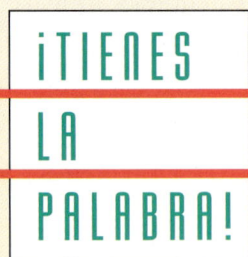

Do the following activities with a partner.

A. **Pensando en el futuro.** Find out your partner's plans for the future by asking

- dónde espera vivir en (*in*) diez años—en una ciudad grande, en una ciudad pequeña o en el campo (*in the country*)
- qué trabajo piensa tener
- si desea tener una familia grande o pequeña

OJO: Practice formulating the questions before you begin the activity. Make the conversation interactive; if you respond to a question first, end your response by saying *¿y tú?*

B. **Invitación.** Act out the following scene with a partner.

Estudiante A (la persona que hace la fiesta):

You are having a party. You see your friend in the library and want to invite him or her.

1. Greet your friend. (Use appropriate gestures.)
2. Say that you are having a party and invite your friend to come.
3. Answer your friend's questions about the party.
4. Suggest that your friend bring (*traer*) a beverage to the party.
5. Tell your friend that you will see him or her at the party.

OJO: 2. A good phrase to use here is *Quiero invitarte a...* . 3. Make sure you don't offer any information until your friend asks for it. 4. A good phrase to use here is *¿Puedes traer...?* 5. A good phrase to use here is *¡Hasta el sábado!* (if the party will be on Saturday).

Estudiante B

You are studying in the library, and a friend comes over and greets you.

1. Return the greeting. (Use appropriate gestures.)
2. Accept your friend's invitation to a party.
3. You need to know where the party will be, on what day, and at what time. Ask questions to find out.
4. Agree to take (*llevar*) a beverage to the party.
5. Thank your friend for the invitation.

OJO: A good phrase to use here is *Me gustaría ir...* .

OTRA VUELTA

Play instructor tape, 2 min.

Listen again to the conversation between Elena and Marcos that you heard at the beginning of this *etapa*. Write down the following information.

- what Marcos says to express his pleasure that Elena is in his biology class
- what Elena says to explain why she is not good at history
- what time Elena's next class is

COMENTARIO CULTURAL

Use of *tú* and *usted*, *vosotros* and *ustedes*

You may have noticed that when the subject pronouns and the verb forms were presented earlier that in the singular there are two different forms for "you": one labeled "familiar," the *tú* form, and one labeled "formal," the *usted* form. This means that whenever you speak with anyone you must decide which verb forms to use. Although usage varies somewhat from country to country, normally you use *tú*, that is, the familiar form of address, with your social equals: classmates and other college students, family members, and other friends. In general, any nonfamily members whom you would likely call by their first name—even if you are meeting them for the first time—can safely be addressed with the familiar forms in Spanish. With other adults, you should use the more formal *usted* form of address. Also, when you are in doubt about which form to use, choose *usted*; it is better to appear overly formal than overly familiar.

If you are speaking to more than one person at the same time, then you must use a plural form of "you." In all of Latin America, in fact in all Spanish-speaking countries except for Spain, the plural of both *tú* and *usted* is *ustedes*, and the familiar versus formal distinction disappears. In Spain, however, the familiar plural forms *vosotros* and *vosotras* are used as the plural of *tú*. This means that if every individual in the group you are speaking to would be addressed as *tú*, the group should be addressed with *vosotros/-as*. Otherwise, the formal *ustedes* is used.

Since the *ustedes* form is so widely used in the Spanish-speaking world, it is the one that will be practiced orally in **Entradas**. The *vosotros/-as* forms will be given in verb conjugations and will appear in some printed and spoken passages so that you can learn to recognize them.

You may want to tell your students about the use of the *vos* form in many parts of Latin America. This is a form that is used in lieu of *tú* as the familiar form of address. Although the use of *vos* is often associated with Argentina, in fact its use is spreading and is found in all Latin American countries in varying degrees.

Actividad. For each of the verb forms in the sentences that follow, indicate whether the form belongs to the pronoun *vosotros* or *ustedes*. Then, name at least one country where you might be likely to hear the statement.

1. **Trabajan** mucho, pero **tienen** tiempo libre los fines de semana, ¿verdad?
2. ¿**Veis** televisión por la noche, o **salís** con los amigos?
3. **Odiáis** muchos deportes, pero **practicáis** el tenis.
4. ¿**Van** a los partidos de béisbol con frecuencia? ¿**Cenan** después en un restaurante cerca del estadio?

DE INTEGRACIÓN

A. Mi autobiografía. Write a short autobiographical statement like the ones in the *Leer* section of the second *etapa*. Be sure to include

- your name
- where you are from
- your interests (*Me gusta*[*n*]...)
- what your major is (*Estudio*...) or what you plan to major in (*Pienso estudiar*...)

B. Mis compañeros de clase. Now introduce yourself to the rest of the class, using the autobiographical statements as a guide. (Do not read them word-for-word!) The listeners will take notes about their classmates, using an outline like the one that follows.

Nombre:

Dirección:

Intereses:

Estudios:

C. Mi horario de clases. Write out your class schedule in Spanish, giving the days, times, and course numbers, for example, *Español 101*.

CH. Entrevista. Interview a partner in the class to find out

- at what time he or she leaves home (or the dorm) in the morning
- at what time he or she likes to study
- if he or she drinks coffee in the cafeteria and, if so, at what time

D. Entrevista. Interview your partner to find out

- su día favorito
- dos actividades que hace en su día favorito
- dos actividades que **no** le gustan y cuándo tiene que hacerlas

Actividades de integración

El jugo es muy popular en la América Latina. Se toman los jugos puros o mezclados (mixed) con agua o con leche. También se sirven las frutas frescas en estas tiendas (shops).

VOCABULARIO

Bebidas y refrescos
Drinks and refreshments

agua (f)   *water*
agua mineral   *mineral water*
azúcar (m)   *sugar*
café (m)   *coffee*
cerveza (f)   *beer*
copa (f)   *wine glass*
crema (f)   *cream*
jugo (m)   *juice*
jugo (m) de manzana   *apple juice*
jugo (m) de naranja   *orange juice*
leche (f)   *milk*
limón (m)   *lemon*

refresco (m)   *soft drink*
taza (f)   *cup*
té (m)   *tea*
vaso (m)   *glass*
vino (m)   *wine*
vino (m) blanco   *white wine*
vino (m) tinto   *red wine*

beber   *to drink (usually alcoholic beverages)*
tomar   *to drink (either alcoholic or nonalcoholic beverages)*

¿Quieres (tomar un café)?   *Would you like (to have a cup of coffee)?*

Me gustaría mucho.   *I'd like to very much.*

La universidad
The university

biología (f)   *biology*
ciencias (f pl) políticas   *political science*
conferencia (f)   *lecture*
contabilidad (f)   *accounting*
curso (m)   *course*
economía (f)   *economics*

facultad (f) college, school of a university
historia (f) history
horario (m) schedule
informática (f) computer science
laboratorio (m) (de lenguas) (language) laboratory
matemáticas (f pl) math
psicología (f) psychology
química (f) chemistry
semestre (m) semester
tarea (f) homework

aprender to learn
enseñar to teach

Palabras interrogativas
Question words

¿Cuál? Which (one)? / What?
¿Cuándo? When?
¿Cuánto/-a? How much?
¿Cuántos/-as? How many?
¿Dónde? Where?
¿Por qué? Why?
¿Qué? What? / Which?

La comida
Meals

almuerzo (m) lunch
cafetería (f) cafeteria
cena (f) dinner
cocina (f) kitchen
comedor (m) dining room
desayuno (m) breakfast
plato (m) plate, dish; food (course, meal)

almorzar (ue) to have lunch
cocinar to cook
comer to eat
preparar to prepare

Deportes y actividades
Sports and activities

baile (m) dance
baloncesto (m) basketball
béisbol (m) baseball
fin (m) de semana weekend
fútbol (m) soccer
fútbol (m) americano football
invitación (f) invitation
tenis (m) tennis
tiempo (m) libre free time

bailar to dance
correr (en maratones) to run (in marathons)
descansar to rest, relax
esquiar en el agua to water ski
esquiar en la nieve to ski
invitar to invite
jugar (ue) to play
nadar to swim

El tiempo y la hora
Telling time

ayer yesterday
hoy today
mañana tomorrow
semana (f) week

¿Qué hora es? What time is it?
Es la... / Son las... It is . . . o'clock.
¿A qué hora... ? At what time . . . ?

El trabajo
Work, job

multinacional (f) multinational company
programa (m) bilingüe bilingual program

Palabras descriptivas
Descriptive words

alegre glad
contento/-a happy
difícil hard, difficult
fácil easy
imposible impossible
nervioso/-a nervous, anxious

Palabras enumerativas
Enumerative words

primero/-a first
segundo/-a second
tercero/-a third
cuarto/-a fourth
quinto/-a fifth

Planes y deseos
Plans and desires

desear (+ inf.) to want (to do something)
esperar (+ inf.) to hope (to do something)
pensar (ie) (+ inf.) to plan to (do something)
querer (ie) (+ inf.) to want (to do something)
tener ganas de (+ inf.) to want to, to feel like (doing something)

Expresiones de tiempo, lugar, modo y cantidad
Expressions of time, place, manner, and quantity

antes de before
despacio slowly
después de after

hasta   *until*
rápido   *quickly*

Otras expresiones útiles
Other useful expressions

Cálmate.   *Settle down.*
Claro.   *Of course.*
Déjame ver (tu tarea).   *Let me see (your homework).*
¡Manos a la obra!   *Let's get to work!*
Me encanta(n)…   *I love . . .*
Me gusta(n)…   *I like . . .*
Me interesa(n)…   *I am interested in . . .*
(El inglés) me mata.   *(English) is killing me.*
No es para tanto.   *It's not so bad as all that.*
No te preocupes.   *Don't worry.*
Odio…   *I hate . . .*
¡Oye!   *Hey! (to get someone's attention)*
¡Qué casualidad!   *What a coincidence!*
¡Qué suerte!   *What (good) luck!*
Soy fatal para (la historia).   *I'm terrible at (history).*
Ya verás.   *You'll see.*

Otros verbos y expresiones verbales
Other verbs and verbal expressions

ayudar   *to help*
cerrar (ie)   *to close*
colgar (ue)   *to hang (up) (a picture or a telephone)*
comenzar (ie)   *to begin, start*
conducir   *to drive*
conocer   *to know or to meet (a person)*
dar   *to give*
decir   *to say, tell*
encontrar (ue)   *to find*
hacer   *to do, make*
matar   *to kill*
odiar   *to hate, detest*
oír   *to hear*
poder (ue)   *to be able*
poner   *to place, put*
saber   *to know (a fact)*
salir   *to depart, leave*
soñar (ue)   *to dream*
traer   *to bring*
venir (ie)   *to come*
ver   *to see*
volver (ue)   *to return, go back*

VOCABULARIO PERSONALIZADO

Día tras día

Capítulo 3

COMMUNICATIVE OBJECTIVES

In this chapter, you will learn several ways to

- recount a sequence of events
- discuss daily activities
- talk about the weather
- express preferences
- tell where things are located
- describe people and objects
- make comparisons
- make a phone call

PRIMERA ETAPA

A mí me gusta madrugar...

ENTRADA

Play instructor tape, 1 min.

Una emisión de radio

You are about to hear part of a radio broadcast. Listen carefully to see if you can find the following information.

- what time of day it is
- what the broadcaster is talking about

1. Este programa de radio es
   a. por la mañana
   b. por la tarde
   c. por la noche
2. ¿A qué hora comienza?
   a. A las 7h
   b. A las 13h
   c. A las 21h
3. ¿De qué habla el locutor (*announcer*)?
   a. De las noticias (*news*) nacionales
   b. De los deportes
   c. Del tiempo (*weather*)

ANTES DE LEER

Since the purpose of pre-reading activities is to prepare students by asking them to access their background knowledge of the subject, the exercises are designed to be done in English. At the discretion of the teacher, however, students could be instructed to carry out the tasks in Spanish.

Preparación

One of the characteristics of well-organized people is that they plan their use of time carefully.

Make a list in English of at least four activities that you would need to include in your weekend schedule on a regular basis.

1.
2.
3.
4.

READING STRATEGY 3

Read for specific information

Regardless of whether we read for pleasure or for information, there is usually a purpose for our reading. For example, we may be looking for a particular telephone number or the departure time of a train or plane. In this case, we do not read the entire telephone directory or train or plane schedule because we can focus on the specific information we need to know, ignoring many details that are not so important to us at that time. When reading for specific information, let your purpose for reading guide you to the information you seek and remember that you do not have to understand every word of the text to obtain this information.

| Play student tape, 1 min. |

Estudiar y practicar

la actuación	*performance*
el conjunto	*musical group*
limpiar	*to clean*
llamar	*to call*
la misa	*mass* (*Catholic religious service*)
pasar	*to spend* (*time*)

LEER

Look at the list of things that Paco wants to do over the weekend. As you read the list, look for answers to the following questions.

1. ¿Por qué escribe Paco **CONCIERTO** en letras mayúsculas (*capital letters*)?
2. ¿Prefiere Paco estudiar por la tarde o por la noche?

```
             POR HACER
SÁBADO:   ☐ 9:00 a.m. lavar la ropa
          ☐ 11:00 a.m. limpiar el cuarto
          ☐ 1:30 p.m. biblioteca — cálculo
          ☐ 5:00 p.m. escribir a papá
          ☐ 8:00 p.m. CONCIERTO
DOMINGO:  ☐ 11:00 a.m. misa
          ☐ 2:00 p.m. biblioteca
                ☐ historia
                ☐ inglés
```

Paco has invited Elena to the concert. She answers with a note. As you read it, look for answers to the following questions.

1. ¿Va Elena con Paco al concierto o no?
2. ¿Qué planes tiene Elena para el fin de semana?

> Paco,
> Lo siento, pero ya tengo planes. Esta tarde Marcos y yo vamos a jugar al tenis si no hace mucho calor, y por la noche vamos a ir al cine. ¿Quizás en otra ocasión?
> Elena

DESPUÉS DE LEER

Actividad 1: Planes para el fin de semana. Read Paco's list and Elena's note again and check the activities that each plans to do this weekend.

Planes de Paco

_____ ir a un concierto
_____ jugar al tenis
_____ estudiar
_____ ir al cine con Elena

Planes de Elena

_____ ir a un concierto
_____ jugar al tenis
_____ estudiar
_____ ir al cine con Marcos

Actividad 2: Verificar. Read the announcement of the *concierto* and respond to the following statements.

HOY, GRAN CONCIERTO

El Conjunto de Cámara de la Ciudad de México que dirige el maestro Benjamín Juárez, se presentará hoy a las 8:00 de la noche en concierto de gala en el Teatro de la Ciudad.

Esta orquesta integrada por veintiocho músicos está compuesta por solistas de las mejores orquestas de México.

Entre el programa de coros y orquestas, está la actuación de la gran pianista, Silvia Navarrete, en el concierto K271 de W. A. Mozart.

Los jóvenes Amigos de la Cultura Musical A.C. dirigido por Antonio de la Borbolla, colaborando en la difusión cultural, hace esta invitación al público amante de la buena música, para que asista al concierto.

Primera etapa

1. El concierto se presenta en el Teatro Benjamín Juárez.	Sí	No
2. Hay más de veinte músicos en la orquesta.	Sí	No
3. Marcos y Elena van al cine con Paco.	Sí	No
4. Paco va a estudiar durante el fin de semana.	Sí	No
5. Paco quiere ir al concierto con Elena.	Sí	No

This activity recycles information from Chapter 2, third etapa.

Actividad 3: Una invitación. Write a brief note inviting a friend to the concert in the advertisement presented in *Actividad 2*. Include the following information.

OJO: Remember that you learned vocabulary for extending invitations in Chapter 2, third etapa.

- who organized the concert
- the day and time of the concert
- where it is to be held
- which orchestra will be playing
- which composer will be featured
- why you think the concert will be good

VENTANILLA AL MUNDO HISPÁNICO   Answering the Telephone

Many times, invitations are extended and accepted over the phone instead of in writing. The way in which one answers the phone differs from country to country. *¡Bueno!* or *¿Bueno?* is common in Mexico, while in Colombia you are more likely to hear *¿Aló?* In Spain, people answer the phone by saying *¡Diga!* If you call a company or small business, you are likely to hear *¿A la orden?* (May I help you?). Sometimes, the caller is asked *¿De parte de quién?* (Who is calling, please?), to which the response would be *Habla* [name] (This is [name] speaking).

AUMENTAR EL VOCABULARIO

Stem-changing -ir verbs are introduced in the Investigar la gramática section of this etapa.

la actuación	performance
el conjunto	musical group
conseguir (i, i)	to get, obtain
en otra ocasión	some other time
limpiar	to clean
llamar	to call
Te habla (Paco).	This is (Paco).
¿Puedo hablar con _____?	May I speak with _____?
¿De parte de quién?	May I ask who's calling?

mentir (ie, i)	to lie
la mentira	lie
la verdad	truth
decir la verdad	to tell the truth
¿(no es) verdad?	isn't that so? right?
la misa	mass (*Catholic religious service*)
la iglesia	church
la sinagoga	synagogue
el servicio religioso	religious service
pasar	to spend (*time*)
¡Que lo pases bien!	(*I hope you*) Have a good time!
pedir (i, i)	to ask for, request
preferir (ie, i)	to prefer
quizás	perhaps, maybe
seguir (i, i)	to follow, continue
sentarse (ie)	to sit down
sentir (ie, i)	to be sorry, regret
Lo siento mucho.	I'm very sorry.
¡Qué lástima!	What a shame/pity!
siempre	always
nunca	never
el sueño	dream
el tiempo	weather
llover (ue)	to rain
la lluvia	rain
nevar (ie)	to snow
la nieve	snow
el pronóstico del tiempo	weather forecast

OJO: Remember that you learned *soñar (con)* (to dream [about]) in Chapter 2.

LLAMAR POR TELÉFONO

el teléfono (el aparato)

descolgar (ue)

marcar el número

sonar (ue) el teléfono

contestar

dejar un recado

colgar (ue)

This activity uses the indicative since it is a description of the process rather than a list of commands.

*A short TPR activity could be added here, using the list of statements the students develop. Commands could either be presented in the familiar or changed to the polite form, at the discretion of the teacher. It is **not** necessary to discuss imperatives in order to do this activity.*

Instrucciones para usar el teléfono público. Imagine that you are writing a "survival manual" for Spanish-speaking students who have no knowledge of English. Write a brief description of the step-by-step process that would be involved in using a pay telephone. The first two steps are provided, to get you started.

1. Primero, usted descuelga el teléfono.
2. Al oír el tono, deposita una moneda.
3. Entonces...

Si la persona que contesta no es la persona con quien usted desea hablar...

4.

Si la persona con quien desea hablar no está en casa...

5.
6.

El uso de tu propio teléfono

1. ¿Dónde está el teléfono en tu casa?
2. Por lo general, ¿quién contesta el teléfono en tu casa? ¿Y en tu cuarto en la residencia?
3. ¿Quién es la persona que te llama con más frecuencia?
4. Si una persona te habla mal por teléfono, ¿qué haces?
5. Si la persona que llamas no está en casa, ¿generalmente llamas más tarde o dejas un recado? ¿Por qué?
6. ¿Te gusta dejar un recado en un contestador automático (*answering machine*)? ¿Por qué sí o por qué no?

USO PRÁCTICO DEL ESPAÑOL ¿Qué tiempo hace?

The way to find out what the weather is like outside at the moment is to ask, *¿Qué tiempo hace ahora?* The responses to the question often use the form *hace* as well.

Hace (muy) buen tiempo.	*It is (very) nice out.*
Hace (muy) mal tiempo.	*It is (very) bad out.*
Hace (mucho) fresco.	*It is (very) cool.*
Hace (mucho) calor.	*It is (very) hot.*
Hace (mucho) sol.	*It is (very) sunny.*
Hace (mucho) frío.	*It is (very) cold.*
Hace (mucho) viento.	*It is (very) windy.*

If it is raining or snowing, an expression with *está* is used instead.

Está lloviendo.	*It is raining.*
Está nevando.	*It is snowing.*
Está lloviznando.	*It is drizzling.*

If you want to talk about what the weather will be like in the future, you can use the *ir a + infinitivo* construction that you learned in Chapter 1.

Hace sol hoy pero mañana **va a llover**.   *It's sunny today but tomorrow **it's going to rain.***

Ponerlo a prueba

Use these drawings to teach new vocabulary (*las montañas, la nieve, patinar, el abanico, sudar*).

A. ¿Qué tiempo hace? In the space below each drawing, write the expression that best describes the weather you see.

_____   _____

B. Poner en orden. Paco has gotten his schedule for the weekend all out of order. Put the items back in the order in which he wanted to do them. Use his list of things to do in the preceding *Leer* section as the basis for your response.

_____ ir a misa   _____ lavar la ropa
_____ limpiar el cuarto   _____ ir al concierto
_____ estudiar inglés   _____ estudiar historia
_____ escribir a la familia

Extra activity: Now describe how Paco's weekend will be.

C. El fin de semana de Paco. According to his plan for the weekend, Paco has scheduled time to write to his parents on Saturday afternoon at 5:00. Here is a portion of his letter. Help him complete it.

> Me _____ los fines de semana aquí porque tengo mucho _____ libre. Los sábados por lo general _____ la ropa, limpio _____ y _____ en la biblioteca. Por la _____ no _____ al cine con mis amigos, porque prefiero ir a un _____ en el centro. Los _____ voy a _____ a las once de _____, porque me _____ dormir hasta las diez. Les escribo más la semana que viene. ¡Hasta entonces!
>   Reciban un abrazo
>   fuerte de su hijo,
>   Paco

CH. Preguntas personales. Answer the following questions about your own personal schedule.

1. Por lo general, ¿qué haces los fines de semana? Menciona tres actividades.
2. ¿Cuál es tu actividad favorita?
3. ¿Qué tienes que hacer los fines de semana (por obligación)?
4. ¿Cuándo limpias tu cuarto?
5. ¿Qué te gustaría hacer este fin de semana que no haces normalmente?
6. Cuando tienes ganas de salir los sábados por la noche, ¿adónde vas? ¿Qué haces?

OJO: Figure out as much as you can from the context, even if you don't know all of the words.

D. Ir al cine. Look at the portion of the movie page of *El País,* a Madrid newspaper, and answer the following questions about it.

1. ¿Cuál es el número de teléfono del Palacio de la Música 3?
2. ¿Cuántas veces (*times*) por día se presenta *Dirty Dancing*? ¿A qué horas?
3. Si quieres ir al cine Palafox, ¿en qué estación de metro (*subway*) bajas (*get off*)?
4. ¿Para qué películas hay restricciones?
5. ¿Qué película ganó (*won*) nueve premios *Oscar*?

Many additional questions can be based on this movie schedule: *¿Cuál es una película de Agatha Christie? ¿Qué cines están cerca de la estación de metro Callao? ¿Cuál es la dirección del cine Roxy? ¿Dónde ponen la película Best Seller?* etc.

Madrid 1. (1) / Plaza del Carmen, 3; Centro / ☎ 521 56 94 / *Metro* Sol. *Parking*.
—**El imperio del sol.** La última película dirigida por Steven Spielberg. Para todos los públicos. 4.15, 7.15, 10.15.
Palacio de la Música 1. (3) / ☎ 521 62 09 / Gran Vía, 35; Centro / *Metro* Callao.
—**Dirty dancing.** Para todos los públicos. 4.30, 7.15 y 10.15.
Palacio de la Música 2. (3) / ☎ 521 62 09 / Gran Vía, 35; Centro / *Metro* Callao.
—**4 cachorros para salvar.** La última producción de Walt Disney. Para todos los públicos. 4.35, 7.20 y 10.20.
Palacio de la Música 3. (3) / ☎ 521 62 09 / Gran Vía, 35; Centro / *Metro* Callao.
—**Tres hombres y un bebé.** Para todos los públicos. 4.30, 7.15 y 10.15.
Palacio de la Prensa. (3) / ☎ 521 99 00 / Plaza de Callao, 4; Centro / *Metro* Callao.
—**Cita con la muerte.** Peter Ustinov, Lauren Bacall. ¡Un filme de Agatha Christie! Tolerada. 4.30, 7 y 10.
Palafox. (1) / ☎ 446 18 87 / Luchana, 15; Chamberí / *Metro* Bilbao / El mejor cine de Europa.
—**El último emperador.** Dirigida por Bernardo Bertolucci. Con John Lone y Peter O'Toole. Una gran superproducción en 70 mm., con el nuevo equipo de sonido Integral Sound. Galardonada con nueve *oscars*. Laborables: 7 y 10.15. Sábados y festivos: 4, 7 y 10.15. Autorizada para todos los públicos.

Paz. (2) / ☎ 446 45 66 / Fuencarral, 125; Chamberí / *Metro* Bilbao.
—**Best seller.** Con Jame Woods, Brayan Dennehy. Un frío asesino y un famoso detective unidos para combatir la corrupción y el crimen. No recomendada a menores de 18 años. Laborables, 7 y 10.15. Miércoles, sábados y festivos, 4.30, 7 y 10.15.
Pompeya. (2) / ☎ 247 09 45 / Gran Vía, 70; Centro / *Metro* Plaza de España.
—**En busca del águila,** de Philippe Mora. De nuevo la aventura con Kathleen Turner y Rutger Hauer. 5.20, 7.30 y 10.15. Tolerada.
Rex. (3) / ☎ 247 12 37 / Gran Vía, 43; Centro / *Metro* Santo Domingo.
—**La familia.** Nominada al *oscar* como mejor película extranjera. 6 premios David de Donatello. Dirigida por Ettore Scola. Con Vittorio Gassman, Fanny Ardaud, Stefania Sandrelli. "Maravillosamente simple, simplemente maravillosa". Apta. Pases: 5, 7.30 y 10.15.
Rialto. (3) / ☎ 247 55 04 / Gran Vía, 54; Centro / *Metro* Santo Domingo.
—**La que hemos armado.** No recomendada menores 13 años. Horario: 4.30, 7 y 10.15. Miércoles, día del espectador.
Roxy A. (3) / ☎ 446 16 24 / Fuencarral, 123; Chamberí / *Metro* Bilbao.
—**Pasodoble.** Fernando Rey, Juan Diego, Antonio Resines. ¡Divertidísima! 4.30, 7 y 10.
Roxy B. (2) / ☎ 446 16 23 / Fuencarral, 123; Chamberí / *Metro* Bilbao.

INVESTIGAR LA GRAMÁTICA Stem-Changing -ir Verbs in the Present Tense

As you saw in Chapter 2, stem-changing verbs have a vowel change in the stem that is **just before** the ending. In the present tense, this change occurs in the *yo, tú, él/ella/usted,* and *ellos/ellas/ustedes* forms.

The stem vowels of **-ir** verbs, and the changes they undergo, are: $e \rightarrow ie$ or $e \rightarrow i$; $o \rightarrow ue$ or $o \rightarrow u$; or $e \rightarrow i$ and $e \rightarrow i$. The second change shown occurs in other tenses that you will learn later.

Here are three model verbs.

preferir (ie, i) (*to prefer*)

prefiero	preferimos
prefieres	preferís
prefiere	prefieren

dormir (ue, u) (*to sleep*)

duermo	dormimos
duermes	dormís
duerme	duermen

servir (i, i) (*to serve*)

sirvo	servimos
sirves	servís
sirve	sirven

Luisa prefiere dormir una siesta después de almorzar, pero yo nunca **d**uermo por la tarde.
¿**S**irvo la ensalada ahora, o prefieres comerla más tarde?

Here are some other frequently used stem-changing *-ir* verbs. You have already seen some and you should learn the others now. Remember to learn the change along with the meaning. There are additional stem-changing *-ir* verbs in the *Aumentar el vocabulario* section of the second *etapa* of this chapter.

OJO: The *-se* at the end of *divertirse* indicates that it is a reflexive verb. You will learn about these verbs in the second *etapa*.

$e \rightarrow ie, i$

divertirse	*to have a good time, to enjoy oneself*
mentir	*to lie*

$o \rightarrow ue, u$

morir	*to die*

OJO: The conjugation for *seguir* and *conseguir* has a spelling change in the *yo* form to preserve the hard "g" sound: *sigo, consigo.*

$e \rightarrow i, i$

conseguir	*to get, obtain*
corregir	*to correct*

OJO: The conjugation for *reír* preserves the accent mark throughout: *río, ríes, ríe, reímos, reís, ríen.*

OJO: *Decir* is another *e → i, i* verb in the present tense, although it is irregular in other tenses that you will learn later.

despedirse (de)	to say good-bye (*to*)
pedir	to request, ask for
repetir	to repeat
reírse (de)	to laugh (*at*)
seguir	to follow
sonreír	to smile

Ponerlo a prueba

A. Combinaciones. Make as many truthful sentences as you can by using one element from each column. Be careful to make all necessary changes in the verbs you use.

Yo	preferir	trabajar mucho
Mis amigos y yo	dormir	hasta las once los fines de semana
Mi amigo/-a	pedir perdón	cuando ofender a otra persona
Mi hermano/-a	sonreír	cuando jugar al baloncesto
Mis amigos	seguir	las reglas (*rules*) de la universidad

OJO: *Pedir perdón* means "to apologize."

B. Más fotografías. Marcos's young neighbor Rafaelito has decided to capture some moments of family life on film. Help him write the captions for his pictures.

1. En esta foto mi mamá _____ la comida. (servir)

2. Mi papá _____ para la foto. (sonreír)

3. Adriana _____ porque quiere la galleta (*cookie*). (mentir)

4. Nosotros _____ más pastel (*cake*) porque está delicioso. (pedir)

5. Papá y Luisita _____ en el sofá (dormir)

6. Mamá es maestra; aquí _____ la tarea de su clase. (corregir)

OJO: Use *y* or *pero* in your response, according to whether your preference is the same or different. Notice that the subject pronoun *yo* is used for emphasis.

C. **Las preferencias.** People are different. Compare your preferences to those of the people mentioned here.

Modelo: Nelson duerme seis horas por noche, y/pero yo...
Nelson duerme seis horas por noche, pero yo duermo ocho.

1. Mis amigos siempre piden café, y/pero yo...
2. Antonio sonríe mucho, y/pero yo...
3. María Concepción siempre dice todo lo que (*everything that*) piensa, y/pero yo...
4. Mis amigos siempre consiguen trabajos interesantes para el verano (*summer*), y/pero yo...
5. Álvaro siempre sirve nachos y refrescos cuando hace una fiesta, y/pero yo...
6. Marta y Raúl juegan al tenis, y/pero Julio y yo...
7. José María repite mucho sus chistes (*jokes*) y es muy aburrido, y/pero yo...
8. Edelberto siempre sigue las reglas (*rules*) de la universidad, y/pero yo...
9. Javier miente mucho y nunca dice la verdad, y/pero yo...

CH. **Más sobre las preferencias.** Divide into groups of three or four. Ask each other which alternative he or she prefers. Then report your group's preferences back to the class. If there is consensus in the group on any of the items, you can report to the class: *El grupo prefiere...* or *Preferimos...*

Modelo: los sábados o los domingos
Prefiero los sábados.
Carlos prefiere los domingos.

1. madrugar (*get up early*) o dormir hasta las once
2. el calor excesivo o el frío excesivo
3. las clases difíciles pero interesantes o las clases fáciles pero aburridas
4. dejar un recado por teléfono con una persona o con un contestador automático

D. **Encuesta: la comida.** Use the following form to survey one of your classmates on the topic of food.

Pregunta	Respuesta
1. En tu casa, ¿quién sirve la comida?	_____ mi mamá
	_____ mi papá
	_____ yo
	_____ (otra) _____
2. Cuando comes en un restaurante, ¿qué pides para tomar con la comida?	_____ agua
	_____ leche
	_____ refresco
	_____ cerveza
	_____ vino
	_____ (otra) _____
3. Cuando sales a comer, ¿a qué restaurante vas?	_____
4. ¿Con quién(es) vas generalmente?	_____
	_____
	_____
5. Por lo general, ¿prefieres comer en casa, en la universidad o en un restaurante?	_____ en casa
	_____ en la universidad
	_____ en un restaurante

¡TIENES LA PALABRA!

Do the following activities with a partner.

A. **Compañero/-a de cuarto.** You are interviewing new students to pair them up as roommates. Interview your partner to find out

- si prefiere la música rock o la música clásica
- si estudia en la biblioteca o en su cuarto
- si madruga
- si hace mucho ruido
- si prefiere tener televisor en el cuarto o no

OJO: Before you begin, practice formulating the questions.

B. Hablar por teléfono

Estudiante A

1. Call your friend. Say the number aloud to yourself as you dial.
2. Ask for your friend.
3. Identify yourself.
4. Leave the message that you will call back at 9:00 that night.
5. Say good-bye.

Estudiante B

1. Answer the phone.
2. Ask who is calling.
3. Say that the person is not there. Ask if the caller wants to leave a message.
4. Repeat the message and say good-bye.

OTRA VUELTA

Play instructor tape, 1 min.

Listen again to the weather report that you heard at the beginning of this *etapa*. Answer the following questions.

1. En el momento de la emisión, la temperatura está a _____ grados.
2. La temperatura durante el día va a llegar a _____ grados.
3. ¿Qué tiempo va a hacer durante el día?

COMENTARIO CULTURAL

Answering the Telephone

In Spanish, when you call one of your friends on the phone the first thing you are likely to say when someone answers is ¿*Con quién hablo*? (With whom am I speaking?) or ¿*Quién habla*? (Who is speaking?). When speaking in English in the United States, such behavior is unacceptably rude. The person who is calling is felt to be intruding on the recipient's private space; the person called is the only one who is entitled to ask, "Who's calling?" In much of the Hispanic world, however, when you call people, even at their home, the chances are that someone other than a family member will answer. In that case, the notion of intrusion does not apply, and the behavior is routine. This is a good example of what we mean when we say that knowing a language is more than just knowing what the words mean. All communication takes place in a sociocultural setting, and understanding the culture is just as important in learning to communicate and interpret what you see and hear as is knowing the grammar and vocabulary.

SEGUNDA ETAPA

"¿Tienes planes para el fin de semana?"

ENTRADA

Play instructor tape, 2 min.

"Vamos a salir esta noche"

Raquel and her friend, David, are planning to go out. As you listen to their conversation, try to figure out

- where they decide to go
- what time they decide to go

1. ¿Qué piensan hacer Raquel y David?
   a. ir al cine
   b. cenar en un restaurante
   c. visitar a sus amigos

2. ¿A qué hora van?
   a. a las 4:30
   b. a las 7:30
   c. a las 7:15

EMPEZAR A ESCUCHAR

Play student tape, 2 min.

Leer

tarde	late
madrugar	to get up early
me despierto	I wake up
temprano	early
estar de vuelta	to be back
calladito/-a	very quiet (*person*); very quietly
dormilón/-ona	sleepyhead
desayunar	to eat breakfast
¿Me esperas?	Will you wait for me?
tener prisa	to be in a hurry

Repetir

Listen to your student tape and repeat the words and phrases you hear.

Identificar

On a separate sheet of paper, write in a column the words and phrases in Spanish from the preceding list. You will hear some sentences on your tape. Whenever you hear one of these words or phrases, write next to it the number of the sentence in which it appears. Each sentence will be read twice. You may stop and start the tape as often as you wish.

Escribir

You will hear some sentences in Spanish. Each one will be read twice. Write them down as you listen, starting and stopping the tape as needed.

Reconocer

Each of the sentences you have just written contains one or more of the words and phrases from the preceding list. Read the sentences carefully and underline as many of the words and phrases from the list as you can find. As you read, make any necessary corrections in your sentences.

ESCUCHAR

Play student tape, 1 min.

Episodio 1: La rutina diaria de Elena

Enfoque comunicativo

You are about to hear Elena and her roommate Alicia talk about their habits and daily routines. What differences in their lifestyles come out in their conversation? Look for information about

- what time they like to get up in the morning
- Alicia's reaction to Elena's schedule

Elena se levanta a las:	5:30	6:00	6:30	7:00	7:30
Alicia se levanta a las:	5:30	6:00	6:30	7:00	7:30
La reacción de Alicia:	entusiasmo		horror		

Enfoque lingüístico

As you listen to the conversation again, write down

- two statements Elena makes to indicate that she likes to get up early
- two exclamations Alicia uses to express her reaction

ESCUCHAR

Play student tape, 1 min.

Episodio 2: La rutina de Alicia

Enfoque comunicativo

Alicia and Elena continue to talk, trying to arrange their morning schedules. As you listen, try to figure out

- Elena's reaction to Alicia's morning schedule
- what they decide to do together

> La reacción de Elena:
>   a. positiva   b. negativa
> Las dos amigas van a
>   a. correr   b. desayunar   c. estudiar

Enfoque lingüístico

As you listen to the conversation again, write down

- the exclamation Elena uses to express her reaction to Alicia's schedule
- how Elena says she doesn't mind waiting for Alicia

VERIFICAR

¿Sí o no?

1. Alicia corre todas las mañanas.   Sí   No
2. A Elena le gusta levantarse a las 5:30.   Sí   No
3. Elena se levanta antes que Alicia.   Sí   No
4. Alicia tiene más energía que Elena.   Sí   No
5. Alicia prefiere levantarse a las 7:30.   Sí   No
6. Elena tiene su primera clase a las 8:00.   Sí   No
7. Elena cree que Alicia es una dormilona.   Sí   No

AUMENTAR EL VOCABULARIO

OJO: Stronger terms for requesting silence are, ¡Silencio! and ¡Cállate!

OJO: El despertador is literally a "wake-up agent." You will learn the verb despertarse, "to wake up," in the next visual vocabulary.

OJO: This is a new meaning for esperar (to hope), which you have already learned.

OJO: You already know volver, which is a synonym of regresar.

la barba	beard
callarse	to become silent; shut up
calladito/-a	very quiet (*person*); very quietly
callado/-a	quiet, quietly
tranquilo/-a	quiet (*place*); peaceful
el ruido	noise
ruidoso/-a	noisy
el silencio	silence
desayunar	to have breakfast
cenar	to have the evening meal
el despertador	alarm clock
dormilón/-ona	sleepyhead
empezar (ie)	to begin
esperar	to wait for
¿Me esperas?	Will you wait for me?
estar de vuelta	to be back
regresar	to return

Segunda etapa

Point out daily meal schedules to students, connecting the verbs *desayunar/desayuno, almorzar/almuerzo, comer/comida, cenar/cena.*

madrugar	**to get up early**
la madrugada	dawn
el anochecer	dusk, nightfall
sentirse (ie, i)	**to feel**
temprano	**early**
tarde	late
más tarde	later on
a tiempo	on time
tener prisa	**to be in a hurry**
terminar	**to end**
vestirse (i, i)	**to get dressed**
afeitarse	to shave
desvestirse (i, i)	to get undressed
peinarse	to comb one's hair

OJO: A phrase that means the same thing as *vestirse* is *ponerse la ropa.*

LA RUTINA DIARIA DE ALICIA

OJO: The word *suele* from the verb *soler (ue)* means "is accustomed to" or "usually" and is followed by an infinitive. It is used here so you can see the infinitive forms of the verbs related to daily routine.

OJO: In Latin America *bañarse* means both "to bathe" and "to shower." In Spain *ducharse* is used for "to shower."

Point out that *lavarse* can be applied to other parts of the body. For example, *lavarse la cabeza, lavarse la cara, lavarse las manos.*

Alicia suele **despertarse** a las 7:15.

Alicia suele **levantarse** a las 7:30.

Alicia suele **bañarse (ducharse)** a las 7:35.

Alicia suele **vestirse** a las 7:50.

Alicia suele **desvestirse** a las 11:00 de la noche.

Alicia suele **lavarse los dientes** a las 11:05 de la noche.

Alicia suele **acostarse** a las 11:20 de la noche.

Alicia suele **dormirse** a las 11:21 de la noche.

Ventanilla al Mundo Hispánico

"Corro solamente cinco kilómetros los días de clase"

The Hispanic world uses the metric system for both weights and measures. Distances are measured in *metros,* about the same distance as a yard. A *kilómetro* is 1000 *metros,* which is approximately 0.6 miles (*millas*). Metros are divided into **centímetros**. There are 2.54 **centímetros** in an inch. Remember that the prefix *kilo-* always indicates a multiple of 1000; for example, *un kilogramo,* which is usually shortened to *un kilo,* is 1000 *gramos,* or about 2.2 pounds (*libras*).

Similarly, the Hispanic world measures temperature on the Celsius scale (often called the centigrade scale, because the word "centigrade" means "divided into 100 parts") rather than Fahrenheit. The formula for conversion from centigrade to Fahrenheit is $(9/5 \times$ degrees centigrade$) + 32$. To convert from Fahrenheit to centigrade the formula is $5/9 \times ($degrees Fahrenheit $- 32)$. A normal body temperature of 98.6° Fahrenheit is 37° centigrade. Here is the way it would be calculated.

From Fahrenheit to centigrade

$5/9 \times (°F - 32)$ = °C $5/9 \times 66.6$ = °C

$5/9 \times (98.6 - 32)$ = °C 37 = °C

Water boils at 100° centigrade. To find the equivalent Fahrenheit temperature, we would calculate as follows.

From centigrade to Fahrenheit

$(9/5 \times °C) + 32$ = °F $180 + 32$ = °F

$(9/5 \times 100) + 32$ = °F 212 = °F

Thus we have calculated that 37° on the Celsius scale is the equivalent of 98.6° Fahrenheit, and 100° Celsius is 212° Fahrenheit. Here are some more examples.

Centigrade		Fahrenheit
32°	=	90° (Hace calor.)
10°	=	50° (Hace fresco.)
–8°	=	18° (Hace frío.)

Preguntas. Answer the following questions.

1. Si una persona corre cinco kilómetros, ¿cuántas millas son?
2. Si una persona pesa (*weighs*) 150 libras, ¿cuántos kilos son?
3. Si la temperatura está a 77 grados Fahrenheit, ¿cuántos grados centígrados son?
4. Si una persona mide 6 pies, ¿cuántos centímetros son?

Have students calculate their height in metros/centímetros *(1" = 2.54 cm); have them calculate the distance from their homes to the university in* kilómetros.

OJO: You will learn in this *etapa* how to use reflexive verbs. For this activity, just conjugate the verb in the *yo* form and use *me* before it, as in the model.

¿A qué hora? Say at what time you do the following.

Modelo: despertarse   *Me despierto a las siete de la mañana.*

1. despertarse
2. levantarse
3. vestirse
4. lavarse los dientes
5. desvestirse
6. acostarse

USO PRÁCTICO DEL ESPAÑOL   Expresiones con **tener**

Use questions to develop familiarity with these expressions: 1. ¿Qué haces cuando tienes mucho calor en julio y agosto? 2. ¿Qué haces cuando tienes mucho frío en diciembre y enero? 3. ¿Por lo general tienes más hambre por la mañana, por la tarde o por la noche?

You have already learned that *tener* is a useful verb to use to talk about desires (*tener ganas*), to talk about having to do something (*tener que* + *inf.*), and to talk about age (*tener _____ años*). Here are some other useful expressions with *tener.*

Sensaciones físicas
tener calor	to be (*feel*) hot
tener frío	to be (*feel*) cold
tener hambre	to be hungry
tener sed	to be thirsty
tener sueño	to be sleepy

OJO: The expression *tener prisa,* "to be in a hurry," is in the preceding *Aumentar el vocabulario* list.

Emociones
tener envidia	to be envious
tener miedo (de)	to be afraid (*of*)
tener ganas (de)	to feel like (*doing something*)
tener interés (en)	to be interested (*in*)
tener paciencia	to be patient

OJO: With *tener* expressions, we use *mucho/-a* (a lot of) (not *muy* [very]) to increase the intensity of the expression: *Tengo* **mucho** *frío* (I am very cold).

Otra expresión
tener fama	to be famous, well-known

Ponerlo a prueba

OJO: Use your guessing skills; do not be concerned if you do not understand every word.

A. **Definiciones.** Choose the word or expression from the *Aumentar el vocabulario* section that best matches each of the following definitions.

1. levantarse muy temprano
2. una persona que duerme mucho y que se levanta muy tarde
3. comer a las 7:00 o a las 8:00 de la mañana
4. el momento del día cuando cae el sol y comienza a ponerse oscuro
5. después de la hora indicada
6. cuando no hay ruido
7. tener que hacer algo muy rápido

8. un sinónimo de **ponerse la ropa**
9. descripción de un lugar donde hay silencio
10. el contrario de **empezar**

B. **Comentarios y respuestas.** Isabel and Mercedes are talking about their families and friends. For each statement made by Isabel, select the most appropriate response for Mercedes.

Isabel

1. Miguel es muy raro, tiene calor cuando hace mucho frío.
2. Mi abuela tiene 85 años y todavía va al mercado todos los días.
3. Parece que la tía Elena siempre tiene razón en todas las discusiones entre la familia.
4. Andrés no tiene paciencia con su hermanita.
5. La pobre Bertita tiene miedo de la oscuridad.

Mercedes

a. Es muy inteligente, y lee mucho también.
b. Es verdad, dice que no quiere jugar con ella porque ella no sabe nada de sus juegos.
c. Sí, nunca lleva una chaqueta (*jacket*).
ch. Es verdad, cree que hay monstruos en los rincones de su cuarto.
d. Es una persona impresionante, de eso no hay duda.

C. **Poner en orden.** Number the following activities from 1 to 9, according to the order in which you do them on a typical day.

____ almorzar ____ desayunar
____ levantarme ____ vestirme
____ bañarme ____ cenar
____ acostarme ____ estudiar
____ despertarme

Now give a brief summary of your daily routine. For example, *Por lo general, me levanto a las* ____ *de la mañana...*

CH. **Preguntas personales**

1. ¿A qué hora te levantas los días de clase? ¿Los fines de semana?
2. ¿Usas despertador? ¿Te gusta levantarte con la radio o con el ruido del despertador? ¿Para qué hora pones (*set*) el despertador o el radio?
3. ¿A qué hora desayunas?
4. ¿Te gusta almorzar temprano o tarde? ¿Por qué?
5. ¿A qué hora cenas? ¿Dónde cenas y con quién?
6. Si estudias en la biblioteca por la noche, ¿a qué hora estás de vuelta en tu cuarto o en tu casa?

Segunda etapa

Have students practice the pronunciation of *inmediatamente*. Other useful words that are also often mispronounced are *probablemente* and *aproximadamente*.

7. ¿A qué hora terminas la tarea por lo general?
8. ¿Te gusta leer un poco después de acostarte, o te gusta dormirte inmediatamente?

D. ¿Qué te gusta hacer? The weather often has an effect on what we do. Complete the following statements by giving information about yourself.

Modelo: Cuando hace frío, me gusta...
Cuando hace frío, me gusta leer en casa.

This is a recycling of the weather expressions introduced in the preceding *etapa*.

1. Cuando hace frío, siempre...
2. Cuando hace sol, me gusta...
3. Cuando está lloviendo, tengo ganas de...
4. Cuando hace mal tiempo, suelo...
5. Cuando hace buen tiempo, tengo ganas de...
6. Cuando está nevando, me gusta...

Aquí se ve una vista de la selva de Puerto Rico desde el pico que se llama "El Yunque." ¿Qué tiempo hace?

E. Creando mini-diálogos. You and your partner have been invited to audition for a soap opera about student life. Unfortunately, the script is incomplete. Complete these mini-dialogues and practice for your audition. Be as dramatic as possible.

Escenario (Scene) 1

(*Suena el despertador.*)

A: ¡Levántate, _____ , que tienes clase en 30 minutos!

B: ¡Ay, no! No puedo levantarme, quiero dormir más.

Escenario 2

A: (Haces mucho ruido) La, la, la…

B: ¡_____! Tengo dos exámenes mañana.

Escenario 3

A: Vamos a poner _____ para las 5:00. Tengo que _____ mañana para terminar la tarea.

B: ¡Ay, no! Tengo un examen mañana y quiero despertarme _____.

INVESTIGAR LA GRAMÁTICA Los verbos reflexivos

Reflexive verbs in Spanish always appear with the pronouns *me, te, se, nos, os,* or *se*. These pronouns often indicate that the subject of the sentence does something to or for itself. You have already seen some of these forms earlier in this *etapa*.

Siempre **me** levanto muy temprano.	I always get up (*literally, get myself up*) very early.
Alicia **se** baña y **se** viste rápido.	Alicia showers (*lit., bathes herself*) and gets dressed (*lit., dresses herself*) quickly.

The reflexive pronoun always corresponds to the subject of the verb.

Cuando Paco está nervioso, **se** despierta a la madrugada.	When Paco is nervous, he wakes up (*lit., wakes himself up*) early in the morning.
Cuando tengo mucho que hacer, **me** escribo una nota.	When I have a lot to do, I write myself a note.
Siempre **me** encuentro con Marisa en el cine. Qué casualidad, ¿no?	I always run into (*lit., find myself with*) Marisa at the movies. What a coincidence, don't you think?

Very often verbs are used reflexively in Spanish that do not have an obvious reflexive meaning in English. *Encontrarse* is a good example of a word whose reflexive meaning is not obvious to a speaker of English, although it is very clear to a speaker of Spanish that if *encontrar* means "to find," then *encontrarse* would mean "to find oneself" in someone's path or in someone's company.

When a reflexive verb is given as a vocabulary item, the infinitive will always have the reflexive pronoun *se* attached to the end to remind you that it is used reflexively. Many of the verbs that have to do with daily routine are used reflexively in Spanish. Here is the present tense of *bañarse* (to bathe or shower).

me baño	**nos** bañamos
te bañas	**os** bañáis
se baña	**se** bañan

Reflexive pronouns precede the verb when it is conjugated, but are attached to the end of the infinitive. Remember that they always refer to the subject of the verb.

Tengo que levantar**me** temprano, pero mi compañero de cuarto **se** levanta tarde.

Many verbs in Spanish can be used reflexively or nonreflexively, depending on whether the action of the verb is done to the subject of the sentence or to someone else.

Siempre **me despierto** a las 7:00. *I always wake up* (*I wake myself up*) *at 7:00.*

Siempre **despierto** al bebé a las 7:00. *I always wake the baby up at 7:00.*
Siempre **me baño** antes de desayunar. *I always take a shower* (*lit., bathe myself*) *before I have breakfast.*
Siempre **baño** al bebé antes de desayunar. *I always bathe the baby before I have breakfast.*

Some verbs change meaning when used reflexively. This is discussed in Chapter 11, third *etapa*.

Once students grasp the notion of reflexivity, you may want to introduce the reciprocal use of reflexives, e.g., *se miran* (they look at each other) and *nos escribimos* (we write to each other).

OJO: Note the relationship between *despertar*, "to awaken" (someone), and *despertador*, "the thing that awakens."

Ponerlo a prueba

A. Un día en la vida de Octavio Palacios. Create sentences from the elements given to talk about Octavio's daily routine.

1. Octavio / poner el despertador / las 7:00
2. Por lo general / levantarse / las 7:30
3. Por eso / tener prisa para bañarse y vestirse
4. No afeitarse porque / tener barba
5. Él y sus amigos / desayunar juntos / la cafetería
6. Octavio / tener clases por la mañana y / estudiar por la tarde

B. Combinaciones. Make as many truthful sentences as you can, using one element from each column.

Yo	levantarse	todos los días
Mi compañero/-a de cuarto	desayunar	tarde los sábados
Mis amigos	salir	los fines de semana
Mis amigos y yo	bañarse	por la mañana
	lavarse los dientes	por la noche

C. ¡Dormilón! Luis has a reputation for partying when he should be sleeping, and sleeping when he should be doing other things. His roommate is at his wit's end. Complete the paragraph to find out what he says to Luis.

El compañero habla: Luis, eres imposible. Cuando _____ (**sonar**) el despertador por la mañana, tú no _____ (**levantarse**). ¡Por decir la verdad, no _____ (**despertarse**)! Ya sé que _____ (**acostarse**) muy tarde por la noche o, mejor dicho, muy temprano por la madrugada, pero esta rutina tiene que cambiar (*to change*). Si no _____ (**levantarse**) a las 7:00, si no _____ (**bañarse**) a las 7:15, si no _____ (**vestirse**) a las 7:30, no puedes llegar a tu clase de las 8:00. Y tú _____ (**saber**) que necesitas esa clase para graduarte (*to graduate*). ¡Por favor, Luis, que ya _____ (**ser**) las 7:45!

CH. Encuesta. You are doing a survey on personal hygiene for a company that manufactures such items as soap, perfume, and deodorant. Luckily you do the survey by phone and it is completely anonymous, since some of the questions are rather personal. Your friend has agreed to allow you to practice on him or her. Use the *usted* form in your questions to practice asking them as you will in your survey.

Modelo: *¿Con qué frecuencia se lava Ud. los dientes?*

OJO: You would always use *usted* in speaking to a stranger on the telephone, especially in a professional capacity, such as a telephone survey.

OJO: For women, you can ask *¿Con qué frecuencia se depila Ud?* (How often do you shave your legs?)

Pregunta	*Todos los días*	*Por lo general*	*A veces*	*Nunca*
1. bañarse con agua fría				
2. lavarse los dientes				
3. afeitarse				
4. peinarse				
5. lavarse el pelo				
6. usar jabón (*soap*) natural				
7. usar perfume o agua de colonia				
8. usar desodorante líquido				

D. Las actividades en tu casa. Answer the following questions about your home life.

1. ¿Quién se levanta temprano para trabajar?
2. ¿Quién madruga para estudiar?
3. ¿Quién despierta a los demás (*others*) generalmente?
4. ¿Quién lava la ropa de los demás?
5. ¿Quién se duerme cuando mira la televisión?
6. ¿Quién se acuesta muy temprano?

Do the following activities with a partner.

A. La rutina. Interview your partner to find out

- a qué hora se levanta los días de clase
- si le gusta madrugar
- a qué hora se levanta los fines de semana
- qué prefiere hacer los sábados
- si le gusta desayunar

B. Encuesta psicológica. A psychology student has created a survey to develop a psychological profile of students of Spanish. You think the survey is strange, but the student is your friend, and you agree to administer it to two people in your Spanish class. Use the following form to record the responses you receive.

OJO: Use the spaces to record the responses of your two friends.

Los estudiantes de español

Pregunta	Estudiante A	Estudiante B
¿De qué tienes fama entre tus amigos?		
¿En qué tienes más interés, en tus estudios o en otra cosa?		
¿De qué tienes miedo, hablando francamente?		
¿En qué circunstancias tienes mucha paciencia? ¿Y poca paciencia?		

Since this is a confidential survey, be sure to refer to your respondents as *Estudiante A* and *Estudiante B* if you report the results to your class.

OTRA VUELTA

Play instructor tape, 2 min.

Listen again to the conversation between Raquel and David that you heard at the beginning of this *etapa*. As you listen, fill in the chart with the information you hear. Some clues are included to get you started.

Película	Cine	Horas
1. El imperio del _____	_____	4:00, _____, 10:15
2. La _____	_____	_____, _____, 10:15

COMENTARIO CULTURAL

Actividades y pasatiempos en el mundo hispánico

Leisure-time activities throughout the Spanish-speaking world are many and varied. They typically involve groups of friends or whole families doing things and going places together. Young people enjoy going to concerts and discotheques. On special occasions you can expect to go to elaborate *fiestas* with lots of food and drink, dancing, and animated conversation. Outings with family or friends often include going to the movies, *el cine,* either to the *vespertina,* the late afternoon show, or to the *nocturna,* the late show. Other times people go to the theater, *el teatro,* to enjoy a live show.

In both cities and small towns, neighborhood parks abound, and people of all ages look for an excuse to go for walks or sit on benches in the parks and talk about everything from international politics to the latest gossip. Often older men gather in the parks and spend their time talking and playing dominoes.

Many people enjoy a regular program of physical fitness, and walking, jogging, and bicycle riding are very popular activities. Although fitness centers and gyms are increasing in popularity and availability, the people generally prefer outdoor activities. Team sports, especially baseball, *el béisbol,* and soccer, *el fútbol,* enjoy enormous popularity.

Los pasatiempos en tu ciudad o pueblo natal (*home town*). Do the following statements apply to the city or town where you grew up? Respond *sí* or *no*.

1. Los jóvenes (*young people*) van a las discotecas los fines de semana.   Sí   No
2. Hay conciertos en los parques durante el verano.   Sí   No
3. Los padres llevan a los niños a la vespertina.   Sí   No
4. Los grupos de amigos se reúnen (*get together*) para hablar de la política.   Sí   No
5. El ejercicio es muy popular. Hay muchas personas que corren en los parques y en las calles (*streets*).   Sí   No

 ¡A arreglar el cuarto!

ENTRADA

Play instructor tape, 2 min.

Un anuncio de radio

You will hear a radio announcement for a furniture store that is having a big sale. As you listen, try to identify the following pieces of information.

Nombre:
Dirección:
Horas:
Se venden (*They sell*):

1.
2.
3.

ANTES DE ESCRIBIR

WRITING STRATEGY 3

Organize your descriptions

When you are asked to describe a person, a place, an object, or an activity, you first have to make some decisions. What aspect(s) are you going to highlight? What is the purpose of your description? Before you begin to write a description, spend some time planning your approach. When describing a person, for example, decide whether you will focus on the person's physical appearance, personality, or biographical data, or perhaps include some information in each category. You can often make your descriptions more interesting by weaving biographical information into your descriptive statements.

Preparación

Descriptions of people can include information about physical characteristics, personality, interests, and activities. Imagine that you are writing to your family

OJO: You can do this prewriting activity in English or, if you refer to the *Estudiar y practicar* list below, in Spanish.

about a new friend you have made. Write the information you would include under each of the following categories.

El físico (Physical characteristics)

1.
2.
3.
4.

La personalidad / Otros rasgos (Other characteristics)

1.
2.
3.
4.

Intereses / Actividades

1.
2.
3.
4.

Now go back over your list and look for relationships among the characteristics you have written. For example, the physical characteristic "athletic" might be related to an interest in a particular sport. Write some additional notes about any relationships you find.

Play student tape, 1 min.

Estudiar y practicar

OJO: Remember other words you have learned to describe people: *amable, simpático/-a, aburrido/-a, moreno/-a* (dark-skinned). Since descriptive words like these characterize people, use the verb *ser* with them.

OJO: You learned these words to describe hair color in Chapter 1. Remember that you say *es pelirrojo/-a* and *es rubio/-a,* but you say *tiene el pelo castaño, tiene el pelo negro.*

El físico
alto/-a	tall
bajo/-a	short
delgado/-a	thin, slender
de mediana estatura	average (height)
flaco/-a	skinny
gordo/-a	fat, heavy
guapo/-a	handsome, nice-looking
pelirrojo/-a	red-haired
el pelo castaño	brown hair
el pelo negro	black hair
rubio/-a	blond

La personalidad / Otros rasgos
abierto/-a	open
agradable	nice, agreeable

OJO: Study tip: Learn these words and the ones in the upcoming *Uso práctico del español* section by grouping them according to general meaning.

antipático/-a	*unfriendly*
celoso/-a	*jealous*
cómico/-a	*funny, comic*
generoso/-a	*generous*
reservado/-a	*reserved*
serio/-a	*serious*
tacaño/-a	*stingy*

ESCRIBIR

La descripción de un amigo (una amiga)

Using the notes and lists you have made, write a description of your new friend in Spanish. Remember that you have a double purpose: (1) to paint a verbal picture of this individual, and (2) to explain why you like him or her.

DESPUÉS DE ESCRIBIR

A. **Analizar la descripción.** Exchange descriptions with a partner. Read your partner's description and notice how it has been organized. What categories has your partner used, and what information is given under each category? Briefly outline your partner's description.

B. **Descripción enfocada** (*focused*). Imagine now that you are looking around a large, crowded room for the friend you have described. Looking at your description, do the following.

1. Bracket the phrases and sentences that would be helpful in this situation. Notice what parts would **not** be helpful.
2. What other information would you need if you were to describe to somebody else what your friend looks like? (Write in Spanish if you can; otherwise, use English.)
   a.
   b.
   c.

VENTANILLA AL MUNDO HISPÁNICO   Las telenovelas

The popularity of *las telenovelas* (soap operas) is a phenomenon that is common to both the United States and the Spanish-speaking world. One difference between them is that U.S. soap operas are a relatively new phenomenon at night, whereas they are commonly shown during prime time in Hispanic countries. *Las telenovelas* are the most recent addition to the *novela* category: *radionovelas* and *fotonovelas* have been popular for some years in Hispanic countries. *Las radionovelas* can be heard on any radio station in the Hispanic world, and *las fotonovelas*, which are pulp magazine stories in a comic-book format, are sold at newsstands and at local neighborhood stores.

AUMENTAR EL VOCABULARIO

abierto/-a — open
   agradable — nice, agreeable
   antipático/-a — unfriendly
   celoso/-a — jealous
   cómico/-a — funny, comic
   generoso/-a — generous
   reservado/-a — reserved
   serio/-a — serious
   tacaño/-a — stingy

alto/-a — tall
   bajo/-a — short
   delgado/-a — thin, slender
   gordo/-a — fat, heavy
   guapo/-a — handsome, nice-looking
   de mediana estatura — average (height)

arreglar — to arrange
   mover (ue) — to move (furniture)
   quitar — to take away, remove

OJO: The verb *mover* means "to move something," while *mudarse* means "to change residence."

cerca de — near
   al lado de — next to
   debajo de — under
   encima de — on top of
   delante de — in front of
   detrás de — in back of, behind
   dentro de — inside of
   fuera de — outside of
   lejos de — far from

deber (+ infinitivo) — must, should (+ *infinitive*)

estar contento/-a — to be happy
   descontento/-a — dissatisfied, displeased (with something)

funcionar — to function, work, run (*machines*)
   no funciona — out of order; this isn't working (said of a project or machine)

importante — important
   No importa. — It doesn't matter.

la pared — wall (*interior wall, as of a room*)
   el piso — floor
   el rincón — corner

OJO: *El rincón* refers to a corner inside a room, where the walls come together. The corner where two outside walls of a building come together is *la esquina,* which also means "street corner."

OJO: Note that the expression "to be wrong" uses the verb *estar* in Spanish. This is because it represents a condition of the moment.

pelirrojo/-a	*red-haired*
el pelo castaño	*brown hair*
el pelo negro	*black hair*
rubio/-a	*blond*
tener razón	*to be right*
estar equivocado/-a	*to be wrong, in error*

EL CUARTO DE LA RESIDENCIA

For homework, have students make a drawing of their rooms like the one here, labeling the items in the room. They will need this drawing for *Actividad F* that follows.

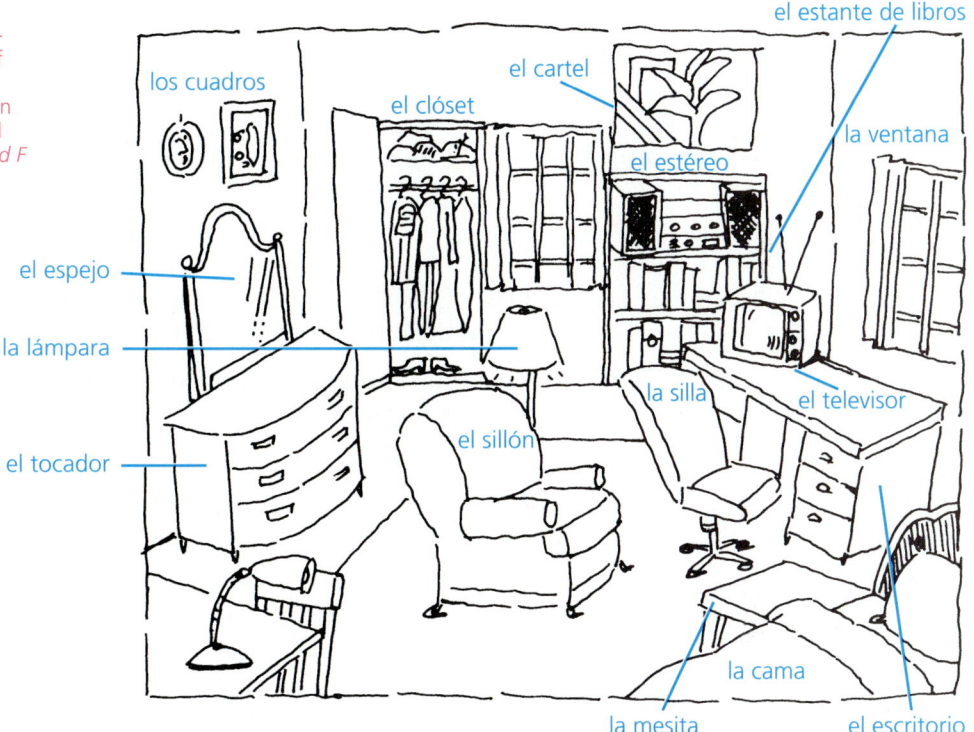

¿Dónde está? Using the prepositions from the *Aumentar el vocabulario* section, say where each of the following items is located.

Modelo: *El escritorio está debajo de la ventana.*

1. el sillón
2. el televisor
3. el cuadro y el cartel
4. la cama
5. el espejo
6. el estéreo

USO PRÁCTICO DEL ESPAÑOL   Más descripciones

Here are some additional adjectives for describing people. Physical characteristics are listed first, followed by more general characteristics.

débil	*weak*
feo/-a	*ugly, unattractive*
fuerte	*strong*
desagradable	*disagreeable, unpleasant*
envidioso/-a	*envious*
optimista	*optimistic*
perezoso/-a	*lazy*
pesimista	*pessimistic*
tímido/-a	*shy*
trabajador(a)	*hardworking*

OJO: Remember the difference between *envidioso/-a* and *celoso/-a*: an *envidioso/-a* desires what others have, while a *celoso/-a* is afraid that others will take away what he or she has.

Ponerlo a prueba

Students should refer to the words in the preceding sections *Estudiar y practicar, Aumentar el vocabulario* and *Uso práctico del español*.

A. Definiciones. Select the best definition for the adjectives listed here. Then, incorporate the definition into a complete sentence, according to the model.

Modelo: rico   una persona que tiene mucho dinero
Una persona que tiene mucho dinero es rica.

1. optimista
2. generoso/-a
3. antipático/-a
4. reservado/-a
5. tímido/-a
6. aburrido/-a
7. envidioso/-a
8. de mediana estatura
9. perezoso/-a
10. feliz

a. una persona que nunca dice nada interesante
b. una persona que siempre está contenta de la vida (*life*)
c. una persona que siempre ve lo positivo
ch. una persona que no es ni alta ni baja
d. una persona que no quiere trabajar
e. una persona que tiene miedo de hablar
f. una persona que ayuda a otras personas
g. una persona que siempre quiere lo que tienen otras personas
h. una persona que no expresa todo lo que siente
i. una persona a quien nadie quiere

B. ¿Cuántos tienes? How many of these items do you have in your room? Where are they located?

Encourage students to report what they actually do or do not have. *No tengo sofá en mi cuarto,* if that is the case.

Modelos: la cama   *Tengo una cama en mi cuarto. Está en el rincón.*
el sofá   *No tengo sofá en mi cuarto.*

1. la silla
2. el sofá
3. el cuadro
4. el cartel
5. el escritorio
6. la lámpara

7. el tocador
8. el espejo
9. el estéreo
10. el estante de libros

C. Poner en orden. Place the items in each group in order according to the criterion given.

1. **tamaño** (*size*)**: pequeño → grande**   el cuadro, la cama, el tocador
2. **utilidad** (*usefulness*) **para guardar** (*store*) **la ropa: más útil → menos** (*least*) **útil**   el piso, el tocador, la silla
3. **para pasar el tiempo libre: me encanta → no me gusta**   mirar las telenovelas, escuchar la música clásica, mirar el noticiario
4. **para sentarme cuando estudio: lugar favorito → menos favorito**   el sillón, la cama, el sofá, el piso
5. **distancia de mi cama: más cerca → más lejos**   la ventana, la mesita, el escritorio, el armario

CH. ¿Dónde está mi libro de español?   Daniel cannot find his *Entradas* book. Look at each of the drawings, and tell him where the book is on each day.

Modelo: *Hoy es lunes. Tu libro está encima del escritorio.*

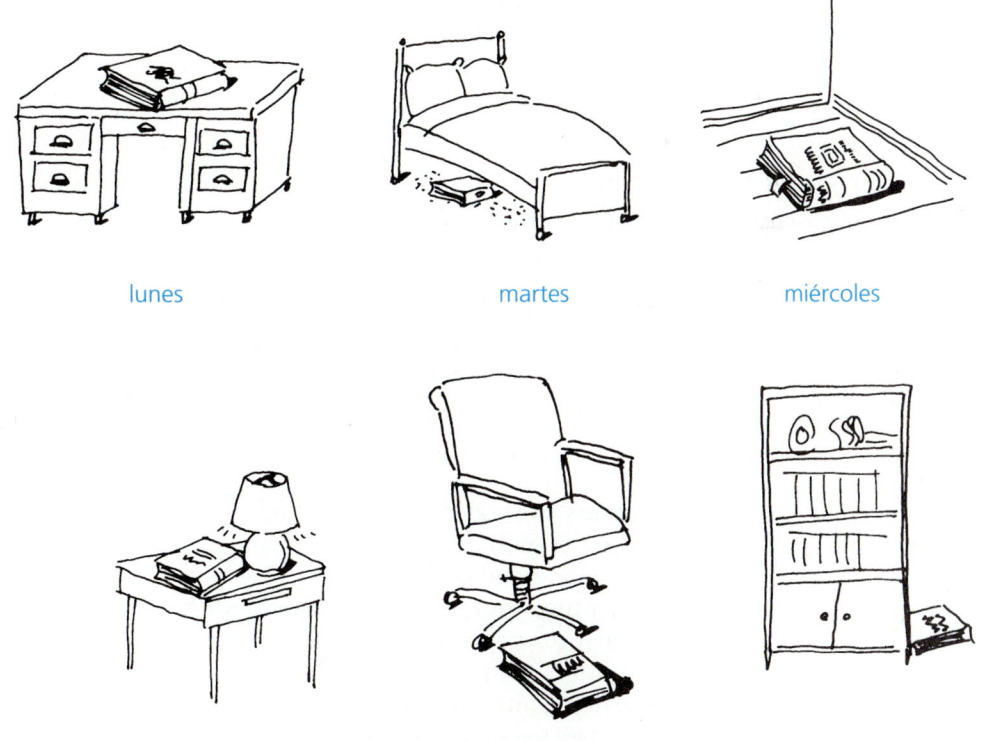

lunes   martes   miércoles

jueves   viernes   sábado

Invite students to expand each question. *¿Qué programas te gustan?* or *¿Cuál es tu programa favorito?*

D. **Preguntas personales**

1. ¿Te gusta mirar la televisión? ¿Escuchar la radio?
2. ¿Cuál de estas dos actividades prefieres?
3. ¿Tienes un televisor o un estéreo en tu cuarto? ¿Dónde están?
4. ¿Tienes cuadros o carteles en las paredes? ¿En el techo (*ceiling*)?
5. ¿Por lo general cuelgas tu ropa? ¿Dónde la cuelgas?
6. Si no cuelgas tu ropa, ¿dónde la pones?
7. ¿Hay mucho polvo en tu cuarto? ¿Dónde hay polvo?
8. ¿Mueves los muebles en tu cuarto con frecuencia? ¿Te gusta reacomodar (*rearrange*) los muebles?

E. **Mini-diálogos.** With a classmate, act out the following mini-conversations. In each one, choose your response from the following list and include whatever additional information seems appropriate. Exchange roles after each mini-conversation.

¡Que lo pasen bien!
Gracias, pero no puedo.
¡Claro que sí!
Gracias, me gustaría.
¡Dormilón/-ona!
Sí, es posible.
¡Qué horror!
¡Fenomenal!

1. —Pienso almorzar en el parque esta tarde. ¿Por qué no vas conmigo?
2. —Ah, ¡viernes por fin! ¡Qué bueno!
3. —Vamos a cenar en Casa Lupita esta tarde, ¿qué te parece?
4. —En mi opinión, esa película es la mejor del año.
5. —Miguel y yo vamos a pasar las vacaciones de Navidad en Ecuador con su familia. Salimos el 21.
6. —¿Más televisión? ¿Por qué no vamos al lago? Hace sol y podemos nadar.

F. **¡Vamos a arreglar el cuarto!** Take out your drawing of your room, and draw the outline of your room on a different sheet of paper. Indicate only the door, windows, and closet. Now give the outline to your partner, and either turn your back or put a barricade between you so that you cannot see what your partner is doing. Explain to your partner where to place the furniture, the pictures, and the posters, using the vocabulary you have just learned. Your partner may ask questions for clarification. After you have finished, see how well you have communicated!

INVESTIGAR LA GRAMÁTICA Las comparaciones

In Chapter 1 you saw how adjectives can be used for simple descriptions. Now you will learn to compare people, places, and things. Comparisons of **inequality** are made when something is better or bigger or less interesting than something else. For these unequal comparisons, use *más... que* or *menos... que*.

Inés es **menos** reservada **que** su hermana Cecilia, ¿verdad?	*Inés is less reserved than her sister Cecilia, don't you think?*
Sí, las dos hermanas son reservadas, pero Cecilia es **más** reservada **que** Inés.	*Yes, the two sisters are reserved, but Cecilia is more reserved than Inés.*

The same formula can be used with nouns to compare quantity or number.

The use of más de *before numbers is introduced in Chapter 10.*

Elena tiene **más** energía física **que** Alicia, pero tiene **menos** disciplina para los estudios **que** su compañera.	*Elena has more physical energy than Alicia, but has less discipline for her studies than her roommate.*

Adverbs and prepositions can be compared the same way.

Ahora el escritorio de Elena está **más** cerca de la ventana **que** su cama.	*Now Elena's desk is closer to the window than her bed is.*
Elena corre **más** rápido **que** los otros miembros de su equipo.	*Elena runs faster than the other members of her team.*

Some adjectives and adverbs have irregular comparative forms.

bueno/-a (adj.); bien (adv.)	mejor
malo/-a (adj.); mal (adv.)	peor

OJO: Remember that when *mejor* and *peor* are adjectives, they must agree in number with the noun they refer to. When they are adverbs, they have only the one form.

El televisor de Alicia funciona **mejor que** su estéreo.	*Alicia's television set works better than her stereo.*
Mis clases este semestre son malas, pero las tuyas son **peores que** las mías.	*My classes this semester are bad, but yours are worse than mine.*

Mayor and *menor* are often used to refer to a person's age.

Carlitos tiene cinco años. Es **mayor que** su hermanito, que tiene cuatro.	*Carlitos is five years old. He is older than his little brother, who is four.*
Joselito es **menor que** su hermano, pero habla **mejor que** él.	*Joselito is younger than his brother, but speaks better than he does.*

Sometimes we want to make a comparison of **equality,** to point out that two things are equal or alike. Use *tan... como* to express equal comparisons with adjectives and adverbs.

Mi hermana es **tan** alta **como** yo.	*My sister is as tall as I am.*
¿Tus clases son **tan** interesantes **como** las mías?	*Are your classes as interesting as mine?*
Nadie corre **tan** rápido **como** Elena, ni se levanta **tan** temprano **como** ella.	*Nobody runs as fast as Elena, nor does anyone get up as early as she does.*

OJO: Notice that the *tanto/-a/-os/-as* form agrees in gender and number with the noun it refers to.

Use *tanto/-a/-os/-as... como* to express equal comparison with nouns.

Josefina tiene **tanto** dinero **como** Eduardo.
Josefina has as much money as Eduardo.

Las mujeres tienen **tantas** responsabilidades **como** los hombres.
Women have as many responsibilities as men.

OJO: The *tanto* form is invariable when it refers to a verb.

Use *tanto... como* to express equal comparison of activities with verbs.

Rafael estudia **tanto como** yo, pero yo saco **mejores** notas **que** él.
Rafael studies as much as I do, but I get better grades than he does.

Ponerlo a prueba

A. Comparaciones. See how many comparisons you can make between the items in the following groups of words.

Modelo: la comida en la cafetería, en el restaurante, en casa (deliciosa)
La comida en la cafetería es más deliciosa que la comida en el restaurante.

or: *La comida en la cafetería es tan deliciosa como la comida en el restaurante.*

When discussing the model in class, give the various possibilities: *más deliciosa que, menos deliciosa que, tan deliciosa como.*

1. la biología, la literatura, la psicología (interesante)
2. estudiar, comer, dormir (agradable)
3. pasar la aspiradora, quitar el polvo, arreglar la cama (trabajo)
4. el coche, la casa, un año en la universidad (costoso/-a)
5. Gabriela Sabatini, tú, el capitán del equipo (*team*) de tenis en tu universidad (juega bien)

OJO: It is easy to guess that *costoso/-a* means "expensive." A synonym for it is *caro/-a.*

B. Más comparaciones. Use your imagination to make comparisons based on the drawings.

Modelo: *El edificio es más grande que la casa.*

1.

2.

3.

4.

C. **En comparación a Bogotá...** Marcos is always talking about Bogotá. How many comparisons can you make between your own hometown and Bogotá, based on what Marcos says?

Modelo: Bogotá es una ciudad muy grande.
Mi ciudad es más pequeña que (tan grande como) Bogotá.

1. Bogotá tiene más de cuatro millones de habitantes.
2. Bogotá tiene muchos lugares de interés para los turistas.
3. En el mes de abril llueve casi todos los días.
4. La vida industrial y comercial de Bogotá es muy activa.
5. Bogotá tiene servicios públicos y medios de transporte muy buenos.
6. El clima es agradable.
7. En general, los habitantes son muy amables.
8. La vida en Bogotá es muy costosa.

CH. **En mi opinión...** Using the adjectives listed, make some comparisons between objects, places, and/or people that you know.

Modelo: inteligente   *Mi hermano es más inteligente que yo.*

1. generoso/-a
2. envidioso/-a
3. divertido/-a
4. aburrido/-a
5. alto/-a
6. grande

D. **Preguntas personales**

1. ¿Tienes hermanos menores? ¿Mayores?
2. ¿Cómo son tus notas en comparación con las de tus amigos/-as? ¿Y en comparación con las de tu compañero/-a de cuarto?
3. ¿Qué fama tiene el equipo de fútbol de tu universidad en comparación con otros de la región?
4. Compara las estaturas (*heights*) de los miembros de tu familia.
5. ¿Cómo comparas tus cursos en cuanto a (*with regard to*) la dificultad? ¿Y en cuanto al interés?

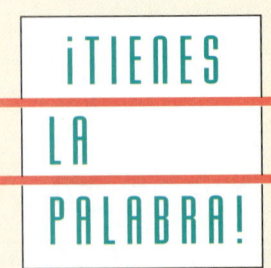

OJO: The student who plays the second role in *A* should ask lots of questions to make the first student describe the friend in as much detail as possible.

OJO: If you are seeking the information in *B*, ask as many questions as possible.

Do the following activities with a partner.

A. **Mi amigo/-a es...** You have become separated from your friend at a party. You see someone you know.

- Greet the person.
- Say that you are looking for your friend.
- Describe your friend. Be sure to mention height, hair color, and eye color.

B. **El horario perfecto.** You are trying to decide about classes for next term. You talk to one of your friends who always seems to know everything.

- Ask for the names of one or two really good courses.
- Ask your friend to describe one of the courses.
- Ask about the professor.

OTRA VUELTA

Play instructor tape, 2 min.

Now listen again to the radio advertisement that you heard at the beginning of this *etapa*. Make a list of all the furniture items that are on sale at the *Mueblería Sánchez*.

COMENTARIO CULTURAL

La casa

Earlier in this chapter you heard a conversation between Alicia and Elena as they rearranged their room. There are several differences between most middle-class homes in Latin America and those in the United States. One is that while bedrooms in the United States usually have recessed closets, it is still somewhat common in Spain and Latin America to find wardrobes, that is, large pieces of furniture that stand against a wall and have room to hang and store clothing and other personal effects. These are called *roperos* or *armarios*.

Other things that would seem unusual to North Americans reflect differences in how Hispanics use their homes and what their cultural values are. For example, while a *patio* is outside in the backyard in the United States, in Hispanic countries it is an open area inside the house that allows for gardens, plants, birds in cages, and sometimes fountains and small sculptures. These areas are reached by passing through one of the rooms of the house, usually the living room.

It is also common to see flat rooftops (*la azotea*) put to good use for washing clothes and hanging them out to dry.

Actividades de integración 143

DE INTEGRACIÓN

Play video

Program 3 *Sones y ritmos* The diversity of regional music

A. **Un anuncio.** Find a full-page ad for a furniture store in your local newspaper. Cover up the prices and the English words for the furniture items. "Convert" the ad into Spanish as follows.

- Label the furniture items in Spanish.
- Choose a Spanish-speaking country, and convert the prices into the currency of that country. Call a local bank or check your university library's copy of the *Wall Street Journal* to get the current exchange rate.

B. **Las actividades diarias.** Write an account of your daily activities. Be sure to include the following information.

- where you live
- what time you get up
- where and when you like to study
- with whom you live
- where and when you eat your meals
- how you spend your free time

C. **Entrevista: El tiempo.** Interview your partner to find out

- where he or she is from
- whether it rains a lot there (*allí*)
- whether it snows a lot
- whether the weather there is good in general
- whether your partner prefers the climate in his or her hometown, or whether the climate in another place (*en otro lugar*) is better

CH. **Mini-drama.** You and your roommate are decorating your room. You want to be sure that your roommate agrees with what you want to do, so you ask

- if you can put your bed under the window
- if your roommate wants the red lamp (really, you want it, instead of the blue one)
- if you can put a poster on the door

D. **Mini-drama.** With a partner, find out his or her account of an ideal day. Report the information to the class.

VOCABULARIO

Llamar por teléfono
To make a telephone call

aparato (m)   telephone
teléfono (m)   telephone

colgar (ue)   to hang up the receiver; to hang
contestar   to answer
dejar un recado   to leave a message
descolgar (ue)   to remove the receiver from the cradle
marcar el número   to dial the number
sonar (ue)   to ring
Te habla (Paco).   This is (Paco). (on the telephone)
¿De parte de quién?   May I ask who's calling?
¿Puedo hablar con... ?   May I speak with . . . ?

El tiempo
The weather

lluvia (f)   rain
nieve (f)   snow
pronóstico (m) del tiempo   weather forecast

llover (ue)   to rain
nevar (ie)   to snow

Hace buen tiempo.   It is nice out.
Hace mal tiempo.   It is bad out.
Hace fresco.   It is cool out.
Hace calor.   It is hot.
Hace sol.   It is sunny.
Hace frio.   It is cold.
Hace viento.   It is windy.
Está lloviendo.   It is raining.
Está nevando.   It is snowing.
Está lloviznando.   It is drizzling.

La rutina diaria
Daily routine

acostarse (ue)   to go to bed
afeitarse   to shave
bañarse   to bathe; to shower
desvestirse (i, i)   to get undressed
dormirse (ue, u)   to go to sleep
ducharse   to shower
lavarse   to wash oneself
levantarse   to get up
peinarse   to comb one's hair
vestirse (i, i)   to get dressed

Expresiones con *tener*
Tener expressions

tener calor   to be (feel) hot
tener envidia   to be envious
tener fama   to be famous, well-known
tener frío   to be (feel) cold
tener ganas (de)   to feel like (doing something)
tener hambre   to be hungry
tener interés (en)   to be interested (in)
tener miedo (de)   to be afraid (of)
tener paciencia   to be patient
tener prisa   to be in a hurry
tener razón   to be right
tener sed   to be thirsty
tener sueño   to be sleepy

Preposiciones
Prepositions

al lado de   next to
cerca de   near
debajo de   under
delante de   in front of
dentro de   inside
detrás de   in back of, behind
encima de   on top of
fuera de   outside
lejos de   far from

Palabras descriptivas
Descriptive words

La personalidad   *Personality*
abierto/-a   open
agradable   nice, agreeable
antipático/-a   unfriendly
celoso/-a   jealous
cómico/-a   funny, comic
generoso/-a   generous
reservado/-a   reserved
serio/-a   serious
tacaño/-a   stingy

El físico   *Physical features*
alto/-a   tall
bajo/-a   short
delgado/-a   thin, slender
gordo/-a   fat, heavy
guapo/-a   handsome, nice-looking
de mediana estatura   average (height)

pelirrojo/-a   red-haired
el pelo castaño   brown hair
el pelo negro   black hair
rubio/-a   blond

Otros rasgos   *Other characteristics*

calladito/-a   very quiet (*person*); very quietly
callado/-a   quiet, quietly
descontento/-a   dissatisfied, displeased (*with something*)
importante   important
ruidoso/-a   noisy
tranquilo/-a   quiet (*place*); peaceful

El cuarto de la residencia y los muebles
Dormitory room and furniture

cama (f)   bed
cartel (m)   poster
clóset (m)   closet
cuadro (m)   framed picture
escritorio (m)   desk
espejo (m)   mirror
estante de libros (m)   bookcase
estéreo (m)   stereo
lámpara (f)   lamp
mesita (f)   night table
pared (f)   wall (*interior, as of a room*)
piso (m)   floor
rincón (m)   corner
silla (f)   chair
sillón (m)   easy chair
televisor (m)   television set
tocador (m)   dresser
ventana (f)   window

Expresiones de la hora
Time expressions

a tiempo   on time
al anochecer   at dusk, nightfall
despertarse   to wake up
en otra ocasión   some other time
madrugar   to get up early
madrugada (f)   dawn
más tarde   later on
nunca   never
quizás   perhaps, maybe
siempre   always
tarde   late
temprano   early

Otros verbos y expresiones verbales

arreglar   to arrange
callarse   to become silent; shut up
cenar   to have the evening meal
conseguir (i, i)   to get, obtain
deber   must, should
decir la verdad   to tell the truth
desayunar   to have breakfast
empezar (ie)   to begin
esperar   to wait for
estar contento/-a   to be happy
estar de vuelta   to be back
estar equivocado/-a   to be wrong, in error
funcionar   to function, work, run (*machines*)
limpiar   to clean
Lo siento mucho.   I'm very sorry.
mentir (ie, i)   to lie
mover (ue)   to move (*furniture*)
no funciona   out of order; this isn't working (*said of a project or machine*)
No importa.   It doesn't matter.
pasar   to spend (*time*)
pedir (i, i)   to ask for, request
preferir (ie, i)   to prefer
quitar   to take away, remove
regresar   to return
seguir (i, i)   to follow, continue
sentarse (ie)   to sit down
sentir (ie, i)   to be sorry, regret
sentirse (ie, i)   to feel
terminar   to end
¿(no es) verdad?   isn't that so? right?
¿Me esperas?   Will you wait for me?
¡Que lo pases bien!   (*I hope you*) Have a good time!
¡Qué lástima!   What a shame/pity!

Otros sustantivos
Other nouns

actuación (f)   performance
barba (f)   beard
conjunto (m)   musical group
dormilón/-ona   sleepyhead
despertador (m)   alarm clock
iglesia (f)   church
mentira (f)   lie
misa (f)   mass (*Catholic religious service*)
ruido (m)   noise
servicio (m) religioso   religious service
silencio (m)   silence
sinagoga (f)   synagogue
sueño (m)   dream
verdad (f)   truth

VOCABULARIO PERSONALIZADO

Haciendo planes

Capítulo 4

COMMUNICATIVE OBJECTIVES

In this chapter, you will learn several ways to

- recount a sequence of events or recent experiences
- make travel plans
- express negation

PRIMERA ETAPA

"¿Qué planes tienes para las vacaciones?"

ENTRADA

Play instructor tape, 2 min.

"¿Tiene Ud. un espejo, por favor?"

You are about to hear a conversation between two people. As you listen, see if you can figure out

- who the people are
- where the conversation takes place

1. ¿Cuál es la relación entre las dos personas?
   a. Son amigos.
   b. Son profesor y estudiante.
   c. Son fotógrafo y cliente.
2. ¿Dónde tiene lugar la conversación?
   a. en un salón de clase
   b. en la casa de la mujer
   c. en un estudio fotográfico

EMPEZAR A ESCUCHAR

Play student tape, 4 min.

Leer

la playa	beach
¡Qué envidia!	I'm green with envy!
la molestia	bother, trouble
de ninguna manera	by no means
estar seguro/-a	to be sure, certain
el (la) invitado/-a	guest
afortunadamente	fortunately
la plata	money (lit., silver)
acompañado/-a	accompanied
divertido/-a	fun, amusing

Repetir

Listen to your student tape and repeat the words and phrases you hear.

Identificar

On a separate sheet of paper, write in a column the words and phrases in Spanish from the preceding list. You will hear some sentences on your tape. Whenever you hear one of these words or phrases, write next to it the number of the sentence in which it appears. Each sentence will be read twice. You may stop and start the tape as often as you wish.

Escribir

You will hear some sentences in Spanish. Each one will be read twice. Write them down as you listen, starting and stopping the tape as needed.

Reconocer

Each of the sentences you have just written contains one or more of the words and phrases from the preceding list. Read the sentences carefully and underline as many of the words and phrases from the list as you can find. As you read, make any necessary corrections in your sentences.

EPISODIO 1: "¡Cómo pasa el tiempo!"

ESCUCHAR

Play student tape, 1 min.

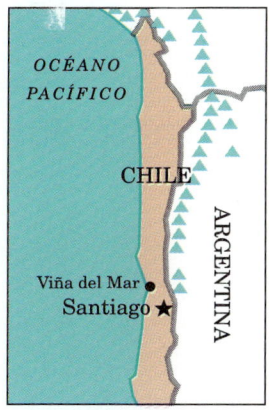

OJO: Viña del Mar is a seacoast resort about 1.5 hours' drive from Santiago. Many *santiaguinos* spend the entire summer (that is, the months that constitute winter in the Northern Hemisphere) there because Santiago is very hot and humid at that time of year.

Enfoque comunicativo

Listen to *Episodio 1* as Alicia, Elena, Marcos, and Paco talk about their plans for Christmas vacation. As you listen, see if you can identify

■ where Alicia, Elena, and Marcos will spend their vacations

¿Qué planes tienen los amigos?

Alicia   a. Bogotá
Elena   b. Santiago
Marcos   c. Guadalajara

Enfoque lingüístico

Listen again to *Episodio 1*, and identify

■ how Elena expresses her desire to go home
■ how Paco expresses his envy of the others' plans

ESCUCHAR

Play student tape, 2 min.

Episodio 2: "¡Es una idea magnífica!"

Enfoque comunicativo

As Marcos and Paco continue to talk, see if you can determine

- what plans Roberto has for the vacation
- why Paco has to spend part of his vacation in El Paso

> 1. ¿Qué planes tiene Roberto?
>   a. viajar a Colombia
>   b. estar con la familia
>   c. visitar a Elena
> 2. ¿Por qué tiene que ir Paco a El Paso?
>   a. Tiene que trabajar para la profesora Suárez.
>   b. Hay una reunión de toda la familia.
>   c. No tiene mucho dinero.

Enfoque lingüístico

Listen again to *Episodio 2* and identify

- two ways that Paco expresses his agreement with Marcos
- the expression that Marcos uses to indicate that his friends have to get ready for their trip

VERIFICAR

¿Sí o no?

1. Elena tiene ganas de volver a su casa en Santiago.	Sí	No
2. Alicia quiere disfrutar (*enjoy*) del verano durante sus vacaciones.	Sí	No
3. Marcos invita a Paco a visitarlo en Bogotá.	Sí	No
4. Roberto piensa pasar las vacaciones en El Paso, Texas.	Sí	No
5. Paco tiene dinero suficiente para pasar sus vacaciones en Colombia.	Sí	No

AUMENTAR EL VOCABULARIO

OJO: *El Día de Todos los Santos,* which falls on November 1, is a religious holiday observed in most Spanish-speaking countries. The night before, *la víspera de Todos los Santos,* is celebrated in the United States as Halloween.

OJO: The word *pascua* is used to refer to a number of religious holidays, including Passover, Easter, Pentecost, and Christmas. Hence, "Merry Christmas" is only one of the several meanings of *Felices Pascuas.*

OJO: *La Jánuca* is also written as *Hanukkah* and may be referred to as *la Celebración de las Luces.*

OJO: *Divertido/-a* is related to *divertirse (ie, i),* "to have fun, have a good time." The opposite of *divertido/-a* is *aburrido/-a,* (boring).

OJO: There is no written accent on the word *anfitriona.* It is like *francesa, alemana, inglesa.*

OJO: Note that *problema* is masculine. Many words that end in *-ma* are masculine: *el programa, el drama, el tema.*

OJO: *La plata* is used in some regions to mean "money." The word *dinero* is used everywhere.

OJO: Remember that you learned the synonym *costoso/-a* in Chapter 3. It may also help you to remember that *barato/-a* and *caro/-a* are antonyms.

acompañado/-a — *accompanied*
   acompañar — *to accompany, go with*
   solo/-a — *alone*
afortunadamente — *fortunately*
   desafortunadamente — *unfortunately*
   ¡Buena suerte! — *Good luck!*
celebrar — *to celebrate*
   el árbol de Navidad — *Christmas tree*
   comprar — *to purchase*
   Día de Todos los Santos — *All Saints' Day*
   Felices Pascuas — *Merry Christmas; Happy Easter*
   Feliz Año Nuevo — *Happy New Year*
   Feliz Navidad — *Merry Christmas*
   (la) Jánuca — *Hanukkah*
   la Navidad — *Christmas*
   la Nochebuena — *Christmas Eve*
   la Nochevieja — *New Year's Eve*
   regalar — *to give a gift*
   el regalo — *gift, present*
de ninguna manera — *by no means, not at all*
   nada — *nothing*
   nadie — *no one, nobody*
   ninguno/-a — *none, not any*
   todo/todos — *everything/everyone*
   toda/todas
divertido/-a — *fun, amusing*
   el (la) invitado/-a — *guest*
   el (la) anfitrión/-ona — *host*
   el (la) huésped(a) — *guest (in a hotel)*
la molestia — *bother, trouble*
   discutir — *to argue, discuss*
   molestar — *to bother, irritate*
   el problema — *problem*
   resolver (ue) — *to solve (a problem)*
la plata — *money (lit., silver)*
   el dinero — *money*
   el oro — *gold*
   rico/-a — *rich, wealthy*
   la riqueza — *wealth*
precioso/-a — *beautiful*
   barato/-a — *inexpensive, cheap*
   bonito/-a — *pretty*
   caro/-a — *expensive, costly*

OJO: Remember that you learned *la envidia* (envy) in Chapter 3. Lovers tend to be *celosos* (afraid of losing what they have), while social climbers tend to be *envidiosos* (craving what others have).

magnífico/-a	wonderful
nuevo/-a	new
quedarse	to stay, remain
¡Qué envidia!	I'm green with envy!
estar celoso/-a	to be jealous
los celos	jealousy
la reunión	reunion, meeting
reunirse con	to meet with, have a meeting with
viajar	to travel
el viaje	trip
hacer un viaje	to take a trip

LAS ESTACIONES DEL AÑO

el verano

Hace sol; hace calor.
ir a la playa

el otoño

Hace fresco.
el ciclismo

el invierno

Hace frío.
esquiar

la primavera

Hace fresco.
el amor, las flores

VENTANILLA AL MUNDO HISPÁNICO — Las estaciones del año

This would be an excellent place to assign projects related to geography of various countries or to talk about the effect that geographic location and features have on life-styles: food, shelter, modes of dress.

The seasons north of the equator are the opposite of those south of the equator—when it is summer in the Northern Hemisphere, it is winter south of the equator, and vice versa. The equator passes through northern Ecuador (this is where the country's name comes from), southern Colombia, and northern Brazil. Areas very near the equator typically have two seasons, each lasting about six months: *la época de lluvia* (the rainy season) and *la época seca* (the dry season). Countries south of the equator—Peru, Bolivia, Paraguay, Chile, Argentina, Uruguay, and most of Brazil—have a seasonal pattern opposite to that of the United States.

Asociaciones. With which season (or seasons) do you associate each of the following items?

1. los exámenes finales
2. los regalos
3. el Día de Todos los Santos
4. la nieve
5. la lluvia
6. las vacaciones
7. ¡Feliz Año Nuevo!
8. las flores nuevas

USO PRÁCTICO DEL ESPAÑOL   Changing Adjectives into Adverbs

Many adjectives can be changed into adverbs by adding the suffix -*mente* to the feminine singular form of the adjective.

agradable → agradablemente
alegre → alegremente
callado → calladamente
difícil → difícilmente
fácil → fácilmente
generoso → generosamente
lento (*slow*) → lentamente
triste (*sad*) → tristemente

OJO: The adverbs that correspond to *bueno/-a* and *malo/-a* are *bien* (well) and *mal* (badly): *Rebeca juega muy bien al tenis, pero yo juego muy mal. Por eso ella no quiere jugar conmigo.*

The feminine singular form of the adjective is always the base for the -*mente* adverb. When the adjective ends in a consonant or -*e*, then -*mente* is added directly to that ending: *feliz* → *felizmente*.

Notice also that if the original form of the adjective requires a written accent mark, then the accent mark is retained in the spelling of the adverb: *débil* → *débilmente*, *rápido* → *rápidamente*, *cortés* → *cortésmente*.

Ponerlo a prueba

A. **Conversaciones.** Complete each conversation by changing the adjectives indicated into adverbs.

Modelo: Julia: Para mí, es difícil comprender al profesor de filosofía.

Carlos: Sí, tienes que escucharlo *activamente* (**activo**) para seguir lo que dice.

1. Elena: Nunca voy a aprender a usar las computadoras. ¡Es imposible!

   Roberto: Cálmate, Elena, si practicas un poco, puedes aprender _____ (**fácil**).

2. Madre: Hijo, apúrate (*hurry up*), por favor. Si no comes más _____ (**rápido**), vamos a llegar tarde al cine.

   Hijo: ¡Pero mamá! Tú comes más _____ (**lento**) que yo. Todavía tienes brócoli en tu plato.

3. Ana: Oye, Nancy, ¿quién es ese chico? Sonríe tan _____ (**tímido**), pero parece (*he seems*) muy simpático.

   Nancy: Sí, lo conozco. Se llama Alfredo Castillo. Sonríe _____ (**reservado**), pero es muy abierto y agradable. Vamos a hablar con él.

4. Esteban: Oye, Luis, vamos al Club Palmeras. Un conjunto nuevo va a tocar.

   Luis: Gracias, pero no puedo ir porque tengo mucha tarea. Me dicen que el guitarrista principal toca _____ (**bueno**), pero canta _____ (**malo**).

B. Definiciones. Choose the word or expression from the *Aumentar el vocabulario* section that is described by each of the following definitions. Then create a sentence for the word that illustrates its meaning.

1. no ser muy costoso
2. una característica de las personas inseguras
3. ir a otro lugar de vacaciones o por negocios
4. pagar dinero para recibir algo nuevo
5. causar problemas a otra persona
6. el contrario de **nada**
7. cuando una persona te visita en tu casa, tú eres esto
8. la fiesta que celebran los judíos en diciembre

C. Preguntas personales

1. Durante las vacaciones, ¿prefieres quedarte en casa o viajar? ¿Por qué?
2. Cuando viajas, ¿a quién visitas? ¿Adónde vas? ¿Con quién?
3. ¿Cuáles son tus planes para las vacaciones de Navidad este año?
4. ¿Cuál es tu estación del año favorita?
5. Menciona tres actividades que haces durante esa estación.
6. ¿Qué estación del año **no** te gusta? ¿Por qué?

7. ¿Celebras la Navidad o Jánuca en tu casa? Menciona dos tradiciones de tu familia.
8. ¿Te gusta celebrar el Año Nuevo? ¿Cómo lo celebras?

CH. Una conversación por teléfono. Paco and Roberto are discussing their vacation plans. Unfortunately, there is a lot of static on the telephone line and they can't hear each other well. See if you can help them by filling in the missing words.

Paco: Hola, Roberto. _____ Paco.

Roberto: Paco, ¿_____?

Paco: Bien, gracias. Mira, pienso ir a una fiesta de _____ esta noche en casa de la profesora Suárez, pero no tengo ganas de ir _____. ¿Me quieres acompañar? Será (*It will be*) un evento _____.

Roberto: A ver, esta noche… No, no puedo. _____, tengo que _____ con unos compañeros de la clase de historia.

Paco: Entiendo. Pues, de todos modos vamos al centro mañana para comprar _____, ¿no?

Roberto: Claro que sí. Pero te digo que no tengo mucha _____.

Paco: ¡Qué va! Ya sé que eres un estudiante _____. Siempre tienes dinero para el cine, para una pizza…

Roberto: ¡Qué fantasía! Pues, nos reunimos mañana a eso de las diez, ¿verdad?

Paco: De acuerdo. Hasta luego.

Roberto: Adiós.

D. Antónimos. Find the word from the *Aumentar el vocabulario* section that is the opposite (*el antónimo*) of the word given. Follow the model.

Modelo: la invitada   El antónimo de **la invitada** es **la anfitriona**.

1. barato
2. afortunadamente
3. solo
4. alguien
5. vender
6. todo
7. el huésped
8. la solución
9. viejo
10. irse

INVESTIGAR LA GRAMÁTICA   El pretérito

El pretérito is one of several past tenses in Spanish. While all of the past tenses in Spanish focus on events or conditions that happened in the past, *el pretérito* creates a picture of a single action, a series of actions, or a condition, all of which were entirely completed within the time the speaker is talking about. For example,

Hablé con él por una hora. — *I spoke to him for an hour.*
(Action that began and ended within a definite time period)

Ayer **limpié** la casa, **preparé** una cena para seis personas y **enseñé** una clase de ejercicio. — *Yesterday I cleaned the house, made a dinner for six, and taught an exercise class.*
(Series of actions, all completed during the time period *ayer*)

Estuve enfermo por una semana. — *I was sick for a week.*
(Condition that began and ended within a definite time period. If you are sick again after that week, the listener understands that it is a different illness, not a continuation of the one that lasted one week.)

When you say *Estudié el chino por cuatro años,* it means that you studied Chinese for four years and then stopped. The activity of studying Chinese is viewed as something that began and was completed in the past. The implication is that you are not studying Chinese now.

You will learn the preterite forms of *-ar* verbs in this *etapa.* The conjugations of *-er* and *-ir* verbs are presented in the next *etapa.*

hablar		trabajar	
habl**é**	habl**amos**	trabaj**é**	trabaj**amos**
habl**aste**	habl**asteis**	trabaj**aste**	trabaj**asteis**
habl**ó**	habl**aron**	trabaj**ó**	trabaj**aron**

Verbs that end in *-car, -gar,* and *-zar* have a spelling change in the *yo* form of the preterite.

buscar → bus**qué,** buscaste, buscó, ...
llegar → lle**gué,** llegaste, llegó, ...
comenzar → comen**cé,** comenzaste, comenzó, ...

Remember that reflexive pronouns go immediately in front of the verb.

— Anoche **me acosté** a las diez. ¿A qué hora **te acostaste** tú?
— Pues, yo **me acosté** más tarde.

Here are some expressions that you can use with the preterite to indicate at what point in the past an action took place.

anoche	*last night*
ayer	*yesterday*
ayer por la mañana/tarde	*yesterday morning/afternoon*
anteayer	*the day before yesterday*
la semana pasada	*last week*
el año pasado	*last year*
una vez (en el pasado)	*once (in the past)*

OJO: Note that the *nosotros* form is the same in the present and the preterite. You can tell the meaning from the context.

Model pronunciation of the preterite forms, paying particular attention to *hablé* and *habló.* Point out the contrast between the preterite form *habló* and the present form *hablo.*

OJO: Note that *comenzar* has no stem change in the preterite. Only *-ir* verbs have a stem change in the preterite.

OJO: Other verbs like *buscar* are *practicar, tocar, explicar.* Other verbs like *llegar* are *jugar, pagar.* Other verbs like *comenzar* are *empezar, almorzar.*

Ponerlo a prueba

A. Transformaciones. Form new sentences according to the cues given.

Modelo: ¿Por qué no cenó **Antonio** con nosotros anoche? (los Méndez)
¿Por qué no cenaron los Méndez con nosotros anoche?

1. Anoche **cenamos** en casa. (yo, la tía de Marcos, ustedes, tú)
2. **Invitamos** a Ángela y a su familia. (los chicos, Anita, él, usted)
3. **Todos** llegaron a las nueve. (Ángela, Tú, Yo, Ellos)
4. **Mamá** preparó una comida deliciosa. (Yo, Tú, Ustedes)
5. **Ángela** nos regaló unas flores (*flowers*) muy bonitas. (Marcos, Ellos, Tú)
6. **Conversé** con los invitados hasta la una. (Nosotros, Mamá, Tú)

OJO: Note that you have to change more than just the verbs.

B. Comentarios y respuestas. Say something new about each person mentioned. Follow the model.

Modelo: Hablo con mi novio/-a todos los días. (Marcos / anoche)
Marcos habló con su novia anoche.

1. Marcos viaja con frecuencia a los Estados Unidos. (La familia de Marcos / el año pasado)
2. La familia de Marcos pasa las vacaciones en Cali. (Nosotros / el verano pasado)
3. Los abuelos acompañan a la familia de Marcos en su viaje. (Tú / el mes pasado)
4. Marcos estudia en los Estados Unidos ahora. (Los primos de Marcos / el semestre pasado)
5. Compró libros todas las semanas. (Marcos / libro de francés / ayer)
6. Marcos celebra la fiesta de la revolución francesa. (Marcos y sus amigos franceses / la semana pasada)
7. Marcos busca un buen restaurante francés. (Nosotros / por cuatro años)
8. Marcos llega a Bogotá hoy. Su familia lo (*him*) busca en la aeropuerto. (Marcos / anoche; Los padres de Marcos / por tres horas)

Extension: Once students have practiced preterite forms with this exercise, have them work in pairs to create a short narration of five to six sentences like the one in Ex. A.

C. La verdad es que... Starting with the phrase *La verdad es que...*, make all the true statements you can using one element from each column. Follow the model.

Modelo: *La verdad es que ayer yo no trabajé nada.*

ayer	yo	trabajar en _____
el fin de semana pasado	mis amigos y yo	cenar en _____
el verano pasado	mi hermano/-a	estudiar en la biblioteca

esta mañana	mis amigos	comprar un(a) _____ nuevo/-a
anoche	mi compañero/-a de cuarto	limpiar _____
una vez	mi familia	llamar a _____ por teléfono

CH. Dímelo todo (*Tell me everything*). You went out for the evening and your grandmother, who is very protective and traditional, wants to know what you did. Answer her questions.

1. ¿Dónde cenaste, Juanito/-a?
2. ¿Bailaron mucho tú y tus amigos?
3. No tomaron mucho, ¿verdad?
4. ¿Quién manejó (*drove*)?
5. ¿A qué hora llegaste a casa?
6. ¿A qué hora te acostaste?
7. ¿Miraste la tele antes de acostarte?

D. Las actividades de ayer. Write a note of five to six sentences telling your partner what you did yesterday. Use one of the following verbs in each of your sentences.

despertarse
levantarse
desayunar
almorzar
estudiar
practicar
nadar
comprar
acostarse

E. Preguntas personales

1. ¿A qué hora te levantas generalmente? ¿A qué hora te levantaste esta mañana?
2. ¿Por cuánto tiempo te quedaste en la cama después de despertarte?
3. ¿Qué tomaste esta mañana con tu desayuno? ¿Cuántas tazas de café tomaste ayer?
4. ¿Ayer estudiaste en tu cuarto o en la biblioteca?
5. ¿Cuál es la última fiesta que tú y tu familia celebraron juntos (*together*)?
6. ¿Compraste una revista o un periódico esta semana? ¿Cuál(es)?

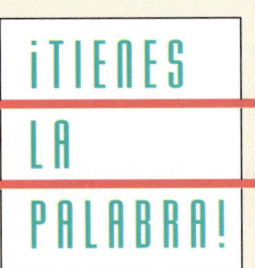

OJO: Use ¿*por qué?* to express the idea of "why?" or "for what purpose?". Remember that in formal situations it is more common to use *usted*.

Do the following activities with a partner.

A. **Un robo en la universidad.** You are a campus police officer. A computer has been stolen from the administration building, Founders Hall, and you are questioning an individual who may be a suspect. You need to know

- whether the individual entered the building last Saturday
- if so, at what time and for what purpose
- if not, at what time the individual ate lunch, and where
- what the student did between 1:00 and 3:00 P.M. on Saturday

B. **Las actividades del invierno.** You work for a sports equipment company that is doing a survey of students' leisure-time winter activities. You are interviewing a student to get the following information about his or her activities last winter. Find out

- whether the student went skiing
- if so, approximately how many times in December, in January, and in February
- when the student last bought new skis (*los esquís*)
- whether the student played in the snow at least (*por lo menos*) once
- what kinds of gifts the student bought for the members of his or her family for Christmas or Hanukkah
- whether the student's family celebrated the holidays at home, or whether they traveled elsewhere

Report the results of your interview to the class.

OTRA VUELTA

Play instructor tape, 2 min.

Listen again to the *Entrada* from the beginning of this *etapa*. Answer the following questions as you listen.

1. ¿Qué necesita la señorita?
2. ¿Adónde va la señorita?
3. ¿Por qué quiere un espejo la señorita?

COMENTARIO CULTURAL

El dinero

All cultures value money, and its importance is reflected in the number of names for money and in the proverbs and expressions that deal with it. In Spanish, *el dinero* is the standard, formal term. One informal word that is often used, particularly in Latin America, is *la plata*. When Paco responds to Marcos's invitation to spend his vacation in Colombia, he says *"Tengo casi toda la plata de mi trabajo"* (I have almost all the money from my job). In Spanish, the word *oro* is also used to express the concept of wealth.

There are a number of expressions in Spanish that relate to money. *El tiempo es oro* is comparable to the English expression "time is money." *Estar nadando en oro* is used to indicate that someone is rolling in money. Another expression, from a well-known verse of a seventeenth-century poem is *Poderoso caballero es don Dinero* (literally, "Sir Money is a powerful gentleman"). This phrase is used in much the same way as the English "money talks."

The verse is from "Letrilla satírica" by Francisco de Quevedo.

Actividad. English also has many words and expressions for money. List at least five words you use or have heard others use.

"Vamos a Colombia"

ENTRADA

Play instructor tape, 2 min.

Haciendo los arreglos

Patricia Laval is making plans for a trip to South America. As you listen to the following telephone conversation, see if you can determine

- what Patricia wants
- what information the official in the office needs

1. ¿Qué quiere Patricia?
   a. sacar una visa
   b. comprar boletos (*tickets*) de avión
   c. conseguir una tarjeta de crédito
2. ¿Qué información necesita el oficial? (Place a check by each item requested.)
   ☐ su nombre   ☐ el nombre de su banco
   ☐ su dirección   ☐ su lugar de nacimiento (*birthplace*)
   ☐ su número de teléfono ☐ su profesión

ANTES DE LEER

READING STRATEGY 4

Read for general information

You often read with a specific objective in mind, but you may need to acquire some general information before attaining that objective. For example, although you wish to enroll in a specific course at the university, you may not know exactly what procedures and requirements are involved. So, you start by reading the university bulletin to get a general overview of the registration process. After the initial reading, you can go back and reread the information that is pertinent to your needs.

[Play student tape, 1 min.]

Preparación

Before traveling to a foreign country we often request pamphlets and brochures that will be helpful in the planning of the trip. List at least three categories of information you would need before taking a trip out of the country.

1.
2.
3.

Estudiar y practicar

comprobar (ue)	*to check, verify*
el equipaje	*luggage*
la etiqueta	*label*
el extranjero	*foreign country*
el (la) extranjero/-a	*foreigner*
la maleta	*suitcase*
el (la) viajero/-a	*traveler*

From the *Leer* section, students might plan a group trip to a country of their choice as a long term activity. In addition to travel information, they could contact the tourism department of the country's embassy for details about the country.

This would be an excellent opportunity to have the class develop a list of things they would need to know and have them contact a travel agency for brochures.

▲ ▲ ▲

LEER

OJO: Look at the activities in the *Después de leer* section before you begin reading. This will give you an idea of the way in which you will report the information that you gather.

Roberto and Paco are planning a trip to Bogotá where they will visit Marcos and his family. They have requested information from a travel agency, and it arrived while Paco was in class. Roberto attaches a note and leaves it on the table for Paco.

As you read the note and the brochure, write down

■ what Paco and Roberto plan to do once they have both read the information

- the advice given regarding the choice of luggage
- the documents Paco and Roberto need to obtain before leaving for Colombia
- safety tips

Paco:
La agencia de viajes nos mandó este folleto que tiene que ver con nuestro viaje a Colombia. Si tienes tiempo, léelo esta tarde y podemos discutirlo mañana. Yo ya lo leí.

Roberto

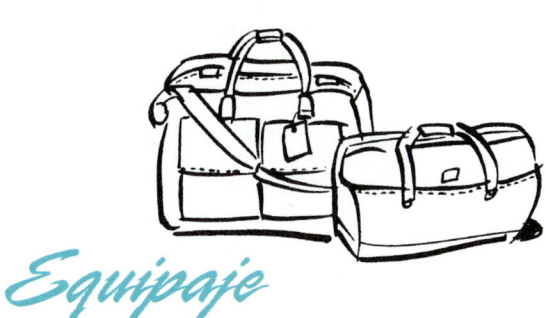

Equipaje

El equipaje varía según el viajero, el tipo de recorrido que va a realizar y el medio de transporte que utilizará. Lo ideal es buscar la combinación apropiada de espacio y resistencia. En general, dos maletas medianas son más fáciles para transportar y manejar que una sola grande. El equipaje debe llevar una etiqueta en la que figure claramente el nombre y dirección del propietario.

Documentos

Si el viaje será al extranjero, hay que comprobar anticipadamente que el pasaporte esté en regla e informarse en el consulado o embajada correspondiente sobre si el país que se va a visitar requiere un visado o certificado de vacuna u otro requisito. También es aconsejable llevar consigo alguna identificación (licencia, credencial escolar o del trabajo) para cualquier caso de emergencia.

DESPUÉS DE LEER

Actividad

1. When does Roberto want Paco to read the note? Why?
2. What two characteristics should one consider when selecting luggage? Who should or should not use different types of luggage and why?
3. What type of health documentation may a traveler need in order to enter some countries?
4. Complete the following chart with information from the brochure.

> *Datos generales*
>
> Tipo de equipaje:
> Número de maletas:
> Tipos de documentos:
> Se obtienen en:
> Para proteger su equipaje:

5. What other advice might you add from personal experience? For example, how would you protect (*proteger*) your documents?

AUMENTAR EL VOCABULARIO

OJO: A visa is a document issued by the host country that permits entry, while a passport is issued by the country where the traveler is a citizen.

aconsejable	*advisable*
aconsejar	*to advise*
apropiado/-a	*suitable*
comprobar (ue)	*to check, verify*
el consulado	*consulate*
el documento	*document*
el certificado de vacuna	*vaccination certificate*
la credencial escolar	*student I.D.*
la licencia	*license*
el pasaporte	*passport*
el requisito	*requirement*
el visado; la visa	*visa*
en regla	*in order*
la embajada	*embassy*
el equipaje	*luggage*
facturar	*to check (luggage)*

Segunda etapa

OJO: *Manejar* also means "to drive a vehicle" and is a synonym of *conducir*, which you learned in Chapter 2.

OJO: See the words for "bus" and "truck" in the *Ventanilla al mundo hispánico.*

OJO: Other words for "car" are *el coche* and *el carro.*

la maleta	suitcase
el maletín	small suitcase; attaché case
la etiqueta	**tag, label**
el domicilio	home address
el (la) propietario/-a	owner
el extranjero	**foreign country; abroad**
el (la) extranjero/-a	foreigner
perder (ie)	**to lose**
guardar	to keep
manejar	**to manage, handle**
el medio de transporte	**means of transportation**
el auto	car
el avión	airplane
viajar	**to travel**
la agencia de viajes	travel agency
el viaje	trip
el (la) viajero/-a	traveler

VENTANILLA AL MUNDO HISPÁNICO — Variantes léxicas en el mundo hispánico

You may be wondering whether the Spanish you are learning will enable you to communicate all over the Spanish-speaking world. It is true that there are vocabulary differences from country to country, but they seldom result in communication problems. For example, "bus" is *el autobús, el ómnibus* or simply *el bus* in most of the Spanish-speaking world, but it is *el camión* in Mexico and *la guagua* in Puerto Rico, Cuba, and the Canary Islands of Spain. Sometimes these differences can lead to confusion, but seldom to a serious breakdown in communication. For example, *camión* means "truck" in the rest of Latin America and in Spain, and *guagua* is a small baby in Chile. Usually, however, the context or a quick question can clear up any misunderstanding.

Actividad. If the students in the class are from different parts of the United States, they can interview each other to find out

- qué palabra genérica usas en inglés para Coca-Cola, Sprite, etc.
- qué palabra usas en inglés para el tipo de helado (*ice cream*) que tiene una forma de espiral (*spiral*)
- si pronuncias diferentemente las palabras en inglés *Mary/merry/marry; cot/caught*

The purpose of this activity is to demonstrate that regional differences in vocabulary and pronunciation in English do not cause breakdowns in communication. Here are some regional variations that may be mentioned: 1. tonic, soda, pop, coke; 2. soft-serve, creemie, Carvel, Dairy Queen.

EL CORREO

la carta el sobre la estampilla la dirección el buzón

enviar una carta el buzón el (la) cartero

OJO: A woman mail-carrier (a rarity in the Spanish-speaking world) is *la cartero*.

OJO: *Mandar* is used in Spain rather than *enviar*.

OJO: "Post Office" is expressed as *el correo* or *la casa de correos*.

Cómo enviar una carta. Put the following steps in the correct order to describe what you have to do to write and mail a letter.

_____ comprar una estampilla   _____ ir al correo

_____ buscar papel y pluma   _____ escribir la carta

_____ escribir el nombre y la dirección   _____ poner la estampilla en el sobre
       en el sobre

_____ poner la carta en el buzón

Follow-up activity: Use the same steps as the basis for a story that groups of students make up together.

USO PRÁCTICO DEL ESPAÑOL   *Por* and *para*

This is the introduction to *por* and *para*. A second and more complete treatment is found in Chapter 6, third *etapa*.

The prepositions *por* and *para* are often expressed in English by the word "for." However, in Spanish *por* and *para* cannot be used interchangeably; in fact, they are quite different.

Por is used to express the concepts of "by means of," "through," "in exchange for," "per," "because of," and "during." *Por* focuses on the motive or the force behind an action.

Los jóvenes viajan **por** avión.
Tenemos que pasar **por** las máquinas de seguridad para llegar a nuestra salida.
No pagué mucho **por** el boleto, gracias a Dios.

La velocidad máxima en esta carretera (*highway*) es 80 kilómetros **por** hora.
Tenemos que conducir **por** catorce horas si queremos llegar a Bogotá hoy.

Para is used to express "for," "in order to," and "considering." *Para* tends to focus attention on the goal, destination, or result of the action.

La universidad ofrece un curso especial **para** los extranjeros.
Voy a comprar una cámara **para** sacar fotos.
Para un estudiante del primer año, habla muy bien el español.

Ponerlo a prueba

A. El cuento de Paco y Roberto. Complete the story of Paco and Roberto's trip using *por* or *para* as appropriate.

1. Paco y Roberto van a Colombia _____ visitar el país.
2. Viajan _____ avión.
3. Doña Consuelo prepara la casa _____ recibirlos.
4. Paco está nervioso _____ no saber qué hacer.
5. No tienen que pagar nada _____ su alojamiento mientras están en Bogotá.
6. Van a estar en Colombia _____ más de un mes.
7. Después de su visita a Cali, los jóvenes salen _____ Bogotá.
8. Tienen que hablar con la agencia de viajes _____ saber la hora del vuelo.
9. Antes de salir de Bogotá, Paco quiere comprar regalos _____ sus padres.

B. El viajero bien organizado. Arrange the following activities into the sequence that a well-organized traveler would follow in preparing for a trip.

_____ facturar el equipaje
_____ poner una etiqueta en las maletas
_____ llamar a la agencia de viajes
_____ hablar con el consulado
_____ obtener los documentos necesarios
_____ buscar el número del consulado
_____ escribirles cartas a tus amigos

C. Definiciones. Choose the word or expression from the *Aumentar el vocabulario* section that best matches each of the following definitions.

1. las maletas
2. la persona que posee una cosa
3. el documento que necesitas para ir de un país a otro
4. el documento que prueba (*proves*) que eres estudiante
5. la palabra que significa "otros países"
6. un sinónimo de "la dirección de tu casa"
7. la oficina donde haces las reservaciones de avión, de hotel, etc.

The official headquarters of an ambassador to a foreign country is an embassy. Consulates are the headquarters of official representatives of a country at the rank of consul. Generally, the embassy is located in the capital city of the host nation, and consulates are located in large cities in different parts of the host country. If U.S. citizens travel to Spain, for example, they must get a visa at one of the several Spanish consulates in the United States.

8. el contrario de "dar"
9. decirle a otra persona lo que tú crees que debe hacer

CH. **Asociaciones.** Match the items in column A with the related items in column B.

A

1. viajeros internacionales
2. estudiantes universitarios
3. manejar/conducir un auto
4. las estampillas
5. la etiqueta
6. la embajada

B

a. las cartas
b. el domicilio
c. los pasaportes
ch. la visa
d. las licencias
e. las credenciales escolares

D. **En busca del equipaje.** You have arrived at your destination only to discover that your luggage is nowhere to be found. Fill out the following claim form for the airline so that your baggage can be located.

Nombre: _____ Teléfono: _____
Domicilio:
Tipo de maleta:
Tamaño: pequeño   mediano   grande   Color:
Contenidos:
Itinerario: de _____ a _____, vuelo número _____
              de _____ a _____, vuelo número _____

E. **Preguntas personales**

1. ¿Te gusta más escribir o recibir cartas?
2. ¿Cuántas cartas recibes en una semana típica? ¿Quién te escribe?
3. ¿Con qué frecuencia escribes a casa? ¿Con qué frecuencia llamas a casa?
4. ¿Viajaste durante el año pasado? ¿Adónde?
5. ¿Se extravió tu equipaje alguna vez? ¿Qué pasó?

INVESTIGAR LA GRAMÁTICA   El pretérito

As you learned in the first *etapa*, *el pretérito* is one of several past tenses in Spanish. Earlier, you practiced the preterite forms of verbs that end in *-ar*. Now take a look at verbs that end in *-er* and *-ir*.

Remember that whenever you use a form of *el pretérito,* you are creating a picture of a single action, a series of actions, or a condition (illness, etc.), all of which were completed within the time you are talking about.

Perdí (*action*) mi equipaje en Cali el año pasado. (*action that began and ended in the definite time period of* el año pasado)

Salí a las nueve, **vi** una película excelente y **volví** a casa a las doce. (*series of actions*)

Regular *-er* and *-ir* verbs in the preterite are conjugated as follows.

comer		vivir	
comí	comimos	viví	vivimos
comiste	comisteis	viviste	vivisteis
comió	comieron	vivió	vivieron

Verbs that end in *-er* and *-ir* and have a vowel immediately before the infinitive ending have a spelling change (*-ió* → *-yó* and *-ieron* → *-yeron*) in the *él/ella/Ud.* and *ellos/ellas/Uds.* forms. Some common verbs that fall into this category are *creer, leer, oír,* and all verbs that end in *-uir* (*incluir, construir*).

leer		construir	
leí	leímos	construí	construimos
leíste	leísteis	construiste	construisteis
leyó	leyeron	construyó	construyeron

OJO: Remember that some *-ar* verbs also have spelling changes: *llegué, comencé.* Spelling changes for *-ar* verbs are always in the *yo* form: *Lle**gué** a tiempo, pero Mario, como siempre, lle**gó** tarde.*

OJO: A good technique for remembering such features as spelling changes and stem changes is to keep a set of index cards or pages in your notebook where you write down the verbs that fall into a particular category (e.g., *-er* and *-ir* verbs in the preterite). Practice writing their conjugations and saying them out loud to imprint the special features in your mind.

Ponerlo a prueba

Actividades A–C are similar in format and content to A–C in the first etapa, *but practice different verbs.*

A. Transformaciones. Form sentences with new subjects, according to the cues.

   Modelo: ¿Por qué no comió **Antonio** con nosotros anoche? (los Méndez)
   ¿Por qué no comieron los Méndez con nosotros anoche?

   1. Anoche **decidimos** cenar en casa. (yo, la tía de Marcos, ellos, tú)
   2. **Invitamos** a Ángela y a su familia. (Los chicos, Anita, El hermano de Javier, Ustedes)
   3. **Todos** salieron a las nueve. (El primo de Marcos, Yo, Los estudiantes extranjeros, Nosotros)
   4. **Comimos** comida china. (Los Colón, Tú, Marcos, Yo)
   5. **Decidimos** ir al cine después de cenar. (Yo, Los chicos, Paco y Roberto)
   6. **La señora de Colón** dejó su dinero en casa y volvió para recogerlo. (Yo, Nosotros, Los amigos de Marcos, El tío Alfredo)

B. Comentarios y respuestas. Say something new about each person mentioned. Follow the model.

   Modelo: Como con mis amigos todos los días. (Marcos / anoche)
   Marcos comió con sus amigos anoche.

1. La familia de Marcos vive en Bogotá. (Los abuelos de Marcos / por cincuenta años)
2. Comen pescado los viernes. (Marcos / el viernes pasado)
3. Salen de vacaciones para Cali. (Nosotros / el verano pasado)
4. Envían tarjetas a todos sus amigos. (Marcos y sus amigos / la semana pasada)
5. Ven a los Rodríguez en Bogotá. (¿Tú / el año pasado?)
6. Paco vive en los Estados Unidos ahora. (Nosotros / el semestre pasado)

C. La verdad es que... Empieza con la expresión **La verdad es que...** y crea todas las oraciones posibles, usando un elemento de cada columna. Sigue el modelo.

Modelo: *La verdad es que ayer yo no trabajé nada.*

Ayer	yo	comer en _____
El fin de semana pasado	mis amigos y yo	insistir en ir al cine
El verano pasado	mi hermano/-a	dormir en la biblioteca
Esta mañana	mi compañero/-a de cuarto	leer la lección
Anoche	mis amigos	descubrir un restaurante estupendo
Una vez	mi familia	conocer a una persona famosa

CH. Querido diario. You have just returned from a super weekend and you are now writing an account of the experience in your daily journal. Mention the following points as you record your experience.

1. ¿A qué hora llegaste?
2. ¿Dónde cenaste la primera noche? ¿Con quién?
3. ¿Qué comiste?
4. ¿Qué hiciste después de la cena?
5. ¿Qué compraste en el viaje? ¿Para quién?
6. ¿Qué más hiciste durante el fin de semana?
7. ¿Por qué fue tan especial la experiencia?

D. Preguntas personales

1. ¿Dónde pasaste las vacaciones el año pasado?
2. ¿Qué equipaje llevaste contigo?
3. ¿Qué información buscas en las etiquetas cuando compras ropa?
4. Menciona tres documentos que llevas contigo generalmente.

Do the following activities with a partner.

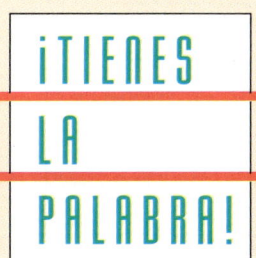

A. Entrevista: Los viajes. Interview your partner to find out

- si conoce otro país
- qué idioma se habla allí
- si hay que tener un pasaporte para viajar allí
- dónde se puede sacar el pasaporte

B. En el consulado. With a partner, create and act out the conversation according to the instructions.

Estudiante A: Empleado/-a

1. Exchange greetings.
2. Ask how you can help.
3. Inquire about the purpose of the visit.
4. Ask for the student's name, address, and nationality.
5. Explain that you will send the student some documents to sign.

Instruct the students to invent a trip if they have not been to another country.

Estudiante B: Estudiante

1. Exchange greetings.
2. Explain that you need a visa to travel to the United States.
3. Explain that you want to study in the United States. Say for how long.
4. Give the requested information.
5. Thank the clerk and say good-bye.

OTRA VUELTA

Play instructor tape, 2 min.

Listen again to the *Entrada* of this *etapa* and the telephone conversation between Patricia and the official at the consulate. Using the following form as a model, record the information that she gives him.

REPUBLICA DE CHILE
MINISTERIO DE RELACIONES EXTERIORES

CEDULA CONSULAR PARA TURISTAS

SOLICITANTE DE LA VISA

PRIMER APELLIDO	SEGUNDO APELLIDO	NOMBRES	SEXO(m/f)	FECHA DE NACIMIENTO

DOMICILIO HABITUAL (Calle, N°, Depto., País)

PAIS DE NACIMIENTO	NACIONALIDAD LEGAL	PROFESION U OCUPACION
N° DEL PASAPORTE O DOCUMENTO VISADO	**PAIS OTORGANTE DEL PASAPORTE**	**MOTIVO DEL VIAJE**

FAMILIARES MENORES DE 18 AÑOS INCLUIDOS EN EL PASAPORTE

NOMBRE COMPLETO DEL FAMILIAR	NACIONALIDAD	SEXO(m/f)	FECHA DE NACIMIENTO

SOLICITUD DE VISA DE TURISMO

AL SEÑOR CONSUL DE CHILE EN ....

El infrascrito, arriba identificado, viene en solicitar el otorgamiento de una Visa de Turismo para sí y para los miembros de su familia que se detallan en la presente Solicitud.

DECLARACION: Declaro estar en conocimiento de que durante mi estada en Chile no podré desarrollar actividades remuneradas ni podré intervenir en su política interna ni en actos contrarios a su Constitución Política o a las Leyes, Decretos y demás disposiciones que rijen en su territorio.

_____   _____
Fecha   Firma del Solicitante

CONTROL DE ENTRADA

Firma, Fecha de Entrada y Sello

VISACION CONSULAR

NUMERO ACTUACION	PLAZO DE DURACION DE LA VISA
DERECHOS CONSULARES	**FECHA DE LA VISACION**

En virtud de la Autorización dada en Circ. Res. 183/83 se concede la Visación de Turismo solicitada, con validez para entrar a Chile por una sola vez dentro del plazo de 90 días a contar de esta fecha.

Firma y Sello del CONSUL

USO OFICIAL

FECHA DE ENTRADA	VENCIMIENTO VISA

COMENTARIO CULTURAL

Los chicanos

Roberto and Paco are getting ready to visit Colombia. They speak Spanish fluently, even though they were born and raised in the United States and are U.S. citizens. *Chicanos* are U.S. citizens of Mexican ancestry. The term *chicano* came into use in the United States in the 1960s and connotes racial and cultural pride. Mexicans and Mexican-Americans are the most numerous group of Spanish-speaking residents in the United States, comprising about 55 percent of the total number of Hispanics.

Many Mexican-Americans have ties to the United States that go back to the 1600s and 1700s, long before the land on which they lived became part of the United States. Following the political and military battles that resulted in the transfer to the United States of most of the land that is now Arizona, California, Colorado, Nevada, New Mexico, Texas, Utah, and Wyoming, most of the 75,000 Spanish-speaking people living in those territories became U.S. citizens. Many of them and their descendants, however, have continued to think of the border as a political, but not a cultural, reality. The issue is still a sensitive one, particularly in Mexico itself.

Actividad. How much do you know about Mexican-American culture? Are the following statements true or false?

1. Sí, 2. No, 3. No, 4. Sí.

1. Los chicanos celebran muchas fiestas mexicanas, como el Cinco de Mayo y la Fiesta de Nuestra Señora de Guadalupe.   Sí   No
2. Las fiestas del Cinco de Mayo celebran la independencia de México.   Sí   No
3. Todos los chicanos hablan español.   Sí   No
4. Los chicanos por lo general siguen las tradiciones culinarias (*food customs*) de sus antepasados mexicanos.   Sí   No

TERCERA ETAPA

"Vamos a hacer las maletas"

ENTRADA

Play instructor tape, 2 min.

En la aduana

You will hear a conversation between two people. As you listen, try to figure out

- where the conversation takes place
- what country the two speakers are in

> 1. ¿Dónde tiene lugar esta conversación?
>   a. en un aeropuerto
>   b. en una tienda
>   c. en una estación de trenes
> 2. ¿En qué país están?

ANTES DE LEER Y ESCRIBIR

Preparación

When traveling to another country, you usually have to go through immigration (*inmigración*) and customs (*hacer aduana*). The process often includes filling out a form (*tarjeta de entrada*), showing some documentation, answering questions, and perhaps opening your luggage for inspection. Thinking about your own travel experiences or scenes of border crossings you may have encountered in books or on television or film, list, in either Spanish or English, some of the questions that a traveler entering another country is likely to be asked.

1.
2.
3.
4.

Think of the key words and phrases (in English if you do not know them in Spanish) that you will have to know to understand the questions and respond to them, words like *el pasaporte, la tarjeta de turismo,* and *la visa.* Refer to the second *etapa* for some of this key vocabulary.

1.   5.
2.   6.
3.   7.
4.   8.

ESCRIBIR

The *Tarjeta de entrada a Colombia* on page 175 is an actual form that all travelers who enter that country must fill out. Read through Writing Strategy 4 before beginning *Actividad A.*

A. Llenar el formulario. Fill out the *Tarjeta de entrada* form. For the purposes of this activity, you can choose to be a Colombian resident returning home after a trip or a resident of another country who is arriving in Colombia. The questions and tips that follow the form (on pages 175 and 176) will help you fill it out, so read and respond to the questions first.

WRITING STRATEGY 4

Learn to paraphrase

In Chapter 2 you practiced linking your sentences together to create a smoother piece of writing. Another way to unify your paragraphs is by paraphrasing, so that your sentences sound natural. For example, if you are asked *¿Cuál es el motivo de su visita a Colombia?*, it will sound very stilted and unnatural to reply, in either written or spoken language, *El motivo de mi viaje a Colombia es el turismo.* Instead, you will want to paraphrase the words of the question and respond *Estoy en Colombia como turista,* or *Estoy en Colombia para conocer el país.*

---

1. **Apellido** (pregunta 1) significa *surname*. ¿Por qué se usa aquí el plural **apellidos**? ¿Qué significa **nombres completos**? ¿Cuántos nombres tienes?

OJO: Refer to the *Comentario cultural* in Chapter 2, third *etapa*.

2. El país de residencia (6) es el país donde vives permanentemente. ¿Esto significa que eres ciudadano/-a (*citizen*) de ese país?

3. La fecha de nacimiento (7) es la fecha de tu cumpleaños. El verbo es **nacer,** *to be born.* Escribe aquí otra manera de preguntar ¿**Cuál es su fecha de nacimiento?**_____

4. Aprendiste en la segunda etapa un sinónimo de la expresión **en el exterior** (9). ¿Cuál es?

5. ¿Qué significa **tránsito** (9)? Recuerda que es un motivo (*reason*) para entrar a Colombia.

6. Un sinónimo de **dirección prevista** (10) es **dirección preseleccionada.** ¿Qué dirección buscan las autoridades?

7. **Empresa** (11) significa lo mismo que **aerolínea. Terrestre, marítima** y **fluvial** representan otras maneras de llegar al país. ¿Qué significan?

   Terrestre: _____   Marítima: _____   Fluvial: _____

B. En la aduana. Now imagine that you have been asked to write in narrative form the information contained in the *Tarjeta de entrada a Colombia.* Write a sentence for each entry on the form, trying wherever possible to paraphrase the printed information. (See Writing Strategy 4 for an example of paraphrasing.) On a separate sheet of paper, write your fourteen sentences. When you have finished, read them all together to make sure that you have written a coherent paragraph.

VENTANILLA AL MUNDO HISPÁNICO   Hacer aduana

All countries have customs and immigration offices to control the entry of persons and goods. Tourists may take into the country items for their personal use, as well as modest gifts. When a traveler's luggage is searched, customs officials are looking for multiple items that might be intended for sale, for illegal items, such as firearms or drugs, and food and vegetable products, which are usually barred because they might harbor parasites or molds that could endanger local agricultural production.

Actividad. The message of the ad on page 177 is intended for travelers who will enter Colombia. As you read it, answer the following questions.

1. ¿Quién escribió este mensaje? ¿Por qué?
2. ¿Qué es **la broca?** ¿Es un animal o una planta?
3. ¿Qué problema causa la broca?
4. ¿Por qué es peligroso (*dangerous*) traer empaques usados a Colombia?

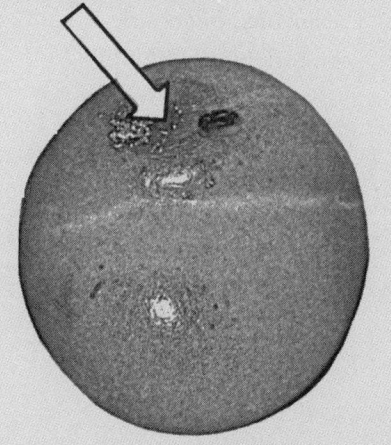
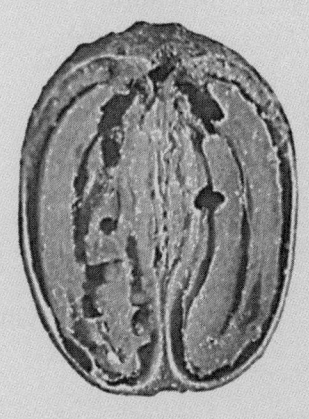

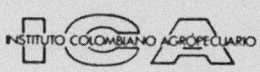

AUMENTAR EL VOCABULARIO

OJO: *Pasar aduana* can also be used.

The words *factura* and *recibo* have different meanings, although they may serve the same function. *La factura* is the invoice, or the bill of sale from the seller requesting or registering payment. When it is stamped "paid," it means that the item has been paid for, and it can then serve as a receipt, or *recibo*. A *recibo* is any document that indicates an item has been paid for.

OJO: The word *probar* also means "to try out" or "to taste," as in *probar un poco de tu helado* (to taste a bit of your ice cream).

OJO: To ask a friend what size shirt or jacket or pants he or she wears, you ask *¿Qué talla usas?* See Chapter 7, first *etapa,* for phrases used in shopping.

OJO: A woman pilot is *la piloto*. Positions such as *cartero* and *piloto,* which are still held only by men in the Spanish-speaking world, do not yet have recognized feminine forms.

la aduana	customs
el (la) aduanero/-a	customs agent
hacer aduana	to pass through customs
la cámara	camera
la foto	photograph
sacar fotos	to take pictures
la escala	intermediate stop, stopover (*on a trip*)
hacer escala	to make a stop
el vuelo directo	direct flight (*no plane change, possible stops*)
el vuelo sin escalas	nonstop flight
la factura	invoice, bill of sale
la cuenta	bill (*in restaurant*)
el impuesto	tax
el recibo	receipt
hacer la maleta	to pack
la bolsa	bag, purse
la mochila	knapsack, backpack
llevar	to wear, to carry
hacer juego con	to go well with
probar (ue)	to try on (*clothing*)
quedar bien/mal	to fit well/poorly
la talla	size (*of clothing*)
el precio	price
costar (ue)	to cost
la liquidación	(clearance) sale
la rebaja	discount, sale
el vuelo	flight
el asiento	seat
aterrizar	to land
la azafata	flight attendant (*Spain*)
el boleto (de ida y vuelta)	(round-trip) ticket
el cinturón (de seguridad)	(seat) belt
despegar	to take off
el (la) piloto	pilot
la (puerta de) salida	departure gate

LAS PRENDAS DE VESTIR

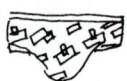
el traje de baño
las sandalias
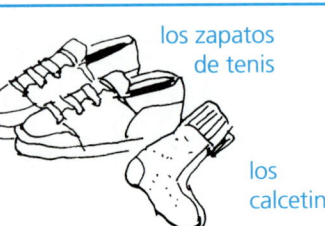
los zapatos de tenis
los calcetines

Tercera etapa

OJO: Some additional words for **La ropa interior:** *las bragas* (women's underpants), *los calzoncillos* (men's undershorts), *la camiseta* (tee shirt), *el sostén* (bra), *el suspensorio* (jockstrap), *la combinación* (full slip), *el medio fondo* or *las enaguas* (half-slip), *las medias* (stockings), *las pantimedias* (pantyhose).

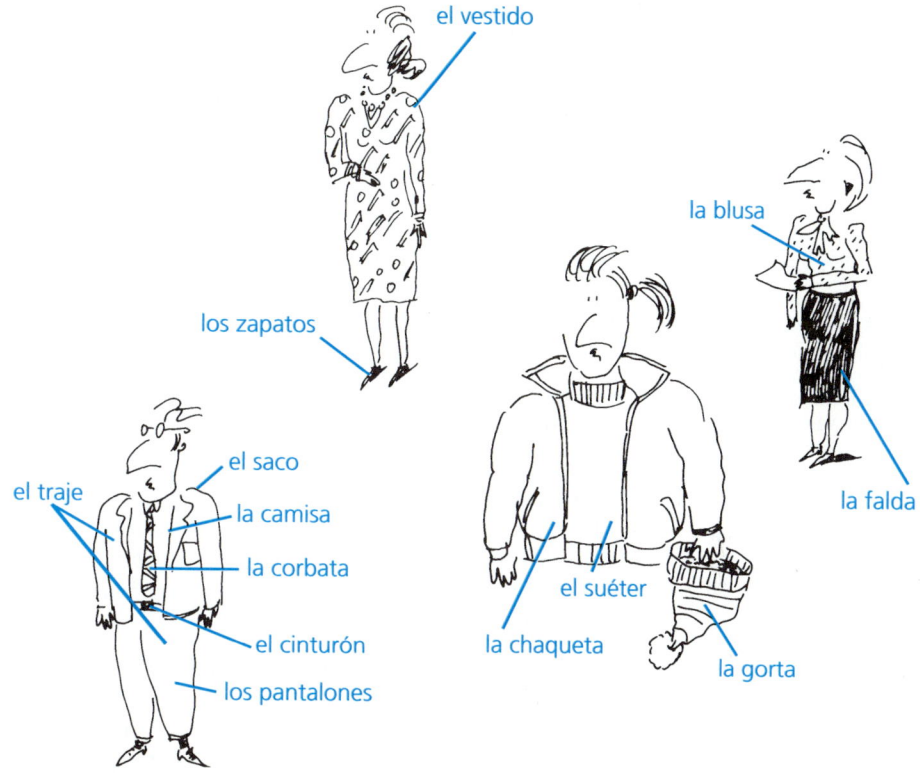

¿Ropa de hombre o de mujer? Indicate if the following articles of clothing are for *hombres* (H), for *mujeres* (M), of if they are worn by both sexes (HM).

1. el traje
2. los pantalones
3. las sandalias
4. la falda
5. la camisa
6. la blusa
7. la corbata
8. los calcetines
9. los zapatos de tenis
10. el abrigo

USO PRÁCTICO DEL ESPAÑOL Affirmative and Negative Expressions

You have already seen that the easiest way to make a Spanish sentence negative is to place the word *no* immediately before the verb.

Quiero ir a Colombia este año, pero **no** puedo.

Spanish has other negative words as well, which are paired with their affirmative opposites in the chart that follows.

OJO: *Jamás* is a more emphatic form of *nunca*. Sometimes the two are used together to give even greater emphasis: *¡Nunca jamás voy a hablar con él!* (I'll never ever speak to him again in my life!)

OJO: Shorten *alguno* and *ninguno* to *algún* and *ningún* before masculine singular nouns. Make sure that the form of *alguno* and *ninguno* agrees with the noun it refers to.

Affirmative		*Negative*	
siempre	always	nunca, jamás	never
una vez	once		
a veces	sometimes		
o… o	either … or	ni… ni	neither … nor
también	also	tampoco	neither
algo	something	nada	nothing
todo	everything, all		
alguien	someone, somebody	nadie	no one, nobody
alguno/-a	some, someone, any	ninguno/-a	none, no one

Negative words can go before or after the verb. If they go after the verb, include the word *no* before the verb.

No entró **nadie** por esa puerta.
Nadie entró por esa puerta.
No one entered through that door.

¿Mario **no** baila **nunca**? ¿Por qué?
Mario never dances. Why not?

No sé. Me dice que **nunca** aprendió.
I don't know. He tells me that he never learned.

Notice that you can have two or more negative words in a Spanish sentence.

Paco **no** fue a la fiesta. Alfredo **no** fue **tampoco**.
Paco didn't go to the party. Alfredo didn't go either.

Herlinda es muy tímida. **No** me dice **nunca nada**.
Herlinda is very shy. She never says anything to me.

Alguien and *nadie* always refer to people. Use the **personal *a*** before them when they are direct objects. Use the same personal *a* construction before *alguno* and *ninguno* when they refer to people.

Franco es amigo de todo el mundo, pero yo no conozco **a** nadie.
Franco is everyone's friend, but I don't know anybody.

Es la hora de la clase, pero no veo **a** ninguno de mis compañeros.
It's time for class to start, but I don't see any of my classmates.

OJO: The plural forms *ningunos/-as* are hardly ever used in Spanish. If the sentence is negative, usually the singular form is used.

OJO: If you and your traveling companion have nothing to declare, your response will contain three negative words.

OJO: If you don't have either of these items, use the expression *ni… ni*.

OJO: Remember that the forms of *ninguno* are almost always singular.

Ponerlo a prueba

A. En la aduana. Contesta las preguntas que te hace el agente de aduana.

Agente: ¿Tiene Ud. algo que declarar?
Tú: _____

Agente: ¿Y su compañero?
Tú: _____

Agente: ¿Trae Ud. armas (*weapons*) o drogas?
Tú: _____

Agente: ¿Tiene Ud. algunas plantas?

Tú: _____

Agente: ¿Ud. piensa alojarse (*stay*) en un hotel o viene a visitar a alguien en nuestro país?

Tú: _____

Agente: Eso es todo. Muchas gracias y bienvenidos a nuestro país.

B. Definiciones. Place the number of the word or expression from the list beside its definition.

1. el cinturón de seguridad
2. el boleto
3. la mochila
4. la liquidación
5. el abrigo
6. despegar

_____ cuando se vende a un precio muy reducido

_____ la prenda de vestir que se usa cuando hace mucho frío

_____ lo que se compra para ir en avión

_____ esto protege a los pasajeros de avión o de auto

_____ cuando el avión se separa de la tierra

_____ un tipo de maleta pequeña que usan los estudiantes para llevar los libros

Follow-up: 1. Have students make sentences incorporating the words and their definitions to practice circumlocution. 2. Have them work in groups of three to incorporate all six words into a humorous paragraph.

C. ¿Cómo se viaja en avión? Place the following activities in the proper sequence for making a trip by air.

_____ entrar en el avión

_____ escuchar las instrucciones del (de la) azafata

_____ comprar el boleto

_____ ir al aeropuerto

_____ despegar

_____ buscar la salida para el vuelo

_____ darle el boleto al (a la) agente

_____ buscar el asiento correcto y sentarse

Follow-up writing assignment: Write the story of an imaginary plane trip, incorporating the steps in this activity and adding more details.

Antes de salir de Bogotá por avión hay que pagar los impuestos de viaje.

OJO: The expression for being light (in weight) is *ligero/-a*.

OJO: To express the idea of returning an item, such as a book (to the library) or something you have bought (to the store), use *devolver*.

CH. Preguntas personales

1. Cuando viajas, ¿prefieres los vuelos con escala o sin escala? ¿Por qué?
2. ¿Te gusta llevar una maleta muy grande y pesada (*heavy*) o varias maletas pequeñas? ¿Por qué?
3. En tu opinión, ¿cuáles son las cinco cosas esenciales para un viajero (una viajera)?
4. ¿Siempre llevas una cámara? ¿De qué te gusta sacar fotos?
5. Cuando vas de compras, ¿buscas las liquidaciones y las rebajas? ¿Por qué sí o por qué no?
6. ¿Siempre pides la factura o el recibo cuando compras algo? ¿Por qué es importante tener el recibo?
7. ¿Usas una mochila para llevar tus libros? ¿Por qué?
8. ¿Cual es la diferencia entre un vuelo directo y un vuelo sin escalas?

D. ¡Qué combinaciones más locas! Create a sentence in which you describe the color combination for each of the following drawings. *¡Usa la imaginación!*

Modelo: *La señora de Molina lleva un vestido verde y zapatos rojos cuando va al trabajo.*

Sra. de Molina
para ir al trabajo

Luis
para correr
por la mañana

Prof. Santana
para enseñar

María Teresa
para ir al cine

Tercera etapa

E. **Hacer la maleta.** You are planning a trip to an exclusive tropical resort. Unfortunately, your luggage restrictions are quite severe, and you can only take one small suitcase. Name the items of clothing that you will take, and explain the reason for taking each one.

Modelo: *traje de baño—Llevo un traje de baño para nadar en el mar.*

F. **Estar de mal humor.** Elena is in a bad mood today and can't find anything good to say to Alicia. They are talking about Carlos, one of Elena's friends. Take Elena's role and respond negatively to Alicia's comments and questions.

Modelo: Alicia: Carlos estudia mucho, ¿verdad?

Elena: *Creo que sí, pero nunca tiene buenas notas.*

1. Alicia: Pues, me dicen que es muy inteligente y que también es muy simpático.

    Elena:

2. Alicia: ¡Qué negativa estás hoy! ¿Tienes algún problema?

    Elena:

3. Alicia: ¿Qué te pasa? ¿Te molesta algo?

    Elena:

4. Alicia: ¿Estás enojada (*angry*) con alguien?

    Elena:

5. Alicia: ¿Vas a salir con Carlos esta noche?

    Elena:

6. Alicia: Entonces, ¿quieres hacer algo?

    Elena:

7. Alicia: ¡Ay, chica, no puedo más (*I can't take any more of this*)! Te invito a salir y me dices que no. ¿Qué te pasa?

    Elena:

G. **Encuesta.** Talk to other members of the class and write the names of appropriate individuals in the spaces.

1. _____ siempre estudia por la noche.

    _____ nunca estudia por la noche.

2. _____ jamás estudia por la mañana.

    _____ casi (*almost*) siempre estudia por la mañana.

3. _____ habla con todo el mundo (*everyone*) en la cafetería.

    _____ no habla con nadie en la cafetería.

OJO: Remember that *el problema* is masculine.

OJO: The verb *molestar* (to bother) works like *gustar*. To respond, you say *No, no me molesta nada* or *Sí, me molesta...*

Help students get started by modeling possible questions: *¿Quién siempre estudia por la noche? Antonio, ¿con qué frecuencia estudias por la noche?*

OJO: Remember that *jamás* is a more emphatic form of *nunca*. The person who says *Jamás estudio por la mañana* is probably a night owl who is appalled by the idea of getting up early to study.

4. _____ nunca escucha música latina.
   _____ a veces escucha música latina.
   _____ siempre escucha música latina.
5. _____ busca trabajo, y _____ busca trabajo también.
   _____ no busca trabajo ni _____ tampoco.
6. _____ fuma (*smokes*) y bebe.
   _____ ni fuma ni bebe.

INVESTIGAR LA GRAMÁTICA   Más sobre el pretérito

Earlier in this chapter you learned when to use the preterite and how to form the preterite of regular verbs. Here are some common verbs that are irregular in the preterite. Note that the *yo* and *él/ella/usted* forms are not stressed on the last syllable and therefore do not have a written accent.

One group of verbs has a *u* in the stem.

OJO: Two other verbs in this group are *andar* (*anduv-*) (to walk) and *caber* (*cup-*) (to fit).

OJO: To avoid confusion between *poner* and *poder* in the preterite, remember that *poder* and its preterite forms (*pude, pudiste,* etc.) all have the letter *d*.

Infinitive	Stem	Forms of the preterite
estar	estuv-	estuve, estuviste, estuvo, estuvimos, estuvisteis, estuvieron
poder	pud-	pude, pudiste, pudo, pudimos, pudisteis, pudieron
poner	pus-	puse, pusiste, puso, pusimos, pusisteis, pusieron
saber	sup-	supe, supiste, supo, supimos, supisteis, supieron
tener	tuv-	tuve, tuviste, tuvo, tuvimos, tuvisteis, tuvieron

A second group of verbs has an *i* in the stem.

OJO: Note the spelling change in *hizo*.

OJO: *Querer* also has a change of meaning in the preterite. *Quise* means "I tried (but didn't succeed)." It means "I wanted" in the sense of "I made an (unsuccessful) effort."

Infinitive	Stem	Forms of the preterite
hacer	hic-	hice, hiciste, hizo, hicimos, hicisteis, hicieron
querer	quis-	quise, quisiste, quiso, quisimos, quisisteis, quisieron
venir	vin-	vine, viniste, vino, vinimos, vinisteis, vinieron

A third group of verbs has a *j* in the stem. Note that the *ellos/ellas/Uds.* form ends in *-eron*.

OJO: Other verbs in this group are *traducir* (to translate) and *reducir* (to reduce).

OJO: Note that *decir* also has an *i* in the stem.

Infinitive	Stem	Forms of the preterite
conducir	conduj-	conduje, condujiste, condujo, condujimos, condujisteis, condujeron
decir	dij-	dije, dijiste, dijo, dijimos, dijisteis, dijeron
traer	traj-	traje, trajiste, trajo, trajimos, trajisteis, trajeron

OJO: Note that *ir* and *ser* have the same forms in the preterite. Context makes it easy to tell them apart.

OJO: *Dar* is irregular because it has the endings of an *-er* or *-ir* verb.

OJO: Some verbs have two different stem changes. The preterite is the first time that you have seen the second stem change in use. Only *-ir* verbs are affected because *-ar* and *-er* verbs have only one stem change, for example, *jugar* (*ue*), *perder* (*ie*).

The last group of irregular verbs has one-syllable infinitives.

Infinitive	Forms of the preterite
ir	fui, fuiste, fue, fuimos, fuisteis, fueron
ser	fui, fuiste, fue, fuimos, fuisteis, fueron
dar	di, diste, dio, dimos, disteis, dieron

The only stem-changing verbs that change in the preterite are those that end in *-ir*, like *dormir* (*ue, u*) and *mentir* (*ie, i*). In the preterite, these verbs use the **second** stem change listed. It occurs only in the *él/ella/usted* and *ellos/ellas/ustedes* forms.

dormir (**ue, u**)
dormí   dormimos
dormiste   dormisteis
durmió   durmieron

mentir (**ie, i**)
mentí   mentimos
mentiste   mentisteis
mintió   mintieron

OJO: Study tip: Keep a list of these verbs handy. Conjugate them aloud frequently to remember the sound of the stem change.

You already know the following *-ir* stem-changing verbs.

despedirse (i, i)   divertirse (ie, i)   morir (ue, u)
seguir (i, i)   sentirse (ie, i)
repetir (i, i)
pedir (i, i)
servir (i, i)
vestirse (i, i)

Ponerlo a prueba

A. **¿Qué pasó ayer?** Paco and Roberto spent the whole day getting ready for their trip. Combine the following sentence elements to say what they did.

Modelo: amigos / ir / centro / mañana
Los amigos fueron al centro por la mañana.

1. Roberto / levantarse temprano
2. amigos / no poder usar el auto de Paco
3. (Ellos) tener / tomar el autobús / ir al centro
4. Primero / hacer unos arreglos / agencia de viajes
5. Entonces / decidir comprar unos regalos / familia de Marcos
6. En la tienda / ver / unos amigos de la universidad
7. Todos / almorzar / restaurante en el centro
8. Paco / pedir / hamburguesa / pero los otros / pedir / ensalada de pollo (*chicken salad*)
9. ¡Qué vergüenza! Roberto / no llevar / cartera. Paco / tener que invitarlo (*pay for him*)

OJO: Remember to use the *a personal* when the direct object of the verb is a person.

10. Paco y Roberto / divertirse con sus amigos / pero no hacer todos sus trámites (*business*)

Extension: Have students incorporate their responses into a paragraph.

B. ¡Qué suerte la de ganar el premio gordo! Yolanda won the lottery and spent the first six months of last year traveling all over Latin America. Say what she did in each country she visited.

Modelo: enero / México / visitar el Museo de Antropología
En enero fue a México y visitó el Museo de Antropología.

enero	México	aprender a bailar el jarabe tapatío, el baile nacional de México; asistir a una corrida de toros (*bullfight*)
febrero	Puerto Rico	divertirse en la playa; conocer El Morro, un fuerte (*fort*) construido por los españoles en el siglo (*century*) XVI
marzo	Costa Rica	ir a los parques nacionales; perder su tarjeta de crédito
abril	Ecuador	hacer una excursión a las Islas Galápagos; escribir un reportaje turístico para *El Universo,* un periódico de Guayaquil
mayo	Perú	ver el lago (*lake*) Titicaca, el lago navegable más alto del mundo; volver dos veces a Machu Picchu
junio	Paraguay	aprender unas palabras de guaraní, una lengua indígena; comprar unas mantillas de ñandutí, el encaje (*lace*) famoso del país

C. La verdad es que... Empieza con la expresión **La verdad es que...** y crea todas las oraciones posibles, usando un elemento de cada columna. Sigue el modelo.

Modelo: *La verdad es que ayer no hice la tarea.*

OJO: You say *el fin de semana pasado* because *pasado* agrees with the masculine word *fin.*

Ayer	yo	hacer la tarea
El fin de semana pasado	mis amigos y yo	ir al cine
El verano pasado	mi hermano/-a	estudiar en la biblioteca
Esta mañana	mi compañero/-a de cuarto	poder terminar la tarea
Anoche		comer en un restaurante
Una vez	mis amigos	hacer un viaje a...
Anteayer	mi familia	dormirse muy tarde
	mis tíos	

CH. Preguntas personales

1. ¿Qué cursos tuviste el semestre/trimestre pasado? ¿Cuántas horas al día tuviste que estudiar? ¿Cómo saliste en los exámenes?

2. ¿Cuándo fue la última fiesta que hiciste? ¿Cuántas personas asistieron, más o menos? ¿Qué contribuyeron tus amigos a la fiesta?
3. ¿Cuándo fue la última vez que saliste a comer a un restaurante? ¿Con quién(es) fuiste? ¿Se divirtieron?
4. ¿Qué hiciste anoche? ¿Miraste la televisión? ¿Qué programa te gustó más? ¿Cuánto tiempo pasaste delante del televisor?
5. Anoche al acostarte, ¿dónde pusiste tu ropa? ¿Y tus libros?

D. Imagínate (padres e hijos). Like all parents, Hispanic parents tend to be more conservative and traditional than their children. In this situation, one person takes the role of the parent, and the other takes the role of the young person. The parent begins each exchange with a question.

Modelo: estar / anoche   Padre/Madre: *¿Dónde estuviste anoche?*
Joven: *Fui a una fiesta excelente.*

1. con quién / salir
2. adónde / ir después de la fiesta
3. a qué hora / venir a casa
4. quién / conducir
5. cómo / conducir
6. cómo / poder llegar tan tarde
7. a qué hora / acostarse
8. por qué / hacer tanto ruido esta mañana
9. por qué / no dormir más

E. Curiosidad. Your roommate got back from a party at 3:00 A.M. You couldn't go to the party because you were studying for an exam. You are very curious about the party and what went on there. Using the phrases from *Actividad D* as a guide, ask your roommate about the party.

Do the following activity with a partner.

Usando la memoria. Interview a classmate to find out the last time he or she did the following.

- ir al zoológico
- dormirse antes de las 9:00 de la noche
- comer un helado de chocolate
- ver una película cómica
- seguir los consejos de sus padres

Ahora descubre quién de la clase

- nunca ha visitado un zoológico
- nunca ha comido un helado de chocolate
- siempre sigue los consejos de sus padres

OTRA VUELTA

Play instructor tape, 2 min.

Now listen again to the conversation between the traveler and the customs agent and list

- dos cosas que la señora tiene en su maleta
- dos cosas mencionadas por el aduanero que ella **no** tiene

COMENTARIO CULTURAL

¿Es más formal la vida en los países hispanos?

Is life more formal in Spain and Latin America than in the United States? Travelers to Latin America probably should take a few more formal outfits in addition to their casual tourist clothing if they plan to spend a considerable amount of time with *colombianos*. Although customs are changing in most parts of the Spanish-speaking world, particularly in the larger cities, it is still true that people dress more formally there than in the United States. Young girls wear very fashionable pants everywhere, but older women tend to wear pants much less often than in the United States. For men, the *guayabera*, a loose-fitting dress shirt that is worn outside the trousers, is quite popular, especially at lower altitudes, where the climate is very hot. Some school children, from their early years through *el bachillerato*, or high school, wear either a uniform or a standard outfit—dark skirts for girls or pants for boys and a white blouse or shirt. Pants are unacceptable as school dress for girls, as are jeans for boys.

Belisario Betancur, president of Colombia 1982–1986, wears a guayabera *as he walks through the streets of Cartagena.*

Even though fashion is becoming more international as a result of modern advances in telecommunications, it is usually best to observe local customs for style and formality of dress. And when in doubt, it is preferable to err on the side of formality.

Answers to *Comentario cultural* activity: 1. inappropriate (I) 2. appropriate (A) 3. I 4. I 5. A 6. Either, depending on whether they have plans to socialize.

Preguntas. Based on the reading, indicate whether or not the clothing given for each situation would be appropriate in most Latin American countries.

1. A woman attends mass in jeans and heavy shoes because she is going on a hike afterward.
2. A young man wears a jacket and tie on a date. He and his friend are going out to dinner and to a play.
3. A young man attends a baptism in shorts because it is very hot that day.
4. A group of tourists visits the *Museo del Oro* in Bogotá wearing shorts.
5. A young woman wears a dress to meet a (male) friend's parents for the first time.
6. Paco and Roberto arrived in Colombia wearing jeans and tee shirts.

ACTIVIDADES DE INTEGRACIÓN

Play video

Program 4 *Personajes inolvidables* Mini-portraits of famous people

A. **¡A conocernos!** Write a description of someone in the class. Include details about

- appearance/clothing
- personality
- academic program
- interests

B. **Mis vacaciones.** Think about a vacation that you have taken, or the most recent school vacation. Write a paragraph about your activities, including one or two sentences for each day you were on vacation.

C. **Los preparativos.** A friend of yours is going to Mexico on a family vacation. With a partner, enact the following conversation. Ask

- when they are leaving
- how long they are going to stay
- whether your friend is going to take a bathing suit
- whether your friend is going to take a camera
- whether your friend and his or her family are going to visit the beaches in Cancún

CH. Entrevista. Habla con un compañero (una compañera) de la clase para descubrir

- cuándo fue la última vez que fue de compras
- qué cosas compró
- a qué hora volvió a casa
- cuánto dinero gastó (gastar: *to spend*)
- cuándo piensa ir de compras otra vez

Después de concluir la entrevista, informa a la clase sobre las actividades de tu compañero/-a.

D. "Su pasaporte, por favor." Act out the following scene with a partner.

> *Estudiante A: Aduanero/-a*
>
> You are a customs agent at the airport in Lima, Perú. A traveler approaches. You ask questions to find out
>
> - where the traveler was born
> - the traveler's permanent address
> - the purpose of his or her trip
> - how long he or she plans to stay in Perú
> - whether he or she is bringing in any alcoholic beverages or plants (*plantas*)
>
> After asking your questions, you end the interaction.

OJO: *Nacer* means "to be born."

> *Estudiante B: El (la) turista*
>
> You have just arrived in Lima, Perú, and must go through customs. In answer to the agent's questions, you give information about
>
> - your birthplace
> - your permanent address
> - the purpose of your trip
> - how long you plan to stay in Perú
> - whether you have any alcoholic beverages or plants (*las plantas*) in your luggage

Actividades de integración

E. **"Abra las maletas, por favor."** Act out the following scene with a partner.

OJO: You should use the verb *salir de*.

Estudiante A: Aduanero/-a

You are a Spanish-speaking customs agent at Kennedy Airport in New York. The office has been instructed to check all luggage for illegal imports. A traveler comes to your station. You are polite, but very thorough. Act suspicious.

- Ask the traveler to open his or her luggage.
- Find out when the traveler left the United States.
- There are five cameras in one of the suitcases. Ask the traveler where he or she bought the cameras, and why there are so many.
- Ask for invoices to prove that the cameras were purchased in the United States.
- The traveler has a plastic bag at the bottom of one of the suitcases. Ask him or her to open it.
- Tell the traveler that he or she may close the suitcases.

Estudiante B: El fotógrafo (la fotógrafa) profesional

You are a professional photographer who has been on assignment abroad and are returning to the United States. You are questioned by the customs agent in Kennedy Airport in New York.

- In answer to the agent's question, say when you left the United States.
- Explain that you need several cameras for your work.
- The agent thinks that you bought the cameras abroad to sell them in the United States. Say where in the United States you bought them and show the invoices to prove it.
- The agent asks you to open a plastic bag. Explain that they are gifts for your children.
- Act polite, but a bit impatient. You worked hard on a long assignment and are eager to get home to your family.

VOCABULARIO

Fiestas
Holidays

árbol (m) de Navidad   *Christmas tree*
Día de Todos los Santos   *All Saints' Day*
Jánuca (f)   *Hanukkah*
Navidad (f)   *Christmas*
Nochebuena (f)   *Christmas Eve*
Nochevieja (f)   *New Year's Eve*
regalo (m)   *gift, present*

celebrar   *to celebrate*
regalar   *to give a gift*

Felices Pascuas   *Merry Christmas; Happy Easter*
Feliz Año Nuevo   *Happy New Year*
Feliz Navidad   *Merry Christmas*

Dinero y compras
Money and Shopping

dinero (m)   *money*
oro (m)   *gold*
plata (f)   *money (lit., silver)*
riqueza (f)   *wealth*

barato/-a   *inexpensive, cheap*
bonito/-a   *pretty*
caro/-a   *expensive, costly*
precioso/-a   *beautiful*
rico/-a   *rich, wealthy*

Problemas
Problems

celos (m pl)   *jealousy*
molestia (f)   *bother, trouble*

discutir   *to argue, discuss*
estar celoso/-a   *to be jealous*
estar seguro/-a   *to be sure, certain*
molestar   *to bother, irritate*
resolver (ue)   *to solve (a problem)*

¡Qué envidia!   *I'm green with envy!*

Estaciones del año
Seasons of the year

invierno (m)   *winter*
otoño (m)   *fall*
primavera (f)   *spring*
verano (m)   *summer*

Los viajes
Travel

aduana (f)   *customs*
el (la) aduanero/-a   *customs agent*
agencia (f) de viajes   *travel agency*
anfitrión/-ona (m/f)   *host*
asiento (m)   *seat*
auto (m)   *car*
avión (m)   *airplane*
azafata (f)   *flight attendant*
boleto (m) (de ida y vuelta)   *(round-trip) ticket*
bolsa (f)   *bag, purse*
cámara (f)   *camera*
certificado (m) de vacuna   *vaccination certificate*
cinturón (m) (de seguridad)   *(seat) belt*
consulado (m)   *consulate*
credencial (f) escolar   *student I.D.*
documento (m)   *document*
domicilio (m)   *home address*
embajada (f)   *embassy*
escala (f)   *intermediate stop, stopover (on a trip)*
equipaje (m)   *luggage*
etiqueta (f)   *tag, label*
extranjero (m)   *foreign country*
extranjero/-a (m/f)   *foreigner*
foto (f)   *photograph*
huésped(a) (m/f)   *guest (in a hotel)*
impuesto (m)   *tax*
invitado/-a (m/f)   *guest*
licencia (f)   *license*
maleta (f)   *suitcase*
maletín (m)   *small suitcase*
medio (m) de transporte   *means of transportation*
mochila (f)   *knapsack, backpack*
pasaporte (m)   *passport*
el (la) piloto   *pilot*
puerta (f) de salida   *departure gate*
viaje (m)   *trip*
viajero/-a (m/f)   *traveler*
visado (m); visa (f)   *visa*
vuelo (m)   *flight*
vuelo (m) directo   *direct flight*
vuelo (m) sin escalas   *nonstop flight*

aterrizar   *to land*
despegar   *to take off*
facturar   *to check (luggage)*

hacer aduana *to pass through customs*
hacer escala *to make a stop*
hacer la maleta *to pack*
hacer un viaje *to take a trip*
sacar fotos *to take pictures*
viajar *to travel*

Actividades
Activities

ciclismo (m) *cycling*
esquiar *to ski*
ir a la playa *to go to the beach*

La ropa
Clothes

abrigo (m) *overcoat*
blusa (f) *blouse*
botas (f pl) *boots*
camisa (f) *shirt*
chaqueta (f) *jacket*
corbata (f) *tie*
cinturón (m) *belt*
falda (f) *skirt*
gorra (f) *cap*
guantes (m pl) *gloves*
liquidación (f) *(clearance) sale*
pantalones (m pl) *pants*
precio (m) *price*
rebaja (f) *discount, sale*
saco (m) *coat, sports jacket*
suéter (m) *sweater*
talla (f) *size (of clothing)*
traje (m) *suit*
traje de baño (m) *bathing suit*
vestido (m) *dress*

hacer juego con *to go well with*
llevar *to wear, carry*
probar (ue) *to try on (clothing)*
quedar bien/mal *to fit well/poorly*

El correo
Mail

buzón (m) *mailbox*
carta (f) *letter*
cartero (m/f) *letter carrier*
dirección (f) *address*
estampilla (f) *stamp*
sello (m) *stamp*
sobre (m) *envelope*

enviar (mandar) una carta *to send (mail) a letter*

Negación y afirmación

jamás *never*
una vez *once*
a veces *sometimes*

o... o *either . . . or*
ni... ni *neither . . . nor*

también *also*
tampoco *neither*

algo *something*
nada *nothing*
todo *everything, all*
todo/todos *everything, everyone*

alguien *someone, somebody*
nadie *no one, nobody*

de ninguna manera *by no means, not at all*
ninguno/-a *none, not any*
alguno/-a *some, someone, any*

Palabras útiles
Useful words

Sustantivos
amor (m) *love*
cuenta (f) *bill (in restaurant)*
factura (f) *invoice, bill of sale*
flor (f) *flower*
propietario/-a (m/f) *owner*
recibo (m) *receipt*
requisito (m) *requirement*
reunión (f) *reunion, meeting*

Verbos
acompañar *to accompany, go with*
aconsejar *to advise*
comprar *to purchase*
comprobar (ue) *to check, verify*
costar (ue) *to cost*
extraviarse *to get lost*
guardar *to keep, take care of*
manejar *to manage, handle*
perder (ie) *to lose*
quedarse *to stay, remain*
renovar (ue) *to renew*
reunirse con *to meet with, have a meeting with*

Otra palabras y expresiones
acompañado/-a *accompanied*
aconsejable *advisable*
afortunadamente *fortunately*
apropiado/-a *suitable*
¡Buena suerte! *Good luck!*
desafortunadamente *unfortunately*
divertido/-a *fun, amusing*
en regla *in order*
magnífico/-a *wonderful*
nuevo/-a *new*
solo/-a *alone*

VOCABULARIO PERSONALIZADO

A conocer la vecindad

Capítulo 5

COMMUNICATIVE OBJECTIVES

In this chapter, you will learn more ways to
- give and seek information
- order food in a restaurant
- make generalizations and recommendations
- talk about the past
- express preferences, likes, and dislikes

PRIMERA ETAPA

La pensión de doña Josefina

ENTRADA

Play instructor tape, 3 min.

OJO: A *pensión* is a boardinghouse where rooms are rented by the week or month. Usually the guests eat at least the main meal of the day together in the dining room. Meals are eaten family style, that is, several diners who may not already know each other eat at the same table. The food is placed on the table and the guests serve themselves. See the *Comentario cultural* in this *etapa* for additional information about lodging in Spain and Latin America.

En busca de alojamiento

Paco and Roberto have arrived in Cali, Colombia, and are looking for lodging. Because they are traveling on a limited budget, they hope to obtain a room in a *pensión*. Listen to the conversation between the two young men, and the subsequent telephone call to the *dueña* (owner) of the *pensión*. As you listen, see if you can determine

- the name of the owner of the *pensión*
- whether the *pensión* is located close to or far from the downtown area
- what meals are included in the price

La pensión Restrepo

Nombre de la dueña:

La pensión está...

Comidas incluidas:

EMPEZAR A ESCUCHAR

Play student tape, 3 min.

Leer

al lado de	*next to*
el (la) cirujano/-a	*surgeon*
el (la) contador(a)	*accountant*
el (la) gerente	*manager*
el (la) huésped(a)	*guest (in a hotel)*
jubilado/-a	*retired*
la modista	*dressmaker, seamstress*
mudarse	*to move (change residence)*
el (la) periodista	*journalist*
el (la) vecino/-a	*neighbor*

Repetir

Escucha la cinta y repite lo que oyes.

Identificar

En una hoja aparte, escribe en una columna las palabras y frases de la lista anterior de Leer. Vas a oír algunas oraciones. Cada vez que oigas una de estas palabras o frases, apunta el número de la oración al lado de la palabra. Cada oración se leerá dos veces.

Escribir

Vas a oír unas oraciones, cada una leída dos veces. Escríbelas al escucharlas.

Reconocer

Ahora, lee otra vez las oraciones que acabas de escribir. Cada una contiene una o más de las palabras y frases de la lista anterior de Leer. Al releerlas, subraya todas las palabras y frases que vienen de la lista. Mientras lees, haz todas las correcciones necesarias.

Beginning with this chapter, some of the direction lines are in Spanish. For the most part, these occur in activities to which the students are already accustomed.

ESCUCHAR

Play student tape, 1 min.

Episodio 1: En la pensión

Enfoque comunicativo

Paco and Roberto decide to rent a room in the *Pensión Restrepo*. When they arrive, doña Josefina receives them and starts to tell them about her other guests, as well as some of her neighbors. As you listen, look at the following list and associate the people with their occupations.

Los huéspedes y los vecinos de doña Josefina

Persona	Profesión
Fernando	periodista
Josué	profesor jubilado (profesora jubilada)
Sr. Pedroza	
Sr. Lima	
Sra. Valdivia de Castillo	cirujano/-a
Dr. Meléndez	estudiante
	modista

Enfoque lingüístico

Listen again to what doña Josefina says and write down

- the word that doña Josefina uses as she begins to speak
- how she explains where señora Valdivia de Castillo's house is located

ESCUCHAR

Play student tape, 1 min.

Episodio 2: Más vecinos de doña Josefina

Enfoque comunicativo

Doña Josefina continues to talk about her neighbors, but it is clear that Paco and Roberto are interested in one person in particular. As you listen to their conversation, try to figure out the name and occupation of that person.

> Nombre:
>
> Hija de:
>
> ¿Trabaja o es estudiante?

Enfoque lingüístico

Listen again to Roberto and doña Josefina's conversation and note

- the words Roberto uses to ask if Sr. and Sra. Meléndez have a daughter
- the words Roberto uses to express his interest in her

VERIFICAR

¿Sí o no?

1. Josué y Fernando son estudiantes universitarios.   Sí   No
2. El señor Lima es un periodista jubilado.   Sí   No
3. La familia Meléndez acaba de mudarse de Popayán a Cali.   Sí   No
4. Roberto tiene ganas de conocer a Carmencita Meléndez.   Sí   No
5. La señora de Meléndez trabaja en un banco.   Sí   No
6. Los Gaitán, los vecinos nuevos, tienen dos hijos.   Sí   No

Ventanilla al mundo hispánico — Los nombres de pila (*first names*)

OJO: Men's names also reflect the Roman Catholic tradition, for example, Joseph, Paul, and, in Spanish, *Jesús*. It is not uncommon for a man to have the name of the Virgin Mary or some other typically female name as part of his name: *Jesús María, José María, José Asunción.*

Have students discuss this question in small groups. Extension: Ask students to make a list of the three most popular women's names and the three most popular men's names. Have groups compare lists.

En español muchos nombres de mujer se basan en las tradiciones y creencias de la religión católica. Los nombres como **Lourdes, Guadalupe, María del Carmen** y **María** son, según el catolicismo, nombres de lugares donde la Virgen María apareció, o son nombres de las personas a quienes se les apareció. Otros nombres comunes de mujer son **Encarnación** (*Incarnation*), **Rosario** (*Rosary*), **Concepción** (*Conception*) y **Natividad** (*Nativity*).

No son solamente los hispanos los que les dan a sus hijos nombres basados en la religión. En inglés los nombres como *Hope, Faith, Charity, Grace* y *Prudence* reflejan una tradición de darles a las hijas nombres de las virtudes puritanas de la época colonial de los Estados Unidos.

Pregunta. Todos los nombres de pila mencionados arriba son nombres de mujer. ¿Puedes pensar en nombres de hombre (en español o en inglés) relacionados con la tradición católica u otra tradición religiosa?

AUMENTAR EL VOCABULARIO

OJO: The term *la cirugía* is used to refer to surgery as a medical specialty, but is **not** used in the same way that we use the word in English to refer to an operation. In Spanish, we would say *Ella va a tener una operación* to express the idea that she is going to have surgery.

OJO: *El barrio,* a synonym for *la vecindad,* is used in Latin America. In the United States it often refers to an urban neighborhood populated by Hispanics.

In addition to its meaning of "garden," *el jardín* is often used to refer to the yard surrounding a house.

el (la) cirujano/-a	*surgeon*
el (la) enfermero/-a	*nurse*
enfermo/-a	*sick*
el (la) médico/-a	*doctor*
la operación	*operation*
operar	*to operate*
el (la) contador(a)	*accountant*
el (la) dueño/-a	*owner*
el (la) gerente	*manager*
jubilado/-a	*retired*
jubilarse	*to retire*
la modista	*seamstress*
el sastre	*tailor*
mudarse	*to move* (*change residence*)
el (la) periodista	*journalist*
el periódico	*newspaper*
la revista	*magazine*
la vecindad; el vecindario	*neighborhood*
el jardín	*garden*
el patio	*courtyard, yard*

LA VECINDAD DE DOÑA JOSEFINA

Within the context of this lesson, *la señal* is used to refer to signs that relate to traffic, whereas *el letrero* is more specifically a sign that provides information or publicity, such as a billboard, a public notice, or a poster.

OJO: Remember that you have already learned *el rincón*. *La esquina* is an exterior corner, where two buildings or streets come together. *El rincón* is an interior corner inside a room, courtyard, or other enclosure.

OJO: Infinitives are often used in signs and other written instructions. Can you figure out what these signs mean? *No fumar. No pisar el césped. No escupir. No correr.*

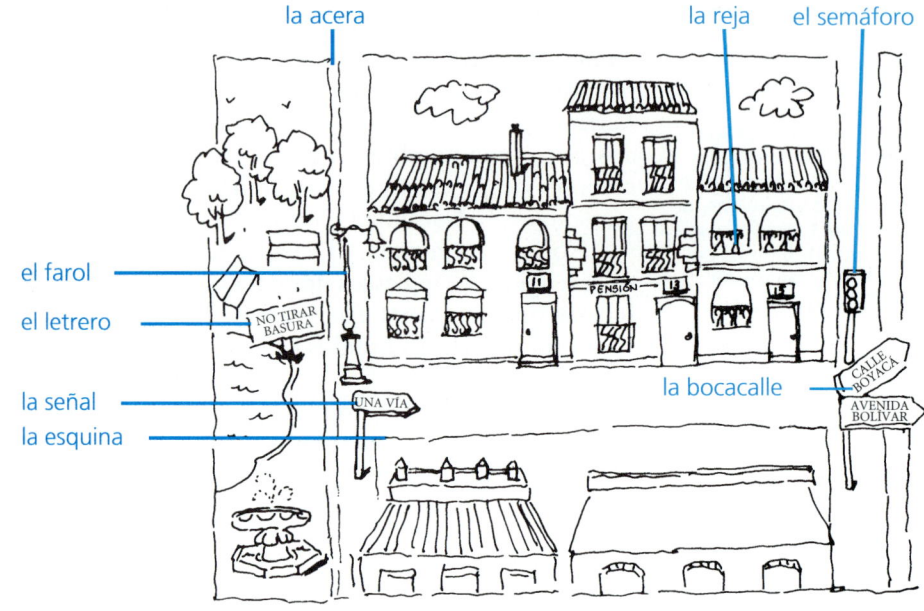

This activity recycles the prepositions introduced in the third *etapa* of Chapter 3.

Actividad. Contesta las preguntas a continuación, basando tus respuestas en el dibujo (*drawing*) y en los Episodios.

1. ¿Dónde está la pensión de doña Josefina?
2. ¿Cuál es la casa de los Meléndez?
3. ¿Dónde vive la modista?
4. ¿Cómo está controlado el tráfico aquí?
5. ¿Cómo protegen (*protect*) los residentes sus casas contra el robo?
6. ¿Cuántos letreros hay en la vecindad? ¿Cuáles son?
7. ¿Dónde está el farol?

USO PRÁCTICO DEL ESPAÑOL   The Present Perfect

The present perfect tense is used to talk about events that happened in the past but bear directly on the present moment. It corresponds to English constructions such as "I have spoken" and "I have arrived."

Conozco a Carmencita Meléndez, pero no **he conocido** a su hermano.
I know Carmencita Meléndez, but I have not met her brother.

Hemos hablado, pero todavía no **hemos salido.**
We have talked, but we haven't gone out yet.

—¿Te **has lavado** las manos, Carlitos?
—Sí, mamá, y me **he lavado** la cara también.
—¿**Has visto** a tu hermana?
—No, mamá, pero **ha llamado**. Viene a las siete.

Have you washed your hands, Carlitos?
Yes, Mom, and I've washed my face, too.
Have you seen your sister?
No, Mom, but she (has) called. She is coming at 6:00.

The present perfect is referred to as a compound tense because it is made up of two parts: a present tense form of the auxiliary verb *haber* and the past participle of the main verb. The verb *haber* is irregular.

he comido *I have eaten*	**hemos** comido *we have eaten*
has comido *you have eaten*	**habéis** comido *you have eaten*
ha comido *you/he/she have/has eaten*	**han** comido *you/they have eaten*

To form the past participle, remove the *-ar*, *-er*, or *-ir* ending from the infinitive and add *-ado* for *-ar* verbs and *-ido* for *-er* and *-ir* verbs.

hablar → habl → habl**ado**
comer → com → com**ido**
vivir → viv → viv**ido**

The following verbs have irregular past participles.

abrir	abierto
cubrir (*to cover*)	cubierto
decir	dicho
describir (*to describe*)	descrito
descubrir (*to discover*)	descubierto
escribir	escrito
hacer	hecho
morir (ue, u)	muerto
poner	puesto
romper (*to break*)	roto
ver	visto
volver (ue)	vuelto

OJO: Notice that *describir* and *escribir* follow the same conjugation pattern. Other similar patterns occur with *cubrir* and *descubrir,* and *volver* and *devolver*.

The past participle can also be used as an adjective. Just as with other adjectives, it must agree with the noun it describes in both number and gender.

El examen no está **terminado** todavía.
Durante el examen los libros se quedan **cerrados**.
Las ventanas no deben estar **abiertas**.
Tenemos **puesto** el aire acondicionado.

The exam is not finished yet.
During the exam the books remain closed.
The windows should not be open.
We have the air conditioner on.

¡OJO! Whenever a reflexive verb is used in the perfect tense, the reflexive pronoun is placed in front of the auxiliary verb.

El niño **se ha puesto** la pijama, pero no **se ha acostado** todavía.

The little boy has put on his pajamas, but he has not gone to bed yet.

Ponerlo a prueba

> The *Investigar la gramática* section of this *etapa* reviews the uses and meanings of the preterite. Ask students to return to this exercise and repeat it using preterite forms.

A. Una carta a mamá. Paco is writing his mother to tell her everything that he and Roberto have done so far on their trip. Write part of his letter for him, according to the cues given.

Modelo: llegar a Cali   *Hemos llegado a Cali.*

1. encontrar una pensión excelente
2. conocer a la dueña, doña Josefina
3. cenar con los otros huéspedes
4. dormir bien
5. no ver la vecindad todavía
6. hacer planes para conocer la ciudad
7. oír hablar mucho de la historia de Cali
8. (Roberto) les escribir a sus padres también

B. Las profesiones. According to the description, what is the profession or working status of each person?

Modelo: Carmencita estudia en la Preparatoria del Sagrado Corazón. Es…
Es estudiante.

> **OJO:** Remember that Spanish does not use an article in statements that identify people's jobs: *es estudiante, es profesora.*

1. Inés trabaja en un hospital. Ayuda a los enfermos. Es…
2. Rafael escribe artículos para un periódico. Es…
3. El Dr. de la Vega se especializa en la cirugía plástica. Es…
4. La señora de Echegaray hace unos vestidos preciosos. Es…
5. El Dr. Ledesma ya no trabaja porque tiene 80 años. Está…
6. Pedro es jefe (*boss*) de un grupo de empleados en la compañía. Es…
7. El señor Bermejo hace los mejores trajes de la ciudad. Es…

> Follow-up: Have students look up occupation titles for their parents or other family members and prepare a one-line description of those jobs. The other students can guess the occupation in English (if necessary), and then the student and/or you can supply the occupation in Spanish.

C. Preguntas personales

1. ¿Qué clase de trabajo hacen tus padres?
2. ¿Tus hermanos trabajan o estudian?
3. En tu familia, ¿cómo se llama el periódico que Uds. leen con más frecuencia?
4. ¿A qué revistas te suscribes? ¿y tu familia?
5. Cuenta algo interesante de uno de los vecinos de tu familia.

Primera etapa

6. ¿A cuál de los vecinos conoces mejor? ¿Dónde vive este vecino (esta vecina) en relación a (*with regard to*) tu casa?
7. ¿Cómo es tu vecindad?
8. ¿Conoces bien a tus vecinos de la residencia o solamente un poco?

CH. ¡A ti te toca! Use the dictionary to find the words you need to talk about the professions of members of your family. In pairs, interview your partner about his or her family and report to the class. Be sure to include the following information.

- **cuál** es el parentesco (padre, tía, etc.)
- **qué** clase de trabajo hacen
- **dónde** viven las personas

D. Tu vecindad. Prepare a brief description of your neighborhood or your dorm. ¿*Quiénes son los vecinos* **a un lado, al otro lado, enfrente** *y* **detrás** *de tu casa?*

INVESTIGAR LA GRAMÁTICA   Otra visita al pretérito

You have seen that the preterite in Spanish is used to refer to events or conditions that took place wholly within the time frame you are talking about, regardless of how long or short a duration the event or condition had.

Ayer a las doce del día **llamé** a mi mamá. El teléfono **sonó** solamente una vez y ella **contestó**. Eso me **pareció** raro porque normalmente los domingos ella trabaja afuera, en el jardín de la casa.

It is very important to understand the difference between "wholly completed in the past" and "wholly completed at the time in the past that you are talking about." In Chapter 6 you will begin to learn how to use another past tense, *el imperfecto*. At that time you will see the notion of something not being over and done with at the time you are talking about. Use the preterite when you want to view the event or condition as a complete, unanalyzed unit.

The focus of the preterite on the completeness of an event or condition results in a different shade of meaning for some familiar verbs when they are used in the preterite.

OJO: Take a minute to think through the logic of the special shade of meaning the verbs in the table have in the preterite. Being acquainted (*conocer*), being able (*poder*), wanting (*querer*), and knowing (*saber*) are not actions, but states or conditions. If we "compress" these states into the single moment when they began, we can think of them as actions that initiate the state or condition. Being acquainted (*conocer*) with someone, for example, began with the action of meeting that person for the first time; knowing (*saber*) a piece of information began with the act of discovering it for the first time.

Verb	Meaning	Meaning in the preterite
conocer	to know, be acquainted with	to meet for the first time
poder	to be able	to accomplish (affirmative)
		to fail at something (negative)

Verb	Meaning	Meaning in the preterite
querer	to want	to try or intend to do something (*but be unsuccessful*) (affirmative) to refuse (negative)
saber	to know	to find out, discover, learn

Conocí a Margarita Castañeda en la fiesta. ¿La **conoces**?
Por la lluvia, no **pude** encontrar un taxi. Finalmente decidí caminar y llegué empapado.
Ayer en la reunión **supimos** el nombre del jefe nuevo, pero no lo **conocimos**. **Quiso** asistir, pero no **pudo**.

I *met* Margarita Castañeda at the party. *Do you know her?*
Because of the rain, I *was unable to* find a taxi. Finally I decided to walk, and I arrived completely drenched.
Yesterday at the meeting *we learned* the name of the new boss, but we *didn't meet* him. He *tried/wanted* to attend, but *was unable* to.

OJO: Note the use of *por* in the phrase *por la lluvia*, "on account of the rain."

Finally, the preterite is used with the expression *hace* to mean "ago."

El jefe comenzó a trabajar aquí **hace dos meses**, pero todavía no ha tenido una reunión general.

The boss started to work here ***two months ago****, but he has still not held a general meeting.*

Ponerlo a prueba

A. La fiesta que no resultó. Verónica had a party, but most of the guests she invited did not go. The next day her friends called to offer their excuses. Complete their sentences according to the model.

Modelo: Yo no pude ir porque _____ (**tener**) que estudiar.
Yo no pude ir porque tuve que estudiar.

1. David no pudo ir porque su hermano _____ (**usar**) el coche.
2. Rafael y Pablo no pudieron ir porque _____ (**tener**) que llevar a su madre a la casa de la abuela.
3. Catalina no pudo ir porque sus padres no le _____ (**permitir**) salir.
4. Osvaldo no pudo ir porque su padre le _____ (**pedir**) ayuda con un proyecto en la casa.
5. Nancy y Teresa no pudieron ir porque _____ (**estar**) en el campo todo el fin de semana.
6. Linda no pudo ir porque _____ (**ponerse:** *to become*) enferma ayer por la tarde.
7. Javier no pudo ir porque su perro _____ (**morirse**).

B. ...pero nos fue imposible. The following people have had a very frustrating day. Using the verb *querer,* find out what happened to each.

1. Bárbara y yo _____ ir al cine, pero nos fue imposible.
2. Tú _____ estudiar toda la tarde, pero te fue imposible.
3. Eliana _____ llamarte, pero le fue imposible.
4. Yo _____ llamar a Eliana también, pero me fue imposible.
5. Ustedes _____ salir a un restaurante, pero les fue imposible.

C. Un robo. Completa la siguiente historia.

El detective habla: La señora Téllez _____ (**llamar**) esta mañana a las ocho en punto. Ella _____ (**decir**): —Necesito una investigación. Hay ruidos extraños en la casa. —El jefe me _____ (**mirar**). Yo _____ (**levantarse**) de la silla, _____ (**poner**) mi café en la mesa, _____ (**buscar**) mi revólver y _____ (**salir**). _____ (**Llegar**) a la casa de los Téllez a las 8:14 en punto. _____ (**Llamar:** *to knock*) a la puerta. La señora Téllez _____ (**abrir**) la puerta. —Muchas gracias. Usted ha _____ (**venir**) muy rápido, —me _____ (**decir**). Yo _____ (**entrar**) en la casa y le _____ (**preguntar**) a la señora, —¿ _____ (**Escuchar**) Ud. ruidos ahora? ¿De dónde _____ (**venir**)? —La señora no _____ (**tener**) que responder; ella y yo _____ (**oír**) unos ruidos que venían (*were coming*) del dormitorio de enfrente. —La puerta está _____ (**cerrar**), —le dije. —Voy a entrar.—

CH. Completar el cuento. Imagine that you are the detective. Finish the story in five more sentences, including the following information.

1. what you did
2. what you saw
3. what you did then
4. what Sra. Téllez did
5. how the situation was resolved

Remember to make each of your sentences a completed action.

D. Cuéntame de tu viaje. Imagine that you have taken one of the trips described in the advertisement on page 206. Tell your partner about it. Include the following information.

- a qué hora saliste de casa
- por qué aerolínea viajaste
- qué lugares visitaste
- si alquilaste (alquilar: *to rent*) un coche
- qué lengua habló el guía
- cuánto tiempo duró el viaje
- a qué hora volviste a casa

OJO: *USD* = United States dollars.

E. ¿Qué han hecho? ¿Qué no han hecho? Talk about each of the following drawings, saying what the individuals in them have done and what they have not done.

F. Preguntas personales

1. ¿Dónde naciste?
2. ¿Qué trajiste a clase hoy en tu mochila?
3. ¿A qué hora viniste a clase hoy? ¿Llegaste temprano, a tiempo o un poco tarde?
4. Por lo general, ¿están bien organizados tus profesores? Y tú, ¿estás bien organizado/-a?
5. ¿A qué hora te acostaste anoche? ¿Cuánto tiempo dormiste?
6. La última vez que fuiste al cine, ¿qué película viste?
7. ¿En qué año aprendiste a conducir? ¿Quién te enseñó?

¡TIENES LA PALABRA!

Haz las siguientes actividades con un compañero (una compañera).

A. Los momentos culminantes. Interview a partner about

- the best (*el mejor*) concert he or she has heard
- the best (*la mejor*) movie he or she has seen
- the best (*el mejor*) book he or she has read

B. ¿Qué pasó en la fiesta? Tu amigo/-a fue a una fiesta, pero tú no pudiste ir. El día después llamas a tu amigo/-a para saber

- quiénes estuvieron allí
- qué sirvió el anfitrión (la anfitriona) para comer y beber
- si bailó mucho y con quién(es)
- si conoció a amigos nuevos
- si pasó algo interesante en la fiesta

OTRA VUELTA

Play instructor tape, 3 min.

Paco and Roberto have prepared a list of the things they are looking for in a *pensión*. Listen to the *Entrada* again and mark *Sí* if doña Josefina's *pensión* has them. If they are not mentioned, mark *No*.

La pensión Restrepo

camas sencillas	Sí	No
almuerzo incluido	Sí	No
cena incluida	Sí	No
en el centro	Sí	No
precios baratos	Sí	No
habitaciones con baño particular	Sí	No
entrada exterior	Sí	No

COMENTARIO CULTURAL

El alojamiento

En España y en la América Latina los turistas y otros viajeros pueden escoger entre varias posibilidades de alojamiento. La mayoría de los centros urbanos tienen **apartamentos** para visitas largas y **hoteles** para visitas más breves. También se puede conseguir alojamiento y comida en hoteles más pequeños y modestos, conocidos en diferentes países como **posadas, hostales** o **mesones.** Para visitas más largas hay **pensiones,** quizás la posibilidad más barata de todas. Los precios y la calidad de los lugares de alojamiento varían bastante, y por lo tanto siempre es buena idea investigar varios lugares antes de tomar una decisión definitiva.

En España, varios castillos, conventos y haciendas se han convertido en **paradores,** elegantes lugares donde el público puede cenar o pasar algunas noches. Estos lugares son de especial interés para los huéspedes que quieren aprender algo de la historia y la arquitectura de España. Muchas librerías y agencias de turismo mantienen listas de paradores, posadas y pensiones.

A continuación se dan algunas expresiones útiles.

Quisiera alquilar una habitación.

Necesitamos reservaciones para _____ noches.

¿Se puede pagar con tarjeta de crédito o con cheques de viajero?

¿En qué piso está la habitación?

¿Hay baño completo en la habitación?

¿Tenemos que compartir (*share*) el baño?

Preguntas. Imagínate que quieres alquilar una habitación en un hotel en Bogotá. ¿Cuáles son tres preguntas (además de las de arriba) que puedes hacerle al empleado del hotel?

OJO: It is quite common in Latin America and Spain for hotel guests to leave their keys at the desk when they go out. This is a convenience for guests, as well as a security measure.

La cliente le pide la llave al dependiente en la recepción, antes de subir a su habitación.

SEGUNDA ETAPA

Conociendo la vecindad

ENTRADA

Play instructor tape, 3 min.

En el restaurante

César and his friend Elena are dining at an elegant restaurant. As you listen to their conversation, try to figure out what they are ordering.

OJO: Don't worry if you can't understand exactly what César and Elena are ordering. Use your guessing skills to figure out phrases such as *término medio* and *al vapor*. Consult the end-of-chapter vocabulary only if absolutely necessary.

Una noche en el Restaurante Estrella del Mar

¿Qué van a comer César y Elena? Escribe **C** (César) o **E** (Elena) al lado de lo que pide cada uno.

_____ Sopa de hongos _____ Arvejas
_____ Sopa de ajo _____ Bróculi
_____ Ensalada de aguacate _____ Chuletas de cerdo
_____ Ensalada de lechuga y tomate _____ Langosta al vapor
_____ Arroz _____ Bistec
_____ Papas fritas _____ Pollo asado

ANTES DE LEER

Use visual clues

Knowing **what** you are reading often enables you to guess the meaning of unfamiliar words and expressions. One of the first things to notice about something you are about to read is what it looks like. Are there any pictures, drawings, or other visual clues telling what the selection is about? Remember to look at these types of nonverbal hints that may help you anticipate the content of what you are about to read.

Preparación

When a person travels to an unfamiliar city, one of the easiest ways to locate needed services is through the telephone directory (*la guía telefónica*). List at least three services or articles that you might find by consulting *la guía telefónica*.

OJO: The word *guía* has more than one meaning. *La guía* is a guidebook or directory and *el (la) guía* is a person who serves as a guide.

1.
2.
3.

Play student tape, 1 min.

Estudiar y practicar

el arreglo	*arrangement*
la jardinería	*garden shop, nursery*
la marca	*brand*
el pastel	*pastry*
la relojería	*shop that sells watches*
la sucursal	*branch office*
el surtido	*assortment, selection*

LEER

As you read the following advertisements taken from a telephone directory, make a list of the types of stores, the items sold, the services offered, and the words the vendors use to describe their goods and services.

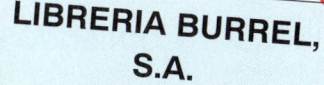

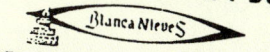

DESPUÉS DE LEER

Escribe el tipo de tienda, los productos que venden, los servicios que ofrecen y las palabras que usan los vendedores para describir sus productos y servicios.

Tienda	*Producto*	*Servicio*	*Descripción*

Ventanilla al mundo hispánico — Comiendo en casa o en la calle

OJO: The expression *en la calle* means "away from home," not necessarily "in the street."

Si eres invitado/-a en una casa en el mundo hispánico hay algunas costumbres muy comunes en casi todas partes que debes saber. La comida principal, o la comida fuerte, se come por la tarde, más o menos a las dos. Muchas veces las responsabilidades del trabajo u otras consideraciones hacen imposible que todos los miembros de la familia coman todas las comidas del día juntos. Sin embargo, todos tratan de estar en casa para la comida de la tarde. Incluso, no se llama a esta comida **el almuerzo,** sino **la comida.** Es cuando todos tratan de estar reunidos para comer y conversar. Es también la comida más grande y más formal del día.

Toda la familia se sienta a comer y nadie se levanta de la mesa antes que los otros. Después de comer muchas veces hay un período muy agradable que se llama **la sobremesa.** Durante la sobremesa todos hablan juntos. No sólo se habla de la vida de los familiares, sino también de la política o de cualquier otro tema que se presente.

Cuando una familia o un grupo de amigos come en un restaurante, se siguen las mismas normas. La gente no come con tanta prisa como en los EEUU, y una comida con su sobremesa puede durar varias horas.

This activity can be treated as a paired activity, where students ask each other questions; or, students can fill out the chart for homework and compare their responses in small groups. Discussion topic: Implications for family life of the fast-food approach to meals versus the relaxed approach.

Actividad. ¿Se parecen tus costumbres a las del mundo hispánico?

Costumbre del mundo hispánico	Frecuencia en mi familia		
	(Casi) Siempre	A veces	(Casi) Nunca
Comer la comida fuerte a las dos			
Todos los miembros de la familia comen juntos.			
Todos se quedan a la mesa durante la comida.			
Hay conversación en la mesa después de la comida.			

AUMENTAR EL VOCABULARIO

OJO: A candy shop is also *la confitería.*

el arreglo	*arrangement*
el bocadillo	*snack*
la calidad	*quality*
el diseño	*design*
dormir la siesta	*to take a nap*
la dulcería	*candy shop*
la jardinería	*garden shop*
la joyería	*jewelry store*

Segunda etapa

OJO: *La tintorería* comes from the noun *el tinte*, meaning the dye used to change the color of cloth. Literally, *la tintorería* would mean a dyer's shop.

la librería	bookstore
la mueblería	furniture store
la relojería	shop that sells watches
la sucursal	branch office
la tintorería	dry cleaners
lavar (limpiar) en seco	to dry-clean
la zapatería	shoe store
hacer compras	**to make purchases**
ir de compras	to go shopping
la marca	brand
el surtido	assortment, selection
el hogar	**house; home**
único/-a	only

LOS PRODUCTOS Y LAS TIENDAS

En la panadería
el pan (*bread*)
el panecillo (*roll*)
el pan dulce (*sweet bread*)

En la papelería
las hojas de papel (*sheets of paper*)
el sobre (*envelope*)
la tinta (*ink*)

En la lechería
la leche (*milk*)
el queso (*cheese*)
la mantequilla (*butter*)
los huevos (*eggs*)
el yogur (*yogurt*)

En la florería
la flor (*flower*)
un ramo de flores (*bouquet*)
la planta (*plant*)

En la pastelería
el pastel (*layer cake*)
la torta (*cake*)
los dulces (*sweets*)

En la carnicería
la carne de res (*beef*)
el cerdo (*pork*)
el pollo (*chicken*)
el pavo (*turkey*)
el jamón (*ham*)

En la pescadería
el pescado (*fish*)
los camarones (*shrimp*)
las almejas (*clams*)
la langosta (*lobster*)
los mariscos (*shellfish*)

Hacer compras. Lupita has to go shopping. Indicate which store she will go to in order to buy what she needs.

Modelo: Lupita necesita pan.   *Va a comprar pan en la panadería.*

1. Lupita busca un pastel de chocolate.
2. Lupita necesita yogur y huevos.
3. Lupita necesita unos sobres.
4. El vestido de Lupita está manchado (*stained*).
5. Lupita quiere comprar una planta para su abuela.
6. Lupita necesita unos panecillos.
7. Lupita quiere preparar un arroz con pollo esta noche.
8. Lupita necesita cordones para sus zapatos de tenis.
9. Lupita quiere comprar un collar (*necklace*) de perlas para el cumpleaños de su madre.
10. Lupita necesita una mesita para su dormitorio.

USO PRÁCTICO DEL ESPAÑOL   Tiendas y vendedores

In some instances, *peluquería* is used to mean barber shop.

OJO: *Pulque* is a mildly intoxicating drink that indigenous groups in Mexico had when Cortez arrived there. It is made by fermenting the juice of the agave plant. Because *pulque* cannot be stored except under refrigeration, and even then only for a rather short period of time, it is available only where it is made in the countryside, or in the *pulquerías,* where it is sold "fresh."

In Spanish, words are often made up of prefixes, roots, and suffixes. Knowing the meanings of prefixes and suffixes helps you determine the complete meaning of new words you may encounter. For example, because *-ería* is a suffix that denotes the place where an item is sold, you can guess that a *zapatería* would be a place that sells shoes, and that a *florería* would sell flowers. Similarly, because the ending *-ero/-a* indicates one who makes or sells a product, you can identify a *zapatero/-a* as a shoemaker and a *panadero/-a* as a baker.

Actividad.   Using the suffix clues from the *Uso práctico,* identify each of the following.

cantinero   pulquería
mueblería   sardinero
jardinero   tortillería
peluquería (Hint: the word *peluca* means "wig")

Ponerlo a prueba

A. **Definiciones.**   Match the words and phrases in the right-hand column with their definitions in the left-hand column.

1. la tienda donde se venden lápices
2. la tienda donde se compran las tortas, las galletas y otros dulces

a. dormir la siesta
b. la tintorería
c. la papelería

3. ir de tienda en tienda
4. descansar después de comer
5. el negocio donde hacen la limpieza en seco

ch. hacer compras
d. la pastelería

B. Clasificaciones. Organize the food items in the following categories: *productos lácteos* (*L*); *carne* (*C*); *mariscos* (*M*); and *dulces* (*D*).

_____ el pavo   _____ la torta   _____ el queso
_____ las almejas   _____ el yogur   _____ las galletas
_____ el cerdo   _____ el jamón   _____ la langosta
_____ el pastel

C. Preguntas personales

1. ¿Cuál te gusta más, la carne o el pescado?
2. ¿Te gusta la carne? ¿Qué tipo te gusta más? ¿Qué carne **no** te gusta?
3. ¿Prefieres el yogur con fruta o sin fruta?
4. ¿Cuál es tu sándwich favorito? ¿En qué consiste?
5. ¿Hay una buena pastelería cerca de la universidad? ¿Qué compras allí?
6. ¿Qué venden en la librería de tu universidad, además de libros?
7. La tintorería que usas, ¿ofrece servicio rápido? ¿Cuesta más? ¿Ofrece otros servicios, además de limpiar la ropa?
8. En el verano, ¿generalmente llevas zapatos de tenis o sandalias?
9. ¿Te gusta dormir la siesta? ¿De qué hora a qué hora?

CH. Pensamientos y planes. What are these people thinking of? What will they do?

¿En qué piensa Esteban? ¿Adónde va para comprarlo?

¿Qué ha hecho Mercedes? ¿Qué problema tiene ahora? ¿Cómo va a resolverlo?

¿Cómo está el niño? ¿Qué quiere hacer la madre?

Remind students that this activity uses the present perfect tense that was presented in the first *etapa*.

D. ¿Qué han hecho? Several friends show up at your door, each one carrying a package. Try to guess where each person has been and what he or she did there. ¡Usa la imaginación!

Modelo: Miguel tiene un libro.
Miguel ha ido a la librería y ha comprado un diccionario bilingüe español-inglés.

1. Sarita y Amalia traen un pastel.
2. Jorge tiene su traje envuelto (*wrapped*) en plástico.
3. Arturo tiene un paquete de camarones.
4. Laura tiene una torta de chocolate.
5. Alicia tiene un par de zapatos nuevos.
6. Alfredo y Enrique traen un ramo de flores.

INVESTIGAR LA GRAMÁTICA   El complemento directo

The direct object (*el complemento directo*) is the word or phrase that usually answers the question "What?" or "Whom?" with respect to the verb.

Rafael compró **un periódico** y **lo** leyó.
Manuela decidió ver **la película nueva que ponen en el Cine Rex** y **la** vio anoche.
Ramón buscó a **Manuela** en el cine y **la** encontró fácilmente.

Rafael bought a newspaper and read it.
Manuela decided to see the new film they are showing at the Rex Theater and she saw it last night.
Ramón looked for Manuela in the theater and found her easily.

OJO: When the direct object is a person, the personal *a* is absorbed into the direct object pronoun.

You can see that the first part of each example answers, respectively, the questions, "What did Rafael buy," "What did Manuela decide to see," and "Whom did Ramón look for." The second part of each sentence tells what happened next.

As you can see from these examples, when the direct object (the "what" or the "whom") has already been mentioned earlier in the sentence (*el periódico, la película nueva, Manuela*), a direct object pronoun is used in the second part of the sentence to avoid repeating the noun.

The form of the direct object pronoun depends on the noun that it replaces.

Singular
me me
te you (fam.)
lo you (form.), him, it (m)
la you (form.), her, it (f)

Plural
nos us
os you (fam.)
los you (form.), them (m/f)
las you (form.), them (f)

Direct object pronouns are placed directly in front of a conjugated verb.

—¿Tienes mi **lápiz** y **papel**?
—Sí, pero no **los** veo ahora.

*Do you have my **pencil** and **paper**?*
*Yes, but I don't see **them** now.*

Segunda etapa

—Pues, ¿no **los** usaste anoche? *Well, didn't you use **them** last night?*
—Sí. Creo que **los** dejé en mi escritorio. *Yes, I think I left **them** on my desk.*

OJO: Tip: Put pronouns (direct object, reflexive, etc.) in front of conjugated verb forms or after infinitives and gerunds.

In the case of infinitives (*-r* forms) or gerunds (*-ndo* forms, which you will learn about in Chapter 6), the direct object pronouns are either attached at the end of the infinitive or gerund or are placed in front of the auxiliary verb.

Tengo una manzana. Tengo que comer**la** ahora porque tengo mucha hambre. *I have an apple. I have to eat it now because I am really hungry.*

Tengo una manzana. **La** tengo que comer ahora porque tengo mucha hambre.

No puedes comer**la** ahora; el profesor va a ver**te**. *You can't eat it now; the teacher will see you.*

No **la** puedes comer ahora; el profesor **te** va a ver.

Tienes razón. Voy a comer**la** después de la clase. *You're right. I'll eat it after class*

Tienes razón. **La** voy a comer después de la clase.

Ponerlo a prueba

Have students identify the noun to which each pronoun refers.

A. ¿Dónde están? Nelson is a forgetful type and never remembers where anything is. Each time he asks, give him the same response, following the model.

Modelo: ¿Dónde está mi libro?   *No sé, tienes que buscarlo.*

1. ¿Dónde están mis boletos? El concierto es esta noche.
2. ¿Dónde está mi toalla? Quiero ducharme.
3. ¿Dónde está el jabón (*soap*)? Quiero lavar la ropa.
4. ¿Dónde están las manzanas? Tengo hambre.
5. ¿Dónde están los bocadillos que compré anoche? Pienso llevarlos a la fiesta esta noche.
6. ¿Dónde están los sobres que me dio Lupita? Tengo que mandar unas cartas.
7. ¿Dónde está la pluma que puse en la mesa? La necesito.
8. ¿Dónde está la guía telefónica? Quiero llamar a la pastelería.

B. Escenas en el consulado. Francisco is in the consulate because he needs a visa to study in the United States. Use the pronoun that corresponds to the direct object in each sentence.

Modelo: Francisco busca información.   *Francisco la busca.*

1. Francisco espera a la oficial.
2. La oficial ayuda a Francisco.

3. Francisco necesita la visa para estudiar en los Estados Unidos.
4. Francisco saca su tarjeta de identidad.
5. Francisco lee los papeles.
6. Francisco firma los papeles.

C. Las instrucciones. María Elena is getting ready for a party and her sister is helping. Give instructions to the sister, according to the model.

Modelo: ¿Y los platos? ¿Qué hago con ellos? (lavar)
Bueno, debes lavarlos ahora, por favor.

1. ¿Y las sillas? ¿Qué hago con ellas? (poner en la sala)
2. ¿Y los discos? ¿Qué hago con ellos? (poner al lado del tocadiscos)
3. ¿Y las bebidas? ¿Qué hago con ellas? (poner en el refrigerador)
4. ¿Y la ensalada? ¿Qué hago con ella? (poner en el refrigerador también)
5. ¿Y la sala? ¿Qué hago con ella? (limpiar)
6. ¿Y las toallas? ¿Qué hago con ellas? (colgar en el baño)

CH. No te oigo bien. In each of the following situations you are not sure you heard the other person's question correctly, so you repeat the essential information before responding. Follow the model, adding new information in each situation.

Modelo: —¿Tienes mi libro? —¿Tu libro? No, no...
—No, no lo tengo. Creo que Marta lo tiene.

1. —¿Dónde vas a pasar las vacaciones?
   —¿Las vacaciones? Voy a...
2. —¿Piensas ver a Julio allí?
   —¿A Julio? No, no pienso...
3. —¿Necesitas pasaporte y visa?
   —¿Pasaporte y visa? Sí,...
4. —¿Y los abuelos? ¿Acompañan a la familia?
   —¿Nuestros abuelos? No, no...
5. —¿Dónde está Felipe? ¿Tiene los boletos para el concierto?
   —¿Los boletos? Sí,...

D. Diálogos. The following dialogues illustrate what happens when direct object pronouns are **not** used. As you notice, the language sounds very artificial. Work with a partner to see if you can make these dialogues sound more natural by replacing the direct object nouns with pronouns wherever possible.

1. En casa
   —¡Federico, limpia tu cuarto ahora mismo!

—¡Ay, mamá, no quiero limpiar mi cuarto ahora! Estoy escuchando el estéreo.

—Quiero que apagues (*I want you to turn off*) el estéreo inmediatamente.

—¡Ay, mamá! No quiero apagar el estéreo ahora.

2. En la residencia estudiantil

—¿Adónde vas, Sofía?

—Al centro, con Carolina Pérez. ¿Conoces a Carolina Pérez?

—No, no conozco a Carolina Pérez. ¿Vas a recoger a Carolina Pérez?

—Sí, ¿por qué?

—¿Puedes dejar mi chaqueta en la tintorería?

—Sí, cómo no. ¿Para cuándo quieres la chaqueta?

—Necesito la chaqueta para el viernes. Muchas gracias, Sofía.

Divide into groups of three and prepare the following conversations.

A. En el restaurante.   (Para tres personas.) A y B son amigos y entran en un restaurante. C es el mesero (la mesera).

1. A asks the waiter (C) for a table for two.
2. B adds that they want a table near the window.
3. C says that there is a table.
4. A and B thank the waiter.

B. Hablando con el mesero (la mesera).   A y B son los clientes; C es el mesero (la mesera). Si es posible, usen accesorios (*props*).

1. C offers A and B menus.
2. A and B thank C.
3. A asks B what he or she plans to order.
4. B asks A for a recommendation.
5. A and B give their orders to C.

OTRA VUELTA

Play instructor tape, 3 min.

Now listen again to the conversation between César and Elena that you heard at the beginning of this *etapa*. Make a list of three complimentary things that the couple says to each other about their night out.

COMENTARIO CULTURAL

La vida escolar

El español y el inglés usan diferentes palabras para describir los diferentes tipos de escuelas. Es más, no hay gran uniformidad de terminología entre los países hispanohablantes. Algunos tipos de escuela que son comunes en los EEUU, como *middle school* y *community college,* no existen en el mundo hispánico. Por lo tanto, no hay palabras para ellos en español. Otras escuelas, como **la escuela primaria,** sí existen en los países hispánicos, pero ofrecen programas diferentes a los de las *elementary schools* en los EEUU. En los países hispánicos las escuelas primarias pueden incluir los grados 1 a 8. Las clases por lo general son más grandes que en los EEUU y el proceso de instrucción es más tradicional, con más énfasis en la memorización y la recitación.

Hay varios términos para *high school,* es decir, los grados 9 a 12. Uno que se usa mucho, **el colegio,** es a veces confuso para las personas de habla inglesa. Si la escuela prepara a los estudiantes para la universidad, es posible que se llame **la preparatoria.** El término más generalizado para *high school* es **la escuela secundaria.** En algunos países de la América Latina se usa el término **el liceo** para referirse a una escuela secundaria pública.

En México la escuela primaria abarca los grados 1 a 6. Después viene la escuela secundaria (grados 7 a 9), y finalmente la preparatoria o **el bachillerato** (grados 10 a 12).

Las nociones de *college* y *university* se expresan indistintamente en español con la palabra **universidad.** Con cualquiera de estas palabras, sin embargo, si estás hablando en español acerca del sistema educativo de los EEUU, vas a tener que explicar lo que quieres decir y no depender de ninguna traducción directa del inglés.

This builds on the information presented in the *Ventanilla al mundo hispánico* section of Chapter 2, first *etapa*.

¿Dónde estudian? Paco and Roberto are discussing their friends and relatives. Indicate what type of school each one attends.

Modelo: La hermanita de Elena tiene 10 años.
Estudia en la primaria, ¿verdad?

1. Carmencita Meléndez tiene 17 años.
2. Jorge Plata tiene 22 años y quiere ser veterinario.
3. El nieto de la profesora Suárez tiene siete años y vive en Monterrey.
4. Fernando y Josué tienen 19 y 20 años, respectivamente.
5. Alma Cuevas vive en San Antonio y está en el décimo (*tenth*) grado.

TERCERA ETAPA

La cita con Carmencita

ENTRADA

Play instructor tape, 2 min.

En el restaurante Casa María

Roberto and Carmencita have been to see the movie *Lo que el viento se llevó* and are now seated in *Casa María* preparing to order their meals. As you listen, notice

- what they order for their main course
- what they decide on for dessert

Una noche en Casa María

¿Qué piden Roberto (**R**) y Carmencita (**C**)?

Menu prices are in Colombian pesos. You may want to have students check the exchange rate table on page 243 and calculate the cost of items in U.S. dollars.

The next section is based on this menu. The *Entrada* is optional, but using it will familiarize students with the items on the menu before they begin the following activities.

MENU

Entradas
Cóctel de frutas	1085
Espárragos con mayonesa	930

Sopas
Sopa de ajo	1165
Sopa de cebolla a la francesa	775
Consomé	930

Ensaladas
Ensalada de lechuga y tomate	620
Ensalada de aguacate	1000
Ensalada rusa	930

Legumbres
Arvejas	695
Bróculi	850
Zanahorias	620

Carnes y aves
Bistec a la parrilla	4650
Chuletas de cerdo con frutas	3100
Pollo asado	2480

Pescado y mariscos
Camarones con salsa verde	3410
Langosta al vapor	4960
Lenguado al horno	4805
Trucha a la parrilla	2635

se sirve con arroz o papas fritas

Postres
Flan	930
Helados	1000
Sorbete de limón	930
Torta de chocolate	1240

ANTES DE LEER Y ESCRIBIR

Play student tape, 1 min.

OJO: These vocabulary items are the headings from the menu. You already know *el pescado* (fish) and *los mariscos* (shellfish).

Estudiar y practicar

el ave (f)	*poultry*
la carne	*meat*
la ensalada	*salad*
la entrada	*appetizer*
la legumbre	*vegetable*
el postre	*dessert*
la sopa	*soup*

Preparación

Now look at the menu selections more carefully. See how many entries you can figure out. Some are cognates (*cóctel de frutas, bróculi*), and others may be words you already know (*flan, camarones*). Write down one or two items for each menu category whose meaning you know, items that you would order if you were dining in *Casa María*.

OJO: Consult the vocabulary list at the end of this chapter only if absolutely necessary. Remember that you do not need to understand every item on the menu at this point, but only one or two that you like in each category.

Entradas:

Sopas:

Ensaladas:

Legumbres:

Carnes y aves:

Pescado y mariscos:

Postres:

WRITING STRATEGY 5

In order to impress on your students the importance of writing and rewriting, you may want to devote some class time to the initial preparation of a composition and then to a rewrite.

Work on writing and rewriting

In the Reading Strategy of Chapter 4, second *etapa*, you were advised to read over the material twice—the first time to get an overview, and the second time to find specific information. A similar strategy is helpful in writing. For your first draft, write down everything you want to say, no matter how inelegant it might seem. Then, using your dictionary as needed, go over it again until you have written what you want to say. Your third approach to your text will be to check for mechanics—subject-verb and noun-adjective agreements, correct verb tenses, spelling, and accent marks. Then put your paper aside for several hours, or overnight. When you go back to it with a fresh eye, look at each idea, and decide whether to add more detail. Make sure that your paper is coherent, with a logical succession of main ideas and supporting information. Finally, check one more time for mechanics before you turn in your *obra maestra* (masterpiece).

ESCRIBIR

Imagine that you and a companion ate last night at *Casa María* and that you are writing a report on the restaurant for a Spanish-language newspaper at your col-

Tercera etapa

OJO: Because you will write about these events as being over and done with, be sure to use the preterite.

lege or university. Write the report as a well-organized narration and include the following information.

- adónde fuiste y con quién
- cuándo fueron
- qué pediste
- qué pidió tu compañero/-a
- cómo estuvo (*tasted*) la comida
- cómo fue el servicio
- cuánto costó la comida

AUMENTAR EL VOCABULARIO

OJO: To order your steak rare, ask for it *poco cocido*; medium is *término medio*; well-done is *muy cocido*.

OJO: Some other words you may find useful are *el ave*, poultry; *a la parrilla*, grilled; *al horno*, baked; *asado/-a*, roasted; *los espárragos*, asparagus; *el hongo*, mushroom.

OJO: Another word for "appetizer" is *el entremés*.

OJO: The names of foods often vary from one country to another. For example, other words you may hear for "mushroom" are *el champiñón* and *la seta*. Another word for "peas" is *los guisantes*.

OJO: The verb *probar* also means to try on clothes. *La prueba,* a quiz or test, is literally a trial of one's skill or knowledge.

la carne — meat
   el bistec — steak
   la chuleta (de cerdo) — (pork) chop
   el lomito — loin (of beef or pork)
la entrada — appetizer
la legumbre — vegetable
   el aguacate — avocado
   las arvejas — peas
   el brócoli — broccoli
   la ensalada — salad
   las judías — green beans
   la lechuga — lettuce
   la zanahoria — carrot
el (la) mesero/-a — waiter
picante — spicy, hot
   soso/-a — bland, flavorless
el postre — dessert
   el flan — caramel custard
   el helado — ice cream
probar (ue) — to taste
la sopa — soup
la trucha — trout
   el lenguado — sole

VENTANILLA AL MUNDO HISPÁNICO   La comida del mundo hispánico

Muchas personas piensan que todos los hispanohablantes comen el mismo tipo de comida, y que todas las comidas de origen español son picantes. Las dos ideas son incorrectas. Cada país del mundo hispánico tiene sus propias comidas regionales y nacionales. Hay gran variedad de ingredientes y condimentos que se añaden a la comida de cada lugar. Generalmente los productos locales influyen sobre el tipo de comida de cada lugar; quienes viven cerca del mar tienen platos que incluyen pescado y mariscos y quienes viven en el interior del país cuentan con productos que crecen en su región.

Las dos recetas siguientes ilustran las diferencias culinarias entre los países del mundo hispánico.

Paella a la valenciana (para 6 a 8)

Ingredientes

500 g de arroz	12 almejas
un pollo pequeño o una langosta mediana	2 pimientos rojos (frescos o de conserva)
200 g de lomo	100 g de cebolla
100 g de salchichas	2 o 3 dientes de ajo
300 g de calamares	2 decilitros de aceite
150 g de langostinos	2 ramitos de perejil
200 g de guisantes frescos	5 o 6 hebras (*thread, fiber*) de azafrán
200 g de tomate (fresco o de conserva)	5 g de pimentón
	4 tazas de agua
100 g de judías verdes	2 tazas de arroz

Póngase la paella al fuego con el aceite y fríase el pollo, el lomo y las salchichas, todo cortado a trozos. Una vez fritos, se sacarán de la paella, y en ella se pondrá la langosta y los calamares (cortados a trozos), los langostinos y las almejas (que previamente se habrán abierto). Una vez fritos se retiran también de la paella, donde se pondrá la cebolla muy picada y los dientes de ajo aplastados. Cocínese durante unos minutos, agregando seguidamente los tomates y pimientos mondados y sin pepitas. Cocínese todo unos minutos más, sazonándolo con sal y pimentón, añadiéndole luego toda la fritada (carnes y pescados), que se dejará cocer un poco más antes de añadir el agua que previamente se habrá calculado a razón de 2 tazas escasas de agua por cada taza de arroz. Añádanse las judías verdes, que se habrán hervido previamente. Combínense un diente de ajo, las hebras de azafrán y el perejil y póngase también en el guiso. Échese el arroz. A medio cocer se revuelve un poco con una cuchara de madera, se adorna con unos langostinos y unas tiritas de pimiento encarnado, y ya no se toca más hasta que termine de cocer.

Antes de servirlo se deja en reposo cerca del fuego durante diez minutos, añadiendo perejil picado muy fino.

OJO: Do not be concerned if you don't understand the recipe completely. Use your knowledge of cooking to figure out what the verbs mean.

Tercera etapa

> ### *Caldo tlalpeño (para 4)*
>
> Ingredientes
>
> Litro y medio de caldo de pollo   2 cucharadas de cebolla picada
> 1 cucharada de cilantro picado   1 chile serrano picado
> 2 tazas de arroz blanco cocido   sal y aceite
> 1 aguacate en rodajas
>
> En una cucharada de aceite en una cacerola sofría la cebolla, sin dorarse. Añada el arroz y fríalo ligeramente. Agregue el caldo hirviendo y sazone con sal.
>
> Haga hervir la sopa durante diez minutos, y luego, al servirla, póngale el cilantro, el aguacate y el chile serrano picado.

LOS CONDIMENTOS

la salsa de tomate
la mostaza

la sal

la pimienta

el ajo

la cebolla

el aliño

el aceite, el vinagre

¿Qué condimentos usas?   Indicate which condiments you use when you eat the following foods.

1. una hamburguesa
2. la ensalada
3. las papas fritas
4. los huevos
5. el bróculi
6. la pizza

USO PRÁCTICO DEL ESPAÑOL   Más sobre el verbo **gustar**

The purpose of this Uso práctico and Actividad A that follows is to give a limited, controlled introduction to indirect object pronouns and to focus on the problematic gustar construction. Ordinarily we do not include translation exercises in Entradas, but in this case we take a cognitive approach in order to address directly the error that arises from English interference.

You saw in Chapter 2 that the verb *gustar* and some other verbs that indicate a personal reaction to something (*encantar, interesar*) have a structure different from the usual **subject + verb + object**:

Me **encantan** los mariscos.   *I love seafood.*
No me **gusta** la carne de res; tiene mucha grasa.   *I don't like beef; it has a lot of fat.*

With these verbs, the subject is the topic of interest or attention (in these examples, *los mariscos* and *la carne de res*). As you can see, the verb *encantan* in the first example is plural because it agrees with *los mariscos*. In the second example, *gusta* is singular because it agrees with *la carne de res*.

In the *Investigar la gramática* section of this *etapa* you will learn how to use indirect object pronouns, and you will understand more about the structure of these *gustar* sentences. Here is an example.

Me gusta el pollo.

Literally, this sentence means "Chicken is pleasing to me." *Me*, or "to me," is the indirect object because it answers the question, To whom? with respect to the verb *gustar*.

The indirect object pronoun that means "to him," "to her," and "to you (*usted*)" is *le*. As you can see, using the pronoun by itself can be ambiguous.

No **le** gusta el pollo.

Who doesn't like chicken? It is not clear. To avoid ambiguity, you need to add the phrase *a* + **noun/name** in addition to the indirect object pronoun *le*.

A Miguel no **le** gusta el pollo.   *Miguel does not like chicken.*
A Cristina no **le** gustan los mariscos.   *Cristina does not like seafood.*

Ponerlo a prueba

A. **Entre gustos no hay disputa** (*There's no accounting for taste*). Express the following in Spanish. Remember that the verb is singular when the subject is an infinitive or even a series of infinitives.

1. I am very interested in Mexican cuisine (*la cocina*).
2. Do you like Mexican food, Sra. Hurtado?
3. My aunt does not like spicy food, although she loves tortillas with cheese.
4. My friend Luis is a good cook (*cocinero*); he loves to prepare Mexican dishes.
5. I don't like his enchiladas, but I do like his garlic soup.

Tercera etapa **227**

OJO: The word *el pez* is a fish in its natural state. *El pescado* is a food item. Note that it literally means "fished," from the verb *pescar*.

B. **Definiciones.** Choose the word or expression from the *Aumentar el vocabulario* section that best matches each of the following definitions.

1. dos líquidos que se usan en la preparación del aliño
2. un pez (*fish*) que se encuentra en los lagos (*lakes*)
3. la persona que sirve la comida en un restaurante
4. un postre frío que se hace con leche, huevos y azúcar
5. dos legumbres que se encuentran comúnmente en las ensaladas
6. una legumbre de olor y sabor tan fuertes que irrita los ojos de la persona que la corta
7. el primer plato que se come en un restaurante
8. una legumbre larga, delgada y verde

C. **Preguntas personales**

1. Cuando comes en un restaurante, ¿generalmente pagas en efectivo (*in cash*) o con una tarjeta de crédito?
2. ¿Qué tipos de comida te gustan más?
3. ¿Piensas cenar en un restaurante la semana que viene? ¿Adónde piensas ir?
4. En la comida que preparan tus padres en casa, ¿qué condimentos usan? ¿Es popular el ajo en tu casa?
5. ¿Pones aliño en la ensalada? ¿Qué tipo de aliño prefieres?
6. ¿Has trabajado alguna vez de mesero/-a? En tu opinión, ¿cuál es el aspecto más difícil del trabajo?

Have students extend the mini-dialogues into longer conversations.

CH. **En el restaurante.** Complete the following mini-dialogues that take place in a restaurant.

1. Pidiendo la comida

   Mesera: ¿Qué desean esta noche?
   Esposa: ¿ _____ ?
   Mesera: Ah, el plato del día es _____ .
   Esposa: Suena riquísimo/-a. Por favor, ¿ _____ ?

2. Durante la comida

   Esposo: ¿Me puedes pasar _____ y _____ ? El pescado está un poco soso.
   Esposa: Sí, cómo no. Todo está delicioso, ¿verdad?

OJO: Note that the *esposa* uses *estar* to comment about the food. This means that she likes how it has been prepared, and how her particular portion tastes.

3. Viene la mesera

   Mesera: Cómo está todo?
   Esposa: Muy rico, gracias. Pero ¿me puede traer _____ para las papas fritas?

Point out *las rejas, las plantas,* and *el patio* that students have already learned. Explain the system of forks to rate restaurants (*el símbolo de cuatro tenedores significa un restaurante excelente*) and point out that this is *un restaurante de tres tenedores.* Have students guess what a *hostelería* is.

En los patios de muchos restaurantes los clientes pueden sentarse al sol o a la sombra.

INVESTIGAR LA GRAMÁTICA   El complemento indirecto

The indirect object (*el complemento indirecto*) of a verb usually indicates the person who, for better or worse, is affected by the action of the verb. Very often the indirect object answers the question "To whom?" or "For whom?" with respect to the verb.

The forms of the *complemento indirecto* are as follows:

me	(to/for) me		**nos**	(to/for) us
te	(to/for) you		**os**	(to/for) you
le	(to/for) him/her/you		**les**	(to/for) them/you

Roberto **le** dio unas flores a Carmencita.   *Roberto gave Carmencita some flowers.*
El mesero **nos** sirvió una ensalada riquísima.   *The waiter served us a delicious salad.*

Indirect objects are almost always used with verbs of communication (*decir, informar, escribir*), verbs of asking (*pedir, preguntar*), verbs of counseling (*recomen-*

Tercera etapa

dar, sugerir [to suggest]), and verbs of giving (*dar, regalar, servir*). As with other pronouns you know, indirect object pronouns are attached to infinitives.

—Paco, quiero pregunta**rte** algo. Quiero regalar**le** algo a Carmencita. ¿Qué **me** recomiendas?
—¿Por qué no **le** regalas unas flores? Hay una florería en la esquina.

Sometimes it is necessary to clarify to whom the indirect object pronoun refers. To do this, you add a phrase consisting of the word *a* plus the identifying noun or pronoun. For example, in the preceding exchange, Roberto says: —*Quiero regalarle algo a Carmencita.* He has to add the phrase *a Carmencita*, because the pronoun *le* in *Quiero regalarle algo* could mean "I want to give **him** something," "I want to give **her** something," or "I want to give **you** something." In the absence of a context, we do not know to whom the pronoun *le* refers. In contrast, when Paco responds, *¿Por qué no le regalas unas flores?*, it is clear from the context that *le* refers to Carmencita.

Sometimes you want to focus attention on the person affected rather than on the action, or to make a contrast between one person and another.

A ti te encantan los mariscos, pero **a mí** no **me** gustan nada.

This sentence would be comprehensible and correct without the clarifying phrases *a ti* and *a mí*. The phrases emphasize the contrast between the tastes of the two people.

When you use the clarifying phrase *a* + **noun/pronoun,** remember that you must also use the indirect object pronoun. The clarifying phrase is optional, but almost always if there is an indirect object in your sentence, the indirect object pronoun is obligatory.

OJO: Here are the forms of the pronouns to be used in the clarifying phrase **a + pronoun**:
a mí   a nosotros/-as
a ti   a vosotros/-as
a él   a ellos
a ella a ellas
a usted a ustedes

These forms are the same as the forms of the subject pronouns with the exception of *mí* and *ti*. Note that *ti* never has a written accent.

OJO: There are three indirect object pronouns in the cartoon. Identify them and explain to yourself how they are used. Hint: *Quedar bien* means "to fit, go well," and has the same structure as *gustar*. If you like the way a sweater fits you, you would say *Me queda bien este suéter.*

Expansion: Have students say what they will really give these people or others for their birthdays. Follow-up: Have students give each other "gifts" with the phrase *"X, te regalo este Y."* The giver should add a sentence describing the gift, its use, or the reason for selecting it. The receiver should respond appropriately.

Ponerlo a prueba

A. **Los regalos.**   Imagine that these people are your relatives or friends. What will you give them for their next birthday?

Modelo: tu hermanito de doce años
A mi hermanito le voy a regalar una pelota de béisbol.

1. tu hermanito de doce años
2. tus tíos que viven en Alaska
3. tu abuela
4. unos amigos que viven en Los Ángeles
5. tu padre
6. dos primos que estudian español
7. tus vecinos
8. una amiga que va a Puerto Rico

a. un libro de cocina
b. una planta
c. una pelota de béisbol
ch. una foto de tu familia
d. un gato o un perro
e. un traje de baño
f. un pastel de chocolate
g. una copia de *Entradas*

B. **"No les voy a regalar..."** Now indicate what you will **not** buy for each person, and say why. Note that you can say either *no voy a darle* or *no le voy a dar*.

Modelo: *A mi hermanito de doce años no voy a darle un traje de baño porque no sabe nadar.*

C. **Un día con la abuelita.** Rosalinda loves her grandmother. What does she do when she visits her?

Modelo: leer el periódico   *Le lee el periódico.*

1. llevar unos regalitos
2. preparar el café
3. servir el almuerzo
4. dar las noticias de la familia
5. limpiar la sala
6. prometer volver otro día

OJO: Formulate your questions as follows: *¿Te gusta(n)...?* Respond in a complete sentence to each question.

CH. **Encuesta: La comida.** You work part-time for a market research firm and have a survey to administer to your friends. Find one other person and ask the questions needed to fill out the following brief survey.

Producto		
los postres en general	Sí	No
el helado	Sí	No
las frutas	Sí	No
el yogur	Sí	No
la combinación de yogur con fruta	Sí	No

Now report to the class on your partner's responses. After a number of people have reported, decide as a group whether to recommend that the company produce *Yofruta*, a fruit-flavored frozen yogurt product (*yogur congelado con fruta*).

La fiesta de sorpresa. Two friends are planning a surprise party for a third friend, Mariluz. Develop the following telephone conversation with a partner.

Estudiante A
1. Call your friend on the phone. Greet him or her.
2. You are in charge of the food. Find out if your friend knows what kind of food Mariluz likes.
3. Thank your friend for the suggestions.
4. Respond to the question, since you know what kind of music Mariluz likes.
5. Suggest a date to get together (*reunirse*) to go over the plans.

Estudiante B
1. Answer the phone. Respond to the greeting.
2. Respond to the question, since you know what kind of food Mariluz likes.
3. You are in charge of the music. Find out if your friend knows what kind of music Mariluz likes.
4. Thank your friend for the suggestions.
5. Agree on a date to get together to go over the plans.

OTRA VUELTA

Play instructor tape, 2 min.

Now listen again to the conversation between Roberto and Carmencita that you heard at the beginning of this *etapa*. As you listen, write down

- the specials that the waiter recommends
- how the waiter asks if they are ready to order
- two phrases that can be used to order food or drink

COMENTARIO CULTURAL

El pan

Cuando en los Estados Unidos usamos la palabra en inglés *bread*, pensamos primero en el pan blanco, cortado en rebanadas (*slices*) uniformes, y envuelto en plástico. Ese tipo de pan existe en la América Latina y en España, aunque no es muy común. Se llama **pan de molde.** Cuando un hispanohablante usa la palabra **pan,** probablemente está pensando en un pan relativamente largo y grueso (*thick*) (más or menos de 12 a 30 cm de largo y de 5 a 8 cm de grueso) que no se hizo en un molde, que no está partido en rebanadas y que no se vende envuelto en plástico. Ya que este tipo de pan está hecho de harina (*flour*), levadura (*yeast*) y agua solamente, se compra y se come el mismo día.

Estas dos palabras, **el pan** y *bread,* son un buen ejemplo de cómo se relacionan la lengua y la cultura. No es suficiente traducir (*translate*) y decir que **pan** significa lo mismo que *bread;* es también importante comprender lo que la palabra **pan** significa culturalmente para un hispanohablante.

Actividad. Trabajando con tu profesor(a) o en grupos pequeños, piensa en otras palabras que tienen connotaciones diferentes en inglés y en español. **La fiesta** es un buen ejemplo para comenzar.

Play video

Program 5 *Ricos sabores*
Regional foods and dishes

A. **¿Un restaurante excelente?** Choose a restaurant that you know well (a local hangout, or even McDonald's, or the cafeteria of your college or university). Write a short review of the restaurant, describing

- the variety of food
- the quality of the food
- the service
- the atmosphere (*el ambiente*)

B. **Una noche en Casa María.** Refer to the menu at the beginning of the third *etapa.* Imagine that two friends are eating there. Write a very brief one-act play, entirely in dialogue, in which the diners order their meal, the waiter brings it, and something unexpected happens.

C. **Mini-drama.** A friend of yours has just moved to your neighborhood and needs information on life there. Answer his or her questions about

- si hay una buena panadería
- hasta qué hora están abiertas las tiendas
- dónde está la tintorería

CH. **Cosas prestadas.** With a partner, develop the following telephone conversation.

Actividades de integración

Estudiante A

1. Call your friend on the phone. Greet him or her.
2. Ask how your friend is.
3. Ask your friend if he or she can lend (*prestar*) you his or her car.
4. Explain why you need the car.
5. Thank your friend and say good-bye.

Estudiante B

1. Answer the phone.
2. Respond to the pleasantries.
3. Find out why your friend needs your car.
4. Agree to lend (*prestar*) your car.
5. Say good-bye.

D. Un trabajo para el verano. Act out the following scene with a partner. A university student has an appointment with the placement counselor (*el consejero o la consejera*) to discuss a summer job.

El consejero (La consejera)

1. Greet the student.
2. Ask what type of work the student has thought about.
3. Find out whether the student has done this type of work before.
4. Give the student an application (*una solicitud*) to fill out.

El (La) estudiante

1. Greet the counselor.
2. Tell the counselor what type of work you have thought about.
3. Talk about your work experience.
4. Take the application and thank the counselor for his or her help.

VOCABULARIO

Las tiendas y sus productos

carnicería (f)   *butcher shop*
ave (f)   *poultry*
bistec (m)   *steak*
carne (f)   *meat*
carne (f) de res   *beef*
cerdo (m)   *pork*
chuleta (f) (de cerdo)   *(pork) chop*
jamón (m)   *ham*
lomito (m)   *loin (of beef or pork)*
pavo (m)   *turkey*
pollo (m)   *chicken*

dulcería (f)   *candy shop*
flan (m)   *caramel custard*
helado (m)   *ice cream*
postre (m)   *dessert*

florería (f)   *flower shop*
flor (f)   *flower*
jardinería (f)   *garden shop, nursery*
planta (f)   *plant*
ramo (m) de flores   *bouquet of flowers*

joyería (f)   *jewelry store*

lechería (f)   *dairy*
huevo (m)   *egg*
leche (f)   *milk*
mantequilla (f)   *butter*
queso (m)   *cheese*
yogur (m)   *yogurt*

librería (f)   *bookstore*

mueblería (f)   *furniture store*

panadería (f)   *bakery, bread store*
pan (m)   *bread*

pan (m) dulce   *sweet bread*
panecillo (m)   *roll*

papelería (f)   *stationery store*
hoja (f) de papel   *sheet of paper*
sobre (m)   *envelope*
tinta (f)   *ink*

pastelería (f)   *pastry shop*
dulces (m pl)   *sweets*
pastel (m)   *layer cake, pastry*
torta (f)   *cake*

pescadería (f)   *fish store*
almeja (f)   *clam*
camarones (m pl)   *shrimp*
langosta (f)   *lobster*
langostina (f)   *prawn*
lenguado (m)   *sole*
mariscos (m pl)   *shellfish*
pescado (m)   *fish*
trucha (f)   *trout*

relojería (f)   *shop that sells watches*

tintorería (f)   *dry cleaners*
lavar (limpiar) en seco   *to dry-clean*

zapatería (f)   *shoe store*

Las legumbres
Vegetables

aguacate (m)   *avocado*
arvejas (f pl)   *peas*
bróculi (m)   *broccoli*
ensalada (f)   *salad*
espárragos (m pl)   *asparagus*
hongo (m)   *mushroom*
judías (f, pl)   *green beans*

lechuga (f)   *lettuce*
zanahoria (f)   *carrot*

Los condimentos
Condiments

aceite (m)   *oil*
ajo (m)   *garlic*
aliño (m)   *salad dressing*
azafrán (m)   *saffron*
cebolla (f)   *onion*
mostaza (f)   *mustard*
pimienta (f)   *pepper*
sal (f)   *salt*
vinagre (m)   *vinegar*

Las profesiones

cirujano/-a (m/f)   *surgeon*
contador(a) (m/f)   *accountant*
dueño/-a (m/f)   *owner*
enfermero/-a (m/f)   *nurse*
gerente (m/f)   *manager*
médico/-a (m/f)   *doctor*
mesero/-a (m/f)   *waiter*
modista (f)   *dressmaker, seamstress*
periodista (m/f)   *journalist*
sastre (m)   *tailor*

La vecindad/ El vecindario
The neighborhood

acera (f)   *sidewalk*
bocacalle (f)   *intersection*
esquina (f)   *corner*
farol (m)   *streetlight*
jardín (m)   *garden*

letrero (m)   (*information*) *sign*
patio (m)   *courtyard, yard*
reja (f)   *grillwork*
semáforo (m)   *traffic light*
señal (f)   *traffic sign*
vecino/-a (m/f)   *neighbor*

Sustantivos útiles

arreglo (m)   *arrangement*
bocadillo (m)   *snack*
calidad (f)   *quality*
diseño (m)   *design*
entrada (f)   *appetizer*
hogar (m)   *house; home*
huésped(a) (m/f)   *guest* (*in a hotel*)
invitado/-a (m/f)   *guest* (*in a home*)

marca (f)   *brand*
operación (f)   *operation*
periódico (m)   *newspaper*
revista (f)   *magazine*
sopa (f)   *soup*
sucursal (f)   *branch office*
surtido (m)   *assortment, selection*

Palabras útiles

a la parrilla   *grilled*
al horno   *baked*
al lado de   *next to*
asado/-a   *roasted*
bien cocido   *well done*
enfermo/-a   *sick*
jubilado/-a   *retired*
picante   *spicy, hot*

poco cocido   *rare*
soso/-a   *bland, flavorless*
término medio   *medium*
único/-a   *only*

Verbos

dormir la siesta   *to take a nap*
hacer compras   *to make purchases*
ir de compras   *to go shopping*
jubilarse   *to retire*
mudarse   *to move* (*change residence*)
operar   *to operate*
probar (ue)   *to taste*

VOCABULARIO PERSONALIZADO

Para orientarnos

Capítulo 6

COMMUNICATIVE OBJECTIVES

In this chapter, you will learn some additional ways to

- seek information
- make travel arrangements
- tell anecdotes and stories
- give directions

Viajeros y huéspedes

ENTRADA

Play instructor tape, 1 min.

Veraneo mexicano

You will hear a conversation between César and Elena. As you listen, see if you can determine

- which of César's relatives lived in Mexico
- what the person used to do in Mexico City
- what the person used to do in Taxco
- what special attraction Acapulco held
- how the person described Guadalajara

El (La) _____ de César vivió en México.

Lugar   *Actividad/Atracción/Descripción*

1. Ciudad de México
2. Taxco
3. Acapulco
4. Guadalajara

EMPEZAR A ESCUCHAR

Play student tape, 3 min.

Leer

¿En qué puedo servirle(s)?	*May I help you?*
hacer los arreglos	*to make arrangements*
por tierra	*by land*
por avión	*by air*
a dos cuadras de	*two blocks away from*
los precios bajos	*low prices*
alquilar	*to rent*
el cheque de viajero	*traveler's check*
firmar	*to sign (signature)*

Repetir

Escucha la cinta y repite lo que oyes.

Identificar

En una hoja aparte, escribe en una columna las palabras y frases de la lista anterior. Vas a oír algunas oraciones. Cada vez que oigas una de estas palabras o frases, apunta el número de la oración al lado de la palabra. Cada oración se leerá dos veces.

Escribir

Vas a oír unas oraciones, cada una leída dos veces. Escríbelas al escucharlas.

Reconocer

Ahora, lee otra vez las oraciones que acabas de escribir. Cada una contiene una o más de las palabras y frases de la lista anterior. Al releerlas, subraya todas las palabras y frases que vienen de la lista. Mientras lees, haz todas las correcciones necesarias.

ESCUCHAR

Play student tape, 2 min.

Episodio 1: ¿Por tierra o por avión?

Enfoque comunicativo

Paco and Roberto are making arrangements to travel to Cartagena from Cali. As you listen to the conversation, see if you can determine

- how they plan to travel
- the cost of the tickets

De Cali a Cartagena

Medio de transporte: Precio de los boletos:

Enfoque lingüístico

Escucha otra vez la conversación y escribe

- la expresión que usa el agente para saludar a Paco y a Roberto
- las dos palabras que usa el agente para referirse al dinero colombiano

ESCUCHAR

Play student tape, 2 min.

Episodio 2: "¿Dónde quieren alojarse?"

Enfoque comunicativo

As the travelers continue their conversation with the travel agent, see if you can determine

- whether they want to stay in the center of the city or near the beach
- how long they plan to stay in Cartagena

La estancia en Cartagena

1. El Hotel Bahía está ____.
   a. en el centro   b. cerca de la playa
2. Van a llegar el ____ del mes.
3. Van a salir el ____ del mes.

Enfoque lingüístico

Escucha otra vez la conversación, y escribe

- cómo pregunta Paco si pueden pagar con cheques de viajero
- cómo Roberto le pregunta a Paco si debe firmar los cheques de viajero

VERIFICAR

In this chapter, more direction lines in the *Enfoque lingüístico* sections and, later, exercises in the *Ponerlo a prueba* sections continue the transition to Spanish when appropriate.

Completa las siguientes oraciones.

1. Roberto y Paco van a la agencia de viajes para...
2. Los amigos deciden viajar en...
3. La moneda nacional de Colombia es...
4. Paco y Roberto van a alojarse en...
5. Los amigos pagan por los boletos de avión con...

AUMENTAR EL VOCABULARIO

a dos cuadras de	two blocks away from
alojarse	to stay temporarily, to have lodging
el alojamiento	lodging
bajo/-a	low
barato/-a	inexpensive
caro/-a	expensive

alquilar	*to rent*
el alquiler	*the rent*
compartir	*to share*
el pago	*payment*
¿En qué puedo servirle(s)?	*May I help you?*
¡Cómo no!	*Of course!*
¡Socorro!	*Help!*
la habitación	*room (with a bed), as in a hotel*
la alcoba	*bedroom*
la pieza	*room*
hacer los arreglos	*to make arrangements*
la agencia de viajes	*travel agency*
el (la) agente	*agent*
la excursión	*tour*
por avión	*by air*
por tierra	*by land*
la sección de fumar	*smoking section*
no fumar	*no smoking*
el humo	*smoke*
Hay de todo.	*There's a lot of variety.*
un poco de todo	*a little bit of everything*
Me está dando hambre.	*I'm getting hungry.*
¡Vamos ya!	*Let's go right now!*

Cada país tiene su moneda nacional.

PAGANDO LA CUENTA

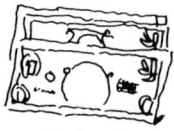
el efectivo

las monedas

los cheques de viajero

pagar a plazos

firmar

cambiar dinero

¿Cómo se paga…? Indica cómo se paga (*one pays*) generalmente en las situaciones siguientes.

- en efectivo
- con cheque
- con cheques de viajero
- con tarjeta de crédito
- a plazos

Modelo: en la tintorería   *En la tintorería generalmente se paga en efectivo.*

1. al taxista
2. para viajar por metro
3. en un restaurante
4. en una agencia de viajes
5. en un hotel
6. para el alquiler de un apartamento
7. en una tienda de ropa
8. al comprar un auto nuevo
9. para estacionar el auto
10. para entrar al cine

Ventanilla al mundo hispánico   El cambio

El valor relativo de las monedas nacionales cambia día a día. La mejor manera de mantenerse al tanto del valor de las distintas monedas del mundo, como por ejemplo el peso de Colombia o la peseta de España, es llamar a un banco o leer la sección de finanzas del periódico. A continuación hay una lista de las monedas nacionales de algunos países de Latinoamérica.

Argentina	el austral	México	el peso
Bolivia	el peso	Panamá	el balboa
Colombia	el peso	Paraguay	el guaraní
Costa Rica	el colón	Perú	el inti (No se usa el sol desde 1988.)
Cuba	el peso		
Chile	el peso		
Ecuador	el sucre	República Dominicana	el peso
El Salvador	el colón		
Guatemala	el quetzal	Uruguay	el peso
Honduras	la lempira	Venezuela	el bolívar

Actividad. Busca en un periódico de esta semana (o llama a un banco local para descubrir) el valor actual (*current*) de todas las monedas de esta lista que puedas encontrar.

USO PRÁCTICO DEL ESPAÑOL Saber y conocer

In the *Entrada* Roberto says to the travel agent: —*No conocemos Cartagena.* (We don't know Cartagena.) The verb *conocer* means "to know" in the sense of being acquainted or familiar with people, places, or things.

—¿**Conoces** a Octavio Chávez? *Do you know Octavio Chávez?*
—Sí, lo **conozco** bien. *Yes, I know him well.*

—¿**Conoces** España? *Have you been to Spain?*
—Sí, mis abuelos viven en Barcelona. *Yes, my grandparents live in Barcelona.*

The verb *saber* means "to know" in the sense of "to have information" or "to know how to do something."

Roberto **sabe** que la tintorería está enfrente del cine. *Roberto knows that the dry cleaners is across from the movie theater.*
Paco **sabe** ir al hotel. *Paco knows how to get to the hotel.*

Point out to students that the question ¿*Conoces España?* also means "Do you know (are you familiar with) Spain?"

OJO: The word "how" in "know how to do/make/drive" is expressed by the verb *saber*. Other high-frequency verbs that include more than one word in the English equivalent are *mirar* (to look at), *buscar* (to look for), *esperar* (to wait for), *escuchar* (to listen to), and *pagar* (to pay for).

Assign for homework; in class, have students compare their answers in pairs, and focus your time only on problem areas.

Ponerlo a prueba

A. Conversaciones entre amigos. Completa las siguientes conversaciones, usando **saber** o **conocer**.

Marta: Estoy buscando a Rodolfo. ¿_____ dónde está?
Pilar: ¿Rodolfo? No lo _____. ¿Quién es?
Marta: Claro que lo _____. Es el novio de Beatriz.
Pilar: En ese caso sí lo _____, pero no _____ dónde está.

Laurencio: Pienso ir a Monterrey durante las vacaciones, pero no _____ nada de la ciudad. ¿La _____ tú?
Federico: Un poco. Estuve allí el verano pasado. ¿Qué quieres _____?
Laurencio: Todo—cómo ir, dónde quedarme, qué debo ver.
Federico: ¡Hombre, tú no _____ nada! ¿Cómo _____ que quieres ir?
Laurencio: No _____, siempre he tenido ganas de _____ la cultura mexicana y Monterrey está relativamente cerca.

Directed exercise: assign as homework.

B. La mudanza. Alonso y Linda Pérez hacen los arreglos para mudarse a Miami. Completa las oraciones con palabras de la lista de Aumentar el vocabulario.

1. Alonso y Linda Pérez no piensan comprar una casa en Miami; han decidido _____ un apartamento.
2. Buscan un apartamento con un alquiler _____ porque no tienen mucho dinero.

3. Además, necesitan dos _____ porque van a _____ el apartamento con Ricardo, el hermano de Alonso.
4. Ricardo vive en Puerto Rico; va a viajar _____ a Miami en diez días.
5. Alonso y Linda han visto un apartamento bien situado—está a tres _____ de la playa, y el autobús que va al centro pasa cerca.

C. Expresiones apropiadas. Escoge la expresión que complete mejor cada situación.

- ¡Vamos ya!
- ¡Cómo no!
- Hay de todo.
- ¡Cálmate, hombre!
- ¡Socorro!

1. El agente de viajes te describe un hotel en Cartagena. Te gusta el hotel y le dices: —Es un hotel estupendo,...
2. Tu amigo está muy nervioso porque no le gusta viajar por avión. Tú le dices:...
3. Después de llegar al hotel, deciden nadar. A tu amigo le coge (*grabs*) una ola (*wave*) grande y no puede respirar (*breathe*). Él grita:...
4. Tu amigo quiere descansar un rato. Después de dos horas, le preguntas si tiene ganas de cenar. Él tiene mucha hambre y responde:...
5. A ti también te está dando hambre, así que le dices:...

CH. Preguntas personales

1. ¿Conoces otro país? ¿Qué país(es) conoces?
2. Cuando viajas, ¿prefieres alojarte en un hotel, o en casa de parientes o amigos? ¿Por qué?
3. Cuando viajas a países extranjeros, ¿es mejor estar con otros norteamericanos o no? ¿Por qué?
4. Cuando haces un viaje, ¿quién hace los arreglos, tú u otra persona?
5. En un vuelo (*flight*) internacional, ¿prefieres sentarte en la sección de fumar o en la de no fumar?
6. ¿Prefieres viajar por avión o por tierra?
7. ¿Cuál es una ventaja de viajar en autobús? ¿Y en avión?
8. ¿Cuál es el lugar más interesante o hermoso que conoces en los Estados Unidos? ¿Y en otro país?

D. Hablando con el agente de viajes. Quieres pasar las vacaciones de Navidad con unos amigos en Bogotá y llamas a una agencia de viajes para hacer los arreglos.

1. ¿Cuáles son tres preguntas que debes hacerle al (a la) agente?
2. ¿Cuáles son tres preguntas que el (la) agente debe hacerte a ti?

INVESTIGAR LA GRAMÁTICA   The Imperfect Tense

In addition to the preterite tense that you first saw in Chapter 4, you also need to learn to use the imperfect tense to talk about the past. Here are the forms of the imperfect.

hablar		comer		vivir	
hablaba	hablábamos	comía	comíamos	vivía	vivíamos
hablabas	hablabais	comías	comíais	vivías	vivíais
hablaba	hablaban	comía	comían	vivía	vivían

Point out that imperfect forms such as hablaba, vivía, or veía will often need an accompanying subject pronoun, because they may refer to yo, él, ella, or usted.

There are only three verbs that are irregular in the imperfect.

ser		ir		ver	
era	éramos	iba	íbamos	veía	veíamos
eras	erais	ibas	ibais	veías	veíais
era	eran	iba	iban	veía	veían

Point out that an imperfect form such as íbamos may be expressed in English as "went," "used to go," "were going," or "would go."

You learned in Chapter 4 that the preterite is used to talk about specific activities or conditions that either began or ended during the time you are talking about.

Una noche **fuimos** al Castillo de San Felipe.
En otra ocasión **comimos** en el Club de Pesca.
Roberto **comió** camarones y después **se enfermó**.

The imperfect is also used to describe activities or conditions that occurred in the past, but they neither began nor ended during the time you are talking about. Use of the imperfect, then, generally indicates one of three things.

1. You are describing a condition that was true, or valid, for the time you are talking about. Furthermore, you are setting the stage to talk about an activity, or you are providing background information.

Cuando **éramos** niños, la casa donde **vivíamos era** muy vieja; **tenía** tres pisos y un enorme jardín.

In this example no action is taking place; the speaker is just describing what the house was like at some time in the past when he or she lived in it.

2. An activity or condition is viewed as being routine or habitual for the time you are talking about. In this case, **no specific instance** of the activity or condition is being referred to.

Los gemelos **hacían** todo juntos; **jugaban, montaban** en bicicleta, y cuando uno **lloraba**, la otra **lloraba** también.

This example means that the twins did everything together routinely or habitually, that is, over and over many times. They used to play together and ride their bikes together, and whenever one cried the other cried too. Note that **no particular instance** of the twins playing, riding their bikes, or crying is being mentioned or singled out. Here is another example of the imperfect used the same way.

Siempre que yo **tenía** un examen en la escuela, la noche anterior **me enfermaba**.

Note once again that the speaker is not referring to any particular instance of having an exam or getting sick. Rather, the speaker is talking about the repetition or habitual nature of these events, which happened many times in the past.

3. The activity or condition was **going on,** that is, it was **in progress,** at the time you are talking about. It neither started nor ended at that time.

Todo **iba** muy bien; todos **bailábamos, comíamos** y **conversábamos.**

This example means that at the time the speaker was talking about, perhaps at a party, everything was going well (a condition); everyone was dancing, eating, and talking (events that were in progress).

You will often want to express a common combination of activities: one activity was in progress when a different activity happened. In this case, use the imperfect to describe the activity that was in progress and the preterite to narrate the other activity that happened.

Anoche, yo **estudiaba** cuando tú me **llamaste.**

This sentence means that the speaker was studying (background information; an activity in progress) when the other person called. The second event took place or began while the first activity was going on.

OJO: Another way of expressing the same idea is to ask the question, "Did something happen or was something going on?" The imperfect is used to express the fact that something was going on, and the preterite is used to express the fact that something happened.

Ponerlo a prueba

A. ¿Qué pasaba cuando llegaron al hotel? Cuando Paco y Roberto llegaron al Hotel Bahía, vieron mucha actividad. Describe lo que vieron, según el modelo.

Modelo: el empleado / hablar por teléfono
*El empleado **hablaba** por teléfono.*

OJO: What is being described here is activity in progress, not the event of making a phone call.

1. un señor / pagar la cuenta
2. dos hombres / cambiar dinero
3. una señora / leer una revista
4. tres niños / comer helado
5. un turista francés / hacer los arreglos para volver a Francia
6. una familia / salir para la playa
7. un empleado / pasar la aspiradora
8. un matrimonio (*couple*) alemán / alquilar un auto

Assign B for homework, with half the class making the *nosotros* transformation and the other half making the *Uds.* transformation. In class, have pairs of students from different groups coach their partners while they work on the transformation they have not already written for homework.

B. Una reunión de amigos. A group of friends gets together at their college reunion and reminisces about their college days. As they listen to Victoria talk, they realize that they could be telling the same story. Take their roles, and tell the story from the following points of view: *nosotros, Uds., tú,* and *Rafaela.*

Modelo: Cuando (yo) **era** estudiante, siempre **me levantaba**...
*Cuando **éramos** estudiantes, siempre **nos levantábamos**...*
*Cuando **Uds. eran** estudiantes, siempre **se levantaban**...*

> **OJO:** The portions of the story that will change are indicated in boldfaced type.

Cuando **era** estudiante, siempre **me acostaba** muy tarde porque **me gustaba** estudiar de noche cuando no **había** tanto ruido en la residencia. Como consecuencia, **me levantaba** diez minutos antes de **mi** primera clase. Cuando sonaba el despertador, **saltaba** (*jumped*) de la cama, **me duchaba** y **me vestía**. **Corría** a **mi** clase, y siempre **llegaba** un poco tarde. **Sabía** que **podía sentarme** en un rincón del aula si **necesitaba** unos minutos más para **despertarme**. A veces el profesor **me hacía** preguntas difíciles para demostrar que él sabía que todavía yo **estaba** medio **dormida**. Pero no **tenía** ganas de cambiar la costumbre de llegar tarde, porque **me** gustaba mucho dormir.

> Another directed exercise that can be easily assigned as homework. If you go over it in class, remind students that the imperfect is used to describe how things were in the past, without focusing on any particular instances or actions.

C. Completar el cuento. Al señor Colón le encanta hablar de su niñez. Pero habla en voz muy baja, y Paco y Roberto no pueden oír ciertas palabras. Mientras describe su juventud, trata de completar la historia.

El Sr. Colon: —Nosotros viv_____ en el interior del país, y luch_____ día y noche contra la naturaleza. Durante la temporada de las lluvias, llov_____ por lo menos dos veces al día y _____ imposible salir de la casa. Si ustedes no han experimentado una tormenta (*storm*) colombiana, no saben el significado de la palabra llover. Pero no _____ nada aburrido. Nosotros, es decir los niños, aprovech_____ esas tormentas para jugar y para escuchar a los adultos. En nuestra familia todo el mundo cont_____ chistes y cuentos, y siempre _____ divertido estar juntos. Mientras llov_____, mi padre y mis tíos repar_____ (reparar: *to repair*) algo, y mi madre y mis tías cos_____ (coser: *to sew*) o trabaj_____ en la cocina. ¡Qué bien olían el pan y las tartas que hac_____ ! Mis hermanos y yo nos acerc_____, tanto para escuchar las historias que cont_____ los adultos como para probar lo que prepar_____. ¡Qué vida más alegre en aquel entonces!

CH. Hablando de la niñez

> Like the *Preguntas personales* earlier in this *etapa,* these questions can be prepared as homework and treated as interviews in class. Encourage the "interviewer" to express interest and ask follow-up questions so that the exchange resembles a conversation. Model phrases for expressing interest and drawing out one's partner.

1. ¿Dónde vive tu familia ahora? ¿Vivían Uds. en el mismo pueblo o ciudad cuando eras niño/-a?
2. ¿Cómo era la casa donde vivías cuando eras niño/-a?
3. ¿Qué te gustaba comer más que nada cuando eras niño/-a?
4. ¿Qué hacías los fines de semana?
5. ¿Dónde pasabas los veranos cuando eras niño/-a? ¿Qué hacías?
6. ¿Viajaban Uds. como familia? ¿Cómo y dónde pasaban las vacaciones?
7. ¿Cómo celebraban Uds. los cumpleaños tuyos y los de tus hermanos?
8. ¿Cuál era la fiesta más importante para tu familia? ¿Cómo la celebraban ustedes?

Primera etapa

In-class activity. Prepare an interview sheet with the statements and guide the students in forming questions based on them: Cuando eras niño/-a, ¿qué hacías cuando no querías ir a la escuela? Have students interview each other, or ask each question of a different classmate. Space can be left on the interview sheet for responses and name of respondent. Before students begin, review with them the phrases from the Uso práctico for expressing repeated actions in the past.

Actividad E can be done as homework or in class, either in pairs or directed by the instructor.

D. ¿Qué hacías cuando...? Pensando en tu niñez, indica qué hacías en las situaciones siguientes.

1. No querías ir a la escuela.
2. Tenías un maestro (una maestra) en la primaria que no te gustaba nada.
3. No querías acostarte.
4. Estabas en casa de un amigo (una amiga) y te servían algo que no querías comer.
5. Hacía mal tiempo y no podías salir.
6. No querías participar en una actividad con tu familia.

E. El pesado (*bore*). You are recounting the trip that you took recently to South America with some friends. However, *el pesado* claims already to have done many times everything you mention. Listed here are the notes you took during the trip. Use these notes to make your statements, and then decide what *el pesado* will say in response.

Modelo: ir a Sudamérica

Tú: *Fuimos a Sudamérica.*

El pesado: *Pues, yo iba a Sudamérica todos los veranos cuando era niño.*

1. hacer una excursión a una mina de sal
2. ver una anaconda en la selva (*jungle*)
3. cruzar el lago Titicaca en barco de vapor
4. pasar una semana en San Andrés y Providencia
5. esquiar en las montañas de Chile
6. comprar ropa indígena en el Perú
7. ir a una fiesta en Cali
8. comer en un restaurante de cuatro estrellas

Use an interview sheet for this in-class activity. Students should circulate freely in the room to find someone who can answer affirmatively to each question. Before you begin, model the questions so that students form them correctly during the activity.

F. Encuesta. Habla con algunos de tus compañeros de clase sobre su niñez. Determina quién

1. caminaba a la escuela primaria y quién tomaba el autobús
2. casi nunca hacía la tarea
3. prefería leer en casa, y quién solía jugar afuera
4. tenía miedo de la oscuridad
5. dormía con la luz prendida
6. abrazaba a su mamá todos los días
7. no ponía atención a los consejos de sus padres

Haz las siguientes actividades con un compañero (una compañera).

A. El anuario (*yearbook*) del colegio. You and a friend are looking through an old yearbook from your senior year in high school. Look at the following pictures and describe to your friend what was happening when the picture was taken. Answer questions your friend may have regarding the photo.

B. Entrevista. Habla con un compañero (una compañera) de la clase para descubrir

- cuáles eran sus actividades favoritas cuando estaba en el colegio
- unos ejemplos de cómo disfrutaba (*enjoyed*) de estos intereses
- si ha continuado con ellos en la universidad

Ahora, cambia los papeles y repite la entrevista. Luego, informa a la clase.

OTRA VUELTA

Play instructor tape, 1 min.

Ahora escucha otra vez la conversación entre Elena y César que escuchaste al comienzo de esta etapa. La cuarta vez que César habla, completa lo que dice.

César: Pues, me dijo que en aquel entonces _____ los museos y los teatros de la ciudad de México, y que _____ compras en los famosos mercados de

Taxco. También siempre que _____ la oportunidad _____ Acapulco y _____ allí en las playas exquisitas.

COMENTARIO CULTURAL

Medios de transporte público

Hay muchas opciones para la persona que quiere desplazarse (*move around*) dentro de una ciudad o entre ciudades en el mundo hispánico. Ya que los sistemas de transporte público son tanto extensos como económicos, la gente tiende a depender más de ellos que de sus propios coches. No existe el estigma social de usar los medios de transporte público que se nota en algunas regiones de los Estados Unidos.

La infraestructura de la mayoría de las ciudades hispánicas no favorece el uso de autos particulares (*private*). Hay poco espacio para estacionamiento y en las

Por lo general, las calles en los pueblos viejos son angostas y atestadas, y pueden causar problemas con la circulación.

ciudades viejas las calles son muy angostas (*narrow*). Por lo general, las familias que tienen auto tienen sólo uno, y éste suele ser pequeño, porque el costo de combustible normalmente es bastante alto. Además, es muy difícil manejar un carro grande por las calles angostas y atestadas (*crowded*). Aunque existen notables excepciones, en la mayoría de los países la distancia entre un lugar y otro dentro de una ciudad, o la que hay entre dos ciudades, no es tan grande como para que el transporte por tren o autobús resulte incómodo.

Además, la mayoría de las ciudades tienen una gran variedad de sistemas de transporte público que hacen innecesario el uso de un automóvil. Los medios de transporte usualmente incluyen rutas extensas de autobuses. Algunas de las ciudades más grandes (por ejemplo, México, D.F.; Lima, Perú; Madrid, España) tienen un metro que conecta el centro y sus alrededores. En muchas ciudades hay vehículos relativamente pequeños que se llaman combinaciones o microbuses, que combinan las funciones de autobús y taxi. Siguen rutas más cortas y controladas que las de los buses, transportan a menos pasajeros y tienen una tarifa fija, sin importar lo lejos que vaya el pasajero.

Para los viajes más largos de una ciudad a otra los pasajeros compran un boleto de autobús con un asiento reservado, como los boletos de avión. En algunos lugares hay diferentes clases o niveles de comodidad y de acuerdo con esto varían los precios de los boletos. Los autobuses de super-lujo muchas veces tienen minibar y baño. A veces se incluye el precio de una comida en el precio del boleto.

Preguntas. Escribe aquí tres razones que explican por qué los habitantes de ciudades del mundo hispánico usan más el transporte público que en los Estados Unidos.

1. 2. 3.

¿Cuáles son las diferencias entre los autobuses y los microbuses o las combinaciones?

	Autobús	Microbús/Combinación
1. Ruta		
2. Tamaño (*Size*)		
3. Tarifa (*Fare*)		

¿Qué voy a tomar? Escoge el medio de transporte apropiado en cada situación.

Answers: 1. ch, 2. a, 3. b, c, 4. c, c

1. ir a la carnicería de la vecindad para comprar la comida de hoy
2. viajar de Cartagena a Cali
3. ir al hospital en el centro
4. ir a la universidad, que está en las afueras de la ciudad

a. un autobús de super-lujo
b. una combinación
c. un autobús
ch. caminar

Conozca Cartagena

ENTRADA

Play instructor tape, 1 min.

Cartagena de Indias, Cartagena del mar…

You are going to hear a radio advertisement promoting tourism to Colombia. Listen for the three reasons that are given to visit Colombia.

Visitar Colombia

Las razones: ¿Sí o no?

1. restaurantes de lujo   Sí   No
2. precios módicos   Sí   No
3. ciudades históricas y bellas   Sí   No
4. montañas y junglas para explorar   Sí   No
5. oportunidades de practicar deportes Sí No
6. playas tropicales   Sí   No

ANTES DE LEER

READING STRATEGY 6

Anticipate and predict content

Have you ever noticed how often you "know" what information is going to be contained in an article, an advertisement, or some other type of text even before you read it? For example, even before you read an article about last night's football game, you know that it will give you information such as who won, the final score, key plays, and the names of some of the outstanding players in the game. Your ability to predict, and the expectation you have for what will be in the selection, enable you to read the article more rapidly and to locate specific information that might be of particular interest to you. Thus, a very useful strategy when reading any selection is to look at the title, a picture, or some other noticeable clue to the content and ask yourself, What information is likely to be in the text? Although it may only take a moment, you will find it very helpful in improving your ability to comprehend what you are about to read.

Capítulo seis   Para orientarnos

Preparación

When you read a brochure or advertisement designed to attract visitors to a city or country, what types of information do you expect to find? What do promoters tend to emphasize in order to attract tourists? Make a list of the kinds of facts and figures that are often contained in publications of this sort. You may find the vocabulary items in the *Estudiar y practicar* section helpful as you prepare your list.

[Play instructor tape, 1 min.]

Estudiar y practicar

al nivel del mar	*at sea level*
el balneario	*bathing or health resort*
el castillo	*castle*
la derrota	*defeat*
en exposición	*on display, on exhibit*
fundar	*to found, establish*
llegar a ser	*to become*
la madera	*wood*
las mercancías	*merchandise*
la mezcla	*mixture*
el museo	*museum*
el paraíso	*paradise*
el puerto	*seaport*
la temperatura promedio	*average temperature*
el ultramar	*overseas*

LEER

As you read the promotional brochure on page 255, look for the following.

- the average temperature in Cartagena
- the year the city was founded
- the name of the founder
- the year Colombia proclaimed its independence from Spain

DESPUÉS DE LEER

A. Datos generales.   Busca la información en el folleto y escribe la respuesta correcta.

> *Cartagena de Indias*
>
> Temperatura promedio: Fundada en el año:
> Nombre del fundador: Año de declaración de la
> Lugares de interés turístico: independencia:

¡Bienvenidos a Cartagena!

Nuestra hermosa ciudad está situada en la región más alegre de Colombia, y prácticamente al nivel del mar. Aquí tenemos un clima ideal: una temperatura promedio de 28 grados centígrados y precipitación anual de solamente 88 centímetros. El sol y las suaves brisas del Mar Caribe hacen de Cartagena un verdadero paraíso en la tierra. Esta encantadora ciudad es una mezcla perfecta de historia fascinante y belleza natural.

La ciudad, llamada oficialmente Cartagena de Indias, fue fundada en el año 1533 por Pedro de Heredia. Durante la época colonial Cartagena pronto llegó a ser el puerto más importante de todo el imperio español de ultramar. De aquí salía para España el oro que recogían los conquistadores y aquí llegaban de regreso muchas mercancías producidas en Europa.

El 11 de noviembre de 1811 los habitantes de Cartagena, cansados de la tiranía y el dominio españoles, declararon su independencia. En 1821, después de la derrota de los españoles por Simón Bolívar, Cartagena fue libre para siempre.

Para que conozcan mejor la ciudad, los invitamos a visitar varios sitios de interés, empezando con la Catedral. Su construcción comenzó en 1575, y duró muchos años. Su interior es solemne y elegante. Su altar central es una obra de arte, elaborado en madera y cubierto de oro.

El enorme y fascinante Castillo de San Felipe, situado dentro del perímetro urbano, fue construido entre 1536 y 1657. Tiene numerosos pasajes secretos, diseñados para movilizar a los soldados sin que fueran vistos. En la noche hay un famoso espectáculo de luz y sonido. ¡Hay que verlo para creerlo!

El Palacio de la Inquisición es otro lugar de interés. Esta hermosa construcción fue terminada en 1776. En las galerías del primer piso se encuentran en exposición artefactos de la Inquisición. Además, en los pisos altos hay otros dos museos: el Museo Antropológico y el Museo Colonial.

Después de una gira por la ciudad, no se pierdan las lindas vistas de Bocagrande, Bocachica y Marbella, nuestros balnearios populares. Otra vez, gracias por su presencia. Conozcan Cartagena, y de parte de todos los cartageneros, ¡bienvenidos!

When you are in a new area, you need help in getting from one place to another. Here are some useful phrases.

To ask for directions

Por favor, ¿me puede decir dónde está...?	Can you please tell me where . . . is?
¿Está lejos?	Is it far?
¿Se puede caminar?	Is it within walking distance?

To understand or give directions

a la derecha	to the right
a la izquierda	to the left
bajar	to go down
doblar	to turn
ir (seguir) derecho	to go straight ahead
pasar por	to pass through, by
seguir (i, i)	to continue, follow
subir	to go up

> Although compass points are not generally used to give directions in the Spanish-speaking world, students may need them to give directions in the United States. Refer students to Chapter 1, third *etapa* for review.

> Note that the present indicative is used here to give directions to persons whom one would address as *usted*. Familiar commands are used more frequently than the indicative to give directions to persons whom one would address as *tú*. Command forms are presented in Chapter 8.

¿Cómo se llega?   Una persona desconocida (*stranger*) te pide información. Refiriéndote al mapa en esta sección explícale a la persona cómo ir de un sitio a otro.

Modelo: del parque a la panadería
Ud. sale del parque a la Avenida Colón y dobla a la izquierda. En la primera esquina, Ud. dobla a la derecha en la Avenida Manzanares. La panadería está a la derecha.

1. de la gasolinera al restaurante
2. de la iglesia a la florería
3. de la zapatería a la tintorería
4. del cine a la confitería
5. de la carnicería a la gasolinera
6. de la florería a la farmacia

Ventanilla al mundo hispánico   Conservando el pasado

En esta etapa ustedes visitaron la Catedral, el Castillo de San Felipe y el Palacio de la Inquisición, edificios muy importantes en la historia de la ciudad de Cartagena. Se encuentran edificios de este tipo en casi todas las ciudades del mundo hispánico, normalmente alrededor de la plaza central, una área que sirve de lugar para que la gente se reúna. En la plaza central de una ciudad es común encontrar flores y arbustos muy bonitos—como por ejemplo en Sevilla, España—fuentes, y monumentos a los héroes militares o figuras literarias del país. La mayoría de las plazas centrales del mundo hispánico tienen también bancos donde la gente puede sentarse a conversar, a leer o a darles de comer a los pájaros. Las plazas centrales de las ciudades están rodeadas de edificios, como por ejemplo, la catedral y los edificios oficiales como la casa de correos, el Palacio de Justicia (donde está la corte) y otras oficinas del municipio. En la Ciudad de México la plaza central se llama el Zócalo. Es una gran área abierta y está pavimentada con piedras grandes. Es allí donde la gente se reúne para oír discursos políticos y ver ceremonias políticas o militares. El Zócalo de la Ciudad de México hoy en día ocupa casi el mismo lugar que ocupaba la plaza central de los aztecas hace más de 500 años.

La plaza central en el mundo hispánico

¿Qué hay en la plaza central?
 a.
 b.
 c.
 ch.
 d.

¿Qué actividades se hacen en la plaza central?
 a.
 b.
 c.
 ch.
 d.

USO PRÁCTICO DEL ESPAÑOL   El presente progresivo

The progressive forms of a verb stress that the action of the verb is in progress right at the moment. The progressive forms are most commonly formed using the verb *estar* followed by the present participle of the main verb.

—¿Qué **estás haciendo,** Roberto?
—Un minuto, que **estoy hablando** por teléfono.

To form the present participle of most verbs, first delete the *-ar, -er,* or *-ir* ending of the infinitive. Then add *-ando* to the stem of *-ar* verbs and *-iendo* to the stem of *-er* and *-ir* verbs.

hablar	→	habl-	→	habl**ando**
comer	→	com-	→	com**iendo**
vivir	→	viv-	→	viv**iendo**

> The stems of some *-ar* verbs end in a vowel, but their endings do not change: *estudiar* → *estudiando.*

When the stem of an *-er* or *-ir* infinitive ends in a vowel, the present participle ending is *-yendo.*

caer	→	ca-	→	ca**yendo**
construir	→	constru-	→	constru**yendo**
leer	→	le-	→	le**yendo**
oír	→	o-	→	o**yendo**
traer	→	tra-	→	tra**yendo**

—¿Qué **estás leyendo**?

—El periódico de hoy. Mira, aquí dice que **están construyendo** una nueva sección del museo.

> This is a good point to review the stem changes in preterite forms. See Chapter 4, third *etapa.*

Stem-changing verbs that end in *-ir* use the second stem change in the present participle.

divertirse (ie, i)	→	divirtiendo
dormir (ue, u)	→	durmiendo
seguir (i, i)	→	siguiendo

The progressive forms are never used to talk about what is going to happen in the future.

Voy al cine esta noche.	I am going to the movies tonight.
¡Salimos mañana!	We're leaving tomorrow!
¿Cuándo vas a graduarte?	When are you graduating?

Ponerlo a prueba

> The title of this activity emphasizes the ongoing nature of the progressive tense.

A. ¡Acción! ¿Cuál será la forma progresiva de los verbos que aparecen a continuación? Crea una oración para cada frase, tratando de crear un contexto unido para las diez frases.

1. estudiar para un examen
2. leer el periódico
3. escribir una carta
4. comprar los libros para el próximo semestre
5. hacer la cama
6. dormir
7. vestirse
8. construir una casita en la playa
9. bajar
10. comer

B. Los preparativos. Explica qué están haciendo Paco y Roberto.

1. 2.

3. (comer)

C. Categorías. Busca dos o tres palabras asociadas con cada categoría en la lista de Aumentar el vocabulario.

1. la confrontación militar
2. el tiempo
3. los metales
4. los monumentos
5. la importación
6. el turismo
7. el museo
8. la madera
9. el balneario
10. el castillo

CH. Explicaciones. Completa las oraciones con palabras o frases de la lista de Aumentar el vocabulario de esta etapa.

1. La tierra que está situada cerca de la costa generalmente está _____. Cuando hay una brisa suave, el _____ del mar es muy agradable al olfato (*sense of smell*).
2. Además de las playas, muchas veces hay monumentos históricos y museos donde no hay que pagar la entrada; es _____.
3. Los _____ de las civilizaciones antiguas que están en _____ son muy interesantes, y _____ a muchos turistas.
4. Hay objetos de _____ y _____, dos metales que se encuentran en la América Latina.
5. La historia de la América Latina cuenta de la _____ de culturas.

6. Cristóbal Colón llegó a las islas del Caribe hace cinco _____.
7. En la _____ de los conquistadores, los indígenas sufrieron por primera vez de enfermedades (*illnesses*) que los españoles llevaron al Nuevo Mundo.

Assign D as homework or use in class. Have students interview each other or work in small groups. Alternatively, ask questions in a whole-group setting.

D. Preguntas personales

1. ¿Cuál es la temperatura promedio en tu región? ¿Cómo es el clima?
2. ¿Qué monumentos históricos hay en tu ciudad? ¿De qué siglo son?
3. ¿Qué artículos comunes de hoy llegarán a ser (*will become*) artefactos históricos en el futuro?
4. ¿Qué mercancías importadas te atraen más? ¿Por qué?
5. ¿Has estado en un balneario alguna vez? ¿Cuál es tu playa favorita?
6. Describe lo que es para ti un balneario ideal, un paraíso en la tierra.
7. ¿Te atraen más las montañas o la playa? ¿Por qué?

In-class activity. Before students begin, brainstorm follow-up questions for one or more of the topics. Review expressions about which listeners have indicated interest.

E. Encuesta: el turismo.
Habla con tus compañeros de la clase para descubrir quién

- ha estado bajo el nivel del mar
- ha visitado un balneario
- ha estado en un castillo

INVESTIGAR LA GRAMÁTICA   Another Look at *por* and *para*

In the second *etapa* of Chapter 4 you learned some of the most common meanings of *por* and *para*. These are reviewed now, and some additional uses are presented.

With expressions of space or time, *por* conveys the notions of "by" or "through" a place, and "during" or "for" a period of time.

Los autobuses que van de Cali a Cartagena pasan **por** muchos pueblos pequeños. Se paran **por** dos horas en Honda y **por** una hora en Magangué para dejar descansar a los pasajeros.

Para expresses the notions of "in order to," "intended for," and "considering."

Para divertirse un poco durante el vuelo a Cartagena Roberto leyó una novela.
Roberto compró un regalo **para** su sobrina.
Para turistas, Roberto y Paco llegaron a conocer bastante bien la ciudad de Cali.

The best way to develop a feel for the uses of *por* and *para* is through extensive listening and reading. Here are a few more examples to help you along.

POR	PARA
Por expresses the notions of	*Para* expresses the notions of
a. "by" or "through" a place, and "during" or "for" a period of time.	a. "in order to," "intended for," and "considering."
Los viajeros que van del norte de California a Texas pasan **por** el estado de Nevada. A veces se paran **por** dos o tres días en Reno para descansar y divertirse. *Travelers who go from northern California to Texas pass through the state of Nevada. Sometimes they stop for two or three days in Reno to rest and have fun.*	**Para** divertirse un poco mientras están en Reno, algunos de los viajeros que tienen suficiente dinero juegan a los naipes. *In order to have a little fun while they are in Reno, some travelers who have enough money gamble (at cards).* Otros compran regalos **para** sus amigos y familia. *Others buy gifts for their friends and family.*
b. "because of," "on account of." **Por** perezoso saliste mal en el examen. *On account of your laziness (Because you're lazy) you did poorly on the exam.*	Dos de mis compañeros de clase pasaron una semana allí, jugando a los naipes. Y **para** estudiantes, gastaron mucho dinero durante aquel período. *Two of my classmates spent a week there, gambling (at cards). And considering they were students, they spent a lot of money during that time.*
c. "by," in the sense of an agent or performer of an action. Los terroristas fueron capturados **por** la Guardia Civil. *The terrorists were captured by the Civil Guard.*	b. "to what purpose," "intended for." ¿**Para** qué son esas pilas? *What are those batteries for?*
ch. "by," in the sense of means (including means of transportation). Los estudiantes viajaron **por** automóvil porque era más económico. *The students traveled by car because it was more economical.*	c. "by" in the sense of a deadline: something must be done **for** or **by** a certain time. Mis padres me dijeron que tengo que estar en casa **para** las seis. *My parents told me that I have to be home by six.*
d. "in exchange for," or with *gracias* meaning "in appreciation for." Muchas gracias **por** invitarme. *Thanks very much for inviting me.*	ch. "to be about to" when used after the verb *estar*. Yo estaba **para** llamarte cuando entraste. *I was about to call you when you came in.*
e. "picking someone up" or "going out in search of something." Me duele mucho la cabeza; voy a la farmacia **por** aspirina. *I have a bad headache; I'm going to the drugstore for aspirin.*	
f. *Por* is also used in a number of idiomatic expressions. (See next page.)	

You may want to remind students that uses **b** and **c** of *para* are extensions of the notion of "intended for."

These three expressions occur less frequently than those listed in the chart. They can be introduced at the instructor's discretion.
por lo menos   *at least*
por si acaso   *just in case*
por lo tanto   *therefore*

por aquí   *around here*
por ejemplo   *for example*
por eso   *that's why*
por fin   *at last, finally*
por lo general   *normally, in general*
por primera/segunda/última vez   *for the first/second/last time*

Ponerlo a prueba

Assign for homework. In class, have students work in small groups to find similar and different responses. Have the groups compete to come up with the most imaginative, outrageous, or culturally appropriate response.

A. La fantasía. Imagínate que estás en los siguientes lugares. Inventa varios propósitos para explicar tu presencia allí.

> **Modelo:** en la universidad
> *Estoy en la universidad para aprender; estoy en la universidad para estudiar; estoy en la universidad para divertirme.*

1. en una fiesta
2. en la tintorería
3. en una discoteca
4. en Cartagena, Colombia
5. en tu pueblo natal (*hometown*)
6. en la playa

In-class activity. Students work in pairs to create mini-dialogues that incorporate the questions.

B. Los niños curiosos. Todo el mundo conoce las famosas preguntas interminables de los niños pequeños. Imagínate que tienes que contestar las preguntas siguientes. ¿Cómo respondes?

1. ¿Por qué tenemos que comer legumbres todos los días? A mí me gustan más el helado y los dulces.
2. ¿Para qué son las toallas? ¿Tengo yo que usarlas?
3. ¿Por qué tengo que acostarme a las nueve?
4. ¿Para qué es el cinturón de seguridad del carro? ¿Por qué tengo que ponérmelo?
5. ¿Por qué no puedo tocar (*touch*) a las personas en la televisión? Puedo verlas y quiero tocarlas también.

Assign as homework. In class, have students quickly compare their answers, and then review. Ask students to explain their reasons for choosing *por* or *para*.

C. Viajando en Colombia. Un joven norteamericano está en Colombia con sus padres. Expresa las oraciones siguientes usando **por** o **para** en lugar de las palabras en negrilla (*boldface*).

1. Mis padres estudian español **con el propósito de** poder conocer mejor a la familia de mi novia.
2. **Antes de** mañana tenemos que decidir si queremos ir a Bogotá.
3. Los padres de mi novia piensan venir **en busca de** nosotros.

Segunda etapa

4. Aprendimos mucho acerca de la historia de Cartagena **a causa de** la excursión que tomamos ayer.
5. La excursión pasa **delante del** Castillo de San Felipe.
6. Cartagena fue el puerto más importante del imperio español **durante** toda la época colonial.
7. En 1821 Cartagena fue liberada **gracias a** la victoria de Simón Bolívar contra los españoles.
8. Caminamos **a lo largo de** toda la ciudad.
9. Compramos unas tarjetas postales **destinadas a** la familia en Chicago.

CH. Información, por favor: ¿por o para? Escribe la palabra apropiada en estas oraciones sobre la historia, y explica por qué se usa.

1. Los moros (*Moslems*) estuvieron en España _____ siete siglos.
2. Fuerton expulsados _____ Fernando e Isabel, los Reyes Católicos.
3. La expulsión fue en 1492, el mismo año en que Cristóbal Colón salió de España _____ las tierras del Este.
4. La conquista de las poblaciones indígenas del Nuevo Mundo _____ los españoles duró _____ pocos años.
5. Según los españoles, conquistaron estas tierras _____ tres razones: oro, rey y religión.
6. En cambio, los grupos de europeos que llegaron a América del Norte salieron _____ tierras nuevas _____ escapar de la persecución religiosa.
7. _____ ser gente mayormente de las ciudades, les fue muy difícil sobrevivir en Nueva Inglaterra y muchos se murieron.
8. Casi toda la población indígena de América del Norte fue destruida _____ la ignorancia y la avaricia (*greed*) de los europeos que pasaron _____ sus tierras.
9. En muchos casos, los nuevos habitantes "compraron" las tierras de los indígenas _____ objetos de poco valor.
10. _____ los indígenas norteamericanos, las injusticias del pasado deben ser corregidas _____ el gobierno de los Estados Unidos.

D. Una encuesta. Hazle preguntas a un compañero (una compañera) de la clase para descubrir la información siguiente.

1. si ha trabajado alguna vez para un miembro de su familia, y si le gusta
2. la última vez que sacó mala nota en un examen, y por qué pasó
3. si prefiere viajar por tren o por avión, y por qué
4. para cuándo tiene que entregar (*hand in*) su próximo ensayo largo, y para qué clase es
5. cuánto tuvo que pagar por sus libros este semestre

¡TIENES LA PALABRA!

A. La historia de la universidad. Busca un folleto o libro sobre tu universidad que tenga información básica sobre su historia. Responde a las preguntas de tu compañero/-a sobre

- cuándo fue fundada
- quién la fundó
- para quiénes era
- cuál fue el primer edificio

B. ¿Dónde está? Imagínate que estás en tu residencia y llegan los padres de un amigo tuyo (una amiga tuya). Sabes que su hijo/-a está en clase. Dales instrucciones con mucho detalle para ir hasta allá, ya que no conocen la universidad.

OTRA VUELTA

Play instructor tape, 1 min.

Ahora escucha otra vez el anuncio publicitario acerca de Cartagena que oíste al comienzo de esta etapa. Al escuchar, apunta la atracción de Cartagena que se asocia con cada sentido.

Cartagena de Indias

Sentido
1. el olfato (*smell*)
2. el tacto (*touch*)
3. la vista (*sight*)

Atracción
a. las discotecas
b. la brisa del Caribe
c. las playas
ch. el mar

COMENTARIO CULTURAL

Las ferias

Los festivales en Colombia, como el Carnaval en Barranquilla, la Feria de Cali o la Feria de Manizales, el concurso de belleza para seleccionar a Miss Colombia y el Festival del Folklore en la ciudad de Ibagué, tienen fama internacional. Todos los países de la América Latina observan sus celebraciones tradicionales, donde el objetivo principal es divertirse o entretener a los visitantes. Tales festivales, sea cual sea su origen, representan una parte importante de la vida hoy en día de las comunidades donde se celebran. Siempre hay mucha celebración y alegría, y siempre tienen grupos musicales que tocan día y noche en las calles, las plazas y los clubes. Hay desfiles con carrozas, corridas de toros, eventos ecuestres, concursos de belleza y bailes que entretienen a todos los que están allí.

Segunda etapa **267**

Actividad. Lee la siguiente lista de actividades y trata de decidir cuáles tienen lugar en Colombia, cuáles ocurren en los Estados Unidos y cuáles pueden pertenecer (*belong to*) a los dos países.

Actividad	¿En Colombia?	¿En Estados Unidos?
corridas de toros		
fuegos artificiales		
desfiles militares		
rodeos		
bandas		
concursos de belleza regionales		
bailes		
bailes folklóricos		
bailes de disfraces		

En muchas de las procesiones en el mundo hispánico figuran imágenes religiosas que representan a la Virgen María o a santos de devoción popular.

TERCERA ETAPA

Servicios y amenidades

ENTRADA

Play instructor tape, 2 min.

The *Entrada* of this *etapa* is more closely related to the task that students will have to perform in the *Hablar y escribir* section than is the case for the *Entradas* of the other *etapas*. You may wish to use one of the following suggestions. 1. Assign the *Estudiar y practicar* words for homework and play the *Entrada* in class the next day; you can do this while you are still working on the previous *etapa*. Then, assign the *Hablar* and *Escribir* sections for the next class. 2. Use the first suggestion but read all or part of the *Entrada* instead of playing the tape. 3. Play the *Entrada* in class and introduce the vocabulary as part of the comprehension activity before assigning the *Hablar* and *Escribir* sections as homework.

En la recepción del Hotel Bahía

Roberto and Paco have just arrived at their hotel in Cartagena. Listen to their conversation with the clerk as they check into the Hotel Bahía, and put the following phrases in order, indicating whether each phrase is said by them (*H* = *huésped*) or by the clerk (*E* = *empleado*). The first phrase is done for you.

En la recepción del Hotel Bahía

1	E	—Buenas tardes, señores. A sus órdenes.
___	___	—No pueden verlo, pero sí pueden oírlo.
___	___	—¿No podemos tener una habitación en el sexto o séptimo piso? Nos molesta el ruido de la calle.
___	___	—Aquí las tengo: dos personas, una habitación, seis noches, a partir de hoy.
___	___	—Lo siento mucho, señores. El hotel está completamente lleno.
___	___	—¡Cómo no! Tenemos lavamanos (*sink*), tina (*tub*) y ducha.
___	___	—Tenemos reservaciones para seis noches.
___	___	—Su habitación está en el primer piso.
___	___	—¿Podemos ver el mar desde la habitación?
___	___	—¿Hay baño completo en la habitación?

ANTES DE HABLAR

Play student tape, 1 min.

Estudiar y practicar

A sus órdenes.	*At your service.*
el baño	(*full*) *bath*
la ducha	*shower*
el lavamanos	(*bathroom*) *sink*

Lo siento mucho.	*I'm very sorry.*
lleno/-a	*full*
la piscina	*pool*
el piso	*floor (level)*
la tina	*bathtub*

Preparación

Imagine that you are a tourist in a nice hotel. You were expecting everything to go well but, unfortunately, you are encountering some problems with your accommodations. Write in Spanish the services and amenities you were expecting, and the problems you are encountering.

Servicios y amenidades	*Problemas*
Mini-bar en la habitación	El mini-bar no funciona.
	No hay mini-bar.
	El mini-bar no tiene refrescos.

HABLAR

Problemas en la recepción. Act out the following scene with a partner.

Turista

1. Greet the clerk. Inquire about your reservation, explaining what you had requested.

2. You are distressed to discover that your reservation has been canceled. It must be a mistake (*un error*). Find a solution to this problem.

3. You then discover several other problems. (You and your partner in this role play should choose one or two of the problems listed here and go into detail about them.)

   ■ Location of the room: You cannot sleep if you hear noise from the street (*el ruido de la calle*).
   ■ Facilities: You asked for a full bath.
   ■ You wanted a view of the ocean (*una vista al mar*), not of the swimming pool.

4. You are firm but not rude, and the clerk is able to make the necessary adjustments. Express your appreciation.

Empleado/-a

1. Greet the guest.
2. You are having trouble finding the reservation. When you find it, you see that it was marked "cancel" (*cancelar*). Luckily, the hotel is not completely full, so you can work out a solution to the problem.
3. You then discover several other problems. (You and your partner in this role play should choose one or two of the problems listed here and go into detail about them.)
   - Location of the room: You have rooms only on the first and second floors (*primer piso, segundo piso*).
   - Facilities: The only available rooms have a sink in the room, but share a bathroom with other guests.
   - The rooms on the ocean side of the hotel are full, except for two that are more expensive.
4. You are firm but always polite, and you and the guest are able to work things out to the guest's satisfaction.

ANTES DE ESCRIBIR

WRITING STRATEGY 6

Communicate forcefully

In Chapter 3 you worked on organizing your descriptions to make then more focused, as well as more interesting. Organization is also the key to communicating forcefully in situations in which you find you must complain about an injustice or about goods and services you have purchased that do not meet your expectations. One organizational strategy, which you will practice in this section, is to start with the statement of the problem as you see it. Then you explain what you mean by recounting what happened that displeased you. Finally, you return to a statement of the problem and your request for a remedy. No matter how you choose to organize your complaint, the key to being forceful is to make a clear and logical statement of the situation as you see it.

Preparación

You are going to write a letter of complaint to the manager of the Hotel Corona. Organize your letter by writing some notes in each of the sections that follow.

El problema:

El relato / ¿Qué pasó?

1.
2.
3.
4.

Consecuencia (*Result*):

ESCRIBIR

Imagine that you have returned from a disastrous vacation at the Hotel Corona. You write a letter to the manager, whom you did not meet because he or she was away on business while you were there. Using your notes, explain to the manager why you will never again return to the Hotel Corona.

OJO: You will learn how to open and close letters in Chapters 10 and 11. For now, use the salutation and greeting given here. They are appropriate for formal business correspondence.

> Estimado señor (Estimada señora):
>
> Acabo de regresar a casa después de una semana muy desagradable en su hotel. Le escribo _____
> _____
>
> Los problemas empezaron cuando llegamos _____
> _____
>
> Finalmente, siento informarle (*I am sorry to inform you*) que, a causa de la experiencia, _____
> _____
>
> Respetuosamente,

AUMENTAR EL VOCABULARIO

a partir de	*beginning with*
A sus órdenes.	*May I help you?* (*lit., at your service*)
agotado/-a	*exhausted, worn out*
cansado/-a	*tired*
descansado/-a	*rested*
el (la) empleado/-a	*clerk*
¡Eso es genial!	*What a great idea!*
largo/-a	*long*
corto/-a	*short* (*in length*)

OJO: *Parecerse a* means "to look alike." "My friend looks like his father" is *Mi amigo se parece a su padre.* "You two look so much alike!" is *¡Ustedes se parecen mucho!*

Lo siento mucho.	I'm very sorry.
lleno/-a	full
vacío/-a	*empty*
más (de)	more (**than**)
menos (de)	*less* (***than***)
parecer	to seem
potable	drinkable
¡Qué flojo/-a eres!	You're so lazy!
la recepción	front desk (**hotel**)
la piscina	*swimming pool*
el piso	*floor* (***level***)

EL BAÑO

Additional useful vocabulary: *maquillarse, pintarse* (to put on makeup); *el maquillaje* (makeup).

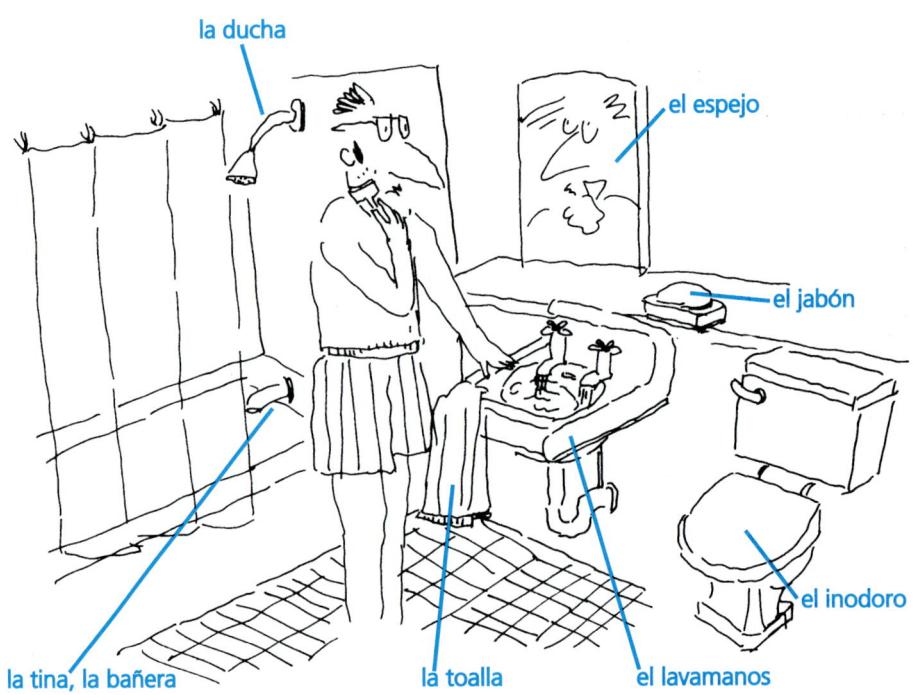

Give students one or more ways to respond: *Para mirarse la cara, el hombre necesita un espejo.*

Frases útiles: ¿*Dónde están los aseos?* ¿*Dónde están los servicios?* (Where is the restroom?); *El inodoro no funciona* (The toilet doesn't flush); *el papel higiénico* (toilet paper)

El arreglo personal. Paco está en el cuarto de baño. Para cada actividad, indica qué necesita.

1. Se mira la cara cuando se afeita.
2. Primero, pone el agua caliente.
3. Se lava bien la cara.
4. Después de afeitarse, se baña.
5. Se seca antes de vestirse.

a. el lavamanos
b. la ducha, la tina
c. la toalla
ch. el espejo
d. el jabón

Ventanilla al mundo hispánico — El agua corriente

Ask students who have traveled to recount where they could and could not drink the water, and what accommodations they had to make: agua mineral, coca-cola, etc.

La disponibilidad de agua corriente en las casas y los hoteles pequeños en muchos pueblos y ciudades pequeñas de la América Latina con frecuencia se hace posible mediante un sistema independiente de recolección y distribución. Un tanque grande que está sobre el tejado del edificio se llena con agua de lluvia, con agua de un camión distribuidor o del sistema municipal. El agua de este tanque después se distribuye por medio de la tubería interna del edificio hasta la cocina, el baño o donde se necesite.

En muchas partes del mundo, los sistemas municipales para la distribución del agua ya están viejos y comunmente el agua ya no se puede tomar, es decir que ya no es potable. Por lo tanto es bastante común encontrar agua embotellada en los hoteles y restaurantes. En los hoteles, si el agua que sale del grifo se puede tomar sin peligro, por lo general cerca del lavamanos del baño hay un letrero pequeño que dice "Agua potable."

Los refrescos y los jugos son muy populares entre los jóvenes de toda latinoamérica.

Preguntas

1. ¿De dónde viene el agua en las casas en algunos pueblos pequeños?
2. Si el agua está en un tanque encima de la casa, ¿cómo va a la cocina y al baño?
3. ¿Has viajado a un lugar donde no podías tomar el agua? ¿Qué tomaste en vez de agua?

INVESTIGAR LA GRAMÁTICA   The Preterite and Imperfect Used Together

You have seen that the preterite (*el pretérito*) is used to talk about events or conditions that are viewed from the speaker's perspective as being completely over and done with **at the time being talked about.** Here is an example of three such events that happen in a series.

Events in a series are usually expressed with the preterite, since the series implies that each event was completed before the next one began.

Esta mañana **me levanté** a las ocho, **me vestí,** y **fui** al museo con Roberto.

The preterite is also used when the events or conditions both begin and end within a specified period of time. It does not matter how long the period of time is, as long as both the beginning **and** end of the event/condition are contained within it.

Estuvieron en el museo **por veinte minutos.**
Los españoles **gobernaron** La Nueva España (México) **por casi trescientos años: de 1519 a 1810.**

The imperfect (*el imperfecto*), however, is used to describe activities or conditions that were habitual or routine in the past. Neither the beginning nor the end of the activity is mentioned.

Cuando Marcos **asistía** al colegio, **participaba** en varias actividades culturales.
Cuando **hacían** fiestas, siempre **invitaban** a la familia y a los amigos.

The imperfect is also used to talk about an activity that was in progress at the time being talked about. If more than one activity is in progress, the imperfect is used for each of them.

Point out to students that the imperfect is used for all of the verbs because all three actions are in progress.

Anoche antes de la fiesta, yo **ponía** la mesa mientras mi compañero de cuarto **lavaba** los platos y otro amigo **preparaba** la ensalada.

OJO: *The imperfect is almost always used to say at what time an activity was taking place because the hour of the day functions as background information for that activity.*

The imperfect and the preterite often occur in the same sentence whenever you wish to say that while one activity was in progress (imperfect) another event took place (preterite).

Mi amigo **preparaba** la ensalada cuando los primeros invitados **llegaron.**
Eran las nueve de la noche cuando **llegaron** los primeros invitados.
Todo el mundo **bailaba** y **conversaba** cuando **entramos** con la comida.
Miguel **bailaba** con Isabel cuando alguien **puso** su canción favorita.

Ponerlo a prueba

Assign as homework. In class, after students have reconstructed the story, have them tell it as a first-person narrative.

A. **Un robo en Madrid.**   Guadalupe Cortés, una de tus amigas, pasó las vacaciones de primavera en España. Cuando estaba en Madrid, tuvo una experiencia muy desagradable. Cuenta su historia.

1. Guadalupe llegar / Madrid por la noche

2. Tener reservación / hotel excelente
3. Esa noche dormir muy bien / porque estar cansada
4. Al día siguiente levantarse temprano / bañarse / desayunar
5. Después de desayunar decidir ir / Museo del Prado
6. El museo no estar lejos de su hotel, así que / decidir ir a pie
7. Haber mucha gente en la calle / porque ser las dos de la tarde
8. De repente (*Suddenly*) / ella darse cuenta de tener una mancha grande en el vestido
9. Poner la bolsa en el suelo / y empezar a limpiárselo
10. En ese momento aparecer un hombre / tomar su bolsa / empezar a correr
11. ¡Qué desgracia! / Lupita perder su dinero
12. Afortunadamente / tener cheques de viajero
13. Ir a la oficina de American Express / los empleados ayudarla esa misma tarde

OJO: Business establishments, offices, and schools in Spain generally close for two or three hours starting at 1:30 or 2:00 in the afternoon. Then the streets are filled with people traveling to their homes or to restaurants or cafeterias for the main meal of the day (*la comida*).

B. La niñez de Silvia. Lee los dos párrafos siguientes una o dos veces para ver de qué se tratan. Después léelos de nuevo, completándolos con la forma apropiada de los verbos entre paréntesis (imperfecto o pretérito).

¡OJO! Hay que prestar atención al contexto.

Cuando Silvia (**ser**) niña, su familia (**vivir**) en San Diego, California, en un barrio tranquilo. Silvia (**asistir**) a la escuela, (**jugar**) con sus amigos y en general (**llevar**) una vida sin aventuras. Cuando la niña (**tener**) diez años, sus padres, que (**ser**) médicos, (**decidir**) mudarse a Guatemala por dos años porque (**querer**) trabajar en un pueblo aislado. Según los médicos guatemaltecos, el pueblo no (**tener**) servicios médicos.
   De repente, la vida de Silvia y de su hermana (**cambiar**) radicalmente. Ya no (**haber**) tiempo de jugar; (**tener**) que poner todos sus juguetes y libros en cajas (*boxes*) y hacer las maletas. En junio de ese año Silvia (**despedirse**) de sus amigos y (**salir**) con su familia para Guatemala.

C. ¿Comprendiste? Ahora contesta las preguntas siguientes acerca de los dos párrafos de arriba.

1. ¿Dónde vivía la familia de Silvia?
2. Describe el barrio.
3. ¿Cómo era la vida de Silvia?
4. ¿Qué decisión tomaron los padres de Silvia?
5. ¿Cuándo tomaron esa decisión y por qué?

Do as a paired or small-group activity in class. Encourage students to create several sentences for each person.

CH. El apagón (*blackout*). Fíjate en el dibujo de una familia grande. Cuenta lo que hacía cada persona cuando se apagaron las luces.

D. El primer día de trabajo. Use the following form to interview a partner about his or her first day at a job with a regular salary. First, you and your partner should work together to formulate a question for each of the ten topics. Then take turns interviewing each other.

Encuesta: el primer día del primer trabajo

Nombre del investigador (de la investigadora):

Nombre del entrevistado (de la entrevistada):

Fecha de la entrevista:

Tema	*Pregunta*
1. Lugar del trabajo	
2. Tipo de trabajo	
3. Edad cuando empezó a trabajar	

Tercera etapa

4. Horas normales del trabajo
5. Ropa para el trabajo
6. Emociones del primer día
7. Lo que dijo el jefe
8. Lo que hizo el primer día
9. Horas del primer día
10. Diferencias entre el primer día y los otros días

OJO: Organiza tus ideas antes de empezar, y ¡cuidado con el imperfecto y el pretérito!

In-class activity. This can be the basis of an in-class or out-of-class writing activity also.

E. **Informe sobre las experiencias.** Ahora escribe el relato del primer día de trabajo de tu compañero/-a, usando la información que conseguiste en la Actividad D.

F. **¿Qué pasó ayer?** Describe lo que pasó en cada dibujo. Tu descripción debe tener dos partes: (1) lo que hacía la gente en cada dibujo cuando (2) ocurrió algo inesperado (*unexpected*). Da todos los detalles que puedas.

OJO: Palabra útil: el lagarto = *lizard*.

¡TIENES LA PALABRA!

Haz las siguientes actividades con un compañero (una compañera).

A. Encuesta sobre la niñez. Entrevista a un compañero (una compañera) de la clase y apunta la información que recibas para después comunicársela a la clase.

¿Con qué frecuencia?
Cuando eras niño/-a...

                          siempre   a menudo   a veces   casi nunca   nunca

1. jugar al béisbol / al fútbol / al tenis / al _____
2. ir a la biblioteca para sacar libros
3. leer en vez de ver televisión
4. obedecer a sus padres
5. sacar buenas notas en la primaria / el colegio
6. hacerse daño en un accidente (pedir detalles)

B. Llegando al hotel. Act out the following scene with a partner.

Turista

1. Greet the clerk.
2. Inquire about a room for three nights. You are traveling with a friend.
3. You would like to have a view of the ocean.
4. Ask about price. Find out if breakfast is included.
5. Ask about mode of payment (credit card, traveler's checks, and so on). Inquire about checkout time.

Before students begin the activity, brainstorm what questions they will ask. A response sheet set up as a grid, with activities listed on the left side of the page and the frequencies across the top, would allow students to check off their partners' responses.

As preparation, review with students (or have them review for homework) this chapter for phrases used in a transaction between a tourist and hotel clerk.

Empleado/-a

1. Greet the guest.
2. Inquire about room preferences.
3. The hotel is rather full, so you are not able to give the guest everything that he or she desires.
4. Answer the guest's questions about price and breakfast.
5. Answer the guest's questions about mode of payment and checkout time. Wish the guests a pleasant stay.

Variation: Have pairs of students work together on a single description of a movie or television program. After a few minutes of preparation, each pair describes its program or film to the rest of the class to see if they can guess it.

C. Un programa inolvidable. Selecciona a alguien con quien hablar. Piensa en un programa de televisión (o en una película) que hayas visto recientemente y descríbele a tu compañero/-a la acción de un episodio (o de la película). Tu compañero/-a tiene que identificar el programa o película que describes. Después, a tu compañero/-a le toca hacer la descripción y tú tienes que identificar el programa o película. ¡OJO! Cuenta el episodio en el pasado y ten cuidado con el uso del pretérito y del imperfecto.

OTRA VUELTA

Play instructor tape, 2 min.

Ahora escucha otra vez la conversación entre Roberto, Paco y el empleado del Hotel Bahía que está al comienzo de esta etapa. Al escuchar, completa el resumen (*summary*) que está a continuación.

En el Hotel Bahía

El empleado les ofrece a Roberto y a Paco una habitación en el _____ piso. Los amigos prefieren cambiar al _____ o _____ piso porque no les gusta el _____ de la calle. Desafortunadamente, no hay otras _____ disponibles; el hotel está completamente _____. Además, las habitaciones en los pisos altos son mucho más _____, y Roberto y Paco necesitan una habitación a un precio _____ .

COMENTARIO CULTURAL

Las leyendas religiosas

Se puede ver este águila (eagle) de piedra, símbolo de luz y poder para los indígenas precolombinos, cerca de San Agustín, Colombia.

Capítulo seis   Para orientarnos

En su viaje a Colombia, Paco y Roberto van a visitar las ciudades de Cali, Cartagena y Bogotá, pero hay otras partes muy bonitas e interesantes de Colombia que no van a conocer. Una de estas partes es el Departamento de Boyacá, situado en el interior del país, al noroeste de la ciudad de Bogotá.

Las mayores concentraciones de la población de Colombia se encuentran en la costa del Mar Caribe y en las regiones mineras. Las poblaciones pequeñas que se encuentran en el altiplano, tales como muchos pueblos de Boyacá, han sufrido relativamente pocos cambios a través de la historia colonial y moderna del país o como resultado del proceso de la industrialización.

Los descubrimientos arqueológicos más recientes indican que los primeros pobladores del altiplano de Boyacá llegaron allí hace unos 12.000 años. Unos quinientos años antes de la llegada de los españoles al Nuevo Mundo la civilización indígena que ocupaba la región era la de los *chibchas*. Una de las leyendas de los chibchas, la leyenda de Bochica, tiene mucho en común con el cuento bíblico de Noé y el diluvio universal.

Según la leyenda chibcha, hubo un período en que los chibchas dejaron de seguir su religión y desobedecieron las tradiciones que dictaban sus actividades diarias. Así es que ofendieron a sus dioses, y abandonaron a su dios principal, el Sol. Para castigar (*punish*) a los chibchas, el Sol abrió los cielos y mandó muchísima lluvia a la Tierra. Los chibchas tuvieron que subir a la parte más alta de las montañas para salvarse de la inundación (*flood*). Desde allí rezaron para que el Sol tuviera piedad de ellos y para que se secara la tierra. El Sol los perdonó y les mandó a Bochica, un dios que tenía la barba y el pelo largos y grises. Bochica tiró su bastón hacia el sureste; se dividieron las montañas, salieron las aguas y la tierra volvió a su estado anterior de fertilidad. Según la leyenda, Bochica se quedó con los chibchas; les enseñó a hilar (*spin*) la lana y el algodón y a hacer ropa.

OJO: Tiró su bastón: *threw his cane.*

A. Pon (*Put*) en orden cronológico los eventos de la leyenda de los chibchas.

____ Los chibchas no seguían las tradiciones de su religión.

____ El Sol les mandó al pueblo a Bochica, un dios especialmente para ellos.

____ Todo el mundo subió a las montañas para no morir del diluvio (*flood*).

____ Bochica vivió con los chibchas y les ayudó mucho.

____ Abandonaron a sus dioses, hasta (*even*) a su dios principal, el Sol.

____ El Sol perdonó al pueblo.

____ El Sol mandó mucha lluvia. La gente tuvo que escaparse.

____ Los chibchas querían volver a su religión y rezaron mucho a su dios, el Sol.

B. Todas las culturas, incluso los grupos locales y pequeños, tienen sus leyendas. Escribe una leyenda relacionada con los grupos, individuos o instituciones siguientes.

1. George Washington
2. tu universidad
3. tu familia o tu grupo étnico

Indica en el mapa más o menos dónde está la región de Boyacá.

DE INTEGRACIÓN

[Play video]

Program 6 *Pasajeros a bordo* Regional and urban transportation

Actividad A reinforces the vocabulary of the second etapa and the structures of the third etapa.

Actividad B reinforces the structure presented in the first etapa of this chapter.

A. Edificios de interés. Write a short description of a historic monument with which you are familiar. Write as though this will be used as part of a flyer about your college or university.

B. Una descripción personal. ¿Has cambiado mucho durante tu vida? Escribe una descripción de ti mismo/-a a la edad de diez años (más o menos), dando detalles acerca de tu familia, tus diversiones, tu personalidad.

C. Llegando al hotel. Act out the following scene with a partner.

> *Turista*
>
> 1. Greet the clerk. Inquire about your reservation, saying how many people are in your party and how many nights the reservation is for.
> 2. Inquire about the location of the room.
> 3. Ask about the facilities in the room.
> 4. Express your appreciation to the clerk.

Empleado/-a

1. Greet the guest.
2. Look up the reservation and verify the information. Everything is in order.
3. Answer the guest's questions about the location of the room and the facilities in it.
4. Acknowledge the guest's compliments and thanks.

CH. Perdone, señor(a). Act out the following scene with a partner.

Turista

You have just checked into your room in a modest hotel and find that there are several problems. Call the desk clerk and mention each one, suggesting a solution in each case.

- There are no lamps.
- There is no hot water.
- You cannot close the window.
- The previous guest has left clothes in the room.

Empleado/-a

You are a desk clerk in a hotel. A new guest calls to complain about several problems. Listen to the guest's complaints and decide what to do. You may wish to use some of the following suggestions.

- You will ask someone to look for a lamp.
- Someone is already working on the hot water problem.
- It is better to keep the window open to catch the ocean breeze.
- You will ask the maid to get the clothes.
- You hope that the guest has a pleasant visit.

D. En una excursión. You are a tourist who is visiting Cartagena and wants to take a tour of the city. With a partner playing the role of the hotel clerk, use

---

1. *Actividades C* and *CH* reinforce the vocabulary and contexts of the third *etapa*.
2. In *Actividad CH*, make sure that the *turista* offers serious and reasonable solutions and that the *empleado/-a* responds adequately to them.

Actividad CH reinforces the vocabulary and contexts of the second and third *etapas*.

Actividad D reinforces the contexts and the structures presented in the first and second *etapas*.

the following cues to get the necessary information. The clerk gives the information requested. Ask the clerk

- whether there are tours of the city
- where they start
- how long they last
- what they cost

E. **Entrevista.** Busca un compañero (una compañera) de la clase que no conozcas bien. Entrevista a esa persona para descubrir

- dónde vivía cuando era niño/-a
- cómo era la casa
- cuántas personas había en la familia
- si alguna vez le pasó algo extraño o fuera de lo común

Prepárate para presentarle a tu compañero/-a a la clase.

VOCABULARIO

¡A viajar!
Let's travel!

agencia (f) de viajes *travel agency*
agente (m/f) *agent*
balneario (m) *bathing or health resort*
excursión (f) *tour*
no fumar *no smoking*
por avión *by air*
por tierra *by land*
sección (f) de fumar *smoking section*

Alojamiento
Lodging

alcoba (f) *bedroom*
alojarse *to stay temporarily, to have lodging*
alquilar *to rent*
alquiler (m) *the rent*
compartir *to share*
habitación (f) *room (with a bed), as in a hotel*
hacer los arreglos *to make arrangements*
pieza (f) *room*
piscina (f) *swimming pool*
piso (m) *floor (level)*
recepción (f) *front desk (hotel)*

El baño
The bathroom

bañera (f) *bathtub*
baño (m) (completo) *(full) bath*
ducha (f) *shower*
espejo (m) *mirror*
inodoro (m) *toilet*
jabón (m) *a bar of soap*
lavamanos (m) *washbasin (sink)*
tina (f) *bathtub*
toalla (f) *towel*

La cuenta y los precios
Bills and prices

bajo/-a *low*
barato/-a *inexpensive*
cambiar dinero *to exchange money*
caro/-a *expensive*
cheques (m pl) de viajero *traveler's checks*
efectivo (m) *cash in bill form*
firmar *to sign*
más (de) *more (than)*
menos (de) *less (than)*

monedas (f pl) *cash in coin form*
pagar a plazos *to pay in installments*
pago (m) *payment*
precio (m) *price*

La historia
History

arma (m) *weapon*
artefacto (m) *relic; artificat*
castillo (m) *castle*
catedral (f) *cathedral*
corona (f) *crown*
derrota (f) *defeat*
en exposición *on display, on exhibit*
época (f) *epoch, era*
exposición (f) *display, exhibition*
guerra (f) *war*
imperio (m) *empire*
libertad (f) *freedom*
museo (m) *museum*
paraíso (m) *paradise*
siglo (m) *century*
torre (f) *tower*
ultramar (m) *overseas*
fundar *to found, establish*

Las direcciones
Giving directions

a dos cuadras de *two blocks away from*
a la derecha *to the right*
a la izquierda *to the left*
bajar *to go down*
doblar *to turn*
ir (seguir) derecho *to go straight ahead*
pasar por *to pass through, by*

seguir (i, i) *to continue; follow*
subir *to go up*

Materias y minerales
Materials and minerals

cobre (m) *copper*
hierro (m) *iron*
madera (f) *wood*

La frecuencia
Frequency

a menudo, mucho *often, a lot*
a veces *sometimes*
casi nunca *seldom (almost never)*
casi siempre *almost always*
con frecuencia *frequently*
de vez en cuando *occasionally*
nunca *never*
poco *a little*
siempre *always*

Palabras para indicar posición
Words that indicate position

a comienzos de *at the beginning of*
a fines de *at the end of*
a partir de *beginning with*
al nivel del mar *at sea level*
situado/-a *situated*
ubicado/-a *situated; located*

Palabras descriptivas
Descriptive words

agotado/-a *exhausted, worn out*
cansado/-a *tired*
corto/-a *short (in length)*
cubierto/-a (de) *covered (with)*
descansado/-a *rested*
diseñado/-a *designed*
gratis *free (no cost)*
largo/-a *long*
libre *free (not busy; not enslaved)*
lleno/-a *full*
potable *drinkable*
vacío/-a *empty*

Sustantivos útiles
Useful nouns

brisa (f) *breeze*
empleado/-a (m/f) *clerk*
humo (m) *smoke*
mercancías (f pl) *merchandise*
mezcla (f) *mixture*
promedio (m) *average*
puerto (m) *seaport*
sentido (m) *sense (physical)*
temperatura (f) *temperature*

Verbos útiles
Useful verbs

atraer *to attract*
construir *to build*
cubrir *to cover*
diseñar *to design*
llegar *to arrive*
llegar a ser *to become*
mezclar *to mix*
parecer *to seem*

Otras palabras y expresiones útiles
Other useful words and expressions

A sus órdenes.   *At your service.*
¡Cómo no!   *Of course!*
¿En qué puedo servirle(s)?   *May I help you?*
¡Eso es genial!   *What a great idea!*
Hay de todo.   *There's a lot of variety.*
Lo siento mucho.   *I'm very sorry.*
Me está dando hambre.   *I'm getting hungry.*
por lo menos   *at least*
¡Qué flojo/-a eres!   *You're so lazy!*
¡Socorro!   *Help!*
un poco de todo   *a little bit of everything*
¡Vamos ya!   *Let's go!*

VOCABULARIO PERSONALIZADO

¡Aquí tienen su casa!

Capítulo 7

COMMUNICATIVE OBJECTIVES

In this chapter, you will learn some new ways to

- ask for and give advice
- talk about what might (or might not) exist or occur
- make purchases
- express desires and influence others

PRIMERA ETAPA

"¿Qué debo hacer?"

ENTRADA

Play instructor tape, 3 min.

"¿Qué precio lleva...?"

You will hear a conversation between Paco, Roberto, and a salesperson. As you listen, identify (1) the items that the clerk suggests, (2) the item that Roberto decides to buy, and (3) the amount he pays for it.

Un regalito para Anita

____ 1. una cinta de música popular   Sí   No
____ 2. una cinta de música tradicional   Sí   No
____ 3. una joya   Sí   No
____ 4. una prenda de vestir   Sí   No
____ 5. un pájaro vivo   Sí   No
____ 6. una estatua   Sí   No
____ 7. Roberto pagó
   a. $8.500
   b. $7.000
   c. $6.500
   ch. $5.500
   d. $5.000

EMPEZAR A ESCUCHAR

Leer

meter la pata	to make a social blunder, "put your foot in your mouth"
tener fama de	to be known for or as
mal educado/-a	ill-mannered, rude
unos consejos	some advice
el cariño	fondness, affection, kindness
descalzo/-a	barefoot

Primera etapa

Play student tape, 2 min.

Repetir

Escucha la cinta y repite lo que oyes.

Identificar

En una hoja aparte, escribe en una columna las palabras y frases anteriores. Vas a oír algunas oraciones. Cada vez que oigas una de estas palabras o frases, apunta el número de la oración al lado de la palabra. Cada oración se leerá dos veces.

Escribir

Vas a oír unas oraciones, cada una leída dos veces. Escríbelas al escucharlas.

Reconocer

Ahora, lee otra vez las oraciones que acabas de escribir. Cada una contiene una o más de las palabras y frases anteriores. Al releerlas, subraya todas las palabras y frases que vienen de la lista. Mientras lees, haz todas las correcciones necesarias.

ESCUCHAR

Play student tape, 1 min.

EPISODIO 1: Las preocupaciones de Paco

Enfoque comunicativo

Roberto and Paco have gone to Bogotá, where they are met by Marcos, who has invited them to stay in his home. Listen to their conversation and try to figure out

- why they are going to leave the luggage in the car
- why Paco is nervous
- the reputation that Paco feels many North Americans have

To develop students' listening and transcription skills further, have them write down the sentence that gives them the information they need to answer each question.

La llegada de los amigos

1. Los amigos dejan el equipaje en el coche porque
   a. la madre de Marcos quiere conocerlos inmediatamente
   b. hay mucho que llevar y necesitan ayuda
   c. no han llegado todavía a la casa de Marcos
2. Paco está nervioso porque
   a. no le gustan las ciudades grandes
   b. tiene miedo de viajar en avión
   c. quiere quedar bien con la familia
3. Según Paco, los norteamericanos tienen fama de ser
   a. mal educados
   b. ricos
   c. generosos

Enfoque lingüístico

Escucha la conversación otra vez y apunta

- ■ la expresión que usa Marcos cuando llegan a su casa
- ■ lo que dice Marcos para calmar a Paco
- ■ las palabras que usa Paco para expresar su preocupación

ESCUCHAR

Play student tape, 1 min.

EPISODIO 2: "¿Puedes darme unos consejos?"

Enfoque comunicativo

As the conversation continues, Marcos gives Paco some advice. As you listen, see if you can determine

- ■ how Paco and Roberto should address Marcos's mother
- ■ when and where they should **not** go barefoot
- ■ where Paco should keep his toiletries

Point out that the use of direct command forms is frequent on the tape only because Paco and Marcos are close friends and because Marcos is giving him advice.

Los consejos de Marcos

1. ¿Cómo deben Paco y Roberto dirigirle la palabra a la madre de Marcos?
   a. doña Consuelo   c. Mamá
   b. Consuelo
2. En la casa de Marcos, ¿dónde se permite andar descalzo?
   a. en el cuarto de baño   c. en ningún sitio
   b. en los dormitorios
3. Paco debe dejar sus cosas
   a. en el baño   c. en su pieza
   b. en la cocina

Enfoque lingüístico

Escucha otra vez el Episodio 2 y apunta

- ■ dos maneras apropiadas de hablarle a la madre de un amigo (una amiga) en Bogotá
- ■ lo que dice Marcos otra vez para calmar a Paco

VERIFICAR

Completa las oraciones.

1. Al llegar, los tres muchachos entran en la casa inmediatamente porque...
2. Paco está nervioso porque...

Have students prepare additional questions or incomplete statements based on the *Episodios* to present to their classmates.

3. Paco quiere que Marcos le dé...
4. Según Marcos, los amigos deben llamar a su madre...
5. Otra recomendación de Marcos es que sus amigos no...
6. Finalmente, después de bañarse hay que...

AUMENTAR EL VOCABULARIO

acostumbrarse a	to be/get accustomed to
la costumbre	custom, habit
andar	to walk
caminar	to walk
ir/venir a pie	to go/come on foot
el balcón	balcony
el cariño	fondness, affection, kindness
cariñoso/-a	affectionate
el odio	hatred
el consejo	a piece of advice
aconsejar	to advise
el (la) consejero/-a	counselor
el quehacer	chore
recomendar (ie)	to recommend
descalzo/-a	barefoot
meter la pata	to make a social blunder, "put your foot in your mouth"
ofender	to offend
tener fama de	to be known for or as
conocido/-a	well-known
mal educado/-a	ill-mannered, rude
tener mala fama	to have a bad reputation

Explain to students that *la pata* is used to refer to the legs of animals, or of furniture, whereas *la pierna* is a human leg. A related expression is *patas arriba* (upside down).

Point out that the opposite of *mal educado* is *bien educado* (well-mannered, polite).

VENTANILLA AL MUNDO HISPÁNICO   "Está en su casa"

OJO: These invitations are rather formal. With someone you address as *tú*, you would say *Estás en tu casa* or *Siéntete como en tu propia casa*.

Have students practice in pairs welcoming each other into their homes. The host's phrase is *Bienvenido/-a, estás en tu casa.*

—Está en su casa.

—Siéntase como en su propia casa.

Cuando le das la bienvenida a un invitado que llega a tu casa, aunque las palabras pueden variar un poco, el mensaje es el mismo: "Mi casa es su casa." No te sorprendas de recibir algún día una invitación por escrito que dice: **La cena será en su casa este viernes a las nueve de la noche....** La cena no va a tener lugar en tu propia casa: la expresión sólo es una forma de ser educado y presupone que tú sabes que "mi casa es su casa".

LA CASA

Give the following definitions and have students respond with the words.
1. el piso superior de una casa 2. el exterior de la casa, generalmente de piedra o de madera 3. la pieza donde los miembros de la familia leen, conversan o miran la televisión 4. lo que se usa para subir a otro piso de la casa 5. el piso inferior de una casa que está debajo de la tierra 6. los dos extremos de una pieza 7. la parte exterior de la casa que la protege contra la lluvia y el frío.

Remind students that *pieza* means a room, but *habitación, dormitorio,* and *alcoba* specifically refer to a bedroom.

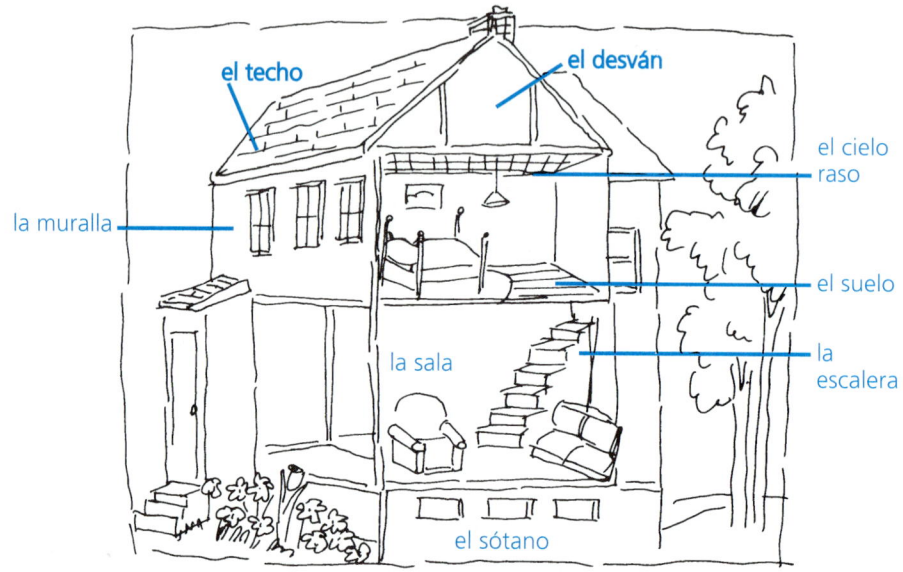

¿Cómo es tu domicilio? Contesta las siguientes preguntas con referencia a tu propia casa o apartamento.

1. ¿Cuántas piezas hay en tu casa?
2. ¿Por dónde entran primero los invitados? ¿La familia entra generalmente por esa misma puerta?
3. ¿Usan Uds. la sala con frecuencia? ¿Cuándo la usan?
4. ¿Cuál es la pieza más popular en tu casa?
5. ¿Cuántos televisores tienen Uds.? ¿En qué piezas se encuentran?
6. ¿Cuántos pisos tiene tu casa? ¿Hay un sótano? ¿Qué tienen Uds. allí?

USO PRÁCTICO DEL ESPAÑOL   Ir de compras

Going shopping when you are in another country is an interesting cultural experience. As you saw in Chapter 5, small specialty stores are the norm in Spanish-speaking countries, so the shopper may go to a number of shops in order to buy, for example, bread, fruit, light bulbs, and soap. As in the United States, large supermarkets containing all of these items are also available. Travelers often wonder how to deal with the issue of bargaining. In an open-air market where you have to ask the vendor for the price of an item, bargaining (*regatear*) is permitted and often expected. In stores, on the other hand, the amounts printed on price tags are fixed prices, just as they are in the United States. Some stores will even post a sign reading *precios fijos,* so that customers will not try to negotiate a lower price. Here are some phrases that are commonly used in shopping.

Vendedor(a)

¿En qué puedo servirle?	Can I help you?
¿Qué talla necesita?	What size (*clothing*) do you need?
¿Qué número calza?	What size shoe do you take?
¿Qué color (*estilo*) prefiere?	What color (*style*) do you prefer?
Lo siento, pero no hay.	I'm sorry, but we don't have any.
Lo siento, pero no nos quedan.	I'm sorry, but we're all out.

Cliente

Busco...	I'm looking for . . .
¿Tienen Uds...?	Do you have . . . ?
¿Cuánto vale (cuesta)?	How much is it?
Es muy caro/-a.	It's very expensive.
¿Se aceptan tarjetas de crédito?	Do you take credit cards?

Ponerlo a prueba

A. Poner en orden. Pon en orden esta conversación entre una dependiente y una cliente.

_____ Normalmente 38 o 40. Depende del vestido.

_____ Busco un vestido para la boda (*wedding*) de mi hija.

_____ Quizás azul o verde. La madre del novio va a llevar un vestido rosado.

_____ Buenos días. ¿En qué puedo servirle, señora?

_____ ¿Y qué color prefiere?

_____ Muy bien, señora, aquí tenemos unos vestidos de su talla. A ver si alguno le gusta.

_____ ¡Qué bien, muchas felicidades! ¿Qué talla necesita?

B. Diferencias culturales. Doña Consuelo va a pensar que los amigos de Marcos son mal educados si hacen ciertas cosas. Indica si los invitados en tu casa pueden hacer estas cosas o no.

1. Los invitados en la casa de Marcos no deben andar descalzos. **En mi casa los invitados...**

2. Los invitados en la casa de Marcos no deben decirle "Consuelo" a su mamá. **En mi casa los invitados...**

3. Los invitados en la casa de Marcos no deben dejar sus toallas en el cuarto de baño. **En mi casa los invitados...**

4. Los invitados en la casa de Marcos no deben usar el mismo jabón que otra persona. **En mi casa los invitados...**
5. Los invitados en la casa de Marcos no deben desayunar en pijama y bata. **En mi casa los invitados...**

C. Preguntas personales

1. ¿En qué situaciones te pones nervioso/-a? (¿En una fiesta, cuando hablas en público, cuando conoces a los padres de tu novio/-a?)
2. ¿Qué consejos les das a tus amigos cuando están de visita en tu casa?
3. En tu opinión, ¿es fácil o difícil ser invitado/-a en la casa de otra persona? ¿Cuáles son algunas situaciones problemáticas?
4. ¿Puedes dar un ejemplo de una actividad o costumbre que te parezca mal educada?
5. ¿Cómo te diriges (*do you address*) a los amigos de tus padres? ¿Y a tus profesores?
6. ¿Eres cariñoso/-a o reservado/-a? ¿Es difícil para ti expresar el cariño?

CH. Pues, yo prefiero...

Estás hablando por teléfono con un amigo (una amiga) que está de vacaciones en otro país. Cada vez que tu amigo/-a describe su experiencia allí, comenta sobre tus propias preferencias en cuanto a la misma cosa.

Modelo: Este hotel no tiene baños en las habitaciones.
　　　　　Pues, está bien, ¿no? Así pagas menos por la habitación.
　　　o: *Pues, yo prefiero tener una habitación con baño privado.*

1. Tenemos que compartir un baño con otros huéspedes.
2. La costumbre es cenar cada noche a las diez.
3. No hay tina de baño, sino ducha solamente.
4. Después de las nueve de la mañana no hay agua caliente.
5. No tenemos champú y usamos el jabón para lavarnos la cabeza.

D. Definiciones.

Escoge la definición o ejemplo que mejor corresponde a las palabras indicadas.

1. andar
2. el balcón
3. el cariño
4. el cielo raso
5. el consejo
6. descalzo
7. el desván

a. el amor
b. ser conocido (por algo)
c. la parte superior que cubre un edificio
ch. ir a pie de un lugar a otro
d. el techo interior de una pieza
e. la parte subterránea de un edificio
f. la advertencia que se da o se recibe acerca de una cosa

8. el sótano
9. el techo
10. tener fama de

g. el espacio entre el techo y el cielo raso
h. un área con suelo y balustrada al exterior de una ventana grande
i. sin zapatos

INVESTIGAR LA GRAMÁTICA   Introducción al subjuntivo

This is a general introduction to the concept of the subjunctive. Explanations of other uses of the subjunctive follow in the third etapa *of this chapter and in later chapters.*

The verb forms (present, preterite, and imperfect) that you have been using, called **indicative** forms, are used to talk about events or conditions that form part of your experience. In that sense, they refer to relatively concrete and specific events or conditions.

A parallel set of present-tense verb forms in Spanish is called the present **subjunctive.** Very little in English usage corresponds to the subjunctive in Spanish, so you will have to spend extra time learning when to use the subjunctive. No single generalization will tell you what the subjunctive "means" in Spanish. Rather, there are about six major uses of the subjunctive that we will take up one at a time. The first one we will examine is used when describing people or things that are not explicitly part of our own experience.

The "Wish List" Subjunctive

We often "describe" people that we have never met or things that we have never seen. This is what we do when we say things like

I want to take a course from a professor **who's an easy grader.**
I'm looking for a house **that has two bathrooms and three bedrooms.**
I have to buy a sweater **that costs less than $35.00.**
Is there anyone here **who can help me?**

In each of these examples, the probability that a professor, house, sweater, or person with these attributes exists is not at issue; it's just that you don't have any **specific** instances of them in your experience. Thus, the descriptive part of each sentence (the part with the attributes) will use the present subjunctive.

Quiero tomar un curso de un profesor **que dé notas altas.**
Busco una casa **que tenga dos baños y tres alcobas.**
Necesito comprar un suéter **que cueste menos de $35.00.**
¿Hay alguien aquí **que pueda ayudarme?**

Compare the preceding sentences with the following.

I want to take a course from Professor Jones, who's an easy grader.
I plan to buy a house (which I saw today) that has two bathrooms and three bedrooms.
I tried on a sweater that costs less than $35.00.
There's someone here who can help you.

In these examples, the professor, the house, the sweater, and the "someone" with the attributes mentioned are already part of your experience—you know, or have seen, the easy grades, the specific house that meets your requirements, the sweater, and the person who can help you. Therefore, the descriptive part of each sentence (the part with the attributes) uses the indicative.

Sometimes we describe people or things that literally do not exist.

There is no one who sings better than Gloria Estefan.
There's nothing here that I like.
In San Diego there are no restaurants that serve Eskimo cuisine.

Obviously, if someone or something with particular attributes is believed not to exist, it cannot form part of the speaker's experience. Thus, the descriptive part of each of these sentences uses the subjunctive.

No hay nadie **que cante** mejor que Gloria Estefan.
No hay nada aquí **que me guste**.
En San Diego, no hay ningún restaurante **que sirva comida esquimal**.

In summary, then, you will use the subjunctive verb forms to describe people or things with attributes that do not form part of your experience or that do not exist.

Forming the Present Subjunctive

For almost all Spanish verbs, the present subjunctive is formed by removing the *-o* from the *yo* form of the present indicative, and adding the following endings.

OJO: Note that *-ar* and *-er* stem-changing verbs follow exactly the same pattern of changes in both the present indicative and the present subjunctive.

hablar → hablo →	hable	hablemos
	hables	habléis
	hable	hablen
pensar → pienso →	piense	pensemos
	pienses	penséis
	piense	piensen
conocer → conozco →	conozca	conozcamos
	conozcas	conozcáis
	conozca	conozcan
salir → salgo →	salga	salgamos
	salgas	salgáis
	salga	salgan

Remind students that the spelling of verb endings in *-car*, *-gar*, or *-zar* is affected by present subjunctive endings. Have students review the spelling of the preterite *yo* form of *buscar, llegar, almorzar*.

You can see that no matter how irregular the original *yo* form is, as long as it ends in *-o*, the formation of the present subjunctive is entirely predictable. The only time you have to learn a special form for the present subjunctive is when the original *yo* form does not end in *-o*. Even then, the endings are predictable.

OJO: A written accent mark is placed on the *yo* and the *él, ella,* and *usted* forms of *dar* to distinguish them from the preposition *de*.

dar → dé, des, dé, demos, deis, den
estar → esté, estés, esté, estemos, estéis, estén

Primera etapa

haber → haya, hayas, haya, hayamos, hayáis, hayan
ir → vaya, vayas, vaya, vayamos, vayáis, vayan
saber → sepa, sepas, sepa, sepamos, sepáis, sepan
ser → sea, seas, sea, seamos, seáis, sean

Stem-changing verbs that end in *-ir* have two stem changes in the subjunctive.

dormir (ue, u)

duerma	durmamos
duermas	durmáis
duerma	duerman

OJO: Study tip: You now know two verb tenses where a second stem change occurs in *-ir* verbs: the present subjunctive, just introduced, and the preterite (*dormí, dormiste, durmió, dormimos, dormisteis, durmieron*), introduced earlier.

Ponerlo a prueba

A. ¿Existe o no existe? You have been eavesdropping on several conversations. Based on the information contained in each sentence, write *Sí* next to it if you are certain that the person or thing with the attributes referred to exists, and *No* if you don't know whether it exists or not.

Conversación A

— Busco una casa en la playa que podamos alquilar este verano.
— Pues una amiga mía ya tiene una. Qué suerte tiene, ¿verdad?

Conversación B

— No conozco a nadie que sepa esquiar.
— Mi primo es un esquiador olímpico.
— ¿Da clases? Quiero encontrar a alguien que me enseñe.
— Si quieres, le preguntaré si tiene tiempo.

Conversación C

— ¿Sabes si hay alguien en nuestra clase que haya visitado Chile?
— Que yo sepa, no, pero mi primo quiere ir este verano.
— Muy bien. Dicen que las montañas son magníficas para esquiar.
— Mi primo espera trabajar allí. Siempre están buscando instructores que hablen más de un idioma.

As a follow-up, have students work in pairs to revise each conversation, making the indefinite references definite and vice versa to the degree that the context allows.

The open-ended nature of the activity will produce more than one correct response in some instances.

B. La vida diaria de la gente. You have decided that one way to gain insight into the daily life of the community you are visiting is to read the classified ads in the local newspaper. Unfortunately, the only copy you have is not clearly printed, and you have to fill in the illegible words and phrases in order to understand what has been written. Complete the following ads as they are likely to read.

Modelo: Estudiante hondureño _____ coche _____ barato y bueno.
Estudiante hondureño busca un coche que sea barato y bueno.

1. Profesora _____ secretaria _____ experiencia con computadoras.
2. Compañía pequeña _____ secretaria _____ leer, hablar y escribir español.
3. Consultorio veterinario _____ estudiante de biología _____ interés en participar en investigaciones científicas.
4. Coleccionista de discos _____ comprar música _____ de origen latinoamericano.
5. Numismático _____ monedas _____ perfil (*profile*) de Simón Bolívar.
6. Grupo musical _____ percusionista _____ tocar música latina.
7. Profesor de inglés _____ asistente _____ español e italiano.
8. Vendedora de libros _____ a alguien _____ leer manuscritos originales.
9. Novelista _____ traductores _____ expertos en novelas históricas.
10. Restaurante _____ meseros _____ trabajar los fines de semana.

C. **Encuesta.** Muchas veces la amistad se basa en los intereses mutuos. Imagínate que te encuentras en un grupo de personas que acabas de conocer. Habla con otros del grupo, diciéndoles lo que buscas, para ver si puedes encontrar a por lo menos dos personas que tengan tus mismos intereses.

Modelo: Busco dos personas que conozcan a una estrella de cine.
(*Nombre*) y (*Nombre*) conocen a una estrella de cine.

o: *No hay nadie en la clase que conozca a una estrella de cine.*

Busco dos personas que...

1. hablar ruso o chino
2. tener más de cuatro hermanos
3. haber nacido en otro país
4. nunca exagerar ni mentir
5. estudiar para ser médico/-a
6. vivir con sus abuelos
7. haber visitado un país de habla española
8. nunca tomar café

CH. **Sumario.** Al terminar tu encuesta, escribe un párrafo para informar a la clase sobre los resultados del trabajo. Puedes incluir oraciones apropiadas para conectar las ideas.

D. **"Quisiera..."** Termina las oraciones de forma original y verdadera.

1. Quisiera pasar las vacaciones en un sitio donde...
2. Quisiera encontrar un trabajo que...

3. Quisiera conocer a una persona que...
4. Quisiera tener amigos que...
5. Quisiera vivir en un sitio donde...
6. Quisiera tener un auto que...

Do this in class as a small-group oral activity, or have students expand it and do it individually as a writing assignment at home.

E. **El amigo (La amiga) ideal.** Piensa en el amigo (la amiga) ideal. ¿Cómo es? Menciona tres o más características. Es una persona que...

1.
2.
3.

F. **Preguntas personales**

1. ¿Qué cualidades buscas en un compañero (una compañera) de cuarto?
2. ¿Tienes preferencias en cuanto a un apartamento? ¿Cuáles son?
3. Una parte importante de la vida estudiantil son las fiestas. En tu opinión, ¿cómo es una buena fiesta?
4. Después de graduarse, muchos estudiantes compran un coche nuevo. La próxima vez que compres un coche, ¿qué clase de coche piensas buscar?
5. Y en cuanto a las características de los vendedores de coches, ¿cuáles prefieres?
6. Puesto que vas a necesitar un buen trabajo para comprar el coche nuevo, ¿qué tipo de trabajo vas a buscar para poder pagar los gastos asociados con este automóvil?

Haz la siguiente actividad con un compañero (una compañera).

Estudiante A: El anfitrión (La anfitriona) (host)

A guest arrives at your home to stay for a few days.

1. Greet your guest and invite him or her in.
2. Ask for your friend's suitcase.
3. Express your pleasure at your guest's arrival.
4. Offer to show your guest to his or her room.

Estudiante B: El invitado (La invitada)

You are a guest in the home of your friends. You want to be sensitive to their schedules and customs.

1. Ask your friends where you should leave your towel and toothbrush.
2. Find out when it would be most convenient for you to shower.
3. Ask what time your friends go to bed and get up in the morning.
4. Find out how you can be helpful while you are there.

OTRA VUELTA

Play instructor tape, 3 min.

Vuelve ahora a la Entrada que escuchaste al comienzo de esta etapa. Escúchala otra vez y apunta la secuencia de precios en el regateo entre Roberto y la dependiente.

La dependiente comienza el regateo al ponerles un precio de _____ .

Roberto hace una oferta de _____ .

La dependiente rebaja el precio a _____ .

Roberto contesta con _____ .

La dependiente dice _____ .

Roberto compra la estatua por _____ .

COMENTARIO CULTURAL

La informalidad formal

En las conversaciones de los Episodios, Marcos trata de tranquilizar a Paco diciéndole que "Aquí todos somos familia. Todo es muy informal." Sin embargo, sus consejos en cuanto a cómo debe portarse su amigo pueden parecer bastante rígidos y formales en comparación con las normas en los Estados Unidos. Cada sociedad tiene ideas, conscientes o inconscientes, sobre qué tipos de comportamiento, de ropa o de lenguaje son apropiados en cada situación. Con tanta variación cultural, una situación que a una persona le parece informal, a otra persona le puede parecer bastante formal.

En general, las relaciones en el mundo hispánico les parecen algo formales a los norteamericanos. También, desde una perspectiva estadounidense, casi todos los encuentros que tienen, ya sean personales o profesionales, parecen realizarse a un paso mucho más lento. Para un norteamericano que viaja por el mundo hispánico es buena idea tratar de vivir un poco más despacio y tratar también de saber cuáles son las normas locales en cuanto a los encuentros sociales y profesionales. Lo mejor es tener un amigo o conocido que comprenda la cultura local. Esta persona puede darle a uno buenos consejos sobre cómo vestirse, cómo invitar a la gente o aceptar una invitación, cómo dar consejos y aceptarlos, y cómo hacer preguntas y conversar un poco antes de llegar al meollo de la cuestión (ir al grano, o, como se dice en inglés, *get to the heart of the matter*).

Situación cultural. Un amigo tuyo te ha invitado a pasar un tiempo de visita con él y con sus padres en su casa en Bogotá. Todas las mañanas tú te levantas, tiendes la cama, arreglas un poco tu cuarto (echas los zapatos, la pijama, la ropa sucia y otras cosas en el clóset). Todas las noches regresas a tu cuarto y ves que el piso está aspirado, y que las cosas que tú echaste al clóset están arregladas. Unos días después tú oyes a la mamá de tu amigo diciéndole a una amiga suya que tú eres muy desordenado con tus cosas. Ya que tú crees que todas las mañanas arreglas y ordenas tu cuarto, no entiendes por qué ella dice que eres desordenado.

¿Cómo interpretas la situación?

a. La mamá de tu amigo cree que todos los norteamericanos son desordenados.
b. La manera en que tú tiendes la cama no se parece a la manera colombiana, y la mamá de tu amigo tiene que tenderla todos los días después de que sales.
c. La mamá de tu amigo considera que el clóset es una parte del cuarto. Por eso ella concluye que si está desordenado el clóset, está desordenado el cuarto.
ch. La mamá de tu amigo espera que tú barras o aspires el piso de tu cuarto voluntariamente todos los días. No le gusta que tú esperes que otra persona lo haga.

Explicación de la alternativa que escogiste:

a. Puede ser que la mamá de tu amigo suponga que todos los norteamericanos son desordenados, pero eso no explica su opinión acerca de tu cuarto.
b. Es importante tender la cama todos los días y tú lo hiciste. Sin embargo, no hay manera colombiana de tender una cama. Esto no explica la actitud de la mamá.
c. En algunas casas los clósets no tienen puertas. Por eso, tienen que mantenerse tan ordenados y arreglados como el resto del cuarto. Si no arreglas tu clóset, no arreglas tu cuarto. Ésta es la respuesta correcta.
ch. Como es el caso también en nuestra cultura, no se espera que los invitados aspiren el piso de su cuarto. Sin embargo, si tú pasas mucho tiempo de visita en una casa de familia y te das cuenta de que las personas de la familia rutinariamente aspiran el piso de su cuarto, entonces está bien que tú te ofrezcas a ayudar. Al fin de cuentas, si es "tu casa", tú también tienes responsabilidades domésticas.

The purpose of this activity is to sensitize students to how easily one can misinterpret a cultural situation, by either consciously or unconsciously applying one's own cultural criteria to "explain" what occurs. Emphasis should be placed on ways in which the guest might have coped with the situation and resolved it, rather than on whether or not students have selected the correct interpretation.

SEGUNDA ETAPA

"Bienvenidos a Bogotá"

ENTRADA

Play instructor tape, 2 min.

Una cena en casa

You are about to hear several friends greet each other as they arrive for a dinner party. As you listen, try to identify

- ■ expressions used by the hostess to greet her guests
- ■ the phrases used to introduce people to each other

Una cena en casa

Saludos

1.
2.

Presentaciones

1.
2.

ANTES DE LEER

READING STRATEGY 7

Preview the internal organization

Sometimes it helps to have an idea of how the information is organized and presented in the material you are reading. Hence an important strategy you can use is to scan the entire selection, noting in particular the title and any subtitles that might be used, section headings, and other words or phrases set in bold print.

Preparación

Roberto is from San Antonio, Texas, and he is pleased to find an article on his city in a magazine that he purchased in Bogotá, Colombia. If you were to write an ar-

Emphasize the importance of formatting, including bold print, subheadings, and pictures, to attract and hold the interest of readers.

ticle to encourage tourists to visit a city you like very much (perhaps your own hometown), what types of information would you include?

1.
2.
3.

How would you organize the information to make people want to read your article?

Play student tape, 1 min.

Estudiar y practicar

los alrededores	surroundings, environs
colmado/-a	filled
contar con	to depend on
la convivencia	living together
disfrutar de	to enjoy
la fogata	the flame of a fire
el paisaje	landscape, scenery
el paseo	walk, pathway
principiar	to begin

Look at the article and write down the title, subtitle, and bold headings in it. Then, write a one-sentence summary of what you think the article will include.

LEER

As you read the article about San Antonio on pages 306 and 307, make a list of three things you would like to see and three things you would like to do should you visit the city.

DESPUÉS DE LEER

You may want to point out to students that *me gustaría* connotes "if I had the opportunity . . ." When the conditional is presented in Chapter 10, remind students of this activity.

Actividad. Escoge tres cosas que te gustaría ver y tres cosas que te gustaría hacer durante una visita a San Antonio.

Me gustaría ver
  a.
  b.
  c.

Me gustaría
  a.
  b.
  c.

SAN ANTONIO: LA CIUDAD DEL RIO

La gran experiencia de estar entre el encanto de lo tradicional y lo moderno

Un paisaje tropical, clima templado, el agua abundante de ríos y manantiales y más de trescientos días al año de brillante sol, se combinan para hacer de San Antonio, Texas y sus alrededores una zona de vegetación exuberante.

La ciudad es también una mezcla de influencias hispanas y americanas, y debe gran parte de su atractivo a la convivencia de grupos de diverso origen cultural, cuyas contribuciones están en su arquitectura, museos y tradiciones.

Fundada por misioneros españoles en 1718, gran parte de las construcciones se conservan intactas como *La Villita*, sitio en donde se establecieron los fundadores, y que hoy es un gran conjunto de tiendas, galerías, talleres de artesanías y artesanos. Otro sitio de tradición es *El Alamo*, en donde el general Santa Anna perdió una batalla en 1836.

DIVERSIONES

La ciudad de San Antonio cuenta con varios parques muy bien conservados e ideales para cualquier actividad como caminar, correr o simplemente tomar el sol.

El más grande es el *Parque Brackenridge*, que incluye el zoológico y cuyos animales están en ambientes especiales preparados para reproducir su medio natural; hay caballerizas, allí puede alquilar hermosos caballos, y disfrutar la frondosidad de los jardines hundidos japoneses. Otra atracción particular es el tren en miniatura que viaja por la periferia del parque.

En el centro de la ciudad, encontrará el latido vital y la verdadera alma de San Antonio, lo que la distingue de todas las demás ciudades de Estados Unidos...*el Paseo del Río*. El atractivo de éste varía de acuerdo a la hora del día en que se visite. Si se desea un ambiente tranquilo que invite a la contemplación, lo ideal son las primeras horas de la mañana.

Ahora bien, hacia el mediodía *Paseo del Río* ya estará colmado de actividad, pues la mayoría de los visitantes deciden ir de excursión en una lancha-taxi, y después descansar tomando una bebida refrescante en los cafés al aire libre. Al anochecer, se transforma en un tapiz de luces centelleantes, sonidos y aromas, con una multitud de diversiones. Puede visitar los centros nocturnos, escuchar música en vivo o presenciar algún espectáculo en el *Arneson River Theater*, un anfiteatro al aire libre en donde el río pasa entre el público y el escenario.

La ciudad también se caracteriza por su excelencia culinaria; hay diversas "tentaciones gastronómicas" para complacer al más exigente paladar con lo más selecto de la cocina internacional.

Los platillos locales también son de reconocida fama, como los churrascos jugosos, cocinados lentamente a la parrilla al estilo texano sobre una fogata de mezquite; carne asada en barbacoa, la especialidad regional llamada "filete empanizado" y la versión de la cocina mexicana conocida como "Tex-Mex".

EVENTOS ESPECIALES

Dependiendo de la fecha en que visite San Antonio, encontrará diversos eventos artísticos y culturales, a través de los cuales captará mejor el auténtico sabor de la ciudad.

En enero y febrero se lleva a cabo el "Gran Festival del Río de Música Campirana" y la "Exhibición de ganado y rodeo". En abril, "La fiesta de San Antonio", es el evento de mayor importancia en la ciudad y se convierte en diez días de hermosas celebraciones.

En mayo principia el "Festival de San Antonio", una fiesta musical en todas sus expresiones. En agosto los visitantes pueden disfrutar del festival "Folklife", que cuenta con la participación de veintiséis importantes grupos culturales.

Por último, el río de San Antonio se viste de gala en diciembre para recibir a la Navidad y el Año Nuevo.

San Antonio le brinda todas las ventajas de una ciudad cosmopolita sin dejar de lado la gracia, el encanto y la hospitalidad que sólo se encuentra en una ciudad pequeña; por eso, visitarla es una experiencia como ninguna otra en el mundo.

AUMENTAR EL VOCABULARIO

You may want to point out to students the expression ¡Esto es el colmo! which is used in situations where an English-speaking person might say "This is the last straw!"

los alrededores — *surroundings, environs*
colmado/-a — *filled*
   colmar — *to heap up, overfill*
   el colmo — *summit, the highest point of something*

contar (ue) con — *to depend on*
convertir (ie, i) — *to convert*
   cambiar — *to exchange money*
   el cambio — *change (from a purchase); exchange rate*
   la casa de cambio — *exchange house*
la convivencia — *living together*
disfrutar de — *to enjoy*
eficaz — *effective, efficient*
establecer — *to establish*
   crear — *to create*
la fogata — *the flame of a fire*
   el fuego — *fire*

el (la) guía	*guide*
la guía	*guidebook*
la guía telefónica	*telephone book*
el paisaje	*landscape, scenery*
el paseo	*walk, pathway*
dar un paseo	*to take a walk*
prestar	*to lend*
pedir prestado/-a	*to borrow*
el préstamo	*loan*
principiar	*to begin*
el valor	*value*

EN LA CASA

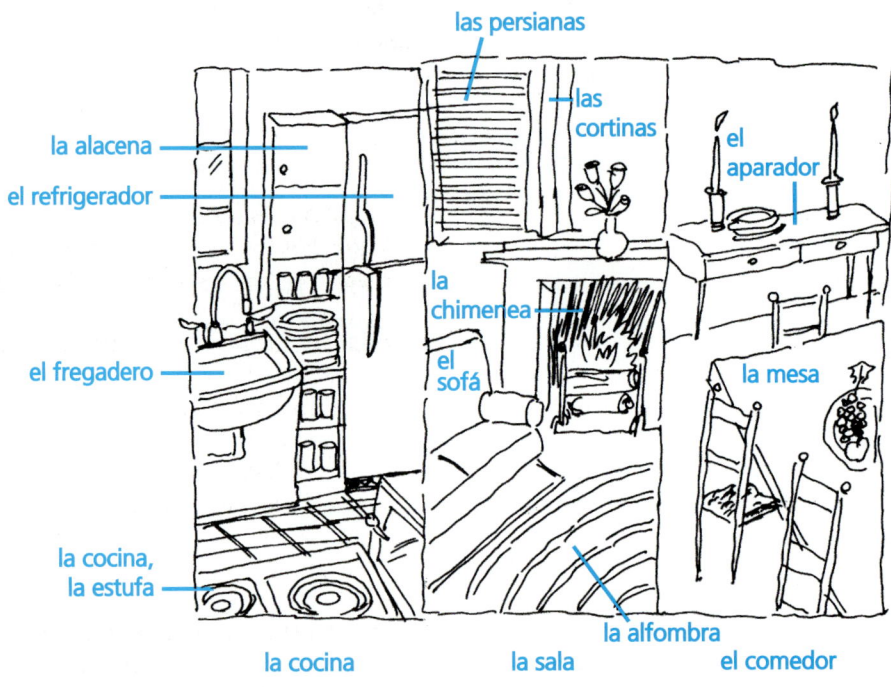

las persianas
las cortinas
el aparador
la alacena
el refrigerador
la chimenea
el sofá
la mesa
el fregadero
la cocina, la estufa
la alfombra
la cocina   la sala   el comedor

En mi casa vivo yo. Escribe un párrafo en el cual describes una casa que conoces. Menciona las cosas incluidas en la lista a continuación.

Modelo: el televisor   *En mi casa el televisor está en la sala.*

1. el sofá
2. el estante
3. las cortinas
4. el refrigerador
5. el fregadero
6. la mesa
7. las persianas
8. el sillón

Follow-up: Listening comprehension activity. Prepare and distribute the floor plan of an apartment, indicating rooms, doors, and windows, but no furniture. Then describe where each piece of furniture is to be placed, and have students draw in the pieces or write in the words. This activity reviews prepositions of location as well as new vocabulary.

VENTANILLA AL MUNDO HISPÁNICO   Las formas diminutivas de los nombres

Point out to students that the diminutive of many other names is formed by adding a diminutive ending to the name itself, as in Juan → Juanito; Sara → Sarita. The topic of diminutives is presented in greater detail in the *Comentario cultural* section in this *etapa*.

In order to carry out this activity, it will be necessary for students to have Spanish names.

En español muchos nombres tienen formas diminutivas, que muchas veces se usan para demostrar cariño hacia las personas. Por ejemplo, en inglés la forma diminutiva de *Barbara* puede ser *Barb, Barbie* o *Bobbie*. Aquí tienes algunas formas diminutivas de algunos nombres comunes en español.

Nombre	Diminutivo	Nombre	Diminutivo
Francisco	Paco/Pancho	Guadalupe	Lupe/Lupita
Guillermo	Memo/Memín	Eduardo	Lalo
Enriqueta	Queta	Rafael	Rafa/Rafita
José	Pepe/Pepito	Carlos	Carlitos

Actividad. Haz una lista de los nombres en español de tus compañeros de clase, y decide si el nombre que usan es una forma diminutiva o no. Si lo es, identifica el nombre original. Si no lo es, determina la forma diminutiva del nombre.

USO PRÁCTICO DEL ESPAÑOL   Los números ordinales

This recycles and builds on information presented as vocabulary in the first *etapa* of Chapter 2, where *primero* through *quinto* were introduced.

Point out that the abbreviation *1º* refers to *primero* and *1ª* to *primera*.

The numbers used to refer to the order in which things are arranged (first, second, third) are called *los números ordinales*. Here are some of the more common ones.

primero/-a [1º; 1ª]
segundo/-a [2º; 2ª]
tercero/-a [3º; 3ª]
cuarto/-a [4º; 4ª]
quinto/-a [5º; 5ª]
sexto/-a [6º; 6ª]
séptimo/-a [7º; 7ª]
octavo/-a [8º; 8ª]
noveno/-a [9º; 9ª]
décimo/-a [10º; 10ª]

OJO: The floors of a house are numbered as in the U.S.: *el primer piso* is the ground floor and *el segundo piso* is the second floor.

In Spanish, apartment and office addresses include the floor number and the number or location of the apartment or office. For example, the address *Galileo 7-3º, Apto. 10* means "7 Galileo Street, third floor, apartment 10." Sometimes the apartment is identified not by number, but by location: *Menéndez Pidal 29-1º der.,* which means "29 Menéndez Pidal Street, first floor, right-hand (*derecho*) side." Office addresses may also include the name of the building, preceded by the abbreviation *Edif.,* for *edificio.* You should also note that *primero,* or "first floor," is one floor above street level. In Spanish-speaking countries you begin counting floors in a building with *la planta baja,* the ground level.

Capítulo siete   ¡Aquí tienen su casa!

Extension: Have students give apartment adresses in the U.S. using the Spanish style: *avenida Collins 3800-12º, Apto. 14* is 3800 Collins Avenue, Apt. 1214.

Ponerlo a prueba

A. Las direcciones.   A continuación hay unas direcciones. Da la interpretación apropiada en cada caso.

Modelo: Galileo 7-3º Apto. 10
La calle Galileo, número 7, tercer piso, apartamento 10

1. Av. Urdaneta 24-5º, Nº 58
2. Casanova 23-1º, Apto. 9
3. Av. Juárez 3, Edif. Iberia, 3º
4. Sucre 17-4º, Nº 12
5. Av. Pedro de Heredia 245, Edif. Avianca, 2º der.

B. Ir de compras.   Llena los espacios con la palabra o expresión apropiada de la lista en la sección de Aumentar el vocabulario.

1. Muchas veces se encuentran lugares de interés en _____ de las ciudades grandes.
2. Durante un viaje, el turista puede ver un _____ que cambia constantemente.
3. Si el turista desea hacer compras en el mercado, primero debe visitar _____ para obtener cierta cantidad de la moneda nacional.
4. También es buena idea saber algo del _____ del artículo que se piensa comprar.
5. Ya que no hay precios fijos en los mercados, el sistema de regatear es muy _____, porque las dos personas establecen un precio aceptable para ambos.
6. Otra cosa que se nota en muchos mercados es la cantidad de vendedores que preparan comida en una parrilla (*grill*) sobre una pequeña _____.
7. Si hace buen tiempo, una buena manera de llegar a conocer un pueblo es _____ por el centro y por la vecindad.
8. Por lo general, el turista puede _____ la amistad de la gente si observa las costumbres y deberes de la cultura que visita.

C. Sinónimos.   Escoge una palabra del vocabulario que tiene el mismo significado que las siguientes.

1. cambiar
2. el precio
3. el líder
4. crear
5. el fuego
6. la estufa
7. el dinero
8. empezar
9. tener confianza en
10. llenísimo

CH. Definiciones. Escoge la definición o ejemplo que mejor corresponde a las palabras indicadas.

1. el ambiente
2. el colmo
3. eficaz
4. establecer
5. la estufa
6. contar con
7. el (la) guía
8. la alacena
9. las persianas
10. el valor

a. se usa para preparar la comida
b. el precio
c. una persona que acompaña a otras para enseñarles el camino o los aspectos interesantes del lugar
ch. crear
d. que hace efecto
e. se usan para cubrir las ventanas
f. la atmósfera
g. el punto más alto (de una montaña)
h. depender de
i. un mueble de la cocina donde se guardan los comestibles y los platos

D. Preguntas personales

1. Por lo general, ¿cómo empiezas tú el día?
2. ¿Cuáles son algunas de las tiendas que hay en los alrededores de tu casa?
3. Menciona algo que nunca le prestas a nadie.
4. Menciona algo que siempre pides prestado a tus amigos.
5. Describe un regalito que compraste recientemente, o que vas a comprar dentro de poco.
6. ¿Cuál es tu cuarto favorito de tu casa? ¿Por qué?

E. ¿Me lo prestas? Make a list of four items you would like to borrow. Then, ask your classmates to lend you the items, and make a list of the person from whom you borrow each item. Don't be surprised if your friend asks you why you want to borrow the item and when you plan to return it. Be prepared!

INVESTIGAR LA GRAMÁTICA — Dos pronombres de complemento con el mismo verbo

Formal commands are discussed in the first etapa of Chapter 8; familiar commands are covered in the second etapa of Chapter 8.

When you have both an indirect object pronoun and a direct object pronoun associated with the same verb, the indirect object pronoun always comes first. This is true whether the pronouns come **before** a conjugated verb or **after** an infinitive, a present participle, or an affirmative command.

Paco compró una artesanía colombiana y quiere mostrár**nosla**.
Doña Consuelo tiene unas fotos de su familia y **me las mostró** anoche. Si tú quieres verlas, ella puede mostrár**telas** esta tarde.

The indirect object pronouns *le* and *les* become *se* when used with the direct object pronouns *lo, la, los, las.*

Doña Consuelo saca el álbum y **se lo** muestra a Paco y a Roberto.
Cuando Roberto viaja, siempre les compra **regalos** a todos sus **amigos**. Por lo general, **se los** regala en una fiesta especial después de su viaje.

Here, what would have been *le* ("to him") becomes *se*. This means that *Yo se lo muestro* when considered by itself can mean "I'm showing it to him / to her / to you (formal, singular or plural) / to them (masculine or feminine)." Only context or a clarifying *a* phrase clears up any possible confusion.

Paco y Roberto quieren ver las fotos y voy a mostrár**selas**.

In this case the context tells us that *se = les = a ellos = a Paco y Roberto.*

—Todos queremos ver las fotos.

—Bueno, voy a mostrár**selas** a ustedes, pero no a los demás.

In this exchange, the second speaker says, "I'll show them to **you,** but not to the rest." Here, the phrase *a ustedes* is necessary for clarity and also to emphasize the contrast between *a ustedes* and *a los demás.*

Ponerlo a prueba

A. ¡No me digas! Lourdes can never believe what other people tell her, and she is always checking to see that she heard correctly. Take Lourdes's role in the following situations.

Modelo: Laura me regaló esta blusa.
Lourdes: ¡No me digas! *¿Te la regaló?* Es preciosa.

1. Álvaro me vendió su coche, porque acaba de comprar otro.
   Lourdes: ¡No me digas! ¿ _____ ? ¡Es un coche estupendo!
2. Lourdes, quiero mostrarte mis fotos.
   Lourdes: ¿Vas a _____ ? ¡Qué bien!
3. Juan Carlos está en el hospital. Vamos a mandarle una tarjeta.
   Lourdes: ¡Qué lástima! Sí, debemos _____ hoy.
4. Mira el suéter que hice para mi sobrinita.
   Lourdes: ¡No me digas! ¿ _____ tú? ¡Es magnífico!
5. Compré un sofá nuevo y tuve que sacar el sofá viejo de la sala. Jorge lo hizo por mí, sin ayuda. Ya sabes que es muy fuerte.
   Lourdes: ¡Qué barbaridad! ¿ _____ solo? Debe ser fortísimo.

6. Voy a decirle a Juanita que ya no voy a prestarle nada.

   Lourdes: De verdad hay que _____ . Siempre te pide cosas y no las devuelve nunca. ¡Es muy distraída (*absentminded*)!

7. Lourdes, me dijeron que el banco les ofreció a ti y a tu hermana un trabajo para el verano.

   Lourdes: Sí, la señora Rodríguez, la directora de personal, _____. ¿Pero quién _____ dijo? ¡Cómo habla la gente, qué vergüenza!

8. Lourdes, la universidad me dio la beca (*scholarship*) que solicité.

   Lourdes: ¡No me digas! ¿ _____ ? ¡Felicitaciones!

This activity can be recycled as a role play and added to the ¡Tienes la palabra! activity in this etapa.

B. Perdone Ud., señorita... You are at customs, on your way to a well-earned vacation at a Caribbean beach resort. Your friends and family have given you gifts for the trip, which you packed without removing them from their original packaging. You did not know that the country you are visiting has very strict laws regarding the importation of any new items that compete with locally made products. The customs officer is questioning you as to why you are bringing these new items into the country. Justify each article, telling the agent why you have the various articles and who gave each of them to you.

Modelo: un traje de baño nuevo
Lo tengo porque mis padres me lo regalaron.

1. una botella de crema bronceadora
2. una blusa de seda (*silk*)
3. un par de pantuflas (*bedroom slippers*)
4. un pijama al estilo chino
5. una botella de champú
6. una cámara
7. una secadora para el pelo
8. un espejo
9. una calculadora
10. un diccionario inglés-español

C. Recomendaciones y consejos. People in some professions are often called on to give advice and recommendations. Put yourself in each situation and respond to the questions that are asked of you.

Modelo: Un guía y una turista en la recepción del hotel
—¿Me recomienda una visita a la catedral?
—*Sí, señorita, se la recomiendo porque es un lugar histórico y la catedral es bonitísima.*

> This is a paried activity. Model one or two responses, if necessary, to give students a better idea of the task: *Se lo recomiendo porque es interesante y el profesor tiene fama de ser excelente.*

Un(a) estudiante y un profesor (una profesora) en la oficina del profesor (de la profesora).

1. ¿Me recomienda el curso de filosofía para el semestre que viene?
2. ¿Cree Ud. que debo incluir estos tres poemas en mi ensayo para su clase?
3. ¿Me permite faltar a clase mañana? Hay un partido de tenis que empieza a las 2:00.

Un(a) cliente y un(a) agente en la agencia de viajes

1. ¿Me recomienda Ud. la excursión de 15 días?
2. ¿Debo cambiar el dinero aquí o en México? ¿Quién puede cambiármelo?
3. ¿Se permite sacar fotos en los museos de la capital?

Un(a) cliente y un empleado (una empleada) en la agencia de empleos

1. ¿Me recomienda la compañía Aerosport? ¿Cómo es?
2. ¿Cree Ud. que van a ofrecerme el puesto?
3. Uds. piensan darme su recomendación, ¿verdad?

¡TIENES LA PALABRA!

En la librería. Haz la siguiente actividad con un compañero (una compañera).

Estudiante A: Vendedor(a)

1. A customer enters the store. Greet the customer and ask if you can help him or her.
2. Ask questions to clarify what kind of novel the customer wants, for example, *novela romántica, novela de suspenso.*
3. Show the customer some books.
4. Tell the customer how much the book costs.

Estudiante B: Cliente

1. Return the greeting. Say that you are looking for a novel to take with you to the beach.
2. Explain your preferences.

3. Choose a book and thank the clerk for his or her help.
4. Ask if credit cards are accepted.

OTRA VUELTA

Play instructor tape, 2 min.

Vuelve ahora a la conversación que escuchaste en la Entrada al comienzo de esta etapa. Escúchala otra vez, y apunta

- un cumplido (*compliment*) que hace uno/-a de los invitados
- una manera de responder a las presentaciones

COMENTARIO CULTURAL

You may want to point out to students that a variation that is sometimes used is *-illo/-illa,* as in *Hermosilla.* In Central America, *-ico/-ica* is used.

El diminutivo

La palabra "diminutivo" quiere decir "pequeño" y los diminutivos se usan mucho más en español que en inglés. Hay muchas terminaciones diminutivas en español, pero las más comunes son **-ito/-ita** y **-cito/-cita**.

Uno de los usos de los diminutivos en español es el de hacer más pequeña una cosa. Así es que "un librito" probablemente sea, en la mente de la persona que lo dice, más pequeño que "un libro", así como se supone que "una casita" es más pequeña que "una casa".

Otro uso importante de los diminutivos es el de demostrar cariño hacia las personas. Así es que si tu nombre es Juan y alguien te llama Juanito, no es porque crea que eres "un pequeño Juan"; te está demostrando cariño. En la sección de Ventanilla al mundo hispánico de esta etapa, hay algunos ejemplos de las formas diminutivas de los nombres.

Uno de los usos más interesantes de los diminutivos es el de suavizar un pedido o un mandato. Por ejemplo, si tú dices, "Dame un vasito de agua, por favor", se oye más suave o más cortés que "Dame un vaso de agua, por favor".

Remind students that the diminutive ending agrees in number and gender with the word that it replaces.

Actividad. ¿Cuál es la palabra base de los siguientes diminutivos?

1. cafecito
2. Carmencita
3. chiquito
4. cochecito
5. hermanito
6. hijita
7. manzanitas
8. mamacita
9. Paquito
10. Adelita

TERCERA ETAPA

Un poco de todo

ENTRADA

Play instructor tape, 1 min.

"Aquí tienen su casa"

Roberto y Paco han llegado a la casa de Marcos en Bogotá, y Marcos les presenta a su madre. Al escuchar esta conversación breve, escribe

- ■ la información que Marcos le da a su madre acerca de sus amigos
- ■ dos frases que doña Consuelo usa para darles la bienvenida

ANTES DE ESCUCHAR Y ESCRIBIR

Play student tape, 2 min.

Ahora vas a escuchar lo que hicieron Paco y Roberto en Cali y Cartagena. Después, vas a ver algunas de las diferencias entre un cuento oral y un cuento escrito.

Estudiar y repetir

bueno...	*well, . . .*
el club campestre	*country club*
el club de pesca	*fishing club, marina*
jugar al golf	*to play golf*
el pase	*pass (entrance permit)*
pues...	*well, . . .*
regatear	*to set a price by bargaining*

Las actividades turísticas. Ahora escucha la conversación entre Roberto, Paco y doña Consuelo, la madre de Marcos. Pon en orden las actividades de los jóvenes e indica si pasaron en Cali o en Cartagena.

Actividades de Paco y Roberto   ¿Cali o Cartagena?

_____ conocer a un ex-gobernador   _____

_____ llegar al Hotel Bahía   _____

_____ jugar al golf y nadar   _____

_____ hacer una presentación en la Universidad del Valle   _____

_____ comer en el Club de Pesca   _____

_____ ver el espectáculo de luz y sonido   _____

Enfoque en la conversación. Ahora escucha otra vez la conversación y escribe

- las frases donde aparecen **pues**... o **bueno**...
- tres ejemplos de interacción entre las tres personas: expresiones de interés, frases para incluir a otra persona en la conversación

1.
2.
3.

WRITING STRATEGY 7

Tell a story

Telling stories is a natural part of many conversations. We also write about our experiences in letters, personal reflections, and more formal essays. Oral language tends to be more informal and unplanned, and the listener can break in to ask a question if the sequence of events is not clear. Writers, on the other hand, have to be more careful in their planning, making sure that they communicate everything clearly the first time. Here are some differences between oral and written narratives.

Oral	Written
Loose organization. Tight logical and chronological sequences are not necessary.	Good organization essential.
Pauses and fillers are natural and expected.	No pauses or fillers (except in dialogue).
Interaction among participants in conversation to express or engage interest.	Writing for a specific audience. Engage reader through use of examples and commentary by narrator.

ESCRIBIR

Think about a trip you have taken. Write out five activities or incidents that were a part of the trip. You may not end up including all five in a written chronological account of your trip, but for the moment put them in chronological order.

1.
2.
3.
4.
5.

Here are some phrases that you can use to link the five events in time.

al día (a la mañana, a la tarde) siguiente	on the next day (*morning, afternoon*)
entonces, pues	then
esa tarde (noche)	that afternoon (*evening*) (*of a day you have already referred to*)
más tarde	later
otro día	on another day

Combine these phrases with the five events you listed to write five sentences about your trip.

1.
2.
3.
4.
5.

Now think of an unusual or funny incident from your trip. It should have some relationship with the five events you have listed, perhaps something that represents your trip as a whole or that points out contrasts from the things you usually do. Jot down some notes about your unusual or funny incident.

You now have the outline of your story. Remember to begin with a paragraph that states what the topic is and what your main point is going to be. Then use your five events and your special incident to paint a verbal picture of your trip.

AUMENTAR EL VOCABULARIO

OJO: A university fraternity or sorority is an example of a *club social*. The words *la fraternidad* and *la sororidad* exist in Spanish, but they most often signify the abstractions "brotherhood" and "sisterhood," not organizations. When the terms are used to refer to organized groups, participation is generally determined by an interest in retaining and sharing religious practices or historical traditions, rather than by a common desire for social interaction. U.S. style fraternities and sororities are not typically found on campuses in Latin America or Spain.

al día (a la mañana, a la tarde) siguiente	on the next day (*morning, afternoon*)
entonces, pues	then
esa tarde (noche)	that afternoon (*evening*) (*of a day you have already referred to*)
más tarde	later
otro día	on another day
el club	club
el club campestre	country club
el club de pesca	fishing club, marina
el club social	social club
el pase	pass (*entrance permit*)
jugar al golf	to play golf
acampar	to camp
campestre	country-like, rural
hacer el esquí acuático	to water-ski

OJO: *Campestre* is an adjective. *El campo* is the noun that means "rural area, country" (as opposed to "city").

hacer el esquí alpino — *to ski (downhill)*
hacer el esquí nórdico — *to ski (cross-country)*
montar a caballo — *to ride a horse*
pescar — ***to fish***
   el pez — *fish (live)*
regatear — ***to set a price by bargaining***

LOS CUBIERTOS

Optional questions: 1. ¿Prefieres las servilletas de papel o las de tela? ¿Por qué? ¿Cuáles son las ventajas y desventajas de cada una? 2. ¿Para qué se usa una copa? ¿Y un vaso? 3. ¿Para qué sirve el platillo? 4. ¿Cuál es la diferencia entre una cuchara y una cucharita? ¿Para qué se usan? 5. ¿Qué hay en el azucarero? ¿Para qué se usa?

OJO: The verb form *pon* is the command "put."

Actividad. Your younger brother is helping you set the dinner table for guests. However, this is his first attempt, and he has no idea what goes where. Tell him where to put each of the following items using the illustration from *Los cubiertos* as a guide.

Modelo: *Pon el plato en la mesa directamente enfrente de la silla.*

1. la servilleta
2. la cucharita
3. el platillo
4. la taza
5. el tenedor
6. el cuchillo
7. la copa

VENTANILLA AL MUNDO HISPÁNICO   La geografía de Colombia

Colombia es el único país de América del Sur que tiene costa tanto del lado del Océano Pacífico como del lado del Mar Caribe. Paco y Roberto visitaron tres de sus ciudades principales. Cartagena está en el norte de Colombia, en la costa del Caribe. Cali, una ciudad de más de 1,5 millones de habitantes, está en el suroeste del país, en un valle fértil en los Andes. Bogotá, la capital de Colombia, está situada en la parte central del país, en un altiplano de los Andes. Está a una altura de 2.600 metros sobre el nivel del mar. Tiene una población de unos cinco millones de habitantes y está a más o menos 2.500 millas al sur de la ciudad de Nueva York en los Estados Unidos.

USO PRÁCTICO DEL ESPAÑOL   Tocando a la puerta

When doña Consuelo greeted her guests in the *Entrada* section at the beginning of the chapter, she said —*Buenos días y bienvenidos,* and then added —*Están en su casa.* This would be an appropriate greeting for friends in most Spanish-speaking homes and an invitation to enter. Other expressions are

¡Pasa! ¡Pasa!	*Come in! Come in!*
¡Adelante!	*Come in!*
¡Siga!/¡Sigue!	*Come in!*

OJO: *¡Siga!* is the *usted* form and *¡Sigue!* is the *tú* form. If you do not know who might be at the door, it is always safer to say *¡Siga! ¡Pasa!* is the *tú* form of *pasar;* the *usted* form is *¡Pase!*

Upon entering, you would say *Gracias* or *Muy amable.* If you are entering a room where a class or a meeting is in progress, a bit more formality is often observed. For example, as a courtesy to the person in charge of the session, you might pause at the door and say

Perdone(n).	*Excuse me.*
Con permiso.	*Excuse me.*
¿Se puede?	*May I come in?*

Responses in these instances would typically be

Pase Ud./Pasa.	*Come in.*
Claro.	*Of course.*
¡Cómo no!	*Of course!*

OJO: Cultural note: If the door of a room is closed, you knock before entering.

In some instances, you may not be invited to enter, either into a home or into a room. In that case, the person inside might say

¿Sí, señor (señora, señorita)?   *Yes?*
Espere Ud. un momento, por favor.   *Wait just a moment, please.*

Ponerlo a prueba

A. ¿Qué vas a decir?   Decide lo que debes decir en las situaciones siguientes.

1. Alguien llama a la puerta de tu casa a las nueve de la noche. Abres la puerta y ves que son dos amigos tuyos. ¿Qué les dices?
2. Alguien llama a la puerta a las dos de la noche. Abres la puerta y ves que es una persona que no conoces. ¿Qué le dices?
3. Estás en una reunión con tus colegas discutiendo algunos asuntos confidenciales. Alguien llama a la puerta de tu oficina para hablar contigo. ¿Qué le dices?
4. Estás dando una sesión de orientación a un grupo de estudiantes internacionales. Uno de los participantes llega tarde, se para en la puerta y pregunta: —¿Se puede?— ¿Qué le dices?
5. Una tarde estás mirando televisión cuando alguien toca el timbre (*rings the doorbell*). Al abrir la puerta, ves que es una amiga de tu mamá. ¿Qué le dices?
6. Eres representante estudiantil en un comité universitario. Llegas un poco tarde a la primera reunión del grupo y ya han empezado. ¿Qué dices?

B. Definiciones y sinónimos.   Escoge la definición o el sinónimo que mejor corresponda a las palabras indicadas.

1. hacer el esquí alpino
2. el pase
3. jugar al golf
4. regatear
5. acampar
6. el pez
7. campestre

a. dormir afuera
b. un documento para entrar gratis
c. participar en un deporte que usa palos de metal
ch. un organismo que vive en los ríos, lagos y mares
d. relacionado con un área rural
e. bajar una montaña en los esquíes
f. entrar en conversación para decidir un precio

C. Situaciones.   De la lista de expresiones que sigue, escoge la mejor respuesta para terminar lo que dice la persona en cada situación.

- No te preocupes.
- Aquí tienen su casa.
- Me encanta el pescado.
- Odio los mariscos.

1. Roberto: Por fin llegamos. Después de tanto tiempo vamos a conocer a tu familia.
   Marcos: Pasen ustedes. _____
2. Paco: ¿Quieres cenar con nosotros esta noche? Pensamos ir al Club de Pesca.
   Mariana: ¡Ay, qué simpático eres! _____.
3. Paco: Conozco un restaurante que sirve carne a la parrilla. Esta noche tengo ganas de comer un biftec enorme.
   Roberto: Pero ya sabes que no me gusta la carne de res.
   Paco: Hombre, _____. Estoy seguro de que sirven también pollo y pescado.
4. Doña Consuelo: ¿Cenaron en algunos lugares interesantes en Cartagena?
   Paco: Sí, señora. ¿Conoce el Club de Pesca? Tiene fama por su langosta a la termidor, pero desgraciadamente _____ _____.

CH. Preguntas personales

1. ¿Cuál es el lugar al que más te gusta ir de vacaciones?
2. ¿Dónde prefieres nadar, en una piscina, en un lago o en el mar? ¿Por qué?
3. En tu opinión, ¿cuál es más difícil de aprender, el esquí alpino o el esquí acuático?
4. En general, el golf y el esquí son deportes que practican los ricos. ¿Por qué?
5. ¿Te gusta acampar? ¿Por qué sí o por qué no?
6. Cuando vas a un restaurante, ¿qué pides generalmente?
7. ¿Cuál prefieres: el pescado, la carne de res o el pollo?
8. ¿Qué prefieres beber con la comida?
9. ¿Sabes cocinar? ¿Cuál es tu especialidad?
10. ¿Quién pone la mesa en tu casa? ¿Qué cubiertos usan los miembros de tu familia en la cena de todos los días?

D. ¿Qué buscas?

Imagínate que estás de viaje en una ciudad desconocida, y no sabes dónde buscar lo que necesitas. Escribe cinco frases que incluyan las palabras claves que aparecen a continuación. Sigue el modelo.

Modelo: cine   *Busco un cine donde pongan películas italianas.*

OJO: Note the use of the subjunctive in this sentence because a movie theater with such attributes is not part of the speaker's experience. Use the same structure (*Busco un...que/donde...*) in your sentences.

1. un museo
2. un club campestre
3. un hotel
4. un restaurante
5. una tienda

INVESTIGAR LA GRAMÁTICA Expressing Desires and Influencing Others

OJO: Study tip: Keep a list on this page or in your notebook of verbs of desire or influence that take the subjunctive, and refer to this list when needed. Some verbs to get you started, in addition to the ones in the paragraph, are *preferir, aconsejar, prohibir, permitir, pedir*.

Earlier in this chapter you learned how to form the present subjunctive and how to use it to talk about things that you have not experienced or seen.

Quiero visitar un museo que **tenga** una exposición de arte precolombino.   *I want to visit a museum that has an exhibition of pre-Columbian art.*

The subjunctive is also used to express the wish that events turn out a certain way, or to indicate that one person is influencing—or trying to influence—the actions of another. Whenever there is a suggestion that someone's wishes or opinions affect what another person does or thinks, then the subjunctive is used. Consider the following paragraph, in which Cristina complains that everyone wants her to study more.

Todos quieren que yo estudie más. Mamá me dice que no vaya al cine con mis amigos los fines de semana. Papá insiste en que pase todo mi tiempo libre en la biblioteca. Mi hermano me aconseja que no mire televisión los días de clase. Mis tíos les recomiendan a mis padres que me quiten el estéreo. ¿Qué hago? Quiero estudiar más, pero es difícil hacer tantos cambios en mi rutina. Voy a decirles a todos que tengan paciencia conmigo.

Notice that most of the sentences in the paragraph follow a particular pattern in which Subject 1 is trying to influence the actions of Subject 2.

Todos quieren que **yo estudie** más.
Papá insiste en que (**yo**) **pase** todo mi tiempo libre en la biblioteca.

In each sentence the subjects are not the same in the two clauses of the sentence: *todos* and *yo* are the subjects in the first sentence and *Papá* and (*yo*) in the second sentence. Note also that the clauses are connected by the word *que*. When the verb in the first clause expresses a desire to influence another, the verb in the second clause will be in the subjunctive.

Notice, however, that if there is only one clause (and therefore only one subject) in the sentence, an infinitive is used.

Quiero estudiar más.

Now go through the paragraph about Cristina's complaints and see how many sentences you can find that follow the pattern of **Subject 1 + verb of desire or influence + *que* + Subject 2 + verb in subjunctive.** Make a list of the verbs in that paragraph that express a desire to influence others.

OJO: The verb *decir* as used in this paragraph is a verb of influence.

Voy a decirles que **tengan** paciencia conmigo.

Compare this sentence to the following two sentences in which *decir* is not used to urge someone to do something, but rather to share information.

Voy a decirles que **tengo** un examen mañana.
Mis padres me dicen que la educación **es** muy importante.

Ponerlo a prueba

A. Todos me dicen algo. Verónica está planeando un viaje a Colombia y varias personas quieren que ella haga algo en particular. Usando los verbos que siguen, imagínate que eres Verónica y escribe la lista de obligaciones que otros te imponen y las sugerencias (*suggestions*) que te hacen.

divertirse	llamar	quedarse	viajar
invitar	pasar	tomar	

1. Mis amigos quieren / verano en Colombia
2. Me dicen / a uno de mis amigos a acompañarme
3. Insisten en / por teléfono antes de salir
4. Me aconsejan / por avión
5. Recomiendan / agua mineral en los hoteles
6. Sugieren / Cali y Bogotá durante el viaje
7. Desean / con ellos por dos o tres semanas
8. Esperan / en las playas y discotecas

B. Quiero que... Estás planeando un viaje con dos amigos, Esteban y Jacinto. Ha llegado el momento de finalizar algunos detalles. ¿Quién debe encargarse (*to take charge*)—tú, Esteban o Jacinto?

Modelo: comprar los boletos
Quiero que Esteban compre los boletos.
o: *Quiero comprar los boletos.*

1. llamar al (a la) agente de viajes
2. hablar con el dueño (la dueña) del apartamento
3. encargarse de la cámara
4. apagar la luz y cerrar el agua
5. sacar toda la comida del refrigerador
6. hacer los arreglos con el (la) taxista

C. Consejos y recomendaciones. Un amigo tuyo va al extranjero por primera vez. ¿Qué le aconsejas (*What advice do you have for him*) para tener un viaje divertido y para evitar problemas?

Modelo: Sugiero que...
Sugiero que no tomes mucho alcohol.

1. Te aconsejo que...
2. Te digo que...
3. Debes...
4. Insisto en que...
5. Te recomiendo que...
6. Espero que...
7. Tienes que...
8. Quiero que...

CH. Las reglas (*rules*). ¿Qué reglas tiene tu universidad con respecto a la vida estudiantil? En grupos de tres, escribe una lista de las actividades que la administración permite, y otra lista de las actividades que prohibe.

Modelo: *Permite que los estudiantes tengan clubes sociales. Prohibe que los estudiantes se queden en las residencias durante el verano.*

D. Preguntas personales

1. Cuando estás en casa, ¿qué quieren tus padres que hagas todos los días? ¿Y los fines de semana?
2. ¿Qué sugieres que haga una persona para prepararse para un examen final en la clase de español?
3. ¿Qué prefieres que hagan tus amigos para celebrar tu cumpleaños?
4. Cuando haces un viaje, ¿qué esperas que haga por ti el (la) agente de viajes?
5. ¿En qué insistes antes de alquilar una habitación en un hotel?

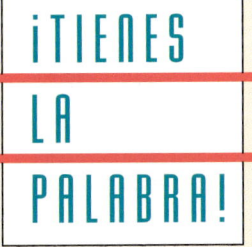

OJO: The travel agent should take an active role in the conversation by introducing complications and asking questions.

OJO: As in *Actividad A* in this section, the travel agent should participate actively in the conversation.

Haz las siguientes actividades con un compañero (una compañera).

A. En la agencia de turismo.
You are in Spain on vacation and want to take a one-day tour of Toledo. You go to a tour agency and make your arrangements with the agent. Act out the following scene, with a partner playing the agent.

- Greet the agent.
- Ask if there are tours from Madrid to Toledo.
- Find out at what time buses leave for Toledo, and when they return.
- Ask how much the tour costs.
- Find out whether you can pay with traveler's checks.
- Tell the agent that you want him or her to make a reservation for you.

B. En la agencia de viajes.
You are interested in a trip to Colombia and go to a travel agency to make the necessary arrangements. Act out the following scene with a partner. You (the traveler) use the cues and your partner (the agent) responds to your questions and requests.

- Find out whether there are tours that include Bogotá, Cali, and Cartagena.
- Ask whether the agent recommends bus or plane travel from one city to the other.
- Find out what the weather is like in Cali at this time of year.
- Ask how long the tour is and how much it costs.
- Have the agent make a reservation for you.

OTRA VUELTA

Play instructor tape, 1 min.

Use of *tú* and/or *usted* between family members varies from country to country. See the Instructor's Manual for further discussion.

Vuelve ahora a la conversación que escuchaste en la Entrada al comienzo de esta etapa. Escúchala otra vez y contesta las siguientes preguntas.

1. ¿Trata Marcos de tú o de usted a su madre?
2. ¿Cómo invita doña Consuelo a los jóvenes a sentarse?
3. ¿Qué dice doña Consuelo para indicar que quiere escuchar las aventuras de los jóvenes?

COMENTARIO CULTURAL

El regateo

Para hacer compras económicas en la América Latina es importante saber regatear. El regateo—así se llama el proceso de regatear—tiene aspectos sociales y también de negocios. Es un vestigio de los tiempos en que no se usaba el dinero para comprar cosas, sino que se intercambiaban artículos de más o menos el mismo valor (un sistema de trueque).

El regateo es más común en los mercados grandes al aire libre. También puede ocurrir en los negocios pequeños, cuando el dueño del negocio es también la persona que trata con el público. Sin embargo, en los almacenes y tiendas grandes, donde los empleados ganan un sueldo fijo, el regateo prácticamente no existe y el sistema es el de precios fijos. En estos casos el cliente paga el precio indicado.

El regateo es un arte y el proceso es verdaderamente complicado. Los párrafos siguientes explican en términos muy simplificados y generales lo que se hace para regatear con éxito.

Primero, el cliente debe tener una idea de cuánto dinero está dispuesto a pagar por el artículo que le interesa. Entonces, cuando el vendedor menciona un precio más alto, el cliente ofrece un precio más bajo del que está dispuesto a pagar. Entonces el vendedor hace otra oferta más baja que la primera, pero más alta que el precio sugerido por el cliente. Finalmente el cliente hace su última oferta y el vendedor la acepta, o bien el cliente se va sin comprar el artículo.

Si piensas regatear es importante tener en cuenta dos ideas. Primero, el cliente no debe hablar mal ni de la calidad del artículo que piensa comprar, ni de la integridad del vendedor. Segundo, el cliente no debe regatear si no tiene un verdadero interés en comprar el artículo. El hacer cualquiera de estas dos cosas no es aceptable y puede crear problemas con el vendedor en el futuro.

Preguntas

1. Menciona un lugar donde generalmente
   a. se hace el regateo _____
   b. no se hace el regateo _____
2. ¿Cuáles son dos reglas culturales acerca del regateo?
   a.
   b.

Actividades de integración

DE INTEGRACIÓN

Play video

Program 7 *Detalles y colores* Detail and color in artistic expression

A. **Una carta.** Tienes un amigo colombiano que dentro de poco tiempo va a visitar a una familia norteamericana. Él te ha escrito pidiéndote consejos sobre lo que debe hacer y lo que no debe hacer mientras está en una casa norteamericana. Escríbele una carta dándole la información que te pide. Menciona costumbres que tienen que ver con el uso del baño, con la ropa (la que es apropiada y la que no lo es, según las circunstancias), con comidas, y con otras costumbres que se te ocurran.

B. **Busco una casa.** Imagínate que te has graduado de la universidad y tienes un puesto muy bueno. Decides comprar una casa. Escribe una descripción de la casa que te gustaría comprar. Usa expresiones como las siguientes.

    Busco una casa que...

    Quiero vivir en una casa que...

C. **Aventuras de compras.** ¿Te ha pasado alguna vez un incidente interesante (bueno o malo) relacionado a las compras? Escribe el cuento, usando el procedimiento explicado en la *Writing Strategy 7*.

CH. **Imagínate (jefes y empleados).** En esta situación, el jefe (la jefa) no estuvo en la oficina ayer. Es un poco fanático/-a en cuanto al trabajo y quiere saber todo lo que ha pasado durante su ausencia. El empleado (La empleada) contesta sus preguntas. Usa tu imaginación para crear (*create*) las preguntas del jefe (de la jefa) y las respuestas del empleado (de la empleada).

Modelo: llegar a la oficina

Jefe/-a: *¿Y a qué hora llegó usted a la oficina?*

Empleado/-a: *Llegué a las 9:00 en punto.*

1. abrir la oficina (¿quién?)
2. poner los documentos (¿dónde?)
3. llamar (¿quién?)
4. hacer los arreglos para mi próximo viaje
5. darle al señor Vargas el informe
6. poder traducir la carta
7. preparar el nuevo contrato

8. ir al banco (¿a qué hora?)
9. decirle a los otros empleados que deben llegar a tiempo
10. (una pregunta original)

D. **La cita.** Con un compañero (una compañera), haz el mini-drama que se propone a continuación.

Estudiante A: El (La) joven

You have arranged a date with a friend. The two of you plan to go to the movies and have something to eat afterward. Because you live at home, your parents want to know all about your social life. Tell your mother or father that you have a date, and answer all their questions. Be as reassuring as possible because you know that your parents are somewhat overprotective.

Estudiante B: El padre o La madre

Your son or daughter has a date. You are somewhat overprotective and want to know everything about it, so you ask your son or daughter

- the name of the friend
- details about the friend's family
- where they are going
- what they are going to do
- what time they will be back

E. **Un invitado (Una invitada) en casa.** A guest has just arrived at your house.

- Invite the guest to sit down in the living room.
- Inquire about his or her trip.
- Offer your guest something to eat or drink.
- Excuse yourself for a moment to prepare the snack.

VOCABULARIO

Los lugares de actividad social
Social gathering sites

club (m) campestre   country club
club (m) de pesca   fishing club, marina
club (m) social   social club

Los deportes
Sports

hacer el esquí acuático   to water-ski
hacer el esquí alpino   to ski (downhill)
hacer el esquí nórdico   to ski (cross-country)

La casa
The house

cielo raso (m)   ceiling; interior roof
chimenea (f)   fireplace
escalera (f)   stairway
estructura (f)   structure
muralla (f)   exterior wall
suelo (m)   flooring
techo (m)   exterior roof

Los espacios
Spaces

balcón (m)   balcony
cocina (f)   kitchen
desván (m)   attic
sala (f)   living room
sótano (m)   basement

Los muebles y los trastos
Furniture and furnishings

alacena (f)   kitchen cupboard
alfombra (f)   rug
aparador (m)   buffet, credenza
cortinas (f pl)   curtains
estufa (f)   stove
fregadero (m)   kitchen sink
persianas (f pl)   venetian blinds
refrigerador (m)   refrigerator
sofá (m)   sofa

La mesa
The table

azucarero (m)   sugar bowl
copa (f)   wine glass
cuchara (f)   tablespoon
cucharita (f)   teaspoon
cuchillo (m)   knife
mantel (m)   tablecloth
platillo (m) / platito (m)   saucer
plato (m)   plate; dish (of food)
servilleta (f)   napkin
taza (f)   cup
tenedor (m)   fork
vaso (m)   water glass (tumbler)

Los números ordinales
Ordinal numbers

primero/-a [1º; 1ª]   first
segundo/-a [2º; 2ª]   second
tercero/-a [3º; 3ª]   third
cuarto/-a [4º; 4ª]   fourth
quinto/-a [5º; 5ª]   fifth
sexto/-a [6º; 6ª]   sixth
séptimo/-a [7º; 7ª]   seventh
octavo/-a [8º; 8ª]   eighth
noveno/-a [9º; 9ª]   ninth
décimo/a [10º; 10ª]   tenth

Las palabras descriptivas
Descriptive words

campestre   country-like, rural
cariñoso/-a   affectionate
caro/-a   expensive
colmado/-a   filled
conocido/-a   well-known
descalzo/-a   barefoot
eficaz   effective, efficient
mal educado/-a   ill-mannered, rude
siguiente   following, next

Los sustantivos útiles
Useful nouns

alrededores (m pl)   surroundings, environs
cambio (m)   change (from a purchase); exchange rate
cariño (m)   fondness, affection, kindness
casa (f) de cambio   exchange house
colmo (m)   summit, the highest point of something
consejero/-a   counselor
consejo (m)   a piece of advice

convivencia (f)   *living together*
costumbre (f)   *custom, habit*
fogata (f)   *the flame of a fire*
fuego (m)   *fire*
guía (m/f)   *guide*
guía (f)   *guidebook*
guía (f) telefónica   *telephone book*
odio (m)   *hatred*
paisaje (m)   *landscape, scenery*
pase (m)   *pass (entrance permit)*
paseo (m)   *walk, pathway*
pez (m)   *fish (live)*
préstamo (m)   *loan*
quehacer (m)   *chore*
valor (m)   *value*

Verbos útiles
Useful verbs

acampar   *to camp*
aconsejar   *to advise*
acostumbrarse a   *to be/get accustomed to*
andar   *to walk*
buscar   *to look for*
cambiar   *to exchange money*
caminar   *to walk*
colmar   *to heap up, overfill*
contar (ue) con   *to depend on*
convertir (ie, i)   *to convert*
crear   *to create*

dar un paseo   *to take a walk*
disfrutar de   *to enjoy*
establecer   *to establish*
ir/venir a pie   *to go/come on foot*
jugar al golf   *to play golf*
meter la pata   *to make a social blunder, "put your foot in your mouth"*
montar a caballo   *to ride a horse*
ofender   *to offend*
pedir prestado/-a   *to borrow*
perdonar   *to pardon; excuse*
pescar   *to fish*
prestar   *to lend*
principiar   *to begin*
recomendar (ie)   *to recommend*
regatear   *to set a price by bargaining*
tener fama de   *to be known for or as*
tener mala fama   *to have a bad reputation*

Otras palabras y expresiones útiles
Other useful words and expressions

¡Adelante!   *Come in!*
al día (a la mañana, a la tarde) siguiente   *on the next day (morning, afternoon)*
bueno…   *well, . . .*
¡Cómo no!   *Of course!*
¿Cuánto vale (cuesta)?   *How much is it?*
¿En qué puedo servirle?   *Can I help you?*
entonces   *then*
Lo siento, pero no hay.   *I'm sorry, but we don't have any.*
Lo siento, pero no nos quedan.   *I'm sorry, but we're all out.*
más tarde   *later*
otro día   *on another day*
¡Pasa! ¡Pasa!   *Come in! Come in!*
pues…   *well, then . . .*
¿Qué color (estilo) prefiere?   *What color (style) do you prefer?*
¿Qué número calza?   *What size shoe do you take?*
¿Qué talla necesita?   *What size (clothing) do you need?*
¿Se aceptan tarjetas de crédito?   *Do you take credit cards?*
¿Se puede?   *May I come in?*
¡Siga! / ¡Sigue!   *Come in!*

A few of the words included in the end-of-chapter vocabulary have been presented previously. They are recycled at this point as a result of the new semantic groupings in which they are included.

VOCABULARIO PERSONALIZADO

"Juventud, divino tesoro..."

Capítulo 8

COMMUNICATIVE OBJECTIVES

In this chapter, you will learn some new ways to

- make polite requests and give commands
- make general statements about what other people say and do
- tell anecdotes and stories
- express how you feel about situations and events
- understand descriptions of experiences others have had in the past
- express doubts, denial, and disbelief regarding situations and events

PRIMERA ETAPA

Cuentos de niños

ENTRADA

Play instructor tape, 2 min.

This *Entrada* provides further practice of structures that have been presented and studied in earlier chapters.

The title of this chapter comes from a poem entitled "Canción de otoño en primavera," written by the Nicaraguan poet Rubén Darío and originally published in *Cantos de vida y esperanza* (Madrid, 1905). The verse is:
Juventud, divino tesoro,
¡ya te vas para no volver!
Cuando quiero llorar, no lloro,
y a veces lloro, sin querer.

"Tenemos una familia pequeña"

In this chapter you are going to learn more about the childhoods of Marcos, Paco, and Roberto. But before you hear their stories, listen to doña Consuelo, Marcos's mother, as she talks about her parents, brother, and two sisters. Listen for the names of her three siblings and the other information that you need to fill in the following chart. The conversation begins as Paco is admiring a family portrait.

La familia de doña Consuelo Santiago de Colón

Miembro de la familia	¿Casado/-a?	¿Dónde vive?
Madre/Padre	sí	Bogotá
Hermano:		
Hermana:		
Hermana:		

EMPEZAR A ESCUCHAR

Play student tape, 3 min.

Leer

los gemelos	twins
mientras	while, during
junto/-a	together
casi	almost
lindo/-a	cute, pretty
orgulloso/-a	proud
el apagón	blackout, power failure
el susto	sudden fright
aprovechar	to take advantage of
besar	to kiss
prender	to turn on (*lights, electrical appliances*)
enojarse	to get angry

Repetir

Escucha la cinta y repite lo que oyes.

Identificar

En una hoja aparte, escribe en una columna las palabras y frases anteriores. Vas a oír algunas oraciones. Cada vez que oigas una de estas palabras o frases, apunta el número de la oración al lado de la palabra. Cada oración se leerá dos veces.

Escribir

Vas a oír unas oraciones, cada una leída dos veces. Escríbelas al escucharlas.

Reconocer

Ahora, lee otra vez las oraciones que acabas de escribir. Cada una contiene una o más de las palabras y frases anteriores. Al releerlas, subraya todas las palabras y frases que vienen de la lista. Mientras lees, haz todas las correcciones necesarias.

ESCUCHAR

Play student tape, 2 min.

Episodio 1: "Aquí están los gemelos"

Enfoque comunicativo

Paco and Roberto are chatting with Marcos and his mother. Doña Consuelo brings out the family photo album to introduce the visitors to some of the other family members. As you listen to the conversation, see if you can determine

- what is special about David and Isabel
- whether Marcos is older or younger than David and Isabel

1. Isabel y David son...
2. Año de nacimiento: David _____ Isabel _____
3. Marcos es (mayor/menor) que sus hermanos.

OJO: Remember that *mayor* and *menor* are used to compare people's ages. Don't confuse them with *mejor,* meaning "better."

Enfoque lingüístico

Escucha otra vez la conversación y apunta

- la exclamación de Roberto cuando ve la foto de los gemelos
- cómo insiste Marcos en que sí le ha dicho a Roberto que sus hermanos son gemelos

ESCUCHAR

Play student tape, 1 min.

This *Episodio* recycles usage of the preterite and imperfect within an oral narrative.

Reference is made in this *Episodio* to *la fiesta de los quince años*. It is described in the next *Ventanilla al mundo hispánico*.

EPISODIO 2: El apagón

Enfoque comunicativo

The group continues to look at the family album. As you listen to the conversation, see if you can determine the sequence of events on the evening of Isabel's *fiesta de los quince años*.

_____ El hermano de Marina se enojó.   _____ Se fue la luz.

_____ Marcos besó a Marina.   _____ Se prendieron las luces.

_____ Marcos y Marina bailaron.

_____ Por fin escampó (*the weather cleared*).

Enfoque lingüístico

Escucha otra vez la conversación en el Episodio 2 y apunta

■ cómo doña Consuelo le pregunta a Marcos si tiene memoria del apagón

■ cómo Marcos expresa la reacción del hermano de Marina

VERIFICAR

Refer students back to the third *etapa* of Chapter 3 for additional descriptive vocabulary.

Escribe dos frases cortas para describir a las siguientes personas, basando tus respuestas en los dos episodios de esta etapa.

1. Doña Consuelo
   a.
   b.

2. Marcos
   a.
   b.

AUMENTAR EL VOCABULARIO

OJO: *Poner* and *encender* are also used when referring to turning on lights and appliances.

OJO: The phrase *aprovechar la oportunidad* is frequently used.

OJO: "To allow" is a new meaning of *dejar*. You learned *dejar un recado* in Chapter 3.

abrazar	to hug, embrace
besar	to kiss
apagar	to turn off (*lights*)
el apagón	blackout, power failure
prender	to turn on (*lights, electrical appliances*)
aprovechar	to take advantage of
casi	almost
dejar	to allow; to leave (*something behind*)
enojarse	to get angry
ponerse furioso/-a	to get furious
los gemelos	twins

Primera etapa

OJO: The verb *nacer* is almost always used in the preterite tense: *nací, naciste, nació, nacimos, nacisteis, nacieron*.

OJO: *Orgulloso/-a* can have both the positive meaning of taking pleasure in others' accomplishments (*Mis padres están orgullosos de mí*) and the pejorative meaning of arrogant, stuck on oneself.

grueso/-a	*thick*
junto/-a	*together*
lindo/-a	*cute, pretty*
mientras	*while, during*
nacer	*to be born*
orgulloso/-a	*proud*
el orgullo	*pride*
pelear	*to fight*
luchar	*to fight*
poner (prestar) atención	*to pay attention*
la primera comunión	*first communion*
el susto	*sudden fright*
asustar	*to frighten*

LA NUEVA TECNOLOGÍA

la computadora

In Spain, a computer is referred to as *el ordenador*. In some regions of Latin America, *el computador* is used.

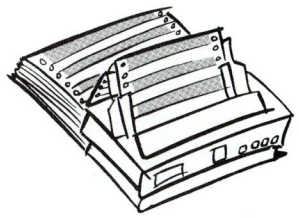

la impresora

la calculadora

la máquina de escribir

el contestador automático

OJO: In Spanish, as in English, the common word for a facsimile machine is *el fax*. The message sent is a *reproducción en facsímil*.

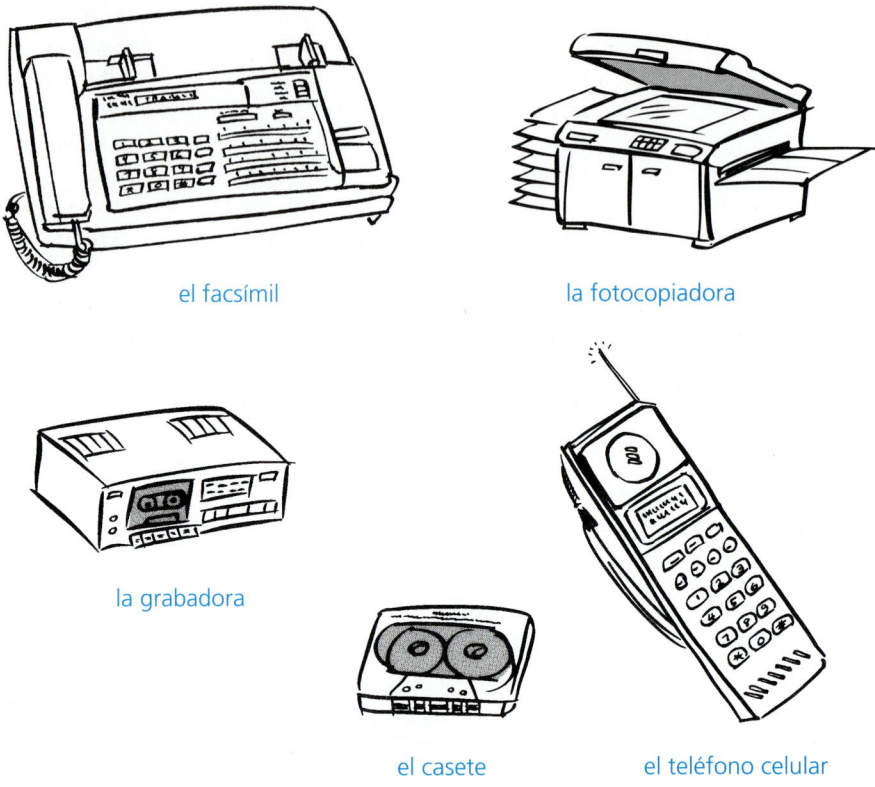

el facsímil

la fotocopiadora

la grabadora

el casete

el teléfono celular

El mundo de la tecnología. A continuación, hay descripciones de varios aparatos que se usan en la oficina o para la comunicación. Identifica el que corresponde a cada definición.

1. Se usa esta máquina para hacer fotocopias.
2. Si una persona te llama y no estás en casa, esta máquina contesta el teléfono.
3. Con este aparato se puede comunicar electrónicamente mientras vuela en un avión.
4. Es una cajita de plástico que contiene una cinta magnética.
5. Se usa esta máquina para grabar y escuchar música y otras cosas.
6. Se usa para multiplicar, sumar, restar y dividir cifras.
7. Este aparato funciona a base del programa que se usa.
8. Con esta máquina se puede mandar electrónicamente una fotografía.
9. Se conecta este aparato a la computadora para poder producir un documento.
10. Se usa para llenar un formulario o para escribir la dirección en un sobre.

Ventanilla al mundo hispánico

La fiesta de los quince años, la quinceañera

Distinguish between the celebration, la fiesta de los quince, and the person celebrating the event, la quinceañera.

Un evento de mucha importancia social en algunas partes del mundo hispánico tiene lugar cuando una muchacha cumple los quince años. Se pone mucho énfasis en la celebración, la cual normalmente es una fiesta en la casa de la joven o en un salón grande de alquiler. En el caso de las familias ricas, los arreglos pueden ser verdaderamente espectaculares e incluyen decoraciones muy elaboradas, una orquesta y un grupo grande de invitados vestidos muy formalmente. La fiesta de los quince años se celebra más comunmente en los países hispánicos del Caribe, México y la América Central, así como en las comunidades hispánicas de los EEUU. En otras partes se celebran los 18 años especialmente entre las familias de alta clase social y el propósito de estas celebraciones es la presentación de la hija ante la sociedad.

USO PRÁCTICO DEL ESPAÑOL

Polite Requests and Formal Commands

Although formal commands are presented here for both receptive and productive control, in most instances, students at this level should be practicing the use of polite requests instead of using command forms.

OJO: *Podría* is the softened form of *puede*.

OJO: *Quisiera* is the softened form of *quiero*.

Point out that formal commands are often replaced in print by infinitives. The section headings in **Entradas** *(Empezar a escuchar, Aumentar el vocabulario) are some examples.*

You want to be especially careful not to appear rude to people whom you address as *usted*. Consequently, you will not often encounter an occasion when you need to use a formal command to order such a person to do something. Instead, you will most likely use a polite request. For example, if you want to ask a waiter to bring another bottle of water, you could say

¿Me hace el favor de traerme otra botella de agua?
¿Me puede (podría) traer otra botella de agua, por favor?
Quisiera otra botella de agua, por favor.

Giving directions is one context in which it is acceptable to use formal commands. Imagine that a stranger asks you where the admissions office is located on your campus. You could say

Siga Ud. derecho por esta calle y **doble** a la derecha en el primer semáforo. **Suba** la colina y **doble** a la izquierda en la calle College. La oficina de admisiones está a la derecha, en la esquina.

Both the affirmative and negative formal commands look the same as the *usted* and *ustedes* forms of the present subjunctive. If you do use a command form, remember that reflexive, direct object, and indirect object pronouns are always attached to affirmative commands, but always precede negative commands. Here are some examples.

No puedo ver el aviso. Por favor, lé**a**me**lo**.

I can't see the sign. Please read it to me.

Nunca devuelve lo que pide prestado. Por favor, escúche**me**, no **le** preste nada.

She (He) never returns what she (he) borrows. Please listen to me, and don't lend her (him) anything.

Ponerlo a prueba

A. Usando el teléfono. Lee estas instrucciones de la guía telefónica. En el margen, al lado de cada mandato subrayado, escribe el infinitivo del verbo.

Consejos para un mejor uso del servicio telefónico

- <u>CONTESTE</u> INMEDIATAMENTE LAS LLAMADAS.

- <u>HABLE</u> CLARAMENTE.
  <u>Procure</u> que su voz sea clara y así evitará repeticiones, <u>recuerde</u> que su voz tiene personalidad.

- <u>SEA</u> CORTES AL HABLAR POR TELEFONO.

- <u>ORGANICE</u> SUS LLAMADAS.
  Organice sus pensamientos y <u>escríbalos</u>, <u>haga</u> notas y <u>sígalas</u> cuando llame.

- <u>PREPARE</u> SUS LLAMADAS.
  Tenga a la mano lápiz y papel, así como la documentación necesaria del asunto que va a tratar.

- <u>CUIDE</u> SU APARATO TELEFONICO.
  <u>No lo golpee</u>. Es frágil, el calor y la humedad le hacen daño; <u>no jale</u> los cordones. <u>Manténgalo</u> siempre en buen estado, <u>límpielo</u> solo con agua y jabón, nunca <u>use</u> alcohol. En caso de descompostura <u>llame</u> al 05.

B. Más problemas con Mario. Mario is not only rude to his friends; his brusque way of speaking is offensive to people whom he should treat with respect. Restate his remarks in a more polite way.

1. (por teléfono a la tía de Marcos) Quiero hablar con Marcos. Llámelo.
2. (a la recepcionista del médico) Hágame una cita con el médico para esta tarde.
3. (a la profesora Suárez) No nos dé tarea este fin de semana.
4. (al camarero) Tráigame el menú, tengo prisa.
5. (a la empleada de la pastelería) Deme una torta de chocolate.
6. (a la abuela de su amigo) No apague la luz, estamos leyendo aquí.

7. (al empleado de la agencia de viajes) Resérveme dos asientos en la excursión de esta tarde.

C. **Los anuncios de radio.** Trabajando en grupos de tres, inventen dos o tres oraciones acerca de cada producto o actividad que se menciona a continuación. Usen mandatos formales para recomendarle al público que use el producto o que participe en la actividad.

1. viajar a Colombia con la Agencia Díaz
2. hacer una excursión al teatro con la clase para ver una obra en español
3. asistir a un concierto de rock en la universidad
4. comprar el libro *Entradas*
5. probar el helado "Super-Cremoso"
6. usar un jabón super-fuerte para lavar la ropa

CH. **Sinónimos.** Indica la palabra de la lista de Aumentar el vocabulario que quiere decir lo mismo que cada frase de la siguiente lista.

1. la interrupción momentánea de la luz eléctrica
2. un sacramento de la Iglesia Católica para los niños de siete u ocho años
3. aparato de comunicación que se encuentra en muchos automóviles en los EEUU
4. llegar al mundo
5. dos hijos que nacen el mismo día y que tienen la misma madre
6. un sentimiento de miedo que ocurre de repente (*suddenly*)
7. una persona que tiene una opinión excesivamente buena de sí misma

D. Preguntas personales

1. ¿Dónde naciste? ¿En qué año?
2. ¿Te llevas (*Do you get along*) bien con tus hermanos? ¿Qué hacen Uds. juntos?
3. ¿Hay gemelos en tu familia? ¿Y entre tus amigos? ¿Quiénes son?
4. ¿Te gustaría tener un hermano gemelo o una hermana gemela? ¿Por qué?
5. ¿Tienes un álbum de fotos de la familia? ¿Tienes una foto favorita en un álbum o en tu cuarto? Descríbela.
6. ¿Estás orgulloso/-a de alguien de tu familia? ¿Por qué?
7. ¿Van muchos invitados a tu casa? ¿Quiénes te visitan con más frecuencia?
8. ¿Qué máquinas de comunicación tienes en tu casa? ¿Y en la residencia?
9. ¿Qué pasa si estás trabajando con una computadora y hay un apagón?

E. Encuesta.

Habla con algunos de tus compañeros de clase para identificar a una persona que corresponda a cada una de las siguientes categorías. Si esa persona no existe, puedes decir: "No hay nadie".

1. Es gemelo/-a.
2. Tiene hermanos gemelos (hermanas gemelas).
3. Tiene un(a) pariente que es también su mejor amigo/-a.
4. Estaba en un lugar público alguna vez cuando hubo un apagón.
5. Nació en otro país.
6. Nunca pelea con sus hermanos.
7. El plátano es su fruta favorita.
8. Vive cerca de sus abuelos.

F. Ven y te los presento.

Un amigo o una amiga piensa visitarte durante las vacaciones. Pero antes de que llegue, quieres decirle algo de tu familia. Prepara unos apuntes (*notes*) sobre

- quiénes viven en tu casa
- la apariencia física y la personalidad de los miembros de la familia
- sus gustos y preferencias

INVESTIGAR LA GRAMÁTICA   Expressing Generalizations

OJO: Notice that these sentences are meant to refer to everybody. That's why they are called generalizations.

The basic formula of *ser* + **adjective** + **infinitive** is used to make broad generalizations.

Para llevar una vida sana **es importante comer** bien. También **es necesario dormir** lo suficiente.

When you want to apply such a generalization to a particular case, situation, or individual, then you use two phrases connected by *que*. In many sentences of this type, the subjunctive is used.

Es importante **que comamos** bien si queremos llevar una vida sana.
It's important for us to eat (that we eat) well if we want to have a healthy life.

También es necesario **que durmamos** bien.
It's also necessary for us to sleep well.

The subjunctive is used with all of these expressions when they are applied to specific individuals and situations.

Other common adjectives used with *ser* to make generalizations are the following.

es absurdo	it is absurd, ridiculous
es bueno/malo	it is good/bad
es (poco) común	it is (not very) common
es (im)posible	it is (im)possible
es interesante	it is interesting
es mejor	it is better
es peligroso	it is dangerous
es preciso	it is necessary
es preferible	it is preferable
es terrible	it is terrible
es urgente	it is urgent, pressing

Here are some examples of sentences using these phrases.

Generalization

Es importante llevar una vida activa.
It's important to lead an active life.

Es peligroso montar en bicicleta de noche en la ciudad.
It's dangerous to ride a bicycle in the city at night.

Generalization applied to an individual

Es importante que Ud. haga ejercicio, Sr. Cárdenas.
It's important for you to exercise, Mr. Cárdenas.

Joselito, **es peligroso** que montes en bicicleta sin tu casco.
Joselito, it's dangerous for you to ride a bicycle without a helmet.

OJO: In the examples, notice how the infinitive is used when the word *que* is not present and how the subjunctive form of the verb is used with *que*.

Ponerlo a prueba

A. Combinaciones. Make as many truthful sentences as you can by using one element from each column.

Modelo: *Es absurdo que mis amigos estudien el sábado por la noche.*

Es absurdo	yo	estudiar el sábado por la noche
Es urgente	mis amigos y yo	demorar (*delay*) en hacer la tarea
Es divertido	mi hermano/-a	cantar y bailar los fines de semana
Es malo	mi compañero/-a de cuarto	comer muchos dulces
Es peligroso	mis amigos	pagar siempre con tarjeta de crédito

B. **Recomendaciones.** What advice would you give the following people?

Modelo: Paco ha invitado a unos amigos a casa.
Paco, es importante que prepares algo para comer.

1. Roberto ha invitado a Carmencita a salir con él.
2. Doña Josefina ha decidido visitar a su hija la semana entrante.
3. Josué ha sacado muy malas notas este semestre.
4. El doctor Meléndez no ha tomado ni un día de vacaciones este año.
5. Los señores Gaitán han llegado a Cali recientemente.
6. Los padres de Carmencita no le han permitido salir sola.
7. Paco le ha recomendado a Roberto un restaurante bueno y caro.
8. Roberto y Paco han visitado Cali.

C. **Hablando con el médico.** Al señor Castañeda no le gustan las recomendaciones de su médico, el doctor Pérez. Usa las expresiones con **ser** de la sección de Investigar la gramática y completa la conversación que aparece a continuación.

Dr. P: _____ que Ud. deje de (*stop*) fumar. _____ para la salud.

Sr. C: Pero, doctor, _____ que deje de fumar. Llevo 40 años fumando cigarrillos.

Dr. P: Pero _____ que me escuche, es por la salud de los pulmones y el corazón.

Sr. C: Ya sé que los cigarrillos son muy peligrosos. ¿ _____ fumar una pipa, y no cigarrillos?

Dr. P: Algunas personas creen que la pipa es mejor porque no se aspira el humo. En mi opinión _____ fumar cigarrillos, pero los dos son malos y usted debe evitarlos.

Sr. C: _____ que usted me haga esa recomendación, porque usted no es adicto como yo.

CH. **Explicaciones.** ¿Estás de acuerdo con las siguientes generalizaciones acerca de viajar? Explica tu punto de vista.

1. Es divertido viajar solo/-a.
2. Es preciso hacer todos los planes antes de empezar el viaje.
3. Es bueno visitar muchos países en cada viaje.
4. Es imposible conocer a muchas personas durante un viaje.
5. Es preferible probar muchas comidas diferentes.
6. Es peligroso salir solo/-a de noche.
7. Es fácil conocer los museos de las ciudades grandes.
8. Es común caminar mucho cuando uno viaja.

Primera etapa **343**

Have the class take notes on what they agree or disagree about while each group reports its findings. Encourage students to express differences of opinion.

D. ¿Qué pasa en esta universidad? En pequeños grupos, pónganse de acuerdo sobre las condiciones que existen en su universidad. Deben discutir lo siguiente.

1. Es bueno que en esta universidad...
2. Es terrible que en esta universidad...
3. Es posible que en el futuro...
4. Es urgente que la administración...
5. Es ridículo que...

Ahora presenten un reporte oral a la clase sobre sus opiniones.

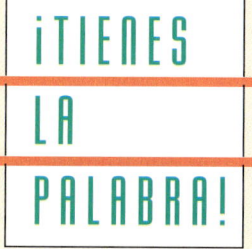

¡TIENES LA PALABRA!

This activity is best done in groups. After students have had time to create their stories, they can read them to the rest of the class. The purpose of the activity is to recycle usage of the preterite and imperfect tenses by having students narrate and describe in the past.

A. Imaginación y fantasía. Tú y tus amigos estaban caminando por la calle cuando, de repente, vieron un OVNI (Objeto Volador No Identificado = *UFO*) en el parque. Se abrió una puerta y bajó una familia entera de extraterrestres. Describe lo que Uds. vieron y lo que pasó después.

B. Familias parecidas. Haz una lista de algunos datos o características de tu familia. Luego, habla con tus compañeros de clase para ver si puedes encontrar a alguien con quien tengas algo en común. Al identificar a esta persona, haz una lista de las semejanzas y diferencias entre las dos familias.

Bosquejo

I. Número de personas en la familia y sus profesiones u oficios
II. Lugares de nacimiento
   A. del padre
   B. de la madre
   C. de los niños
III. Características físicas
   A. del padre
   B. de la madre
   C. de los niños
IV. Características de la personalidad
   A. del padre
   B. de la madre
   C. de los niños

Follow up: Develop a complete list on the board by collecting recommendations from each group. Encourage students to approach the task seriously and help them phrase their responses so that they use the vocabulary they control, rather than looking up a lot of words in the dictionary.

C. Recomendaciones para el nuevo estudiante. Con un compañero (una compañera) de la clase, prepara una lista de recomendaciones generales para los estudiantes que no tienen ninguna experiencia universitaria.

Modelo: *Es mejor llegar a la universidad* (campus) *dos o tres días antes del primer día de clase.*

OTRA VUELTA

Play instructor tape, 2 min.

Vuelve ahora a la Entrada que escuchaste al comienzo de esta etapa. Escúchala otra vez y contesta las siguientes preguntas.

1. De los dos hermanos, ¿doña Consuelo es la menor o la mayor?
2. ¿Cuáles son las profesiones de los tres hermanos?

   Jorge _____   Luz María _____
   Graciela _____

COMENTARIO CULTURAL

An excellent short story that reflects the concept of *la familia* is "No oyes ladrar los perros" by the Mexican author Juan Rulfo.

La familia

El concepto de "la familia" varía de cultura a cultura. En los EEUU, por ejemplo, "la familia" generalmente incluye sólo a los padres y sus hijos, o lo que se llama "la familia inmediata" o "nuclear"; para referirse a los demás familiares se usa la palabra *relatives*. En muchos países hispánicos, la unidad básica de "la familia" es más extensa e incluye a los abuelos, los tíos abuelos (*great-aunts and great-uncles*), los tíos, los primos y los sobrinos. Cuando alguien dice que la familia viene a comer, es muy importante saber el contexto cultural. ¡Puede ser que lleguen tres personas o que lleguen quince!

No se considera extraño el que vivan en la misma casa otras personas además de los padres y sus hijos. Asimismo, los padres esperan que sus hijos ya adultos vivan en la casa familiar hasta que se casen o acepten un trabajo en otra ciudad. Aunque las costumbres están cambiando poco a poco, sobre todo en las ciudades más grandes, en general los hijos adolescentes o adultos no se van de la casa para vivir en otra parte solos o con amigos. En realidad, son tan independientes como los jóvenes norteamericanos, pero su independencia no se manifiesta en el deseo de vivir separados de sus padres y sus hermanos.

Point out that it is quite common for a North American who has a Hispanic friend to be welcomed into the latter's family if he or she visits their home city.

Cuando un joven se va de la casa de sus padres para vivir en otra parte, las relaciones familiares siguen siendo muy estrechas. Es muy común que uno considere a sus familiares como sus mejores amigos—por ejemplo, a un primo, una tía, un sobrino. Cuando uno viaja por el país se espera que, siempre sea posible, se quede en casa de algún familiar y no en un hotel. Sería muy mala educación no aceptar la invitación de algún familiar para quedarse en su casa. La misma hospitalidad se les extiende también a los amigos de los familiares. Este es otro ejemplo de la idea de que "mi casa es su casa".

Diferencias. Usa el cuadro que aparece a continuación para apuntar las diferencias mencionadas en el Comentario cultural entre el concepto de "la familia" en la cultura hispana y la anglo-americana.

La familia hispana	La familia anglo-americana

Actividad. Determina el valor cultural que se refleja en cada una de las siguientes situaciones.

Modelo: La abuela prepara una comida para la familia (25 personas) todos los domingos.
La familia se reúne con frecuencia.

1. Carolina tiene 28 años y es enfermera. Todavía vive en casa con sus padres, su abuela y sus cuatro hermanos menores.
2. Graciela vive en Cali. Cada vez que tiene un problema y necesita a alguien con quien hablar, llama a su hermana en Bogotá.
3. Cuando Rita se entera de que sus amigas Victoria y Mariana van a visitar Santiago de Chile, insiste en que se alojen con su familia, aunque ella no va a estar allí, y sus amigas no conocen a su familia.
4. La profesora Suárez va a un congreso en Nueva York y la universidad ha ofrecido pagarle dos noches en el hotel con los demás participantes. Ella prefiere quedarse con su prima que vive cerca de la ciudad.
5. Olga y Cecilia, que son primas, han decidido alquilar un apartamento cerca de la universidad en vez de vivir en casa con sus padres. La familia está muy preocupada.

Marginal notes:
Because students have limited control of Spanish at this point, they should not be expected to go beyond a simple statement that explains or interprets the situations. Emphasize the idea that culture is quite complex and that an awareness that differences do exist is the first step in coming to a greater understanding and tolerance of those differences, whatever they may be.

Because this activity calls on students to interpret cultural values, it may work better to form small groups and have each group deal with one of the five situations.

Un niño travieso

ENTRADA

Play instructor tape, 3 min.

Un juego peligroso

Escucha mientras Paco cuenta la historia de un accidente que le ocurrió cuando era niño y pon los eventos en orden cronológico.

El accidente

__1__ Subí al segundo piso del establo.
____ Y perdí el conocimiento.
____ Por fin me quitaron el yeso.
____ Pues conté hasta cien con los ojos cerrados.

OJO: La lista continua.

_____ Estuve con el brazo enyesado por unas semanas.
_____ Me caí por la escalera.
_____ Abrí los ojos y empecé a buscar a mis amigos.
_____ Mis hermanos tuvieron que buscar al médico.
_____ Una niña me pegó con un palo y se me partió el brazo otra vez.
_____ Se me partieron el brazo izquierdo y la clavícula.

ANTES DE LEER

READING STRATEGY 8

Identify sentence segments

Sometimes, sentences in Spanish seem to be very long. However, upon close examination they are usually made up of several pieces of information linked together. One strategy you can use to deal with these longer sentences is to look for meaningful groups of words within the sentence.

Preparación

What do you know about dreams? Were you ever frightened by a dream as a child? Do you remember your dreams when you wake up? What causes us to dream? There are lots of superstitions and folk wisdom about dreams. For example, some people say that if you dream you are falling off a cliff and don't wake up before you hit bottom, you will die in your sleep. Make a list of at least three things that you have heard about dreams, then share your list with the class.

1.
2.
3.

[Play student tape, 1 min.]

Estudiar y practicar

agitado/-a	agitated, disturbed
atardecer	to become late afternoon
el cordón	cord, string
lograr	to gain; to succeed
el recuerdo	memory; souvenir
sin embargo	nevertheless

soñar (ue)   to dream
las tinieblas   complete darkness

▲▲▲▲
LEER

Gabriel García Márquez (1928–   ), the world-renowned Colombian author and winner of the 1982 Nobel Prize for Literature, is famous for his ability to manipulate language and for his evocative descriptions of people, places, and objects, many of which exist simultaneously in the worlds of reality and fantasy. One of his most famous novels is *Cien años de soledad* (*One Hundred Years of Solitude*), a novel that has been widely read in translation throughout the world.

OJO: Remember that long sentences can be treated as several short segments. For example, the first sentence in the reading selection is *Mi recuerdo más vivo y constante no es el de las personas sino el de la casa misma de Aracataca donde vivía con mis abuelos.* How could you divide this sentence into four shorter segments?
1.
2.
3.
4.

Students should divide the sentence as follows. *1. Mi recuerdo más vivo y constante 2. no es el de las personas 3. sino el de la casa misma de Aracataca 4. donde vivía con mis abuelos.*

In the *Entrada* of this chapter, you heard the narrator tell about something that happened to him as a child. In the reading selection that follows, one of the most famous writers of Colombia, Gabriel García Márquez, talks about a dream he used to have. As you read, note at least three features of the recurring dream he describes.

Gabriel García Márquez

Los suyos

—Mi recuerdo más vivo y constante no es el de las personas sino el de la casa misma de Aracataca donde vivía con mis abuelos. Es un sueño recurrente que todavia persiste. Más aún: todos los días de mi vida despierto con la impresión, falsa o real, de que he soñado que estoy en esa casa. No que he vuelto a ella, sino que estoy allí, sin edad y sin ningún motivo especial, como si nunca hubiera salido de esa casa vieja y enorme. Sin embargo, aun en el sueño, persiste el que fue mi sentimiento predominante durante toda aquella época: la zozobra (*uneasiness*) nocturna. Era una sensación irremediable que empezaba siempre al atardecer, y que me inquietaba aun durante el sueño hasta que volvía a ver por las hendijas de las puertas la luz del nuevo día. No logro definirlo muy bien, pero me parece que aquella zozobra tenía un origen concreto, y es que en la noche se materializaban todas las fantasías, presagios y evocaciones de mi abuela. Esa era mi relación con ella: una especie de cordón invisible mediante el cual nos comunicábamos ambos con un universo sobrenatural. De dia, el mundo mágico de la abuela me resultaba fascinante, vivía dentro de él, era mi mundo propio. Pero en la noche me causaba terror. Todavia hoy, a veces, cuando estoy durmiendo solo en un hotel de cualquier lugar del mundo, despierto de pronto agitado por ese miedo horrible de estar solo en las tinieblas, y necesito siempre unos minutos para racionalizarlo y volverme a dormir. El abuelo, en cambio, era para mi la seguridad absoluta dentro del mundo incierto de la abuela. Sólo con él desaparecía la zozobra, y me sentía con los pies sobre la tierra y bien establecido en la vida real. Lo raro, pensándolo ahora, es que yo quería ser como el abuelo—realista, valiente, seguro—, pero no podía resistir a la tentación constante de asomarme al mundo de la abuela.

DESPUÉS DE LEER

This excerpt provides an excellent opportunity to point out how the imperfect is used to describe the past.

> El recuerdo es...
>
> El sueño es...
>
> El autor interpreta el sueño diciendo que la sensación que sentía representaba su relación con...

A. Preguntas específicas

1. ¿Cómo era la casa de los abuelos de García Márquez?
2. ¿Cuándo empezaba y cuándo terminaba el miedo que sentía?
3. Según el autor, ¿qué causaba el miedo?
4. ¿En qué sentido era diferente la "magia" durante el día?
5. ¿Qué representa el abuelo para García Márquez?

B. Preguntas personales

1. ¿Cuál es uno de los recuerdos más vivos de tu niñez? ¿Todavía te causa el mismo efecto? ¿Cuál es?
2. ¿Hay algún pariente u otro adulto que te haya impresionado muchísimo? ¿Quién es y qué influencia ha tenido en tu vida?
3. ¿Puedes recordar algún lugar especial de tu juventud? Descríbelo.
4. Describe una experiencia—o buena o mala—que tuviste de niño/-a.

C. Un paso más. Escribe una descripción (¡en español, por supuesto!) de por lo menos dos párrafos de un lugar o de una persona que recuerdas de tu niñez o juventud.

AUMENTAR EL VOCABULARIO

Point out the relationships of these words to mañana, tarde.

a menudo	*often*
agitar	*to agitate*
agitado/-a	*agitated, disturbed*
molestar	*to bother*
el alba	*dawn*
amanecer	*to dawn*
atardecer	*to become late afternoon*
la oscuridad	*darkness*
las tinieblas	*complete darkness*
caerse	*to fall down*

Segunda etapa

> Point out to students that the English word "lasso" comes from *el lazo,* "knot."

el cordón	cord, string
la soga	rope
el cuerpo	body
la cadera	hip
la cintura	waist
la clavícula	collarbone
la espalda	back
el estómago	stomach
el muslo	thigh
darse cuenta (de)	to realize
imaginarse	to imagine
lograr	to gain; to succeed
partir	to break (*apart*)
compartir	to share
repartir	to distribute, divide up
pegar	to hit
hacerse daño	to get hurt, be injured
el recuerdo	memory; souvenir
sin embargo	nevertheless
además (de)	besides, in addition to
soñar (ue)	to dream
el sueño	dream
travieso/-a	mischievous
bien educado/-a	well-mannered, polite
el yeso	plaster (*cast*)
enyesado/-a	set in a cast

> Point out to students that *partir* is used with bones and *romper* is used with objects.

VENTANILLA AL MUNDO HISPÁNICO   Expresiones de emoción

En la Entrada de esta etapa, doña Consuelo expresa su reacción al cuento de Paco diciendo, "¡Qué mala suerte! ¡Qué desgracia!" Tales expresiones de emoción se usan para indicar una reacción espontánea, ya sea positiva o negativa, a un evento. Aunque hay variaciones regionales, la mayoría de las expresiones que se dan a continuación son comunes en todos los países del mundo hispánico.

Reacciones positivas

¡Qué bello/-a!	How beautiful!
¡Qué buena suerte!	What good luck!
¡Qué rico/-a!	How wonderful! How delicious!
¡Qué sorpresa!	What a surprise!

Reacciones negativas

¡Qué barbaridad!	How awful!
¡Qué desgracia!	What terrible luck!

¡Qué horror!   How horrible!
¡Qué lástima!   What a shame! What a pity!
¡Qué lata!   What a pain (bother)!
¡Qué mala suerte!   What bad luck!
¡Qué susto!   How scary!
¡Qué vergüenza!   How embarrassing!

Follow-up: Have students perform some of the conversations in pairs; the class provides appropriate expressions of emotion.

Actividad. Escribe dos diálogos que presenten contextos apropiados para una reacción positiva y una reacción negativa. En cada caso, la expresión emotiva sería (*would be*) el próximo turno.

Modelo: A: *¿Sabes lo que me pasó ayer?*
B: *No, ¿qué te pasó?*
A: *Pues, estaba en mi coche. Conducía rápido, porque iba a casa de Eduardo para ver el partido. Y un policía me cogió en la calle First. Tengo que pagar $65 por andar a 45 en vez de 25.*
B: *¡Qué lata!*

LAS PARTES DEL CUERPO

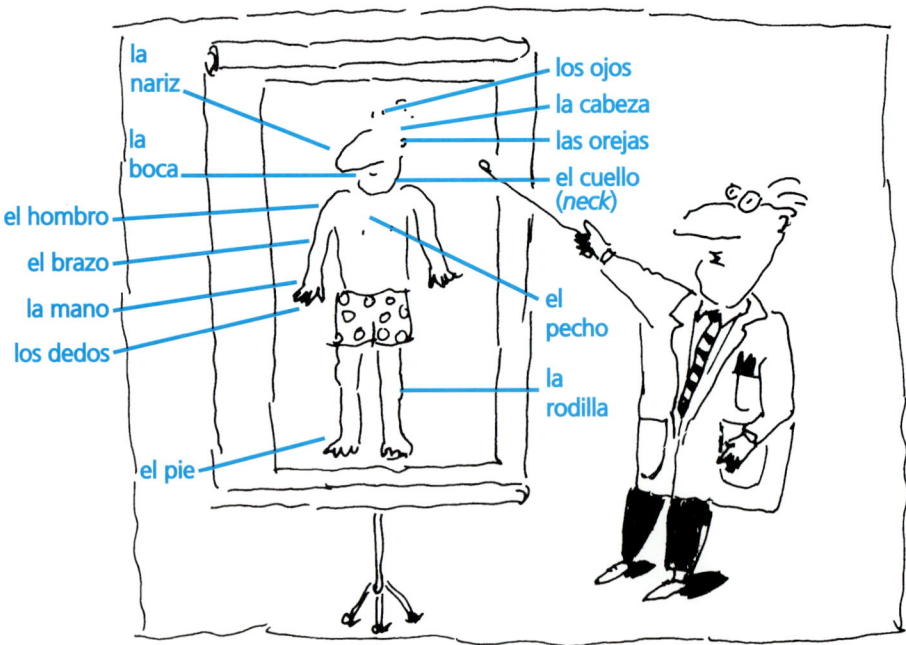

Asociaciones. Indica qué parte(s) del cuerpo te viene(n) a la mente cuando piensas en las actividades siguientes.

Modelo: ir a un museo de arte moderno
Pienso en los ojos—para ver los cuadros.

1. entrar en una panadería o en una pastelería
2. comprar zapatos nuevos
3. levantar pesas (*weights*) en el gimnasio
4. ponerse la corbata (hombres)
5. ponerse un abrigo
6. buscar una moneda que se cayó al césped

USO PRÁCTICO DEL ESPAÑOL   Familiar Commands

The commands here and in the third etapa *of this chapter are presented for 1) production with high-frequency uses and phrases, and 2) recognition. Stress production of indirect and softened commands.*

In Chapter 7 you learned that the subjunctive can be used to influence the actions of others. For example, if you want a friend to get to your house before 8:00, you could say

Es importante que **llegues** antes de las ocho.	*It's important for you to arrive before eight.*
Quiero que **llegues** antes de las ocho.	*I want you to arrive before eight.*

You can also state your wishes more directly by using *mandatos,* or commands. For people whom you address as *tú,* you can say

Por favor, **llega** antes de las ocho.   *Please, arrive before eight.*

You might also say the following to a friend or a child.

Pide una hamburguesa, son ricas aquí.	*Order a hamburger; they are delicious here.*
Por favor, **come** más despacio, no tenemos prisa.	*Please eat more slowly; we're not in a hurry.*

Notice that the form for the affirmative familiar command looks the same as the *él, ella, usted* form of the present tense of regular verbs. Direct commands can sound rude, however, so it is often wise to soften them either by including *por favor* or by stating them indirectly as questions. For example, if you want someone to speak more loudly, you can say

Por favor, habla más alto. No te oigo.	*Please, speak up. I can't hear you.*
¿Puedes hablar más alto, por favor? No te oigo.	*Can you speak louder, please? I can't hear you.*

A few common verbs have an irregular affirmative familiar command.

decir	**di**		hacer	**haz**
ir(se)	**ve**(**te**)		poner(se)	**pon**(**te**)
salir	**sal**		ser	**sé**
tener	**ten**		venir	**ven**

OJO: Note that reflexive, direct object, and indirect object pronouns are attached to the end of the verb (*Ponte el abrigo; Dime todo*). This is true for the **affirmative** commands only.

OJO: The familiar commands that are irregular in the affirmative (*sal, ven, pon,* and so on) are regular in the negative (*no salgas, no vengas, no pongas*).

Some familiar commands are commonly used with friends and children without the connotation of rudeness or bossiness.

¡**Ven** acá, hija, y **date** prisa! — Come here, child, and hurry!
Tenme esto, por favor. — Please hold this for me.
Oye, ¿has visto a David? — Hey, have you seen David?
Ponte el abrigo, que hace frío. — Put your coat on; it's cold out.
Dime (**Cuéntame**) todo. — Tell me everything.

A **negative** command is used to tell someone **not** to do something. The negative familiar commands use the *tú* form of the present subjunctive.

No **salgas** ahora, por favor. — Please don't go out now.
No me **llames** esta noche, no voy a estar en casa. — Don't call me tonight; I won't be home.

Use negative commands sparingly, since they, too, can be interpreted as rude. You can soften them by adding some explanation or by using a verb of influence instead. For example, if you want to tell a friend to avoid a particular restaurant, you could say

No vayas a ese restaurante, la comida es malísima.
Te aconsejo que **no vayas** a ese restaurante.
¿Por qué vas a ese restaurante? Es malísimo.
No debes ir a ese restaurante, es malísimo.
Siempre les digo a mis amigos que **no vayan** a ese restaurante porque los meseros son muy antipáticos.

Ponerlo a prueba

Encourage students to add details for personalization and humor: *Sé bueno o no puedes ir.*

A. Padres y niños. Usando los mandatos familiares y las indicaciones (*cues*) que aparecen a continuación, decide lo que diría (*might say*) un padre o una madre a su hijo/-a.

Modelo: acostarse   ¡Acuéstate ahora mismo!

1. venir acá
2. decirnos la verdad
3. lavarse las manos
4. ponerse las botas
5. ser bueno
6. no hacer ruido
7. hacerlo ahora mismo
8. darse prisa
9. mirar esto
10. no salir ahora

Act. B, Follow-up 1: Have students give instructions for other similar activities, such as using a phone card, writing a check, or preparing for a party.
Act. B, Follow-up 2: For each affirmative instruction, have a student add a negative or softened command: *Ve al banco, pero es mejor que vayas durante el día, no por la noche; Ve al banco pero no vayas por la noche, no es seguro.*

B. Las instrucciones. Tu amigo/-a no sabe cómo usar una tarjeta bancaria para sacar fondos de su cuenta. Explícale paso por paso (*step by step*) lo que debe hacer.

Modelo: ir al banco   Ve al banco.

1. sacar la tarjeta de tu bolsa
2. tener cuidado de meter la tarjeta correctamente

3. marcar tu número de identificación personal
4. indicar cuánto dinero quieres sacar
5. tomar el dinero
6. sacar tu tarjeta del cajero automático

C. ¡Sssh! ¡No digas eso! Mario tiene la mala costumbre de usar mandatos con sus amigos y de decirles exactamente lo que piensa. Expresa nuevamente cada mandato para que resulte más suave o más cortés.

Modelo: Marta, dame un café.
Marta, ¿me puedes dar un café, por favor?

1. Rafael, no comas ese helado, es para Isabel.
2. ¡Apaga el televisor ahora mismo!
3. Beatriz, no te pongas esa blusa, es muy fea.
4. No invites a Samuel a tu fiesta, siempre bebe demasiado.
5. Tráeme el cuaderno rojo que está en la mesa.
6. Búscanos otras dos sillas.
7. ¡No fumes aquí!
8. Escribe la composición hoy, la tienes que entregar mañana.

CH. Definiciones. Indica a qué palabra de la lista de Aumentar el vocabulario corresponden las definiciones siguientes.

1. un sinónimo de muchas veces
2. la parte del cuerpo que incluye los ojos, las orejas, la nariz y la boca
3. un niño que siempre hace lo que no debe hacer
4. dividir algo en partes para dárselas a varias personas
5. lo que se usa para inmovilizar un hueso partido
6. lo que pasa muchas veces si tienes un accidente
7. la falta de luz
8. muchas veces es una fantasía
9. la parte del cuerpo entre la cabeza y la clavícula
10. la parte posterior del cuerpo entre los hombros y la cintura

D. Preguntas personales

1. De niño/-a, ¿eras travieso/-a o bien educado/-a? ¿Había un niño travieso (una niña traviesa) en tu familia?
2. ¿Había un niño travieso (una niña traviesa) en tu escuela cuando eras más joven? ¿Qué hacía? ¿Cómo lo (la) trataba el maestro (la maestra)?
3. Cuando eras niño/-a, ¿de qué tenías miedo?
4. ¿Qué hacías por la tarde después de las clases?

5. ¿Te partiste el brazo u otra parte del cuerpo alguna vez? ¿Qué te pasó? ¿Lo tuviste enyesado? ¿Por cuánto tiempo?

6. Cuando eras niño/-a, ¿molestabas a tus hermanos, o ellos te molestaban a ti? ¿Pasaba esto con frecuencia?

7. ¿Te gustaba compartir tus juguetes (*toys*) con tus hermanos y tus amigos? ¿Cuál era tu juguete favorito?

E. **Las reacciones.** Álvaro y Norberto están hablando de las últimas noticias de sus amigos. Después de cada noticia, indica la reacción probable del otro, usando las expresiones de la Ventanilla al mundo hispánico de esta etapa.

To make this activity more communicative, have Student 1 respond to the reaction of Student 2.

Modelo: Lourdes me dijo que ayer se cayó cuando montaba a caballo.
Reacción: *¡Qué horror! ¿Qué le pasó?*

1. La mamá de Alejandra le mandó tres cajas de bombones.
   Reacción:
2. Lucía me dijo que un hombre la asaltó en la calle y le robó la bolsa.
   Reacción:
3. ¿Oíste que el primo de Esteban se casó el sábado pasado?
   Reacción:
4. ¿Has visto las fotos del nuevo sobrino de Georgina?
   Reacción:
5. Me imagino que has oído lo de Eduardo, ¿verdad?
   Reacción:

F. **¿Cuál es la diferencia entre...?**

1. el alba y la oscuridad
2. un niño travieso y un niño bien educado
3. un cordón y una soga
4. amanecer y anochecer
5. el brazo y la pierna

INVESTIGAR LA GRAMÁTICA   The Subjunctive with Expressions and Verbs of Emotion

In the first *etapa* of this chapter you saw how we use the subjunctive with expressions of the form **ser** + **adjective** + **que,** whenever a broad generalization is applied to a particular individual.

Es absurdo que no vengas todos los días a la clase de español.
Es preferible que te quedes en casa estudiando.

These expressions, as well as *es terrible que, es triste que,* and others, allow us to express our emotions about some situation or event outside of ourselves. There are many other verbs and expressions that serve the same communicative function.

Paco **está contento de que haya** vuelos a Cartagena todos los días.
Roberto **tiene miedo de que el viaje en autobús sea** muy largo.
Sentimos mucho que no puedas ir a Colombia con nosotros.

Expressions like *estar contento de que, tener miedo de que,* or *sentir que* allow us to express our emotional reaction to some event outside ourselves. The external event or situation that causes us to feel the emotion is expressed in the subjunctive. Here are some more things that Cristina's family members might have said to her in Chapter 7 when they were trying to get her to be a better student.

Es importante que saques mejores notas este año.
Es terrible que no estudies más.
Es triste que tengamos tantos problemas contigo.
Es preferible que no tengas estéreo en tu cuarto.
Reconocemos que **es una lástima que no puedas** salir con tus amigas, pero **es mejor que vayas** a la biblioteca.

The preceding examples all use expressions with *ser*. The following examples show other verbs and expressions that allow us to express our emotions.

Nos sorprende que tengamos que castigarte.
Tu papá y yo **sentimos que no comprendas** que tienes que aplicarte más a tus estudios.
No nos gusta que tengas estos problemas.
Nos enoja que no pongas atención.

Ponerlo a prueba

A. **Un viaje esperado.** Determine whether or not the subjunctive is used in the following sentences. Identify (a) who is expressing the emotion, (b) who is being influenced by the feeling, and (c) the verb or expression that denotes emotion.

Modelo: Siento mucho que tengas que volver a casa antes de las 11:00.
Who is expressing the emotion: *Yo*
Who is being influenced: *tú*
Verb or expression of emotion: *sentir*
Use of subjunctive: *sí*

1. Espero pasar el verano en México.
2. Ojalá que uno de mis amigos me acompañe.
3. En realidad, tengo miedo de viajar solo.
4. Mis amigos me dicen que es preferible que vayamos durante el mes de julio.
5. Temo que no haya tiempo para viajar a Oaxaca, donde viven mi prima y su familia.

Haz las siguientes actividades con un compañero (una compañera).

A. Encuesta. ¿Qué opinas si...? Habla con cuatro o cinco compañeros/-as de la clase, preguntándoles cómo reaccionarían (*would react*) frente a las circunstancias mencionadas.

- Suben los precios de las comidas en las cafeterías.
- Bajan la matrícula por primera vez desde hace diez años.
- Van a cortar la electricidad en la universidad el lunes que viene.
- Van a cancelar todos los exámenes finales este semestre.

Organiza las respuestas que recibes bajo las categorías de positiva y negativa. Luego, informa a la clase.

B. Pues, de aquí... Con un compañero (una compañera) de la clase, identifica un lugar popular que conozcas muy bien (por ejemplo, una peluquería, una panadería, una discoteca), pero no se lo digas a tu compañero/-a. Luego, dale oralmente las instrucciones necesarias a tu amigo/-a para ir allá.

C. Encuesta. Temores y esperanzas. Habla con dos de tus compañeros/-as de la clase, pidiéndoles información sobre una cosa que teman y algo que esperen. Luego, informa a la clase.

OTRA VUELTA

Play instructor tape, 3 min.

Escucha otra vez la anécdota que contó Paco en la Entrada de esta etapa y apunta

- cómo doña Consuelo lo anima a Paco a continuar su cuento
- cómo Paco expresa la idea de *faint, pass out*

COMENTARIO CULTURAL

In the *Entrada* section in this *etapa,* Paco describes a game that he used to play with his friends. The following *Comentario cultural* provides students with additional information about children's games in some Hispanic countries. Emphasize the similarities, as well as the differences.

Juegos y actividades de los niños

Los juegos y otras diversiones de los niños son una parte importante de la juventud. Además de su valor recreativo y físico, a través de ellos los niños aprenden las normas de interacción social apropiadas para su cultura: los conceptos sobre lo que se considera justo o injusto, bueno o malo, honesto o deshonesto. Los juegos desarrollan habilidades sociales enseñando conceptos tales como el de tomar turnos, seguir reglas y otros procedimientos. En algunos juegos se interpretan diferentes papeles, en los cuales los niños "practican" el comportamiento de los adultos en determinadas situaciones. En fin, se puede decir que hasta cierto punto los juegos y otras diversiones de los niños reflejan su cultura.

Algunos juegos son comunes tanto en los países hispánicos como en los

An interesting topic to discuss among students is the purpose that games serve in terms of conveying cultural values and rules of behavior.

Mexican children trying to decide who is "it" in a game might perform this version of "One Potato…" *Tin, Marín, dedó, pingüé, Cúcara, mácara, títere fue, Yo no fui, fue Teté, Pégale, pégale que ella fue.*

Another favorite children's rhyme used in greetings is: *¿Qué te pasa, Calabaza?* The answer is: *Nada, nada, Limonada.*

1. dominoes 2. checkers 3. Chinese checkers 4. Parcheesi 5. jigsaw puzzles 6. chess

Estados Unidos. El fútbol se juega mucho en América Latina y en España, y el béisbol es muy popular en toda la región del Caribe. Los niños saltan a la cuerda (*jump rope*), juegan rayuela (*hopscotch*) y pelota (*catch*), y juegan a los bandidos (*cops and robbers*). Los juegos que se practican dentro de la casa incluyen jugar con las muñecas (*playing with dolls*) y varios juegos de mesa—el Monopolio, los naipes (*cards*), las damas (*checkers*), el ajedrez (*chess*), el dominó y los rompecabezas (*puzzles*). Algunas actividades son propias de regiones más específicas. Por ejemplo, la piñata—una olla hecha de barro o una figura de cartón decorada, llena de dulces, juguetes y monedas—es común en Centroamérica, en México y en el suroeste de los EEUU. En las fiestas, sobre todo de cumpleaños, se cuelga la piñata con una cuerda y los niños, que tienen los ojos vendados, tratan de romperla con un palo.

Actividad. A continuación hay una lista de juegos de mesa (*table and board games*). Identifica los equivalentes en inglés, luego habla con un compañero (una compañera) de la clase sobre un recuerdo tuyo de la niñez relacionado con uno de estos juegos.

1. el dominó
2. las damas
3. las damas chinas
4. Parqués
5. los rompecabezas
6. el ajedrez

Roberto, el hijo modelo

ENTRADA

Play instructor tape, 3 min.

Roberto talks about his childhood, following up the story of Paco's accident recounted in the *Entrada* of the second *etapa*.

"Nunca me pasó nada por el estilo…"

Ahora Paco y Roberto hablan de la juventud de Roberto. Mientras escuchas, identifica dónde vivía Roberto y qué hacía para pasar el tiempo. Además, apunta dos actividades mencionadas por los jóvenes.

La niñez de Roberto

Ciudad:
Barrio:
Diversiones:

Las actividades

de Paco

1.

2.

de Roberto

1.

2.

ANTES DE HABLAR Y ESCRIBIR

Preparación

Casi todos nosotros tenemos anécdotas acerca de los automóviles, por ejemplo un incidente de cuando éramos niños, cómo y cuándo aprendimos a manejar, un accidente que vimos o tuvimos. Piensa en una experiencia tuya relacionada con los coches y usa el espacio a continuación para organizarla.

Cuándo:

Dónde:

Descripción del coche / de las circunstancias:

Qué pasó:

1.

2.

3.

Cuál fue el resultado final:

HABLAR

Ahora, con un compañero (una compañera) de la clase, haz las dos actividades siguientes.

1. Cuéntale al compañero (a la compañera) la experiencia.
2. Ayúdense (*Help each other*) a decidir por qué la experiencia es interesante. ¿Por qué es digna de contarse (*worth telling*)? ¿Es divertida, o emocionante (*exciting*) o te ayudó a ser más responsable?

Tercera etapa

WRITING STRATEGY 8

Give your story a point

You learned in Chapter 7 some of the differences between spoken and written stories. All narratives about personal experiences, to be interesting to your listener or reader, should have a point—some reason that the story is being conveyed. Often, this has to do with the events being unusual in some way—funny, frightening, or contrary to your expectations. You need to communicate this as you are recounting the narrative. You can tell your reader directly what the point of the story is by writing, for example, *...y entonces algo muy sorprendente pasó.* Your other alternative is to embed the surprise element in your narrative by the words you choose: *...y cuando lo vi allí en el parque, grité espontáneamente, "¡Martín, te quiero con locura!"* Your stories should communicate your point in several ways, for example, by telling your reader directly, using a direct quote, or choosing adjectives that communicate an emotion.

ESCRIBIR

Ahora convierte tu cuento oral en una narrativa escrita. Lee otra vez la *Writing Strategy* 7 en la tercera etapa del Capítulo 7. Acuérdate de comunicarle bien a tu público por qué tu cuento es interesante.

AUMENTAR EL VOCABULARIO

el aceite	oil
agregar	to add
algo por el estilo	something like that
nada por el estilo	nothing like that
el barrio	neighborhood
el bate	baseball bat
el balón	ball (*large, as for soccer, basketball*)
la canasta, el cesto	basket (*for basketball*)
la cancha	court, playing field
la pelota	ball (*small, as for tennis, baseball*)
la raqueta	racquet
la red	net
el cambio	change (*one for another*)
competir (i, i)	to compete
el (la) conformista	conformist
el (la) rebelde	rebel
construir	to build
la diversión	recreation, pastime

OJO: Remember that *conformista* and *rebelde* are also adjectives.

llevarse (con)	to get along (with)
portarse bien/mal	to behave well/badly
tratar	to treat (a person well, badly)
recorrer	to cover a distance
tapar	to cover (up), to put the lid or cork on
el corcho	cork
la tapa	lid

EL AUTOMÓVIL

1. Add words as needed: *el embrague, la caja de cambios, el parachoques, los faroles, el guardafango.* 2. *La llanta = el neumático; una llanta pinchada = una llanta rota.*

Point out that both *parabrisas* and *limpiaparabrisas* take the masculine singular article.

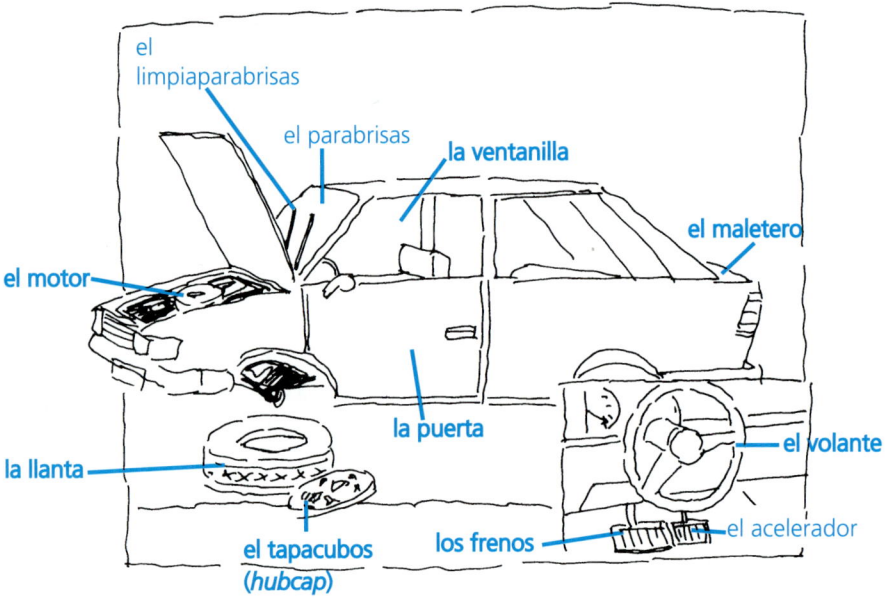

VENTANILLA AL MUNDO HISPÁNICO   El fútbol

En los países de habla española, así como en el resto del mundo, la palabra "fútbol" se refiere a lo que en los EEUU se llama *soccer*. El fútbol es probablemente el deporte que más se juega en todo el mundo. Cada cuatro años se juegan una serie de eliminatorias para determinar al campeón mundial de fútbol. Esta competencia se llama "la Copa Mundial del Fútbol". En 1992 el Mundial se celebró por primera vez en los Estados Unidos.

El término que se refiere a lo que los estadounidenses llaman *football* es "el fútbol americano". Hay que tener cuidado con la terminología para no confundir a la gente.

USO PRÁCTICO DEL ESPAÑOL   Making Impersonal Statements

Point out the difference between "you/they" used impersonally with se and used personally to mean tú/ustedes.

English has several words that can be used to refer to people in general rather than to anyone in particular, especially when talking about how things are generally done: **one, you, they, people.** In Spanish, one way that impersonal statements can be made is by placing *se* in front of the third-person forms of the verb.

Se dice que la vida nocturna en Cartagena es muy buena.	People/They say that the night life in Cartagena is very good.
Es verdad. **Se puede** salir a comer, **se puede** bailar...	It's true. You/One can go out to eat, go dancing...

Se + third-person plural form of the verb is used when the noun that follows is in the plural.

Se oye música fabulosa en las discotecas.	You can hear fabulous music in the discos.
También **se ven** unas parejas que bailan divinamente.	One can also see some couples who dance beautifully.
Se come bien en ese restaurante.	One eats well at that restaurant.
Se sirven unos platos increíbles.	They serve some incredible dishes.

Ponerlo a prueba

A. Imagínate. Una estudiante de intercambio acaba de llegar y tienes la responsabilidad de explicarle algunas costumbres norteamericanas.

Modelo: la ropa que se lleva   *Aquí se lleva ropa informal.*

This activity can be done in pairs, with one student asking the questions (¿A qué hora se abren las tiendas?) and the other student responding.

1. las horas de abrir y cerrar las tiendas
2. los medios de transporte público
3. lo que se hace los fines de semana
4. las horas de trabajo
5. las horas de las clases
6. las horas de las comidas
7. lo que se come de desayuno, de almuerzo y de cena
8. los lugares por donde se puede pasear sin problema
9. los lugares por donde no se debe pasear
10. lo que se hace en una fiesta típica

B. Definiciones. Indica a qué palabra de la lista de esta etapa corresponden las siguientes definiciones.

1. una persona que siempre hace lo que esperan los demás
2. poner un corcho en una botella

3. una vecindad
4. el área donde se juega al tenis
5. la parte del coche donde se ponen las cosas cuando uno va de viaje
6. una parte ornamental del coche que es de metal

C. **Opiniones.** Completa las oraciones siguientes de acuerdo con tu opinión.

1. Prefiero un coche pequeño (grande) porque...
2. Los coches de dos (de cuatro) puertas son preferibles porque...
3. Una ventaja de tener un maletero grande es...
4. Es recomendable saber cambiar una llanta pinchada porque...
5. Los limpiaparabrisas deben funcionar bien porque...
6. Prefiero (No prefiero) los coches en los que se puede subir y bajar las ventanillas automáticamente porque...

CH. **Preguntas personales**

1. ¿Cómo era el barrio en donde vivías de niño/-a?
2. ¿Cuáles eran tus diversiones favoritas?
3. ¿Cómo te portabas en la escuela cuando eras niño/-a?
4. ¿Cuáles eran tres actividades que tus padres no te dejaban hacer?
5. ¿Tu familia ha vivido siempre en el mismo lugar, o ustedes se han mudado? Explica.
6. Si tienes coche, o tu familia tiene coche, descríbelo.
7. ¿Cómo es para ti el coche ideal?
8. ¿Tuviste una llanta pinchada alguna vez? ¿Qué hiciste? Describe las circunstancias.
9. Para ti, ¿cuáles son los problemas asociados con ser dueño de un coche?

D. **Las relaciones familiares.** Completa las oraciones siguientes, de acuerdo con tu experiencia personal.

1. Cuando era niño/-a, mis padres siempre se enojaban cuando...
2. El barrio donde vivíamos era aburrido (interesante) porque...
3. Yo me llevaba bien con mis amigos porque...
4. Cuando aprendí a manejar, mis padres me permitían usar el coche si...
5. Cuando era niño/-a mi travesura (*prank*) favorita era...

E. **¿Conformista o rebelde?** Piensa en la descripción de una persona, real o imaginaria, que sea un "hijo modelo" (una "hija modelo") o el opuesto, un "hijo rebelde" (una "hija rebelde"). Prepárate para describir a esa persona, para ver si tus compañeros pueden identificarla como "conformista" o "rebelde".

INVESTIGAR LA GRAMÁTICA

Expressing Certainty versus Uncertainty, Doubt, Denial, and Disbelief

In these examples, doubt and disbelief are being expressed about events and conditions in the present and the future. To express doubt in the present about events in the past, the present perfect subjunctive is used: Dudo que Leonor le haya prestado dinero a Miguel. Es imposible que haya tenido confianza en una persona tan irresponsable.

Doubt, uncertainty, and disbelief are part of everyone's experience. The subjunctive is used to talk about things we doubt, deny, or do not believe.

The following conversation might take place between two friends.

— No puedo prestarte dinero, Miguel. **Dudo** que me lo **devuelvas.**

— ¿Por qué, Leonor? **¿Es posible** que no **confíes** (confiar: *to trust*) en mí?

— ¡No sólo es posible, sino cierto! Tienes buen corazón, Miguel, pero **no creo** que **seas** muy responsable.

Miguel and Leonor have used some common expressions of doubt in their conversation. If Miguel were to defend his character by denying what Leonor has said, the conversation might continue in this way.

— Leonor, **es imposible** que me **hables** así. Soy muy honesto y honrado, ¿no?

— Siento decirte esto, Miguel, pero **no es verdad** que **devuelvas** lo que te prestan. Mi cuaderno de biología por ejemplo…

— Pero eso no es lo mismo. Se me perdió (*I lost it*). **Estoy seguro** que no **voy** a perder el dinero que me vas a prestar.

Here are the most common expressions of doubt, denial, and disbelief.

dudar	no es verdad
es dudoso	es imposible
quizás, posiblemente	no creer, no pensar
(no) es posible	no estoy seguro/-a
no es cierto	negar (*to deny*)

In Spanish, *creer* and *pensar* in the affirmative express certainty, while *no creer* and *no pensar* express doubt.

— **No creo** que Carolina **venga.** Vamos a salir sin ella.

— Pues, Mario **piensa** que **viene** pronto, que hay mucho tráfico. Por mi parte, quisiera esperar unos minutos más.

Ponerlo a prueba

Ask students to convert the sentences from ciertas to dudosas (or vice versa).

A. ¿Cierto o dudoso? Lee las oraciones siguientes y decide si la persona expresa certeza (**C**) o duda (**D**) frente a la situación.

1. Dudo que Julia salga con Javier.
2. Pues, es verdad que a ella le encanta bailar.

3. Tienes razón, y no creo que Javier sepa bailar.
4. No sé. Es verdad que nunca lo he visto bailar.
5. Dice que no sabe bailar, pero no creo que diga la verdad.
6. Pero no hay duda de que es un atleta formidable: corre, nada y esquía como un ángel.
7. Así que es posible que sepa bailar.
8. ¿Quién sabe? ¡Lo que sí es seguro es que no sabemos nada acerca del caso!

This activity can be structured as a debate. Focus on the statement of opposing opinions.

B. En tu opinión... ¿Qué opinas acerca de las declaraciones siguientes? Usa una de estas expresiones al contestar.

(No) Creo que... Es posible que...
(No) Dudo que... Es imposible que...
(No) Niego que... (No) Es verdad que...
(No) Estoy seguro/-a de que...

1. Los niños traviesos siempre tienen problemas más tarde en la vida.
2. Los niños traviesos también son los más imaginativos.
3. Jugar a las escondidas es un juego muy peligroso.
4. La niñez es la época más feliz de la vida.
5. Los niños siempre prefieren los juegos activos, mientras que las niñas son más tranquilas.
6. Los gemelos tienen mucha suerte; siempre tienen un compañero (una compañera) y mejor amigo/-a.
7. Es mejor ser hijo único (hija única) que tener hermanos.
8. La rebelión de los hijos adolescentes contra sus padres es una etapa natural del proceso de maduración.

Note that there are various ways to contradict the niño travieso. Students working in pairs can create mini-diálogos for each situation.

C. Cuidando al niño travieso. ¡Qué mala suerte! Estás cuidando al hijo de unos amigos de tus padres. Es un niño travieso que trata de convencerte de que sus padres se lo permiten todo. Pero tú no le crees todo lo que te dice. Responde a las declaraciones del niño usando una expresión de duda, negación o certeza.

Modelo: Mis padres me dejan comer helado en la sala.
Dudo que tus padres te dejen comer helado en la sala.
o: *Estoy seguro/-a que tus padres no te dejan comer helado en la sala.*

1. En esta casa se puede ver televisión hasta las tres de la madrugada.
2. No tengo que lavarme la cara antes de acostarme.
3. Siempre como diez galletas antes de acostarme.
4. Mis padres quieren que me acueste en el sofá, no en mi cama.
5. No puedo acostarme ahora; mi abuela me va a llamar desde Cali.

6. Mi hermana y yo siempre jugamos al béisbol en la casa.
7. No puedo acostarme porque hay un fantasma en mi cuarto.
8. Mis padres me permiten pegarle a mi hermana; dicen que ella es antipática.

This activity is best done in groups of three.

CH. **La fiesta de los quince años.** Esta noche es la fiesta de los quince de María Luisa Sandoval. La señora de Sandoval está muy nerviosa y está hablando con sus dos hermanas acerca de los detalles. Su hermana Adriana es optimista y la otra, Ofelia, es pesimista. Para cada preocupación que expresa la señora de Sandoval, da las reacciones posibles de las dos hermanas.

Modelo: ¿Y las flores? ¿Están bien?
Adriana: *Sí, están preciosas. No te preocupes, hermana.*
Ofelia: *No sé, están casi muertas ya. Dudo que las puedas usar esta noche.*

1. ¿Y la comida? No sé si hay bastante.
2. ¿Les gusta cómo están decoradas las mesas?
3. Estoy preocupada por la misa antes de la fiesta. Ojalá que los niños no lloren.
4. ¿Qué pasa si no va el padre Juan José a la fiesta? Lo he invitado.
5. ¿Y la música? Espero que la orquesta sea buena.
6. Sé que a toda la familia le encanta bailar. Espero que haya espacio suficiente.
7. ¿Qué hago si otra mujer tiene el mismo vestido que yo?
8. ¿Y nuestro primo Raúl? ¿Qué hago si bebe demasiado vino y se pone (*becomes*) antipático?

Haz las siguientes actividades con un compañero (una compañera).

A. **Pensando en un automóvil nuevo.** Imagínate que vas a comprar tu primer auto. Tu amigo/-a ya tiene auto, así que le pides consejos. Pregúntale

- cómo es su auto
- cuándo lo compró
- cuántas millas ha recorrido
- qué problemas ha tenido con él
- qué te recomienda: un automóvil nuevo o uno de segunda mano

This can also be used as a writing activity.

OJO: *La lista continúa.*

B. **Un recuerdo de la niñez.** ¿Te acuerdas de un incidente en que te hiciste daño? Cuéntale a un compañero (una compañera) de la clase

- qué te pasó
- cuántos años tenías

- dónde ocurrió el incidente
- qué daño te hiciste
- qué hiciste

Luego informa a la clase.

OTRA VUELTA

Play instructor tape, 3 min.

Vuelve ahora a la Entrada que escuchaste al comienzo de esta etapa. Escúchala otra vez y contesta las preguntas siguientes.

1. ¿En qué ciudades ha vivido la familia de Roberto?
2. ¿Cuáles son tres actividades que Roberto hacía cuando era niño?
3. Según Roberto, ¿por qué se llevaba bien con sus amigos?
4. ¿Qué tipo de estudiante era Roberto?
5. Por otra parte, ¿cómo era la niñez de Paco?
6. En tu opinión, ¿cuál de los dos es el hijo modelo?

OJO: Paco habló de su niñez en la Entrada de la segunda etapa.

COMENTARIO CULTURAL

The wide cultural variation in the United States is seen in the activities, behavior, and living patterns of families. In many ethnic communities in the United States, family life is similar to the picture of family life in Hispanic countries presented here. Point out to students that patterns of family life are changing everywhere, in Hispanic countries as well as in the United States. The variation and rate of change are both so great that any generalization will have many exceptions.

Criar a los niños

La forma de criar a los niños varía de cultura en cultura. La cantidad de tiempo que los niños pasan con sus padres, las actividades que comparten los adultos y los niños, la lengua que los adultos usan con los niños (y viceversa) son algunas de las diferencias principales.

Muchos niños en las culturas hispánicas crecen rodeados de un enorme número de parientes. Con frecuencia los abuelos y otros parientes solteros viven en la misma casa, y los tíos y los primos viven cerca. Las niñeras no son tan comunes, ya que los familiares o a veces las criadas, que también suelen vivir en la casa, cuidan a los niños.

También es común ver a las familias con sus bebés en los restaurantes, los cines y en misa. Los niños, que oyen miles de veces la frase "Pórtate bien" durante su niñez, crecen con la idea de que ellos de verdad se portarán bien en tales circunstancias. Es más, los padres por lo general toleran el ruido y la desorganización ocasionados por los jóvenes.

Los niños y sus padres casi siempre se tutean. Hoy en día un padre que regaña a su hijo quizás use la forma de **usted** para dar más énfasis a sus palabras, así como un padre estadounidense usa a veces el nombre completo del niño.

Actividad. You might well see the following scenes in parts of the Spanish-speaking world. Indicate for each one whether it would be found *siempre* (S), *a veces* (V), or *nunca* (N) in the area where you live.

1. Una familia—padre, madre, abuela y tres niños—está paseándose en un parque el domingo por la tarde. Todos están vestidos elegantemente, los hombres con saco y corbata y las mujeres con vestidos bonitos.
2. En una fiesta para celebrar el santo o el cumpleaños de una niña de ocho años están presentes veinte miembros de la familia.
3. Un matrimonio está cenando en un buen restaurante con sus cuatro hijos de 7, 5, 3 y 2 años de edad.
4. Un matrimonio joven va al cine con su bebé de seis meses.

Play video

Program 8 *Juegos y diversiones* Traditional games and pastimes

A. **Un cuento divertido.** Escribe un cuento sobre algo divertido que te haya pasado. En tu cuento debes incluir

- la situación: dónde estabas, cuándo ocurrió y una descripción de las circunstancias
- los eventos: qué pasó
- por qué fue divertido el incidente. Puedes incluir diálogo, monólogo interior, comentarios directos al lector.

B. **Agente de seguros** (*insurance*). Imagínate que eres un(a) agente de seguros. Escribe una descripción del carro de un cliente después de haber chocado con un camión lleno de basura (*garbage*). Tienes que describirlo detalladamente, para que la compañía sepa cuánto deben pagar. A continuación hay un dibujo que preparaste poco después del accidente.

C. ¿Cómo se organiza una fiesta? Haz una lista de las cosas que se hacen para organizar una fiesta, usando las siguientes palabras de transición.

Modelo: Primero... *Primero se escoge la fecha.*

1. Segundo
2. Tercero
3. Cuarto
4. Quinto
5. Luego (*Then, Next*)
6. Después
7. Entonces (*Then, Next*)
8. Luego
9. Finalmente

CH. Lo cierto, lo dudoso y lo imposible. You are a news reporter for a local radio station. With your group, prepare a story about the accident shown in *Actividad B*. Include some things that you are sure about, some things that are doubtful, and some things that you believe are impossible. Select a *locutor* and "broadcast" your report to the rest of the class.

D. Mini-drama: Conflictos en el trabajo. En pequeños grupos, representen los papeles que se indican a continuación.

Estudiante A: Jefe/-a
Estudiante B: Empleado/-a
Estudiante C: Quejón/-ona (*Complainer*)

El (La) Estudiante A le da al (a la) Estudiante B por lo menos cinco instrucciones para el día de trabajo. Cada vez que el jefe le da una instrucción al empleado (a la empleada), el (la) Estudiante C, que está observando la conversación, hace un comentario que explica lo que el jefe (la jefa) acaba de decir.

Modelo: A: *Por favor, ¿me puede preparar este informe antes de las 11:00?*
B: *Sí, señor(a), sin problema.*
C: *¡Dios mío, le dice que prepare el informe en dos horas!*

E. Una visita al mecánico (a la mecánica). Role play the following situation.

> *Estudiante A: Dueño/-a del auto*
>
> You are having trouble with your car and have taken it to the garage. You take out your list and tell the mechanic
>
> - the windshield is broken
> - the windshield wipers don't work
> - there are vibrations (*vibraciones*) in the steering wheel
> - there is a strange smell in the trunk
>
> Find out whether the garage will repair your car, and how long it will take.

Estudiante B: Mecánico/-a

A customer comes in with an old car and a long list of problems.

- As you listen to what is wrong with the car, express your concern.
- Ask how the problems happened and when they started.
- You aren't sure what is wrong with the car, so you try to avoid talking about when it will be ready.

VOCABULARIO

El automóvil

aceite (m) *oil*
acelerador (m) *accelerator*
frenos (m pl) *brakes*
limpiaparabrisas (m) *windshield wiper*
llanta (f) *tire*
maletero (m) *trunk (of a car)*
motor (m) *motor, engine*
parabrisas (m) *windshield*
puerta (f) *door*
tapacubos (m) *hubcap*
ventanilla (f) *side (door) window*
volante (m) *steering wheel*

El cuerpo humano

boca (f) *mouth*
brazo (m) *arm*
cabeza (f) *head*
cadera (f) *hip*
cintura (f) *waist*
clavícula (f) *collarbone*
cuello (m) *neck*
cuerpo (m) *body*
dedos (m pl) *fingers*
espalda (f) *back*
estómago (m) *stomach*
hombro (m) *shoulder*
mano (f) *hand*
muslo (m) *thigh*
nariz (f) *nose*
ojos (m pl) *eyes*
orejas (f pl) *ears*
pecho (m) *chest*
pie (m) *foot*
rodilla (f) *knee*

Día y noche

alba (m) *dawn*
amanecer *to dawn*
atardecer *to become late afternoon*
oscuridad (f) *darkness*
soñar (ue) *to dream*
sueño (m) *dream*
tinieblas (f pl) *complete darkness*

Expresiones de emoción

Reacciones negativas
¡Qué barbaridad! *How awful!*
¡Qué desgracia! *What terrible luck!*
¡Qué horror! *How horrible!*
¡Qué lástima! *What a shame! What a pity!*
¡Qué lata! *What a pain (bother)!*
¡Qué mala suerte! *What bad luck!*
¡Qué susto! *How scary!*
¡Qué vergüenza! *How embarrassing!*

Reacciones positivas
¡Qué bello/-a! *How beautiful!*
¡Qué buena suerte! *What good luck!*

¡Qué rico/-a!   How wonderful! How delicious!
¡Qué sorpresa!   What a surprise!

La nueva tecnología

calculadora (f)   calculator
casete (m)   cassette
computadora (f)   computer
contestador (m) automático   telephone answering machine
facsímil (m)   fax machine
fotocopiadora (f)   photocopy machine
grabadora (f)   tape recorder
impresora (f)   printer
máquina (f) de escribir   typewriter
teléfono (m) celular   cellular telephone

Generalizaciones

es absurdo   it is absurd, ridiculous
es bueno/malo   it is good/bad
es (poco) común   it is (not very) common
es (im)posible   it is (im)possible
es interesante   it is interesting
es mejor   it is better
es peligroso   it is dangerous
es preciso   it is necessary
es preferible   it is preferable
es terrible   it is terrible
es urgente   it is urgent, pressing

Palabras relacionadas con los deportes

balón (m)   large ball (basketball)
bate (m)   baseball bat
canasta (f), cesto (m)   basket (for basketball)
cancha (f)   court, playing field
diversión (f)   recreation, pastime
pelota (f)   small ball (tennis ball, baseball)
raqueta (f)   racquet
red (f)   net

Palabras descriptivas

agitado/-a   agitated, disturbed
bien educado/-a   well-mannered, polite
enyesado/-a   set in a cast
grueso/-a   thick
junto/-a   together
lindo/-a   cute, pretty
orgulloso/-a   proud
travieso/-a   mischievous

Otras palabras y expresiones útiles

a menudo   often
además (de)   besides, in addition (to)
algo por el estilo   something like that
casi   almost
mientras   while, during
nada por el estilo   nothing like that
sin embargo   nevertheless

Sustantivos útiles

apagón (m)   blackout, power failure
barrio (m)   neighborhood
cambio (m)   change (one for another)
conformista (m/f)   conformist
corcho (m)   cork
cordón (m)   cord, string
gemelo/-a (m/f)   twin
orgullo (m)   pride
primera comunión (f)   first communion
rebelde (m/f)   rebel
recuerdo (m)   memory; souvenir
soga (f)   rope
susto (m)   sudden fright
tapa (f)   lid
yeso (m)   plaster (cast)

Verbos útiles

abrazar   to hug, embrace
agitar   to agitate
agregar   to add
apagar   to turn off (lights)
aprovechar   to take advantage of
asustar   to frighten
besar   to kiss
caerse   to fall down
compartir   to share
competir (i, i)   to compete
construir   to build
darse cuenta (de)   to realize
dejar   to allow; to leave (something behind)
enojarse   to get angry
hacerse daño   to get hurt, to be injured
imaginarse   to imagine
lograr   to gain; to succeed
luchar   to fight
llevarse (con)   to get along (with)
molestar   to bother
nacer   to be born
partir   to break (apart)
pegar   to hit
pelear   to fight
poner (prestar) atención   to pay attention

Vocabulario

ponerse furioso/-a *to get furious*
portarse bien/mal *to behave well/badly*
prender *to turn on (lights, electrical appliances)*
recorrer *to cover a distance*
repartir *to distribute, divide up*
tapar *to cover (up), to put the lid or cork on*
tratar *to treat (a person well, badly)*

VOCABULARIO PERSONALIZADO

¡Dios mío! ¿qué te pasa?

Capítulo 9

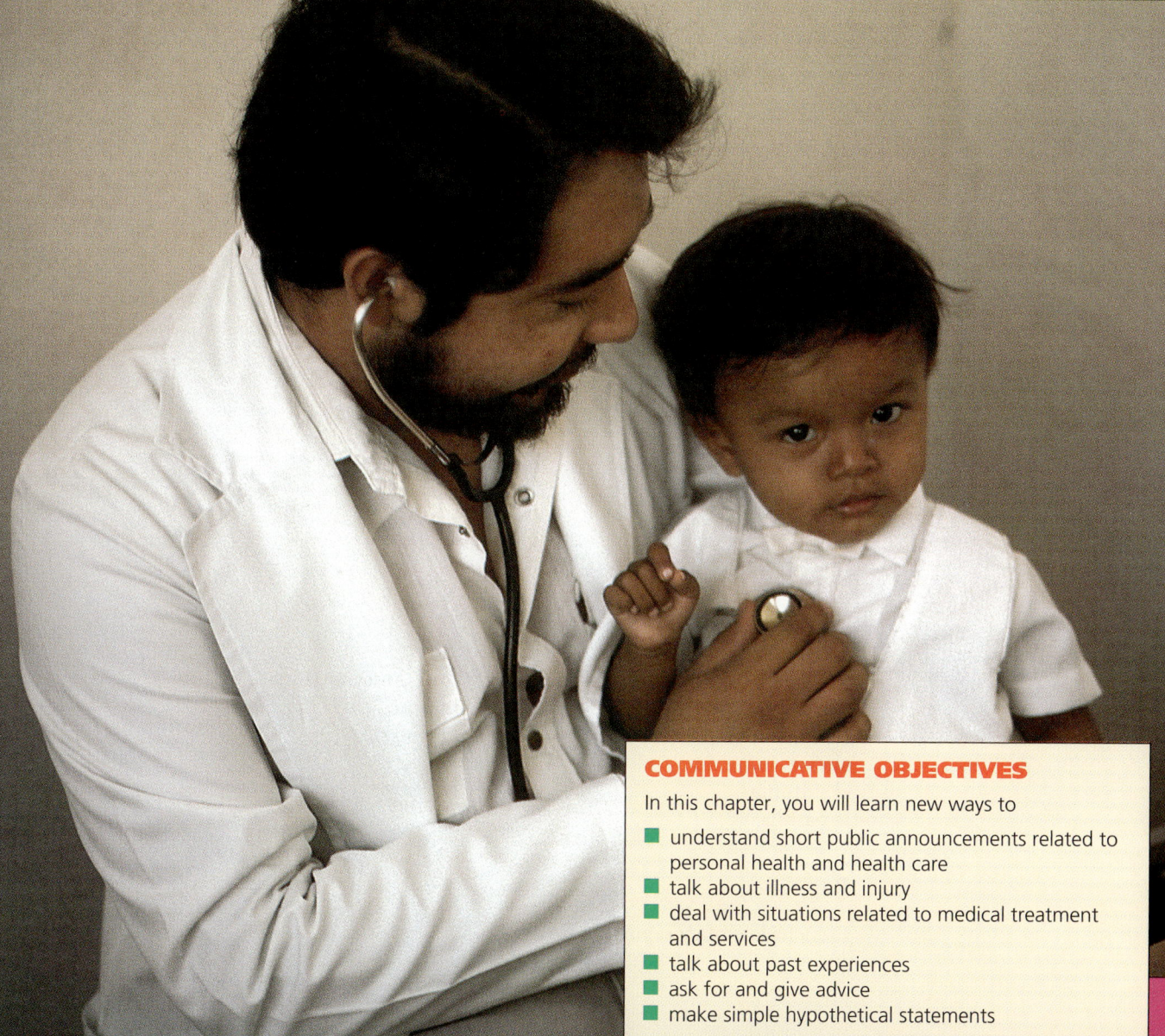

COMMUNICATIVE OBJECTIVES

In this chapter, you will learn new ways to

- understand short public announcements related to personal health and health care
- talk about illness and injury
- deal with situations related to medical treatment and services
- talk about past experiences
- ask for and give advice
- make simple hypothetical statements

PRIMERA ETAPA

"¿Te sientes mal?"

ENTRADA

Play instructor tape, 1 min.

Se abre la Clínica Buena Vista

Listen to the following announcement about the opening of a new medical clinic, and see if you can determine

- the hours the clinic will be open
- two of the services and facilities available
- the telephone number

Clínica Buena Vista

Horas:

Servicios: 1.
            2.

Teléfono:

EMPEZAR A ESCUCHAR

Play student tape, 2 min.

Leer

la fiebre	fever
¡Esto es el colmo!	This is the last straw!
tomar(le) el pelo (a uno)	to tease, "pull (someone's) leg"
recetar	to prescribe
aliviar	to relieve
el síntoma	symptom
la pastilla	pill

Repetir

Escucha la cinta y repite lo que oyes.

Identificar

En una hoja aparte, escribe en una columna las palabras y frases anteriores. Vas a oír algunas oraciones. Cada vez que oigas una de estas palabras o frases, apunta el número de la oración al lado de la palabra. Cada oración se leerá dos veces.

Escribir

Vas a oír algunas oraciones, cada una leída dos veces. Escríbelas al escucharlas.

Reconocer

Ahora lee otra vez las oraciones que acabas de escribir. Cada una contiene una o más de las palabras y frases anteriores. Al releerlas, subraya todas las palabras y frases que vienen de la lista. Mientras lees, haz todas las correcciones necesarias.

ESCUCHAR

Play student tape, 1 min.

Episodio 1: "¿Qué te pasa, Susana?"

Enfoque comunicativo

Susana, la hermana menor de Elena, ha ido a visitarla a la universidad. Susana no se siente bien. Al escuchar la conversación entre las dos hermanas, trata de averiguar

- cuándo tiene lugar la conversación
- qué le pasa a Susana
- por qué, según Susana, se siente mal

El problema de Susana

1. Esta conversación tiene lugar
   a. por la mañana   b. por la tarde   c. por la noche
2. ¿Cuál es el problema de Susana? (Hay más de una respuesta posible.)
   ____ Le duele el estómago.
   ____ Le duele la cabeza.
   ____ Tiene una fiebre muy alta.
   ____ Tiene mucho sueño.
3. Según Susana, ¿cuál es la causa del problema?
   a. algo que comió   b. el agua   c. un virus

Enfoque lingüístico

Escucha otra vez el Episodio 1 y escribe

- una frase que Susana usa para decir que se siente mal
- la expresión que usa Elena para indicar que no está de acuerdo con el autodiagnóstico de Susana

Students should be able to figure out the meaning of *autodiagnóstico.*

ESCUCHAR

Play student tape, 1 min.

Episodio 2: "¿Y si me muero antes de las 9:00?"

Enfoque comunicativo

Elena y Susana siguen hablando. Al escucharlas, intenta averiguar

- lo que Elena le recomienda a Susana como alivio inmediato
- lo que Elena promete hacer más tarde, después de las 9:00

> *Las sugerencias de Elena*
>
> 1. Como alivio inmediato, Susana debe...
>   a. llamar al médico
>   b. comer algo
> 2. Más tarde, Elena promete...
>   a. tomar aspirina
>   b. tratar de dormir

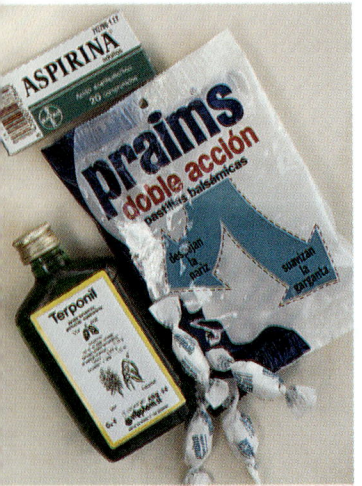

Hay muchas marcas de medicina que se puede comprar en una farmacia.

Enfoque lingüístico

Escucha otra vez el Episodio 2 y escribe

- las palabras que Elena usa para decirle a Susana que tome aspirina
- la recomendación que Elena le hace a Susana sobre el comer y el beber

VERIFICAR

Completa las oraciones.

1. A Susana le duele...
2. Según los amigos de Susana, ella no debía...
3. Elena cree que la enfermedad de Susana fue causada por...
4. La noche anterior Susana bebió...
5. Después de las nueve, Elena va a...
6. Elena le recomienda a Susana que...

Ventanilla al mundo hispánico   ¡No tomes el agua!

A los turistas de los Estados Unidos que visitan otros países, con frecuencia se les aconseja que no tomen el agua. Este es un buen consejo para cualquier persona que viaje de un país a otro, como lo demuestra la experiencia que tuvo Susana cuando se enfermó mientras visitaba a su hermana Elena en los Estados Unidos.

Hay varios factores que pueden causar el malestar estomacal, incluyendo los cambios de clima, de altitud, el cambio del horario rutinario y el nivel de estrés, o sea, de tensión nerviosa. Sin embargo, algunas veces la causa directa del malestar estomacal es el agua o la comida. Esto se debe a que los intestinos de cada persona están acostumbrados a ciertas bacterias en el agua de su propio país o región, y cuando se viaja a otro país o región, las bacterias de esa área, que son inofensivas para los habitantes de la región, pueden causar problemas serios a los visitantes. Este malestar temporal se conoce con el nombre de "mal de turista", o sencillamente "turista".

AUMENTAR EL VOCABULARIO

OJO: In some countries, carbonated drinks, including sparking water, may be referred to as *una gaseosa*.

el agua mineral — *mineral (bottled) water*
　el agua destilada — *distilled water*
　el agua corriente — *running water*
aliviar — *to relieve*
　el alivio — *relief*
　la aspirina — *aspirin*
　el calmante — *tranquilizer, painkiller*
　calmar — *to calm*
　mejorarse — *to get better (health)*

OJO: *El colmo* is related to the English word "culmination." You already learned the literal meaning in Chapter 7.

el colmo — *height (as in finishing touch, last straw)*
　el colmo de lo ridículo — *the height of the ridiculous*
　¡Esto es el colmo! — *This is the last straw!*
　¡No puedo más! — *I can't stand any more!*
chocar (con) — *to crash, bump (into)*
recetar — *to prescribe*
　la inyección — *injection*
　la medicina — *medicine*
　la pastilla — *pill*
　la receta — *prescription*
　el remedio — *medicine; remedy*

OJO: You have already learned that *la receta* means "recipe." In a medical context, you might think of a "recipe" for medicine as a prescription.

el síntoma — *symptom*
　el dolor — *pain*
　los escalofríos — *chills*

la fiebre	*fever*
hinchado/-a	*swollen*
la piel	*skin*
la presión sanguínea	*blood pressure*
el resfriado	*cold*
la tos	***cough***
toser	*to cough*
vomitar	*to vomit*
tomar(le) el pelo (a uno)	***to tease, "pull someone's leg"***
malcriado/-a	***spoiled; impolite***

LOS ÓRGANOS DEL CUERPO HUMANO

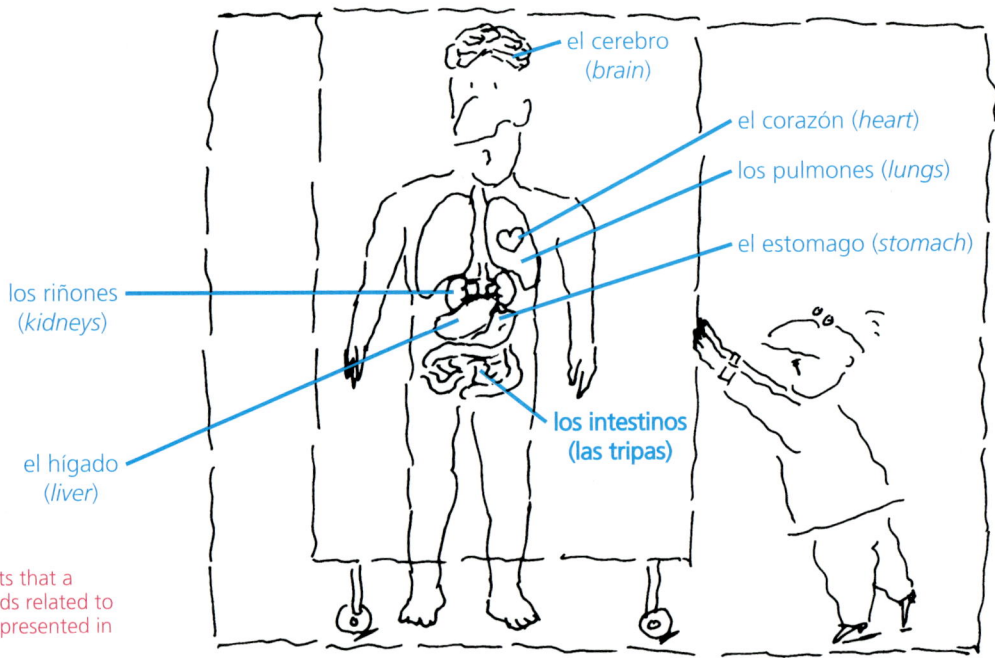

Remind students that a number of words related to the body were presented in Chapter 8.

1. el hígado 2. el cerebro 3. los pulmones 4. el estómago 5. la piel

¿Qué le pasa? Eres médico/-a. Los síntomas de las personas siguientes indican varios problemas. En cada caso, indica qué parte del cuerpo está afectada y di lo que debe hacer el (la) paciente.

1. Jorge no se siente bien, y tiene la piel y los ojos amarillos.
2. A Silvia le duele constantemente la cabeza y está mareada.
3. Octavio fuma y tose mucho por la mañana.
4. Cristina siente dolores inmediatamente después de comer.
5. Tres niños pasaron todo el día en la playa sin ponerse la camisa.

USO PRÁCTICO DEL ESPAÑOL Emphasizing Ownership or Possession

In the second *etapa* of Chapter 1, you learned to use the adjectives *mi, tu, su, nuestro/-a,* and *vuestro/-a* to express possession. Another set of possessive adjectives in Spanish is similar to the possessives **mine, yours, his, hers, ours,** and **theirs** in English.

mío/-a	*mine*	nuestro/-a	*ours*
tuyo/-a	*yours (fam.)*	vuestro/-a	*yours (pl fam.)*
suyo/-a	*yours (form.), his, hers*	suyo/-a	*yours (pl form.), theirs*

This second group of possessive adjectives is used to emphasize ownership. If you wished to take the statement *Mi coche es blanco* and change it to emphasize the fact that it is **yours**, rather than that it is **white**, you would say *El coche blanco es mío.* Remember that possessives, like all adjectives in Spanish, agree in both gender and number with the item possessed.

Emphasis on description
Nuestra clínica es **grande**.
Tu medicina es **costosa**.

Emphasis on possession
La clínica grande es **nuestra**.
La medicina costosa es **tuya**.
Estas pastillas no son **mías**; ¿son **tuyas**?
Octavio es el único que fuma aquí; estos cigarrillos serán (*must be*) **suyos**.

Ponerlo a prueba

A. ¿De quién es? Indica a quién pertenece (*belongs*) cada cosa mencionada, poniendo énfasis en la persona a quien le pertenece la cosa más que en la cosa.

Modelo: (yo) la receta   *La receta es mía.*

1. (nosotros) el agua mineral
2. (Susana) las pastillas
3. (las hermanas) la suerte
4. (los médicos) la culpa (*fault, blame*)
5. (tú) el síntoma
6. (ellos) los instrumentos
7. (Carlos y yo) la responsabilidad
8. (ustedes) la oportunidad
9. (Jorge) las aspirinas
10. (él) el calmante

B. Clasificaciones. Pon las palabras siguientes en la categoría apropiada: síntomas (S) o remedios (R).

____ vomitar   ____ la inyección   ____ la pastilla
____ el dolor   ____ la aspirina   ____ el calmante
____ los escalofríos ____ la fiebre   ____ la tos

OJO: Useful vocabulary: *estornudar,* to sneeze; *estar constipado/-a,* to have a head cold; *sonar (ue) las narices,* to blow one's nose.

C. Preguntas personales

1. ¿Te gusta tomar aspirina u otro remedio para aliviarte el dolor de cabeza? ¿Por qué sí o por qué no?
2. ¿Hay algunas comidas que te dan dolor de estómago? ¿Cuáles son?
3. ¿Estuviste alguna vez en el hospital? ¿Qué tenías?
4. Cuando eras niño/-a, ¿qué hacías cuando estabas enfermo/-a?
5. ¿Quién te cuidaba? ¿Qué hacía esa persona?
6. ¿Sufres de los resfriados a menudo? ¿Cuáles son tus síntomas?
7. Cuando sientes mucha tensión en tu vida, ¿qué síntomas tienes generalmente?
8. Algunas personas dicen que es mejor comer ligeramente (*lightly*) seis veces al día, en vez de las tres comidas diarias. ¿Cuál es tu opinión?
9. ¿Sueles desayunar? ¿Por qué es bueno para la salud comer por la mañana?

CH. ¡Te toca a ti! Busca en el diccionario las palabras que necesites para hablar de una enfermedad que tuviste cuando eras más joven. En grupos de dos, averigua la información siguiente acerca de tu compañero/-a y da un pequeño informe a la clase.

The report can be oral and/or written.

- **qué** enfermedad era
- **cuántos** años tenías
- **cuáles** eran tus síntomas
- **qué** tuviste que hacer para curarte

INVESTIGAR LA GRAMÁTICA   More on Stem-Changing Verbs

OJO: Study tip: Write out the conjugations of the verbs in this *Investigar la gramática* section for the present indicative, present subjunctive, and preterite. Use different-colored pens to mark the first and second stem changes and spelling changes. Add verbs to the list as you come across them.

As you have already seen, verbs like *contar* (ue) and *entender* (ie) and other *-ar* and *-er* stem-changing verbs change o → ue and e → ie only in the present indicative and the present subjunctive, whenever the stem vowel is stressed.

Present indicative		*Present subjunctive*	
cuento	contamos	cuente	contemos
cuentas	contáis	cuentes	contéis
cuenta	cuentan	cuente	cuenten
entiendo	entendemos	entienda	entendamos
entiendes	entendéis	entiendas	entendáis
entiende	entienden	entienda	entiendan

— Elena me dice que Susana todavía está mal. Es posible que le **duela** el estómago porque comió demasiado anoche.

— Puede ser. Pero espero que no nos **cuente** todos los detalles de su problema.

— Es posible que ella no **entienda** lo desagradable que es.

— Pues, a mi parecer, sí lo sabe, pero le encanta discutirlo.

Verbs like *apagar* and *agregar*, which you learned in Chapter 8, have a spelling change in the present subjunctive to retain the hard *g* sound: *apague, apagues, apague, apaguemos, apaguéis, apaguen*. *Jugar* (*ue*) has both a stem change and a spelling change in the present subjunctive: *juegue, juegues, juegue, juguemos, juguéis, jueguen*. Notice that the spelling change is needed in all forms to keep the hard *g* sound and that the stem change (in boldface type) follows the same pattern as for the verbs *contar* and *entender* just presented.

Stem-changing verbs that end in -*ir*, such as *dormir* (*ue, u*) and *mentir* (*ie, i*), have the same changes as the -*ar* and -*er* verbs in the present indicative and present subjunctive, and they also have a second change. These verbs change *o* → *u* and *e* → *i* in the *él/ella/usted* and the *ellos/ellas/ustedes* forms of the preterite, in the *nosotros/-as* and *vosotros/-as* forms of the present subjunctive, and in the -*ndo* form (*el gerundio*).

> Point out that while the *o* → *ue* and *e* → *ie* change depends on the stem vowel being stressed, the *o* → *u* and *e* → *i* change depends on there being no /-i-/ in the following syllable.

> **OJO:** *Durmamos, durmáis* in the present subjuncctive, *durmió, durmieron* in the preterite, and *durmiendo* in the gerund represent the second stem change.

Present indicative		Present subjunctive		Preterite		Gerund
duermo	dormimos	duerma	durmamos	dormí	dormimos	durmiendo
duermes	dormís	duermas	durmáis	dormiste	dormisteis	
duerme	duermen	duerma	duerman	durmió	durmieron	
miento	mentimos	mienta	mintamos	mentí	mentimos	mintiendo
mientes	mentís	mientas	mintáis	mentiste	mentisteis	
miente	mienten	mienta	mientan	mintió	mintieron	

— Jorge, el doctor recomienda que **duermas** más—siete u ocho horas.

— Es imposible que nosotros **durmamos** tanto, Luisa. Tenemos que trabajar, estudiar y cuidar la casa.

> **OJO:** Note the use of the subjunctive with *Es imposible*. See Chapter 8, third *etapa*.

Finally, -*ir* stem-changing verbs like *pedir* (*i, i*) and *seguir* (*i, i*) have the stem change *e* → *i* as both the first and second change.

Present indicative		Present subjunctive		Preterite		Gerund
pido	pedimos	pida	pidamos	pedí	pedimos	pidiendo
pides	pedís	pidas	pidáis	pediste	pedisteis	
pide	piden	pida	pidan	pidió	pidieron	

> **OJO:** Like *jugar*, verbs such as *seguir* have spelling changes in addition to the stem changes. Since the combination *gi* is a soft *g* sound, a *u* is added to preserve the hard *g* sound. Note that *u* is added to all forms of *seguir* in the preterite: *seguí, seguiste, siguió, seguimos, seguisteis, siguieron*.

Ponerlo a prueba

A. En la Clínica Buena Vista. Imagínate que eres médico/-a en la Clínica Buena Vista. Tienes estas recomendaciones para los pacientes que te visitan.

1. (para la señora Tenorio) —Señora, le recomiendo que usted _____ (**dormir**) más. Y es importante que usted le _____ (**pedir**) más ayuda a la familia. Está completamente exhausta y debe descansar.

2. (para el señor Ayala) —Señor, le recomiendo que _____ (**divertirse**) más. Creo que usted sufre de estrés. Específicamente, es necesario que usted _____ (**comenzar**) a disfrutar (*enjoy*) de la vida, no sólo trabajar. Le recomiendo que _____ (**practicar**) un deporte, que _____ (**jugar**) con sus niños y que _____ (**reírse**) más. Ésta es mi receta.

3. (para Carlitos, un niño de 10 años) —Bueno, Carlitos, vamos a ver si podemos cambiar un poco tu dieta. Es necesario que _____ (**desayunar**) y _____ (**almorzar**) bien, porque son las comidas más importantes del día. Y no quiero que les _____ (**pedir**) dulces a tus amigos en la escuela; prefiero que _____ (**comer**) frutas si tienes hambre durante el día. Es importante que _____ (**cambiar**) tus costumbres ahora, porque si no, vas a tener mayores problemas en el futuro.

B. Deseos para el futuro. Trinidad está pensando en su clase de biología. Es difícil, y el profesor es un poco problemático. Trinidad espera que los problemas se alivien. Completa sus pensamientos, siguiendo el modelo.

Modelo: La tarea es imposible.   Ojalá que *sea* más fácil esta noche.

1. El profesor casi nunca repite los puntos importantes. Ojalá que los _____ (**repetir**) hoy.

2. Nunca me siento bien en esta clase, de tanto concentrarme. Quizás yo _____ (**sentirse**) mejor esta semana.

3. El profesor casi siempre nos pide la tarea. Ojalá que no nos la _____ (**pedir**) hoy, porque yo no pude hacerla anoche.

4. Si nos pide la tarea, quizás no la _____ (**corregir**) pronto, para darme tiempo de hacerla.

5. El profesor casi nunca se ríe en la clase, es muy serio. Ojalá que _____ (**reírse**) o que por lo menos _____ (**sonreírse**) hoy, porque si no, la clase es muy aburrida.

6. A veces mi amigo Horacio se duerme cuando habla el profesor. Ojalá que ni Horacio ni yo _____ (**dormirse**) durante la clase. ¡Qué vergüenza si el profesor se da cuenta!

7. Horacio siempre me pide comida, porque no almuerza sino hasta después de la clase. Ojalá que hoy _____ (**almorzar**) antes de llegar a clase.

8. En fin, la clase no es muy divertida. Ojalá que (nosotros) _____ (**divertirse**) un poco hoy.

C. Una noche extraña. Raúl tuvo una noche diferente de lo normal. Completa las oraciones siguientes para descubrir lo que pasó.

1. Raúl no suele asistir a las fiestas grandes porque no le gusta el ruido, pero anoche...
2. Los amigos de Raúl generalmente no sirven mucha comida en sus fiestas, pero anoche...
3. Raúl generalmente se aburre en las fiestas porque no le gusta bailar, pero anoche...
4. Además (*In addition*), a Raúl no le gusta que sus amigos le cuenten chismes (*gossip*), pero anoche...
5. Generalmente Raúl no se divierte en las fiestas, pero anoche...
6. Cuando la gente le pregunta si está divirtiéndose, suele mentir y decir que sí, pero anoche...
7. Muchas veces se sienta en una silla y no habla con nadie, pero anoche...
8. Suele despedirse del anfitrión de la fiesta e irse muy temprano, pero anoche...

CH. Una aventura en la vida de Héctor Vásquez. Usando los verbos que aparecen a continuación, completa la historia de Héctor sobre su aventura.

OJO: You can use the verbs more than once.

bañarse	dormirse	seguir
comenzar	llegar	tomar
contar	mentir	vestirse
despedirse	reírse	volver
despertarse	salir	

Esta mañana yo _____ a las siete, como siempre. _____ y _____. Después de desayunar, _____ de mi mamá y _____ para el trabajo. Como me había acostado (*I had gone to bed*) muy tarde, _____ en el autobús y pasé mi parada (*stop*). ¡Qué vergüenza! Cuando _____, el autobús ya estaba a dos millas de mi parada. Cuando yo le _____ mi problema al conductor, éste _____ y _____ a conducir. Por fin pude bajar y _____ otro autobús para volver al centro. Cuando _____ a mi trabajo, les _____ mi aventura a mis colegas. —No te creemos, estás _____, —me dijeron. Como (yo) no pude convencerlos, _____ de ellos, fui a mi escritorio y _____ a trabajar.

OJO: As you complete *Actividad D,* pay particular attention to which verbs have a stem change (*cambio de raíz*) and why. Refer back to the explanation in the *Investigar la gramática* section as necessary.

D. A ti te toca. Ahora tú vas a contar la aventura de Héctor, empezando así: Esta mañana Héctor **se despertó** a las siete...

¡TIENES LA PALABRA!

The role plays in *¡Tienes la palabra!* are becoming more difficult. Encourage students to rely on what they know and to recast the language of the instructions into familiar expressions and structures: *Un conductor venía por la derecha, el otro venía por la izquierda. El primero no prestaba atención y chocó con el segundo.*

Students may need to know *frenar* (to brake). Point out the relationship to *los frenos,* which they learned in Chapter 8, third *etapa*.

Haz las siguientes actividades con un compañero (una compañera).

A. **Un accidente de coche.** Entrevista a un compañero (una compañera) de la clase sobre un accidente de automóvil que haya visto o que haya tenido. Debes preguntarle

- dónde ocurrió
- cuándo ocurrió y a qué hora
- quiénes eran los conductores
- qué hicieron los conductores para causar el accidente
- si había heridos

El compañero (La compañera) contesta las preguntas y después ustedes dos informan a la clase.

B. **Mal de turista.** You are a tourist in South America and get sick one night. You call the front desk of the hotel and ask for help.

- Identify yourself and explain your problem.
- Say how you think you got sick.
- Ask for the name of a doctor whom you can call at night.
- Ask the clerk for a temporary remedy.

Your partner, who plays the role of the desk clerk, will express sympathy, answer your questions, and offer some advice.

OTRA VUELTA

Play instructor tape, 1 min.

Escucha otra vez la Entrada al principio de esta etapa y contesta las preguntas siguientes acerca de la Clínica Buena Vista.

1. ¿Cuál es la dirección de la clínica?
2. ¿Qué otros servicios se mencionan?
   a. _____ b. _____ c. _____

COMENTARIO CULTURAL

Los curanderos (*healers*)

Cuando los españoles llegaron al Nuevo Mundo, varias civilizaciones de las Américas tenían tratamientos médicos bien desarrollados que incluían la cirugía y el uso de plantas medicinales para curar enfermedades. Los curanderos de estas civilizaciones usaban sus conocimientos acerca del valor medicinal de algunas plantas para curar a los enfermos y pasaban este conocimiento de generación a generación. Esto se hacía normalmente por medio de un proceso de enseñanza en el cual el curandero o curandera escogía y educaba a su sucesor(a). Dada la importancia del poder curativo de las plantas medicinales para el bienestar de la sociedad y el gran conocimiento que estos curanderos tenían, ellos eran y siguen siendo figuras muy respetadas en su cultura.

La confianza en los curanderos no se limita a las culturas indígenas o a las personas incultas, ni tampoco a los tiempos del pasado remoto. De la misma manera en que alguien en los Estados Unidos podría recetarte un consomé de pollo para curarte de un resfriado, una persona en Colombia tal vez te recete un té de manzanilla (*chamomile*) para combatir el malestar estomacal, o toronjil (*lemon balm* [*an herb*]) para calmarte los nervios.

La ciencia moderna ha comprobado el valor de muchos tratamientos a base de plantas, tales como el uso de la quinina para combatir diversos tipos de fiebres tropicales, o el uso de la sávila (*aloe*) para el tratamiento de problemas de la piel. Las compañías farmacéuticas continúan experimentando con remedios naturales en un esfuerzo por identificar los ingredientes activos que tienen valor curativo.

En toda América Latina, y también en aquellas partes de los Estados Unidos donde hay una población hispánica considerable, uno puede encontrar a un curandero (una curandera), y también una botánica—un lugar donde se venden remedios naturales. A causa del efecto positivo de muchos tratamientos naturales, la confianza en las plantas medicinales es bastante generalizada en el mundo hispánico. A pesar de sus limitaciones, las plantas medicinales constituyen una defensa importante en contra de muchas enfermedades, especialmente cuando no hay otras posibilidades de obtener tratamiento médico.

Actividad 1. Completa las siguientes oraciones de acuerdo con este Comentario cultural.

1. Si una persona desea ser curandero o curandera, aprende ese arte...
2. Los curanderos de las civilizaciones indígenas gozaban de (*enjoyed*) una fama...
3. Dos hierbas que se mencionan aquí son..., que sirve para..., y..., que sirve para...
4. Hoy en día... también tiene(n) interés en los remedios naturales.
5. Una botánica, que se puede encontrar en..., es...

Actividad 2. Contesta las preguntas que aparecen a continuación.

1. En tu familia, ¿se usan remedios que no sean los "oficiales" de la profesión médica? ¿Cuáles son?
2. ¿Conoces un remedio "folklórico" para los síntomas siguientes?
   a. el dolor de cabeza
   b. el hipo (*hiccups*)
   c. el resfriado

SEGUNDA ETAPA

"¡Me duele todo el cuerpo!"

ENTRADA

Play instructor tape, 2 min.

Tres nuevos médicos en la Clínica Buena Vista

Listen to the radio spot announcing the addition of three new doctors to the staff of the Clínica Buena Vista. As you listen to the announcement, see if you can understand

- the full name of each doctor
- their office hours

Tres médicos nuevos en la Clínica Buena Vista

Doctor(a)	Horas de consulta
1. Dr.	
2. Dra.	
3. Dra.	

ANTES DE LEER

READING STRATEGY 9

Note the key point in each paragraph

When the text you are reading has several paragraphs, it is very helpful to take notes (either on paper or in your mind) as you read. This strategy will help you organize the information as you obtain it, so that you will have a better understanding of the entire passage. In addition, if you have written your notes, you have an excellent basis for review. It is not necessary, nor sometimes even a good idea, to take extensive notes. A better strategy in many cases is to write down the one or two key points in each paragraph.

Segunda etapa

Preparación

Have you ever considered the long-term benefits of sports, rather than simply recognizing their entertainment value? List one health advantage for each of the following sports.

Deporte	Ventaja
el tenis	
el golf	
el béisbol	
el ciclismo	
la natación	

Play student tape, 1 min.

OJO: You have already seen the word *la piscina* for "swimming pool." In Mexico, *la alberca* is more common.

Estudiar y practicar

la alberca	*swimming pool*
apenas	*scarcely*
el clavado	*dive*
deslizarse	*to slip, slide*
empaparse	*to get soaked*
nocivo/-a	*noxious, poisonous*
nutrir	*to nourish*

LEER

If you had to argue (*en español, ¡claro!*) in support of swimming as a sport that promotes health, what three points would you make?

1. 2. 3.

Now, for each reason that you have given, provide an example or illustration (*también en español*) to support what you have said.

a. b. c.

As you read "Nadar: algo más que un buen deporte" (page 390), make notes on the arguments the writer uses to support his opinion regarding the benefits that one derives from swimming.

DESPUÉS DE LEER

Ventajas que se derivan de la natación

Para la salud	Para la belleza
1.	1.
2.	2.
3.	3.

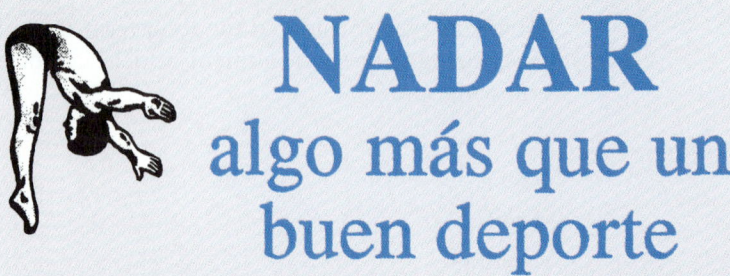

NADAR
algo más que un buen deporte

Por Gertrudis Majcen

Contéstate con sinceridad: ¿no te gustaría, en este preciso instante, echarte de cabeza al agua y nadar tranquilamente unos 10 o 15 minutos? No importa que no nades bien, o que tus vacaciones todavía estén distantes, o que tener una alberca disponible, en casa o en algún club, sea algo difícil. Pero confiesa que te gustaría deslizarte sobre el agua, braceando acompasadamente, dejándote empapar con la suave caricia líquida.

Nadar, aunque no lo hagas como una campeona olímpica, es, en efecto, una de las actividades físicas más completas y tonificantes, y su práctica exige un aprendizaje sencillo y un equipo que, según se van reduciendo las medidas de los trajes de baño, cada vez es más pequeño. En cambio, sus ventajas son muchas: en primer lugar, cual quier estilo de natación proporciona mayor agilidad y fortaleza muscular, a la vez que mejora la coordinación motora y favorece la fundación respiratoria (aún para las muchas mujeres que todavía no consiguen dejar de fumar).

En segundo lugar, nadar —de preferencia en agua no muy fría— mejora la circulación sanguínea y estimula el funcionamiento del corazón y los grandes vasos arteriales, aumenta la oxigenación de la sangre y por lo tanto ayuda a nutrir los tejidos.

El agua, por su parte, tiene un efecto benéfico sobre la piel, que se hidrata y desintoxica, liberándose de las nocivas toxinas que la afean y desmejoran. Y si eres de las apenadísimas víctimas del acné, alégrate porque según recientes estudios, la práctica regular de la natación parece contribuir a mejorar la apariencia de estas molestas lesiones de la piel.

En cuanto al mejoramiento de la sulueta, hay que advertir que la natación, como ningún otro deporte, tiene efectos mágicos: la práctica regular ayuda a delinear la figura y a reducir los excedentes grasos. Eso sí, este resultado debe acompañarse de una dieta balanceada y un estilo de vida más higiénico, porque de lo contrario la mejoría será fugaz y apenas perceptible.

Y si estas ventajas para la salud y la belleza no son suficientes para convencerte, piensa en la delicia de jugar libremente en el agua, de echarte un precioso clavado y de sentirte segura y sin temores aunque bajo tus pies haya 20 metros de agua. Porque debes confesarlo. si no sabes nadar es un poco triste estarse sentada al borde de la alberca o remojarse apenas en la parte menos profunda, con miedo de caminar un poco más allá, donde ya no haces pie.

Actividad. Now, read the selection once more and identify the main idea in each paragraph. **Do not copy the entire sentence.** Just make a note of the key words, so that you can express the ideas in your own way later.

OJO: In the phrase *ideas clave*, note that it is *ideas* that reflects number, not the word *clave*.

Párrafo	Ideas clave
1	
2	
3	
4	
5	
6	

Ventanilla al mundo hispánico   La farmacia

In some countries the *farmacia* is called a *botica*.

En España y también en muchos países latinoamericanos cuando es necesario comprar medicinas se va a una farmacia. Por lo general, la farmacia no es una sección de un supermercado. Es una tienda especializada, en el sentido de que solamente venden medicinas y otros productos relacionados con la salud y a veces con la belleza, como cosméticos, pasta dentífrica y vitaminas. Las tiendas que venden tanto medicinas como otros productos que no tienen nada que ver con la salud no son comunes en la mayoría de los países de habla española.

Actividad. Indica cuáles de los productos se puede comprar en una farmacia.

1. alcohol medicinal
2. aspirina
3. calmante
4. cerveza
5. leche
6. polvos (*face powder*)
7. pastillas
8. medicina recetada por un médico
9. ropa
10. helado

AUMENTAR EL VOCABULARIO

la alberca	*swimming pool*
el clavado	*a dive*
empaparse	*to get soaked*
el antiséptico	*antiseptic*
el antibiótico	*antibiotic*
la penicilina	*penicillin*
apenas	*scarcely*
la herida	*wound, injury*
herir (ie, i)	*to wound, to injure*
lastimarse	*to injure oneself*
nocivo/-a	*noxious, poisonous*
nutrir	*to nourish*
los primeros auxilios	*first aid*
torcer (ue)	*to twist*
cojear	*to limp*
tratarse de	*to have to do with*
estar relacionado/-a con	*to be related to*
tener que ver con	*to have to do with*
la venda	*bandage*
la curita	*small bandage (Band-Aid)*

OJO: Related term: *la nutrición*.

LOS ESTADOS FÍSICOS

deslizarse (*to slip*)

estar hecho/-a pedazos
(*to be falling apart*)

el equilibrio

Point out to students the relationship between *mar*, *marinero/-a*, *marisco*, and *mareado/-a*.

jadear (*to pant, gasp for breath*)

mareado/-a

perder el conocimiento

volver en sí

pisar

tropezar

USO PRÁCTICO DEL ESPAÑOL Keeping Track of Previous Information

As you know, in Spanish, subjects are routinely omitted in sentences where the context makes it clear what the subject of a verb is.

Paco no va a la fiesta porque tiene otro compromiso.

The same thing also happens to a noun whose meaning is clear from the context. Whenever a noun is implied by the context, it is omitted, leaving everything else the way it would be if the noun were still there. For example, Patricia asks Elena

—¿Qué vestido me pongo, **el rojo** o **el azul**? — What dress should I wear, the red one or the blue one?

The word *vestido* is omitted because it is understood from the context. This also happens when you use possessive pronouns in place of a noun that has already been mentioned.

¿Qué vestido prefieres, **el mío** o **el suyo**? — Which dress do you prefer, mine or hers?
¿En qué casa tendremos la fiesta, en **la tuya** o **la nuestra**? — In which house will we have the party, yours or ours?

Sometimes a noun can be modified by a group of words (a clause) rather than just one adjective.

¿Qué vestido me pongo, **el que** compré ayer o **el que** siempre me pongo para ir a fiestas? — Which dress should I wear, the one that I bought yesterday or the one that I always wear when I go to a party?

Whenever you see *el que...*, *la que...*, *los que...* or *las que...*, you should be able to discover from the context what the missing noun is.

The case of *lo que...* is a little different. Its equivalent in English is "what" or "that which." Rather than replace a single noun, *lo que* replaces an entire thought or event.

No me gustó **lo que** hiciste. — I didn't like what you did.
Lo que no entiendo es cómo pudiste llegar tan temprano. — What I don't understand is how you were able to arrive so early.

Ponerlo a prueba

A. Opiniones sobre la vida universitaria. Con un compañero (una compañera) de la clase, prepara una serie de preguntas y respuestas según el modelo.

Modelo: los coches grandes versus los coches pequeños

A: ¿Prefieres los coches grandes o los pequeños?

B: Prefiero los pequeños porque son más económicos.

1. las universidades grandes versus las universidades pequeñas
2. la vida que llevas aquí versus la vida que llevabas en la casa de tus padres

3. los deportes de equipo versus los deportes individuales
4. la comida picante versus la comida no picante
5. las fiestas organizadas versus las fiestas improvisadas

B. ¿De qué hablas? Alicia y Patricia están hablando después de la fiesta. Completa el diálogo, indicando lo que podría decir Alicia para aclarar (*to clarify*) los comentarios de Patricia. Usa **el que, la que, lo que**.

Modelo: Patricia: ¿Viste al muchacho con quien bailé toda la noche?
Alicia: ¿*El que no bebía nada? Sí, me fijé en él.*

Patricia: Creo que es amigo de Roberto, ¡y tan guapo!
Alicia: Es guapo, sí, pero no tan guapo como _____ llegó después.
Patricia: ¿Oíste lo que me dijo sobre una de las invitadas?
Alicia: No, pero no debes creer todo _____ oyes en estas fiestas.
Patricia: Sí, lo sé, pero me habló de la colombiana pelirroja.
Alicia: ¿_____ llevaba el vestido de seda (*silk*) y bailó toda la noche?
Patricia: La misma. Me dijo que es una estrella de cine en su país.
Alicia: Pues, es posible. De todas las invitadas, era _____ más y mejor bailaba.

C. Sinónimos y definiciones. Indica la palabra de Aumentar el vocabulario que quiere decir lo mismo que cada una de las palabras o frases siguientes.

1. perder el equilibrio
2. una venda pequeña
3. no caminar bien a causa de una pierna o un tobillo lastimado
4. recuperarse de un estado de inconsciencia
5. respirar rápidamente y con dificultad
6. las técnicas que se usan en casa para ayudar a una persona enferma o herida
7. un líquido o crema que se le pone a una herida para limpiarla
8. dar de comer

CH. ¿Qué necesitas? Indica cuál es más útil en cada situación y cómo se usa.

un antibiótico   una venda
un antiséptico   un yeso
una curita   un experto en primeros auxilios

1. Te cortaste el dedo con un cuchillo en la cocina. No es nada serio, pero estás sangrando.
2. Estabas esquiando, te caíste y parece que se te partió la pierna. No puedes moverla.

3. Te caíste en la calle y tienes graves heridas en las dos rodillas.
4. Tienes que limpiar una herida antes de cubrirla con una venda.
5. Estás enfermo/-a, con fiebre y dolores de espalda. El médico te dice que tienes una infección de los riñones.

D. **Preguntas personales**

1. ¿Qué haces cuando te duele la cabeza?
2. Cuando tienes un resfriado, ¿es mejor comer mucho o poco? ¿Por qué?
3. ¿Crees que hay algunos tipos de comida que pueden curar un resfriado, tales como la sopa de pollo o el jugo de naranja?
4. ¿Cuál es el peor accidente que sufriste cuando eras niño/-a?
5. ¿Qué sabes acerca de los primeros auxilios? ¿A quién has ayudado?
6. ¿Has perdido el conocimiento alguna vez, o has estado con alguien a quien esto le haya pasado? ¿Qué hiciste?
7. ¿Crees que las vitaminas son importantes para mantener la salud? ¿Por qué?
8. ¿Usas tu cinturón de seguridad cuando manejas? ¿Siempre? ¿Estás a favor o en contra del uso obligatorio de los cinturones de seguridad? ¿Por qué?

E. **¿Qué pasó?** Los dibujos que aparecen a continuación representan los momentos previos a un accidente. Describe lo que **pasaba** cuando **ocurrió** cada uno de los tres accidentes.

Modelo: *La mujer corría con su perro. De repente el perro vio un gato interesante. El perro empezó a correr detrás del gato, la mujer tropezó en el camino, se cayó y se le torció el tobillo.*

INVESTIGAR LA GRAMÁTICA The Imperfect Subjunctive

Point out to students that they already know *quisiera*, an imperfect subjunctive form that is used for polite requests.

Point out to students that the imperfect subjunctive also occurs in conditional sentences that are contrary to fact: *Viajaría por Europa si gozara de buena salud.* This usage will be explained in Chapter 11, first *etapa*.

The same uses you have learned for the present subjunctive also apply to the imperfect (past) subjunctive.

Quiero que vayas conmigo. *I want you to go with me.*
Quería que fueras conmigo. *I wanted you to go with me.*
Quiero ver una casa que tenga piscina. *I want to see a house that has a swimming pool.*
Quería ver una casa que tuviera piscina. *I wanted to see a house that had a swimming pool.*
Es dudoso que venga. *It's doubtful that he will come.*
Era dudoso que viniera. *It was doubtful that he would come.*

The forms of the imperfect subjunctive all come from the *ellos* form of the preterite. If you know your regular and irregular preterite verb forms, learning the imperfect subjunctive forms will be very easy for you. To form the imperfect subjunctive of any verb, *-ar*, *-er-*, or *-ir*, regular or irregular, stem-changing or not, first drop the *-ron* from the *ellos* form of the preterite. Then add the following endings.

– ra	– ramos
– ras	– rais
– ra	– ran

OJO: The *nosotros* form will have an accent mark on the vowel immediately preceding the *-ramos*, as in *habláramos, comiéramos, viviéramos*.

Because these endings are the same for all verbs, you need remember only the irregularities in the verb stems and the accent mark in the *nosotros* form.

habla**ron** → habla**ra**, habla**ras**, habla**ra**, hablá**ramos**, habla**rais**, habla**ran**
comie**ron** → comie**ra**, comie**ras**, comie**ra**, comié**ramos**, comie**rais**, comie**ran**
vivie**ron** → vivie**ra**, vivie**ras**, vivie**ra**, vivié**ramos**, vivie**rais**, vivie**ran**
hicie**ron** → hicie**ra**, hicie**ras**, hicie**ra**, hicié**ramos**, hicie**rais**, hicie**ran**
dije**ron** → dije**ra**, dije**ras**, dije**ra**, dijé**ramos**, dije**rais**, dije**ron**
durmie**ron** → durmie**ra**, durmie**ras**, durmie**ra**, durmié**ramos**, durmie**rais**, durmie**ran**
fue**ron** → fue**ra**, fue**ras**, fue**ra**, fué**ramos**, fue**rais**, fue**ran**

Again, note that verbs with an irregular stem or with a stem change in the *ellos* form of the preterite carry that same stem through all the forms of the imperfect subjunctive.

Ponerlo a prueba

A. Un congreso sobre la salud. Alicia fue a un congreso sobre la salud. Al volver, le contó a Elena lo que aprendió. Completa sus comentarios, escogiendo el indicativo o el subjuntivo.

OJO: You will see the verb *decir* several times in this activity. Remember that it can be used to convey information or to give a recommendation or an order. It takes the subjunctive only in this second case.

Review with students the uses of the subjunctive that are demonstrated here, especially the use of *decir* that can convey both information (indicative) or influence (subjunctive).

El congreso fue muy interesante. Aprendí bastante; a ver si recuerdo los puntos más importantes.

Primero, en cuanto a la piel, nos (**habló, hablara**) un especialista en dermatología. Dijo que el sol (**es, sea**) el mayor enemigo de la piel. Nos recomendó a todos que (**protegíamos, protegiéramos**) la piel contra el sol, que (**usábamos, usáramos**) siempre cremas bloqueadoras.

Otro médico nos dio una charla sobre la relación entre la salud y la dieta. Dijo que (**evitábamos, evitáramos**) la grasa (*fat*) en la comida, cosa que es difícil de hacer aquí en la universidad. Dijo que la grasa (**puede, pueda**) causar enfermedades del corazón. Sugirió que (**comimos, comiéramos**) más frutas y verduras porque (**tienen, tengan**) fibra y vitaminas. Otra cosa muy interesante (**fue, fuera**) su comentario sobre el agua. Dijo que en general no (**tomamos, tomemos**) suficiente agua, y que debemos tomar más, ya que el agua (**es, sea**) muy importante para la salud general.

This exercise can be converted into a paired activity, in which Student A converts the sentence to a question, and Student B answers it: A: *¿Qué era necesario en el pasado?* B: *Era necesario que conserváramos la salud.*

B. Para vivir con buena salud. Algunas cosas en la vida no cambian. Cambia estas oraciones al pasado, empezándolas con la frase **En el pasado...**

Modelo: Los padres esperan que sus hijos miren menos televisión.
En el pasado, los padres esperaban que sus hijos miraran menos televisión.

1. Es necesario que conservemos la salud.
2. Las madres quieren que sus hijos coman verduras y frutas.
3. En las revistas se nos aconseja que evitemos los dulces.
4. Los médicos les dicen a los jóvenes que duerman por lo menos ocho horas por noche.
5. Los maestros prefieren que sus estudiantes estén a la alerta para aprender más y mejor.
6. Es aconsejable que hagamos ejercicio todos los días.
7. Los entrenadores (*coaches*) insisten en que los atletas corran ocho kilómetros por día para mantenerse en buena forma.
8. Arreglan los horarios para que los atletas trabajen más por la mañana, cuando no hace tanto calor.

1. Have students go into detail, so that they produce several sentences with similar structures about each drawing. 2. Have students in pairs create *mini-diálogos* about one or more drawings.

C. Las instrucciones. Estas situaciones son muy conocidas. En cada una de ellas, explica lo que le dijo una persona a la otra.

1. ¿Qué le dijo la madre a la niña?
2. ¿Qué le dijo la esposa al esposo?
3. ¿Qué le dijo el médico a la paciente?
4. ¿Qué le dijo el niño a la niña?

OJO: Usa el subjuntivo cuando se trata de obligación, duda, voluntad o emoción. Usa el indicativo cuando se trata de dar información bien definida. Al terminar debes tener un párrafo lógico.

Have students interview each other using the incomplete sentences as prompts for questions. Then have students write a paragraph that incorporates the information learned about the partner.

Model one or two sentences so that students understand that they have to pose, and answer, the questions with careful attention to structure.

CH. Las obligaciones de la niñez. Primero, lee todas las oraciones incompletas que están a continuación. Segundo, termínalas de acuerdo con tus experiencias cuando eras niño/-a.

1. Cuando yo era niño/-a, mis padres siempre querían que...
2. Nunca permitían que (yo)...
3. Pero siempre dejaban que mi hermano/-a (mis hermanos/-as)...
4. Para explicar, siempre decían que...
5. A pesar de sus explicaciones, yo...
6. Por fin la cuestión se resolvió cuando...

D. Encuesta. Ponte de pie y habla con otros miembros de la clase para encontrar una persona que corresponda con las oraciones que aparecen a continuación.

Modelo: (pregunta posible) *¿Insistían tus padres en que comieras frutas y verduras?*

Busca una persona...   *Nombre*

1. cuyos (*whose*) padres insistían en que trabajara todos los veranos cuando asistía a la escuela secundaria   _____
2. a quien se le partió la pierna o el brazo una vez   _____

Busca una persona...	Nombre
3. en cuya (*whose*) familia se hablaba mucho de la salud	_____
4. cuyos padres siempre querían que hiciera más ejercicio	_____
5. cuyos padres siempre le decían, cuando era más joven, que apagara el televisor	_____

¡TIENES LA PALABRA!

Haz las siguientes actividades con un compañero (una compañera).

A. Una llamada al médico (a la médica)

Estudiante A: Paciente

While running, you stepped on a rock and fell. You call the doctor's office to make an appointment.

1. Identify yourself.
2. Say that you need an appointment immediately.
3. Explain how the accident happened.
4. Say when it happened, and explain that your ankle is swollen and painful.
5. Agree to an appointment time.
6. Thank the receptionist and say good-bye.

Estudiante B: Recepcionista

You answer the phone in the doctor's office.

1. Greet the patient.
2. Explain that the doctor's schedule is completely filled.
3. Ask how and when the accident happened.
4. Ask about the current condition of the patient's ankle.
5. Set up an appointment time.
6. Say good-bye.

The directions are in English in this activity so that students will have to select the appropriate vocabulary on their own.

If students have trouble expressing "the doctor's schedule is completely filled," encourage them to recast the idea into familiar expressions and structures: *El doctor (La doctora) está muy ocupado/-a esta semana. ¿Quiere Ud. verlo/-a el lunes próximo?*

Instruct the student who plays the role of the ambulance dispatcher to ask questions to gather as much detail as possible from the caller.

B. Un caso urgente. Estás solo/-a en casa. Estás arreglando un estante de libros y de repente todos los libros y el estante se te caen encima. No puedes mover la pierna derecha. Afortunadamente el teléfono está cerca y llamas una ambulancia.

- Identifícate.
- Explica qué te pasa.
- Dale tu dirección.

OTRA VUELTA

Play instructor tape, 2 min.

Escucha otra vez el anuncio sobre la Clínica Buena Vista que escuchaste al comienzo de esta etapa, e identifica las especialidades de los tres médicos nuevos.

Doctor/-a *Especialidad*

_____ Dr. Mauricio Garcés a. psiquiatría
_____ Dra. Marta Martínez de Velasco b. cardiología
_____ Dra. Ana María León c. pediatría
 ch. cirugía de los ojos
 d. dermatología

COMENTARIO CULTURAL

El hospital y la clínica

En Latinoamérica se puede recibir tratamiento médico en hospitales, clínicas, consultorios y algunas veces en la casa. El sentido de las palabras que se usan para describir el sistema de salud pública varía de país en país. Los términos que se usan en este Comentario cultural son válidos para Colombia. Tal vez tu profesor o profesora haya tenido experiencia con otros países y pueda decirte cuáles son los términos apropiados para ellos.

En Colombia, "los hospitales" ofrecen servicios médicos a bajo costo o gratis. Forman parte del sistema de Seguro Social y en ellos cualquier colombiano tiene el derecho de pedir servicios médicos. Generalmente son bastante grandes y las instalaciones médicas varían considerablemente de un hospital a otro, de acuerdo con los recursos técnicos y financieros de la región. Este sistema socializado de servicios públicos de salud garantiza que cualquier persona tenga acceso a algún tipo de tratamiento médico que de otra manera no podría pagar. También hay hospitales militares que proveen servicios gratis a los soldados y otros militares.

"Las clínicas" generalmente son particulares, tienen menos personal y son más pequeñas que los hospitales. A menudo las clínicas están equipadas con tecnología más moderna y típicamente ofrecen servicio a clientes internados. Es más costoso recibir tratamiento médico en una clínica que en un hospital ya que por ser instituciones particulares no reciben ningún subsidio del gobierno. El alto costo de los servicios médicos trae como resultado que haya menos pacientes, y

OJO: Other Latin American countries may have a different distribution of medical facilities. In Costa Rica, for example, the hospitals are better equipped than the smaller *clínicas*.

muchas personas opinan que debido a esto hay una relación más estrecha y personal entre los médicos y sus pacientes.

"Los consultorios", que son las oficinas de los médicos, ofrecen sólo tratamientos externos, es decir, tratamientos para las personas que no están internadas en un hospital o en una clínica. Normalmente un consultorio consiste en una sala de recepción, una sala de reconocimiento médico (*examining room*) y la oficina privada del médico. Si un paciente necesita tratamiento especializado, el médico hace los arreglos para que admitan al paciente en un hospital o en una clínica. Muy de vez en cuando los médicos hacen visita al domicilio, sobre todo en casos de emergencia. No obstante, esto es cada vez menos común, ya que la gente va utilizando más las ambulancias y otros servicios para el tratamiento de enfermedades y heridas.

"Información, por favor." Usando el formulario que está a continuación, escribe uno o dos puntos clave para las tres facilidades médicas que se describen en el Comentario cultural.

Facilidad médica	*Descripción* (*puntos clave*)
El hospital	1.
	2.
La clínica	1.
	2.
El consultorio	1.
	2.

"¿Qué número marcas?" A continuación hay varios anuncios de servicios médicos. ¿A quién o a qué empresa llamarías en las siguientes situaciones?

1. Tu gato no quiere comer nada.
2. Se te acaban de romper los lentes.
3. Tienes un dolor de garganta constante.
4. Estás deprimido/-a y no puedes comer ni dormir.
5. Necesitas adelgazar (*lose weight*).
6. Te tienen que sacar un diente.

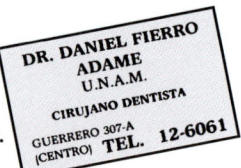

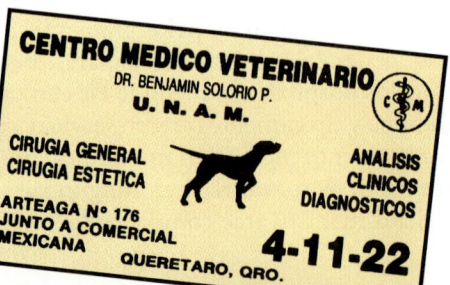

TERCERA ETAPA

Enfermedades y hospitales

ENTRADA

Play instructor tape, 2 min.

"¡Peligro!"

Listen to the following public service announcement regarding a health hazard. As you listen, try to determine

- whether the hazard is related to air pollution, food, or water
- two precautions one should take as a result

1. Este anuncio se trata de un problema con
   a. la contaminación del aire
   b. mariscos contaminados
   c. la contaminación del agua

2. Para evitar problemas, se le recomienda a la gente que
   a. no salga de su domicilio durante el día
   b. no compre ni coma mariscos
   c. use solamente agua mineral o destilada

ANTES DE LEER Y ESCRIBIR

Play student tape, 1 min.

Estudiar y practicar

el agradecimiento	*gratitude, appreciation*
el aparato	*equipment, machine*
la barrera	*barrier, fence*
el cupón	*coupon*
la intervención quirúrgica	*operation*
merecer	*to deserve*
poner al corriente	*to inform*
el tumor cerebral	*brain tumor*

Preparación

El título del texto en esta sección es "Carta-testimonio de una madre americana". Sin leer la carta que aparece a continuación, trata de adivinar algo sobre su propósito (*purpose*) y contenido.

1. ¿Cuál es la función principal de un testimonio?
   a. informar
   b. persuadir
   c. criticar
2. Piensa en los testimonios que conoces. ¿Quién los escribe (o pronuncia), y de qué se tratan?
3. Ya has estudiado el vocabulario anterior, así que sabes que la carta-testimonio trata sobre una persona que tiene un tumor cerebral.
   - ¿Puedes adivinar la relación entre la "madre americana" que escribe la carta y la persona enferma?
   - Explica tu respuesta.

Ahora lee la carta y contesta las siguientes preguntas.

CARTA-TESTIMONIO DE UNA MADRE AMERICANA

Si se trata de la salud, 5.000 Km. no es mucha distancia.

Si usted también cree, como la señora Rubin, que la distancia no debe ser una barrera para conseguir lo mejor para los suyos, póngase en contacto con nosotros enviándonos el cupón y le informaremos más ampliamente.

"Mi hijo Gregory, de 22 años, duerme en su cama de la Clínica Universitaria de Navarra. Somos de New Jersey. ¿Cómo nos encontramos en Pamplona, tan lejos de nuestro hogar?.

Hace ocho años se le detectó a mi hijo Greg un tumor cerebral. No era maligno. Recibió radioterapia y después de un año de recuperación se reintegró a la vida normal.

En enero del pasado año, Greg sufrió una convulsión. La intervención quirúrgica que se le practicó en New York, descubrió un nuevo tumor, pero, esta vez, maligno.

Consultamos a los mejores médicos de New York. Recomendaron un tratamiento de quimioterapia y radiación. Al mismo tiempo, un especialista de Filadelfia nos puso al corriente de una técnica que se utiliza en Europa, especialmente en Pamplona, España. Nos comentó los excelentes resultados obtenidos por la Clínica Universitaria de Navarra. Nos habló de la Clínica desde dos puntos de vista, el tecnológico y el humano.

Por fin vinimos a España. Hoy pienso si es posible comparar la Clínica Universitaria con los hospitales americanos. Ciertamente nuestros hospitales, nuestros médicos, nuestra tecnología, es excelente. Nuestra experiencia con la profesión médica americana ha sido muy buena pero... la Clínica de Pamplona merece, en mi opinión, una consideración muy especial.

Tras conocer la Clínica pude comprobar el excelente equipo médico, auxiliado por modernos e impresionantes aparatos. En pocas palabras tengo completa confianza en las posibilidades técnicas del Centro. Pero, ¿qué decir del aspecto humano?. Tanto la atención al enfermo como a los acompañantes es diferente. Es algo especial.

Por el momento, sólo tenemos esperanza y gratitud por el tratamiento y la asistencia recibidos.

La Clínica Universitaria de Navarra, su espíritu, sus expertos en Medicina, pero, sobre todo, la calidad humana de cada uno de sus componentes, merecerán nuestro eterno agradecimiento."

Mrs. Elisabeth Rubin, New Jersey - USA

Carta-testimonio de una madre americana

1. ¿Qué tratamientos tuvo Greg Rubin antes de ir a la Clínica Unive Navarra?
   a.　　　　　　　　b.　　　　　　　　c.
2. ¿Cómo se ente　　　ró (*found out*) la famili
3. Escribe dos frases que comparan la Clínica Unive　　　rsitaria d hospitales norteame　　　ricanos, según (*according to*) la señ

OJO: If you need to refresh your memory on making comparisons, see Chapter 3, third *etapa*.

Tema	Comparación
El aspecto tecnológico	
El aspecto humano	

WRITING STRATEGY 9

Transfer thought to language

Becoming more proficient in Spanish means, in part, learning how to think in Spanish rather than in English. An important part of this process is getting used to transferring your thoughts directly into familiar Spanish phrases and sentences, rather than translating English words into Spanish words. In the following activity, for example, think first about what you want to write, and then go immediately to phrases in Spanish that you feel confident in using. As an illustration, if you want to ask Greg what it was like to be sick at age fourteen when all of his friends were out having fun, **do not** think of each word in English and try to render it in Spanish. This kind of direct translation almost never gives you idiomatic Spanish. Instead, think about what the question is really asking. Then it will be obvious that you can phrase your question "What was it like" as *¿Cómo te sentías cuando...?* Note that this strategy is important for both writing and speaking.

ESCRIBIR

1. Escribe cinco preguntas que te gustaría hacerle a Greg. Recuerda que él tenía catorce años cuando se le descubrió el primer tumor y que ahora tiene veintidós.
   a.
   b.
   c.
   ch.
   d.

OJO: Strategy: Reread the Writing Strategy. Make sure you understand what the letter says, and then figure out a simple way to write Greg's medical history so you are not copying the letter.

2. Imagínate que eres Greg Rubin. Escribe un párrafo acerca de tu historia médica. Usa la información que aparece en la carta-testimonio, pero escríbela en tus propias palabras de una forma más sencilla.

3. Al lado de la carta se hace referencia a un cupón que se puede mandar a la Clínica Universitaria de Navarra para pedir información. Diseña (*Design*) ese cupón.

Ventanilla al mundo hispánico   Cuando alguien estornuda...

Muchas culturas tienen una manera especial de reaccionar cuando alguien estornuda. En las culturas hispánicas la reacción más común es decir "¡Salud!" o "Jesús". Después, la persona que acaba de estornudar normalmente responde "Gracias". (No se dice "¡Perdón!" al estornudar como se dice *"Excuse me"* en inglés.) Si alguien estornuda varias veces seguidas, la persona que normalmente dice "¡Salud!" después de la serie de estornudos dice "¡Salud, dinero y amor!" Los que normalmente dicen "¡Jesús!" dicen "¡Jesús, María y José!" En todo caso, la más importante de todo esto es que si tú estornudas en un país de habla española alguien va a decirte algo, y tú siempre debes responder "Gracias".

AUMENTAR EL VOCABULARIO

el agradecimiento	*gratitude, appreciation*
el aparato	*equipment, machine*
la barrera	*barrier, fence*
el cupón	*coupon*
el diagnóstico	*diagnosis*
afirmar	*to affirm*
la enfermedad	*illness*
la alergia	*allergy*
desmayarse	*to faint, pass out*
la gripe	*flu*
el sarampión	*measles*
el SIDA	*AIDS*
la varicela	*chicken pox*
la estatura	*height*
pesar	*to weigh*
el peso	*weight*
estornudar	*to sneeze*

OJO: *La operación* and *la intervención quirúrgica* are synonyms. Remember that you learned *el cirujano (la cirujana)* in Chapter 5.

OJO: A synonym for *dar puntos* is *suturar (una herida)*.

OJO: *Esterilizar* has a spelling change in the present subjunctive and the preterite. It is conjugated like *comenzar*.

OJO: *Secar* has the same spelling changes as *buscar*.

OJO: *Merecer* is conjugated like *conocer: merezco, mereces,* and so on.

la intervención quirúrgica	*operation*
la anestesia	anesthesia
dar puntos	to stitch a wound
desinfectar	to disinfect
esterilizar	to sterilize
mojar	to moisten
secar	to dry
tomar una muestra de sangre	to take a blood sample
el ligamento	*ligament*
el músculo	muscle
el tendón	tendon
merecer	**to deserve**
poner al corriente	**to inform**
ponerse en contacto (con)	to get in touch/contact (with)
el tumor cerebral	*brain tumor*
benigno/-a	benign
maligno/-a	malignant

EN LA SALA DE EMERGENCIA

La camilla = stretcher. *La camilla de ruedas* = gurney.

la sala de espera

El técnico le saca una radiografía al paciente.

Encourage students to go into as much detail as possible.

En la sala de emergencia. Imagínate que trabajas en una sala de emergencia. ¿Qué procedimiento recomiendas en cada caso?

1. El paciente fuma dos paquetes de cigarrillos por día. Tose mucho y le duelen los pulmones.
2. Una mujer está mareada y se siente muy débil. Se ha desmayado dos veces en las últimas 24 horas.
3. Traen a un hombre en una camilla. Se hirió una pierna en un accidente de motocicleta. La herida no es grave, pero está llena de gravilla (*gravel*).

USO PRÁCTICO DEL ESPAÑOL — Another Verb Like *gustar*: Me duele, me duelen

OJO: Make sure you remember the indirect object pronouns: *me, te, le, nos, os, les.*

Earlier you learned about *gustar* and other verbs that have the same structure: *fascinar, encantar, interesar.*

Me encantan el jazz y el rock, pero no **me interesa** mucho la música clásica.
A Mónica **le gustan** todas las ciencias, pero prefiere la física porque **le fascinan** las matemáticas.

OJO: Reminder: *doler* means "to feel pain." If something causes you pain, you might say *Estos zapatos me molestan*, or *me hacen doler los pies.*

The verb *doler* (*ue*) functions structurally the same way as *gustar*.

Me duele el estómago.   *My stomach hurts.*
¿Te duelen los pies?   *Do your feet hurt?*

The indirect object pronoun refers to the person who is experiencing the pain.

Me duele la cabeza.   *My head hurts.*
Paco fue al hospital; **le dolía mucho el brazo.**   *Paco went to the hospital; his arm hurt a lot.*

OJO: Sometimes the *a + persona* phrase is used for contrast or emphasis, even when the referent is clear from the context: *Todos estamos enfermos hoy; a Juanita le duele la cabeza y a mí me molesta el estómago.* The phrase *a Juanita* is needed to clarify to whom the *le* refers, but *a mí* just emphasizes the contrast between the speaker's symptoms and Juanita's.

In the second example, it is clear from the context that the *le* in *le dolía el brazo* refers to Paco. As with other indirect object pronouns, when the context is not clear, the phrase *a + persona* is added for clarification.

A Juanita le duele la cabeza.   *Juanita's head hurts.*

Remember that the verb is singular or plural in agreement with the **source** of the feeling, not with the person experiencing it. An athlete and her doctor might have the following conversation.

— Así que le **duelen** las dos rodillas, ¿verdad?

— Sí, doctor, pero me **duele** mucho más la derecha que la izquierda.

Ponerlo a prueba

A. ¿Qué te duele(n)? Imagínate que has participado en las actividades siguientes. Di qué parte(s) del cuerpo te duele(n); si puedes, añade más detalles.

Modelo: Compraste zapatos nuevos que te han resultado incómodos.
Compré estos zapatos nuevos, caminé dos millas con ellos y ahora me duelen mucho los pies.

1. Ayer tocaste piano por seis horas.
2. No te diste cuenta de que el café estaba tan caliente y empezaste a tomarlo.
3. Corriste en un maratón esta mañana.
4. Cortaste cebollas para hacer una tortilla española.
5. Comiste muchísimo anoche.
6. Anoche dormiste en un hotel y la cama no era nada cómoda. Además, la almohada (*pillow*) era más grande y más dura que la tuya en casa.

OJO: A *tortilla española* is a Spanish omelette, which consists of eggs, onions, and potatoes.

B. Sinónimos y definiciones. Indica la palabra de la lista en Aumentar el vocabulario que significa lo mismo que cada una de las siguientes palabras o frases. Después, emplea cada palabra o frase en una oración interesante. ¡Usa la imaginación!

1. poner agua en algo
2. la opinión del médico (de la médica) acerca de la condición del paciente (de la paciente)
3. limpiar una herida
4. una frontera común entre los terrenos (*property*) de dos vecinos
5. un procedimiento común en un examen médico
6. el procedimiento que se usa para cerrar una herida profunda
7. una enfermedad asociada con la niñez
8. lavar algo en agua muy caliente para matar los microbios
9. un sinónimo de "canceroso"
10. un sinónimo de "informar"

C. ¿Cuál es más grave? Según tu opinión, pon las enfermedades y condiciones en orden de gravedad, de la menos grave (1) a la más grave (8).

_____ tener el hombro dislocado
_____ partirse el tobillo
_____ sufrir de la varicela
_____ sufrir del SIDA
_____ tener insomnio
_____ tener alergia al polen de varias plantas
_____ tener la presión sanguínea un poco alta
_____ herir los ligamentos de la rodilla

Ahora formen grupos de tres personas. Compara el orden de tu lista con el de tus compañeros. Trata de convencerlos de que tu orden es el mejor.

CH. Preguntas personales

1. ¿Tuviste el sarampión o la varicela cuando eras niño/-a? ¿Qué recuerdas de la experiencia?
2. ¿Qué otras enfermedades tuviste cuando eras más joven?
3. Cuando no te sientes bien, ¿prefieres ir al consultorio del médico (de la médica) o a la sala de emergencia? ¿Por qué?
4. Cuando vas a la enfermería o a la clínica de la universidad, ¿hay mucha gente en la sala de espera? ¿Por cuánto tiempo tuviste que esperar la última vez que fuiste allí?
5. ¿Cuánto mides? ¿Quién es la persona más alta de tu familia? ¿La más baja? ¿Cuánto miden estas personas?
6. ¿Cuándo fue la última vez que alguien te midió la presión sanguínea? ¿Cuándo te sacaron una muestra de sangre?
7. ¿Tuviste alguna vez una herida en la que tuvieran que darte puntos? Explica los detalles.
8. En tu opinión, ¿cuál es peor—partirse un tobillo o herir los ligamentos y tendones del tobillo?
9. Si una persona usa muletas o una silla de ruedas, ¿puede vivir cómodamente donde vives tú? ¿Por qué sí o por qué no?
10. ¿Es accesible este salón de clase a la gente que usa silla de ruedas? En general, ¿es esta universidad accesible a la gente inválida (*disabled*)?

D. Ahora tú eres el médico (la médica).
Vamos a suponer que eres médico/-a y que tus pacientes vienen a tu consultorio con los siguientes síntomas. Receta algo en cada situación.

Modelo: Paciente: ¡Ay, doctor/-a! ¡Me duele horriblemente la cabeza!
Tú: *Pues, tome dos aspirinas y baje el volumen del radio.*

1. —Hace tres días que tengo fiebre.
2. —Me duele la pierna derecha y tengo el tobillo hinchado.
3. —Tosí toda la noche y no pude dormir ni un minuto.
4. —Me desperté vomitando y siento unos dolores de estómago horribles.
5. —Hace una semana que no tengo apetito; me siento muy débil.

INVESTIGAR LA GRAMÁTICA More on the "Wish-List" Subjunctive

As you saw in the first *etapa* of Chapter 7, the subjunctive is used to describe someone or something that is not yet part of your personal experience. This might mean that whatever you are describing is merely indefinite, literally nonexistent, or has simply not yet been experienced. Whether you use the present or the imperfect subjunctive depends on the time you are talking about: the present subjunctive is used for present or future time and the imperfect subjunctive is used for past time.

Búscame un libro **que cueste menos de treinta dólares.**	*See if you can find me a book that costs less than $30.00.*
No pude encontrar un libro **que costara menos de treinta dólares.** Entonces, te compré uno que costó treinta y uno con cincuenta.	*I couldn't find a book that cost less than $30.00, so I bought you one that cost $31.50.*
Necesitaba un compañero de cuarto **que hablara ruso.**	*I needed a roommate who spoke Russian.*
Vamos a ver si encontramos un profesor **que tenga tiempo para hablar con nosotros.**	*Let's see if we can find a professor who has time to talk with us.*

In a conversation, it is very common for one person to ask a question using the subjunctive and for the other to answer using the indicative.

— ¿Conoce usted a **alguien que repare carros japoneses?**

— ¡Cómo no! Aquí nuestros mecánicos no **hacen** otra cosa.

Note that the question needs the subjunctive because it asks about someone with attributes that may or may not exist. The response uses the indicative because it refers to specific mechanics known to the speaker who have the desired attributes. The person who responds might continue the conversation by denying (and therefore using the subjunctive) that there is a better repair shop in town.

— Tenemos muy buena fama en toda la ciudad. **No hay otro taller que le dé** tan buen servicio como nosotros.

Ponerlo a prueba

A. ¿Y en la clínica vieja?   Acaban de abrir una clínica nueva en la calle Lavaca. Dos amigos hacen comparación entre la clínica nueva y una vieja que ya no existe. Toma tú el papel del amigo (o de la amiga) que habla del pasado. Sigue el modelo.

Modelo: — En la clínica nueva hay una secretaria que trabaja de 8:00 a 5:00.
— *¡Magnífico! En el pasado no había nadie que trabajara de 8:00 a 5:00.*

1. En la clínica nueva hay un médico que se especializa en alergias.
2. En la clínica nueva hay una enfermera que ayuda a los pacientes.
3. En la clínica nueva hay un contador que se encarga de (*is in charge of*) los asuntos financieros.
4. En la clínica nueva hay un médico que hace operaciones sencillas.
5. En la clínica nueva hay una secretaria que escribe cartas y contesta el teléfono.
6. En la clínica nueva hay una señora que va por la noche para limpiar.
7. En la clínica nueva hay un señor que recoge a los pacientes que no pueden llegar solos.
8. En la clínica nueva hay muchos pacientes que están muy contentos.

B. Pero en la Clínica Mala Vista... En el mismo barrio hay otra clínica pero es mala. No tiene el personal (*personnel*) abundante y competente que tiene la clínica nueva. Repite la Actividad A, pero esta vez tú te quejas de lo que **no** tiene la Clínica Mala Vista.

Modelo: — En la clínica nueva hay una secretaria que trabaja de 8:00 a 5:00.
— *¡Qué envidia! En la Clínica Mala Vista no hay nadie que trabaje de 8:00 a 5:00.*

C. ¿Hay alguien aquí que...? En grupos de cinco o seis, averigua si hay alguien en tu grupo que llene los siguientes requisitos.

1. tener un coche pequeño
2. saber cambiar una llanta pinchada
3. tocar el violín
4. estudiar música latina
5. conocer personalmente a un(a) artista profesional
6. sacar buenas notas en todos los cursos
7. querer ser médico/-a
8. pensar estudiar para abogado/-a

Ahora informa a la clase, siguiendo el modelo.

Modelo: *Sí, hay una persona en nuestro grupo que toma el café negro y sin azúcar. Es Patricia.*

o: *No, no hay nadie en nuestro grupo que tome el café negro sin azúcar.*

OJO: You can ask either a direct question to a specific member of the group —*Marta, ¿tomas el café negro sin azúcar?*—or you can ask a general question of the whole group: *¿Hay alguien aquí que tome el café negro sin azúcar?* Remember to use the subjunctive for the general question, since the person you are looking for is not yet known to you.

OJO: Remember that *el (la) artista* in item 5 refers to any kind of fine arts performer: musician, painter, actor, and so on.

CH. **Buscar un buen médico (una buena médica).** Encontrar un buen médico (una buena médica) a veces es difícil. Rafael, que se preocupa mucho de la salud, le cuenta a su amigo el tipo de médico/-a que buscaba. Toma tú el papel de Rafael, y haz oraciones de acuerdo con el modelo.

Modelo: tener su consultorio cerca de mi casa
Buscaba un médico que tuviera su consultorio cerca de mi casa.

1. contestar muchas preguntas sin quejarse
2. hablar conmigo por teléfono si tenía preguntas
3. abrir su consultorio temprano por la mañana
4. trabajar los sábados
5. hacer radiografías en el consultorio
6. especializarse en cardiología
7. ser experto en el diagnóstico
8. lavarse las manos con frecuencia y también usar guantes de plástico
9. esterilizar los instrumentos todos los días
10. dar puntos en el consultorio

D. **El médico (La médica) ideal.** ¿Qué buscas tú en un médico (una médica)? Con un compañero (una compañera) de la clase, hagan una lista de los cinco criterios más importantes de los cuales los dos están de acuerdo.

Queremos un médico (una médica) que...

1.
2.
3.
4.
5.

Ahora, comparen su lista con las de otros compañeros de la clase para ver cuáles son los criterios más frecuentes.

E. **Preguntas personales.** Cuando eras niño/-a ¿había alguien en tu familia o entre tus amigos que fuera así?

1. tomarse para sí mismo lo mejor de todo
2. ser siempre muy generoso/-a con los demás
3. siempre ayudar con los quehaceres de la casa
4. sonreír o cantar cuando hacía los quehaceres domésticos
5. siempre jugar contigo
6. compartir los juguetes (*toys*) contigo

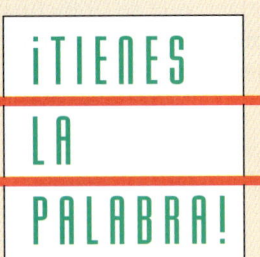

¡TIENES LA PALABRA!

Do in class as a small group oral activity, or have students expand it and do it individually as a writing assignment at home.

Haz las siguientes actividades con un compañero (una compañera).

A. **¡Pero, doctor(a)!**

Estudiante A: El (La) paciente
Your doctor has just given you a physical examination and is now prescribing a number of necessary changes in your lifestyle in order to improve your health. Unfortunately, your doctor seems to feel that almost everything you like to do is unhealthy. As the doctor advises you, explain why you think you should **not** follow the recommendations. Remember, it is **your** health that is involved, not that of your doctor!

Estudiante B: El doctor (La doctora)
You have just finished giving your patient a physical examination, and now must convince him (her) to make some drastic changes in his (her) lifestyle. Recommend at least five habits or activities that the patient must change, and emphasize the importance of each change. Keep in mind that your patient is well known for being a "party animal," so these changes are not going to be agreed to without some very good arguments on your part. Ultimately, however, it is the patient's life, not yours, that will be shortened if these destructive practices continue, so you cannot force the changes on him (her).

B. **El estudiante y su salud.** Con un compañero (una compañera) de la clase, prepara una lista de actividades positivas y otra de actividades negativas que la universidad puede distribuir a los estudiantes del primer año que piden información sobre la salud personal. Deben recordar que sus lectores son estudiantes, y que no van a aceptar facilmente las recomendaciones que limitan sus actividades sociales. Así, debes preparar un comentario breve para acompañar a cada recomendación. Al terminar las listas, escríbelas en la pizarra para poder compartirlas con la clase.

OTRA VUELTA

Play instructor tape, 2 min.

Escucha otra vez el anuncio que oíste en la Entrada al comienzo de la tercera etapa. Al escuchar, escribe los cuatro síntomas de la toxificación de los mariscos contaminados que se mencionan.

Síntomas de toxificación

1.
2.
3.
4.

COMENTARIO CULTURAL

Kilómetros and *grados centígrados* are discussed in the *Ventanilla al mundo hispánico* of Chapter 3, second *etapa*.

Más sobre las medidas métricas

Aunque el sistema métrico es el sistema oficial de los Estados Unidos, la gran mayoría de la gente sigue usando el sistema de pulgadas (*inches*), yardas, onzas, libras, etc. Si una persona mide un metro con sesenta y cinco centímetros, al estilo norteamericano esto equivale a medir *five foot five* o sencillamente *five five*.

Para convertir las medidas tradicionales norteamericanas en medidas métricas hay que expresarlas en pulgadas y multiplicar por 2,54. Si nuestra amiga mide cinco pies con cinco pulgadas, o sea 65 pulgadas, calculamos que mide un metro con sesenta y cinco centímetros. En números redondos, un pie (doce pulgadas) equivale a 30 cm (en realidad 30,48 cm).

Aprendiste en el Capítulo 3 que en el sistema métrico el peso se expresa en kilogramos. Si el médico le pregunta a una paciente cuánto pesa, puede que ella contesta "Peso 54 kilos". Cincuenta y cuatro kilos (= kilogramos) equivalen a 119 libras en el sistema norteamericano. Ya que cada kilo equivale a 2,2 libras, para convertir las libras en kilogramos hay que dividir las libras por 2,2. Obviamente, si ya sabes el peso de una persona en kilos, multiplicas el peso por 2,2 para saber cuánto pesa en libras.

Actividad. Contesta las siguientes preguntas usando las medidas métricas.

1. ¿Cuánto mides?
2. ¿Cuánto te gustaría medir?
3. Un hombre pesa 185 libras. ¿Cuánto pesa en kilos?
4. Una niña de cinco años pesa 45 libras. ¿Cuánto pesa en kilos?

DE INTEGRACIÓN

Play video

Program 9 *Remedios tradicionales y modernos* Traditional and modern health care

The directions are in English so that the students will have to select the appropriate vocabulary.

A. **Las instrucciones del médico (de la médica).** You have had major surgery and are leaving the hospital today. You write down your doctor's instructions so you won't forget anything that you are supposed to do or not do. Write a note to yourself in Spanish, reminding yourself that the doctor told you

- not to use the stairs more than once a day
- not to drive for ten days
- to get plenty of rest
- not to return to work or school for four weeks

B. **Carta-testimonio de un estudiante universitario.** Imagine that you are either so pleased with your current educational experience or so unhappy with it that you are moved to write a *carta-testimonio* in Spanish and send it to prospective students. Model your letter after the letter written by Gregory Rubin's mother in the *Antes de leer y escribir* section of this *etapa*. Be sure to include a story or anecdote that illustrates your extreme pleasure or displeasure, and follow it up with recommendations to prospective students. Begin your letter with the general salutation *Estimado/-a estudiante* and write as though you were addressing yourself to a student who has shown interest in attending your college or university.

C. **Un problema en la agencia de modelos.** You are the owner of a very successful modeling agency. However, a number of your models (both male and female) recently have been gaining so much weight that you must now impose some rules regarding nutrition and exercise. See how many rules you can generate in Spanish, beginning with either *Deben...* or *No deben...*

Assign a third student to each group who has the task of recounting the story of the purchase.

CH. **En la farmacia.** You need some first-aid supplies. Go to the pharmacy and ask the clerk for help. You need Band-Aids, bandages, and antiseptic cream. You don't have much money with you; ask what everything costs so you are sure to have enough to pay for what you need.

Your partner, who plays the role of the clerk, is very curious and asks a lot of questions: what you use the items for, whether there has been an accident at your home, and so on.

D. **Una llamada de emergencia.** A university student is very ill. A friend offers to call the infirmary and talk to the nurse.

Vocabulario

Estudiante A: Amigo/-a

1. Identify yourself and ask to speak to the doctor or a nurse.
2. Explain that your friend is very sick: vomiting, high fever, chills, and severe abdominal cramps.
3. Ask what you should do.
4. Arrange an appointment with the doctor. Insist on an appointment soon, even though the doctor's schedule is full.
5. Thank the nurse and say good-bye.

Estudiante B: Enfermero/-a

1. Greet the caller. Offer to help, since the doctor is with a patient.
2. Ask for the friend's symptoms.
3. Offer suggestions for immediate relief.
4. Make an appointment for the friend to see the doctor. It may be difficult, because the doctor's schedule is quite full.
5. Offer the caller encouragement and say good-bye.

VOCABULARIO

Accidentes y los estados físicos

cojear *to limp*
chocar (con) *crash, bump (into)*
deslizarse *to slip, slide*
desmayarse *to faint, pass out*
equilibrio (m) *balance*
estar hecho/-a pedazos *to be falling apart, to be a wreck*
hinchado/-a *swollen*
jadear *to pant, gasp for breath*
lastimarse *to injure oneself*
mareado/-a *dizzy; nauseated*
perder (ie) el conocimiento *to lose consciousness*
pisar *to step on*
torcer (ue) *to twist*
tropezar *to trip*
volver en sí *to regain consciousness*

Enfermedades y condiciones médicas

benigno/-a *benign*
diagnóstico (m) *diagnosis*
dolor (m) *pain*
enfermedad (f) *illness*
escalofríos (m pl) *chills*
fiebre (f) *fever*
gripe (f) *flu*
maligno/-a *malignant*
resfriado (m) *cold*
SIDA (m) *AIDS*
sarampión (m) *measles*
síntoma (m) *symptom*
tos (f) *cough*
toser *to cough*
tumor (m) cerebral *brain tumor*
varicela (f) *chicken pox*
vomitar *to vomit*

Medicinas y remedios

alergia (f) *allergy*
anestesia (f) *anesthesia*
antibiótico (m) *antibiotic*
antiséptico (m) *antiseptic*
aspirina (f) *aspirin*
calmante (m) *tranquilizer, painkiller*
curita (f) *small bandage (Band-Aid)*
inyección (f) *injection*
medicina (f) *medicine*
pastilla (f) *pill*
penicilina (f) *penicillin*
receta (f) *prescription*
recetar *to prescribe*
remedio (m) *medicine, remedy*
venda (f) *bandage*

Los órganos del cuerpo humano

cerebro (m) *brain*
corazón (m) *heart*
estómago (m) *stomach*
hígado (m) *liver*
intestinos (m pl) *intestines*
ligamento (m) *ligament*
músculo (m) *muscle*
piel (f) *skin*
pulmones (m pl) *lungs*
riñones (m pl) *kidneys*
tendón (m) *tendon*
tripas (f pl) *guts*

La sala de emergencia

camilla (f) *stretcher*
herida (f) *wound, injury*
herir (ie, i) *to wound, to injure*
intervención (f) quirúrgica *operation*
muletas (f pl) *crutches*
radiografía (f) *X ray*
recepcionista (m/f) *receptionist*
sala (f) de espera *waiting room*
silla (f) de ruedas *wheelchair*

Otras palabras y expresiones relacionadas con la salud

dar puntos *to stitch a wound*
desinfectar *to disinfect*
estatura (f) *height*
esterilizar *to sterilize*
estornudar *to sneeze*
nocivo/-a *noxious, poisonous*
nutrir *to nourish*
pesar *to weigh*
peso (m) *weight*
presión (f) sanguínea *blood pressure*
primeros auxilios (m pl) *first aid*
sacar una muestra de sangre *to take a blood sample*

Sustantivos útiles

agradecimiento (m) *gratitude, appreciation*
agua (f) corriente *running water*
agua (f) destilada *distilled water*
agua (f) mineral *mineral (bottled) water*
alberca (f) *swimming pool*
alivio (m) *relief*
aparato (m) *equipment, machine*
barrera (f) *barrier, fence*
clavado (m) *dive*
colmo (m) *height (as in finishing touch; last straw)*
cupón (m) *coupon*

Verbos útiles

afirmar *to affirm*
aliviar *to relieve*
calmar *to calm*
empaparse *to get soaked*
estar relacionado/-a con *to be related to*
mejorarse *to get better (health)*
merecer *to deserve*
mojar *to moisten*
poner al corriente *to inform*
ponerse en contacto (con) *to get in touch/contact (with)*
secar *to dry*
tener que ver con *to have to do with*
tomar(le) el pelo (a uno) *to tease, "pull someone's leg"*
tratarse de *to have to do with*

Otras palabras y expresiones útiles

apenas *scarcely*
el colmo de lo ridículo *the height of the ridiculous*

Vocabulario

¡Esto es el colmo! *This is the last straw!*

malcriado/-a *spoiled, impolite*

¡No puedo más! *I can't stand any more!*

VOCABULARIO PERSONALIZADO

¡A divertirnos!

Capítulo 10

COMMUNICATIVE OBJECTIVES

In this chapter you will learn some new ways to
- extend, accept, and decline invitations
- ask for and give advice
- make explanations, narrate and describe events
- talk about future and conditional occurrences

PRIMERA ETAPA

Una fiesta norteña

ENTRADA

Play instructor tape, 2 min.

Invitación a una recepción

En este capítulo vas a aprender a invitar a la gente, a aceptar invitaciones y a rechazarlas. Vas a escuchar dos conversaciones: la primera entre Teresa, una estudiante universitaria y su amigo Lorenzo, y la segunda entre Teresa y una profesora suya. Al escuchar, llena el formulario que aparece a continuación con la información que Teresa le da a cada persona acerca del motivo de la fiesta, la fecha, la hora y el lugar.

La fiesta de Teresa

Sitio: Hora:

Fecha: Motivo:

EMPEZAR A ESCUCHAR

Play student tape, 3 min.

Leer

tener el gusto de...	to have the pleasure of . . .
se llevará a cabo...	it will take place (will occur) . . .
debido a	due to
el compromiso	commitment, obligation
previo/-a	previous
si me hiciera el favor de...	if you would please (do me the favor of) . . .
saludar	to greet

Repetir

Escucha la cinta y repite lo que oyes.

Identificar

En una hoja aparte, escribe en una columna las palabras y frases anteriores. Vas a oír algunas oraciones. Cada vez que oigas una de esas palabras o frases, apunta el número de la oración al lado de la palabra. Cada oración se leerá dos veces.

Escribir

Vas a oír unas oraciones, cada una leída dos veces. Escríbelas al escucharlas.

Reconocer

Ahora, lee otra vez las oraciones que acabas de escribir. Cada una contiene una o más de las palabras y frases de la lista en esta sección de Leer. Al releerlas, subraya todas las palabras y frases que vienen de la lista. Mientras lees, haz todas las correcciones necesarias.

ESCUCHAR

Play student tape, 2 min.

Episodio 1: "¿Qué invitación? ¿A qué?"

Enfoque comunicativo

La profesora Suárez ha invitado a algunos de sus estudiantes a una fiesta. Entre los invitados están Paco y Roberto. Cuando llega la invitación, Roberto está en la casa de un amigo, así que Paco lo llama por teléfono para darle la noticia. Tú vas a escuchar a Paco leyéndole la invitación a Roberto. Trata de descubrir

- el motivo de la fiesta
- dónde y a qué hora será la fiesta

Fiesta norteña

Motivo de la fiesta: _____

Dónde se llevará a cabo: _____

Cuándo se llevará a cabo: _____

Cómo responder: Box 321 _____

Enfoque lingüístico

Escucha otra vez la conversación y apunta

- la frase que se usa para hacer la invitación
- la expresión que se usa para indicar el lugar de la fiesta
- la expresión que usa Roberto para indicar cuándo va a volver a casa

424 Capítulo diez ¡A divertirnos!

LEER

EPISODIO 2: "Es usted muy amable..."

Enfoque comunicativo

Después de hablar de la invitación, Paco y Roberto le escriben una nota de respuesta a la profesora Suárez. Lee la nota y trata de descubrir

- por qué Paco no puede asistir a la fiesta
- cómo Roberto va a acordarse de la dirección y de la fecha de la fiesta

Point out to students that invitations are rarely declined, and refer them to the Comentario cultural *section at the end of this* etapa.

> 5 de abril
>
> Estimada profesora Suárez:
>
> Es usted muy amable por invitarnos a la reunión planeada para el día 12, y Roberto ya ha apuntado la fecha en su calendario. Por mi parte, siento mucho no poder ir, debido a que tengo un compromiso previo. Si me hiciera el favor de saludar a los estudiantes de mi parte y de explicarles que no puedo asistir, se lo agradecería mucho.
>
> Le agradecemos mucho su invitación.
>
> Respetuosamente,
> Paco Méndez
> Roberto Hernández

La respuesta a la invitación

1. Paco no puede ir a la fiesta porque
   a. ya tiene otro compromiso
   b. ya tiene planes para salir con su novia
   c. tiene que trabajar con los estudiantes latinoamericanos

2. Roberto se acordará de la fecha de la fiesta porque
   a. la ha aprendido de memoria
   b. ve a la profesora Suárez todos los días
   c. ha escrito la información en su calendario

Enfoque lingüístico

Lee la carta otra vez y apunta

- dos maneras de expresar el agradecimiento
- una expresión que se puede usar para no aceptar una invitación

VERIFICAR

Contesta las siguientes preguntas.

1. ¿Cuál de los jóvenes abre la carta de la profesora Suárez?
2. Según Roberto, ¿qué es una "fiesta norteña"?
3. ¿Dónde se llevará a cabo la fiesta?
4. ¿Cuál es el motivo de la fiesta?
5. Después de decidir si van o no, ¿qué tienen que hacer los invitados?
6. ¿Por qué no puede asistir Paco?
7. ¿Qué hace Roberto para recordar la fecha?

AUMENTAR EL VOCABULARIO

OJO: Note that *asistir* is a false cognate. "To help" is *ayudar*.

OJO: *El compromiso* also means engagement to be married.

Gracias, muy amable is an abbreviated expression, taken from *Gracias, es usted muy amable.* It is an appropriate response to a compliment.

agradecer	**to acknowledge a favor** (*to appreciate*)
la carta de agradecimiento	thank-you letter
asistir a	**to attend**
el compromiso	**commitment, obligation**
el cumplido	**compliment**
Gracias, muy amable.	Thanks, it's nice of you to say that.
de parte de	**on behalf of**
debido a	**due to**
hacer el favor de	**please**
si me hiciera el favor de…	if you would please (*do me the favor of*) …
llevarse a cabo	**to take place**
se llevará a cabo…	it will take place (*occur*) …
el motivo	**reason, motive**
con el motivo de	for the purpose of
previo/-a	**previous**

rechazar	to refuse (*an invitation*); to reject
saludar	to greet
tener el gusto de...	to have the pleasure of ...

Ventanilla al mundo hispánico   "Te invito..."

En la mayoría de los países hispanohablantes una invitación para salir, por ejemplo a un restaurante o a una función social, conlleva la noción de que la persona que ofrece la invitación va a pagar. Cuando dos amigos se encuentran en un bar o en un restaurante, un simple **"Te invito"** identifica a la persona que pagará en esa ocasión. Queda entendido que la otra persona "invitará", o sea, pagará la próxima vez. Estando en un bar o en un café con un grupo de amigos, la norma es que una persona diferente compre cada "ronda" de bebidas y no que una sola persona pague todas las bebidas durante toda la noche. Cuando te invitan en América Latina o en España, es muy ofensivo insistir en pagar tu parte de la cuenta. Por el otro lado, cuando tú has invitado a una persona a comer o a ir al cine, no te sorprendas de que esa persona no haga el menor esfuerzo para pagar su comida o su entrada. Hay que tener en cuenta que este sistema recíproco que se sigue en el mundo hispánico reparte los costos con la misma eficacia (y con más discreción) que la costumbre de dividir una cuenta u otros gastos en el momento de pagar.

Preguntas

1. Imagínate que un joven colombiano o uruguayo invita a un amigo a salir a tomar un café o a cenar. Según la Ventanilla, ¿cuál es la obligación del amigo que invita? ¿El invitado tiene también una obligación? ¿Cuál es?
2. ¿Cuáles son una diferencia y una semejanza entre el sistema norteamericano del *Dutch treat* y el sistema de la cultura hispánica explicado en la Ventanilla?

CORRESPONDENCIA COMERCIAL: SALUDOS Y DESPEDIDAS

	Saludos	*Despedidas*
Más formal	Muy señor mío (señora mía):	Su servidor(a),
	Distinguido/-a... :	Respetuosamente,
		De usted muy atentamente,
		Suyo/-a muy atentamente,

| Menos formal | Estimado/-a... : | Cordialmente, |
| | | Atentamente, |

The greetings and closings are arranged in order from more formal to less formal. Any of the closings can, however, be used with any of the greetings.

Saludos y despedidas. Escoge un saludo y una despedida apropiados para cada una de las situaciones siguientes.

This activity involves only the selection of the heading and the closing.

Expansion: Have students write one of the letters as an in-class or outside-of-class writing assignment.

1. una carta a un cliente que tiene una cuenta atrasada (Además de ser cliente, tú lo conoces personalmente.)
2. una carta al presidente de una corporación en la cual le pides que patrocine a un estudiante internacional en la universidad
3. una carta al director de una agencia de turismo en la cual tú le das las gracias por toda su ayuda
4. una carta a un ex-profesor tuyo (una ex-profesora tuya) en la cual le pides una carta de recomendación
5. una carta al representante del servicio de reclamos (*customer service*) de la compañía de teléfonos en la cual disputas el saldo de la última cuenta

USO PRÁCTICO DEL ESPAÑOL   *Ojalá* + Subjunctive

Ojalá with the imperfect subjunctive to express a counterfactual desire at the moment of speech (¡Ojalá que estuviera mi hermano aquí para ayudarnos!) will be taken up in Chapter 11, first etapa, along with other contrary-to-fact expressions.

Ojalá is a word borrowed from Arabic which in Spanish expresses an especially fervent wish or desire. It is sometimes used by itself with the approximate meaning of, "I certainly hope so!"

—Ayer mi compañero de cuarto tuvo una entrevista para un trabajo nuevo. ¿Crees tú que le darán el puesto?
—**¡Ojalá!** (= **¡Ojalá** que sí!)

Usually, however, *Ojalá* is followed by the subjunctive, just as with other expressions of emotion.

Mañana tenemos el día libre. **¡Ojalá que no llueva!**

Ponerlo a prueba

A. Fiestas y más fiestas. Paco y Roberto piensan preparar una cena para algunos de sus amigos. Mientras hablan, expresan sus deseos en cuanto a ciertos aspectos de la comida y la reunión. Con un compañero (una compañera) representen los papeles de Roberto y de Paco y preparen un diálogo.

Modelo: Paco: (venir todos los que han invitado)
   Paco: *Ojalá que vengan todos los que hemos invitado.*

Roberto: (no olvidar traer discos)
Paco: (Elena preparar quesadillas)
Roberto: (Carlos no llegar con su libro de biología)
Paco: (tener suficiente comida)
Roberto: (el chile colorado no estar demasiado picante)

B. Una invitación por teléfono.   Susana y Elena han decidido hacer una fiesta para celebrar el fin del semestre. Observa los dibujos a continuación y prepara diálogos para acompañarlos.

This activity is meant to be written. Students produce an invitation and two responses, one response accepting and the other declining.

C. Una invitación. Usando las palabras clave, escribe las oraciones que podrías usar en las siguientes situaciones.

1. Escribiendo invitaciones a una fiesta
   a. motivo / fin del semestre
   b. llevar a cabo / viernes / 21 horas
   c. gusto / invitar

2. Aceptando una invitación
   a. amable / invitar
   b. querer / llevar
   c. aceptar / gusto

3. Rechazando una invitación
   a. sentir / fiesta
   b. agradecer / saludar
   c. compromiso / viernes

CH. "Lo siento mucho, pero…" Llena los espacios con las palabras y frases de la lista que está a continuación. Hay que conjugar algunos de los verbos.

compromiso	hacer el favor	saludar
de mi parte	invitar	sentir mucho
decirles	poder	
haberme		

Follow-up: Have students rewrite the paragraph as a third-person narrative for homework: La semana pasada su amiga Alicia le…

La semana pasada mi amiga Alicia me _____ a asistir a un baile, pero no _____ ir porque ya tenía otro _____. La llamé y le pedí que me _____ de _____ a mis amigos _____ y de _____ que _____ no poder asistir. También le di las gracias por _____ invitado.

D. Preguntas personales

1. ¿Cuándo fue la última vez que escribiste una carta de agradecimiento? ¿A quién? ¿Con qué motivo?
2. Menciona una vez que recibiste una carta de agradecimiento. ¿En qué circunstancias?
3. ¿Cuándo fue la última vez que recibiste una invitación por correo? ¿Para qué tipo de actividad era?
4. ¿Cuándo fue la última vez que rechazaste una invitación a una fiesta? ¿Por qué?
5. ¿Qué compromisos tienes para el próximo fin de semana?
6. ¿Cómo sueles responder cuando una persona te agradece algo en que le has ayudado?
7. ¿Qué has hecho recientemente por otra persona?

E. Diálogos. En cada uno de los diálogos, da una respuesta apropiada según el caso.

1. Marta: Ana, te esperamos en casa el sábado por la noche. Vamos a tener un baile.
   Ana: …
2. Pepe: ¡Qué vestido más elegante!
   Teresa: Gracias, Pepe, …
3. Susana: ¡Ay, me duele todo el cuerpo!
   Elena: …
4. Alberto (por teléfono): Quisiera hablar con Mauricio, por favor.
   Criada: …
5. Profesora Suárez: ¿Quieres que les diga que no podrás asistir?
   Paco: Sí, profesora, …

F. Una fiesta de sorpresa. Cuenta la historia de la fiesta de sorpresa para Roberto, basándote en la información que aparece a continuación. Empieza así:

Roberto cenó a las 6:00 y volvió a su cuarto para estudiar. Estaba leyendo su libro de biología cuando…

1. The phone rang.
2. Alicia asked Roberto to come over for a study break.
3. Roberto tried to refuse, but Alicia insisted.
4. Alicia suggested that they could study together.
5. Roberto arrived and knocked on Alicia's door.
6. Alicia told him to come in.
7. All of his friends jumped up and yelled "Surprise!"

> Have students work in groups to create a narrative. As an extension, you might have them write the dialogue of the phone conversation between Roberto and Alicia.

INVESTIGAR LA GRAMÁTICA   Más sobre el imperfecto del subjuntivo

> **OJO:** Refer to Chapters 7 and 8 for the major uses of the subjunctive.

> **OJO:** See Chapter 7, first *etapa* and Chapter 8, third *etapa*.

In Chapter 9 you learned the forms and practiced some of the uses of the imperfect subjunctive. In this *etapa* you will use the imperfect subjunctive in additional contexts.

1. The subjunctive is used to describe places, things, and events that were not or are not within the experience of the speaker.

Hoy voy de compras. Quiero comprar un suéter **que cueste** entre $30 y $40. A ver si puedo encontrar uno **que me guste y que no me ponga** en bancarrota (*bankruptcy*).

Ayer fui de compras. Quería comprar un suéter **que costara** entre $30 y $40, pero no pude encontrar ninguno **que me gustara** a ese precio. Por fin tuve que comprar uno **que costaba** $50.

OJO: See Chapter 7, third *etapa*.

2. The subjunctive is used after verbs that express desires or attempt to influence the behavior of others.

Este semestre nuestro profesor **insiste en que todos hablemos** español. El semestre pasado tampoco **permitió que habláramos** inglés.

Mis padres **quieren que yo pase** las vacaciones de verano en casa, pero prefiero quedarme cerca de la universidad para trabajar.

El verano pasado también no me quedé aquí para trabajar. **Quería que mi familia viniera** a visitarme, pero les fue imposible.

OJO: See Chapter 8, first *etapa*.

3. The subjunctive is used with personal expressions that are applied to particular individuals and situations.

Es importante que Julio consiga un buen trabajo porque tiene muchos gastos en la universidad.

Por eso también **era necesario que él trabajara** durante las vacaciones de primavera. Encontró un trabajo excelente que le gustó mucho.

OJO: See Chapter 8, second *etapa*.

4. The subjunctive is used with expressions and verbs of emotion.

Me alegro mucho de que mi familia piense visitarme este verano. **Fue triste que no pudiéramos** reunirnos el verano pasado.

OJO: *Fue triste* means "it was sad." To express "I was/felt sad," you would say *Estaba triste*.

5. The subjunctive is used after verbs and expressions of doubt and denial.

Mis padres dudan que yo pueda ganar tanto dinero como gané el verano pasado. **No creen que la compañía me permita** trabajar tantas horas por semana.

Mis padres tienen razón. Hablé con mi jefe y él me dijo que **dudaba que pudiera** trabajar más de 45 horas por semana.

OJO: See Chapter 8, third *etapa*.

Ponerlo a prueba

A. **Preparativos para la fiesta.** La profesora Suárez está revisando mentalmente sus preparativos para la fiesta. Siguiendo el modelo, reproduce lo que ella se dijo para sí misma.

Modelo: decir / mi esposo / enviar las invitaciones
Le dije a mi esposo que enviara las invitaciones.

OJO: Remember that *pedir*, "to ask someone for something," takes the subjunctive. *Preguntar*, "to ask a question," takes the indicative.

OJO: In some of the sentences, note that *decir* means "to convey information" and so does not take the subjunctive. Analyze the sentences carefully before you respond.

1. pedir / Margarita / traer sus cintas
2. sugerir / Paco / venir por la tarde para ayudarme
3. pedir / Verónica / hacernos un plato de sus empanadas
4. decir / mi esposo / comprar los refrescos
5. decir / los invitados / llegar después de las ocho
6. decir / Esteban / (yo) querer que / invitar a su novia también
7. decir / los estudiantes / (yo) esperar que / (nosotros) hablar inglés en la fiesta
8. es importante / (yo) tener todo listo el día anterior
9. ojalá que / todos / divertirse en la fiesta

OJO: No tienes que usar siempre el verbo **recomendar.** Puedes sustituirlo por **decir, aconsejar, pedir, insistir en...**

B. **Fuimos a la clínica ayer y el médico nos recomendó...** Toda la familia Rosales fue a la clínica ayer. Di tú lo que el médico les dijo a los miembros de la familia. Sigue el modelo.

Modelo: Danny / comer menos comida con grasa
El médico le recomendó a Danny que comiera menos comida con grasa.

1. Rosita / mirar menos televisión y hacer más ejercicio
2. la abuelita / descansar por la tarde
3. la señora de Rosales / ir al hospital para una radiografía de pecho
4. el señor Rosales / dejar de fumar y bajar de peso
5. Alfredo / seguir con su programa de levantar pesas
6. la tía Norma / leer unos artículos de revista sobre la nutrición
7. el tío Pedro / acordarse de tomar sus pastillas para la presión sanguínea
8. Tomasina / consultar con un cirujano

OJO: Tienes que usar la imaginación.

C. **Las dudas.** Yolanda siempre duda de todo y no quiere creer nada hasta que alguien le demuestre que es la verdad. Expresa las dudas de Yolanda, siguiendo el modelo.

Modelo: el profesor / darnos un examen antes de las vacaciones
Ayer Yolanda dudaba que el profesor nos diera un examen antes de las vacaciones, pero hoy el profesor nos dio un examen de sorpresa.

1. hacer buen tiempo hoy
2. la película nueva / ser tan buena como su favorita, *Lo que el viento se llevó*
3. su amigo / poder terminar su tarea en dos horas
4. servirse / una cena deliciosa en la cafetería
5. su compañera de cuarto / querer acompañarla a una fiesta
6. el libro que buscaba / estar en la biblioteca

CH. **Habla Yolanda.** Imagínate que eres Yolanda y estás expresando las dudas y deseos de la Actividad C. Sigue el modelo y ¡usa tu imaginación!

Modelo: *Dudo que el profesor nos dé examen antes de las vacaciones. ¡Ojalá que no nos dé uno!*

OJO: Vas a usar varias formas de los verbos. Lee con cuidado.

D. **La larga aventura de Evelina buscando un apartamento.** Lee la historia de Evelina y escribe las palabras que faltan.

Evelina decidió buscar un apartamento, porque ya no le _____ (**gustar**) el apartamento donde _____ (**vivir**). Quería un apartamento que _____ (**ser**) más grande y sobre todo que _____ (**tener**) una cocina con más espacio y más luz natural. No le _____ (**gustar**) cocinar en la oscuridad. Durante tres semanas _____ (**buscar**) el apartamento perfecto y no encontró ninguno que le _____ (**parecer**) apropiado. Por fin _____ (**encontrarse**) un día con su amiga Antonia. Antonia le dijo que quería que ella _____ (**conocer**) a su primo Faustino, porque Faustino _____ (**tener**) un apartamento muy lindo y _____ (**pensar**) mudarse a otra ciudad. "¡Qué bueno!" pensó Evelina. "Ojalá que me _____ (**gustar**) el apartamento y ojalá que Faustino _____ (**querer**) mudarse."

Al día siguiente, Evelina y Faustino _____ (**conocerse**). Pero en vez de hablar de apartamentos, los dos _____ (**descubrir**) que _____ (**tener**) mucho en común. Un año después de conocerse, _____ (**casarse**) y ahora los dos _____ (**vivir**) felices en el apartamento de Faustino.

This can be assigned as written homework.

E. Más obligaciones de la niñez. Lee las oraciones incompletas que están a continuación. Después, termínalas de acuerdo con tus experiencias de cuando eras niño/-a. Al final debes tener un párrafo lógico.

1. Cuando era niño/-a, mis padres siempre insistían en que yo...
2. Insistían en eso porque temían que yo...
3. Nunca permitían que (mis hermanos y yo)...
4. Pero no es natural que los niños siempre...
5. Recuerdo una vez que yo...

Haz las siguientes actividades con un compañero (una compañera).

A. Una invitación aceptada

Estudiante A

You are planning a party. Call your friend.

1. Invite him or her to the party.
2. Say when and where the party will be.
3. Say who will be there.
4. Tell him or her what to bring.
5. Say that it is all right to bring a friend.
6. End the conversation.

The role-play directions are in English to avoid giving away the vocabulary. Students should be alerted to the uses of llevar *and* traer *before they begin the role play.* Llevar: *to take something to a place different from where the speaker is located.* Traer: *to bring something to where the speaker is located. Note that this usage is different in English.*

Estudiante B

Your friend calls to invite you to a party.

1. Accept the invitation; you are pleased to be invited.
2. Ask when and where the party will be.
3. Ask who else will be there.
4. Offer to bring something.
5. Ask if you can bring a friend.
6. Thank your friend and say good-bye.

B. Una invitación rechazada

Estudiante A

You are planning a dinner party. You call to invite a friend.

1. Extend the invitation.
2. When your friend refuses, express your regret.
3. Ask if he or she would like to get together another time.

Estudiante B

A friend calls to invite you to a dinner party.

1. You are unable to go. Express your regrets.
2. Explain what your previous commitment is.
3. Suggest another time and place to get together.

Actividad C is a paired activity in which one of the students will be the caller and the other will be the person called. The activity should last no more than two or three minutes, then the roles should be reversed. You may want to have students sit back-to-back so that they cannot give visual cues to one another.

C. ¡Ven a una fiesta! Muy de repente decidiste hacer una fiesta. Ahora que unos amigos han llegado y la fiesta está en marcha, tú llamas a otro amigo (otra amiga), le dices lo que está pasando y lo (o la) invitas a participar. Con un compañero (una compañera), hagan los dos papeles de anfitrión/-ona e invitado/-a e inventen la conversación telefónica.

OTRA VUELTA

Play instructor tape, 2 min.

Vuelve ahora a la Entrada que escuchaste al comienzo de esta etapa. Escúchala otra vez y llena el formulario que aparece a continuación.

> **Las invitaciones**
>
> Dos expresiones para hacer una invitación:
>   a.
>   b.
>
> Una expresión para aceptar una invitación:
>
> Una expresión para rechazar una invitación:

COMENTARIO CULTURAL

La puntualidad

Desde el punto de vista latinoamericano o español, la mayoría de los estadounidenses parecen ser muy puntuales. Sin embargo, el concepto de lo que es la puntualidad depende de la cultura de uno: en diferentes culturas, la puntualidad se define y se entiende de diferentes maneras. Lo que se considera "llegar tarde" en una sociedad puede considerarse "llegar a tiempo" en otra. La mayoría de las reuniones sociales, por ejemplo, los bailes o las fiestas en casa de alguien, comienzan más tarde en el mundo hispánico que en los Estados Unidos, y sólo se acaban cuando la última persona haya salido. Casi nunca se especifica la hora en que termina una invitación, ya que hacer tal cosa sería el colmo de la mala educación.

En el caso de un coctel o de una fiesta que se celebra en una casa particular, no es raro que los primeros invitados lleguen media hora o hasta una hora después de la hora anunciada en la invitación, ni que los invitados sigan llegando hasta mucho más tarde. En realidad, es muy posible que los anfitriones no estén listos para recibir a los invitados a la hora citada, o como se dice en español, a las personas que llegan **a la hora americana**. En vista de esto, no es necesario rechazar una invitación sólo porque tienes otro compromiso para la misma noche a menos que tu compromiso te ocupe toda la noche. En vez de rechazar la invitación, lo más probable es que una persona cumpla con su otro compromiso y llegue más tarde a la fiesta.

Si en vez de una fiesta la invitación es para una comida más bien formal, es muy importante llegar a la hora anunciada, porque la comida estará preparada para servirse a esa hora. Otros eventos que normalmente comienzan a la hora anunciada son los cines y los vuelos de avión. En estos casos, si no llegas a tiempo, pierdes la función o el avión te deja.

¿Se hace o no se hace? Indica si las siguientes acciones son aceptables o inaceptables en un contexto cultural hispánico y explica por qué.

1. Llegas 30 minutos antes de la hora anunciada para una fiesta para ayudar a los anfitriones a organizar todo.
2. Invitas a unos funcionarios del Partido Liberal a una recepción que se celebrará desde las ocho hasta las once de la noche.

3. Appropriate. You would simply go to the party after you and your associate have parted for the evening. 4. Appropriate. As long as guests are present, the host is expected to continue providing for them. 5. Inappropriate. Coffee and/or tea may be provided, but no suggestion should be made that it is being served because it is time to leave.

3. Aceptas una invitación a una fiesta la misma noche que tienes cita con un colega para tomar algo y hablar de negocios.
4. Ofreces más bocadillos y bebidas a los invitados, aunque ya son las tres de la madruga y algunos invitados ya se han ido.
5. Les dices a los invitados que vas a preparar café para que puedan llegar bien a su casa.

Guía cultural. Con base en la información de este Comentario cultural y tus respuestas a la Actividad anterior, escribe

■ una lista de "reglas sociales" para anfitriones e invitados hispánicos
■ una lista correspondiente para anfitriones e invitados norteamericanos

Reglas sociales

Anfitriones hispánicos
1.
2.
3.
4.

Anfitriones norteamericanos
1.
2.
3.
4.

Invitados hispánicos
1.
2.
3.
4.

Invitados norteamericanos
1.
2.
3.
4.

SEGUNDA ETAPA "¿Qué me pongo?"

ENTRADA

Play instructor tape, 1 min.

"¡Qué fiesta más divertida!"

Vas a escuchar una conversación entre dos personas. Están hablando acerca de una fiesta reciente. Al escuchar la conversación, trata de descubrir

- el motivo de la fiesta
- quiénes asistieron
- algunas cosas que hicieron los invitados en la fiesta

Apuntes sobre la conversación

El motivo de la fiesta:

Los invitados:

Las actividades:

ANTES DE LEER

READING STRATEGY 10

Recognize relationships between words and phrases

One of the characteristics of connected text, that is, text in which sentences are joined to form paragraphs, is that relationships between phrases and sentences are established. For example, when the word "if" connects two thoughts, the reader knows that some condition is being imposed as a prerequisite to whatever is being reported: "If (When) you receive an invitation that concludes with R.S.V.P., you should respond immediately." This establishes a condition under which a response is necessary and connects the receipt of an invitation with the act of responding. In Spanish, words that indicate this type of relationship include *si, cuando, pero, en vez de,* and *al contrario.*

Preparación

Vamos a suponer que se te pidió que le explicaras a una persona que no conoce las normas de tu cultura algunas de las reglas que hay que respetar al ser invitado a cenar en la casa de alguien. Haz una lista de tres cosas que se considerarían "buena educación" y tres que se considerarían "mala educación" las cuales el invitado debe tener en cuenta.

Recomendado

1. dar las gracias por la invitación
2.
3.
4.

No recomendado

1. no responder a la invitación
2.
3.
4.

Estudiar y practicar

denotar	to signify
estar al tanto (de)	to be up-to-date, current
evitar	to avoid
la pareja	couple; other member of a couple
el rato	short period of time
tener en cuenta	to take into account, bear in mind

LEER

Al leer el artículo, subraya las palabras que parecen establecer relaciones condicionales entre las frases.

Modelo: <u>Cuando</u> la inviten a una fiesta, a una cena o a un coctel, tenga en cuenta todos los detalles que denotan que usted está al tanto de la etiqueta y que, además, es una persona con buenos modales.

LOS "SÍ" Y LOS "NO" DE LA ETIQUETA...

Cuando la inviten a una fiesta, a una cena o a un coctel, tenga en cuenta todos estos detalles que denotan que usted está al tanto de la etiqueta y que, además, es una persona con buenas maneras...

● Responda prontamente. Si la invitación se la hacen por teléfono y es extensiva a su esposo o a su pareja, dígale a la anfitriona que en cuanto consulte con él le confirmará su asistencia.

● Hágale saber a su anfitriona que usted va a ir con un compañero para que la invitación incluya a ambos y para que no cuente con usted como posible pareja de otro hombre que vaya solo.

● Si no va a asistir, dígalo inmediatamente. Bastará con un: "Lo siento, tengo un compromiso".

SI LA INVITAN A UNA CENA
● Lleve un pequeño regalo.

SI LA INVITACION ES A UN COCTEL
● Vaya a saludar a la anfitriona en cuanto llegue.
● Preséntese usted misma a los otros invitados si la anfitriona está ocupada o no se encuentra cerca.

DESPUES DE LA FIESTA
● Envíe una nota de agradecimiento o llame por teléfono al día siguiente y hágale saber el rato tan agradable que pasó.

● Si realmente le agradó la fiesta, corresponda con una invitación similar. Pero si no, evítese pasar otra velada poco agradable.

● Si lleva de regalo algo de comer o una botella de vino, no espere que la anfitriona lo sirva. Y si lleva un ramo de flores, ofrézcase para ponerlas usted misma en un jarrón y así la anfitriona no tendrá que abandonar a sus otros invitados mientras lo hace.

● Comparta con los demás, no pase la noche exclusivamente con su pareja.

● No vaya a encender el televisor o el tocadiscos, eso le corresponde a la dueña de la casa, si ella lo desea.

● Nunca ponga a la anfitriona en el compromiso de decirle a qué otras personas ha invitado, además de usted.

● No asuma que puede asistir con su pareja si solamente la han invitado a usted.

● Una vez que acepte la invitación, no trate de evadirse del compromiso.

DESPUÉS DE LEER

Follow-up activities: 1. In groups, decide which three rules are most important. Debate between groups. 2. Arrive at principles of "etiquette"—what really matters and what is just "form." 3. Group work: Have the students invent a new set of etiquette rules and explain when these rules are applied. Have them create an outrageous new etiquette, the more creative the better.

The term "con buenas maneras" found in the first paragraph of the reading selection is an anglicism—a word "created" in Spanish from the English expression. The appropriate term is *persona de buenos modales* or *persona educada*.

A. Condiciones y resultados. En las columnas apropiadas, apunta por lo menos cinco ejemplos de palabras clave entre una condición y un resultado.

Palabra clave	*Condición*	*Resultado*
Cuando	la inviten a una fiesta, cena o coctel	tenga en cuenta detalles que denotan que está al tanto de la etiqueta

You may want to point out that in the United States, it is often considered bad manners to rest your left hand on the table if you are not using it to cut your food. (It should remain in your lap.) In some other countries, it is considered bad manners **not** to leave your left hand on the table. Similarly, in the United States we expect to find the napkin to the left of the plate when the table is set. In Colombia, for example, it is usually placed on the right.

B. Buenos modales. Considera otra vez la lista de reglas de la etiqueta de tu cultura que preparaste antes de leer el artículo. Cuenta el número de ejemplos que apuntaste que también están incluidos en el artículo. Luego, añade las reglas del artículo que no tienes todavía en tu lista.

C. Normas arbitrarias. Las normas de la etiqueta son a veces bastante arbitrarias. Por ejemplo, en muchas partes de los Estados Unidos se considera mala educación mantener el tenedor en la mano izquierda para llevarse la comida a la boca. Si uno quiere cortar un pedazo de carne, uno comienza con el cuchillo en la mano derecha y el tenedor en la mano izquierda; se corta la carne y después se coloca el cuchillo en el plato para poder cambiar el tenedor a la mano derecha. Sólo entonces se puede comer la carne. ¿No te parece ridícula esta costumbre? ¿Qué otras normas se aplican a la etiqueta de la mesa? ¿Son también arbitrarias o tienen alguna razón de ser?

VENTANILLA AL MUNDO HISPÁNICO   Hispanohablantes estadounidenses

Los hispanoparlantes en los Estados Unidos usan varias palabras para referirse a sí mismos. Así como no todos los que hablan inglés son ingleses, no todos los que hablan español son españoles. Por ejemplo, los habitantes de México son **mexicanos**; los de Costa Rica son **costarricenses**; los de Colombia son **colombianos**. Como ya leíste en el Comentario cultural de la Segunda etapa del Capítulo 4, el término **chicano** se refiere únicamente a los ciudadanos de los Estados Unidos de ascendencia mexicana; no incluye a los **cubanos**, a los **puertorriqueños** (también conocidos como **borinqueños**) ni a los de ningún otro grupo hispánico en los Estados Unidos. Si tienes dudas de cómo referirte a alguna persona, lo mejor es sencillamente preguntarle a esa persona, —¿Es usted latino?

Acuérdate de que todos los que viven en el hemisferio occidental son "americanos", no solamente los estadounidenses.

Preguntas

1. ¿Qué término usa la gente hispana en tu región para referirse a sí misma? ¿Hispanos? ¿Latinos? Pregúntales a dos o tres personas si no estás seguro/-a.
2. Hoy en día, cada vez hay más personas que rechazan ciertos términos que antes usaban para identificarse. Algunas personas de ascendencia mexicana prefieren llamarse **mexicano americanos** en vez de **chicanos**. Otros, que antes se decían **latinos** ahora no usan este término. ¿Sabes por qué? ¿Qué especulaciones tienes?

Marginal notes:
1. Have students ask other students and/or faculty members. 2. Some (especially older) Mexican Americans reject the term *chicano* because of its political connotations from the 1960s. Current discomfort with *latino/-a* and also *hispano/-a* comes from the historical and cultural imperialism inherent in the terms, which derive from the Spanish Conquest. This issue is highly subjective and personal, so discussion will not be conclusive.

AUMENTAR EL VOCABULARIO

denotar	*to signify*
estar a gusto	*to be comfortable, at ease*
cómodo/-a	*comfortable*
incómodo/-a	*uncomfortable*
estar al tanto de	*to be up-to-date, current*
la estrella	*star*
el (la) estrella de cine	*movie star*
evitar	*to avoid*
fijarse en	*to notice*
Me he fijado...	*I have noticed . . .*
el (la) hispanohablante	*Spanish-speaking person*
de habla española	*Spanish-speaking*
los modales	*manners*
Es una persona educada.	*He/She has good manners.*
Es una persona de buenos modales.	
la pareja	*couple; other member of a couple*
ponerse	*to become; to wear*
estrenar	*to wear or use for the first time*
puesto que	*since, given that*
¡Qué va!	*Don't be ridiculous!*
¡No seas tonto/-a!	*Don't be a fool.*
¡Vaya!	*Go on, you're joking.*
¡Ay! ¡No exageres!	*What an exaggeration.*
¡Qué va! Eso no es nada.	*That's not important.*
el rato	*short period of time*

OJO: A synonym is *hispanoparlante*. Both literally mean "one who speaks Spanish."

OJO: To have bad manners is expressed as *ser mal educado/-a*. Note that *la educación* in this context is a false cognate. It means "upbringing," not formal education in school.

recordar (ue)	to remember
se me ocurre (que)...	it occurs to me (that)...
sea lo (el, la) que sea...	whatever it might be...
tener en cuenta	to take into account, bear in mind

EXPRESIONES LLAMATIVAS

¡Cuidado!   ¡Mira!

¡Cálmate!   ¡No exageres!
¡Tranquilo!

Actividad. Explica lo que pasa en los dibujos. En cada uno, explica por qué la persona usa la expresión indicada.

USO PRÁCTICO DEL ESPAÑOL   El tiempo futuro

You have already learned a number of ways to talk about future time in Spanish. The most common way, especially when the future event or situation is relatively close to the present moment, is simply to use the present tense.

Mañana **comienzan** las vacaciones. **Salimos** para la casa de mis padres a las 8:00 de la mañana.

In Chapter 2, you learned that certain verbs can be combined with infinitives to refer to the future.

Pensamos quedarnos con ellos cuatro días y después **esperamos** pasar otros tres días en las montañas. **Vamos a** acampar en un lugar muy aislado que tiene un lago magnífico.

You have also seen that the present subjunctive often refers to the future because it is used to express desires, doubts and other emotions about things that will or may happen subsequently.

Ojalá que no haya problemas con el vuelo. También **espero que haga** buen tiempo.

Spanish also has a future tense that is used when the anticipated event or situation is viewed as relatively distant from the present moment. All verbs use the same set of endings for the future tense and most verbs add these endings directly to the infinitive.

hablar		comer		vivir	
hablar**é**	hablar**emos**	comer**é**	comer**emos**	vivir**é**	vivir**emos**
hablar**ás**	hablar**éis**	comer**ás**	comer**éis**	vivir**ás**	vivir**éis**
hablar**á**	hablar**án**	comer**á**	comer**án**	vivir**á**	vivir**án**

Los estudiantes internacionales **llegarán** en el verano. Primero **se presentarán** en una sesión de orientación, y luego **comenzarán** sus clases.

A few verbs have irregular stems in the future, but the endings are all exactly the same as above.

Querer (querré, querrás...) also has an irregular stem, but is rarely used in the future and need not be practiced.

decir → dir**é**, dir**ás**, dir**á**, dir**emos**, dir**éis**, dir**án**
haber → habré, habrás...
hacer → haré, harás...
poder → podré, podrás...
poner → pondré, pondrás...
saber → sabré, sabrás...
salir → saldré, saldrás...
tener → tendré, tendrás...
venir → vendré, vendrás...

Two Spanish proverbs that use the future tense are: *Dime con quién andas y te diré quién eres* **and** *Será lo que deba ser.*

—**Pondremos** la lista de invitados cerca del teléfono.

—Sí, y así **podremos** apuntar a quienes **vendrán**.

The future tense is often used to "wonder" about what's happening at the present time.

| Veo que no está en clase hoy la profesora. ¿**Estará** enferma? | *I see that the teacher isn't in class today. I wonder if she's sick.* (*Do you think she's sick?*) |

The future tense is also used to speculate on the cause or reason for a present state of affairs.

| Sí. Está mal del estómago. **Será** algo que comió anoche. | *Yes. She has an upset stomach. It's probably something she ate last night.* |

Ponerlo a prueba

In addition to new vocabulary, this exercise recycles use of the subjunctive from Chapter 7, third *etapa*.

A. Así te aconsejo. Un amigo tuyo que acaba de llegar a los Estados Unidos se preocupa bastante de la etiqueta estadounidense. Acaba de recibir una invitación a una cena en casa de uno de sus profesores. Te pregunta qué debe hacer para demostrarle a su profesor que es una persona educada. Lee las situaciones a continuación y dile lo que debe hacer o lo que **no** debe hacer en cada situación.

Modelo: Un profesor mío me ha invitado a cenar en su casa.
Pues, te aconsejo que respondas pronto a la invitación.

1. Pienso llevar un ramo de flores.
2. Quiero saber quiénes más van a asistir.
3. Espero que pongan unos discos nuevos.
4. Quiero conocer a todos los otros invitados.
5. Ojalá que consideren que soy una persona con buenos modales.
6. Quiero que mi profesor me conozca muy bien.
7. Espero pasar un rato muy agradable en la cena.
8. No sé si habrá algo más interesante para hacer este fin de semana o no.

B. ¿Qué debo hacer si...? Tu amigo todavía está preocupado con la cena. Dile lo que debe (o **no** debe) hacer si ocurre lo siguiente.

Modelo: si me invitan a cenar
Si te invitan a cenar, responde pronto a la invitación.

1. si no voy a asistir
2. si la invitación es a un coctel
3. si paso un rato agradable
4. si me encanta la fiesta
5. si **no** me pasa nada agradable
6. si llevo un ramo de flores
7. si no conozco a nadie en la fiesta
8. si no hay música
9. si no sé quiénes más van a asistir
10. si acepto la invitación y luego decido que no quiero asistir

C. ¿En qué situación estamos? Lee estos comentarios y decide en qué situaciones se podría oírlos.

Modelo: —Lo siento, pero no puedo. Tengo un compromiso previo.
Acabo de invitar a mi amigo a una fiesta.

1. —No quiero ver esa película. La actriz no me gusta nada.
2. —Claro que te recuerdo. ¿No nos conocimos en casa de David?

Segunda etapa **445**

Remind students that percentages are spoken as *por ciento*.

3. —El 15% de los estudiantes en esta universidad son hispanohablante.
4. —Voy a estrenar mi traje nuevo esta noche. Maricarmen va a presentarme a sus padres.
5. —Me estoy poniendo un poco nerviosa. Pronto vendrán los invitados.

CH. Mini-diálogos. Con un compañero (una compañera) de la clase, preparen conversaciones basadas en las situaciones mencionadas en la Actividad C. La oración original de la actividad debe ser una de las líneas de la conversación.

D. Imagínate. Has recibido una invitación a una fiesta formal y elegante que tendrá lugar a finales del mes. Quieres que un amigo tuyo (una amiga tuya) te acompañe, pero no quiere ir. Trata de convencerlo/la. Fíjate en el dibujo de la fiesta (tu imagen mental) e imagínate que le tienes que describir el escenario a tu amigo/-a para convencerlo/la a asistir.

Modelo: *Habrá muchos invitados.*

¿Qué le dirás en cuanto a...

1. los invitados?
2. la ropa que llevarán las mujeres?
3. la ropa que llevarán los hombres?
4. lo que harán los invitados?
5. lo que hará la anfitriona toda la noche?
6. tu reacción a la fiesta en general?

E. ¿Qué pasará después? Aquí están algunos de los invitados la mañana después de la fiesta. Describe el estado físico de cada uno/-a y lo que estará haciendo según el dibujo.

Modelo: *Roberto no se sentirá muy bien, pero a las doce menos cuarto de la mañana tendrá que levantarse. Le quedan quince minutos de descanso.*

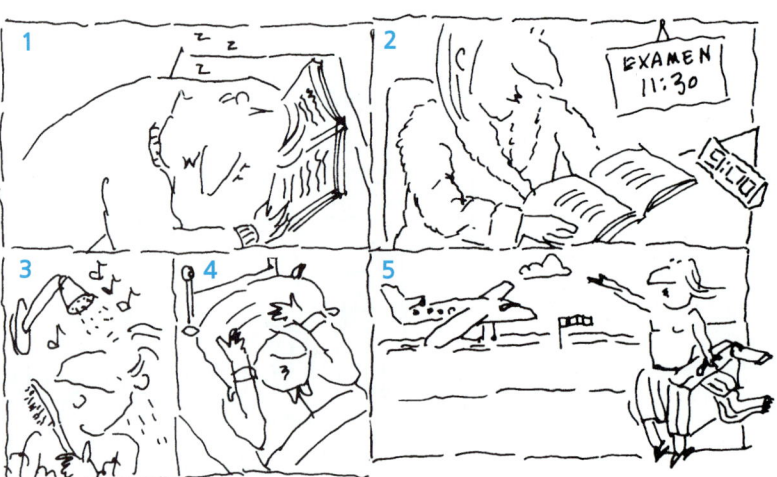

1.
2.
3.
4.
5.

F. Preguntas personales

1. Para ti, ¿qué es lo más difícil de ser anfitrión/-ona de una fiesta?
2. Menciona algo raro que hayas visto en una fiesta recientemente.
3. Cuando quieres vestirte formalmente, ¿qué ropa te pones?
4. ¿Qué es lo más agradable que recuerdas de las fiestas de tu niñez?
5. Ahora que eres adulto/-a, ¿qué prefieres hacer en una fiesta?
6. En tu opinión, ¿qué se necesita para tener una buena fiesta?
7. Y para ti, ¿cómo se arruina una fiesta?

INVESTIGAR LA GRAMÁTICA El condicional

The conditional tense is used to talk about what someone **would** do or what **would** happen under some set of circumstances.

Evelina creía que la universidad le **daría** una beca para continuar sus estudios.	*Evelina thought the university would give her a scholarship to continue her studies.*
Le **gustaría** estudiar negocios internacionales. **Empezaría** el semestre que viene y **terminaría** en dos años.	*She would like to study international business. She would start next semester and would finish in two years.*

The conditional is also used in indirect quotations in which someone reports what another person said in the past.

El médico me dijo que me **recetaría** un antibiótico y que **me sentiría** mejor dentro de seis horas.	*The doctor told me that he would prescribe an antibiotic and that I would feel better in six hours.*
Yo llamé a mi jefe para decirle que no **iría** a la oficina y que **volvería** a llamarlo mañana.	*I called my boss to tell him that I would not go to the office and that I would call him again tomorrow.*

For verbs that are regular in the conditional tense, the endings, which are the same for all verbs, are added directly to the infinitive.

hablar		comer		vivir	
hablaría	hablaríamos	comería	comeríamos	viviría	viviríamos
hablarías	hablaríais	comerías	comeríais	vivirías	viviríais
hablaría	hablarían	comería	comerían	viviría	vivirían

Querer (querría, querrías...) also has an irregular stem, but is almost never used in the conditional and need not be practiced.

The verbs that have irregular stems in the future have the same stems in the conditional, but the endings are exactly the same as above.

decir	→	diría, dirías, diría, diríamos, diríais, dirían
haber	→	habría, habrías...
hacer	→	haría, harías...
poder	→	podría, podrías...
poner	→	pondría, pondrías...
saber	→	sabría, sabrías...
salir	→	saldría, saldrías...
tener	→	tendría, tendrías...
venir	→	vendría, vendrías...

Ponerlo a prueba

A. Si yo fuera (*If I were*) rico/-a. Vamos a suponer que has ganado la lotería y que de repente tienes muchísimo dinero. ¿Qué harías? Usa las siguientes frases para imaginar tu nueva vida. Empieza todas tus oraciones con la frase **Si yo fuera rico/-a...**

1. comprar un coche
2. viajar a Latinoamérica

3. ir a la playa, a las discotecas, ...
4. (no) poner dinero en el banco
5. tener dos casas, una en..., y la otra...
6. dar una parte del dinero a...

OJO: The future tense form of *hay* is *habrá*.

B. **¿Cómo será la excursión?** Los señores Almagro quieren pasar las vacaciones en Colombia y tienen muchas preguntas para el agente de viajes. Ayúdales a hacerlas, usando en cada pregunta un elemento de cada columna.

Modelo: *¿Cuánto costará el viaje?*

Follow-up: Have students take the role of the travel agent and answer the questions.

¿Cuánto	alojarse	en la capital?
¿Cuántos días	ir	el viaje?
¿Dónde	costar	primero?
¿Será posible	tener que	en la playa?
¿Qué documentación	pasar	en cada lugar?
¿Cuándo	estar por una semana	llevar?

C. **¿Qué dijo?** Elena cuidó a Susana cuando estaba enferma. Tú estás contando más tarde todo lo que Elena dijo, de acuerdo con el modelo.

Modelo: Elena dice que llamará al médico.
Elena dijo que llamaría al médico.

Expansion: Have students in turn mention something they are planning to do. Other students follow up with a report: *María dijo que...*

1. Elena dice que le dará a Susana dos pastillas de Mejoral.
2. Elena dice que le hará una taza de té.
3. Elena dice que su mamá recomendará un poco de agua mineral también.
4. Elena dice que Susana se sentirá mejor dentro de poco.
5. Elena le dice a Susana que el médico la verá en su consultorio a las 10:30.
6. Elena dice que saldrán de la casa a las 10:15.
7. Elena dice que Patricia vendrá para llevarlas al consultorio.
8. Elena dice que no habrá mucha gente en el consultorio a esa hora.

CH. **¿Qué hora será?** Conoces muy bien el horario de María Luisa, así que puedes adivinar a qué hora hace las actividades siguientes. Sigue el modelo.

Modelo: Es muy temprano y María Luisa está levantándose.
Serán las seis de la mañana.

1. María Luisa está entrando en su primera clase.
2. Está almorzando con sus amigos.
3. Está caminando hacia la biblioteca para estudiar con su amiga Mónica.
4. Llega tarde. Hace media hora que Mónica está esperándola.

5. Están saliendo de la biblioteca, después de estudiar mucho para un examen de economía.

6. María Luisa está en su cuarto, hablando por teléfono con sus padres.

7. Está de camino a la piscina; va a nadar.

D. **El mundo del futuro.** Imagínate que puedes predecir cómo será el mundo del futuro. Descríbelo.

1. En el mundo del futuro, todo el mundo tendrá...
2. Las escuelas serán muy diferentes; por ejemplo, ...
3. Habrá muchos cambios sociales. Por ejemplo, los médicos...
4. Comprar y preparar la comida será totalmente diferente porque...
5. En cuanto al transporte y los problemas del petróleo, ...

E. **El horóscopo.** Lee el párrafo que corresponda a tu signo del zodíaco y decide cuáles son tres cosas que harás hoy o mañana para cumplir con las predicciones. Entrevista a un compañero (una compañera) de la clase sobre sus planes, e informa a la clase.

EN EL CIELO

El Amor

por Daisy Trinidad

El amor nace y crece en el fondo del corazón. Hay tantas maneras de sentir y mostrar esta profunda emoción que uno se podría pasar toda la vida probándolas. En el zodíaco, cada signo tiene su propia forma, su estilo preferido de amar.

ARIES Quédate tranquilo hasta el 3 de enero. Mientras que tu planeta regente Marte está en retroceso, tu vida y tus planes están en el aire. No te enojes si tus proyectos no se realizan tan rápidamente como quieres. Ten paciencia. Las estrellas indican que tu año nuevo empezará con una poderosa explosión. En el amor, también tienes que tener cierta paciencia. Los arianos prefieren un amor fuerte, intenso y rápido.

TAURO ¡Este fin de año tú no eres tímido! Quieres festejar, celebrar y compartir con tus amigos y familiares hasta la madrugada. Está bien, pero trata de no ganar peso ni de abusar del alcohol. ¡Cuida tu salud y saluda a 1991! El amor, para los taureanos, es celebrar la belleza y la gracia. Tienes mucho cariño y calor y siempre estás listo para otro amor. Pero cuando estás en pareja, mantienes una relación estable y fiel.

GEMINIS Normalmente dices lo que piensas en cualquier ocasión. Pero ahora, cuando alguien (especialmente tu pareja) te pregunta algo, las palabras te faltan. No te preocupes. Esta debilidad transitoria desaparecerá después de la primera semana de enero. La lengua es tu zona erógena. Te gusta hablar de amor—antes, mientras y después. Para ti la música y las palabras de amor son como caricias.

(pasa a la próxima página)

ILUSTRACION POR ANDREA ARROYO

CANCER Hay tensión en tu vida, mientras los planetas Saturno, Neptuno y Urano estén opuestos a tu sol. Afortunadamente, Saturno saldrá de tu zona peligrosa en pocos meses. Venus, el planeta del amor y la alegría, se queda en tu sector del cielo en diciembre, dándote un descanso. Cáncer es el más cariñoso de los signos astrales y el más tímido. No puedes hacer el amor si no te sientes seguro, confortable y querido.

LEO Los leos que nacieron en el mes de julio pueden sentir un doble golpe de suerte este fin de año; los otros deben esperar a la primavera si quieren ganar la lotería. Pero las estrellas te favorecen en la salud y en el trabajo. El amor del leo es un amor orgulloso, celoso y a veces exhibicionista. Tú no puedes hacer el amor en las sombras cuando estás enamorado. La tuya es una pasión pública.

VIRGO Tendrás que enfrentarte con una persona que no está de acuerdo con tus ideas o planes. Aunque tú no eres argumentativa, ahora vale la pena luchar contra la oposición. Tú tienes razón, y en poco tiempo, tus oponentes van a cambiar de opinión. Los nativos de Virgo, conservadores en el amor, son también los conocedores del zodíaco. Tú gozas del amor en todos sus detalles, desde la ropa de tu pareja hasta el color y la textura de las sábanas.

LIBRA Tu situación hogareña mejorará antes del fin de año, y pasarás una Navidad rodeado de familia y amigos. Poco después, podrías viajar hacia otros países, otras aventuras. No trates asuntos legales hasta el fin de febrero, y no viajes sin un seguro de salud. Si el amor fuera política, los libras serían embajadores. Sabes mantener tu pareja feliz pero te aburres; conoces una persona muy bien y ya quieres conocer a otra.

ESCORPION Te sientes poderoso porque Júpiter y Plutón están bien puestos para ti y tu carrera. ¡Cuidado! Júpiter te hace sentir confiada cuando hay peligro a tus espaldas. Antes que empieces tus grandes proyectos, mira adelante y atrás. Los escorpiones sienten el amor y el sexo con una pasión que no tienen otros signos del zodíaco. Tu amor es fuerte, sagrado, muy físico y misterioso aun para tí mismo.

SAGITARIO Después de una Navidad feliz con tus familiares, posiblemente en un país exótico, deberás atender a tus asuntos financieros. No te gusta pensar en esas cosas, pero un espíritu libre tiene que hacer cosas prácticas de vez en cuando. Los sagitarios, caprichosos en el amor, no gustan de restricciones, leyes, ni personas dominantes, a menos que este sea tu juego preferido.

CAPRICORNIO Profundos cambios en tu punto de vista y tu filosofía personal te convertirán en un ser maduro y sabio, y tus amigos notarán la diferencia. Te pueden encantar las disciplinas chinas e indúes; pero no seas tan serio durante las fiestas del fin del año. También en el amor tiendes a ser demasiado serio. Muchas veces, los capricornios pasan años sin un amor. Pero cuando al fin caen, lo hacen como si fuera un terremoto.

 ACUARIO Tu carrera que parece llena de desafíos y decepciones, cambiará en pocos meses. Ahora tienes mucha energía y debes usarla para adelantar proyectos que tengas con tu pareja o asociados. Trata de enfocarte y de mantener tu disciplina. La comunicación a todos los niveles es muy importante para ti en el amor. Quieres saber todo de tu amante y a la misma vez eres un buen y simpático consejero para él o ella.

 PISCIS Tus amigos quieren tu atención. Ayúdalos, goza de su compañía, pero ten cuidado de amigos falsos. Eres muy generoso, pero en el mundo de hoy no se puede confiar en cualquiera. Los piscis buscan el amor ideal. Cuando estás enamorado, te sacrificas para mantener tus ilusiones. Pero la realidad te dice que el amor es una decepción, un engaño. Para ser feliz tienes que aprender que nunca el amor temporal puede ser ideal.

Haz las siguientes actividades con un compañero (una compañera).

A. ¡A la onda!

Estudiante A

Eres locutor de una emisora (*station*) de radio. Cada día llamas a alguien por teléfono para hacerle una serie de preguntas sobre tal o cual cosa. Esta vez, las preguntas tienen que ver con la etiqueta. Pregúntale su opinión sobre lo siguiente.

1. diferentes maneras de rechazar una invitación
2. posibles regalos apropiados y no apropiados para llevar a una anfitriona
3. el tipo de traje o vestido que se debe llevar a una fiesta que no es ni formal ni completamente informal
4. distintas maneras de despedirse de una fiesta si se quiere salir temprano
5. cómo sugerir a la anfitriona que cambie el tipo de música que está tocando

Estudiante B

Acabas de recibir una llamada telefónica del locutor de un programa de radio muy popular. Te hace una serie de preguntas sobre la etiqueta. Contesta las preguntas que te hace, diciéndole lo que opinas.

B. Así será. Con un compañero (una compañera) de la clase, discute tus opiniones sobre lo siguiente.

1. la vida social que esperas tener este año
2. lo fácil o difícil que son tus clases este año
3. la necesidad de conseguir un trabajo después de terminar los estudios
4. la importancia del español en relación a este trabajo
5. las diferencias entre la vida actual y la vida en el año 2000

OTRA VUELTA

Play instructor tape, 1 min.

Vuelve ahora a la Entrada que escuchaste al comienzo de esta etapa. Escúchala otra vez y describe brevemente la ropa que llevaba la anfitriona.

COMENTARIO CULTURAL

Las fiestas

Hay mucha gente que se supone, muchas veces equivocadamente, que *a party* es lo mismo que "una fiesta". En español la palabra "fiesta" implica ciertas cosas: un número bastante grande de invitados, bocadillos y bebidas, probablemente un buffet más tarde (ya que hay demasiadas personas para que se sirva una comida formal con todos sentados en una mesa) y sobre todo, música bailable. Por lo general, si falta una o más de estas características, el evento no se llama "una fiesta" sino "una reunión" o quizás "una tertulia".

Aunque algunas *parties* norteamericanas se parecen a las fiestas latinoamericanas, la palabra en inglés indica una variedad más amplia de reuniones y actividades sociales, las cuales en español se llamarían "comidas" (*dinner parties*) o "cocteles" (*cocktail parties*) y que no son sinónimos de "fiestas".

En español, la palabra "fiesta" también se usa para referirse a *holidays,* sean éstas seculares o religiosas. Si mañana tienes el día libre puedes decir "Mañana es día festivo" o "Mañana es día de fiesta" sin implicar que va a haber fiesta. La expresión "fiesta nacional" por lo general se refiere al día de la independencia: el 2 de mayo en España (que celebra la independencia del dominio francés), el 4 de julio en los Estados Unidos, el 5 de julio en Venezuela, el 9 de julio en Argentina, el 20 de julio en Colombia, el 16 de septiembre en México y el 19 de septiembre en Chile (tradicionalmente es también el día de las elecciones chilenas).

You may want to assign specific countries for students to look up, so that you get a more widespread pattern of holidays.

Actividad. Select a Spanish-speaking country, look it up in an encyclopedia, and make a list of its major national holidays. Bring your list to class, compare it with the lists compiled by your classmates, and see if there are certain dates that a number of countries have in common for important *fiestas*.

TERCERA ETAPA

La correspondencia personal

ENTRADA

[Play instructor tape, 3 min.]

"Hola, mami..."

Pablo Martinelli, un joven de Buenos Aires, ha viajado a los Estados Unidos a visitar a su hermano, Jorge, que estudia veterinaria en la universidad. Escucha la conversación entre Pablo y su mamá, que está en Buenos Aires. Para cada tema de la lista a continuación, escriba una pregunta que ella le hace a él.

Las preguntas de la Sra. de Martinelli

1. Salud:
2. Nuevos amigos:
3. Comida:
4. Idioma:
5. Regreso:

ANTES DE LEER Y ESCRIBIR

[Play student tape, 1 min.]

Estudiar y practicar

el (la) aguafiestas	"party pooper," "wet blanket"
darle las gracias (a alguien)	to thank (someone)
defenderse (ie)	to manage; to survive
en cuanto a	regarding, concerning
extrañar	to miss, long for (people, places)
impedir (i, i)	to hinder; to impede
Le (Te) ruego que...	I beg you to . . .

Preparación

Lee la carta que está a continuación y apunta la información siguiente:

■ cómo Susana empieza y termina la carta y por qué selecciona el saludo y la despedida que usa

Saludo: _____

Despedida: _____

■ dos maneras de expresar el agradecimiento
   1. _____
   2. _____

OJO: The formulaic expression "...el detalle que usted tuvo para conmigo..." expresses "the thoughtfulness you showed towards me..."

■ dos detalles que Susana incluye para darle a la carta un tono personal y sincero
   1. _____
   2. _____

---

14 de abril

Estimada profesora Suárez,

Quiero darle las gracias por haberme invitado a la fiesta del día 12 pasado que hizo para los estudiantes latinos, aunque yo no soy una de ellos. Me sentí completamente a gusto y me divertí muchísimo. Me gustó mucho estar con un grupo de hispanohablantes, ya que en los pocos días que llevo aquí en los Estados Unidos he aprendido muy poco inglés. En efecto, esta noche estoy invitada a otra fiesta, pero esta vez Elena y yo seremos las únicas latinas. De verdad, no sé cómo me voy a defender.

En todo caso, de nuevo le agradezco el detalle que usted tuvo para conmigo y le ruego que usted acepte mi sincero agradecimiento por todo lo que hizo para incluirme en el grupo de sus amigos y sus alumnos.

Suya muy atentamente,
Susana Rodríguez
(hermana de Elena)

Write thank-you notes

Writing a good thank-you note is an important social skill in many cultures. If you analyze Susana's letter above, you will see that it has all of the necessary ingredients:

- a salutation and closing at the appropriate level of formality
- an expression of thanks in the first paragraph, accompanied by some supporting detail
- a closing paragraph in which the appreciation is repeated and good wishes are extended

ESCRIBIR

Ahora imagínate que tu profesor/-a de español ha invitado a la clase a cenar para celebrar el final del semestre. Escríbele una carta de agradecimiento después de la cena, siguiendo la guía de la *Writing Strategy 10*.

Una carta personal

Primero vas a leer la carta que Susana le escribe a su madre después de estar en los Estados Unidos por casi dos semanas. Fíjate bien en los tres o cuatro temas principales de la carta. ¿Cuáles son?

OJO: The order in which the date is written calls for first the day and then the month, as in *19 de abril 1993*. It is not uncommon to use a Roman numeral for the month, 19/IV/93.

OJO: *La pasó muy bien* and *se divirtió mucho* both mean "she had a good time."

19 de abril

Queridísima mamita:

Espero que la presente los encuentre bien a todos y que no se hayan olvidado de mí. ¡Imagínate que ya he pasado casi dos semanas aquí con Elena! Primero que nada te cuento que Elena y yo estamos divinamente bien. No debes preocuparte por nada. Una vez que se me quitó el ataque de "turista" que me dio recién llegada, me he sentido muy bien. En cuanto al tobillo de Elena, sigue enyesado, pero eso no le impide que vaya a donde quiera. Hace una semana, por ejemplo, fuimos a una fiesta que una profesora de la universidad dio para un grupo de estudiantes latinos. Nos divertimos mucho y aunque Elena no pudo bailar nada, la pasó muy bien. Dos días después fuimos a otra fiesta en el apartamento de uno de los amigos de Elena. ¡No te imaginas lo aburrida que me pareció!

OJO: *Unos aguafiestas.* Note that the word *aguafiestas* is invariable: singular and plural, masculine and feminine.

> Tú sabes que en una fiesta lo más importante es que la gente sea simpática y la música bailable. Pues estos estudiantes norteamericanos son unos aguafiestas. Para ellos, una "fiesta" no es más que una oportunidad de sentarse a hablar y a tomar cerveza y vino. Nadie quiso bailar y como yo casi no hablo inglés, me sentí completamente aislada del grupo.
>
> En cambio, a Elena todo le pareció de lo más normal y divertido. Parece que desde que ella está aquí se ha acostumbrado mucho a la vida y la cultura norteamericanas. Sobre gustos no hay nada escrito, ¿verdad?
>
> Estoy muy contenta aquí, pero también estoy lista para regresar a casa, porque los extraño a todos, especialmente a ti. Me alegro de poder estar en Guadalajara para celebrar tu santo. Recibe un abrazo de tu hija que tanto te quiere,
>
> *Susana*

Point out the use of the plural adjective *norteamericanas* to modify the compound object nouns *vida* and *cultura*.

OJO: See the *Ventanilla al mundo hispánico* section for an explanation of the *día del santo*.

Actividad

1. En una hoja aparte, escribe un bosquejo (*outline*) de la carta de Susana. Divídelo en secciones según las tres o cuatro ideas principales que hayas identificado en la carta. ¿Qué detalles incluye Susana en cada sección?

Note that students only outline the letter here. They will actually write this letter in *Actividad D* of *Investigar la gramática* in this *etapa*.

2. Ahora te toca a ti. Imagínate que vas a escribirle una carta a tu familia (¡en español, por supuesto!). Prepara el bosquejo de la carta que vas a escribir.

AUMENTAR EL VOCABULARIO

OJO: *En cuanto a* is used to introduce a thought: *En cuanto al tobillo de Elena...*

OJO: Examples: *Ayer tuve que faltar a la reunión porque mi hija estaba enferma.*

OJO: *Faltar* (to be lacking) and *hacer falta* have the same structure as *gustar*: *Le hace falta un vestido,* but *Le hacen falta botas nuevas.*

acostumbrarse a	to get used to
el (la) aguafiestas	"party pooper;" "wet blanket"
alejado/-a de	removed or apart from
no cabe duda	(*there is*) no doubt
De eso no me cabe duda.	I don't doubt it at all.
cansarse de	to become tired of
darle las gracias (a alguien)	to thank (*someone*)
defenderse (ie)	to manage; to survive
Me defiendo en español.	I "get by" in Spanish.
en cuanto a	regarding, concerning
envidiable	enviable
estar listo/-a	to be ready to do something
extrañar	to miss, long for (*people, places*)
faltar	to miss (*a meeting, an appointment*); to be lacking
hacer falta	to lack; to need

Tercera etapa

OJO: *El castellano* is used instead of *el español* in some parts of Latin America, especially Argentina and Uruguay, to refer to the language spoken in Spain and Spanish America.

el idioma	*language (e.g., Spanish, English)*
la lengua	*language; tongue*
el castellano	*Spanish (lit., Castilian)*
¡Imagínate!	*Imagine that! (used as a "filler")*
impedir (i, i)	*to hinder; to impede*
impedido/-a	*disabled*
inválido/-a	*disabled*
rogar (ue)	*to beg, plead*
Le (Te) ruego que...	*I beg you to . . .*

VENTANILLA AL MUNDO HISPÁNICO — El día del santo

OJO: In Spanish-speaking cultures, first names may be chosen to honor a relative, perhaps a parent, an uncle, a grandparent, or simply because the name is popular at the time.

En la carta que Susana le escribe a su mamá, le dice que estará en Guadalajara para celebrar **el santo** de su mamá. En el calendario de los países católicos cada día se asocia con el nombre de uno o más santos. El santo, o el día del santo de una persona, es el día designado para el santo que tiene el mismo nombre. Ya que el nombre de pila de la mamá de Susana es Carmen, ella celebra el día del santo el 16 de julio, o sea, el día de la Virgen del Carmen. Los que llevan el nombre José celebran su santo el 19 de marzo; los que se llaman Juan lo celebran el 24 de junio, etc. Es común, sobre todo entre familiares y amigos íntimos, mandar una tarjeta o un pequeño regalo no sólo para el cumpleaños sino también para el santo de la persona.

Actividad. Busca la fecha de tu santo, usando un libro de referencia de la biblioteca, o consultando con amigos hispanos o con la parroquia (*parish*) católica cerca de la universidad. Si tu nombre no corresponde al de ningún santo (ninguna santa), usa tu segundo nombre o adopta otro nombre que te guste.

CORRESPONDENCIA PERSONAL: SALUDOS Y DESPEDIDAS

OJO: The word *íntimo* means "close" as in "close friends," rather than the meaning in English of "intimate."

	Saludos	*Despedidas*
Informal	Querido/-a...	Cariñosamente
		Con todo cariño de tu buen amigo/-a
Más personal (buenos amigos)	Mi muy querido/-a...	Abrazos
		Recibe un abrazo de
		Besos
Íntimo	Queridísimo/-a...	...te quiere
		...te adora

Actividad. En cada una de las situaciones siguientes, decide cuáles serían el saludo y la despedida más apropiados.

1. una carta a tu prometido/-a
2. una carta a un amigo (una amiga) pidiéndole la nueva dirección de otro amigo (otra amiga)
3. una nota a un amigo (una amiga) animándole a participar en un congreso profesional
4. una nota a un amigo (una amiga) de toda la vida que acaba de anunciar su compromiso matrimonial (*engagement*)
5. una nota a un amigo (una amiga) que vive en otra ciudad pidiéndole información sobre un concierto que se llevará a cabo allí
6. una carta de agradecimiento a un amigo (una amiga) que hizo una fiesta magnífica el fin de semana pasado

---

USO PRÁCTICO DEL ESPAÑOL   Más que y más de

In Chapter 3 you learned how to make comparisons using the expressions *más ... que* and *menos ... que*.

Tengo **menos** dinero **que** tiempo.
Creo que mi vida universitaria es **más** interesante y **más** divertida **que** mi vida cuando estaba en el colegio.
Tengo **más** tiempo libre **que** la mayor parte (*majority*) de mis amigos. Salgo **más** frecuentemente **que** ellos.

In these examples, nouns (*dinero, tiempo*), adjectives (*interesante, divertida*), and adverbs (*frecuentemente*) are being compared. *Más que* is also used in the expressions *más que nunca* (more than ever), *más que nada* (more than anything), and *más que nadie* (more than anyone).

A Antonio le fascina la arqueología ahora **más que nunca.**
Más que nada, quiere trabajar de voluntario en una excavación.

An exception to the use of *más que* and *menos que* occurs if the expression is used immediately before a number. Then the word *de* is used instead of *que*.

Desde febrero Antonio ha escrito **más de veinte cartas** buscando una excavación que le pueda pagar los gastos del vuelo.

Regarding *Actividad A:*
In Chile the greatest north-south distance is 2,650 miles (4,265 kilometers), and the greatest east-west distance is 265 miles (427 kilometers).

Total land area in Brazil is 3,286,487 square miles (8,511,965 square kilometers).

The tallest peak in the Andes, as well as in the Western Hemisphere, is Aconcagua, which has a height of 22,831 feet (6,959 meters). It is located in Argentina, about 65 miles (105 kilometers) from Santiago de Chile.

Ponerlo a prueba

A. Lección de geografía. A continuación hay algunas oraciones. Completa cada una con **más de** o **más que,** según el caso.

1. La extensión de Chile es de _____ 4.200 kilómetros de norte a sur.
2. El área del Brasil es de _____ 8.511.000 kilómetros cuadrados.
3. El pico más alto de los Andes tiene una altura de _____ 6.900 metros.
4. Para mantener la economía, Colombia depende _____ nada de la exportación del café.
5. Con una población de _____ 5.000.000 habitantes, Bogotá es la ciudad más grande del país.
6. _____ nada, a los bogotanos les preocupa el crecimiento casi incontrolable de su ciudad.

B. Definiciones. Da una definición en español de las palabras siguientes.

Modelo: imaginarse   *usar la imaginación para pensar en algo*

1. acostumbrarse
2. el aguafiestas
3. el castellano
4. defenderse
5. extrañar
6. estar listo/-a
7. faltar
8. impedir
9. rogar

C. Entre amigos. Usando las palabras y frases de Aumentar el vocabulario, escribe oraciones originales que describan por lo menos a cinco de tus compañeros de la clase. Si es necesario, habla con ellos para confirmar si lo que dices es verdad.

Modelo: *Felipe tiene un amigo que es aguafiestas.*

CH. Preguntas personales

1. ¿Tuviste problemas para acostumbrarte a la universidad? Explica.
2. Si invitas a un aguafiestas a una fiesta, ¿qué haces con él o ella?
3. ¿De qué te cansas rápidamente? ¿En qué actividades puedes participar por mucho tiempo sin cansarte?
4. ¿Cuál es la característica más envidiable de tu mejor amigo/-a?
5. ¿Qué o a quién extrañas cuando estás en la universidad?
6. ¿Cuántos idiomas hablas? ¿Cuáles son?

D. ¿Estás a favor o en contra? ¿Estás de acuerdo con las opiniones siguientes? ¿Por qué sí o por qué no? Defiende tu opinión.

1. Las fraternidades son organizaciones sociales importantes en las universidades. Las personas que se oponen a ellas no son más que aguafiestas.

2. Todos los edificios de esta universidad deben tener acceso fácil para las personas inválidas, cueste lo que cueste (*no matter what it costs*).
3. Los estudiantes que faltan a tres clases deben suspender (*fail*) el curso.
4. En las clases de español se debe prohibir completamente el uso del inglés. Si no, los estudiantes nunca aprenderán a defenderse en esa lengua.
5. Si a un estudiante le hace falta una semana extra para escribir un ensayo, el profesor (la profesora) debe dársela sin preguntar por qué necesita más tiempo.
6. No hay duda de que los estudiantes de hoy en día leen relativamente poco, por la importancia que se le da a la televisión en nuestra sociedad.

E. **Entrevista: Una fiesta diferente.** Entrevista a un compañero (una compañera) de la clase sobre una fiesta a la que haya asistido y que haya sido diferente de las fiestas comunes y corrientes (*ordinary*). Pídele detalles sobre, por ejemplo,

- el motivo de la fiesta
- cuándo fue
- dónde se llevó a cabo
- por qué y cómo fue diferente de otras fiestas

INVESTIGAR LA GRAMÁTICA   Verbos que tienen preposiciones

Four of the most common prepositions in Spanish are *a, con, de,* and *en*. In addition to their standard meanings, these same prepositions are often used with specific verbs whenever these verbs are followed by an infinitive. The first expression of this type that you learned, as a way to talk about future time, was *ir + a + infinitivo:* **Voy a estudiar** en la biblioteca esta noche. Several other verbs also use the preposition *a* when an infinitive follows.

El profesor comenzó la clase a las 2:00 en punto.
El profesor **comenzó a enseñar** la clase a las 2:00 en punto.
Empecé mi tarea a las 9:30.
Empecé a escribir mi tarea a las 9:30.
La profesora Jiménez enseña español. Hace unas semanas nos **enseñó a usar** el pretérito. Algunos de mis compañeros de la clase nunca lo aprendieron, pero yo **aprendí a usarlo** bien casi todo el tiempo.
Mi profesora ayuda a todos sus alumnos; **nos ayuda a entender, a leer, a escribir** y a **hablar** español.
Muchas veces ella nos invita a su oficina.
Muchas veces ella nos **invita a estudiar** en su oficina.

Somewhat fewer verbs use the preposition *con* when they are followed by an infinitive.

Mi primo quiere casarse con una mujer que conoció en Cancún cuando estaba allí de vacaciones.
Sueña todas las noches; **sueña con casarse** con ella.

OJO: Remember that the personal *a* is used before a direct object that is a person or something that is being personified: *No veo el perro,* but *Quiero mucho a mi perro.*

OJO: The expression *soñar con* is also used when that verb is followed by a noun: *Mi primo sueña con esta mujer todas las noches.*

The expression *contar con* means "to depend/rely on," whether it is followed by an infinitive or not.

Necesito que alguien me ayude a hacer la tarea. ¿Puedo **contar contigo**?

Many common verbs use the preposition *de* whether they are followed by an infinitive or not.

Anoche, **me di cuenta de** que no había empezado (*I had not begun*) mi ensayo de historia. No sé por qué, pero nunca **me acuerdo de** los ensayos hasta última hora.
Pero todavía tengo la posibilidad de cumplir con esta obligación. Durante tres días no **dejaré de leer** y **escribir** sobre la revolución mexicana.
Traté de **olvidarme del** ensayo por unas horas para descansar, pero fue imposible. ¡Estoy obsesionado! **Estoy seguro de** que saldrá bien.

OJO: Study tip: Make a list of verbs and their prepositions, and add to it as you come across more verbs.

The preposition *en* is used with the following verbs:

confiar en:	**Confío en** que saldrás bien en el examen final.
consentir (ie, i) en:	Carmencita **consintió en ir** al restaurante con Roberto.
entrar en:	Antes de registrarse en el hotel, Paco y Roberto **entraron en** la habitación y vieron que tenía baño completo.
insistir en:	¡Qué conflicto! Nosotros **insistimos en hablar** inglés y el profesor **insiste en** que hablemos español.
pensar (ie) en:	Roberto pasa todo su tiempo libre **pensando en** Carmencita.
tardar en:	La profesora Suárez no está en este momento, pero no **tardará en llegar**.

Ponerlo a prueba

This activity practices the preposition uses from this section of *Investigar la gramática,* as well as uses students have seen throughout the book.

A. **Una cita importante.** Completa el cuento que aparece a continuación escogiendo las preposiciones adecuadas. Si no se usa una preposición, pon la marca *x* en el espacio en blanco.

1. Esta noche Luis piensa _____ llamar _____ su amiga Rosaura.
2. Quiere invitarla _____ cenar.
3. Van _____ taxi porque Luis no tiene coche; está _____ el taller (*repair shop*).
4. Puesto que Luis acaba _____ mudarse a la ciudad y no es de aquí, no conoce los restaurantes.
5. Pero se acuerda _____ uno que es muy bueno.
6. Rosaura consintió _____ ir, pero tiene que volver _____ casa _____ las ocho porque tiene mucha tarea.
7. Luis se alegra _____ que ella vaya _____ él.
8. Luis le regala _____ Rosaura un ramo _____ flores.
9. Los dos se divierten mucho y esa noche Rosaura sueña _____ Luis.
10. Ella decide _____ llamarlo al día siguiente.

Capítulo diez ¡A divertirnos!

B. **¿Dónde y con quién?** A continuación hay una lista de actividades. Para cada actividad, di dónde aprendiste a hacerla (si es que la haces) y quién te la enseñó.

Modelo: leer   *Aprendí a leer en la escuela, en el primer grado. La maestra me enseñó.*

1. afeitarse (hombres) / maquillarse (mujeres)
2. bailar
3. cocinar
4. conducir
5. escribir
6. vestirse
7. hablar otro idioma (¿cuál?)
8. nadar

This activity reviews prepositions of location introduced in earlier chapters.

C. **En la agencia de bienes raíces.** Eres agente de bienes raíces y un(a) cliente te ha llamado para pedirte información sobre una casa que está en venta. Descríbele la casa, usando las preposiciones siguientes: **a la derecha de, a la izquierda de, cerca de, lejos de, detrás de, dentro de, encima de** y **debajo de.**

CH. **Respondiendo a una carta.** Imagínate que eres la madre o el padre de Susana, y que acabas de recibir la carta que vimos en la sección Leer y escribir de esta etapa. Escribe cinco preguntas que vas a hacerle a Susana en tu próxima carta, usando en cada pregunta una de las preposiciones que se explican en esta sección de Investigar la gramática.

1.
2.
3.
4.
5.

Ahora busca un compañero (una compañera) de la clase. Cada persona hará sus preguntas y contestará las preguntas del otro o de la otra.

D. **Una carta a la familia.** Usando como modelo la carta de Susana a su madre y también tu bosquejo, escribe una carta a casa o a un amigo tuyo (una amiga tuya) contándole de tu vida en la universidad.

¡TIENES LA PALABRA!

Haz las siguientes actividades con un compañero (una compañera).

A. **Aguafiestas**

Estudiante A: Anfitrión/-ona

You have invited someone you do not know well to a party at your house and it is clear that he or she is not having a good time. Try to en-

Directions for *Actividades A* and *B* are in English, so that students will have to supply the appropriate vocabulary.

gage the person in conversation, offer food and drink, invite him or her to dance—everything you can think of to make the person happy and comfortable. After trying your best, you may politely excuse yourself.

Estudiante B: Aguafiestas

You are at a party with people you don't know well, and you are not having a good time. Your host tries to make you feel comfortable, but by now you are in a terrible mood and refuse to be cheered up. Be as negative as possible about anything that is suggested to you.

B. **Una disculpa.** You have missed your appointment with a friend to have lunch. You call your friend to explain. With a classmate taking the role of your friend, enact the following:

- Identify yourself and greet your friend.
- Apologize. Explain why you missed the appointment.
- Arrange a new appointment.

OTRA VUELTA

Play instructor tape, 3 min.

Vuelve ahora a la Entrada que escuchaste al comienzo de esta etapa. Escúchala otra vez y apunta por lo menos una respuesta que Pablo da a las preguntas de su madre en las categorías mencionadas a continuación.

Salud: Idioma:
Nuevos amigos: Regreso:
Comida:

COMENTARIO CULTURAL

Expresiones de cortesía

Hay varias expresiones en español que podrían traducirse al inglés como *Excuse me,* pero las expresiones en español no son intercambiables. Cada una tiene una connotación distinta. "Por favor", que ya has aprendido con el significado de *please,* puede usarse para llamarle la atención de una persona. De esta manera la expresión "por favor" se usa para iniciar un pedido.

Por favor, ¿puede usted decirme dónde queda la biblioteca?

Para decir *Excuse me* en el sentido de pedir permiso para hacer algo (irse de la mesa o de un grupo de amigos, por ejemplo), en español se dice "Con permiso".

Para decir *Excuse me* después de hacer algo inesperado o accidental, se dice "Perdón". Por ejemplo, si por alguna razón tienes que salir de un teatro, comienzas diciendo "Con permiso" a cada persona que molestas al salir. Si al tratar de pasar le pisas el pie a alguien, le dices "¡Ay, perdón!"

Actividad. Piensa en los siguientes incidentes y decide qué forma de decir *Excuse me* es la más indicada.

1. Llegas a una puerta justo cuando otra persona se acerca por el otro lado.
2. Chocas con alguien y esa persona derrama su bebida.
3. Tratas de pasar por enfrente de alguien que ya está sentado en un cine.
4. Quieres pedirle a tu profesor(a) que te conteste una pregunta.
5. Te despides de un grupo de amigos en la cafetería.

Play video

Program 10 *Creencias y celebraciones* Religious holidays and celebrations

A. Te invito. Escríbele una carta a un amigo (una amiga) invitándolo/-la a una fiesta en tu casa. Incluye la información clave: el motivo de la fiesta, cúando y dónde se llevará a cabo, y otros datos importantes.

B. Lo siento... Acabas de recibir una invitación a un coctel honrando a un profesor tuyo que se jubila. No podrás asistir a causa de un examen final que tienes el día siguiente. Escríbele al anfitrión (a la anfitriona) rechazando la invitación, pero de una forma delicada, sin decir precisamente por qué no puedes asistir. No te olvides de expresar tu agradecimiento por haber sido invitado/-a.

C. Una fiesta. Escribe una descripción de una fiesta a la que hayas asistido recientemente. (¡Si es necesario, puedes cambiar los nombres para proteger a los inocentes!)

CH. Lo siento mucho, pero... Un amigo (Una amiga) te llama por teléfono y te invita a cenar. Desafortunadamente, tienes otro compromiso. Con tu compañero (compañera), representen (*act out*) la escena siguiente.

- Explícale el problema a tu amigo/-a.
- Dale las gracias por la invitación.
- Arregla otra fecha para reunirte con él o ella.

The stimuli in *Actividad D* are in English to avoid providing students with the vocabulary.

D. Una invitación. Con un compañero (una compañera), representen la escena siguiente. Estás planeando una fiesta para darle la bienvenida a un amigo mexicano que ha llegado de Guadalajara. Llamas por teléfono a un amigo (una amiga) para invitarlo/-la. En la conversación debes incluir la información siguiente.

- when it is
- where the party will be
- how to get there (Give directions to the party's location.)
- what time it starts
- who else is invited
- what you intend to wear (your friend doesn't know what to wear)
- that your friend can bring records or tapes of Latin American music

E. ¡A comer! Con dos compañeros de la clase representen la escena siguiente. Una pareja colombiana que recién ha llegado a los Estados Unidos recibe una invitación a una cena *pot luck*. Como no saben qué significa, llaman a su único amigo norteamericano (única amiga norteamericana) y le preguntan qué es *pot luck* y qué deben hacer para participar. Su amigo norteamericano (amiga norteamericana) les explica el término y les da la información cultural necesaria para que los colombianos se diviertan en la cena.

VOCABULARIO

Despedidas

Abrazos (m pl)   *Hugs*
Atentamente   *Attentively*
Besos   *Kisses*
Cariñosamente   *Affectionately*
Con todo cariño   *With affection*
Cordialmente   *Cordially*
De usted muy atentamente   *Attentively yours*
Recibe un abrazo de   *With hugs from*
Respetuosamente   *Respectfully*
Su servidor(a)   *Your servant*
Suyo/-a muy atentamente   *Attentively yours*
...te adora   *... adores you*
...te quiere   *... loves you*

Expresiones llamativas

¡Ay! ¡No exageres!   *What an exaggeration!*
¡Cálmate!   *Calm down!*
¡Cuidado!   *Be careful!*
¡Imagínate!   *Imagine that!* (used as a "filler")
¡Mira!   *Look!*
¡No seas tonto/-a!   *Don't be a fool!*
¡Qué va!   *Don't be ridiculous!*
Eso no es nada.   *That's not important.*
¡Tranquilo!   *Calm down!*
¡Vaya!   *Go on, you're joking!*

Saludos

Distinguido/-a...   *Distinguished...*
Estimado/-a...   *Esteemed...*
Mi muy querido/-a...   *My very dear...*
Muy señor(a) mío/-a: *Dear Sir/Madam,*
Queridísimo/-a...   *Beloved...*
Querido/-a...   *Dear...*

Sustantivos útiles

aguafiestas (m/f, s/pl)   "party pooper"; "wet blanket"
carta (f) de agradecimiento   thank-you letter
castellano (m)   Spanish (Castilian)
compromiso (m)   commitment, obligation
cumplido (m)   compliment
estrella (f)   star
estrella (m/f) de cine   movie star
idioma (m)   language (e.g., Spanish, English)
lengua (f)   language; tongue
motivo (m)   reason, motive
rato (m)   short period of time

Verbos útiles

acostumbrarse a   to get used to
agradecer   to acknowledge a favor (to appreciate)
asistir a   to attend
cansarse de   to become tired of
darle las gracias (a alguien)   to thank (someone)
defenderse (ie)   to manage; to survive
denotar   to signify
estar a gusto   to feel comfortable, at ease
estar al tanto de   to be up-to-date, current
estar listo/-a   to be ready to do something
estrenar   to wear or use for the first time
evitar   to avoid
extrañar   to miss, long for (people, places)
faltar   to miss (a meeting, an appointment); to be lacking
fijarse en   to notice
hacer falta   to lack; to need
impedir (i, i)   to hinder; to impede
llevarse a cabo   to take place
ponerse   to become; to wear
recordar (ue)   to remember
rechazar   to refuse (an invitation); to reject
rogar (ue)   to beg, plead
saludar   to greet
tener el gusto de   to have the pleasure of
tener en cuenta   to take into account

Otras palabras y expresiones útiles

con el motivo de   for the purpose of
de parte de   on behalf of
debido a   due to
en cuanto a   regarding, concerning
hacer el favor de   please
más que nada   more than anything
más que nadie   more than anyone
más que nunca   more than ever
No cabe duda.   (There is) no doubt.
puesto que   since, given that
se llevará a cabo...   it will take place (occur) . . .
se me ocurre (que)   it occurs to me (that)
sea lo (el, la) que sea   whatever it might be
si me hiciera el favor de...   if you would please (do me the favor of) . . .

Palabras descriptivas

alejado/-a de   removed or apart from
amable   nice (said of a person)
cómodo/-a   comfortable
de habla española   Spanish-speaking
envidiable   enviable
hispanohablante (m/f)   Spanish-speaking person
impedido/-a   disabled
incómodo/-a   uncomfortable
íntimo/-a   very close, intimate
inválido/-a   disabled
previo/-a   previous

VOCABULARIO PERSONALIZADO

¿Qué me aconsejas?

Capítulo 11

COMMUNICATIVE OBJECTIVES

In this chapter, you will learn several new ways to
- ask for and give advice
- speculate about the future
- make simple hypothetical statements
- talk about unplanned occurrences

PRIMERA ETAPA — Las mentiras piadosas

ENTRADA

Play instructor tape, 2 min.

"Dime lo que debo hacer…"

Vas a oír una conversación telefónica entre dos amigas. Al escucharla, apunta los datos y las características personales de Enrique y de Mariano.

Datos y características personales	*Enrique*	*Mariano*
¿interesante o aburrido?		
¿extrovertido o introvertido?		
edad		
carrera		
pasatiempos		

EMPEZAR A ESCUCHAR

Play student tape, 3 min.

Leer

el asunto	*matter; issue*
hacer bromas	*to make jokes*
matricularse	*to register for a course*
copiar	*to copy*
hacer trampa	*to cheat*
fracasar	*to fail*
echar	*to throw out*
la culpa	*fault; blame*
la incertidumbre	*uncertainty*
la mentira piadosa	*white lie*

Repetir

Escucha la cinta y repite lo que oyes.

Identificar

En una hoja aparte, escribe en una columna las palabras y frases anteriores. Vas a oír algunas oraciones. Cada vez que oigas una de esas palabras o frases, apunta el número de la oración al lado de la palabra. Cada oración se leerá dos veces.

Primera etapa

Escribir

Vas a oír unas oraciones, cada una leída dos veces. Escríbelas al escucharlas.

Reconocer

Ahora lee otra vez las oraciones que acabas de escribir. Cada una contiene una o más de las palabras y frases de la lista en la sección de Leer de esta etapa. Al releerlas, subraya todas las palabras y frases que vienen de la lista. Mientras lees, haz todas las correcciones necesarias.

ESCUCHAR

Play student tape, 1 min.

EPISODIO 1: Un asunto bastante serio

Enfoque comunicativo

Marcos habla con su amigo César acerca de un problema ético: si debe o no debe decir la verdad. Al escuchar la conversación, determina

- si el problema es serio
- cuál es la reacción de César

> *El problema de Marcos*
> 1. Según Marcos, se trata de un problema...
> 2. La primera reacción de César es que siempre...
> 3. Antes de dar su opinión, César quiere...

Enfoque lingüístico

Escucha la conversación otra vez y apunta

- las palabras que usa César para ofrecer su consejo
- la manera en que Marcos expresa la incertidumbre

ESCUCHAR

Play student tape, 2 min.

EPISODIO 2: El dilema de Marcos

Enfoque comunicativo

La conversación continúa. Al escucharla, determina

- cuál es el problema
- cuál es la reacción de César

> *El dilema de Marcos*
>
> 1. Escribe un resumen del dilema de Marcos.
>
> 2. ¿Cuál es la reacción de César?

Enfoque lingüístico

Al escuchar la conversación otra vez, apunta

- las tres expresiones que usa Marcos para establecer la secuencia cronológica de los acontecimientos de su historia
- las expresiones que Marcos usa para presentar las dos alternativas

VERIFICAR Contesta las siguientes preguntas.

1. ¿Qué pasó con la tarea de Marcos?
2. ¿Qué hizo su compañero de clase con la tarea?
3. ¿Por qué se preocupa tanto Marcos por si debe decirle la verdad al profesor o no?
4. ¿Qué quiere Marcos que César haga?
5. ¿Qué consejos le da César a su amigo?

AUMENTAR EL VOCABULARIO

OJO: *Contar un chiste* is "to tell a joke," while the series of words related to *broma* have to do with practical jokes or tricks.

OJO: *La broma pesada* is a "practical joke." Although it refers to something more extreme in Spanish than in English, the adjective *pesado* describes boring or uninteresting things or people.

OJO: A *carrera* is a field of study, such as engineering, while an *especialización* is an area within the field of study, such as mechanical engineering.

el asunto	matter; issue
el tema	theme
la broma	joke
el (la) bromista	entertaining person; practical joker
en broma	in fun
en serio	seriously
hacer bromas	to joke; to play a trick
la carrera	career; major field of study
la culpa	fault; blame
culpable	at fault, guilty of something
culpar	to blame (*someone*)
tener la culpa	to be at fault
echar	**to throw out**
echar(le) la culpa (a alguien)	to cast blame on (*someone*)
echar flores	to flatter

el piropo	*a flattering comment*
fracasar	**to fail**
tener éxito	*to succeed*
hacer trampa	**to deceive, to cheat**
copiar	*to copy*
engañar	*to trick; to deceive*
engañoso/-a	*deceitful*
malicioso/-a	*malicious*
la incertidumbre	**uncertainty**
la mentira piadosa	*white lie*
matricularse	**to register** (*for a course*)
salir bien	**to do well; to turn out well**
salir mal	*to do poorly; to turn out badly*
temer(se)	**to fear**
cobarde	*cowardly*
miedoso/-a	*fearful*
valiente	*brave*

LAS NOTAS (CALIFICACIONES) ESCOLARES

Explain that in some instances the numbers 1–5, 1–7, 1–10, or 1–20 are used to grade scholastic performance. As in our own system, there is a minimum satisfactory grade on each scale, and grades that fall below that are considered failing. On the 1–7 scale, for example, any score from 4 down to 1 is "failing."

Explain that grades in a course are frequently assigned on the basis of a single, final examination, rather than calculated on the basis of numerous scores assigned over a longer period of time. This makes examination time particularly stressful for students, since the score on a single examination may determine whether or not they are permitted to continue their studies.

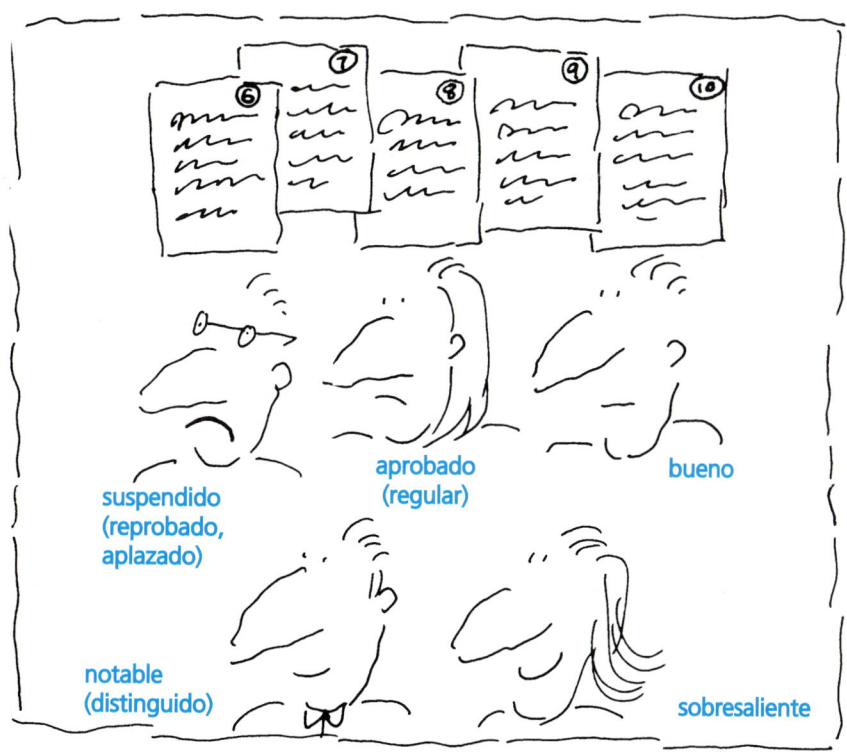

suspendido (reprobado, aplazado)
aprobado (regular)
bueno
notable (distinguido)
sobresaliente

En el mundo hispánico, generalmente se usa un sistema de calificaciones numérico. Las notas constituyen un sistema que va de 1 a 10.

Sé tú el intérprete. Trabajas con una compañía que ha recibido una solicitud de empleo de un hombre recién llegado de Latinoamérica. El director (La directora) de la compañía no entiende el español y te pide que interpretes los cursos y calificaciones que aparecen en la solicitud. ¿Cuáles serían los equivalentes de estas notas en los Estados Unidos?

Asignatura	*Nota*
Matemáticas	sobresaliente
Contabilidad	aprobado
Gerencia	bueno
Francés	notable
Inglés	aprobado
Finanzas	suspendido

Ventanilla al mundo hispánico   El individuo frente al grupo

En los Episodios de esta etapa Marcos tiene que enfrentarse con un dilema: si debe decirle a su profesor algo que va en contra de su compañero de la clase y que le puede hacer daño, o si no debe decirle nada y asumir él mismo la responsabilidad. La razón por la cual esta situación le causa un dilema a Marcos es que, por lo general, en la mayoría de las sociedades hispánicas la unidad del grupo es más importante que el éxito personal. Como resultado, es muy probable que un individuo asuma la responsabilidad si cree que la consecuencia de no hacerlo es que otro miembro del grupo quede mal.

En *Fuenteovejuna,* un famoso drama del siglo XVI escrito por Lope de Vega, un pueblo entero acepta la responsabilidad de haber ofendido a un miembro de la nobleza en vez de confesar qué individuo lo había hecho en realidad.

USO PRÁCTICO DEL ESPAÑOL   Use of the Infinitive as a Noun

The infinitive form of a verb is sometimes used as a noun, that is, as a subject, a direct object, or the object of a preposition.

Correr es bueno para la salud. *Running is good for one's health.*
Me gusta **correr.** *I like to run. / I like running.*
Pero no es divertido **caerse.** *But it's no fun to fall. / But falling is no fun.*

Primera etapa

¡OJO! Always use the infinitive after a preposition.

El médico hizo el diagnóstico **después de ver** las radiografías.

The doctor made the diagnosis after seeing the X-rays.

Elena esperó dos días **antes de llamar** al médico.

Elena waited two days before calling the doctor.

Ponerlo a prueba

A. Proposiciones filosóficas. Completa las oraciones. ¿Estás de acuerdo con ellas?

1. _____ es vivir.
2. Ver es _____.
3. Buscar es _____.
4. _____ es aprender.
5. Jugar es _____.
6. _____ es saber.
7. _____ es _____.

a. ganar
b. estudiar
c. creer
ch. leer
d. amar
e. encontrar
f. ?

B. Definiciones. Usa tu habilidad para adivinar a fin de escoger una palabra o frase de Aumentar el vocabulario en esta etapa que puedas asociar con estas definiciones.

1. el contrario de salir bien
2. no tener éxito
3. hacer salir
4. perverso, cruel
5. tener miedo
6. decir un piropo
7. una persona que hace bromas
8. una nota excelente

C. ¡A escribir! Usa las siguientes palabras para escribir oraciones originales.

1. en broma
2. en serio
3. copiar
4. la culpa
5. engañar
6. el asunto
7. echar flores
8. hacer trampa

CH. Preguntas personales

1. ¿Alguna vez has fracasado en una clase? ¿Qué pasó?
2. En cuanto a tus clases, ¿qué es lo que temes más?
3. ¿Qué se le debe hacer a alguien que copia en una clase?
4. ¿Qué haces tú si alguien quiere copiar tu tarea? ¿Te ha pasado alguna vez? Explica.

5. ¿Crees que alguien te haya hecho trampa recientemente? ¿Qué te hizo?
6. ¿Has dicho una mentira piadosa alguna vez? En qué circunstancias?

INVESTIGAR LA GRAMÁTICA   Stating Conditions and Hypotheses

Statements of conditions or hypotheses usually take the form of "If X, then Y." For example, a doctor might say to a patient,

Si Ud. sigue estas instrucciones, pronto se sentirá mejor.	If you follow these instructions, you will feel better soon.
Si Ud. no trabaja de noche, dormirá más.	If you don't work at night, you will sleep more.

In these examples, which are conditions, the doctor does not imply that the patient either will or will not follow the instructions or change working hours. The combination of a present tense verb in the *si* (if) clause and a future tense verb in the *resultado* (result) clause means that **if** the patient follows the instructions, **then** the result of feeling or sleeping better will certainly occur.

In more hypothetical statements, particularly when the speaker believes the stated condition to be false or virtually impossible, the speaker speculates that one set of circumstances (expressed in the *si* clause) would bring about certain results (expressed in the *resultado* clause).

> Point out that you can change the order of the ideas without changing the meaning: *Ud. se sentiría mejor si siguiera estas instrucciones; Podría dormir más si no trabajara de noche.*

Si siguiera estas instrucciones, **se sentiría** mejor.	If you followed these instructions, you would feel better.
Si no trabajara de noche, **podría dormir más.**	If you didn't work at night, you would sleep more.

In these statements, the imperfect subjunctive is used in the *si* clause and the conditional tense is used to give the result. For example, a doctor and patient might have the following exchange.

—Si Ud. **durmiera** más, **tendría** más energía.	If you slept more, you would have more energy.
—Doctor, **podría** dormir más si no **trabajara** de noche, pero es muy difícil descansar durante el día.	Doctor, I could sleep more if I didn't work at night, but it is hard to rest during the day.
—Pues, sí, entiendo. Pero también **dormiría** mejor si **hiciera** más ejercicio.	Well, yes, I understand. But you would also sleep better if you exercised more.
—Puede ser. Entonces, si hago ejercicio esta noche, lo llamaré a usted mañana y se lo diré.	That might be true. So if I exercise tonight, I'll call you tomorrow and tell you about it.

In summary, the imperfect subjunctive and the conditional tense are used to refer to

1. conditions that are contrary to fact

Si yo **fuera** profesor, **daría** notas muy altas.	If I were a professor, I would give very high grades.

2. hypotheses that are considered extremely unlikely or literally impossible

Si te lo **pidiera**, ¿me **dejarías** copiar tu tarea?	*If I asked, would you let me copy your assignment?*

As an additional example, a mother might say to her child,

Hijito, si **pruebas** esto, **descubrirás** que te gusta, ya **verás**.	*Son, if you try this, you'll find you like it, you'll see.*

The implication here is that the mother is sure the child will like the new food. Compare with the following sentence.

Todo el mundo me dice que si lo **probara, me gustaría,** pero no lo creo.	*Everybody says that if I tried it, I would like it, but I don't believe it.*

The implication here is that the speaker is highly doubtful that he or she will like the unfamiliar food. The subjunctive indicates that the speaker has no intention of trying it.

Ponerlo a prueba

1. Expansion: Have students work in pairs to continue the conversation. 2. Follow-up: Have students change the uncertain sentences to fact, and the factual sentences to speculation.

A. ¿Cierto o incierto? Lee las siguientes oraciones y decide si indican posibilidad (*P*) o imposibles (*I*).

1. Vamos a la Galería Fronteras esta tarde. Si sales con nosotros, verás unos cuadros magníficos.
2. Si me sintiera mejor, iría con mucho gusto, pero me duele mucho la espalda.
3. Bueno, pensamos ir otra vez el sábado. Si estás mejor, puedes acompañarnos. ¡La exposición es una maravilla!
4. ¡Ay, mujer! ¿Cómo sabes? Hablas como si ya conocieras las obras.
5. No hablemos más. Si no te doliera tanto la espalda, no me estarías criticando.
6. ¿Por qué no salimos un rato? Si vamos al club, podrás meterte al *jacuzzi* un rato.
7. Gracias, pero no quiero. El médico me dice que si guardo cama esta semana, la semana que viene estaré mejor y podré hacer de todo.

OJO: The expression *como si* is always followed by the imperfect subjunctive because its meaning indicates that whatever is to follow is clearly contrary to fact.

B. El dilema de Marcos. Las respuestas a las siguientes preguntas cuentan la historia del dilema de Marcos como si pasara en el futuro. Contesta las preguntas para reconstruir la historia.

Modelo: Si un compañero quisiera ver su tarea, ¿qué haría Marcos?
Si un compañero quisiera ver su tarea, Marcos se la mostraría.

1. Si Marcos se la mostrara, ¿qué haría el compañero?
2. Si el compañero la copiara, ¿cómo reaccionaría Marcos?
3. Si el profesor pidiera la tarea, ¿qué harían los estudiantes?

4. Si el profesor leyera las tareas, ¿qué pensaría?
5. Si Marcos necesitara consejos, ¿qué haría?
6. Si el amigo de Marcos también fuera amigo del compañero, ¿qué le aconsejaría a Marcos?
7. Si tú estuvieras en la situación de Marcos ahora, ¿qué harías?

C. **¡Ay, si no tuviéramos que estudiar...!** Ya es la temporada de los exámenes y los estudiantes preferirían estar en otro lugar. Construye por lo menos ocho oraciones hipotéticas utilizando un elemento de cada columna.

Modelo: *Si no tuviéramos que estudiar, bailaríamos toda la noche.*

Condición

1. (No) tenemos que estudiar.
2. (No) Hay una prueba de español el lunes por la mañana.
3. Los cursos (no) son tan difíciles.
4. El compañero (La compañera) de cuarto (no) toca tan alto el estéreo.
5. Los vecinos (no) hacen tanto ruido durante la noche.
6. Los libros que necesitamos (no) están en reserva.

Resultado

a. dormir mejor
b. poder estudiar más
c. bailar toda la noche
ch. nunca ir a la biblioteca
d. estar en la playa en este momento
e. leer en el cuarto

CH. **¿Qué pasará?** Elena pasará las vacaciones de primavera en Guadalajara. Está pensando tanto en lo que hará como en lo que podría hacer. Completa sus oraciones.

Modelo: Si vamos al Mercado de la Libertad / comprar una blusa para Alicia
Si vamos al Mercado de la Libertad, compraré una blusa para Alicia.

1. Si consiguiéramos boletos / ir a una función en el Coliseo Arena
2. Si / llevar a mis sobrinitos al parque Agua Azul visitaremos el zoológico
3. Si hay tiempo / tomar el trencito y / ver las marionetas
4. Si Antonio / invitarme al Lago Chapala saldríamos en un barco
5. Si cenáramos en el centro / (yo) le sugerir un restaurante excelente
6. Si hubiera tiempo / poder escuchar a los mariachis también

D. **¿Qué harías?** Termina cada oración de una forma lógica.

1. Si fuera rico/-a...
2. Si no asistiera a la universidad este año...
3. Si tuviera una enfermedad grave...

4. Si pudiera estar en otro lugar en este momento...
5. Si yo..., iría al cine esta noche.
6. Si no... clases hoy, pasaría el día en...
7. Si... sol y calor todos los días, ...
8. Si... presidente de esta universidad, (yo)...

E. **Situaciones difíciles.** Contesta las preguntas que están debajo de cada dibujo.

Expand by redoing as a contrary-to-fact situation: *¿Qué pasaría aquí si el hombre no viera la bicicleta?*

¿Qué pasará aquí...

1. ...si el hombre no ve la bicicleta?
2. ...si la mujer ve lo que va a pasar?
3. ...si el hombre está herido?
4. ...si la mujer es la madre de los niños?

Expand by changing to: *¿Qué pasará si el hombre no tiene dinero ni tarjeta de crédito?*

¿Qué pasaría aquí...

1. ...si el hombre no tuviera ni dinero ni tarjeta de crédito?
2. ...si la mujer no tuviera dinero tampoco?
3. ...si vieran a unos amigos suyos en otra parte del restaurante?
4. ...si la pareja viviera cerca del restaurante?
5. ...si fueran turistas de otro país?

¡TIENES LA PALABRA!

Haz las siguientes actividades con un compañero (una compañera).

A. **¡Necesito ayuda, por favor!** You work for an ambulance service. A call comes in from someone whose child has had an accident; the child has fallen out of a tree. You ask the following:

- when and where the accident took place
- where the child is now
- what the injuries are
- where the family lives

Say that the child should not be moved (*no debe moverse*), and that the ambulance (*la ambulancia*) will be there soon.
    Your partner, who plays the role of the parent, gives the information requested.

B. **¡Un momento!** Preparen el mini-drama que se explica a continuación.

Estudiante A

Your professor has asked you to meet with him or her to explain why your homework assignments are so similar to those of one of your classmates. Although you know that it looks suspicious, you have not been cheating. Explain to the professor

1. that you always turn in your papers when the professor asks for them
2. that you go to the library whenever you can
3. that you do not discuss assignments with your classmates until after you have done them
4. that you hope the professor talks to the other student before he or she decides that you have been cheating

Estudiante B

You are a professor. Two students in one of your classes have regularly handed in suspiciously similar homework assignments. Talk with Student A to determine

1. when he or she turns in the assignments
2. where he or she usually studies

3. when and with whom he or she discusses the assignments
4. what the student thinks you should do about the matter

OTRA VUELTA

Play student tape, 2 min.

Vuelve ahora a la Entrada que escuchaste al comienzo de esta etapa. Escúchala otra vez y contesta las preguntas que aparecen a continuación.

1. ¿Qué problema tiene Rita?
2. ¿Qué datos necesita María Cristina para ayudar a su amiga?
3. Según María Cristina, ¿qué debe hacer Rita?

COMENTARIO CULTURAL

La solidaridad

Los miembros de cada cultura sienten lealtad o solidaridad para con otras personas dentro de su misma sociedad, por ejemplo: la familia (en el sentido amplio de la palabra); los colegas u otras personas que ejercen la misma profesión; los residentes del mismo pueblo, ciudad, estado o país; los que practican la misma religión; los socios del mismo club u otra organización social/profesional; los que hablan el mismo idioma o el mismo dialecto.

Lo que varía de cultura en cultura es la importancia relativa que tiene cualquier relación personal o asociación profesional. Esta percepción de solidaridad, pertenencia o identificación a un grupo influye en muchas de las decisiones que las personas toman: a quién piden consejos, a quién emplean o despiden, quizás hasta dónde una persona decide vivir o a qué universidad decide asistir.

En el mundo hispánico normalmente el compromiso (*commitment*) más fuerte es con la familia. La mayor responsabilidad que siente el hispano es la de asegurarse de que sus familiares estén bien, que no les haga falta nada esencial. Después de la familia, la lealtad se extiende al grupo de amigos. La noción de "amigo" en las culturas hispánicas es algo más amplia y profunda que la de la palabra *friend* en inglés. "Amigo" quizás se expresaría mejor en inglés diciendo *close friend*. Las demás personas con quienes uno se asocia normalmente son "conocidos" (*acquaintances*), "socios" (*associates*), o "colegas" (*colleagues*).

Si una persona tiene un problema personal, normalmente busca consejos primero de algún familiar, y después de uno de sus amigos íntimos. En esto podemos ver que las culturas hispánicas y la norteamericana no son siempre muy diferentes. Por eso, no nos sorprende que Marcos hable de su dilema personal primero con uno de sus amigos y no con su profesor u otra fuente "oficial" de ayuda, tal como un consejero o un decano.

Siempre es bueno tener alguien con quien hablar sobre asuntos personales.

Actividad. ¿A cuál de las siguientes personas le dirías "amigo/-a", "amigo íntimo (amiga íntima)", "conocido/-a", o "socio/-a"?

1. tu jefe en el trabajo
2. un amigo desde que eras niño/-a
3. tu compañero/-a de cuarto de un semestre
4. tu novio/-a
5. un compañero (una compañera) de la clase

SEGUNDA ETAPA — El chisme y la realidad

ENTRADA

¡Aprenda por correo!

Vas a oír una conversación entre una consejera y un estudiante. Hablan de un curso de inglés por correspondencia. Al escuchar la conversación apunta dos ventajas y dos desventajas que menciona la consejera.

Ventajas   *Desventajas*

1.   1.
2.   2.

ANTES DE LEER

Read between the lines

Writers draw on a variety of techniques to make their descriptions more vivid and evocative, to clarify the ideas and viewpoints they want to express, and to generate an emotional reaction on the part of the reader that will support the position the writer is attempting to make. If you were to hear a particular course described as "the grade point destroyer," you would have an immediate awareness of what the course was like, although you knew nothing about the specific content. Literary devices often used by writers to create these images include metaphors (expressions implying a comparison between two different things, as in "a heart of stone"), similes (a statement that one thing is **like** another, as in "as hard as nails"), and analogies (in which the writer depicts one thing in terms of something else which, in a literal sense it is not, as in "life is a journey"). In Spanish, these nonliteral, or figurative, expressions often include *como* and *así como* as indicators that the writer is attempting to create an image, clarify an idea, or solicit support for a particular point of view.

Preparación

The headline of the following article is an excerpt from a conversation. What does the word "Shhhh" suggest about what is being said? Who do you think is speaking? Do you think the speakers are chatting or gossiping? Define the word "gossip." Give two reasons why you think some people gossip, and two reasons why you think they should not do so. Answer the following questions.

1. El título "Shhhh": ¿Qué sugiere acerca del contenido del artículo?
2. En tu opinión, ¿un artículo que lleva este título se dedicará a contar chismes o a analizar un fenómeno social?
3. En tu opinión, ¿qué significan **el chisme** y la actividad de **chismear**?
4. ¿Por qué a la gente le gusta chismear?
   a.
   b.

5. ¿Es malo chismear? ¿Por qué?
   a.
   b.

Play student tape, 1 min.

Estudiar y practicar

alimentar	*to feed*
burlón/-ona	*derisive, mocking*
crecer	*to grow, increase in size*
chismear	*to gossip*
destacarse	*to stand out*
detener	*to detain*
enterarse (de)	*to inform oneself* (*about*); *to find out* (*about*)
el (la) novio/-a	*sweetheart, fiancé(e)*; *groom* (*bride*)
parar	*to stop*

LEER

Mientras lees el artículo, presta (*pay* [lit. *lend*]) atención especial a las expresiones siguientes y decide lo que significa o implica cada una basándote en el contexto en que está usada.

1. El chisme es algo así como un cáncer...
2. ...así como negar nuestra propia existencia.
3. ...el chisme es como el aire...
4. Es una epidemia planetaria...
5. ...se maquilla como si estuviera en pleno desfile de carnaval.

Muchas veces nos han preguntado acerca de nuestros pasatiempos preferidos: bailar, escuchar música, leer, etc. Pero si fuéramos sinceras (y el chisme no tuviera ningún tabú), ¿te imaginas cuántas personas, sin vacilar, responderían: "chismear"?

"Shhh..., no lo digas a nadie, pero te tengo tremendo chisme". Si éste no es el principio de un tema de conversación entre dos amigas, estamos seguras de que es el final. En algún momento de la charla sale a relucir "la televonela" de algún conocido. El chisme es algo así como un cáncer (curable) que debemos atacar a tiempo para que no se extienda.

¿Ya te enteraste? Ahora Raúl está saliendo con otra chica y Marcia... la muy "creída", piensa que él aún suspira por ella... ¡Hum!!!

Si todos (hombres y mujeres) llegáramos a un acuerdo para detenerlo, sería maravilloso. Pero la realidad es otra. Negar la existencia del chisme sería algo así como negar nuestra propia existencia.

Para muchos, el chisme es como el aire que respiran: imprescindible e incontrolable. Lo encontramos en la escuela, el trabajo, la cafetería y hasta en cualquier familia. Es una epidemia planetaria y nadie está inmune a ella. Intentemos clasificarlo:

● **Chismes piadosos:** Podrían clasificarse como "tontos", porque en realidad a nadie le interesan. Ejemplo: "Al fin Rosa consiguió novio". "Anoche me llamó Carlos y le di un plantón", etc. Este tipo de chisme tiene un fin de curiosidad y es inofensivo.

● **Chismes venenosos:** Las personas que utilizan este tipo de comentarios terminan quedándose solas. Son detestables y casi siempre el chisme es inventado o tiene muy poca base. Ejemplo: "Vigila a tu novio, yo creo que está enamorando a Ana".

● **Chismes destructivos:** Los promueven personas bajas y envidiosas. Este tipo de chisme es el peor, porque puede encerrar difamación o tener graves consecuencias. Cuídate de escucharlo y mucho más de repetirlo. Cuando te encuentres ante un comentario de éstos, que puedan destruir moralmente a otra persona, detenlo enseguida. Ejemplo: "Yo creo que fulano usa drogas porque siempre está *ido*".

Como has podido comprobar, en ninguna de sus facetas el chisme es positivo, y la persona que ha hecho de él un hábito, nunca será bien aceptada en ningún grupo. A la larga el chismoso es detectado y termina solo. Sé honesta y evita los comentarios indiscretos acerca de otros. No te hagas eco de ellos y, sobre todo, cuando traten de destruir a otra persona, páralos a tiempo.

● **Chismes burlones:** Son los que utilizan algunas y algunos para resaltar y hacerse los simpáticos delante de un grupo. Ejemplo: "Marta jura que ese corte le queda regio..." "Rosa se maquilla como si estuviera en pleno desfile de carnaval". El fin aquí es criticar y destacar los defectos de un tercero para que los demás se rían y se diviertan.

● **Chismes interesados:** Son algo así como "chismes disimulados para enterarse de algo". Algunas personas los utilizan para ganar amistades, enemistar a unas con otras, o sacar algo a cambio. Son peligrosos y no esconden fines limpios. Además, muchas veces pueden ser inventados. Apártalos de tu vida y no les hagas eco. Ejemplo: "Maribel me dijo que eras una pesada y te lo digo porque yo sí soy tu amiga".

DESPUÉS DE LEER

A. Las variedades del chisme. Según el autor del artículo, hay cinco tipos de chismes. Usando el formulario que aparece a continuación, defínelos y da un ejemplo de cada uno. Después, escribe tanto las causas como los efectos de chismear.

Las variedades del chisme

Los tipos de chismes:

1.
   Definición:
   Ejemplo:
2.
   Definición:
   Ejemplo:
3.
   Definición:
   Ejemplo:
4.
   Definición:
   Ejemplo:
5.
   Definición:
   Ejemplo:

Las causas de chismear:

1.
2.
3.

Los efectos de chismear:

1.
2.
3.

B. Muchas veces los autores usan ejemplos e imágenes (metáfora, símil, analogía) para dar énfasis a sus ideas u opiniones. ¿Cómo reaccionas tú a los ejemplos incluidos en la sección titulada Leer? Considerando la manera en

Segunda etapa

que está escrito el artículo, ¿cuál es la actitud del autor hacia el chisme? Explica tu respuesta.

Actividades C, CH can be given as writing assignments.

C. El artículo se refiere al chisme como si fuera solamente una actividad de las mujeres. ¿Es verdad? ¿De qué chismean los hombres? ¿Qué papel desempeña el chisme en las campañas políticas?

CH. Haz una comparación entre los tipos de chismes mencionados en el artículo y las categorías que se encuentran en la política.

AUMENTAR EL VOCABULARIO

a cambio (de)	*in exchange (for)*
acerca de	*about, concerning*
alimentar	*to feed*
burlón/-ona	*derisive, mocking*
burlarse (de)	*to make fun (of) or joke (about)*
comprobar (ue)	*to confirm*
averiguar	*to verify*
crecer	*to grow, increase in size*
aumentar	*to increase, add to*
chismear	*to gossip*
comprometer	*to compromise*
el chisme	*gossip*
chismoso/-a	*gossipy (adj.); a gossipy person*
deshonrar	*to dishonor*
difamar	*to defame*
la fama	*fame, reputation*
el derecho	*general law, legal right*
la ley	*civil or constitutional law, ordinance*
el pleito	*lawsuit*
poner un pleito	*to sue, take to court*
la regla	*regulation*
destacarse	*to stand out*
relucir	*to shine, excel*
detener	*to detain*
parar	*to stop*
enamorarse (de)	*to fall in love (with)*
enterarse (de)	*to inform oneself (about); to find out (about)*
informarse (de)	*to obtain information (about)*
estar seguro/-a	*to be certain*
el (la) fulano/-a	*so-and-so, John/Jane Doe*
hacerse	*to become; to prepare oneself to be*
el (la) novio/-a	*sweetheart; fiancé(e); groom (bride)*

When the word Derecho is capitalized, it usually refers to law school, as in Facultad de Derecho. An alternative for Facultad de Derecho is Facultad de Leyes.

Generally speaking, Spanish speakers refer to the derecho of an individual, but the ley of a country, as in Tenemos el derecho de ganarnos la vida, pero es contra la ley robar a otros para hacerlo.

Sometimes, this mythical person is given the complete name of Fulano/-a de Tal. A second person would be referred to as Mengano/-a.

la preocupación — concern, worry
sorprender — to surprise
sugerir (ie, i) — to suggest; recommend
tomar una decisión — to make a decision

LA JUSTICIA Y LA CORTE

Lawyers are usually addressed as *Licenciado/-a*. See the *Comentario cultural* of this *etapa*.

El tribunal (el juzgado)

Actividad. Escribe la palabra que corresponde a las definiciones siguientes.

1. el lugar en donde se juzga al criminal
2. el (la) que está acusado/-a de cometer un crimen
3. el (la) que procesa (*prosecutes*) al acusado (a la acusada)
4. el (la) que defiende al acusado (a la acusada)
5. el grupo que decide si el acusado (la acusada) es culpable
6. el (la) que juzga al acusado (a la acusada)
7. los documentos legales que determinan la legalidad de un acto
8. la acción legal que puede iniciar un individuo contra otro
9. las garantías personales que tienen todos bajo un gobierno justo

Ventanilla al mundo hispánico — Las mujeres y el trabajo

Es interesante notar que, a pesar de los muchos estereotipos que existen en cuanto a los dos sexos, la discriminación sexual no es un factor en la selección de estudiantes universitarios en los campos profesionales: derecho, medicina, enseñanza, arquitectura, economía. Aunque pueda haber limitaciones económicas o circunstancias personales que afecten a la gente—sin tener en cuenta su sexo—que determinan si pueden terminar con éxito una carrera universitaria, su admisión a estos programas profesionales generalmente no tiene nada que ver con el sexo del solicitante o aspirante. Por lo tanto, es tan común ver mujeres médicos y abogadas en la América Latina como lo es en los Estados Unidos.

USO PRÁCTICO DEL ESPAÑOL — Talking About Unplanned Occurrences

In describing an accident that happened to you, you might say something like:

Ayer se me torció el tobillo.	I twisted my ankle. (*lit.*, My ankle got twisted.)
Al caerme, también se me cortó la rodilla.	When I fell, I also cut my knee (*lit.*, my knee got cut).

These statements recount events that happened by chance or accident.
 In Spanish, a number of verbs are used in this way when the speaker conveys that the action was unintended and unplanned.

Se me **cayó** el vaso.	I dropped the glass.
Se me **rompió** el plato.	The plate broke.
Se le **torcieron** los dos tobillos.	He twisted both his ankles.
Se les **quebró** el bate.	Their baseball bat broke.
Se me **ocurrió** una idea.	I had an idea.
Se les **olvidaron** las entradas.	They forgot the tickets.
¿Se te **perdió** la cartera? ¡Qué desgracia!	You lost your wallet? How awful!

Note that the verb agrees with the subject of the sentence (*el vaso, el plato, los tobillos,* and so on). The person involved in the action or affected by it is expressed with the indirect object pronoun (*me, te, le, nos, os, les*).

Ponerlo a prueba

A. ¿Qué pasó aquí? Ayer fue un día de mala suerte. Cuenta todo lo que pasó, siguiendo el modelo.

Modelo: Marta rompió dos platos. *A Marta se le rompieron dos platos.*

1. Yo olvidé mis libros en casa.
2. Julia perdió la receta que le dio el médico.
3. Torcí la rodilla en mi clase de ejercicio.
4. Ricardito rompió su juguete favorito.
5. Los niños estaban jugando al béisbol y quebraron su bate.
6. Dejé caer una botella de jugo en la cocina.

B. **¡Que desgracia!** Fíjate en los siguientes dibujos y escribe lo que la persona indicada dice.

Modelo:

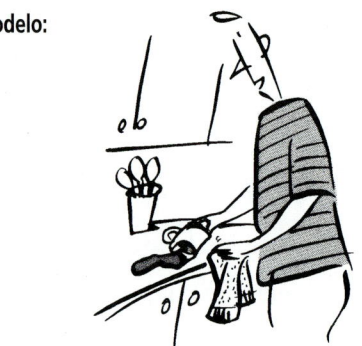

¡Se me rompió la taza!

1.

2.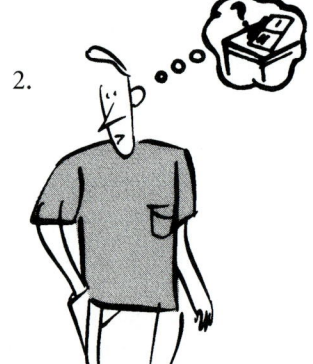

3.

4.

5.

6.

7.

C. Asociaciones. Relaciona la palabra o frase en la columna A con una palabra o frase semejante en la columna B. Luego, con cada palabra escribe una frase que muestre su significado.

A	B
1. alimentar	_____ a. aumentar
2. comprobar	_____ b. cesar
3. crecer	_____ c. dar de comer
4. el derecho	_____ ch. decidir
5. destacarse	_____ d. el enamorado
6. hacerse	_____ e. la justicia y la libertad individual
7. la ley	_____ f. llegar a ser
8. el novio	_____ g. la regla obligatoria
9. parar	_____ h. relucir
10. tomar la decisión	_____ i. verificar

CH. Diferencias importantes. Describe la principal diferencia entre los pares de palabras que aparecen a continuación.

Modelo: la abogada / el acusado
La abogada defiende a su cliente, pero el acusado es el cliente de un abogado (una abogada).

1. los chismes burlones / los chismes venenosos
2. deshonrar / honrar

3. alimentar / dejar morir de hambre
4. crecer / disminuir
5. el (la) juez / el (la) alguacil

D. **Definiciones.** Usa tu capacidad para adivinar a fin de identificar la palabra que corresponde a cada definición.

1. Esta palabra se refiere a una persona que habla mal de otros.
2. Se usa esta palabra para expresar un sentido de intranquilidad.
3. Se usa esta palabra para referirse a una persona no específica.
4. Esta palabra quiere decir "obtener información o datos".
5. Esta palabra se refiere al acto de hacer algo muy notable.
6. Esta palabra se refiere al proceso de madurar.
7. Se puede usar esta palabra para referirse al proceso de destruir la fama de alguien.
8. Esta palabra se usa para decir "causar una reacción de sorpresa".
9. Este término general se refiere a los que se ríen de los otros.

E. **Preguntas personales**

1. Cuenta una experiencia que hayas tenido que tenga que ver con un tribunal o con un abogado (una abogada).
2. ¿Cuáles son algunas características de un buen abogado (una buena abogada)?
3. ¿Te gustaría hacerte abogado/-a? ¿Por qué?
4. En tu opinión, ¿sería más fácil ser abogado/-a o juez? ¿Por qué?
5. ¿Qué opinas tú de los chismes?
6. ¿Qué haces tú cuando alguien te cuenta un chisme?
7. ¿Qué se puede hacer para desanimar (*discourage*) a una persona chismosa?
8. ¿Cuál es la diferencia entre un chisme y una mentira?
9. ¿Cómo te sientes cuando alguien se burla de ti?

INVESTIGAR LA GRAMÁTICA The Subjunctive with Certain Conjunctions

As you will recall, the subjunctive is often used to convey a mood of uncertainty. Sometimes, when we talk about or anticipate events or actions that will take place in the future, there exists this element of uncertainty. The following expressions in Spanish all require the use of the subjunctive.

a menos que	unless
antes (de) que	before
a pesar de que	in spite of
con tal (de) que	provided that, as long as
en caso de que	in case
para que	so that
sin que	without

> Explain to students that in this sense "future" is relative to the time in which an event is being (or was) discussed and when it will (or did) occur. Thus, I can refer to what I was going to do if something else occurred, although the entire sentence is expressed in past time. For example, *Carlos iba a salir temprano a menos que recibiera una llamada de Elena.*
>
> If there is no change of subject, Spanish most often uses *para, sin, antes de,* and *despues de* followed by the infinitive of the verb. *Voy a estudiar para poder ir a Nueva York durante las vacaciones. Anoche estudié por seis horas sin parar. Almorcé antes de salir. Me acosté despues de estudiar.*

Me iban a poner un pleito **a menos que** mi abogado les **escribiera** una carta.
They were going to take me to court unless my lawyer wrote them a letter.

Debes llamar a un abogado **en caso de que** te **pongan** un pleito.
You should call a lawyer in case they take you to court.

El juez llegará a las dos **con tal de que** no **haya** mucho tráfico.
The judge will arrive at two provided that there isn't a lot of traffic.

In the first example, the speaker did not know at the time of speaking whether the lawyer would write a letter. In the last two examples, the speaker does not know whether he or she will be taken to court or whether there will be a lot of traffic.

Compare the preceding statements with the following. Notice the difference in the degree of uncertainty being expressed.

> **OJO:** Notice that the use of the preterite expresses certainty in that it reports on events that took place in the past.

Manejo más rapido **cuando tengo** que llegar temprano.
I drive faster when I have to get there early.

Cuando hace mal tiempo llevo un paraguas a la oficina.
When the weather is bad I take an umbrella to the office.

Comenzaron **en cuanto llegó** el juez.
They began as soon as the judge got there.

Ponerlo a prueba

A. ¿Qué nos dice? Lee cada oración y decide lo que **no** sabemos. ¿Es posible escribir más de una respuesta?

Modelo: Pienso hablar con César a menos que llegue Marcos primero.
No sabemos quién va a llegar primero, Marcos o César.
No sabemos con quién la persona va a hablar.

1. Mis padres me dejarán ir a Nueva York con tal de que saque buenas notas en todos mis cursos este semestre.
2. Pero en caso de que salga mal, tendré que pasar el verano estudiando.
3. Espero que me presten el dinero para que pueda pasar todo el verano aquí.
4. Voy a estudiar mucho para que no tengamos que cambiar planes.
5. Me gustaría salir de vacaciones sin que mis padres me dieran permiso, pero no creo que sea posible.

B. El examen. Termina las frases que aparecen a continuación para formar oraciones completas. Para cada una hay varias posibilidades.

Modelo: Tengo que prepararme bien para el examen final a menos que la profesora...
Tengo que prepararme bien para el examen final a menos que la profesora nos diga que es optativo.

1. Pienso ir a la biblioteca antes de que los otros estudiantes...
2. Voy a almorzar contigo con tal de que...
3. Una amiga me va a llamar temprano para que...
4. No puedo levantarme sin que alguien...
5. Mis amigos me dicen que no haga planes para ir a las montañas con ellos en caso de que...

C. Los consejos. Un amigo tuyo (Una amiga tuya) te ha pedido consejos en cuanto a una beca prestigiosa de la universidad que piensa solicitar. Dale consejos en cuanto a lo siguiente:

Modelo: escribir la solicitud (*application*) a máquina
Debes escribir la solicitud a máquina para que los jueces la lean sin dificultad.

1. pedirle una carta de apoyo (*support*) de tu profesora de inglés
2. entregar la solicitud a tiempo o con anticipación
3. mandar la solicitud por correo o entregarla en persona
4. llamar a la oficina para preguntar si has ganado la beca
5. hablar con un juez, que es profesor tuyo, acerca de tus posibilidades
6. decirles a tus padres que has solicitado la beca

OJO: There may be more than one possible response. See how many plausible responses you can come up with for each phrase.

Follow-up: Have students gather in groups of three or four to see how many conjunctions can be used plausibly for each phrase.

CH. ¡No lo vas a creer! Escoge una expresión de la lista para completar cada oración.

a menos que   en caso de que
a pesar de que   para que
con tal (de) que   sin que

Modelo: Iban a salir a las nueve <u>a menos que</u> empezara la música.

1. Parece que en cualquier clase hay por lo menos un estudiante que intenta hacer trampa en los exámenes _____ no pueda recordar los datos importantes.
2. No lo vas a creer, pero en mi clase de historia hay una chica que siempre copia _____ la esté mirando el profesor.
3. Los otros estudiantes cubren sus trabajos _____ ella no los pueda ver.

4. Una vez durante un examen, ella pidió permiso para ir al baño _____ hubiera oportunidad de consultar el libro.
5. El profesor le dio permiso, _____ dejara su bolsa en la clase.
6. Y ella se puso furiosa, manteniendo que tenía que llevar la bolsa _____ no hubiera papel higiénico en el baño.
7. El profesor la miró, y con una sonrisa, le dijo: —Pues, señorita, le dejo salir _____ acepte nuevas preguntas en el examen al volver.
8. En fin, ella comprendió que no podría hacer trampa _____ lo supiera el profesor y ahora estudia para los exámenes.

The cues in *Actividad A* and *B* are in English so that the students will have to provide the vocabulary.

Haz las siguientes actividades con un compañero (una compañera).

A. **Experiencias nuevas.** El hermano menor de tu mejor amigo está al punto de matricularse en la universidad. Está hablando contigo, pidiéndote consejos acerca de lo que debe hacer—y no hacer—durante su primer año. Contesta sus preguntas, dándole la información que, según tu modo de pensar, es importante. Él quiere saber

- the best place to live and where to look for a place to live
- the best places off campus to eat
- the best night spots
- the best courses to take
- which courses to take as sequels to others
- the most difficult courses
- whether or not a car is a necessity

B. **¡Buen viaje!**

Estudiante A

Acabas de ganar una competencia. El premio es un viaje al Caribe. Afortunadamente, tienes un amigo (una amiga) que hizo el mismo viaje el año pasado. Pídele consejos a tu amigo/-a sobre:

1. the best time of year to go
2. the best type of lodging
3. whether to take cash or credit cards
4. how to find out more details about the trip
5. what will happen at customs

The role of *Estudiante B* is quite specific, which may tempt the students to try to translate the instructions directly into Spanish. Encourage students to focus on responding to the questions their partners ask, rather than including all the details of the printed advice.

Estudiante B

Tu amigo/-a acaba de ganar una competencia y recibió como premio un viaje al Caribe. Puesto que tú hiciste el mismo viaje el año pasado, tú conoces muy bien la región, y puedes darle consejos sobre lo que va a encontrar. Contesta sus preguntas, diciéndole lo siguiente:

1. Any time is good provided that it is not during the rainy season.
2. A large hotel is best in case you want to swim in a pool.
3. Most credit cards are accepted, but cash is needed to make purchases in the markets.
4. The travel agent will contact you with more information before the departure date.
5. You should not open your suitcases at customs unless the agent requests it.

OTRA VUELTA

Play instructor tape, 3 min.

Vuelve ahora a la Entrada que escuchaste al comienzo de esta etapa. Escúchala otra vez y contesta las siguientes preguntas.

1. ¿Es el curso por correspondencia mejor o peor que un curso regular? ¿Por qué?
2. ¿Cuál es la diferencia principal entre los dos?
3. ¿Qué tipo de materiales se usan para enseñar este curso?
4. ¿En qué aspecto del idioma se pone más énfasis?
5. ¿Cuál parece ser la desventaja principal de la clase por correspondencia?
6. En tu opinión, ¿cuál de los dos cursos sería mejor para aprender inglés?

COMENTARIO CULTURAL

El uso de títulos en el tratamiento social de la gente

Como ya hemos visto, los hispanohablantes usan títulos en vez de nombres al dirigirse a otra persona por escrito. Es muy común, por ejemplo, combinar un título de estado civil (Sr., Sra., Srta.) con la profesión de la persona a quien uno se dirige. Así es común ver formas de tratamiento como Sr. Ingeniero, Srta. Licenciada, Sr. Doctor, Sra. Gerente.

El título "Maestro/-a" además de referirse a un profesor (una profesora) de escuela primaria o secundaria, se usa con cualquier persona que se reconoce como un experto en algún arte como la música y la pintura, o un oficio como albañil (*mason*), plomero, mecánico. A los profesores universitarios que tienen su doctorado se les puede decir "Doctor(a)" o "Profesor(a)", siendo este el uso más común.

Las tarjetas de presentación también son muy importantes en América Latina y se usan tanto en situaciones formales de negocios como en las situaciones sociales más informales. En casi todos los tratos comerciales es casi seguro que se intercambiarán tarjetas de presentación, muchas veces como respuesta a la pregunta, —¿Tiene usted una tarjeta?— En los encuentros sociales se intercambian tarjetas si existe la posibilidad de que las dos personas quieran que ponerse en contacto en el futuro.

Actividad. A continuación hay varios ejemplos de tarjetas de presentación. ¿Puedes determinar la profesión de cada persona y qué título usarías al escribirle una carta?

TERCERA ETAPA

Querida Tía Lilia

ENTRADA

"¡Qué vida más cruel!"

Vas a oír una conversación entre Paco y Roberto. Mientras escuchas la conversación, determina

■ por qué está tan preocupado Roberto
■ qué deben pagar Paco y Roberto

- lo que no ha pagado Roberto todavía
- otro gasto que van a tener los dos dentro de poco

1. Roberto está tan triste porque...
2. Paco y Roberto deben pagar...
3. Roberto no tiene dinero para...
4. Dentro de poco los jóvenes tienen que pagar...

ANTES DE LEER Y ESCRIBIR

Play student tape, 1 min.

Estudiar y practicar

la angustia	anguish, despair
caleño/-a	a person from Cali
el comportamiento	behavior
encaprichado/-a	infatuated
espantoso/-a	frightening, terrible
lo antes posible	as soon as possible
medio muerto/-a	half dead
las ojeras	circles under the eyes
resultar	to result in, turn out to be
últimamente	lately, recently

Preparación

The first letter that follows is written to a personal advice newspaper columnist, like "Dear Abby" and Ann Landers in the United States. The writer has a friend, a college student, who has fallen so deeply in love that he cannot function in his daily life. Without looking at either the friend's letter or *Tía Lilia*'s response, try to imagine what the two letters will contain.

La carta de "Preocupado y desesperado":

1.
2.
3.

OJO: Remember that suggestions and advice are often expressed with the subjunctive: *Debe decirle a su amigo que* **haga**.... But when the friend states a fact about life, the indicative is used: *Debe decirle a su amigo que los estudios* **son** *más importantes que el amor.*

La carta de Tía Lilia aconseja que "Preocupado y desesperado" debe:

1.
2.
3.

Tercera etapa **497**

WRITING STRATEGY 11

Explain a situation

Explaining a situation requires two principal ingredients: presenting the facts in an organized manner and expressing one's own feelings in relation to the situation. A clear presentation of the information you want your reader to have is important so that the sequence of events and the current state of affairs are understood. Explaining your own relationship to the situation—your role in it, your feelings about it—is important if you want your reader to interpret the situation as you see it. The more clear and eloquent you are in your explanation, the less likely the reader will be to question your assumptions or disagree with your analysis.

LEER Y ESCRIBIR

As you read the first letter, analyze the strategy the writer uses. How is the letter organized? For each paragraph, first decide whether the writer emphasizes the facts or his feelings. Then write down what aspects of the facts or his feelings the writer mentions.

Carta de "Preocupado y desesperado"

Párrafo 1: ¿Información acerca de la situación o sentimientos personales?

1.   2.

Párrafo 2: ¿Información acerca de la situación o sentimientos personales?

1.   2.

Párrafo 3: ¿Información acerca de la situación o sentimientos personales?

1.   2.

Párrafo 4: ¿Información acerca de la situación o sentimientos personales?

1.   2.

Emphasize the fact that the writer is not using the same expression over and over but is using a variety of ways to refer to el amor: sus sentimientos, la situación, su pasión, su tristeza.

> **Querida Tía Lilia:**
>
> Yo sé que es un poco raro que un hombre escriba para pedirle consejos, pero no tengo otro remedio. Hoy le escribo porque estoy muy preocupado por el estado mental y emocional de mi amigo "Pepe" (no se llama así de verdad). Es más, últimamente me está volviendo completamente loco. Permítame explicarle la situación.

> Resulta que hace unos meses "Pepe" y yo hicimos un viaje a Colombia. Mientras estábamos en Cali, él salió unas cuantas veces con una muchacha caleña que podemos llamar "Rosita" y ahora se cree profundamente enamorado de ella. Está tan terriblemente encaprichado que está a punto de dejar hasta su carrera universitaria. Déjeme darle solamente unos ejemplos de su comportamiento.
>
> Primero, gasta todo su dinero en llamadas telefónicas a Cali y por eso no ha comprado ni la mitad de los libros y otros materiales escolares que necesita para este semestre. Además, parece que ya no puede (o no quiere) concentrarse en sus estudios, porque siempre está pensando en "Rosita". Segundo, prácticamente ha dejado de comer y dormir. Ha bajado unos ocho kilos y tiene unas ojeras espantosas. En fin, se ve medio muerto. Y finalmente, a mí no me deja en paz. No puedo estudiar en mi cuarto porque "Pepe" siempre llega a contarme sus angustias.
>
> Como usted puede ver, el problema no es solamente de "Pepe." Es mío también. Quiero ayudar a "Pepe", pero yo también necesito ayuda urgentemente. Por favor, aconséjeme lo antes posible.
>
> "Preocupado y desesperado"

OJO: Before going on to Tía Lilia's response, read what to look for at the top of page 499.

PREGÚNTESELO A

Tía Lilia

> Querido "Preocupado y desesperado":
>
> ¡Usted de verdad tiene un problema! Usted no me dice mucho acerca de su amigo: cuántos años tiene, cuántas veces ha estado (o se ha sentido) enamorado, etcétera, pero me imagino que "Pepe" es todavía joven y que no ha tenido mucha experiencia con el amor. Los casos como éste son muy difíciles, porque el "enamorado" siempre cree que nadie lo comprende. Es inútil tratar de disuadirlo de sus sentimientos. Lo único que Ud. puede hacer es darle la impresión de aceptar todo lo que dice como si fuera la verdad y ayudarlo a encontrar una manera de enfrentarse a la situación. La mejor terapia consiste en aceptarle a la víctima su pasión y su tristeza y en tratar de ajustar todo a la realidad. Dígale algo así—Mira, amigo. Yo sé que no hay nada más difícil que vivir lejos de la persona de tus sueños, pero si tú y "Rosita" van a casarse, no puedes decirles a sus padres que por quererla tanto te arruinaste la vida, sacrificaste tu carrera y volviste locos a los amigos y a la familia. Dedícate a tu amor y concéntrate en tu carrera para que puedas ser tan buen marido y padre como ella esposa y madre.
>
> Mientras tanto, Ud. debe tomarlo todo con calma. Así, salva usted la carrera de su amigo y la propia también.
>
> *Tía Lilia*

Tercera etapa

In the second letter, notice that *Tía Lilia* has several suggestions for what *"Preocupado y desesperado"* should say and not say to his friend "Pepe." As you read, indicate two pieces of advice that she offers on each side.

Lo que "Preocupado y desesperado" **debe** decirle a su amigo:

1.   2.

Lo que "Preocupado y desesperado" **no debe** decirle a su amigo:

1.   2.

DESPUES DE LEER

Invent a situation that is happening to a friend, and write a letter to *Tía Lilia* in which you ask for advice about how to help your friend. Go back to your analysis of the *"Preocupado y desesperado"* letter and use the structure of his letter as a model for the one you write.

AUMENTAR EL VOCABULARIO

OJO: Remember that *cerca de* means physically near.

OJO: A synonym for *aparentar* is *parecer*.

acerca de	about, concerning
la angustia	anguish; despair
aparentar (ie)	to seem to be
arruinar	to ruin
caleño/-a	a person from Cali
el comportamiento	behavior
conceder	to concede; to grant
dar la impresión de	to give the appearance of
desesperarse	to lose hope
desesperado/-a	desperate
disuadir	to dissuade; to deter
encaprichado/-a	infatuated
espantoso/-a	frightening; terrible
gastar	to spend (*money, not time*)
malgastar	to waste
el hogar	home
inútil	useless
lo antes posible	as soon as possible
mantener	to support; to maintain
medio muerto/-a	half dead
la mitad	half
las ojeras	circles under the eyes
propio/-a	own; of one's own
resultar	to turn out to be
salvar	to save
sobrevivir	to survive
la terapia	therapy

OJO: *Mantener* is conjugated like *tener*.

OJO: The expression *medio muerto* is most often used figuratively to mean "exhausted" or "wiped out."

la tristeza	sadness
últimamente	lately, recently

Ventanilla al mundo hispánico — Asuntos del corazón

Muchos periódicos y revistas en el mundo hispánico ofrecen columnas a través de las cuales la gente puede ponerse en contacto con un posible esposo o esposa, o sencillamente con un posible compañero. Estos breves anuncios normalmente contienen una descripción de la persona que escribe y una de la persona que se busca. Tanto los hombres como las mujeres utilizan estas columnas y siempre es divertido especular sobre cuáles serán los resultados de los anuncios. La que sigue es de una de estas columnas de un periódico de Caracas.

Caballero joven, culto, desea conocer chica de pelo suave y liso, no mal parecida y que viva en Caracas exclusivamente. Escribir con datos al Poeta Misterioso. Sección Correo del Corazón, Apartado 1192, Caracas.

¿Cómo crees que será una respuesta a esta carta?

Writing activity: Have students respond to this anuncio, *either for themselves or for a friend.*

LA CARA Y LOS COSMÉTICOS

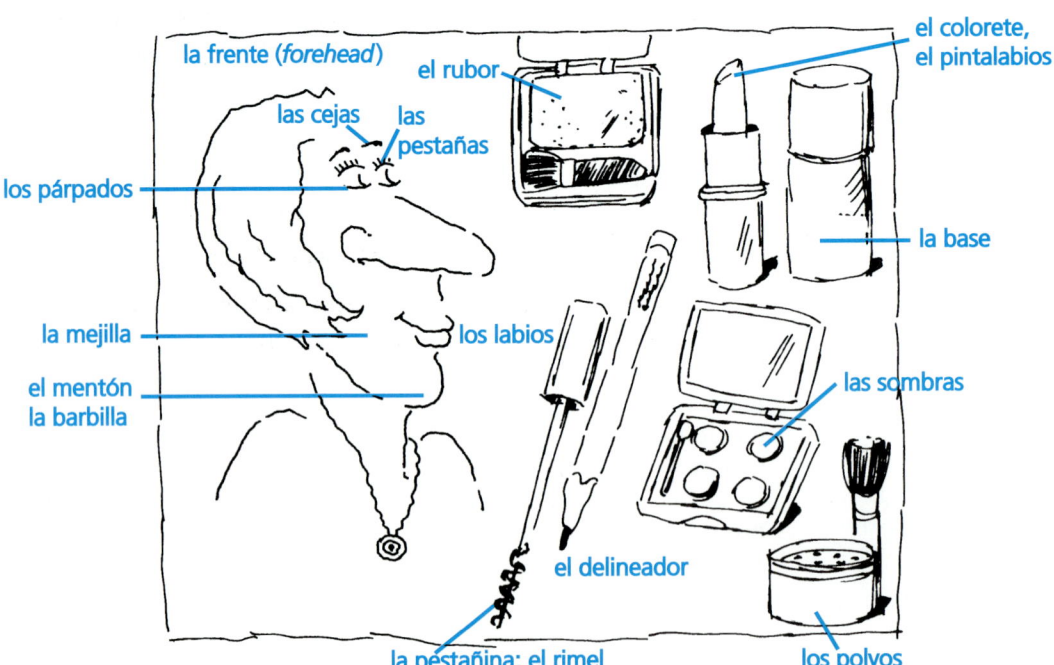

Actividad. Combinar los cosméticos con las facciones de la cara.

1. la mejilla
2. el mentón
3. las pestañas
4. las cejas
5. los párpados
6. la frente
7. los labios

a. el delineador
b. las sombras
c. el colorete; el pintalabios
ch. la base
d. la pestañina
e. los polvos
f. el rubor

USO PRÁCTICO DEL ESPAÑOL Más sobre algunos verbos

As indicated in Chapter 3, some verbs always appear with a reflexive pronoun, while many other verbs may use the pronouns to indicate that the subject of the sentence does something to or for itself. There are other verbs, however, whose meanings change completely when the reflexive pronoun is added. Here are some of those verbs.

dormir	to sleep	dormirse	to fall asleep
hacer	to do, make	hacerse	to become, prepare oneself to be (e.g., médico/-a)
ir	to go	irse	to go away, to leave
poner	to put, place	ponerse	to put on, become (e.g., ponerse furioso/-a)
probar	to try, taste	probarse	to try on
quitar	to remove, take away	quitarse	to take off
volver	to return	volverse	to become (e.g., volverse loco/-a)

Ponerlo a prueba

A. ¿Cuál será? Escoge el verbo apropiado, según el dibujo.

El estudiante
(a) quitó (b) se quitó
el polvo del libro.

La muchacha
(a) pone (b) se pone
una carta en el buzón.

El payaso (*clown*)
(a) pone (b) se pone
los zapatos.

La señora
(a) quita (b) se quita
el abrigo.

La chica
(a) probó (b) se probó
el café.

El muchacho
(a) prueba (b) se prueba
los zapatos.

Los jóvenes
(a) van (b) se van
al cine.

B. ¿Quién podría decirlo?   Aquí hay una serie de oraciones que podría haber dicho a. "Pepe", b. el amigo de "Pepe", o c. La Tía Lilia. En el espacio delante de cada número, pon la letra correspondiente a la persona que probablemente lo hubiera dicho.

_____ 1. ¡No puedo más! ¡Me estás volviendo loco!

_____ 2. No, hombre, no estoy encaprichado. Estoy enamorado.

_____ 3. ¡Tú no me entiendes, mis padres no me entienden, nadie me entiende!

_____ 4. Siento no poder pagarte, pero no me queda ni un centavo.

_____ 5. Mira, amigo, tienes que descansar. Tienes unas ojeras espantosas.

_____ 6. Tiene que aceptar todo lo que dice como si fuera la verdad.

_____ 7. No trate de convencerlo de que este amor va a fracasar, porque no lo va a aceptar.

C. Definiciones. Asocia las definiciones con palabras escogidas de Aumentar el vocabulario.

1. una persona que vive en Cali
2. destrozar
3. una persona que está pálida y que tiene ojeras grandes
4. el lugar en donde vive una persona
5. sistema de tratamiento médico o sicológico
6. la desesperación
7. que causa miedo
8. que no tiene ningún uso
9. ponerse una prenda de vestir para ver si le gusta
10. salir

> Review with students other conjunctions that are useful in creating compound and complex sentences: *sin embargo, además, porque, aunque*. Include the expressions in the *Investigar la gramática* section of the second *etapa*.

CH. "Personalmente creo..." Completa las oraciones que aparecen a continuación. Si estás de acuerdo, completa la oración usando la palabra **y**. Si no estás de acuerdo, usa **pero**.

Modelo: Mis amigos me dicen que todas las cartas que publica la "Tía Lilia" son auténticas, *pero personalmente creo que algunas son inventadas por ella.*

1. El amigo de "Pepe" dice que es poco común que un hombre escriba para pedir consejos, y / pero personalmente...
2. "Pepe" dice que está completamente enamorado de "Rosita", y / pero personalmente...
3. El amigo de "Pepe" cree que el amor a la distancia siempre fracasa, y / pero personalmente...
4. Hay muchos que dicen que un joven de 17 años no puede estar de verdad enamorado, y / pero personalmente...
5. El amigo de "Pepe" cree que es importante tratar de ayudar a su amigo, y / pero personalmente...
6. Según su amigo, el problema no es solamente de "Pepe", y / pero personalmente...
7. Hay muchos que creen que uno tiene que asegurar su carrera antes de casarse, y / pero personalmente...
8. Mucha gente cree que es más fácil tener éxito en la universidad si se está casado, y / pero personalmente...
9. Para muchas personas parece muy importante casarse lo antes posible, y / pero personalmente...
10. La Tía Lilia cree que le ha dado buenos consejos al amigo de "Pepe", y / pero personalmente...

D. Preguntas personales

1. ¿Conoces a alguien que le haya pedido consejos a una persona como "Tía Lilia"? ¿Qué pasó? ¿En qué circunstancias lo harías tú?

2. En tu opinión, ¿son buenos o malos los consejos que se dan en los periódicos?
3. ¿Qué haces cuando alguien te pide consejos?
4. Durante el año académico, ¿de qué te preocupas más?
5. ¿Cuál es una de las ventajas de casarte antes de graduarte? ¿Y una desventaja?
6. ¿Cuál es la diferencia entre estar encaprichado/-a y estar enamorado/-a?
7. ¿Cuáles son algunos "síntomas" que indican que una persona está enamorada?
8. ¿Con quién hablas cuando buscas consejos?

INVESTIGAR LA GRAMÁTICA   Anticipating Events and Actions

You have already learned that very often the present tense is used in simple sentences to talk about future time. In some instances, however, longer sentences can be used which contain references to something that is being anticipated but has not yet happened.

Roberto va a sentirse muy feliz **cuando vea** a Carmencita.	*Roberto is going to feel very happy when he sees Carmencita.*
Va a viajar otra vez a Cali **tan pronto como tenga** el dinero para el boleto.	*He is going to visit Cali again as soon as he has the money for the ticket.*

Here are some common expressions that introduce anticipated actions.

cuando	*when*
después de que	*after*
en cuanto	*as soon as*
tan pronto como	*as soon as*
hasta que	*until*

The meaning of these expressions often calls for the use of the subjunctive because the event named by the speaker has not yet occurred. Consider the following examples, which use the subjunctive.

Paco necesita hablar con Roberto **después de que llegue.**	*Paco needs to talk with Roberto after he arrives.*
Tan pronto como pueda, va a tratar de hacerlo concentrarse de nuevo en sus estudios.	*As soon as he can, he is going to try to make him concentrate again on his studies.*

In the following examples, the indicative is used because the event mentioned by the speaker **has already occurred.** That is, the speaker is recounting a simple statement of fact and is not anticipating any event.

Paco habló con Roberto **después de que llegó.**

Paco spoke with Roberto after he arrived.

Tan pronto como conoció a Carmencita, Roberto se enamoró.

As soon as he met Carmencita, Roberto fell in love.

When talking about events in the past, use the subjunctive to refer to an event that is anticipated but has not yet taken place at the time you are talking about. When no future event is anticipated, the indicative is used.

Se enamoró **en cuanto conoció** a Carmencita.

He fell in love as soon as he met Carmencita.

Pensaba invitarla a cenar **tan pronto como tuviera** tiempo.

He planned to ask her out to dinner as soon as he had time.

Íbamos a confirmar las reservaciones con el restaurante **tan pronto como llegáramos** a casa.

We were going to confirm the reservations with the restaurant as soon as we got home.

Ponerlo a prueba

A. **¿Ya ha ocurrido o no?** Lee cada oración y decide si se refiere a algo que ya ha ocurrido (**O**) o algo que todavía no ha pasado (**N**).

Modelo: Fuimos de compras cuando llegó Miguel. (**O**)

1. Este año hice los arreglos para comprar un retrato especial tan pronto como llegué a la universidad.
2. El artista me va a llamar tan pronto como lo termine.
3. Me dijo que puedo darle el dinero en cuanto lo tenga.
4. Mis amigos tuvieron que esperar hasta que le pagaran para recibir sus retratos.
5. Quiero regalárselo a mis padres sin que lo sepan mis hermanitos.
6. El año pasado ellos adivinaron cuál era mi regalo tan pronto como lo vieron.
7. Este año no voy a mostrarles el paquete hasta que mis padres empiecen a abrir sus regalos.

B. **Nuestro viaje.** Vamos a hacer un viaje tan pronto como terminen las clases este año. Completa el párrafo a continuación para describir nuestros planes.

En cuanto nosotros _____ (**terminar**) el último examen, saldremos para Florida. Cuando _____ (**cansarse**) de manejar tomaremos un café y continuaremos el camino. En cuanto _____ (**ver**) un buen hotel en el camino, pararemos. Al día siguiente, cuando _____ (**despertarse**), seguiremos manejando hasta que _____ (**llegar**) a la playa.

C. **En el aeropuerto.** Imagínate que vas a visitar a tu tía en España durante el verano. Escribe oraciones originales usando los grupos de palabras a continuación, añadiendo otras palabras que sean necesarias para describir el viaje.

Modelo: Mi tía / ir a recoger cuando / llegar
Mi tía me va a recoger cuando llegue.

1. Yo / ir a salir tan pronto como / tener tiempo
2. Yo / pensar darle un regalo cuando / visitar a mi amigo/-a
3. Mis amigos / tener que esperar hasta que / regresar para recibir sus regalos
4. La azafata / esperar hasta que / salir el avión para servir las bebidas
5. Yo / dormir hasta que el avión / aterrizar
6. Los otros viajeros / ir a buscar un hotel cuando / llegar

CH. **Haciendo los planes.** Estás en un restaurante hablando acerca de tus planes para el futuro con un grupo de amigos. Pero hay tanto ruido que es difícil oír todo lo que dicen. Usando los siguientes fragmentos, trata de reconstruir algunas de las oraciones.

Modelo: Me voy a graduar cuando...
Me voy a graduar cuando termine dos asignaturas más.

1. Me voy a casar cuando...
2. Mis padres me van a regalar un coche nuevo cuando...
3. Y los míos me van a pagar un viaje a Sudamérica en cuanto...
4. Oigan, los voy a invitar a una fiesta en cuanto...
5. ¡Ay, queridos amigos! Estaré muy triste cuando...
6. ¿Sabes que Micaela piensa visitar Bogotá el día en que...?
7. Sí. Y también dice que no vuelve hasta que...

D. **¿Fiesta?** Acabas de decirle a un amigo que estás pensando en hacer una fiesta. Ahora todo el mundo te está haciendo preguntas sobre la fiesta, aunque tus planes no son seguros. Contesta las preguntas indicando cierta incertidumbre.

Modelo: ¿Cuándo va a ser la fiesta?
Será tan pronto como lleguen mis amigos colombianos.

1. ¿Vas a invitar a muchas personas?
2. ¿Cuándo vas a empezar a invitarlas?
3. ¿Qué clase de música quieres que llevemos?
4. ¿Hasta qué hora vamos a bailar?
5. ¿Cuándo vas a hacer los preparativos?
6. ¿A qué hora va a empezar la fiesta?

E. **Los consejos.** Con dos o tres compañeros/-as de la clase, prepara una lista de consejos que podrías darle a tu hermanito/-a sobre cómo debe portarse al matricularse en la universidad.

Modelo: *Debes llamar a tu consejero/-a en cuanto llegues.*

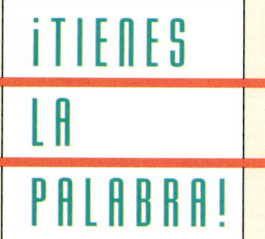

Haz las siguientes actividades con un compañero (una compañera).

Estudiante A

Your roommate is depressed because his girlfriend (or her boyfriend) is going to Mexico for the summer. You decide to call a "hot line" number for assistance and talk to a counselor.

1. Explain the nature of the problem.
2. Say what your roommate is or is not doing.
3. Discuss the effect it is having on you.
4. Ask for advice regarding what you should do to help your roommate.

Estudiante B

You are a volunteer counselor who answers a "hot line" number that people call when they are troubled. This caller insists that his or her roommate has a problem, but you suspect that the caller may be the one who is most in need of advice.

1. Ask what his or her roommate is doing.
2. Find out what problems this causes.
3. Make some recommendations as to how the caller might help his or her roommate.
4. Suggest that the caller contact you again in about a week to tell you what has happened.

OTRA VUELTA

[Play instructor tape, 1 min.]

Vuelve ahora a la Entrada que escuchaste al comienzo de esta etapa. Escúchala otra vez y contesta estas preguntas.

1. ¿Está fastidiado o tranquilo Paco?
2. ¿Cuál es la causa del problema?
3. ¿Cómo reacciona Paco?
4. ¿En qué sentido es el problema de Roberto también el de Paco?
5. ¿Qué consejos le da Paco a Roberto?

COMENTARIO CULTURAL

"¿Qué dirá la gente?"

Una de las causas más comunes de un "malentendido" entre los miembros de una cultura y los viajeros de otras culturas es la suposición inconsciente de que "todo el mundo sabe portarse bien". Sin embargo, todo viajero se da cuenta muy pronto de que las normas de conducta en una cultura no se aplican automáticamente a otras culturas. No existe ningún código universal de buena conducta; cada cultura o subcultura decide por sí sola qué es aceptable y qué no lo es.

En la tercera etapa, la dificultad que tiene Roberto en ajustarse a la ausencia de su querida Carmencita nos hace recordar las diferentes normas en cuanto a las relaciones sociales o románticas en el mundo hispánico y en los Estados Unidos. Si bien en los Estados Unidos puede ser aceptable que una persona invite a otra del sexo opuesto a su apartamento a estudiar, a tomar un cafecito o un refresco, o a ayudar a empacar todo antes de mudarse, tales invitaciones se verían muy mal en América Latina. Allí la regla es que una mujer nunca visita el apartamento o el cuarto de un hombre a menos que haya más personas presentes. El invitar así a alguien del sexo opuesto—o el aceptar tal invitación—representa una invitación abierta y transparente a establecer una relación íntima. Ya que la implicación sexual es tan obvia en estos casos, una invitación por el estilo fácilmente causa un malentendido y representa un insulto. El resultado más probable será que la amistad se acabe ahí mismo.

Otro ejemplo de una costumbre norteamericana que puede verse como inaceptable en las culturas hispánicas puede ocurrir cuando un muchacho joven acompaña a su amiga a la puerta de su casa después de haber salido con ella. En los Estados Unidos es común que la pareja se demore un buen rato a la puerta "despidiéndose". En la mayoría de los países hispánicos es preferible invitar al muchacho a entrar a la casa. Hasta la tendencia que tienen muchas personas a saludar o comenzar una conversación con una persona del sexo opuesto que no conozcan, digamos en un aeropuerto o una cafetería de la universidad, se ve como comportamiento descarado e impertinente. Si quien lo hace es una mujer, esto muchas veces les da a los hombres latinos la idea estereotípica y completamente errónea de que ella está tratando de llamar la atención.

En fin, una conducta aceptable y apropiada es de muchísima importancia para la persona que espere ser aceptada por otra cultura. Para que uno funcione

---

Point out that even within the same culture, what is appropriate in the city may not be appropriate in small towns (for example, an unmarried young woman living in an apartment by herself); what is appropriate for children is not appropriate for young adults; what is appropriate for men may not be appropriate for women, and so on.

Point out that in smaller towns, when a couple stands for a long period at the door, the perception of those who observe the pair might be any of the following: a. one of the pair is a servant and does not have the authority to invite his or her friend inside; b. the visitor is considered "unacceptable" by the people who live there, therefore he or she is not invited inside; c. the woman has loose morals. Although it is inappropriate to invite a person of the opposite sex into one's room or apartment, there is nothing improper about an invitation to the family home.

en otro ambiente cultural es tan importante el saber las expectativas sociales como lo es el saber hablar el idioma.

Actividad. Basándote en la información que se incluye en este Comentario cultural y en los anteriores, trata de determinar si las siguientes conductas se considerarían aceptables en Colombia u otro país hispánico.

Answers: 3, 5, 6, 7, 8, 9 are all appropriate. Point out that the acceptability of item 8 varies from context to context and country to country.

1. reírse y bromear en voz alta en un restaurante
2. caminar descalzo en casa
3. sacar todos tus artículos de uso personal del baño después de bañarte y arreglarte
4. llamar "mamá" a la madre de uno de tus amigos
5. ofrecer un cigarro o un chicle a todos los del grupo antes de tomar uno tú
6. abrir la puerta a alguien que no conoces
7. preguntar por los familiares de un amigo aunque tú no los conozcas personalmente
8. decirle "maestro" a un albañil o a un pintor al hablar con él
9. responder a un cumplido que te ha hecho la mamá de un amigo diciendo, —Gracias, es usted muy amable.
10. especificar en una invitación escrita a qué hora terminará una fiesta

[Play video]

Program 11 *Pueblos indígenas* Pre-Columbian communities in Mexico and Bolivia

A. Así es la vida. Based on your knowledge of your own culture, write a letter in Spanish to a foreign friend who is about to make a first visit to the United States. Give advice about "must-do's" and "taboos," and mention things that should and should not be done with regard to dating customs, table manners, and restaurant behavior in order to be considered polite.

B. Querida Tía Lilia. Find an advice column in the newspaper and read one of the letters. Then, prepare a brief summary in Spanish of the problem that the writer has and the advice that the columnist gives. See if you can accomplish the task using words that you already know, instead of looking up new words in the dictionary.

C. Yo soy la Tía Lilia. Formen grupos de tres personas. Cada grupo debe escribir una carta pidiéndole consejos a la Tía Lilia. Luego, intercambien cartas entre los grupos y escriban respuestas.

CH. ¡A matricularnos! Descríbele a tu amigo/-a el proceso de matriculación de cursos en tu universidad. Para ordenar la descripción debes incluir las palabras **primero, segundo, luego, entonces...** para contar la secuencia.

VOCABULARIO

Notas (Calificaciones) escolares

aprobado (regular) *acceptable*
bueno *good*
notable *very good*
sobresaliente *outstanding*
suspendido (reprobado, aplazado) *suspended; failing*

La justicia

abogado/-a (m/f) *attorney*
acusado/-a (m/f) *defendant*
alguacil (m) *sheriff; constable*
derecho (m) *general law, legal right*
juez (m/f) *judge*
jurado (m) *jury*
juzgado (m) *court of law*
ley (f) *civil or constitutional law, ordinance*
pleito (m) *lawsuit*
regla (f) *regulation*
tribunal (m) *court of law*

Bromas y chismes

broma (f) *joke*
broma (f) pesada *practical joke*
bromista (m/f) *entertaining person; practical joker*
burlarse (de) *to make fun (of), joke (about)*
burlón/-ona *derisive, mocking*
chisme (m) *gossip*
chismear *to gossip*
chismoso/-a *gossipy (adj.); a gossipy person*
en broma *in fun*
en serio *seriously*
hacer bromas *to joke; to play a trick*
hacer trampa *to cheat; deceive; trick*

La cara y los cosméticos

barbilla (f) *beard*
base (f) *base (makeup)*
cejas (f pl) *eyebrows*
colorete (m) *lipstick*
delineador (m) *eyeliner*
frente (f) *forehead*
labios (m pl) *lips*
mejilla (f) *cheek*
mentón (m) *chin*
ojeras (f pl) *circles under the eyes*
párpados (m pl) *eyelids*
pestañas (f pl) *eyelashes*
pestañina (f) *mascara*
pintalabios (m) *lipstick*
polvos (m pl) *powder*
rimel (m) *mascara*
rubor (m) *rouge*
sombras (f pl) *eyeshadow*

Palabras conectivas

acerca de *about, concerning*
a menos que *unless*
antes (de) que *before*
a pesar de que *in spite of*
con tal (de) que *provided that*
en caso de que *in case*
para que *so that*
sin que *without*

Palabras descriptivas

caleño/-a *a person from Cali*
cobarde *cowardly*
culpable *at fault*
desesperado/-a *desperate*
encaprichado/-a *infatuated*
engañoso/-a *deceitful*
espantoso/-a *frightening; terrible*
inútil *useless*
malicioso/-a *malicious*
medio muerto/-a *half dead; exhausted*
miedoso/-a *fearful*
piadoso/-a *merciful; pious*
triste *sad*
valiente *brave*

Verbos útiles

alimentar   *to feed*
aparentar (ie)   *to seem to be*
arruinar   *to ruin*
aumentar   *to add to*
averiguar   *to verify*
comprobar (ue)   *to confirm*
comprometer   *to compromise*
conceder   *to concede; to grant*
copiar   *to copy*
crecer   *to grow, increase in size*
culpar   *to blame*
dar la impresión de   *to give the appearance of*
desesperarse   *to lose hope*
deshonrar   *to dishonor*
destacarse   *to stand out*
detener   *to detain*
difamar   *to defame*
disuadir   *to dissuade; to deter*
echar   *to throw out*
echar flores   *to flatter*
echar la culpa   *to cast blame upon*
enamorarse (de)   *to fall in love (with)*
engañar   *to trick; to deceive*
enterarse (de)   *to inform oneself (about)*
estar seguro/-a   *to be certain*
fracasar   *to fail*
gastar   *to spend*
hacerse   *to become; to prepare oneself to be*
informarse   *to obtain information about*
malgastar   *to waste*
mantener   *to support; to maintain*
matricularse   *to register (for a course)*
parar   *to stop*
resultar   *to turn out to be*
salir bien   *to do well; to turn out well*
salir mal   *to do poorly; to turn out badly*
salvar   *to save*
sobrevivir   *to survive*
sorprender   *to surprise*
sugerir (ie, i)   *to suggest; recommend*
temer(se)   *to fear*
tener éxito   *to succeed*
tener la culpa   *to be at fault*
tomar una decisión   *to make a decision*

Sustantivos útiles

angustia (f)   *anguish; despair*
asunto (m)   *matter; issue*
carrera (f)   *career; major field of study*
comportamiento (m)   *behavior*
culpa (f)   *fault; blame*
fama (f)   *reputation*
fulano/-a (m/f)   *so-and-so, John / Jane Doe*
hogar (m)   *home*
incertidumbre (f)   *uncertainty*
mentira (f) piadosa   *white lie*
mitad (f)   *half*
novio/-a (m/f)   *sweetheart; fiancé(e); groom (bride)*
piropo (m)   *a flattering comment*
preocupación (f)   *concern, worry*
tema (m)   *theme*
terapia (f)   *therapy*
tristeza (f)   *sadness*

Otras palabras y expresiones útiles

a cambio de   *in exchange for*
lo antes posible   *as soon as possible*
propio/-a   *own; of one's own*
últimamente   *lately, recently*

VOCABULARIO PERSONALIZADO

¡Hasta pronto!

Capítulo 12

COMMUNICATIVE OBJECTIVES

In this chapter, you will learn several new ways to

- talk about activities in progress
- express emotions
- anticipate future events
- make plans for staying in touch

PRIMERA ETAPA

"Te quiero más que nunca..."

ENTRADA

Play instructor tape, 2 min.

"¡Ay de mí!"

Ahora vas a escuchar una conversación entre Graciela y su amiga Ernestina. Hace tres años que Graciela sale con Jorge, su novio, y ahora ha surgido un problema serio entre los dos. Escucha la conversación entre las dos amigas para determinar

- adónde Jorge piensa ir y por qué
- qué han dicho los padres de Graciela
- lo que Graciela **no** quiere hacer

Una crisis en la vida de Graciela

¿Qué desean—o **no** desean—Jorge, Graciela y los padres de Graciela? Resume la posición de cada uno.

Jorge:
Graciela:
Los padres de Graciela:

EMPEZAR

Play student tape, 3 min.

Leer

a pesar de	*in spite of*
cargar	*to load*
contar (ue) con	*to count on; to depend upon*
estar enamorado/-a (de)	*to be in love (with)*
mover palancas	*to pull strings*
el salario	*hourly wage*

Repetir

Escucha la cinta y repite lo que oyes.

Identificar

En una hoja aparte, escribe en una columna las palabras y frases anteriores. Vas a oír algunas oraciones. Cada vez que oigas una de esas palabras o frases, apunta el número de la oración al lado de la palabra. Cada oración se leerá dos veces.

Escribir

Vas a oír unas oraciones, cada una leída dos veces. Escríbelas al escucharlas.

Reconocer

Ahora, lee otra vez las oraciones que acabas de escribir. Cada una contiene una o más de las palabras y frases de la lista en la sección anterior de Leer. Al releerlas, subraya todas las palabras y frases que vienen de la lista. Mientras lees, haz todas las correcciones necesarias.

Episodio 1: "Te quiero más que nunca"

Enfoque comunicativo

Las clases han terminado y Roberto le está escribiendo una carta de amor a Carmencita Meléndez, su amiga de Cali. Al leer la carta, busca la siguiente información.

- las noticias de Roberto
- el trabajo que consiguió
- sus planes para el verano

6 de mayo

Adorada Carmencita:

Tengo buenas noticias. Primero, te quiero más que nunca. Segundo, te cuento que afortunadamente me recuperé en los estudios y que terminé el semestre con muy buenas notas en casi todas mis materias, menos biología. Resulta que demoré tanto en empezar a estudiar para ese curso que, a pesar de mis esfuerzos en las últimas semanas, sólo pude sacar como nota final una C (un siete en tu sistema).

Pero lo más importante, mi tesoro, es que es muy posible que nos veamos. Estoy haciendo todo lo posible para que nos veamos de nuevo este verano. Mi papá habló con el gerente de la compañía donde trabaja en San Antonio, y movió palancas para darme un buen empleo a partir del primero de junio. Voy a cargar y descargar camiones de carga con una transportadora de horquilla. Es un trabajo pesado, pero el salario es excelente. Voy a ayudar a mis papás con los gastos de la casa, pero aún así, creo que para la tercera semana de julio voy a poder pasar unos días contigo en Cali. ¡Ay, mi corazón, cuento los minutos que faltan para verte!

OJO: *Una transportadora de horquilla* is a fork lift.

> *La carta de Roberto, primera parte*
>
> 1. ¿Cuáles son las buenas noticias de Roberto?
> 2. ¿Cuál es el trabajo que consiguió Roberto?
> 3. ¿Por qué pudo Roberto conseguir un trabajo tan bueno?

Enfoque lingüístico

Lee la carta otra vez y apunta

- dos expresiones de cariño que usa Roberto
- la expresión que usa para describir cómo su padre le consiguió el trabajo

LEER

Episodio 2: "¡Cómo son los padres!"

Enfoque comunicativo

Sigue leyendo la carta de Roberto a Carmencita y busca la siguiente información.

- la actitud de los padres de Roberto ante su amistad con Carmencita
- por qué Roberto tiene que empacar sus cosas

> Les he contado mucho de ti a mis papás y les he mostrado las fotos que me has mandado, pero todavía no creen que tú y yo seamos novios o que estemos de verdad enamorados. ¡Cómo son los padres! Cuenta con que te quiero y que te extraño muchísimo. No falta mucho para que estemos juntos de nuevo. Ojalá que algún día sea para siempre.
>
> Bueno, vida mía, por ahora tengo que seguir empacando mis cosas. Tengo que mudarme de la residencia mañana por la mañana, y por la tarde voy a San Antonio en avión. Te escribo de nuevo al llegar a casa. Mientras tanto, recibe un abrazo fuerte y el gran amor de tu novio que tanto te quiere
>
> *Roberto*

> *La carta de Roberto, segunda parte*
>
> 1. ¿Cuál es la actitud de los padres de Roberto ante su amistad con Carmencita?
> 2. ¿Por qué tiene Roberto que empacar sus cosas?

Enfoque lingüístico

Lee la carta otra vez y apunta

- ■ la exclamación con la cual Roberto reacciona ante la actitud de sus padres
- ■ cómo expresa Roberto su deseo de casarse con Carmencita en el futuro

VERIFICAR

Las oraciones siguientes son falsas. Corrígelas de acuerdo con la carta de Roberto a Carmencita.

1. Roberto sacó buenas notas en todos sus cursos.
2. Roberto piensa trabajar todo el verano.
3. Roberto trabajará en una oficina.
4. Desgraciadamente, el trabajo no paga mucho, pero es interesante.
5. Roberto está empacando sus cosas porque ya se gradúa de la universidad.

AUMENTAR EL VOCABULARIO

OJO: The expression *pasión ardiente* is found in romantic fiction.

Note new definitions for *contar*. Students learned the meaning "to recount a story" in Chapter 5.

a pesar de	*in spite of*
no obstante	nevertheless
sin embargo	nevertheless
adorado/-a	*adored; very dear*
ardiente	ardent; passionate
cargar	*to load*
descargar	to unload
contar (ue) con	*to count on; to depend upon*
crecer	*to grow (up)*
criarse	to grow up, be raised
de hoy en adelante	*from now on*
echar de menos	*to miss, long for*
extrañar	to miss, long for
empacar	*to crate; pack up*
el esfuerzo	*effort*
estar enamorado/-a (de)	*to be in love (with)*
gozar (de)	*to enjoy something*
la palanca	*lever*
mover (ue) palancas	to pull strings
tener un enchufe / tener palancas	to have connections
el rato	*period of time, while*
al poco rato	shortly after
recuperarse	*to recuperate (health)*

el salario	hourly wage
la jornada	working day
tiempo parcial; jornada parcial	part-time
medio tiempo	half-time
el sueldo	salary

Point out to students the difference between el sueldo *and* el salario, *which is a false cognate.*

VENTANILLA AL MUNDO HISPÁNICO — Los términos cariñosos

Diminutives are also used in families in which children are named after their parents. For example, Carmencita's mother may well be named María del Carmen, and a boy called Danielito might be the son of Daniel.

En el Capítulo 7 aprendiste que se pueden usar los apodos y los diminutivos para expresar afecto y cariño, tanto hacia los niños como hacia los adultos.

En su carta a Carmencita, Roberto usa otros términos de afecto. A continuación se presentan algunas expresiones de amor.

amor mío	mi vida
cariño	vida mía
corazón	querido/-a
mi amor	mi tesoro
mi cielo	amorcito

MÁS PROFESIONES Y OFICIOS

la agente de bienes raíces

el bombero

el camionero

la carpintera

la comerciante

el farmacéutico

El agricultor (la agricultora) is another word for farmer.

los granjeros

la mujer de negocios

la obrera

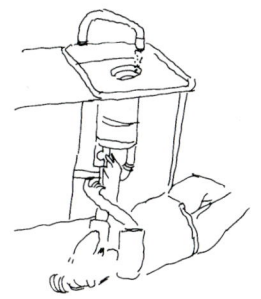
el plomero

El plomero is *el fontanero* in Spain.

Extension: Turn any of these sentences into role plays. Students work in pairs to prepare the role play (call to the service provider, discussion of the problem, arrangements for an appointment) and present it to the class.

Actividad. ¿A quién llamas?

1. Necesitas hacer reparaciones en el techo de tu casa.
2. Hay agua en el piso de la cocina. Parece estar saliendo por debajo del fregadero.
3. Ves un accidente entre un camión y un coche. Hay mucha gasolina en la calle.
4. El médico te ha recetado unas pastillas para tu bronquitis.
5. Piensas hacer renovaciones en la casa. Quieres levantar paredes nuevas en la cocina y construir un garaje.
6. Quieres alquilar un apartamento en una ciudad grande.
7. Necesitas consejos sobre cómo conseguir un empleo en una multinacional.
8. Te cuidas mucho en cuestiones de salud y quieres comprar legumbres y huevos muy frescos.

USO PRÁCTICO DEL ESPAÑOL Repaso del verbo **estar** con el gerundio (**-ndo**) y con el participio pasado (**-do**)

"Progressive" forms consist of the verb *estar* followed by the present participle (the *-ndo*) form. To form the present participle, first delete the *-ar, -er,* or *-ir* ending from the infinitive. Then add *-ando* for *-ar* verbs and *-iendo* for *-er* and *-ir* verbs.

OJO: Remember that *-er* and *-ir* verbs whose stem ends in a vowel spell the present participle *-yendo*: *cayendo, leyendo, construyendo.* Also remember that *-ir* stem-changing verbs show the second change in the present participle: d**u**rmiendo, s**i**rviendo, div**i**rtiéndose.
The present progressive was introduced in Chapter 6, second *etapa*.

Progressive forms stress the ongoing nature of an activity. Unlike in English, progressive forms are never used to talk about what is going to happen in the future.

Salgo para Colombia mañana. **Estoy haciendo** la maleta ahora mismo.
I'm leaving for Colombia tomorrow. I'm packing my bags right now.

Estar followed by the past participle used as an adjective describes a state that results from a previous action.

Abrí la puerta y **está abierta** todavía.
I opened the door and it's still open.

No puedo leer este periódico; **está escrito** en ruso.
I can't read this newspaper; it's written in Russian.

Ponerlo a prueba

A. Un día de mucha actividad. Es un día de mucha actividad para la familia Garza. Forma dos oraciones con los elementos indicados para decir (1) qué están haciendo los miembros de la familia y (2) cuál es el resultado de su acción. Sigue el modelo.

Modelo: Marta / lavar el carro
Marta está lavando el carro. El carro está lavado.

1. Jorge / lavar el carro
2. Patricia / escribir una carta a su abuelo
3. Ignacio / construir una casita para el perro
4. Tomás / abrir todas las ventanas de la casa
5. Raquel / hacer unas galletas de chocolate
6. Cristina / reparar su estéreo
7. Antonio / poner la mesa para la comida
8. La señora de Garza / servir la comida
9. Los niños pequeños / divertirse en el patio
10. La muchacha / planchar la ropa

B. Sinónimos y definiciones. Al lado de cada palabra, escribe un sinónimo o una definición. Después, escribe una oración que incorpore tanto la palabra como su sinónimo o definición.

Modelo: el salario
el dinero que recibe una persona por el trabajo que hace
El salario en este trabajo es muy bajo; trabajo muchísimo, pero me pagan solamente cuatro dólares por hora.

1. de hoy en adelante
2. echar de menos
3. tener un enchufe

4. un rato
5. cargar
6. crecer
7. gozar
8. ardiente

C. **Una carta romántica.** Un amigo tuyo te ha pedido ayuda con una carta que le está escribiendo a su novia. La quiere, pero no es una persona muy romántica y su carta le parece un poco seca. Ayúdale a darle más pasión a la carta. Cambia las palabras y expresiones indicadas, y otras si puedes, para crear una carta llena de sentimientos románticos.

> *Querida Diana:*
>
> *Otra vez te escribo para decirte que **te quiero mucho** y que te echo de menos. **Me gustan** tus cartas y nuestras llamadas telefónicas los fines de semana. Cuando visite tu país este verano quiero pasar **un rato** contigo. Me alegra mucho de que seamos **amigos**, aunque vivamos en diferentes países.*
>
> *Pues, **mi amiga**, ya tengo que irme a la clase de español—la más importante para mí en estos días—y después a la biblioteca. Te escribo de nuevo esta noche cuando termine de estudiar. Recibe **un saludo** de tu novio que siempre **piensa en ti**,*
>
> *Alejandro*

CH. **Preguntas personales**

1. Actualmente, ¿tienes trabajo de tiempo parcial? ¿Cuántos horas por semana trabajas?
2. ¿Qué pueden hacer los hombres o la mujeres de negocios para aumentar su sueldo?
3. ¿Conoces a alguien que pueda mover palancas en la universidad o en el empleo? ¿Puedes pensar en un ejemplo de cuándo lo hizo?
4. Después de un fin de semana muy activo, ¿cuántos días necesitas para recuperarte?
5. A pesar del ruido, ¿hay ventajas asociadas con vivir en una residencia estudiantil? ¿Cuáles son algunas desventajas?
6. ¿Cuáles son las ventajas de vivir en casa con tu familia hasta graduarte de la universidad? ¿Cuáles son las desventajas?
7. ¿A quién extrañas mucho cuando no estás con esa persona?
8. Hay personas que extrañan a sus animales domésticos. ¿Qué opinas de las relaciones tan fuertes entre un animal y su dueño/-a?

INVESTIGAR LA GRAMÁTICA Repaso general del subjuntivo

Here is a summary of the key points about the subjunctive that you have studied in previous chapters.

Expressions using the verb *ser* followed by an adjective and the infinitive express general truisms.

Es importante llegar a tiempo.
Es posible estudiar y divertirse a la vez.
Es necesario sacar buenas notas.

OJO: This use of the subjunctive was first presented in Chapter 8, first *etapa*.

When these general truths are applied to a particular individual or situation, the subjunctive is used in place of the infinitive.

Es importante que tú llegues a tiempo.
Es posible que tengamos un examen mañana.
Es necesario que Roberto saque buenas notas.

OJO: This use of the subjunctive was first presented in Chapter 7, third *etapa*.

The subjunctive is used when one person tries to influence another's actions, either directly or indirectly.

Les dije que leyeran el capítulo con cuidado.
Sugiero que ustedes pasen varias horas en la biblioteca.
Quiero que todos saquen buenas notas.

OJO: See Chapter 8, second *etapa*.

The subjunctive is used to express emotions. The emotion itself is in the indicative; the event or circumstance that evokes the emotion is in the subjunctive.

Siento mucho que no **hayas podido** acompañarnos.
Nos alegramos de que **tengas** otra oportunidad de visitar Cali.
La familia de Marilú deseaba que la celebración de sus quince años **fuera** una experiencia inolvidable.

OJO: See Chapter 11, first *etapa*.

In "if-clauses," the subjunctive is used to talk about situations or events that are contrary to fact or are believed to be impossible.

Si **tuviera** dinero, iría a Colombia.
Alicia cocinaría un plato chino-colombiano si **recordara** la receta.
Si nuestro equipo de fútbol americano **ganara** todos los partidos, sería el campeón nacional.

OJO: See Chapter 7, first *etapa*.

The subjunctive is used to describe people, things, or situations that are not part of one's personal experience and may not even exist.

Roberto y Paco piensan buscar una pensión que **tenga** una habitación con baño.
Alicia quiere encontrar un restaurante que **sirva** comida típica.
No hay nadie que **sepa** hablar todos los idiomas del mundo.

OJO: See Chapter 11, third *etapa*.

In adverbial clauses, the subjunctive is used to refer to something that is anticipated but has not yet happened.

Vamos a cenar **cuando lleguen** los invitados.
Tan pronto como termine con el examen final, estaré de vacaciones.

OJO: See Chapter 8, third *etapa*.

The subjunctive is used to express doubt, denial, and disbelief.

Dudo que **tengamos** suficiente dinero para cenar en ese restaurante.
Niego que mi hermano **sea** el ladrón que la policía busca.
No creo que tú **puedas** terminar a tiempo.

Ponerlo a prueba

A. Por favor... Imagínate que eres gerente de una oficina. Las peticiones (*requests*) que aparecen a continuación están expresadas de una forma bastante brusca. Busca una manera más cortés de expresarlas, empezando con **quisiera** o **me gustaría**.

Modelo: Quiero que me ayudes.
Quisiera que me ayudaras, por favor.
Me gustaría que me ayudaras, si puedes.

Have students add follow-up information to create a context: *Quisiera que me ayudaras, por favor. Si trabajamos juntos, podemos terminar el proyecto hoy.*

1. Ud. tiene que escribir esta carta antes de las cinco.
2. Quedese en casa hasta que termine el informe.
3. Tráigame un café.
4. Búsqueme el archivo (*file*) del Sr. Garcés.
5. Quiero que Ud. lea el informe del Sr. Hinojosa y que me diga si necesita atención inmediata.
6. Llame al carpintero. Quiero que me construya una estantería para libros aquí en esta pared.
7. Dígale a Núñez que su contrato estará listo mañana a las tres.
8. Cuénteme qué pasó en su reunión con Vásquez.

B. Consejos para el trabajo. El padre de Roberto le está dando consejos para que se lleve bien con sus compañeros de trabajo. Completa sus oraciones usando los verbos indicados.

1. Es muy importante que tú _____ (**llegar**) a tiempo todos los días.
2. Es necesario que _____ (**llevar**) tu almuerzo contigo, ya que te dan solamente media hora para comer.
3. Es bueno que _____ (**comer**) con los otros trabajadores para conocerlos mejor.
4. También es importante que _____ (**usar**) sombrero y que _____ (**tomar**) mucha agua durante el día, porque el sol es bastante fuerte por la tarde.
5. Es posible que tu salario _____ (**ser**) un poco más alto que el de los jóvenes que trabajan tiempo parcial. Así que es mejor que no _____ (**decir**) nada acerca de cuánto te pagan.
6. Tampoco es bueno que _____ (**mencionar**) cómo conseguiste el trabajo. No quiero que nadie _____ (**saber**) que yo moví palancas para mi hijo.

C. ¿Qué tipo de empleo buscas? Imagínate que estás a cargo de una encuesta. Inventa una posible respuesta de las personas que se mencionan a continuación. Escoge los verbos de la siguiente lista, usando un verbo diferente para cada oración.

dar	pagar
emplear	permitir
garantizar	producir
hacer	tener
incluir	_____ (verbo que tú seleccionas)

Modelo: carpintero   *Busco trabajo con una compañía que me emplee ahora mismo, porque necesito trabajo urgentemente.*

1. agente de bienes raíces
2. hombre / mujer de negocios
3. estudiante (trabajo para el verano)
4. profesor/-a
5. taxista
6. farmacéutico/-a
7. enfermero/-a
8. consejero/-a

CH. Planes para el futuro. Unos amigos hablan de los planes profesionales de Graciela. Completa lo que dicen, prestando atención tanto al modo de los verbos (subjuntivo/indicativo) como al tiempo (presente, futuro, etc.).

Graciela: Bueno, pienso dedicarme a los negocios. En cuanto _____ (**terminar**) los estudios, _____ (**poder**) conseguir un puesto con una multinacional. Es posible que yo _____ (**empezar**) con un sueldo bastante alto si sigo estudios graduados antes de empezar a trabajar.

Rafael: Pero no creo que te _____ (**aceptar**) para estudios graduados de negocios a menos que _____ (**tener**) ya experiencia en el mundo de los negocios. Creo que tú _____ (**tener**) que trabajar por unos años antes de volver a estudiar.

Yolanda: Quizás _____ (**tener**) razón, Rafael, pero creo que el caso de Graciela _____ (**ser**) diferente, ya que ella _____ (**trabajar**) durante tres veranos con Merrill Lynch.

Graciela: Pero estoy de acuerdo contigo, Rafael. Sería mejor que yo _____ (**buscar**) trabajo después de graduarme, pero la verdad es que me _____ (**encantar**) la vida de estudiante y no quiero abandonarla todavía.

D. La situación de Roberto. ¿Qué opinas de la situación de Roberto? ¿Es bueno establecer una relación romántica con una persona que vive en otro continente? Completa las frases que aparecen a continuación para darle algunos consejos a Roberto.

1. Roberto, creo que sería mejor que tú...
2. En realidad, es malo que tú...
3. En el futuro tú y Carmencita...

4. Y ¿qué va a pasar cuando...?
5. Siento ser tan pesimista, pero dudo que...
6. Si yo estuviera en tu situación, yo...

¡TIENES LA PALABRA!

Haz las siguientes actividades con un compañero (una compañera).

A. **En casa de los Meléndez.** Imagínate que Roberto ha ido a Cali a visitar a Carmencita y que está conversando con sus padres. Formen grupos de dos, en los cuales una persona es Roberto y la otra es el padre o la madre de Carmencita.

Estudiante A: Roberto

1. Greet Dr. and Mrs. Meléndez.
2. Thank them for allowing Carmencita to go out with you.
3. Answer their questions about your summer job.
4. Respond to their concerns about your friendship with their daughter. Explain to them your feelings for Carmencita.
5. Bring the conversation to a close.

Estudiante B: El padre / La madre de Carmencita

1. Greet Roberto, and welcome him to your home.
2. Inquire about his trip.
3. Ask about his summer job.
4. Question him closely about his feelings for Carmencita and his intentions for the future.
5. Express your concerns, explaining conventions of Hispanic culture as appropriate.
6. Bring the conversation to a close.

B. **Un accidente de automóvil.** Hubo un accidente de automóvil. Afortunadamente no es nada grave, pero el carro está en una cuneta (*ditch*) al lado del camino y no se puede sacarlo. El conductor (La conductora) va a una casa cercana a llamar por teléfono para pedir ayuda. El dueño (La dueña) de la gasolinera contesta la llamada telefónica. Con un compañero (una compañera) haz el siguiente mini-diálogo.

Estudiante A: El conductor (La conductora)

1. Explícale al dueño (a la dueña) de la gasolinera cómo ocurrió el accidente.
2. Explícale dónde está tu carro ahora y qué ayuda necesitas.
3. Pregúntale cuánto te va a cobrar. Si el precio te parece demasiado alto, discútelo con él o ella.

Estudiante B: El dueño (La dueña) de la gasolinera

1. Pregúntale cómo ocurrió el accidente. Pídele muchos detalles.
2. Averigua dónde está el automóvil y qué ayuda necesita.
3. Dile cuánto vas a cobrarle. Si se queja, defiende el precio y la alta calidad de tu trabajo.

OTRA VUELTA

Play instructor tape, 2 min.

Vuelve ahora a la Entrada que escuchaste al comienzo de esta etapa. Escúchala otra vez y contesta las siguientes preguntas.

1. ¿Cómo se siente Graciela?
2. ¿Cuál es su conflicto interior?
3. ¿Cómo expresa Ernestina su compasión por la situación de su amiga?

COMENTARIO CULTURAL

Más sobre enchufes y palancas

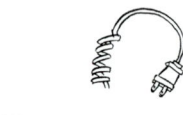

Hablando literalmente, un enchufe es el extremo de un cable eléctrico que se conecta a la pared. Una palanca es una barra larga que una persona usa para poder mover objetos muy pesados.

Coloquialmente, sin embargo, la expresión "tener un enchufe" quiere decir conocer a una persona que tiene influencia y que puede ayudarnos a obtener algo. "Mover palancas" quiere decir aprovechar las buenas conexiones para conseguir un trabajo, un favor, etc. Es decir, si tú tienes un buen enchufe, puedes mover palancas. Estas dos expresiones demuestran el deseo de hacer negocios con gente que ya es conocida. Estas relaciones personales son recíprocas, ya que los amigos que "han movido palancas" por ti algún día van a esperar que tú los ayudes a ellos también.

En el caso de las relaciones que existen entre padres e hijos, normalmente uno no piensa en "enchufes" ni "palancas". Como en todas las culturas del mundo, los padres hacen todo lo posible para ayudar a sus hijos. El énfasis que se pone en la lealtad a la familia dentro de la cultura hispánica quiere decir que los hijos respetan mucho a sus padres y que asumen cada vez más responsabilidad para con ellos cuando son viejos.

Una carta de agradecimiento. Tomando el papel de Roberto en esta etapa, escríbele a tu padre una carta de agradecimiento por haberte ayudado a conseguir tu trabajo de verano.

"Y yo te quiero a ti..."

ENTRADA

Play instructor tape, 2 min.

Un encuentro feliz

Ahora vas a escuchar una conversación entre Pilar y Julia en la cual hablan de la cita que Julia tuvo la noche anterior. Al escuchar, busca la información siguiente.

- el nombre y la profesión del hombre con quien salió Julia
- lo que él le regaló
- adónde fueron a cenar

Apuntes sobre la conversación

Nombre del hombre:
Profesión:
El regalo:
Nombre del restaurante:

ANTES DE LEER

Look for cohesive elements

Words and sentences are connected to form paragraphs that are "logical" in the sense that meaning flows smoothly. Certain words suggest that a phrase elaborates or illustrates (in other words, for example), qualifies or contrasts (however, on the other hand), compares or emphasizes (similarly, of course), enumerates or lists (first, next, then), or reports, synthesizes, or concludes (therefore, in summary, in conclusion). As you read, pay attention to these words, since they are important guides to understanding the passage.

Preparación

It has been said that men and women are social beings who need the presence of their own kind. The need to feel a part of a group or to have a sense of belonging in a particular social environment is important to our mental health. Can you think of instances in which these basic needs can result in overreactions or negative reactions?

Play student tape, 1 min.

Estudiar y practicar

el apoyo	*support*
atraer	*to attract*
insoportable	*intolerable*
madurar	*to mature*
padecer	*to suffer*
superar	*to overcome*

LEER

The title of the article asks the question "Do you suffer from *solofobia*?" What type of condition do you think is being described? As you read, note the definition of this condition given by the author. Also, note why some people suffer *solofobia* and what advice the author gives to help overcome it.

The article comes from a Spanish-language women's magazine and, as a result, is written from a woman's perspective. Do men suffer from *solofobia* too? As you read the article, make note of the concerns and preoccupations that the author mentions and decide whether or not they apply to both sexes.

¿Eres una lapa...? Padeces de Solofobia

Muchas chicas creen que si no están con un hombre al lado... no valen. ¿Eres tú una de ellas? ¡Ten mucho cuidado! Esa sensación de abandono puede hacerte caer en los brazos del primero que encuentres... aunque éste no te convenga.

Carla, de 22 años, es la típica chica que padece de *solofobia*, una terrible sensación de abandono que la hace estar prendida a cualquier brazo masculino. Desde que cumplió 16 años ha tenido infinidad de romances. Ahora sale con un muchacho que, según sus propias palabras, "es totalmente insoportable", pero piensa seguir con él hasta que encuentre a otro sustituto. Ella no puede —ni sabe— vivir si no tiene un enamorado.

¿Dónde está el problema?

Los sicólogos explican que este síndrome se da porque algunas piensan "que sin un chico no somos gente".

Para agravar el problema, entra otro factor: la "edad". Y es que a partir de los 20 años nos empezamos a fijar que el mundo entero consiste de parejas. Y así sucede lo inevitable: caemos en manos de uno de esos "insoportables" que deambulan por este planeta.

Por supuesto, no es extraño que nos sintamos así. Desde pequeñas se nos ha reafirmado el concepto de que las mujeres estamos "completas" cuando tenemos pareja. Jamás se ha dado énfasis al hecho de que también somos personas capaces de sentirnos plenamente satisfechas, realizadas ¡y divertidas! aun cuando estemos solas.

Pero la solofobia comienza a manifestarse desde la adolescencia, pues es en esa época cuando las chicas necesitan reafirmar su sentimiento de que son hermosas, populares y capaces de atraer al sexo opuesto. Y aunque muchas de estas muchachas crecen y maduran en otros aspectos, su nivel de autoconfianza permanece en estado adolescente y les resulta imposible lograr esa independencia emocional.

Teresa, que a los 24 años ya es jefa de una agencia de empleo, admite que aún no ha superado esa etapa: "Siempre quiero realizar todas mis actividades acompañada por un hombre. La simple idea de salir sola al cine, a cenar o a una exposición, me parece ridícula y sin sentido. Para mí, estar sola significa que no soy capaz de interesarle a nadie, y este sentimiento no es precisamente muy agradable".

Este complejo de inferioridad afecta todas las facetas de tu vida. Para comprenderlo mejor, deja que Ana Laura te cuente su caso: "Cuando terminaba con un chico, inmediatamente comenzaba a buscar otro. A menudo, no tenía nada en común con ellos, pero adoptaba sus puntos de vista para mantenerlos interesados en mí. Ahora, todos mis gustos, ideales e intereses están destrozados y no sé en realidad qué es lo que quiero".

Tu verdadero Yo

Si te pasas la mayor parte de tu tiempo haciendo lo imposible para evitar estar sola, eso quiere decir que aún no has desarrollado tu propia personalidad, que necesitas un apoyo. Si es así, debes aprender a conocerte a ti misma, y lo que es más importante, a gustarte a ti misma. La única manera para que puedas lograr esto —y al mismo tiempo mejorar tus relaciones sentimentales en un futuro— es pasando más tiempo a solas y aprendiendo a disfrutarlo.

Irónicamente, cuanto más esfuerzos haces por encontrar un chico con quien salir, más difícil es que aparezca el que realmente te ame y te comprenda. Tratar de adaptarte siempre a las necesidades de los demás, trae como resultado que pierdas lo que TU realmente quieres.

Los sicólogos utilizan una frase muy real que debes recordar: "La única persona con quien tienes que vivir para siempre es contigo misma, por lo tanto, te harás un gran favor si aprendes a conocerte y a 'disfrutarte'".

Beatriz comprendió esta lección gracias a su compañera de cuarto en la universidad. "Mónica era completamente diferente a mí; tenía gran cantidad de amigos con los que compartía sus gustos, pero jamás se desesperaba por formalizar una relación. Además, se sentía feliz de quedarse algunas noches en casa, aunque la invitaran a salir, si en realidad no sentía deseos de estar acompañada. Aprendí muchísimo de ella. El primer paso y el más importante para curarte de la solofobia es reconocer que estar sola no es malo".

Amistad vs. romance

Aunque suene obvio, vale la pena recordar que una de las formas de vencer la solofobia es tratar a los muchachos como personas, no como prospectos amorosos. Los amigos desinteresados te ayudarán en situaciones donde la solofobia puede hacer crisis, por ejemplo, cuando tienes que asistir a una actividad donde todos van acompañados.

Aunque las costumbres sociales establezcan la relación de pareja como el estado ideal para la mujer, no debes dejarte amarrar por los estereotipos. Una pareja saludable y equilibrada es aquélla donde ambos disfrutan de la compañía mutua, sin perder su identidad. Pero de otra forma, uno de los dos estará anulando las expectativas de su compañero y, a la larga, ninguno de los dos será verdaderamente feliz. Y eso, por supuesto, no es lo que tú quieres.

DESPUÉS DE LEER

Read the article a second time and locate the following words in the text. Indicate what relationship these words establish between the ideas expressed.

Cohesive element	Relationship	Explanation
pero	contradiction	Although she finds her boyfriend unbearable, she continues to go out with him.
así	_____	_____
por supuesto	_____	_____
aunque	_____	_____
si	_____	_____
cuanto más	_____	_____
por lo tanto	_____	_____
además	_____	_____

AUMENTAR EL VOCABULARIO

advertir (ie, i)	to warn; to advise
la anticipación	expectation
con anticipación	in advance
atraer	to attract
disminuir	to diminish
empequeñecer	to become smaller
estimar	to esteem
amar	to love
adorar	to adore
menospreciar	to hold in contempt
florecer	to flourish
desarrollar	to develop
el fondo	background
a fondo	in depth
insoportable	intolerable
madurar	to mature
el noviazgo	courtship
padecer	to suffer
pasajero/-a	temporary
superar	to overcome
tener en mente	to take into account
tener presente	to take into account, bear in mind
tomar en serio	to take seriously

OJO: The related noun is *el menosprecio*. A stronger degree of scorn and contempt is *despreciar* and *el desprecio*.

Ventanilla al mundo hispánico

Salir en grupos

Entre muchos jóvenes latinoamericanos es común salir en grupos gran parte del tiempo, en vez de salir solos un joven y su amiga. Algunas de las familias más tradicionales creen que la muchacha debe salir siempre en grupo con sus amigos, sus conocidos o sus compañeros de clase. Aunque ya no es muy común que la pareja de jóvenes tenga que salir acompañada de un pariente o "chaperón", el que dos jóvenes salgan solos en pareja no es tan común en el mundo hispánico como lo es en los Estados Unidos.

LAS RELACIONES PERSONALES

USO PRÁCTICO DEL ESPAÑOL   Fact, Possibility, . . . or Opinion?

One of the most critical decisions that a person must make in a discussion or when reading for information is whether the statements made are factual or not. Pleasant conversations can become problematic if one or another of the parties insists that everything he or she says is factual and that whatever someone in disagreement says is opinion. Conversely, one component of effective conversation skills is the ability to express an opinion in a nonthreatening manner, and by doing so to imply that you are not opposed to changing your position. The importance of context in helping a reader determine meaning has been emphasized throughout the reading strategies presented in *Entradas*. Similarly, common sense or your own life experience will also help you decide whether many of the statements you read and hear are factual, contrary to fact, supposition, or opinion.

Although "facts" are often interpreted according to the point of view of the speaker or the writer, some phrases do clearly signal that a supposition or an opinion—which may or may not be a fact—is being expressed. Listed below are just a few expressions that are commonly used to introduce suppositions and opinions, both in conversation and in writing.

Supposition	*Opinion*
parece que	a mi parecer
se dice	en mi opinión
es posible que	creo que
se supone	sospecho que
aparentemente	según mi modo de pensar
puede ser que	opino que

Ejemplos

Mi tía está muy enojada conmigo. (*statement of fact*)
Aparentemente mi tía está muy enojada conmigo. (*statement refers to an assumed or apparent fact*)
Creo que mi tía está enojada conmigo. (*my opinion regarding the situation*)

Ponerlo a prueba

A. **¿Hecho, suposición u opinion?**   Lee las oraciones que están a continuación, y decide si representan hechos (**H**), suposiciones (**S**) u opiniones (**O**).

1. Muchas personas creen que si no están con otra persona al lado no valen como personas.
2. Aparentemente, Carla no puede ni sabe vivir si no tiene un enamorado.
3. La solofobia comienza a manifestarse desde la adolescencia.

4. La simple idea de salir sola al cine, a cenar o a una exposición, me parece ridícula y sin sentido.
5. Se dice que la única persona con quien tienes que vivir para siempre es contigo misma.

B. Las relaciones. Escoge la frase de la columna a la derecha que mejor corresponda a la expresión de la columna a la izquierda.

_____ 1. los conocidos
_____ 2. los amigos
_____ 3. la pareja
_____ 4. los novios
_____ 5. los recién casados
_____ 6. los casados

a. después de cinco años de matrimonio
b. salen juntos de vez en cuando
c. acaban de ser presentados el uno al otro
ch. hace muchos años que se conocen y salen juntos
d. acaban de salir de la boda
e. están juntos todo el tiempo y quieren casarse

C. En vez de decir... se puede decir... Hay varias maneras de expresar casi cualquier idea o concepto en español. Escoge la palabra o expresión de la columna a la derecha que mejor corresponda a la de la izquierda.

_____ 1. insoportable
_____ 2. crecer
_____ 3. disminuir
_____ 4. enamorados
_____ 5. padecer
_____ 6. tener presente
_____ 7. no permanente
_____ 8. querer mucho
_____ 9. advertir

a. adorar
b. aumentar
c. empequeñecer
ch. sufrir
d. dar consejos
e. pasajero/-a
f. novios
g. tener en mente
h. intolerable

CH. Antónimos. Escoge la palabra o expresión cuyo significado sea el contrario. Luego, escribe una definición breve de la palabra.

1. permanente
2. burlar
3. aceptable
4. aumentar
5. amar

D. Adivinanzas. A continuación hay algunas expresiones basadas en las palabras de Aumentar el vocabulario. A ver si puedes adivinar el significado de cada una, sin usar el diccionario.

Modelo: un amor floreciente   *love in bloom*

1. reservar con anticipación
2. una deuda creciente
3. el desarrollo económico
4. un aumento de sueldo
5. un amor pasajero

E. Preguntas personales

1. ¿Qué te hace falta cuando estás en la universidad?
2. ¿Qué extrañas más de tus años en la escuela secundaria?
3. ¿Quién es la persona más insoportable que has conocido recientemente?
4. ¿A quién estimas mucho? ¿Por qué?
5. ¿Qué materias estudias más a fondo en la universidad?
6. ¿Qué puede hacer un hombre para asegurarse de que florezca una relación con una mujer? ¿Y al revés?

Follow-up: Have students create a sentence for each phrase that illustrates its meaning.

INVESTIGAR LA GRAMÁTICA   Reviewing the Reading Strategies

With each chapter of *Entradas* you have been introduced to a strategy that you can use to become a more effective and efficient reader of Spanish. Here is a list of those strategies.

1. Use your background knowledge of the subject
2. Use your knowledge of context
3. Read for specific information
4. Read for general information
5. Use visual clues
6. Anticipate and predict content
7. Preview internal organization
8. Identify sentence segments
9. Note the key point in each paragraph
10. Recognize relationships between words and phrases
11. Read between the lines
12. Look for cohesive elements

Now, apply these strategies as you complete the activities in the next section.

Ponerlo a prueba

A. ¿Qué sé yo? El título del artículo en esta etapa sugiere que tiene que ver con los individuos que sufren del miedo al abandono. Sobre la base de tu experiencia, o lo que hayas leído sobre el asunto, contesta las siguientes preguntas.

1. ¿Cuáles son algunos síntomas del problema?
2. En tu opinión, ¿es la solofobia una debilidad severa? ¿Por qué?
3. ¿Qué puede hacer una persona para mejorarse?
4. ¿Cómo le pueden ayudar sus amigos a un individuo que padece de esta enfermedad sicológica?
5. ¿Cómo aumenta o disminuye el problema la sociedad o la cultura?

B. Bosquejo (*Outline*) general. Prepara un bosquejo del artículo, empezando con el título y fijándote en las secciones principales del texto. Debajo de cada idea principal incluida en el bosquejo, apunta por lo menos un detalle que explique o apoye la idea.

C. Por ejemplo... La persona que escribió el artículo dio varios ejemplos para convencer al lector. Lee la descripción de lo que pasó con Carla, con Teresa y con Beatriz, y decide qué muestra cada anécdota en términos de la opinión de la persona que escribió el artículo.

CH. Palabras conectivas. Fíjate en el comentario de Beatriz e identifica las palabras que ella usó para dar fluidez a lo que decía. Escribe una lista de estas palabras y compáralas con las que están en la Estrategia de leer de página 528.

> As a follow-up to *Actividad D,* have students exchange letters and write responses. In some instances, it may be a good idea to do this as a paired activity, to allow for peer editing.

D. Querida Tía Lilia. Imagínate que Carla es una amiga tuya y que tú no sabes qué hacer para ayudarla. Escribe una carta a la "Tía Lilia" describiendo el problema de Carla y pidiendo consejos.

¡TIENES LA PALABRA!

Con un compañero (una compañera) de la clase, haz el siguiente mini-drama.

Estudiante A

You call a friend and suggest that the two of you go out for the evening to celebrate the end of the school year. Suggest several things that the two of you could do, and convince your friend to celebrate with you.

> *Estudiante B*
>
> A friend calls you and suggests that the two of you go out for the evening to celebrate the end of the school year. Unfortunately, you have a number of obligations that you must take care of. Each time your friend suggests something, tell him or her what you have to do instead.

OTRA VUELTA

Play instructor tape, 2 min.

Escucha otra vez la Entrada de la segunda etapa y contesta las preguntas que siguen.

1. ¿De dónde es el amigo de Julia?
2. ¿Dónde vive actualmente?
3. ¿Cómo es el amigo?
4. ¿Qué van a hacer Julia y Pilar mañana?

COMENTARIO CULTURAL

Cuando los jóvenes quieren salir en pareja

Las costumbres que existen en los Estados Unidos respecto a cuándo y cómo dos jóvenes pueden salir solos en pareja son bastante diferentes de las de los países hispánicos. Por lo general, en el mundo hispánico los jóvenes comienzan a salir en grupos a la edad de catorce o quince años, más o menos. Esta es la edad a la cual los jóvenes estadounidenses comienzan a salir solos en pareja. En el mundo hispánico la división del grupo de amigos en parejas normalmente ocurre varios años más tarde, después de graduarse de la escuela secundaria, por ejemplo. Aún así, la costumbre de salir en grupo para divertirse es tan fuerte en el mundo hispánico que sigue siendo muy común durante toda la vida.

En el Capítulo 5, Roberto invitó a Carmencita Meléndez a salir al cine con él. Aunque los padres de Carmencita la dejaron ir, insistieron en que fuera a la primera función—que es por la tarde—para que ella regresara a casa antes del anochecer.

Como ya viste en el vocabulario de esta etapa, los hispanoparlantes usan palabras como "amigo/-a" y "buen amigo (buena amiga)" para hablar de una relación que puede ser sólo una amistad o el comienzo de una relación algo romántica, pero no muy bien definida todavía. Una vez que el joven y su "amiga" han descubierto que los une una relación afectiva bastante profunda y seria, empiezan a usar las palabras "mi novio/-a". Las palabras "novio" y "novia" nunca deben emplearse en el sentido de la expresión *boyfriend* o *girlfriend* en inglés, pues estas palabras en español implican una relación mucho más profunda y duradera.

A. Encuesta. ¿Estás de acuerdo con las declaraciones siguientes o no?

1. Los jóvenes no deben salir solos en pareja hasta los 17 años.
2. Los padres deben conocer a la familia de los amigos de sus hijos adolescentes, antes de permitir que sus hijos salgan con ellos.
3. Los jóvenes adolescentes de 14 o 15 años no deben salir por la noche sin su familia.
4. Si los novios viven juntos antes de casarse pueden evitar el divorcio.
5. Es recomendable en algunos casos casarse antes de terminar los estudios universitarios.
6. Los jóvenes deben vivir con sus padres hasta casarse.

B. ¿Estamos de acuerdo? Ahora compara tus respuestas con las de los compañeros de la clase. ¿Dónde hay mayor desacuerdo? En el caso de las declaraciones más polémicas, hagan una lista de las razones a favor y en contra.

TERCERA ETAPA

El gran crisol del mundo

ENTRADA

"¡Que te vaya bien!"

Escucha estas frases de varias conversaciones distintas. Al escucharlas, determina lo que motiva la fiesta y apunta los planes de cada persona.

Una fiesta
Motivo de la fiesta:
Arturo:
Beatriz:
Rodrigo:

ANTES DE LEER Y ESCRIBIR

Play student tape, 1 min.

Estudiar y practicar

las acciones	*stocks, shares*
estorbar	*to hinder, obstruct*
el (la) familiar	*family member*
justo/-a	*fair, just*
las mercaderías	*commodities, merchandise*
perjudicar	*to damage, impair*
el presupuesto	*budget*
el principio	*principle*
provechoso/-a	*advantageous, beneficial*

Preparación

En este capítulo hemos hablado de las relaciones entre los amigos y los enamorados, y de lo importante que es ser justo, honrado y de tomar en cuenta las necesidades del otro. Lo mismo se puede decir de las relaciones en el negocio. Lee el artículo que aparece en la página 539 y apunta en tus propias palabras (es decir, sin copiar) algunas de las pautas (*guidelines*) que nos da el autor.

1.   4.
2.   5.
3.

Possible response (Writing Strategy 12): The guidelines would have become "preachy" if negative consequences had been given for each one. Saving the "consequences statements" for the end gives them greater impact, since they will be foremost in the readers' minds after they complete the article.

Ahora, dale a las pautas que has escrito en orden de importancia, según tus experiencias y tus valores morales. ¿Hay una norma que tú pondrías en la lista que no se haya incluido en el artículo?

WRITING STRATEGY 12

Have an overall plan

Perhaps the most important strategy when you approach any composition task is to have a sense of your mission: What is your goal? Who is your audience? How should you organize the content of what you are about to write? If you look again at "Ética y cortesía en los negocios," you will see that the author's last two pieces of advice are different from the others in having a second sentence that explains the far-reaching negative effects of engaging in particular business practices. Why did he put those two guidelines at the end? Can you fit your hypothesis into a possible overall plan for this article?

ETICA Y CORTESIA EN LOS NEGOCIOS

por Luz Solano Borrero

Desafortunadamente, en la vida contemporánea el dinero tiene un atractivo tan grande que hay personas que llegan a sacrificar su integridad, honradez y reputación a cambio de acumular riquezas en el menor tiempo posible. Es tan fuerte su ambición y el deseo de hacerse ricos rápidamente que se olvidan de los valores morales.

Se dice que el terreno de los negocios es deleznable (*slippery*). Por eso, es necesario tener sumo cuidado. Se requiere actuar correctamente, con prudencia, con lealtad y sin envidia (para evitar un desliz). Además, deben tomarse en cuenta las más elementales normas de la cortesía y de la ética profesional, sin las cuales pueden surgir serios problemas aún entre viejos amigos o familiares cercanos.

Hay principios fundamentales que deben observarse en toda transacción comercial, tales como:

- *No volverse atrás en un negocio cuando se ha dado la palabra, aunque no exista un documento.*

- *No tratar de realizar un negocio tan provechoso para uno que pueda causarle un descalabro* (serious setback) *a otra persona o corporación.*

- *No desacreditar lo que tiene planes de comprar con el objeto de conseguir un precio más bajo de lo justo.*

- *Nunca utilizar a un amigo o a un familiar para hacerle competencia desleal o estorbar los proyectos o negocios de otros.*

- *No aprovecharse de intrigas para adquirir acciones, mercaderías o propiedades a menor precio a costa del sacrificio de los demás.*

- *No valerse de trucos para obtener ganancias exageradas.*

- *No darle al cliente un presupuesto menor para luego, al cerrar el negocio, "ajustarle" un precio más alto.*

- *No menospreciar los artículos o los servicios de otras personas con el propósito de cobrar más por los suyos.*

- *Nunca pagar con un cheque sin fondos. Además de ser un delito penalizado por ley, su nombre y su crédito se perjudicarán.*

- *No haga prometer cosas que no va a poder cumplir. Hacer falsas promesas es faltarle el respeto a los demás.*

ESCRIBIR

Ahora tú vas a escribir un breve artículo siguiendo el formato y el estilo de los comentarios de Luz Solano Borrero sobre los negocios. Sigue las indicaciones que aparecen a continuación.

1. Primero, escoge el tema general y el tema específico que vas a tratar.
2. Después, escribe un primer párrafo en el cual explicarás tu tema y por qué es importante tener ciertas pautas para manejarse bien en él.
3. Tercero, redacta (*draft*) tu lista de consejos.
4. Finalmente, arréglalos en el orden apropiado de acuerdo con tus metas (*goals*).

AUMENTAR EL VOCABULARIO

las acciones	stocks, shares
la Bolsa	stock exchange
el cheque sin fondos	bad check (*one that bounces*)
las mercaderías	commodities, merchandise
el atractivo	attraction
cumplir (con)	to complete; follow through (*on*)
estorbar	to hinder, obstruct
el (la) familiar	family member
justo/-a	fair, just
la lealtad	loyalty
leal	loyal
desleal	disloyal
perjudicar	to damage, impair
el presupuesto	budget
el principio	principle
provechoso/-a	advantageous, beneficial

OJO: The adjective "attractive" is also *atractivo/-a*.

EL MUNDO

OJO: The corresponding adjectives are *africano/-a, antártico/-a, asiátio/-a, australiano/-a, europeo/-a, norteamericano/-a, sudamericano/-a*.

1, 2, 4, 8, Europe; 3, Africa; 5, 6, 9, Asia; 7, South America; 10, North America.

Mira el mapa en la página 541.

Actividad. ¿En qué continente está...?

1. Lituania
2. Grecia
3. Marruecos
4. Polonia
5. Vietnam
6. India
7. Paraguay
8. España
9. Corea
10. México

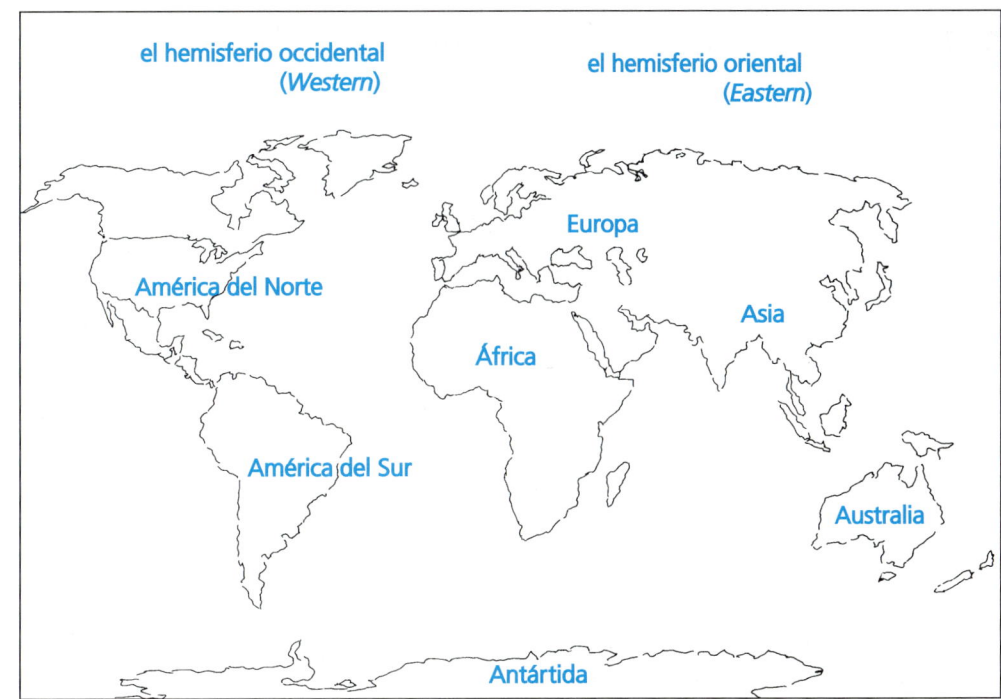

In most schools in Latin America and Spain, North America and South America are counted together as a single continent, *América*.

Ventanilla al mundo hispánico Proverbios y refranes

Los proverbios y refranes son una forma de divertirse con el idioma. Suelen expresar mucha información en pocas palabras. Estas expresiones se usan casi exclusivamente en situaciones familiares o muy informales y forman una parte importante de la conversación de todos los días. Algunos refranes del español son muy similares en su significado a los que tenemos en inglés, aunque a veces las palabras son bastante diferentes.

Give students additional proverbs to understand and find English equivalents for: *No es oro todo lo que reluce, Más vale pájaro en mano que cien volando, No hay mal que por bien no venga.*

Actividad. Identifica la versión en inglés de estos refranes en español.

_____ 1. Más vale tarde que nunca.
_____ 2. No se ganó Zamora en una hora.
_____ 3. A quien madruga, Dios lo ayuda.
_____ 4. De la mano a la boca, se pierde la sopa.
_____ 5. Las paredes oyen.
_____ 6. Gato escaldado del agua fría huye.

a. Once burned, twice shy.
b. Better late than never.
c. Rome wasn't built in a day.
ch. The early bird catches the worm.
d. The walls have ears.
e. There's many a slip 'twixt the cup and the lip.

USO PRÁCTICO DEL ESPAÑOL Los comparativos **mayor** y **menor**

When the comparative adjectives *mayor* and *menor* describe people, they always mean, respectively, "older" and "younger." When used as superlatives (*el [la] mayor, los [las] mayores; el [la] menor, los [las] menores*) they mean respectively, "the oldest" and "the youngest."

Mi hermano **menor** tiene 16 años.	My younger brother is 16 years old.
Mi hermana es tres años **mayor** que yo.	My sister is three years older than I am.
Josué, el **mayor** de mis hermanos, tiene 34 años.	Joshua, the oldest of my brothers and sisters, is 34 years old.

If you need to compare people in terms of size, use *más grande* or *más alto/-a* for "bigger/taller" and *más pequeño/-a* or *más bajo/-a* for "smaller/shorter."

Mi hermano menor es **más grande** que yo.	My younger brother is bigger than I am.

Otherwise, *mayor* means "bigger" or "major," while *menor* means "smaller" or "minor." Here are some common expressions that use these words.

OJO: Adults or people legally of age are *los mayores de edad.*

OJO: *Quepa* is the present subjunctive of *caber.*

No tengo **la menor idea** de lo que quieres decir.	I don't have the faintest / slightest idea of what you mean.
No se les vende alcohol a **los menores de edad.**	Alcohol is not sold to minors.
...para que no te quepa **la menor duda**	. . . so that you won't have any doubts (lit. ". . . so that the smallest doubt won't fit")
Lo hice **sin mayores problemas.**	I did it without any major problems.
El edificio de la Corte Suprema está en **la Plaza Mayor.**	The Supreme Court building is on the main square of the city.

Ponerlo a prueba

A. Relato. Completa el relato que se presenta a continuación.

El día que Ramón _____ (**cumplir**) los 21 años, se levantó feliz. —Por fin soy _____ de edad, —se dijo. Pero con los años vienen _____ (**greater**) responsabilidades también. Como Ramón _____ (**especializarse**) en la economía internacional, tenía que pasar el día trabajando en su proyecto de estadística.

OJO: Remember that a "major field of study" is *la especialidad* and "to major" is *especializarse.*

—No tengo la _____ (**slightest**) idea de cómo empezar—, se dijo. Pues llamó a su amigo Gerardo y le _____ (**pedir**) ayuda. Pero Gerardo estaba ocupado. Su hermano _____ (**younger**) estaba enfermo y Gerardo tenía que quedarse en casa para cuidarlo. Quedaron Ramón y Gerardo en encontrarse en el laboratorio de computación por la tarde. —Ya me siento _____ (**better**),— pensó Ramón. Después Gerardo me ayudará y mientras tanto puedo divertirme. Me alegro de ser _____ (**the youngest**) de mi familia. _____ (**The older ones**) tienen que ocuparse de _____ (**the younger ones**). Por suerte me escapé de eso.

B. **Definiciones.** Da una definición en español de las siguientes palabras.

Modelo: el principio
   Es una idea moral en la cual una persona cree firmemente.

1. provechoso/-a
2. el presupuesto
3. la Bolsa
4. un cheque sin fondos
5. leal
6. Antártida
7. el familiar
8. la acción

C. **¿Qué principio de la ética comercial ha sido violado?** Después de leer las situaciones que aparecen a continuación, indica qué principio de la ética comercial del artículo de Luz Solano Borrero ha sido violado.

1. López le compró a Benítez cuatro televisores para su motel. Cuando Benítez trató de cobrar el cheque de López no pudo, porque López no tenía suficientes fondos en su cuenta corriente.
2. Ramírez contrató a Miranda para que Miranda pasara un día por semana arreglando el jardín, cortando el pasto, etc. Quedó en pagarle semanalmente. Después de la tercera semana, Ramírez le dijo a Miranda que no le iba a pagar semanalmente sino cada dos semanas porque así le era más fácil.
3. Vásquez entró en la Mueblería Sánchez en busca de un sofá. Cuando Vásquez le comentó al vendedor que los precios le parecían muy altos, el vendedor le respondió: —Si los precios son un poquito más altos que los de la competencia es por la calidad. Voy a decirle a usted algo en confianza: no compre sus muebles del Sr. Palacios, porque allí tienen un problema con la humedad en el almacén (*warehouse*) y a los muebles les da un olor...
4. El único supermercado grande de un pueblo pequeño baja tanto sus precios que les quita el negocio a las tiendas de comestibles más pequeñas.
5. Dávila y Torres han llegado a un acuerdo. Durante las negociaciones, Torres quedó satisfecho con el presupuesto pero cuando llegó Dávila con el contrato, Torres vio que Dávila lo había cambiado sin avisarle.

CH. **Preguntas personales**

1. ¿Qué interés tienes en los negocios?
2. Es obvio que el dinero tiene muchos atractivos, pero ¿hay desventajas también en ganar mucho dinero?
3. ¿Cuál es el arreglo comercial o financiero más provechoso que hayas tenido en tu vida?
4. El artículo sobre la ética comercial le recomienda al hombre o a la mujer de negocios que "no haga promesas que no va a poder cumplir". ¿Es siempre válido este principio? ¿Has hecho tú alguna vez una promesa sabiendo que no la ibas a cumplir?

5. ¿Puedes dar un ejemplo de una actividad que es legal, pero que tú consideras en contra de tus principios éticos?

INVESTIGAR LA GRAMÁTICA   Reviewing the Writing Strategies

Throughout *Entradas* you have been developing your abilities to write in Spanish by means of a series of Writing Strategies in each chapter. Here is a list of the topics that have been covered.

1. Organize your information
2. Link your sentences with connecting words
3. Organize your descriptions
4. Learn to paraphrase
5. Work on writing and rewriting
6. Communicate forcefully
7. Tell a story
8. Give your story a point
9. Transfer thought to language
10. Write thank-you notes
11. Explain a situation
12. Have an overall plan

These strategies may be familiar to you from English or writing courses you may have taken in high school or college. The challenge, as you have seen in *Entradas,* is to transfer your writing skills to Spanish and to train yourself to think, plan, and write in Spanish without translating from English. As you continue to study Spanish you will probably focus most on narrative, description, and analysis. One strategy that has not been formally practiced in *Entradas* is using a bilingual dictionary. For the activities that follow, you should have access to a full-sized Spanish-English / English-Spanish dictionary.

Ponerlo a prueba

A. **Conocer el diccionario.**   En la página 545 aparecen algunas definiciones de la palabra "pesar" tomadas de un diccionario bilingüe. Después de leerlas, contesta las preguntas.

1. ¿Qué significa *vt*?
2. ¿Qué significa *vi*?
3. Escribe una frase que ilustre la diferencia entre **pesar** (*vt*) y **pesar** (*vi*).

4. ¿Qué significa (*fig.*)?
5. ¿Qué significa (*CAm*)?
6. ¿Qué significa *nm*?

> **pesar** 1. *vt* **a.** to weigh **b.** to weigh down, be heavy for; **me pesa el abrigo** *the coat weighs me down* **c.** (*fig.*) to weigh heavily on; **le pesa tanta responsabilidad** *so much responsibility bears heavily on him* (or *is a burden to him*) 2. *vi* **a.** to weigh; (Phys) to have weight; **pesa cinco kilos** *it weighs five kilos* **b.** (*CAm, Col, Ven*) to sell meat 3. *nm* **a.** regret; grief, sorrow; **a mi _____** *to my regret* **b. a _____ de** *in spite of, despite*; **a pesar de que no tiene dinero** *in spite of the fact that he has no money*

Use students' errors and difficulties as material for discussing effective dictionary use.

B. **Usando el diccionario: del inglés al español.** Busca en el diccionario el significado en español de las palabras y expresiones que aparecen a continuación y escribe oraciones en español que ilustren su significado.

1. to tan (get darker by lying in the sun)
2. lines (on the face)
3. to look like someone
4. to benefit *vt*
5. heartbeat
6. coffee beans
7. boxing ring
8. rung (as in "The bell has already rung.")

C. **Usando el diccionario: del español al inglés.** Busca en el diccionario el significado en inglés de las palabras y expresiones que aparecen a continuación.

1. salga lo que salga
2. papel (*Cine, Teatro,* etc.)
3. Ojos que no ven, corazón que no siente.
4. poner en marcha atrás
5. camión *nm* (Mex)
6. correr *vt* (CAm, Mex, Ven) a uno
7. pasarse *vr* (fruit)
8. gusto *nm*

CH. **Las palabras en contexto.** En las siguientes oraciones, una palabra o frase aparece en letras cursivas. Usando el diccionario, escoge la palabra más apropiada según el contexto de la oración.

1. I'm going to *take* these books upstairs. Voy a _____ estos libros.
2. I'll *take care* of them later. Más tarde _____ de ellos.
3. Finally my project *is over*! ¡Por fin mi proyecto _____!
4. And yours . . . *How is it coming along*? Y el tuyo, ¿ _____ ?
5. My project *dealt with* environmental issues. Mi proyecto _____ asuntos del medio ambiente.
6. *Let's call it a day.* We can work more tomorrow morning. _____. Podemos continuar mañana por la mañana.
7. This paper *is driving me* crazy. Este ensayo me _____ loco/-a.
8. As soon as I finish the paper, George and I are going *to get together* for dinner. En cuanto yo termine el ensayo, Jorge y yo vamos a _____ para cenar.

¡TIENES LA PALABRA!

Con un compañero (una compañera) de la clase haz los siguientes mini-dramas.

A. Hasta que mejoren las notas...

Estudiante A (*El padre / La madre*)

Report cards have just come out and your teenager's performance has been very poor. As a result, you have decided to impose a few "rules of the house" until the grades improve. You are advising your child of these new rules. Be firm. After all, it's **your** house!

Modelo: *Tienes que hacer la tarea antes de cenar.*

You might suggest that you expect your teenager to:

- eat less junk food (*comida rápida*)
- wash the dishes after supper
- watch educational TV programs
- bring home at least two books each evening
- study for three hours each evening and go to bed before 10:00

Add anything else you can think of that might improve your child's grades.

> **Estudiante B** (*El/La joven*)
>
> You are aware that your report card was bad, but you don't think that so many rules should be laid down, especially since your friends don't have the same rules. Counter your parent's rules by pointing out what **everybody else** or **nobody else** does regarding each rule. Be emotional in your responses. After all, it's **your** free time!
>
> **Modelo:** *¡Ay, mamá (papá), nadie tiene que hacer la tarea antes de cenar!*

B. ¡Que tengas un buen viaje! Un amigo (Una amiga) te llama para decirte lo que va a hacer durante las vacaciones. Hazle preguntas sobre sus planes y decide si les será posible reunirse durante el verano. Si no, pónganse de acuerdo en cuanto a lo que van a hacer para mantenerse en contacto.

OTRA VUELTA

Play instructor tape, 2 min.

Escucha otra vez la Entrada de la tercera etapa y contesta las siguientes preguntas.

1. ¿Dónde vivía Arturo mientras estudiaba en la universidad?
2. ¿Por qué quieren ir a Chile Celso y Esteban?
3. ¿Qué quiere leer Beatriz?

COMENTARIO CULTURAL

Ciudadanos del mundo

La mayoría de los viajeros internacionales pronto se dan cuenta de que, cuando uno va de un país a otro, no solamente cambian los idiomas. En cada país la percepción que tiene la gente del mundo, su sistema de valores, su comportamiento social, su estilo de vestirse, su comida típica y su arquitectura, todo forman parte de la impresión que recibe el viajero de que "aquí las cosas son diferentes".

El mundo está cada vez más interrelacionado debido a las comunicaciones modernas y el contacto personal. Por eso, la gente cambia poco a poco su manera de vivir. Ropa de estilo europeo ya se encuentra en todas partes del mundo. Las técnicas para construir escuelas en México ya se han aplicado en Nepal. El jazz norteamericano se oye en Rusia y en los demás países de Europa oriental. Los jóvenes de Cali, Colombia, se interesan en muchas de las mismas cuestiones importantes que también les son de interés a los jóvenes de Denver, Colorado. Muchas veces comparten también los mismos gustos en el estilo de ropa, en la música popular, etc. En efecto, muchos países extranjeros parecen cada vez menos "extranjeros" y más conocidos y familiares.

Los verdaderos ciudadanos del mundo son los que tienen la habilidad de reconocer las normas sociales locales en otras partes del mundo y ajustarse a ellas sin abandonar sus propios valores. Para estas personas, una nueva cultura les ofrece una oportunidad para aprender cómo otra gente, en otros lugares, soluciona los problemas universales que enfrenta a todo el mundo.

Consejos y sugerencias. Prepara una lista de lo que los estudiantes del primer año en tu universidad deben y no deben hacer para acostumbrarse a la "cultura" del lugar.

Play video
Program 12 *Profesiones y oficios* Traditional and nontraditional professions

A. **Viajemos a...** Describe una visita que hayas hecho a otro país, ciudad o región. No identifiques el lugar de tu viaje, pero descríbelo de tal forma que tu compañero/-a tenga la posibilidad de adivinarlo. Tu compañero/-a te hace preguntas, las cuales debes contestar dando más detalles. Cuando tu compañero/-a identifique tu "lugar secreto", ustedes cambian de papeles y repiten la actividad.

B. **Una carta personal.** En la primera etapa Roberto le escribe una carta a Carmencita contándole lo que ha hecho durante el semestre pasado y dándole una idea de los planes que tiene para las vacaciones. Ahora, escribe tú una carta de dos o tres párrafos narrando lo que has hecho este semestre y hablando de los planes que tienes para el futuro. Imagínate que estás escribiéndole a un buen amigo, buena amiga o a un/-a pariente y emplea los saludos y despedidas apropiados.

OJO: The person playing the role of the little brother or sister should respond to the reactions of the older brother or sister.

C. **El/La cuidaniños.** Imagínate que tienes que cuidar a tu hermano/-a menor de 14 años durante todo el fin de semana, ya que tus padres han salido de viaje. La primera noche ocurre que tu hermana o hermano llega a casa a las 3:00 de la madrugada, aunque tenía que volver para la medianoche. Después de cada excusa que te da, ofrécele tu opinión.

Modelo: Estuve con Carlitos y su familia.
No creo que hayas estado con Carlitos y su familia.

1. Fuimos al cine.
2. La película duró cuatro horas.
3. El coche del papá de Carlitos no arrancó.
4. Tuvimos que caminar a casa.
5. Los padres de Carlitos insistieron en que me quedara un rato más.

6. Me perdí en el parque.
7. ¡Te digo la verdad!
8. (Más excusas y cuentos)

CH. **Está tan claro como el agua.** Muchos dichos se comprenden fácilmente, aunque no tengan equivalente en inglés. En los dichos que aparecen a continuación, trata de identificar los que son equivalentes en los dos idiomas.

1. En boca cerrada no entran moscas.
2. Poderoso caballero es don Dinero.
3. A buen hambre no hay pan duro.
4. Cien refranes, cien verdades.
5. Del árbol caído todos hacen leña.
6. Agua pasada no mueve molino.

a. There is some truth to folk sayings.
b. Money talks.
c. Keep your mouth shut and you won't get into trouble.
ch. Everybody kicks you when you're down.
d. Beggars can't be choosers.
e. Don't cry over spilled milk.

VOCABULARIO

El amor y las relaciones románticas

Sustantivos
atractivo (m)   *attraction*
casados (m pl)   *married couple*
conocido/-a   *acquaintance*
familiar (m/f)   *family member*
matrimonio (m)   *married couple; marriage*
noviazgo (m)   *courtship*
novio/-a   *sweetheart; groom (bride)*
pareja (f)   *couple*
recién casado/-a   *newlywed*

Verbos y expresiones verbales
amar   *to love*
atraer   *to attract*
desarrollar   *to develop*
echar de menos   *to miss, long for*
estar enamorado/-a (de)   *to be in love (with)*
estimar   *to esteem*
extrañar   *to miss, long for*
florecer   *to flourish*
menospreciar   *to hold in contempt*

Adjetivos
adorado/-a   *adored; very dear*
ardiente   *ardent; passionate*

Los continentes
África (f)   *Africa*
América (f) del Norte   *North America*
América (f) del Sur   *South America*
Antártida (f)   *Antarctica*
Asia   *Asia*
Australia   *Australia*
Europa   *Europe*

El trabajo y los negocios

Profesiones
agente (m/f) de bienes raíces   *real estate agent*
bombero/-a   *fire fighter*
camionero/-a   *truck driver*
farmacéutico/-a   *pharmacist*
granjero/-a   *farmer*
hombre/mujer de negocios   *business person*

carpintero/-a carpenter
comerciante (m/f) shopkeeper
obrero/-a laborer
plomero/-a plumber

Las finanzas (Finance)
acciones (f pl) stocks, shares
Bolsa (f) stock exchange
cheque (m) sin fondos bad check (one that bounces)
mercaderías (f pl) commodities, merchandise
presupuesto (m) budget
salario (m) hourly wage
sueldo (m) salary

Verbos y expresiones verbales
cargar to load
descargar to unload
mover (ue) palancas to pull strings
tener un enchufe / tener palancas to have connections

Sustantivos
jornada (f) working day
medio tiempo half-time
palanca (f) lever
tiempo (m) parcial; jornada (f) parcial part-time

Sustantivos útiles

anticipación (f) expectation
apoyo (m) support
esfuerzo (m) effort
lealtad (f) loyalty
principio (m) principle
rato (m) period of time, while

Otras palabras y expresiones útiles

a fondo in depth
a pesar de in spite of
advertir (ie) to warn; to advise
al poco rato shortly after
con anticipación in advance
contar (ue) con to count on; to depend on
crecer to grow (up)
criarse to grow up, be raised
cumplir (con) to complete; follow through (on)
de hoy en adelante from now on
desleal disloyal
disminuir to diminish
empacar to crate; to pack up
empequeñecer to become smaller
estorbar to hinder, obstruct
gozar (de) to enjoy something
insoportable intolerable
justo/-a fair, just
leal loyal
madurar to mature
más que nunca more than ever
no obstante nevertheless
padecer to suffer
pasajero/-a temporary
perjudicar to damage, impair
provechoso/-a advantageous, beneficial
recuperarse to recuperate (health)
sin embargo nevertheless
superar to overcome
tener en mente to take into account, bear in mind
tener presente to take into account, bear in mind
tomar en serio to take seriously

VOCABULARIO PERSONALIZADO

APPENDIX A Regular Verbs

Simple Tenses

Infinitive	Present Indicative	Imperfect	Preterite	Future	Conditional	Present Subjunctive	Past Subjunctive	Commands
hablar *to speak*	hablo hablas habla hablamos habláis hablan	hablaba hablabas hablaba hablábamos hablabais hablaban	hablé hablaste habló hablamos hablasteis hablaron	hablaré hablarás hablará hablaremos hablaréis hablarán	hablaría hablarías hablaría hablaríamos hablaríais hablarían	hable hables hable hablemos habléis hablen	hablara hablaras hablara habláramos hablarais hablaran	habla (no hables) hable hablad (no habléis) hablen
aprender *to learn*	aprendo aprendes aprende aprendemos aprendéis aprenden	aprendía aprendías aprendía aprendíamos aprendíais aprendían	aprendí aprendiste aprendió aprendimos aprendisteis aprendieron	aprenderé aprenderás aprenderá aprenderemos aprenderéis aprenderán	aprendería aprenderías aprendería aprenderíamos aprenderíais aprenderían	aprenda aprendas aprenda aprendamos aprendáis aprendan	aprendiera aprendieras aprendiera aprendiéramos aprendierais aprendieran	aprende (no aprendas) aprenda aprended (no aprendáis) aprendan
vivir *to live*	vivo vives vive vivimos vivís viven	vivía vivías vivía vivíamos vivíais vivían	viví viviste vivió vivimos vivisteis vivieron	viviré vivirás vivirá viviremos viviréis vivirán	viviría vivirías viviría viviríamos viviríais vivirían	viva vivas viva vivamos viváis vivan	viviera vivieras viviera viviéramos vivierais vivieran	vive (no vivas) viva vivid (no viváis) vivan

Compound tenses

Present progressive	estoy estamos estás estáis está están	} hablando	aprendiendo	viviendo
Present perfect indicative	he hemos has habéis ha han	} hablado	aprendido	vivido
Present perfect subjunctive	haya hayamos hayas hayáis haya hayan	} hablado	aprendido	vivido
Past perfect indicative	había habíamos habías habíais había habían	} hablado	aprendido	vivido

APPENDIX B Stem-changing Verbs

Infinitive Present Participle Past Participle	Present Indicative	Imperfect	Preterite	Future	Conditional	Present Subjunctive	Past Subjunctive	Commands
pensar *to think* e → ie pensando pensado	pienso piensas piensa pensamos pensáis piensan	pensaba pensabas pensaba pensábamos pensabais pensaban	pensé pensaste pensó pensamos pensasteis pensaron	pensaré pensarás pensará pensaremos pensaréis pensarán	pensaría pensarías pensaría pensaríamos pensaríais pensarían	piense pienses piense pensemos penséis piensen	pensara pensaras pensara pensáramos pensarais pensaran	piensa no pienses piense pensad (no penséis) piensen
acostarse *to go to bed* o → ue acostándose acostado	me acuesto te acuestas se acuesta nos acostamos os acostáis se acuestan	me acostaba te acostabas se acostaba nos acostábamos os acostabais se acostaban	me acosté te acostaste se acostó nos acostamos os acostasteis se acostaron	me acostaré te acostarás se acostará nos acostaremos os acostaréis se acostarán	me acostaría te acostarías se acostaría nos acostaríamos os acostaríais se acostarían	me acueste te acuestes se acueste nos acostemos os acostéis se acuesten	me acostara te acostaras se acostara nos acostáramos os acostarais se acostaran	acuéstate no te acuestes acuéstese acostaos (no os acostéis) acuéstense
sentir *to be sorry* e → ie, i sintiendo sentido	siento sientes siente sentimos sentís sienten	sentía sentías sentía sentíamos sentíais sentían	sentí sentiste sintió sentimos sentisteis sintieron	sentiré sentirás sentirá sentiremos sentiréis sentirán	sentiría sentirías sentiría sentiríamos sentiríais sentirían	sienta sientas sienta sintamos sintáis sientan	sintiera sintieras sintiera sintiéramos sintierais sintieran	siente no sientas sienta sentid (no sintáis) sientan
pedir *to ask for* e → i, i pidiendo pedido	pido pides pide pedimos pedís piden	pedía pedías pedía pedíamos pedíais pedían	pedí pediste pidió pedimos pedisteis pidieron	pediré pedirás pedirá pediremos pediréis pedirán	pediría pedirías pediría pediríamos pediríais pedirían	pida pidas pida pidamos pidáis pidan	pidiera pidieras pidiera pidiéramos pidierais pidieran	pide no pidas pida pedid (no pidáis) pidan
dormir *to sleep* o → ue, u durmiendo dormido	duermo duermes duerme dormimos dormís duermen	dormía dormías dormía dormíamos dormíais dormían	dormí dormiste durmió dormimos dormisteis durmieron	dormiré dormirás dormirá dormiremos dormiréis dormirán	dormiría dormirías dormiría dormiríamos dormiríais dormirían	duerma duermas duerma durmamos durmáis duerman	durmiera durmieras durmiera durmiéramos durmierais durmieran	duerme no duermas duerma dormid (no durmáis) duerman

APPENDIX C Change of Spelling Verbs

Infinitive Present Participle Past Participle	Present Indicative	Imperfect	Preterite	Future	Conditional	Present Subjunctive	Past Subjunctive	Commands
comenzar (e → ie) *to begin* z → c before e comenzando comenzado	comienzo comienzas comienza comenzamos comenzáis comienzan	comenzaba comenzabas comenzaba comenzábamos comenzabais comenzaban	**comencé** comenzaste comenzó comenzamos comenzasteis comenzaron	comenzaré comenzarás comenzará comenzaremos comenzaréis comenzarán	comenzaría comenzarías comenzaría comenzaríamos comenzaríais comenzarían	**comience** **comiences** **comience** **comencemos** **comencéis** **comiencen**	comenzara comenzaras comenzara comenzáramos comenzarais comenzaran	comienza (no **comiences**) **comience** comenzad (no **comencéis**) **comiencen**
conocer *to know* c → zc before a, o conociendo conocido	**conozco** conoces conoce conocemos conocéis conocen	conocía conocías conocía conocíamos conocíais conocían	conocí conociste conoció conocimos conocisteis conocieron	conoceré conocerás conocerá conoceremos conoceréis conocerán	conocería conocerías conocería conoceríamos conoceríais conocerían	**conozca** **conozcas** **conozca** **conozcamos** **conozcáis** **conozcan**	conociera conocieras conociera conociéramos conocierais conocieran	conoce (no **conozcas**) **conozca** conoced (no **conozcáis**) **conozcan**
construir *to build* i → y; y inserted before a, e, o construyendo construido	**construyo** **construyes** **construye** construimos construís **construyen**	construía construías construía construíamos construíais contruían	construí construiste **construyó** construimos construisteis **construyeron**	construiré construirás construirá construiremos construiréis construirán	construiría construirías construiría construiríamos construiríais construirían	**construya** **construyas** **construya** **construyamos** **construyáis** **construyan**	**construyera** **construyeras** **construyera** **construyéramos** **construyerais** **construyeran**	**construye** (no **construyas**) **construya** construid (no **construyáis**) **construyan**
leer *to read* i → y; stressed i → í leyendo leído	leo lees lee leemos leéis leen	leía leías leía leíamos leíais leían	leí leíste **leyó** leímos leísteis **leyeron**	leeré leerás leerá leeremos leeréis leerán	leería leerías leería leeríamos leeríais leerían	lea leas lea leamos leáis lean	**leyera** **leyeras** **leyera** **leyéramos** **leyerais** **leyeran**	lee (no leas) lea leed (no leáis) lean

APPENDIX C Change of Spelling Verbs (continued)

Infinitive / Present Participle / Past Participle	Present Indicative	Imperfect	Preterite	Future	Conditional	Present Subjunctive	Past Subjunctive	Commands
pagar *to pay* **g → gu** before e pagando pagado	pago pagas paga pagamos pagáis pagan	pagaba pagabas pagaba pagábamos pagabais pagaban	**pagué** pagaste pagó pagamos pagasteis pagaron	pagaré pagarás pagará pagaremos pagaréis pagarán	pagaría pagarías pagaría pagaríamos pagaríais pagarían	**pague** **pagues** **pague** **paguemos** **paguéis** **paguen**	pagara pagaras pagara pagáramos pagarais pagaran	paga (no **pagues**) **pague** pagad (no **paguéis**) **paguen**
seguir (e → i, i) *to follow* **gu → g** before a, o siguiendo seguido	**sigo** sigues sigue seguimos seguís siguen	seguía seguías seguía seguíamos seguíais seguían	seguí seguiste siguió seguimos seguisteis siguieron	seguiré seguirás seguirá seguiremos seguiréis seguirán	seguiría seguirías seguiría seguiríamos seguiríais seguirían	**siga** **sigas** **siga** **sigamos** **sigáis** **sigan**	siguiera siguieras siguiera siguiéramos siguierais siguieran	sigue (no **sigas**) **siga** seguid (no **sigáis**) **sigan**
tocar *to play, touch* **c → qu** before e tocando tocado	toco tocas toca tocamos tocáis tocan	tocaba tocabas tocaba tocábamos tocabais tocaban	**toqué** tocaste tocó tocamos tocasteis tocaron	tocaré tocarás tocará tocaremos tocaréis tocarán	tocaría tocarías tocaría tocaríamos tocaríais tocarían	**toque** **toques** **toque** **toquemos** **toquéis** **toquen**	tocara tocaras tocara tocáramos tocarais tocaran	toca (no **toques**) **toque** tocad (no **toquéis**) **toquen**

APPENDIX D Irregular Verbs

Infinitive Present Participle Past Participle	Present Indicative	Imperfect	Preterite	Future	Conditional	Present Subjunctive	Past Subjunctive	Commands
andar *to walk* andando andado	ando andas anda andamos andáis andan	andaba andabas andaba andábamos andabais andaban	**anduve** **anduviste** **anduvo** **anduvimos** **anduvisteis** **anduvieron**	andaré andarás andará andaremos andaréis andarán	andaría andarías andaría andaríamos andaríais andarían	ande andes ande andemos andéis anden	**anduviera** **anduvieras** **anduviera** **anduviéramos** **anduvierais** **anduvieran**	anda (no andes) ande andad (no andéis) anden
*caer *to fall* **cayendo** caído	**caigo** caes cae caemos caéis caen	caía caías caía caíamos caíais caían	caí caíste **cayó** caímos caísteis **cayeron**	caeré caerás caerá caeremos caeréis caerán	caería caerías caería caeríamos caeríais caerían	**caiga** **caigas** **caiga** **caigamos** **caigáis** **caigan**	cayera cayeras cayera cayéramos cayerais cayeran	cae (no caigas) caiga caed (no caigáis) caigan
*dar *to give* dando dado	**doy** das da damos dais dan	daba dabas daba dábamos dabais daban	**di** **diste** **dio** **dimos** **disteis** **dieron**	daré darás dará daremos daréis darán	daría darías daría daríamos daríais darían	dé des dé demos deis den	diera dieras diera diéramos dierais dieran	da (no des) dé dad (no deis) den
*decir *to say, tell* **diciendo** **dicho**	**digo** **dices** **dice** decimos decís **dicen**	decía decías decía decíamos decíais decían	**dije** **dijiste** **dijo** **dijimos** **dijisteis** **dijeron**	**diré** **dirás** **dirá** **diremos** **diréis** **dirán**	**diría** **dirías** **diría** **diríamos** **diríais** **dirían**	diga digas diga digamos digáis digan	dijera dijeras dijera dijéramos dijerais dijeran	di (no digas) diga decid (no digáis) digan
*estar *to be* estando estado	**estoy** **estás** **está** estamos estáis **están**	estaba estabas estaba estábamos estabais estaban	**estuve** **estuviste** **estuvo** **estuvimos** **estuvisteis** **estuvieron**	estaré estarás estará estaremos estaréis estarán	estaría estarías estaría estaríamos estaríais estarían	esté estés esté estemos estéis estén	estuviera estuvieras estuviera estuviéramos estuvierais estuvieran	está (no estés) esté estad (no estéis) estén

*Verbs with irregular *yo*-forms in the present indicative

v

APPENDIX D Irregular Verbs (continued)

Infinitive Present Participle Past Participle	Present Indicative	Imperfect	Preterite	Future	Conditional	Present Subjunctive	Past Subjunctive	Commands
haber *to have* habiendo habido	he has ha [hay] hemos habéis han	había habías había habíamos habíais habían	hube hubiste hubo hubimos hubisteis hubieron	habré habrás habrá habremos habréis habrán	habría habrías habría habríamos habríais habrían	haya hayas haya hayamos hayáis hayan	hubiera hubieras hubiera hubiéramos hubierais hubieran	
*hacer *to make, do* haciendo hecho	hago haces hace hacemos hacéis hacen	hacía hacías hacía hacíamos hacíais hacían	hice hiciste hizo hicimos hicisteis hicieron	haré harás hará haremos haréis harán	haría harías haría haríamos haríais harían	haga hagas haga hagamos hagáis hagan	hiciera hicieras hiciera hiciéramos hicierais hicieran	haz (no hagas) haga haced (no hagáis) hagan
ir *to go* yendo ido	voy vas va vamos vais van	iba ibas iba íbamos ibais iban	fui fuiste fue fuimos fuisteis fueron	iré irás irá iremos iréis irán	iría irías iría iríamos iríais irían	vaya vayas vaya vayamos vayáis vayan	fuera fueras fuera fuéramos fuerais fueran	ve (no vayas) vaya id (no vayáis) vayan
*oír *to hear* oyendo oído	oigo oyes oye oímos oís oyen	oía oías oía oíamos oíais oían	oí oíste oyó oímos oísteis oyeron	oiré oirás oirá oiremos oiréis oirán	oiría oirías oiría oiríamos oiríais oirían	oiga oigas oiga oigamos oigáis oigan	oyera oyeras oyera oyéramos oyerais oyeran	oye (no oigas) oiga oíd (no oigáis) oigan
poder (o → ue) *can, to be able* pudiendo podido	puedo puedes puede podemos podéis pueden	podía podías podía podíamos podíais podían	pude pudiste pudo pudimos pudisteis pudieron	podré podrás podrá podremos podréis podrán	podría podrías podría podríamos podríais podrían	pueda puedas pueda podamos podáis puedan	pudiera pudieras pudiera pudiéramos pudierais pudieran	

APPENDIX D Irregular Verbs (continued)

*Verbs with irregular yo-forms in the present indicative

Infinitive / Present Participle / Past Participle	Present Indicative	Imperfect	Preterite	Future	Conditional	Present Subjunctive	Past Subjunctive	Commands
*poner to place, put poniendo puesto	pongo pones pone ponemos ponéis ponen	ponía ponías ponía poníamos poníais ponían	puse pusiste puso pusimos pusisteis pusieron	pondré pondrás pondrá pondremos pondréis pondrán	pondría pondrías pondría pondríamos pondríais pondrían	ponga pongas ponga pongamos pongáis pongan	pusiera pusieras pusiera pusiéramos pusierais pusieran	pon (no pongas) ponga poned (no pongáis) pongan
querer (e → ie) to want, wish queriendo querido	quiero quieres quiere queremos queréis quieren	quería querías quería queríamos queríais querían	quise quisiste quiso quisimos quisisteis quisieron	querré querrás querrá querremos querréis querrán	querría querrías querría querríamos querríais querrían	quiera quieras quiera queramos queráis quieran	quisiera quisieras quisiera quisiéramos quisierais quisieran	quiere (no quieras) quiera quered (no queráis) quieran
reír to laugh riendo reído	río ríes ríe reímos reís ríen	reía reías reía reíamos reíais reían	reí reíste rió reímos reísteis rieron	reiré reirás reirá reiremos reiréis reirán	reiría reirías reiría reiríamos reiríais reirían	ría rías ría riamos riáis rían	riera rieras riera riéramos rierais rieran	ríe (no rías) ría reíd (no riáis) rían
*saber to know sabiendo sabido	sé sabes sabe sabemos sabéis saben	sabía sabías sabía sabíamos sabíais sabían	supe supiste supo supimos supisteis supieron	sabré sabrás sabrá sabremos sabréis sabrán	sabría sabrías sabría sabríamos sabríais sabrían	sepa sepas sepa sepamos sepáis sepan	supiera supieras supiera supiéramos supierais supieran	sabe (no sepas) sepa sabed (no sepáis) sepan
*salir to go out saliendo salido	salgo sales sale salimos salís salen	salía salías salía salíamos salíais salían	salí saliste salió salimos salisteis salieron	saldré saldrás saldrá saldremos saldréis saldrán	saldría saldrías saldría saldríamos saldríais saldrían	salga salgas salga salgamos salgáis salgan	saliera salieras saliera saliéramos salierais salieran	sal (no salgas) salga salid (no salgáis) salgan

APPENDIX D Irregular Verbs (continued)

Infinitive Present Participle Past Participle	Present Indicative	Imperfect	Preterite	Future	Conditional	Present Subjunctive	Past Subjunctive	Commands
ser *to be* siendo sido	soy eres es somos sois son	era eras era éramos erais eran	fui fuiste fue fuimos fuisteis fueron	seré serás será seremos seréis serán	sería serías sería seríamos seríais serían	sea seas sea seamos seáis sean	fuera fueras fuera fuéramos fuerais fueran	sé (no seas) sea sed (no seáis) sean
*tener *to have* teniendo tenido	tengo tienes tiene tenemos tenéis tienen	tenía tenías tenía teníamos teníais tenían	tuve tuviste tuvo tuvimos tuvisteis tuvieron	tendré tendrás tendrá tendremos tendréis tendrán	tendría tendrías tendría tendríamos tendríais tendrían	tenga tengas tenga tengamos tengáis tengan	tuviera tuvieras tuviera tuviéramos tuvierais tuvieran	ten (no tengas) tenga tened (no tengáis) tengan
traer *to bring* trayendo traído	traigo traes trae traemos traéis traen	traía traías traía traíamos traíais traían	traje trajiste trajo trajimos trajisteis trajeron	traeré traerás traerá traeremos traeréis traerán	traería traerías traería traeríamos traeríais traerían	traiga traigas traiga traigamos traigáis traigan	trajera trajeras trajera trajéramos trajerais trajeran	trae (no traigas) traiga traed (no traigáis) traigan
*venir *to come* viniendo venido	vengo vienes viene venimos venís vienen	venía venías venía veníamos veníais venían	vine viniste vino vinimos vinisteis vinieron	vendré vendrás vendrá vendremos vendréis vendrán	vendría vendrías vendría vendríamos vendríais vendrían	venga vengas venga vengamos vengáis vengan	viniera vinieras viniera viniéramos vinierais vinieran	ven (no vengas) venga venid (no vengáis) vengan
ver *to see* viendo visto	veo ves ve vemos veis ven	veía veías veía veíamos veíais veían	vi viste vio vimos visteis vieron	veré verás verá veremos veréis verán	vería verías vería veríamos veríais verían	vea veas vea veamos veáis vean	viera vieras viera viéramos vierais vieran	ve (no veas) vea ved (no veáis) vean

The glossaries contain contextual meanings of both productive and receptive vocabulary as used in this text. Featured vocabulary and idiomatic expressions appear in the same forms as they do at the end of each chapter. A number in parenthesis that follows an entry indicates the chapter in which it first appears as active vocabulary. Irregular verbs followed by an asterisk [*] appear in their conjugated forms in the appendix. The following abbreviations are used.

adj	adjective	m	masculine	pl	plural
f	feminine	n	noun	sing	singular

SPANISH-ENGLISH

A

a: a cambio de in exchange for (11); **a comienzos de** at the beginning of (6); **a dos cuadras de** two blocks away from (6); **a fines de** at the end of (6); **a fondo de** in depth (12); **a la derecha** to the right (6); **¿A la orden?** May I help you?; **a la izquierda** to the left (6); **a la parrilla** grilled (5); **a más tardar** at the very latest; **a menos que** unless (11); **a menudo** often, a lot (6); **a partir de** beginning with (6); **a pesar de que** in spite of (11); **¿A qué hora…?** At what time . . . ? (2); **A sus órdenes.** At your service. (6); **a tiempo** on time (3); **a veces** sometimes (4); **A ver…** Let's see . . .
abierto/-a open (3)
abogado/-a (m/f) attorney (11)
abrazar to hug, embrace (8)
Abrazos (m pl) Hugs (10)
abrigo (m) overcoat (4)
abril April (1)
abrir to open (1); **Abre el libro a la página…** Open your book to page . . .
abuela (f) grandmother (1)
abuelo (m) grandfather (1)
abuelos (m pl) grandparents (1)
aburrido/-a boring, bored (1)
acampar to camp (7)
accesorio (m) prop
acciones (f pl) stocks, shares (12)
aceite (m) oil (5); motor oil (8)
acelerador (m) accelerator (8)
acera (f) sidewalk (5)
acerca de about, concerning (11)
acompañado/-a accompanied (4)
acompañar to accompany, go with (4)

aconsejable advisable (4)
aconsejar to advise (4)
acostarse (ue)* to go to bed (3)
acostumbrarse a to get accustomed/ used to (7)
actividad (f) activity (7)
actuación (f) performance (3)
acuático/-a related to water
acusado/-a (m/f) defendant (11)
¡Adelante! Come in! (7)
adelgazar to lose weight
además besides (8); **~ de** in addition to (8)
Adiós good-bye (1)
adorado/-a adored; very dear (12)
adorar to adore (10)
aduana (f) customs (4); **hacer ~** to pass through customs (4)
aduanero/-a (m/f) customs agent (4)
advertir (ie) to warn; to advise (12)
afeitarse to shave (3)
afirmar to affirm (9)
afortunadamente fortunately (4)
África (f) Africa (1)
africano/-a African
agencia (f) **de viajes** travel agency (4)
agente (m/f) agent (6); **~ de bienes raíces** real estate agent (12)
agitado/-a agitated, disturbed (8)
agitar to agitate (8)
agosto August (1)
agotado/-a exhausted, worn out (6)
agradable nice, agreeable (3)
agradecer to acknowledge a favor; to appreciate (10)
agradecimiento (m) gratitude, appreciation (9)
agregar to add (8)
agua (f) water (2); **~ corriente** running water (9); **~ destilada** distilled water (9); **~ mineral** mineral (bottled) water (9)

aguacate (m) avocado (5)
aguafiestas (m/f, s/pl) "party pooper," "wet blanket" (10)
águila (f) eagle
agujero (m) hole
ahora now
aire (m) air
ajedrez (m) chess
ajo (m) garlic (5)
al: ~ anochecer at dusk, nightfall (3); **~ horno** baked (5); **~ lado de** next to (3); **~ nivel del mar** at sea level (6); **~ poco rato** shortly after (12)
alacena (f) kitchen cupboard (7)
alba (f) dawn (8)
albañil (m) mason
alberca (f) swimming pool (9)
alcoba (f) bedroom (6)
alegre glad (2)
alejado/-a de removed or apart from (10)
Alemania (f) Germany (1)
alemán/-ana German (1)
alergia (f) allergy (9)
alfombra (f) rug (7)
algo something (4); **~ por el estilo** something like that (8)
alguacil (m) sheriff; constable (11)
alguien someone, somebody (4)
alguno/-a some, someone, any (4)
alimentar to feed (11)
aliño (m) salad dressing (5)
aliviar to relieve (9)
alivio (m) relief (9)
almacén (m) warehouse
almeja (f) clam (5)
almohada (f) pillow
almorzar (ue) to have lunch (2)
almuerzo (m) lunch (2)
Aló Hello (on the telephone)
alojamiento (m) lodging (6)
alojarse to stay temporarily, to have lodging (6)

alquilar to rent (6)
alquiler (m) the rent (6)
alrededores (m pl) surroundings, environs (7)
alto/-a tall (3)
allí there
amable friendly, kind (1), nice (10)
amanecer to dawn (8)
amar to love (12)
amarillo/-a yellow (1)
ambiente (m) atmosphere (restaurant)
ambulancia (f) ambulance
América (f): ~ **del Norte** North America; ~ **del Sur** South America (12)
americano/-a American (1)
amigo/-a (m/f) friend (1)
amistad (f) friendship (1)
amor (m) love (4)
anaranjado/-a orange (in color) (1)
andar* to walk (7)
anestesia (f) anesthesia (9)
anfitrión/-ona (m/f) host
angosto/-a narrow
angustia (f) anguish; despair (11)
Antártida (f) Antarctica (12)
anteayer day before yesterday
antepasado/-a (m) ancestor
antes de before (2); ~ **que** before (11); **lo ~ posible** as soon as possible (11)
antibiótico (m) antibiotic (9)
anticipación (f) expectation (12); **con ~** in advance (12)
antipático/-a unfriendly (3)
antiséptico (m) antiseptic (9)
anuario (m) yearbook
año (m) year (1); **¿Cuántos años tienes?** How old are you? (1)
apagar to turn off (lights) (8)
apagón (m) blackout, power failure (8)
aparador (m) buffet, credenza (7)
aparato (m) telephone (3); equipment, machine (9)
aparentar (ie) to seem to be (11)
apartado (m) **postal** post office box (1)
apartamento (m) apartment (1)
apellido (m) surname
apenas scarcely (9)
apio (m) celery (8)
aplazado suspended; failing (11)
apoyar to support
apoyo (m) support (12)
aprender to learn (2)
aprobado acceptable (11)
apropiado/-a suitable (4)
aprovechar to take advantage of (8)
aproximadamente approximately
apuntes (m pl) notes
apurarse to hurry

árbol (m) tree; ~ **de Navidad** Christmas tree (4)
archivo (m) file
ardiente ardent; passionate (12)
argentino/-a Argentinian (1)
arma (f) weapon (6)
armario (m) wardrobe (3)
arreglar to arrange (3); **hacer los arreglos** to make arrangements (6)
arreglo (m) arrangement (5)
arruinar to ruin (11)
arte (f) art
artefacto (m) relic; artifact (6)
arvejas (f pl) peas (5)
asado/-a roasted (5)
aseos (m pl) rest rooms
asiento (m) seat (4)
asistir a to attend (10)
aspirina (f) aspirin (9)
asunto (m) matter; issue (11)
asustar to frighten (8)
atardecer to become late afternoon (8)
Atentamente Attentively (10); **De usted muy ~** Attentively yours (10)
aterrizar to land (1)
atestado/-a crowded
atractivo (m) attraction (12)
atraer to attract (6)
aumentar to add to (11); to increase
auto (m) car (4)
automóvil (m) car (8)
avaricia (f) greed
ave (f) poultry (5)
averiguar to verify (11)
avión (m) airplane (4); **por ~** by air, airmail (6)
ayer yesterday (2)
ayudar to help (2)
azafata (f) flight attendant (4)
azafrán (m) saffron (5)
azotea (f) tiled roof
azúcar (m) sugar (2)
azucarero (m) sugar bowl (7)
azul blue (1)

B

bailar to dance (1)
baile (m) dance (2)
bajar to go down (6); to lower
bajo/-a short (3)
balcón (m) balcony (7)
balneario (m) bathing or health resort (6)
balón (m) large ball (basketball) (8)
baloncesto (m) basketball (2)
bancarrota (f) bankruptcy
bañarse to bathe; to shower (3)
bañera (f) bathtub (6)

baño (m) bathroom; ~ **completo** full bath (6)
barato/-a inexpensive, cheap (4)
barba (f) beard (3)
barbaridad: ¡Qué ~! How awful! (8)
barbilla (f) beard (11)
barrera (f) barrier, fence (9)
barrio (m) neighborhood (8)
base (f) base (makeup) (11)
basura (f) garbage
bate (m) baseball bat (8)
beber to drink (2)
bebida (f) beverage, drink
beca (f) scholarship
beige beige (1)
béisbol (m) baseball (2)
benigno/-a benign (9)
besar to kiss (8)
beso (m) kiss (10)
bien well; ~ **cocido** well done (meat) (5); ~ **educado/-a** well-mannered, polite (8)
biblioteca (f) library (1)
bilingüe bilingual (2)
biología (f) biology (2)
bistec (m) steak (5)
blanco/-a white (1)
blusa (f) blouse (4)
boca (f) mouth (8)
bocacalle (f) intersection (5)
bocadillo (m) snack (5)
boda (f) wedding
boleto (m) ticket; ~ **de ida y vuelta** round trip ticket (4)
bolígrafo (m) pen
boliviano/-a Bolivian (1)
bolsa (f) bag, purse (4); **Bolsa** Stock Exchange (12)
bombero/-a (m/f) firefighter (12)
bonito/-a pretty (4)
bosquejo (m) outline
bota (f) boot (4)
botica (f) pharmacy
brasileño/-a Brazilian (1)
brazo (m) arm (8)
brisa (f) breeze (6)
bróculi (m) broccoli (5)
broma (f) joke (11); ~ **pesada** practical joke (11); **en ~** in fun (11); **hacer bromas** to joke; to play a trick (11)
bromista (m/f) entertaining person; practical joker (11)
bueno/-a good (P); **bueno…** well … (7); **¡Bueno!** Hello! (on the telephone); **¡Buena suerte!** Good luck! (4); **Buenas noches.** Good evening. / Good night. (1); **Buenas tardes.** Good afternoon. (1); **Buenos días.** Hello; Good morning. (1)

Glossary

burlarse (de) to make fun (of), joke (about) (11)
burlón/-ona derisive, mocking (11)
buscar to look for (7)
buzón (m) mailbox (4)

C

caballero (m) man, gentleman
caber to fit
cabeza (f) head (8)
cadera (f) hip (8)
caer* to fall
caerse to fall down (8)
café (m) coffee (2)
café brown (1)
cafetería (f) cafeteria (2)
caja (f) box
calculadora (f) calculator (8)
cálculo (m) calculus
caleño/-a a person from Cali (11)
calidad (f) quality (5)
calmante (m) tranquilizer, painkiller (9)
calmar to calm (9); **¡Cálmate!** Settle down! (2); Calm down! (10)
calor (m) heat
calladito/-a very quiet (person); very quietly (3)
callado/-a quiet, quietly (3)
callarse to become quiet; to shut up (3)
calle (f) street (1)
cama (f) bed (3)
cámara (f) camera (4)
camarero/-a (m/f) waiter
camarones (m pl) shrimp (5)
cambiar to change; **~ dinero** to exchange money (6)
cambio (m) change (from a purchase); exchange rate (7); change (one for another) (8); **a cambio de** in exchange for (11)
camilla (f) stretcher (9)
caminar to walk (7)
camión (m) truck
camionero/-a (m/f) truck driver (12)
camisa (f) shirt (4)
campestre country-like, rural (7); **club ~** country club (7)
campo (m) country, countryside
canasta (f) basket (for basketball) (8)
cancelar to cancel
cancha (f) court, playing field (8)
cansado/-a tired (2)
cansarse de to get tired of (10)
capital (f) capital (1)
cargar to load (12)
cariño (m) fondness, affection, kindness (7); **Con todo ~** With affection (10)

Cariñosamente Affectionately (10)
cariñoso/-a affectionate (7)
carne (f) meat; **~ de res** beef (5)
carnicería (f) butcher shop (5)
caro/-a expensive, costly (4)
carpintero/-a (m/f) carpenter (12)
carta (f) letter (1); **~ de agradecimiento** thank you letter (10)
cartel (m) poster (3)
cartera (f) wallet
cartero (m/f) letter carrier (4)
carrera (f) career; major field of study (11)
carretera (f) highway
carro (m) car
casa (f) house (1); **~ de cambio** exchange house (7); **en ~** at home (1)
casados (m pl) married couple (12)
casarse to get married
casete (m) cassette (8)
casi almost (8); **~ nunca** seldom (almost never) (6); **~ siempre** almost always (6)
castaño brown (for hair) (1)
castellano (m) Spanish (lit., Castilian) (10)
castigar to punish
castillo (m) castle (6)
casualidad: ¡Qué ~! What a coincidence! (2)
catedral (f) cathedral (6)
catorce fourteen (1)
cebolla (f) onion (5)
cejas (f pl) eyebrows (11)
celebrar to celebrate (4)
celos (m pl) jealousy (4)
celoso/-a jealous (3)
cena (f) dinner (2)
cenar to have the evening meal (3)
centro (m) center (1)
cerca de near (3)
cerdo (m) pork (5)
cerebro (m) brain (9)
certificado (m) certificate **~ de vacuna** vaccination certificate (4)
cerveza (f) beer (2)
cerrar (ie) to close (1)
césped (m) lawn
cesto (m) basket (for basketball) (8)
ciclismo (m) cycling (4)
cielo raso (m) ceiling
cien, ciento one hundred (1)
ciencias (f pl) **políticas** political science (2)
cinco five (1)
cincuenta fifty (1)
cine (m) movies, cinema
cintura (f) waist (8)
cinturón (m) belt (4); **~ de seguridad** seat belt (4)
cirugía (f) surgery

cirujano/-a (m/f) surgeon (5)
cita (f) date, appointment
ciudad (f) city (1)
ciudadano/-a (m/f) citizen
Claro. Of course. (2)
claro/-a light colored
clase (f) class (P)
clásico/-a classical
clavado (m) dive (9)
clavícula (f) collarbone (8)
clóset (m) closet (3)
club (m) club; **~ campestre** country club (7); **~ de pesca** fishing club; marina (7); **~ social** social club (7)
cobarde cowardly (11)
cobre (m) copper (6)
cocina (f) kitchen (2)
cocinar to cook (2)
cocinero/-a (m/f) cook
coco (m) coconut
coctel (m) cocktail party
coche (m) car
cojear to limp (9)
colega (m) colleague
colgar (ue) to hang (up) (2)
coliflor (f) cauliflower
colmado/-a filled (7)
colmar to heap up, overfill (7)
colmo (m) summit, the highest point of something (7); height (as in finishing touch; "last straw") (9); **el ~ de lo ridículo** height of the ridiculous (9)
colocar to place, put
colombiano/-a Colombian (1)
colorado/-a red
colorete (m) lipstick (11)
collar (m) necklace
comedor (m) dining room (2)
comenzar (ie)* to begin, start (2)
comer to eat (2)
comerciante (m/f) shopkeeper (12)
cómico/-a funny, comic (3)
comida (f) food, meal (1); **~ rápida** junk food
como as; like; **~ si** as if
cómo how; **¿Cómo está(s)?** How are you?(1); **¡Cómo no!** Of course! (6); **¿Cómo se dice…?** How do you say…?; **¿Cómo te llamas?** What's your name? (P)
cómodo/-a comfortable (10)
compañero/-a de cuarto roommate (1)
compartir to share (6)
competir (i, i) to compete (8)
comportamiento (m) behavior (11)
comprar to purchase (4); **hacer compras** to make purchases (5)
comprobar (ue) to check, verify (4); to confirm (11)

comprometerse to make a commitment (11)
compromiso (m) commitment, obligation (10); **~ de matrimonio** wedding engagement
computadora (f) computer (8)
comunión (f) communion (8); **primera ~** first communion
con with; **~ anticipación** in advance (12); **~ el motivo de** for the purpose of (10); **~ frecuencia** frequently (6); **Con permiso.** Excuse me (asking for permission). (1); **~ tal (de) que** provided that (11)
conceder to concede; to grant (11)
concierto (m) concert
condimento (m) condiment (5)
conducir to drive (2)
conferencia (f) lecture (2)
conformista (m/f) conformist (8)
congreso (m) congress, symposium
conjunto (m) (musical) group (3)
conocer* to be familiar with, acquainted with (a place); to meet; to know a person (1); **¿Conoces… ?** Have you ever been to (a place)?
conocido/-a (m/f) acquaintance (12); (adj) well-known (7)
consecuencia (f) result, consequence
conseguir (i, i) to get, obtain (3)
consejero/-a counselor (7)
consejo (m) a piece of advice (7)
construir* to build (6)
consulado (m) consulate (4)
contabilidad (f) accounting (2)
contador(a) (m/f) accountant (5)
contar (ue) to tell; to count; **~ con** to depend upon (7); **~ un chiste** to tell a joke
contento/-a happy (2)
contestar to answer (3)
contestador (m) **automático** answering machine
continuar to continue
conversación (f) conversation (1)
conversar to converse (1)
convertir (ie, i) to convert (7)
convivencia (f) living together (7)
copa (f) wine glass (2)
copiar to copy (11)
corazón (m) heart (9)
corbata (f) (neck) tie (4)
corcho (m) cork (8)
cordialmente cordially (10)
cordón (m) cord, string (8)
corona (f) crown (7)
cortés courteous, polite (1)
cortina (f) curtain (7)
corto/-a short (in length) (6)

corregir (i, i) to correct
correo mail (4); **correos** (m) post office
correr to run
correspondencia (f) correspondence (1)
corriente ordinary; **agua ~** running water (9); **poner al ~** to inform (9)
coser to sew
costar (ue) to cost (4); **¿Cuánto cuesta?** How much is it? (7); **cueste lo que cueste** no matter what it costs
costarricense Costa Rican (1)
costoso/-a costly, expensive
costumbre (f) custom, habit (7)
crear to create (7)
crecer to grow, increase in size (11); to grow up (12)
credencial (f) **escolar** student I.D. (4)
crema (f) cream (2)
criarse to grow up; to be raised (12)
cruce (m) **de camino** intersection
cuaderno (m) notebook, workbook (P)
cuadra block (6)
cuadro (m) framed picture (3)
¿cuál? which (one)? / what? (2)
¿cuándo? when? (2)
¿cuánto/-a? how much? (2); **¿cuántos/-as?** how many? (2); **¿Cuánto vale (cuesta)?** How much is it? (7); **¿Cuántos años tienes?** How old are you? (1); **en cuanto a** regarding, concerning (10)
cuarenta forty (1)
cuarto (m) room, bedroom (1)
cuarto/-a quarter, fourth (2)
cuatro four (1)
cuatrocientos/-as four hundred (1)
cubierto/-a (de) covered (with) (6)
cubrir to cover (6)
cuchara (f) tablespoon (7)
cucharita (f) teaspoon (7)
cuchillo (m) knife (7)
cuello (m) neck (8)
cuenta (f) bill (in a restaurant) (4)
cuerda (f) string
cuerpo (m) body (8)
¡Cuidado! Be careful! (10)
culpa (f) fault; blame (11); **echar la ~** to cast blame upon (11)
culpable at fault (11)
culpar to blame (11)
cumpleaños (m) birthday
cumplido (m) compliment (10)
cumplir to complete; to follow through (on) (12)
cuneta (f) ditch
cuñado/-a brother-/sister-in-law
cupón (m) coupon (9)
curandero/-a (m/f) healer
curita (f) small bandage (Band-Aid) (9)
curso (m) course (2)

CH

champiñón (m) mushroom
chaqueta (f) jacket (4)
charlar to chat (1)
cheque (m) checks; **~ de viajero** traveler's check (6); **~ sin fondos** bad check (one that bounces) (12)
chico/-a boy/girl (1)
chile (m) **colorado** red chili pepper
chileno/-a Chilean (1)
chimenea (f) fireplace (7)
chino/-a Chinese
chisme (m) gossip (11)
chismear to gossip (11)
chismoso/-a gossipy (adj); a gossipy person (11)
chiste (m) joke; **contar (ue) un ~** to tell a joke
chocar (con) crash, bump (into) (9)
chuleta (f) **de cerdo** pork chop (5)

D

dama (f) lady
damas (f pl) checkers; **~ chinas** Chinese checkers
dar* to give (2); **~ la impresión de** to give the appearance of (11); **~ puntos** to stitch a wound (9); **~ un paseo** to take a walk (7); **darse cuenta (de)** to realize (8); **darse la mano** to shake hands
de of; from; **¿De dónde eres?** Where are you from? (1); **¿De parte de quién?** May I ask who's calling? (3); **~ habla española** Spanish-speaking (10); **~ hoy en adelante** from now on (12); **~ lujo** luxurious (6); **De nada.** You're welcome.; **~ ninguna manera** by no means, not at all (4); **~ parte de** on behalf of (10); **~ repente** suddenly; **~ usted muy atentamente** Attentively yours (10); **~ vez en cuando** occasionally (6)
debajo de under (3)
deber must, should (3)
debido a due to (10)
débil weak (3)
décimo/-a tenth (7)
decir* to say, tell (2); **~ la verdad** to tell the truth (3)
declarar to declare
dedo (m) finger (8); **~ de pie** toe
defenderse (ie) to manage; to survive (10)
dejar to allow; to leave (something behind) (8); **~ un recado** to leave a message (3); **~ de** to stop (doing something); **Déjame ver (tu tarea).** Let me see (your homework). (2)

Glossary

delante de in front of (3)
delgado/-a thin, slender (3)
delicioso/-a delicious
delineador (m) eyeliner (11)
demorar to delay
denotar to signify (10)
dentro de inside (3)
deporte (m) sport (2)
derecho/-a right; **a la ~** to the right (6)
derecho (m) legal right (11)
derrota (f) defeat (6)
desafortunadamente unfortunately (4)
desagradable disagreeable, unpleasant
desanimar to discourage
desarrollar to develop (12)
desayunar to have breakfast (3)
desayuno (m) breakfast (2)
descalzo/-a barefoot (6)
descansar to rest, relax (1); **descansado/-a** rested (6)
descargar to unload (12)
descolgar (ue) to remove the telephone receiver from the cradle (3)
descontento/-a dissatisfied, displeased (with something) (3)
describir to describe
descubrir to discover
desear (+ inf) to want (to do something) (2)
desesperado/-a desperate (11)
desesperarse to lose hope (11)
desgracia: ¡Qué ~! What terrible luck! (8)
deshonrar to dishonor (11)
desinfectar to disinfect (9)
desleal disloyal (12)
deslizarse to slip, slide (9)
desmayarse to faint, pass out (9)
despacio slowly (7)
despedida (f) farewell (1); goodbye, closing (of a letter) (10)
despedirse (i, i) to say good-bye (3)
despegar to take off (airplane) (4)
despertador (m) alarm clock (3); **poner el ~** to set the alarm clock
despertarse (ie) to wake up (3)
después de after (2)
destacarse to stand out (11)
destilado/-a distilled; **agua ~** distilled water
desván (m) attic (7)
desvestirse (i, i) to get undressed (3)
detener to detain (11)
detrás de in back of, behind (3)
devolver to return (an item)
día (m) day (1); **Buenos días.** Hello; Good morning. (1); **Día de Todos los Santos** All Saints' Day (4)
diagnóstico (m) diagnosis (9)

diciembre December (1)
diez ten (1)
difícil difficult (2)
dinero (m) money (4); **cambiar ~** to exchange money (6)
dirección (f) address; direction (1)
dirigirse to address
discutir to argue, discuss (4)
diseñar to design (6)
diseño (m) design (5)
disfamar to defame (11)
disfrutar de to enjoy (7)
disminuir to diminish (12)
distinguido/-a distinguished (10)
distraído/-a absent-minded
disuadir to dissuade; to deter (11)
diversión (f) recreation, pastime (8)
divertido/-a fun, amusing (4)
divertirse (ie, i) to have a good time, to enjoy oneself
doblar to turn (6)
doce twelve (1)
documento (m) document (4)
doler (ue) to hurt (feel pain)
dolor (m) pain (9)
domicilio (m) home address (4)
domingo (m) Sunday
¿dónde? where? (2)
dormilón/-ona sleepyhead (3)
dormir (ue, u)* to sleep (3); **~ la siesta** to take a nap (5)
dormirse (ue, u) to go to sleep (3)
dormitorio (m) bedroom (1)
dos two (1)
doscientos/-as two hundred (1)
ducha (f) shower (6)
ducharse to shower (3)
duda (f) doubt
dudar to doubt
dueño/-a (m/f) owner (5)
dulce (adj) sweet; **dulces** (m pl) sweets (5)
dulcería (f) candy shop (5)

E

economía (f) economics (2)
ecuatoriano/-a Ecuadorian (1)
echar to throw out (11); **~ de menos** to miss, long for (12); **~ flores** to flatter (11); **~ la culpa** to cast blame upon (11)
edad (f) age (1)
edificio building
educado/-a: mal ~ ill-mannered, rude (7)
efectivo (m) cash in bill form (6)
eficaz effective, efficient (7)
egipcio/-a Egyptian
Egipto Egypt

ejercicio (m) exercise (P)
él he (1)
ella she (1)
ellos/-as they (1)
embajada (f) embassy (4)
emergencia (f) emergency; **sala de ~** emergency room (9)
emocionante exciting
empacar to crate; to pack up (12)
empaparse to get soaked (9)
empequeñecer to become smaller (12)
empezar (ie) to begin (3)
empleado/-a (m/f) clerk (6)
en in; on; **~ broma** in fun (11); **~ casa** at home (1); **~ caso de que** in case (11); **~ cuanto a** regarding, concerning (10); **~ efectivo** in cash; **~ exposición** on display, on exhibit (6); **~ la calle** away from home; **~ mi opinión** in my opinion (1); **~ negrilla** boldface; **~ otra ocasión** some other time (3); **~ regla** in order (4); **~ relación a** with regard to; **~ serio** seriously (11)
enamorarse (de) to fall in love (with) (11)
encaje (m) lace
encantado/-a pleased to meet you (1)
encantar to love (2)
encaprichado/-a infatuated (11)
encargarse de o take charge of
encima de on top of (3)
encontrar (ue) to find (2)
encontrarse (ue) (con) to encounter, come across
encuesta (f) poll (1)
energía (f) energy
enero January (1)
enfermedad (f) illness (9)
enfermero/-a (m/f) nurse (5)
enfermo/-a sick (5)
enfocado/-a focused
engañar to trick; to deceive (11)
engañoso/-a deceitful (11)
enojado/-a angry
enojarse to get angry (8)
ensalada (f) salad (5)
enseñar to teach (2); to show
enterarse (de) to inform oneself (about) (11)
entonces then (7)
entrada (f) entrance (1); appetizer (5)
entrar to enter (1)
entregar to hand over, hand in
entremés (m) appetizer
entrenador(a) (m/f) coach
entrevista (f) interview
enviar to send; **~ una carta** to send (mail) a letter (4)
envidia (f) envy; **¡Qué ~!** I'm green with envy! (4)

envidiable enviable (10)
envidioso/-a envious
envolver (ue) to wrap
enyesado/-a in a cast (8)
época (f) epoch, era (6)
equilibrio (m) balance (9)
equipaje (m) luggage (4)
equipo (m) team
equivocado/-a wrong, in error
error (m) mistake, error
escala (f) stopover (on a trip) (4); **hacer ~** to make a stop (4); **vuelo sin escalas** non-stop flight
escalera (f) stairway (7)
escalofríos (m pl) chills (9)
escolar school-related
escribir to write (P)
escritorio (m) desk (3)
escuchar to listen
escupir to spit
esfuerzo (m) effort (12)
espacio (m) space (7)
espalda (f) back (8)
espantoso/-a frightening; terrible (11)
España Spain (1)
español (m) Spanish (P)
español(a) (m/f) Spaniard
espárragos (m pl) asparagus (5)
especialización (f) major field of study
espejo (m) mirror (3)
esperanza (f) hope
esperar to hope (2); to wait for (3); **sala de espera** waiting room (9)
espinacas (f pl) spinach
espiral spiral
esquí (m) ski; skiing; **~ acuático** water skiing (7); **~ alpino** downhill skiing (7); **~ nórdico** cross-country skiing (7)
esquiar to ski (4); **~ en el agua** to water ski; **~ en la nieve** to ski (in the snow) (2)
esquina (f) corner (exterior) (5)
establecer to establish (7)
estación (f) season (4)
estado (m) state
Estados Unidos (m pl) United States (1)
estadounidense person from the U.S. (1)
estampilla (f) stamp (4)
estante (m) **de libros** bookcase (3)
estar* to be (1); **~ a gusto** to be comfortable, at ease (10); **~ al tanto de** to be up-to-date, current (10); **~ celoso/-a** to be jealous (4); **~ contento/-a** to be happy (3); **~ de vuelta** to be back (3); **~ enamorado/-a (de)** to be in love (with) (12); **~ equivocado/-a** to be wrong, in error (3); **~ hecho/-a pedazos** to be falling

apart, to be a wreck (9); **~ listo/-a** to be ready to do something (10); **~ relacionado/-a con** to be related to (9); **~ seguro/-a** to be certain (4)
estatura (f) height (9)
este (m) east (1)
estéreo (m) stereo (3)
esterilizar to sterilize (9)
estimar to esteem (12); **estimado/-a** esteemed (10)
estómago (m) stomach (8)
estorbar to hinder, obstruct (12)
estornudar to sneeze (9)
estrella (f) star; **estrella (m/f) de cine** movie star (10)
estrenar to wear or use for the first time (10)
estructura (f) structure (7)
estudiante (m/f) student (1)
estudiar to study (1)
estufa (f) stove (7)
etiqueta (f) tag, label (4)
Europa (f) Europe (12)
evitar to avoid (10)
excursión (f) tour (6)
exposición (f) display, exhibition (6)
extranjero (m) foreign country (4); **extranjero/-a** (m/f) foreigner (4)
extrañar to miss, long for (people, places) (10)
extraviarse to get lost (4)

F

fácil easy (2)
factura (f) invoice, bill of sale (4)
facturar to check (luggage) (4)
facultad (f) college, school of a university (2)
falda (f) skirt (4)
faltar to miss (a meeting, an appointment); to be lacking (10)
fama (f) reputation (11); **tener ~ de** to be known for or as (7)
familia (f) family (1)
familiar (m/f) family member (12)
farmacéutico/-a (m/f) pharmacist (12)
farmacia (f) pharmacy
farol (m) street light (5)
fascinante fascinating
favorito/-a favorite
febrero February (1)
fecha (f) date (1)
feliz happy; **Felices Pascuas** Merry Christmas; Happy Easter (4); **Feliz Año Nuevo** Happy New Year (4); **Feliz Navidad** Merry Christmas (4)
fenomenal terrific, sensational (3)
feo/-a ugly, unattractive

fiebre (f) fever (9)
fiesta (f) party; **~ de disfraz** costume party
fijarse en to notice (10); **¡Fíjate!** Imagine that! (1)
filosofía (f) philosophy
fin (m) purpose (1); end; **~ de semana** weekend (2); **a fines de** at the end of (6)
finanzas (f pl) finances (12)
fino/-a thin
firma (f) signature
firmar to sign (6)
física (f) physics
físico (m): **el ~** physical features (3)
flan (m) caramel custard (5)
flojo/-a: **¡Qué ~ eres!** You're so lazy (6)
flor (f) flower (4); **echar flores** to flatter (11)
florecer to flourish (12)
florería (f) flower shop (5)
fluvial fluvial
fogata (f) the flame of a fire (7)
fortaleza (f) firmness
foto (f) photograph (4)
fotocopiadora (f) photocopy machine (8)
fracasar to fail (11)
francés/-esa French (1)
Francia France (1)
fraternidad (f) brotherhood
frecuencia (f) frequency (6); **con ~** frequently
frecuentemente frequently
fregadero (m) kitchen sink (7)
frenar to brake
frenos (m pl) brakes (8)
frente (f) forehead (11)
fresa (f) strawberry
fresco (m) coolness
frijoles (m pl) beans
frío (m) coldness
fuego (m) fire (7)
fuera de outside (3)
fuerte (m) fort; strong (3)
fugaz fleeting, likely to go away
fulano/-a (m/f) so-and-so, John/Jane Doe (11)
fumar to smoke; **sección (f) de (no) fumar** (no) smoking section (6)
funcionar to function, work, run (machines) (3); **No funciona.** Out of order. / This isn't working. (3)
fundar to found, establish (6)
fútbol (m) soccer (2); **~ americano** football (2)

G

galleta (f) cookie
ganar to win

Glossary

gaseosa (f) sparkling water, soft drink
gastar to spend (11)
gemelo/-a (m/f) twin (8)
generoso/-a generous (3)
gerente (m/f) manager (5)
gesto (m) gesture
ghaneano/-a Ghanian
gimnasio (m) gym
gordo/-a fat, heavy (3)
gorra (f) cap (4)
gozar (de) to enjoy something (12)
grabadora (f) tape recorder (8)
gracias thank you (1)
grado (m) degree
graduarse to graduate
gramo (m) gram
grande big, large (1)
granjero/-a (m/f) farmer (12)
gratis free (no cost) (6)
gripe (f) flu (9)
gris gray (1)
grueso/-a thick (8)
guante (m) glove (4)
guapo/-a handsome, nice-looking (3)
guaraní (m) Guaraní (language); (m/f) member of the Guaraní tribe
guardar to keep, take care of (4)
guatemalteco/-a Guatemalan (1)
guerra (f) war (6)
guía (f) guidebook (7); (m/f) guide (7); ~ **telefónica** telephone book (7)
guisantes (m pl) peas
gustar to like, be pleasing
gusto (m) pleasure; **estar a** ~ to be comfortable (10); **Mucho** ~. Pleased to meet you.; **tener el** ~ **de** to have the pleasure of (10)

H

haber* to have
habichuelas (f pl) string beans
habitación (f) room (with a bed), as in a hotel (6)
hablar to speak (P)
hace: ~ **buen tiempo** it's nice out (3); ~ **mal tiempo** it's bad out (3); ~ **calor** it's hot (4); ~ **fresco** it's cool (4); ~ **frío** it's cold (4); ~ **sol** it's sunny (4)
hacer* to do, make (2); ~ **aduana** to pass through customs (4); ~ **bromas** to joke; to play a trick (11); ~ **compras** to make purchases, shop (5); ~ **el favor de** please (10); ~ **escala** to make a stop (4); ~ **falta** to lack, need (10); ~ **juego con** to go well with (4); ~ **la maleta** to pack (4); ~ **los arreglos** to make arrangements (6); ~ **trampa** to cheat; to deceive; to trick (11); ~ **un viaje** to take a trip (4)
hacerse to become; to prepare oneself to be (11); ~ **daño** to get hurt, to be injured (8)
harina (f) flour
hasta until (2); **Hasta luego.** See you later. (1)
hay there is; there are; **Hay de todo.** There's a lot of variety. (6); **¿Hay preguntas?** Are there any questions?
helado (m) ice cream (5)
herida (f) wound, injury (9)
herir (ie, i) to wound, injure (9)
hermanastro/-a (m/f) stepbrother/stepsister
hermano (m) brother (1); **hermana** (f) sister (1); **hermanos** (m pl) siblings (1)
hierro (m) iron (6)
hígado (m) liver (9)
hilar: to spin (thread)
hinchado/-a swollen (9)
hispano/-a Hispanic (1)
hispanohablante (m/f) Spanish-speaking person (10)
historia (f) history (2)
hogar (m) house; home (5)
hoja (f) leaf; ~ **de papel** sheet of paper (5)
hola hello (P); **hola** hi (1)
hombre (m) man (1); ~ **de negocios** businessman (12)
hombro (m) shoulder (8)
hondureño/-a Honduran (1)
hongo (m) mushroom (5)
hora (f) hour; **¿A qué hora…?** At what time . . . ? (2)
horario (m) schedule (2)
horno: al ~ baked (5)
horror: ¡Qué ~**!** How horrible! (8)
hoy today (2); **de** ~ **en adelante** from now on (12)
huésped/-a (m/f) guest (in a hotel) (4)
huevo (m) egg (5)
humo (m) smoke (6)

I

idea (f) idea
idioma (m) language (10)
iglesia (f) church (3)
igualmente the same here; likewise (1)
imaginarse to imagine (8); **¡Imagínate!** Imagine that! (10)
impedido/-a disabled (10)
impedir (i, i) to hinder; to impede (10)
imperio (m) empire (6)
importante important (3)
imposible impossible (2)
impresionante impressive (1)
impresora (f) printer (8)
impuesto (m) tax (4)
incertidumbre (f) uncertainty (11)
incómodo/-a uncomfortable (10)
inesperado/-a unexpected
información (f) information
informarse to obtain information about (11)
informática (f) computer science (2)
ingeniería (f) engineering
ingeniero/-a (m/f) engineer
Inglaterra England (1)
inglés/-esa English (1)
inmediatamente immediately
inodoro (m) toilet (6)
insoportable intolerable (12)
inteligente intelligent (1)
interesante interesting (1)
intervención (f) **quirúrgica** operation (9)
intestinos (m pl) intestines (9)
íntimo/-a very close, intimate (10)
inundación (f) flood
inútil useless (11)
inválido/-a disabled; handicapped (10)
invernal winter (adj) (7)
invierno (m) winter (4)
invitación (f) invitation (2)
invitado/-a (m/f) guest (in a home) (4)
invitar to invite (2)
inyección (f) injection (9)
ir* to go; ~ **a la playa** to go to the beach (4); ~ **al cine** to go to the movies (1); ~ **al grano** to get to the heart of the matter; ~ **de compras** to go shopping (5); ~ **derecho** to go straight ahead (6); ~ **a pie** to go on foot (7)
irse to go away (1)
Italia Italy (1)
italiano/-a Italian (1)
izquierdo/-a left; **a la** ~ **izquierda** to the left (6)

J

jabón (m) a bar of soap (6)
jadear to pant, gasp for breath (9)
jamás never (4)
jamón (m) ham (5)
Jánuca (f) Hanukkah (4)
japonés/-esa Japanese
jardín (m) garden (5)
jardinería (f) garden shop; nursery (5)
jefe/-a (m/f) boss
jornada (f) working day (12); ~ **parcial** part-time (12)
joven (m/f) young person (1)
joyas (f pl) jewelry
joyería (f) jewelry store (5)

Glossary

jubilarse to retire (5); **jubilado/-a** retired (5)
judías (f pl) green beans (5)
juego (m) game; **juegos** (m pl) **de mesa** table/board games; **hacer ~ con** to go well, match (4)
jueves (m) Thursday
juez (m/f) judge (11)
jugar (ue) to play (2); **~ a los bandidos** to play cops and robbers; **~ al golf** to play golf; **~ con las muñecas** to play dolls; **~ pelota** to play catch; **~ rayuela** to play hopscotch
jugo (m) juice (2); **~ de manzana** apple juice (2); **~ de naranja** orange juice (2)
juguete (m) toy
julio July (1)
junio June (1)
junto/-a together (8)
jurado (m) jury (11)
justicia (f) justice (11)
justo/-a fair, just (12)
juzgado (m) court of law (11)

K

kilogramo (m) kilogram
kilómetro (m) kilometer

L

labio (m) lip (11)
laboratorio (m) **(de lenguas)** (language) laboratory (2)
lácteo/-a dairy
lado (m) side; **al ~ de** next to (3)
lagarto (m) lizard
lago (m) lake
lámpara (f) lamp (3)
langosta (f) lobster (5)
langostina (f) prawn (5)
lápiz (m) pencil (P)
largo/-a long (6)
lastima: ¡Qué ~! What a shame! (8)
lastimarse to injure oneself (9)
lata (f) tin can; bother; **!Qué lata!** What a pain! (4)
latino/-a Latin American
latinoamericano/-a Latin American
lavamanos (m) washbasin (sink) (6)
lavar (limpiar) en seco to dry clean (5)
lavarse to wash oneself (3); **~ los dientes** to brush one's teeth (3)
leal loyal (12)
lealtad (f) loyalty (12)
leche (f) milk (2)
lechería (f) dairy (5)
lechuga (f) lettuce (5)
leer* to read (P)
legumbre (f) vegetable (5)
lejos de far from (3)
lengua (f) language; tongue (10)
lenguado (m) sole (fish) (5)
letra (f) letter; **~ mayúscula** capital letter; **~ minúscula** lower-case letter
letrero (m) (information) sign (5)
levadura (f) yeast
levantar to lift, raise; **~ pesas** to lift weights; **levantarse** to get up (3)
ley (f) law (11)
libertad (f) freedom (6)
libra (f) pound
libre free (not busy; not enslaved) (6)
librería (f) bookstore (5)
libro (m) book (P)
licencia (f) license (4)
liceo (m) high school
ligamento (m) ligament (9)
ligero/-a light in weight
limón (m) lemon (2)
limpiaparabrisas (m) windshield wiper (8)
limpiar to clean (3)
lindo/-a cute, pretty (8)
liquidación (f) (clearance) sale (4)
locutor(a) (m/f) announcer
lograr to gain; to succeed (8)
lomito (m) loin (of beef or pork) (5)
lucha (f) fight; **~ libre** wrestling
luchar to fight (8)
luego then, next
lugar (m) place; **~ de nacimiento** birthplace
lunes (m) Monday (2)
luz (f) light

LL

llamar to call (3); to knock
llanta (f) tire (8)
llave (f) key
llegar to arrive (1); **~ a ser** to become (6); **~ al meollo** to get to the heart of the matter
lleno/-a full (6)
llevar to wear, carry (4)
llevarse (con) to get along (with) (8); **~ a cabo** to take place (10)
llover (ue) to rain (3)
lluvia (f) rain (3)

M

madera (f) wood (6)
madrastra (f) stepmother
madre (f) mother (1)
madrugada (f) dawn (3)
madrugar to get up early (3)
madurar to mature (12)
maestro/-a (m/f) teacher
magnífico/-a wonderful (4)
mal educado/-a ill-mannered, rude (7)
malcriado/-a spoiled, impolite (9)
maleta (f) suitcase (4); **hacer la ~** to pack (4)
maletero (m) trunk (of a car) (8)
maletín (m) small suitcase (4)
malgastar to waste (11)
malicioso/-a malicious (11)
maligno/-a malignant (9)
malo/-a bad (P)
manchado/-a stained
mancha (f) stain
mandar to send (4)
manejar to manage, handle, (4); drive
mano (f) hand (8); **darse la ~** to shake hands; **¡Manos a la obra!** Let's get to work! (2)
mantel (m) tablecloth (7)
mantener to support; to maintain (11)
mantequilla (f) butter (5)
manzana (f) apple (5)
mañana tomorrow (2); (f) morning (1)
mapa (m) map (1)
maquillaje (m) make-up
maquillarse to put on makeup (11)
máquina (f) machine; **~ de escribir** typewriter (8)
mar (m) sea, ocean
marca (f) brand (5)
marcar: ~ el número to dial the number (3)
mareado/-a dizzy; nauseated (9)
marisco (m) seafood; shellfish (5)
marítimo/-a maritime
martes (m) Tuesday
marzo March (1)
matar to kill (2)
matemáticas (f pl) math (2)
materno/-a maternal
matricularse to register (for a course) (11)
matrimonio (m) married couple; marriage (12)
mayo May (1)
mayor older; **~ parte** (f) majority
Me está dando hambre. I'm getting hungry. (6)
mediano/-a average (3); **de mediana estatura** average height
medicina (f) medicine (9)
médico/-a (m/f) doctor (5)
medio/-a half; **medio muerto/-a** half dead; exhausted (11); **medio tiempo** half-time (12)

Glossary

XVII

medio (m) **de transporte** means of transportation (4)
mejilla (f) cheek (11)
mejor better
mejorarse to get better (health) (9)
menor younger
menos (de) less (than) (6); **a ~ que** unless (11); **echar de ~** to miss, long for (12); **¡Menos mal!** That's a relief! / It's a good thing! (1)
menospreciar to hold in contempt (12)
mentir (ie, i) to lie (3)
mentira (f) lie (3); **~ piadosa** white lie (11)
mentón (m) chin (11)
menudo: a ~ often, a lot (6)
mercaderías (f pl) commodities, merchandise (12)
mercancías (f pl) merchandise (6)
merecer to deserve (9)
mes (m) month (1)
mesa (f) table (7)
mesero/-a (m/f) waiter (5)
mesita (f) night table (3)
meta (f) goal
meter to put; **~ la pata** to make a social blunder (7)
metro (m) meter; subway
mexicano/-a (m/f) Mexican (1)
mezcla (f) mixture (6)
mezclar to mix (6)
miedo (m) fear; **tener ~ (de)** to be afraid of (3)
miedoso/-a fearful (11)
mientras while, during (8)
miércoles (m) Wednesday
mil one thousand (1)
millón million (1)
mirar to look, watch (1)
misa (f) mass (3)
mitad (f) half (11)
mochila (f) knapsack, backpack (4)
modista (f) dressmaker, seamstress (5)
mojar to moisten (9)
molestar to bother, irritate (4)
molestia (f) bother, trouble (4)
moneda (f) coin (6)
montar a caballo to ride a horse (7)
morado/-a purple (1)
moreno/-a dark-skinned
morir (ue, u) to die
moro/-a (m/f) Moslem, Moor
mostaza (f) mustard (5)
mostrar (ue) to show
motivo (m) reason, motive (10); **con el ~ de** for the purpose of (10)
motor (m) motor, engine (8)
mover (ue) to move (furniture) (3); **~ palancas** to pull strings (12)

muchacho/-a (m/f) child (1)
mucho/-a a lot (P)
mudarse to move (change residence) (5)
mueblería (f) furniture store (5)
muebles (m pl) furniture (7)
muestra (f) sample
mujer (f) woman (1); **~ de negocios** businesswoman (12)
muletas (f pl) crutches (9)
multinacional (f) multinational company (2)
muñeca (f) wrist; doll
muralla (f) exterior wall (7)
músculo (m) muscle (9)
museo (m) museum (6)
música (f) music
muslo (m) thigh (8)
muy very; **Muy bien, gracias.** Very well, thank you. (1); **~ hecho/-a** well-done (meat); **Muy señor/-a mío/-a...** Dear Sir/Madam . . . (10)

N

nacer to be born (8)
nacimiento (m) birth
nacionalidad (f) nationality (1)
nada nothing (4); **~ por el estilo** nothing like that (8)
nadar to swim (2)
nadie no one, nobody (4)
naipes (m pl) playing cards
naranja (f) orange
nariz (f) nose (8)
Navidad (f) Christmas (4); **Feliz Navidad** Merry Christmas (4)
negrilla (f) boldface type
negro/-a black (1)
nervioso/-a nervous, anxious (2)
nevar (ie) to snow (3)
ni... ni neither . . . nor (4)
nieto/-a grandchild
nieve (f) snow (3)
ninguno/-a none, not any (4)
nocivo/-a noxious, poisonous (9)
nocturna (f) late show (movies)
noche (f) night (); **Buenas noches.** Good evening. / Good night. (1); **Noche vieja** (f) New Year's Eve (4); **Nochebuena** (f) Christmas Eve (4)
nombre (m) **de pila** given (first) name
noreste (m) northeast (1)
noroeste (m) northwest (1)
norte (m) north (1)
norteamericano/-a North American
nosotros/-as we (1)
notable very good (11)
notas (f) **(calificaciones) escolares** academic grades (11)
noticias (f) news
novecientos/-as nine hundred (1)
noveno/-a ninth (7)
noventa ninety (1)
noviazgo (m) courtship (12)
noviembre November (1)
novio/-a (m/f) sweetheart; fiancé(e); groom/bride (11)
nueve nine (1)
nuevo/-a new (4)
número number
nunca never (3); **más que ~** more than ever (10)
nutrición (f) nutrition
nutrir to nourish (9)

O

o... o either . . . or (4)
obrero/-a (m/f) laborer (12)
obtener to obtain, get
octavo/-a eighth (7)
octubre October (1)
ochenta eighty (1)
ocho eight (1)
ochocientos/-as eight hundred (1)
odiar to hate, detest (2)
odio (m) hatred (8)
oeste (m) west (1)
ofender to offend (7)
oficina (f) office
oído (m) hearing
oír* to hear (2)
ojeras (f pl) circles under the eyes (11)
ojos (m pl) eyes (8)
ola (f) wave
olfato (m) sense of smell (6)
olor (m) smell, odor
olvidarse de to forget
once eleven (1)
operación (f) operation (5)
operar to operate (5)
optimista optimistic
opuesto opposite
orden: A sus órdenes. At your service. (6)
ordenado/-a orderly
ordenador (m) computer (8)
orejas (f pl) ears (8)
orgullo (m) pride (8)
orgulloso/-a proud (8)
orientación (f) orientation
oro (m) gold (4)
oscuridad (f) darkness (8)
oscuro/-a dark (1)
otoño (m) fall (4)
otro/-a other, another
OVNI (m) UFO
oye hey (2)

P

padecer to suffer (12)
padrastro (m) stepfather (1)
padre (m) father (1)
padres (m pl) parents (1)
pagar* to pay; ~ **a plazos** to pay in installments (6); ~ **en efectivo** to pay cash
pago (m) payment (6)
país (m) country (1)
paisaje (m) landscape, scenery (7)
palabra (f) word; ~ **clave** key word
palanca (f) lever (12); **tener palancas** to have connections (12)
pan (m) bread (5); ~ **dulce** sweet bread (5)
panadería (f) bakery, bread store (5)
panameño/-a Panamanian (1)
panecillo (m) roll (5)
pantalones (m pl) pants (4)
pantuflas (f pl) bedroom slippers
papel (m) paper (P); ~ **higiénico** toilet paper
papelería (f) stationery store (5)
para for; ~ **que** so that (11)
parabrisas (m) windshield (8)
parada (f) stop (bus, taxi)
paraguayo/-a Paraguayan (1)
paraíso (m) paradise (6)
parar to stop (11)
parecer to seem (6)
parecerse a to look like
pared (f) wall (interior) (3)
pareja (f) couple (12)
pariente (m/f) relative (1)
párpados (m pl) eyelids (11)
parte (f) part; **de ~ de** on behalf of (10); **mayor ~** (f) majority
partir to break (apart) (8); **a ~ de** beginning with (6)
parrilla (f) grille; **a la ~** grilled (5)
parroquia (f) parish
pasado mañana day after tomorrow
pasajero/-a temporary (12)
pasaporte (m) passport (4)
pasar to pass, go in (1); to spend (time) (3); ~ **por** to pass through, by (6)
pasatiempo (m) hobby, interest (1)
pase (m) pass (entrance permit) (7)
paseo (m) walk, pathway (7); **dar un ~** to take a walk (7)
pasillo (m) hallway, corridor (1)
paso (m) step; ~ **por paso** step by step
pastel (m) layer cake, pastry (5)
pastelería (f) pastry shop (5)
pastilla (f) pill (9)
pata (f) foot (of an animal); **meter la ~** put your foot in you mouth (7); **patas arriba** upside down
paterno/-a paternal

patinar to skate
patio (m) courtyard, yard (5); ~ **delantero** front yard
pauta (f) guideline
pavo (m) turkey (5)
payaso (m) clown
pecho (m) chest (8)
pedir (i, i)* to ask for, request (3); ~ **prestado/-a** to borrow (7)
pegar to hit (8)
peinarse to comb one's hair (3)
pelear to fight (8)
película (f) movie, film
peligroso/-a dangerous
pelirrojo/-a red-haired (3)
pelo (m) hair (1); ~ **castaño** brown hair (3); **tomarle el ~ (a uno)** to tease, "pull someone's leg" (9)
pelota (f) small ball (tennis ball, baseball) (8)
peluca (f) wig
penicilina (f) penicillin (9)
pensar (ie)* to think (1); ~ **(+ inf.)** to plan to (do something) (2)
pensión (f) boarding house
peor worse
pepino (m) cucumber
pequeño/-a small, little (1)
perder (ie) to lose (4); ~ **el conocimiento** to lose consciousness (9)
perdonar to pardon; to excuse (7); **¡Perdón!** I'm sorry! (P)
perezoso/-a lazy (3)
perfil (m) profile
periódico (m) newspaper (5)
periodismo (m) journalism
periodista (m/f) journalist (5)
perjudicar to damage, impair (12)
permitir to let, allow
pero but (1)
persianas (f pl) venetian blinds (7)
persona (f) person; ~ **desconocida** stranger
personal (m) personnel
personalidad (f) personality (3)
pertenecer to belong to
peruano/-a Peruvian (1)
pesado/-a (m/f) bore; (adj) heavy
pesar to weigh (9); **a ~ de que** in spite of (11)
pesas (f pl) weights; **levantar ~** to lift weights
pescadería (f) fish store (5)
pescado (m) fish (5)
pescar to fish (7)
pesimista pessimistic
peso (m) weight (9)
pestañas (f pl) eyelashes (11)

pestañina (f) mascara (11)
petición (f) request
pez (m) fish (live) (7)
piadoso/-a merciful; pious (11); **mentira** (f) **piadosa** white lie
picante spicy, hot (5)
pie (m) foot (8); **dedos del ~** toes
piel (f) skin (9)
pierna (f) leg
pieza (f) room (6)
piloto (m/f) pilot (4)
pimienta (f) pepper (condiment) (5)
pimiento (m) pepper (vegetable)
pintalabios (m) lipstick (11)
pintarse to put on make-up
pintar to paint; **pintarse** to put on make-up
pintura (f) paint; painting
piropo (m) a flattering comment (11)
pisar to step on (9)
piscina (f) swimming pool (6)
piso (m) floor (3); floor (level of a building) (6)
plan (m) plan
planchar to iron
planta (f) plant (5); ~ **baja** ground floor
plata (f) silver; money (4)
platillo (m) saucer (7)
platito (m) saucer (7)
plato (m) plate, dish; food (course, meal) (2); dish (of food) (7)
playa (f) beach (4)
pleito (m) lawsuit (11)
plomero/-a plumber (12)
pluma (f) pen (P)
poco a little (6); **al ~ rato** shortly after (12)
poco cocido/-a rare (meat) (5)
poder*(ue) to be able (2)
polvos (m pl) powder (11)
pollo (m) chicken (5)
poner* to place, put (2); ~ **al corriente** to inform (9); ~ **el despertador** to set the alarm clock; ~ **atención** to pay attention (8)
ponerse to become; to wear (10); ~ **en contacto (con)** to get in touch/contact (with) (9); ~ **furioso/-a** to get furious (8); ~ **la ropa** to get dressed
por: ~ **avión** by air (6); ~ **favor** please (P); ~ **lo menos** at least (6); **¿por qué?** why? (2); ~ **tierra** by land (6)
porque because
portarse bien/mal to behave well/badly (8)
postre (m) dessert (5)
potable drinkable (6)

Glossary

XIX

potente powerful
practicar to practice; ~ deportes to play sports (1)
precio (m) price (4)
precioso/-a beautiful (4)
preferir (ie, i) to prefer (3)
pregunta (f) question (P)
preguntar to ask questions
prenda (f) de vestir article of clothing
prender to turn on (lights, electrical appliances) (8)
preocupación (f) concern, worry (11)
preparar to prepare (2)
presentar to introduce (1)
presión (f) sanguínea blood pressure (9)
préstamo (m) loan (7)
prestar to lend (7); ~ atención to pay attention (8)
presupuesto (m) budget (12)
previo/-a previous (10)
primavera (f) spring (season) (4)
primero/-a first (2)
primeros auxilios (m pl) first aid (9)
primo/-a (m/f) cousin (1)
principiar to begin (7)
principio (m) principle (12)
probablemente probably
probar (ue) to taste (5)
probarse (ue) to try on (4)
problema (m) problem (4)
procesar to prosecute
producto (m) product (5)
profesor(a) (m/f) professor (P), teacher
programa (m) bilingual program (2)
promedio (m) average (6)
pronóstico (m) del tiempo weather forecast (3)
pronto soon
propietario/-a (m/f) owner (4)
propio/-a own; of one's own (11)
propósito (m) purpose
proteger to protect
provechoso/-a advantageous, beneficial (12)
prueba (f) proof
psicología (f) psychology (2)
puerta (f) door (1); ~ de salida departure gate (4)
puerto (m) seaport (6)
pues well, then (7)
puesto que since, given that (10)
pulgada (f) inch
pulmones (m pl) lungs (9)

Q

quedar: ~ bien/mal to fit well/poorly (4)
quedarse to stay, remain (4)
quehacer (m) chore (7)
queja (f) complaint
quejón/-ona (m/f) complainer
querer (ie)* to want (2); to love
queso (m) cheese (5)
¿quién? who? (1)
química (f) chemistry (2)
quimoterapia (f) chemotherapy
quince fifteen (1)
quinientos/-as five hundred (1)
quinto/-a fifth (2)
quitar to take away, remove (3)
quitarse la ropa to get undressed
quizás perhaps, maybe (3)

R

radiación (f) radiation
radiografía (f) X ray (9)
ramo (m) (de flores) bouquet (of flowers) (5)
rápido quickly (2)
raqueta (f) racquet (8)
rasgo (m) characteristic (3)
rato (m) short period of time (10); (a) while (12); al poco ~ shortly after (12)
ratón (m) mouse
rayuela (f) hopscotch
rebaja (f) discount, sale (4)
rebajar to lower
rebanada (f) slice
rebelde (m/f) rebel (8)
recepción (f) front desk (hotel) (6)
recepcionista (m/f) receptionist (9)
receta (f) prescription (9)
recetar to prescribe (9)
recibir to receive
recibo (m) receipt (4)
recién casado/-a (m/f) newlywed (12)
reclamo (m) claim
recomendar (ie) to recommend (7)
recordar (ue) to remember (10)
recorrer to cover a distance (8)
recuerdo (m) memory; souvenir (8)
recuperarse to recuperate (health) (12)
rechazar to refuse (an invitation); to reject (10)
red (f) net (8)
redactar to draft
reducir to reduce, lower
refresco (m) soft drink (2)
refrigerador (m) refrigerator (7)
regalar to give a gift (4)
regalo (m) gift, present (4)
regatear to set a price by bargaining (7)
región (f) region
regla (f) regulation (11); rule; en ~ in order (4)
regresar to return (3)
regular acceptable (11)
reír (i, i)* to laugh
reírse (de) (i, i) to laugh at (3)
reja (f) grillwork (5)
relacionado/-a con related to (9)
reloj (m) watch
relojería (f) watch shop (5)
relucir to shine, excel
remedio (m) medicine, remedy (9)
renovar (ue) to renew (4)
reparar to fix
repartir to distribute, divide up (8)
repetir (i, i) to repeat
reprobado suspended; failing (11)
requisito (m) requirement (4)
reservado/-a reserved (3)
resfriado (m) cold (9)
residencia (f) residence hall, college dormitory (1)
resolver (ue) to solve (4)
respetuosamente respectfully (10)
respirar to breathe
resultado (m) result, outcome
resultar to turn out to be (11)
resumen (m) summary
reunión (f) reunion, meeting (4)
reunirse con to meet with, have a meeting with (4)
revista (f) magazine (5)
rico/-a rich, wealthy (4)
rimel (m) mascara (11)
rincón (m) corner (interior) (3)
riñones (m pl) kidneys (9)
río (m) river
riqueza (f) wealth (4)
rodilla (f) knee (8)
rogar (ue) to beg, plead (10)
rojo/-a red (1)
romper to break
ropa (f) clothing
ropero (m) wardrobe
rosado/-a pink (1)
rubio/-a blond (1)
rubor (m) rouge (11)
rueda (f) wheel
ruido (m) noise (3)
ruidoso/-a noisy (3)

S

sábado (m) Saturday
saber* to know (a fact) (2)
sabor (m) flavor
sacar: ~ fotos to take pictures (4); ~ una muestra de sangre to take a blood sample (9)
saco (m) coat, sports jacket (4)
sal (f) salt (5)

sala (f) living room (7); **~ de emergencia** emergency room (9); **~ de espera** waiting room (9); **~ de reconocimiento** examining room
salario (m) hourly wage (12)
salida (f) exit (1)
salir* to leave (1); to depart (2); **~ bien** to do well; to turn out well (11); **~ mal** to do poorly; to turn out badly (11)
saltar to jump; **~ la cuerda** to jump rope
salud (f) health (9)
saludar to greet (10)
saludo (m) greeting (1); greeting (in a letter) (10)
salvadoreño/-a Salvadoran (1)
salvar to save (11)
sandía (f) watermelon
sangre (f) blood
sarampión (m) measles (9)
sastre (m) tailor (5)
sea lo (el, la) que sea whatever it might be (10)
secar to dry (9)
sección (f) **de (no) fumar** (no) smoking section (6)
seda (f) silk
seguir (i, i)* to follow, continue (3)
según according to
segundo/-a second (2)
seguro/-a certain (11)
seis six (1)
seiscientos/-as six hundred (1)
selva (f) jungle
sello (m) stamp (4)
semáforo (m) traffic light (5)
semana (f) week (2); **fin** (m) **de ~** weekend (2); **~ que viene** next week
semestre (m) semester (2)
sentarse (ie) to sit down (3)
sentido (m) sense (physical) (6)
sentir (ie, i)* to be sorry, regret (3); **Lo siento mucho.** I'm very sorry. (3)
sentirse (ie, i) to feel (3)
señal (f) traffic sign (5)
señor (m) man (1); gentleman; sir
señora (f) woman (1); lady (married or widowed); wife; ma'am
señorita (f) young, unmarried woman (1); miss
septiembre September (1)
séptimo/-a seventh (7)
ser* to be (1); **~ (de)** to be from
serio/-a serious (3); **en serio** seriously (11)
servicio (m) religious service (3)
servicios (m pl) rest rooms
servilleta (f) napkin (7)
servir (i, i) to serve

sesenta sixty (1)
sesión (f) session
seta (f) mushroom
setecientos/-a seven hundred (1)
setenta seventy (1)
sexto/-a sixth (7)
si if
SIDA (m) AIDS (9)
siempre always (3)
siesta (f) nap; **dormir la ~** to take a nap (5)
siete seven (1)
siglo (m) century (6)
siguiente following, next (7)
silencio (m) silence (3)
silla (f) chair (3); **~ de ruedas** wheelchair (9)
sillón (m) easy chair (3)
simpático/-a nice (1)
sin embargo nevertheless (8)
sin que without (11)
sinagoga (f) synagogue (3)
síntoma (m) symptom (9)
situado/-a situated (6)
sobre (m) envelope (4)
sobresaliente outstanding (11)
sobrevivir to survive (11)
sobrina (f) niece (1)
sobrino (m) nephew (1)
socio (m/f) associate
sociología (f) sociology
¡socorro! help! (6)
sofá (m) sofa (7)
soga (f) rope (8)
sol (m) sun
solamente only
soler (ue) to be accustomed to, have the habit of
solicitud (f) application
solo/-a alone (4)
sombras (f pl) eyeshadow (11)
sonar (ue) to ring (3)
sonreír (i, i) to smile
soñar (ue) to dream (2)
sopa (f) soup (5)
sororidad (f) sisterhood
sorprender to surprise (11)
sorpresa (f) surprise
soso/-a bland, flavorless (5)
sótano (m) basement (7)
su servidor(a) your servant (10)
subir to go up (6)
sucursal (f) branch office (5)
sudar to sweat, perspire
sueldo (m) salary (12)
suelo (m) floor (7)
sueño (m) dream (3)
suerte (f) luck; **¡Buena ~!** Good luck! (4)

suéter (m) sweater (4)
sugerencia (f) suggestion
sugerir (ie, i) to suggest; to recommend (11)
superar to overcome (12)
sur (m) south (1)
sureste (m) southeast (1)
suroeste (m) southwest (1)
surtido (m) assortment, selection (5)
suspender to fail
suspendido suspended; failing (11)
sustantivo (m) noun
susto (m) sudden fright (8)
suyo/-a muy atentamente attentively yours (10)

T

tacaño/-a stingy (3)
tacto (m) sense of touch
talla (f) size (of clothing) (4)
taller (m) repair shop
tamaño (m) size
también also (1)
tampoco neither (4)
tapa (f) lid (8)
tapacubos (m) hubcap (8)
tapar to cover (up), to put the lid/cork on (8)
tardar to delay; **a más ~** at the very latest
tarde (f) afternoon (1); late
tarea (f) homework (2)
taza (f) cup (2)
té (f) tea (2)
teatro (m) theater
tecnología (f) technology (8)
techo (m) roof (7)
teléfono (m) telephone (3); **~ celular** cellular telephone (8)
telenovela (f) soap opera
televisor (m) television set (3)
tema (m) theme (11)
temer(se) to fear (11)
temperatura (f) temperature (6)
temprano early (3)
tendón (m) tendon (9)
tenedor (m) fork (7)
tener* to have (1); **~ calor** to be (feel) hot (3); **~ el gusto de** to have the pleasure of (10); **~ en cuenta** to take into account (10); **~ en mente** to take into account, bear in mind (12); **~ envidia** to be envious (3); **~ éxito** to succeed (11); **~ fama** to be famous, well-known (for/as) (3); **~ frío** to be (feel) cold (3); **~ ganas de** to feel like (doing something) (2); **~ hambre** to be hungry (3); **~ interés**

(en) to be interested in (3); **~ la culpa** to be at fault (11); **~ mala fama** to have a bad reputation (7); **~ miedo (de)** to be afraid (of) (3); **~ paciencia** to be patient (3); **~ palancas** to have connections (12); **~ presente** to take into account, bear in mind (12); **~ prisa** to be in a hurry (3); **~ que** to have to (do something) (1); **~ que ver con** to have to do with (9); **~ razón** to be right (3); **~ sed** to be thirsty (3); **~ sueño** to be sleepy (3); **~ un enchufe** to have connections (12)
tenis (m) tennis (2)
terapia (f) therapy (11)
tercero/-a third (2)
terminar to end (3)
término medio medium (cooked) (5)
terreno (m) property
terrestre earthly
tía (f) aunt (1); **~ abuela** (f) great-aunt
tiempo (m) weather (3); **a ~** on time (3); **~ libre** free time (2); **~ parcial** part-time (12)
tienda (f) store (5)
tierra (f) land
tímido/-a shy (3)
tina (f) bathtub (6)
tinieblas (f pl) complete darkness (8)
tinta (f) ink (5)
tinte (m) dye
tintorería (f) dry cleaners (5)
tío (m) uncle (1); **tíos** (m pl) aunt and uncle (1); **~ abuelo** (m) great-uncle
tirar to throw
toalla (f) towel (6)
tocador (m) dresser (3)
tocar* to touch; **~ el timbre** to ring the doorbell
todo everything, all (4); **~ el mundo** (m) everyone; **~ lo que** everything that; **todos** everything, everyone (4)
tomar to take (2); to drink (2); **~ en serio** to take seriously (12); **~ una decisión** to make a decision (11); **~ una muestra de sangre** to take a blood sample (9); **tomar(le) el pelo (a uno)** to tease, "pull someone's leg" (9)
torcer (ue) to twist (9)
torta (f) cake (5)
torre (f) tower (6)
tos (f) cough (9)
toser to cough (9)
trabajar to work (1)
trabajo (m) work, job (2)
traducir to translate
traer* to bring (2)
tragar to swallow

traje (m) suit (4); **~ de baño** bathing suit (4)
trámite (m) transaction
tranquilo/-a quiet (place); peaceful (3)
¡tranquilo! calm down! (10)
transportadora (f) **de horquilla** fork lift
traspatio (m) back yard
trastos (m pl) furnishings (7)
tratar to treat (a person well, badly) (8)
tratarse de to have to do with (9)
travieso/-a mischievous (8)
trece thirteen (1)
treinta thirty (1)
tres three (1)
trescientos/-as three hundred (1)
tribunal (m) court of law (11)
tripas (f pl) guts (9)
triste sad (11)
tristeza (f) sadness (11)
tropezar to trip (9)
trucha (f) trout (5)
tú you (familiar sing) (1)
tumor (m) **cerebral** brain tumor (9)

U

ubicado/-a situated; located (6)
últimamente lately, recently (11)
ultramar (m) overseas (6)
un(a) a(n), one (P)
una vez once (4)
único/-a only (5)
universidad (f) university (1)
uno/-a one (1)
unos/-as some (P)
uruguayo/-a Uruguayan (1)
usted you (formal, sing) (1)
ustedes you (formal/familiar, pl) (1)
útil useful
utilidad (f) usefulness
uva (f) grape

V

vaca (f) cow
vacío/-a empty (6)
vacuna (f) vaccination
valer to be worth
valiente brave (11)
valor (m) value (7)
Vámonos. Let's leave. / Let's get going. (1); **¡Vamos ya!** Let's go! (6)
varicela (f) chicken pox (9)
vaso (m) glass (2); water glass (tumbler) (7)
vecindad (f) neighborhood (5)
vecindario (m) neighborhood (5)
vecino/-a (m/f) neighbor (5)
veinte twenty (1)

venda (f) bandage (9)
vender to sell
venezolano/-a Venezuelan (1)
venir (ie)* to come (1); **~ a pie** to come on foot (7)
ventaja (f) advantage
ventana (f) window (1)
ventanilla (f) side (door) window (8)
ver to see (1); **A ver…** Let's see . . .
verano (m) summer (4)
verdad (f) truth (3); **¿(No es) verdad?** Isn't that so? Right? (3)
verdadero/-a true
verde green (1)
vergüenza (f) embarrassment (8)
vespertina (f) late afternoon show
vestido (m) dress (4)
vestirse (i, i) to get dressed (3)
vez (f) time, occasion; **a veces** sometimes (4); **de ~ en cuando** occasionally (6)
viajar to travel (4)
viaje (m) trip (4); **hacer un ~** to take a trip (4)
viajero/-a (m/f) traveler (4); **cheque de ~** traveler's check (6)
vibración (f) vibration
vida (f) **estudiantil** student life (1)
viejo/-a old, elderly
viento (m) wind
viernes (m) Friday
vinagre (m) vinegar (5)
vino (m) **blanco** white wine (2)
vino (m) **tinto** red wine (2)
vino (m) wine (2)
visa (f) visa (4)
visado (m) visa (4)
vista (f) sight; **~ al mar** ocean view
vivir to live (1)
volante (m) steering wheel (8)
volver (ue) to return, go back (2); **~ en sí** to regain consciousness (9)
vomitar to vomit (9)
vosotros/-as you (familiar, pl) (1)
vuelo (m) flight; **~ directo** direct flight (4); **~ sin escalas** nonstop flight (4)

Y

yeso (m) plaster (cast) (8)
yo I (1)
yogur (m) yogurt (5)

Z

zanahoria (f) carrot (5)
zapatería (f) shoe store (5)
zapato (m) shoe
zozobra (f) uneasiness; anxiety

ENGLISH-SPANISH

A

a(n), one un(a)
able: poder (2)
about acerca de (11)
absent-minded distraído/-a
accelerator acelerador (m) (8)
acceptable aprobado, regular (11)
accompanied acompañado/-a (4)
accompany acompañar (4)
according to según
accountant contador(a) (m/f) (5)
accounting contabilidad (f) (2)
acknowledge a favor agradecer (10)
acquaintance conocido/-a
add agregar (8); ~ to aumentar (11)
addition: in ~ to además de
address dirección (f) (1)
adore adorar (10)
advance: in ~ con anticipación (12)
advantage ventaja (f); to take ~ of aprovechar (8)
advantageous provechoso/-a (12)
advice consejo (m) (7)
advisable aconsejable (4)
advise aconsejar (4)
affection cariño (m) (7)
affectionate cariñoso/-a (7)
affectionately cariñosamente (10)
affirm afirmar (9)
afraid miedoso/-a (11); to be ~ of tener miedo (de) (3)
Africa África (f) (1)
after después de (2)
afternoon tarde (f) (1); become late afternoon atardecer (8); Good afternoon. Buenas tardes. (1); late ~ (dusk) atardecer (m) (3)
age edad (f) (1)
agent agente (m/f) (6)
agitate agitar (8)
agitated agitado/-a (8)
AIDS SIDA (m) (9)
air aire (m); by ~ por avión (6)
airplane avión (m) (4)
alarm clock despertador (3); to set the ~ poner el despertador
all todo (4), All Saints' Day Día de Todos los Santos
allergy alergia (f) (9)
allow dejar (8), permitir
almost casi (8); ~ always casi siempre (6); ~ never casi nunca (6)

alone solo/-a (4)
also también (1)
always siempre (3)
American americano/-a (1)
amusing divertido/-a (4)
ancestor antepasado/-a
anesthesia anestesia (f) (9)
angry enojado/-a; get ~ enojarse (8)
anguish angustia (f) (11)
announcer locutor(a) (m/f)
answer contestar; answering machine contestador (m) automático
antibiotic antibiótico (m) (9)
antiseptic antiséptico (m) (9)
anxiety zozobra (f) (8)
anxious nervioso/-a
apartment apartamento (m) (1)
appetizer entrada (f) (5)
apple manzana (f) (8); ~ juice jugo (m) de manzana (2)
application solicitud (f)
apply makeup maquillarse
appreciate agradecer
appreciation agradecimiento (m) (9)
approximately aproximadamente
April abril (1)
ardent ardiente (12)
Argentinian argentino/-a (1)
argue discutir (4)
arm brazo (m) (8)
arrange arreglar (3)
arrangement arreglo (m) (5); make arrangements hacer los arreglos (6)
arrive llegar (1)
art arte (f)
artifact artifacto (m) (6)
ask: ~ for pedir (i, i) (3); ~ a question preguntar
asparagus espárragos (m pl) (5)
aspirin aspirina (f) (9)
associate socio/-a (m/f)
assortment surtido (m) (5)
At your service. A sus órdenes. (6)
at: at fault culpable (11); at home en casa (1); at least por lo menos (6); at sea level al nivel del mar (6); at the beginning of a comienzos de (6); at the end of a fines de (6); at the very latest a más tardar
attend asistir a (10)
attentively atentamente (10); attentively yours De usted muy atentamente (10), Suyo/-a muy atentamente (10)
attic desván (m) (7)
attorney abogado/-a (11)

attract atraer (6)
August agosto (1)
aunt tía (f) (1)
autumn otoño (m) (4)
average (height) mediano/-a (3)
average promedio (m) (6)
avocado aguacate (m) (5)
avoid evitar (10)
awful: How ~! ¡Qué barbaridad!; ¡Qué horror! (8)

B

back espalda (f) (8); back yard traspatio (m); be ~ estar de vuelta (3); in ~ of detrás de (3)
backpack mochila (f) (4)
bad malo/-a (P)
bag bolsa (f) (4), saco (m)
baked al horno (5)
bakery panadería (f) (5)
balance equilibrio (m) (9)
balcony balcón (m) (7)
ball pelota (f); ~ (large, e.g., basketball) balon (m) (8)
bandage venda (f) (9); small ~ (Band-aid) curita (f) (9)
bank banco (m)
bankruptcy bancarrota (f)
barefoot descalzo/-a (7)
bargain regatear (7)
barrier barrera (f) (9)
base (makeup) base (f) (11)
baseball béisbol (m) (2); ~ bat bate (m) (8)
basement sótano (m) (7)
basket (for basketball) canasta (f) (8); cesto (m) (8)
basketball baloncesto (m) (2)
bat bate (m) (8)
bathe bañarse (3)
bathing/health resort balneario (m) (6)
bathtub bañera (f) (6); tina (f) (6)
Be careful! ¡Cuidado! (10)
be estar; ser (1); ~ from ser de (1)
beach playa (f) (4)
beans frijoles (m pl); string ~ habichuelas (f pl) (5), judías (f pl) (5)
beard barba (f) (3); barbilla (f) (11)
beautiful precioso/-a (4)
because porque
become llegar a ser (6); ponerse (10); hacerse (11)
bed cama (f) (3)
bedroom dormitorio (m) (1); alcoba (f) (6)

beef carne (f) de res (5)
beer cerveza (f) (2)
before antes de (2); antes (de) que (11)
beg rogar (ue) (10)
begin comenzar (ie) (2); empezar (ie) (3); principiar (7); **at the beginning of** a comienzos de (6); **beginning with** a partir de (6)
behalf: on~ of de parte de (10)
behave well/badly portarse bien/mal (8)
behavior comportamiento (m) (11)
behind detrás de (3)
beige beige (1)
belong to pertenecer
beloved queridísimo/-a (10)
belt cinturón (m) (4); **seat ~** cinturón de seguridad (4)
beneficial provechoso/-a (12)
benign benigno/-a (9)
besides además (8)
better mejor
big grande (1)
bilingual bilingüe (2)
bill: ~ of sale factura (f) (4); **(restaurant) ~** cuenta (f) (4)
biology biología (f) (2)
birthday cumpleaños (m)
black negro/-a (1)
blackout apagón (m) (8)
blame culpa (f) (11); culpar (11); **cast ~ upon** echar la culpa (11)
bland soso/-a (5)
block cuadra (f) (6)
blond rubio/-a (1)
blood sangre (f); **~ pressure** presión (f) sanguínea (9)
blouse blusa (f) (4)
blue azul (1)
boarding house pensión (f)
body cuerpo (m) (8)
boldface (type) negrilla (f)
Bolivian boliviano/-a (1)
book libro (m)
bookcase estante (m) de libros (3)
bookstore librería (f) (5)
boot bota (f) (4)
boring; bored aburrido/-a (1)
born: be ~ nacer (8)
borrow pedir prestado/-a (7)
boss jefe/-a (m/f)
bother molestar (4); molestia (f) (4); **What a ~ / pain!** ¡Qué lata! (8)
bouquet (of flowers) ramo (m) de flores (5)
box caja (f)
boy chico (1)
brain cerebro (m) (9); **~ tumor** tumor (m) cerebral (9)
brake frenar; **brakes** frenos (m pl) (8)

branch office sucursal (f) (5)
brand marca (f) (5)
brave valiente (11)
Brazilian brasileño/-a (1)
bread pan (m) (5); **~ store** panadería (f) (5); **sweet ~** pan dulce (5)
break romper; **~ apart** partir (8)
breakfast desayuno (m) (2); **have ~** desayunar (3)
breathe respirar
breeze brisa (f) (6)
bride novia (f) (11)
bring traer (2)
broccoli brócoli (m) (5)
brother hermano (m) (1); **brother-in-law** cuñado (m)
brotherhood fraternidad (f)
brown café (1); **brown (for hair)** castaño (1)
brush one's teeth lavarse los dientes (3)
buffet aparador (m) (7)
build construir
building edificio (1)
but pero (1)
butcher shop carnicería (f) (5)
butter mantequilla (f) (5)
by: ~ air por avión (6); **~ land** por tierra (6); **~ no means** de ninguna manera (4)

C

cafeteria cafetería (f) (2)
cake torta (f) (5)
calculator calculadora (f) (8)
calculus cálculo (m)
call llamar (3)
calm calmar (9); **Calm down!** ¡Cálmate! (10)
camera cámara (f) (4)
camp acampar (7)
cancel cancelar
candy shop dulcería (f) (5)
cap gorra (f) (4)
capital capital (f) (1)
car auto (m) (4); automóvil (m) (8); carro (m); coche (m)
caramel custard flan (m) (5)
career carrera (f) (11)
careful: Be careful! ¡Cuidado!
carpenter carpintero/-a (m/f) (12)
carrot zanahoria (f) (5)
case: in ~ en caso de que (11)
cash (in bill form) efectivo (m) (6)
cassette casete (m) (8)
cast (for broken bones) yeso (m) (8); **in a ~** enyesado/-a (8)
castle castillo (m) (6)

cathedral catedral (f) (6)
cauliflower coliflor (f) (8)
ceiling; interior roof cielo raso (m) (7)
celebrate celebrar (4)
celery apio (m) (8)
center centro (m) (1)
century siglo (m) (6)
certain: be ~ estar seguro/-a (11)
chair silla (f) (3); **easy ~** sillón (3)
change cambiar; **(from a purchase)** cambio (m) (8)
characteristic rasgo (m) (3)
chat charlar (1)
cheap barato/-a
cheat hacer trampa (11)
check (luggage) facturar (4)
check cheque (m); **bad ~ (one that bounces)** cheque (m) sin fondos (12); **traveler's ~** cheque de viajeros
checkers (game) damas (f pl)
cheek mejilla (f) (11)
cheese queso (m) (5)
chemistry química (f) (2)
chemotherapy quimoterapia (f)
chest pecho (m) (8)
chicken pollo (m) (5)
chicken pox varicela (f) (9)
child muchacho/-a (m/f) (1)
Chilean chileno/-a (1)
chills escalofríos (m pl) (9)
chin mentón (m) (11)
Chinese chino/-a
chore quehacer (m) (7)
Christmas Navidad (f) (4); **~ Eve** Nochebuena (f) (4); **~ tree** árbol (m) de Navidad (4)
church iglesia (f) (3)
circles under the eyes ojeras (f pl) (11)
citizen ciudadano/-a (m/f)
city ciudad (f) (1)
claim reclamo (m)
clam almeja (f) (5)
class clase (f)
classical clásico/-a
clean limpiar (3)
clerk empleado/-a (m/f) (6)
clock reloj (m); **alarm ~** despertador (m) (3)
close (near) cerca de (3); **(intimate)** íntimo/-a (10)
close (shut) cerrar (ie) (1)
closet clóset (m) (3)
clothing ropa (f); **article of ~** prenda (f) de vestir
clown payaso (m)
club club (m); **country ~** club campestre (7); **fishing ~** club de pesca (7); **social ~** club social (7)
coach entrenador(a) (m/f)

Glossary

coat abrigo (m) (4); saco (m) (4)
cocktail cóctel (m)
coconut coco (m) (8)
coffee café (m) (2)
coin moneda (f) (6)
cold resfriado (m) (9); **be ~** tener frío (3); **coldness** frío (m)
collarbone clavícula (f) (8)
colleague colega (m/f)
Colombian colombiano/-a (1)
comb one's hair peinarse (3)
come venir (1); **Come in.** Pasa./Adelante./Siga./Sigue. (7); **~ on foot** venir a pie (7)
comfortable cómodo/-a (10); **be ~** estar a gusto (10)
commitment compromiso (m) (10); **to commit oneself** comprometerse
communion comunión (f); **first ~** primera comunión (8)
compete competir (i, i) (8)
complainer quejón/-ona
complaint queja (f)
compliment cumplido (m) (10); piropo (m) (11)
computer ordenador (m); computadora (f) (8)
computer science informática (f) (2)
concede conceder (11)
concern preocupación (f) (11)
concerning en cuanto a (10); relacionado/-a con (9)
concert concierto (m)
condiment condimento (m) (5)
confirm comprobar (ue) (11)
conformist conformista (m/f) (8)
connections: have ~ tener palancas, tener un enchufe (12)
construct construir (6)
consulate consulado (m) (4)
contact ponerse en contacto (con) (9)
continue seguir (i, i) (3); continuar(a)
conversation conversación (f) (1)
converse conversar (1)
convert convertir (ie, i) (7)
cook cocinar (2); cocinero/-a (m/f)
cookie galleta (f)
coolness fresco (m)
copper cobre (m) (6)
copy copiar (11)
cord cordón (m) (8)
cordially cordialmente (10)
cork corcho (m) (8)
corner: exterior ~ esquina (f) (5); **interior ~** rincón (m) (3)
correct corregir (i, i)
correspondence correspondencia (f) (1)
corridor pasillo (m) (1)
Costa Rican costarricense (1)

costly costoso/-a; caro/-a (4)
cough tos (f) (9); toser (9)
counselor consejero/-a (m/f) (7)
country país (m) (1); **~ club** club (m) campestre (7); **foreign ~** extranjero (m)
country-like campestre (7)
countryside campo (m)
couple: married ~ casados (m pl) (12), matrimonio (m) (12); **(married or unmarried)** pareja (f) (12)
coupon cupón (m) (9)
course curso (m) (2)
court: ~ of law juzgado (m) (11); tribunal (m) (11); **(playing field)** cancha (f) (8); **courtyard** patio (m) (5)
courteous cortés (1)
courtship noviazgo (m) (12)
cousin primo/-a (m/f)(1)
cover (up) tapar (8)
cover cubrir (6); **~ a distance** recorrer (8)
covered (with) cubierto/-a (de) (6)
cow vaca (f)
cowardly cobarde (11)
crash (into) chocar (con) (9)
cream crema (f) (2)
create crear (7)
cross-country skiing esquí (m) nórdico (7)
crown corona (f) (6)
crutches muletas (f pl) (9)
cucumber pepino (m)
culinary culinario/-a
cup taza (f) (2)
curtain cortina (f) (7)
custom costumbre (f) (7)
cute lindo/-a (8)
cycling ciclismo (m) (4)

D

dairy lácteo/-a; lechería (f) (5)
damage perjudicar (12)
dance bailar (1); baile (m) (2)
dangerous peligroso/-a
dark oscuro/-a (1); **get ~** anochecer (8)
darkness oscuridad (f) (8); **complete ~** tinieblas (f pl) (8)
date: (calendar) fecha (f) (1); **(appointment)** cita (f)
dawn madrugada (f) (3); alba (m) (8); amanecer (8)
day día (m) (1); **~ after tomorrow** pasado mañana; **~ before yesterday** anteayer; **every ~** todos los días; **working ~** jornada (f) (12)
Dear... Querido/-a... (10); **Dear Sir/Madam...** Muy señor/-a mío/-a... (10)
deceitful engañoso/-a (11)

deceive engañar (11); hacer trampa (11)
December diciembre (1)
decision decisión (f); **make a ~** tomar la decisión (11)
declare declarar
defame disfamar (11)
defeat derrota (f) (6)
defendant acusado/-a (m/f) (11)
degree grado (m)
delay tardar, demorar
delicious delicioso/-a
depend upon contar (ue) con (7)
derisive burlón/-ona (11)
describe describir
deserve merecer (9)
design diseñar (6); diseño (m) (5)
designed diseñado/-a (6)
desk escritorio (m) (3)
despair angustia (f) (11)
desperate desesperado/-a (11)
dessert postre (m) (5)
detain detener (11)
develop desarollar (12)
diagnosis diagnóstico (m) (9)
dial marcar (el numero) (3)
die morir (ue, u)
difficult difícil (2)
dining room comedor (m) (2)
dinner cena (f) (2); **eat ~** cenar
disagreeable desagradable
discourage desanimar
discover descubrir
discuss discutir (4)
dishonor deshonrar (11)
disinfect desinfectar (9)
disloyal desleal (12)
display exposición (f) (6)
dissatisfied (displeased) descontento/-a (3)
dissuade disuadir (11)
distilled destilado/-a; **~ water** agua (f) destilada (9)
distinguished distinguido/-a (10)
distribute repartir (8)
disturbed agitado/-a (8)
ditch cuneta (f)
dive clavado (m) (9)
dizzy mareado/-a (9)
do hacer (2); **~ badly** salir mal (11); **~ well** salir bien (11)
doctor médico/-a (m/f) (5)
document documento (m) (4)
door puerta (f) (1)
dormitory: college ~ residencia (f) (1)
doubt duda (f); **There is no ~.** No cabe duda. (10)
downhill skiing esquí (m) alpino (7)
draft redactar
dream soñar (ue) (2); sueño (m) (3)

dress vestido (m) (4)
dresser tocador (m) (3)
dressmaker modista (f) (5)
drink beber (2); **(beverage)** bebida (f); **soft ~** refresco (m) (2)
drinkable potable (6)
drive conducir (2)
dry secar (9); **~ clean** lavar (limpiar) en seco (5); **~ cleaners** tintorería (f) (5)
due to debido a (10)
during mientras (8)
dye tinte (m)

E

early temprano (3); **get up ~** madrugar (3)
ears orejas (f pl) (8)
earthly terrestre
east este (m) (1)
easy fácil (2); **~chair** sillón (m) (3)
eat comer (2)
economics economía (f) (2)
Ecuadorian ecuatoriano/-a (1)
efficient eficaz (7)
effort esfuerzo (m) (12)
egg huevo (m) (5)
Egypt Egipto
Egyptian egipcio/-a
eight ocho (1)
eighth octavo/-a (7)
eight hundred ochocientos/-as (1)
eighty ochenta (1)
either ... or o... o (4)
eleven once (1)
embarrassing: How ~! ¡Qué vergüenza! (8)
embassy embajada (f) (4)
embrace abazar (8)
emergency emergencia (f)
empire imperio (m) (6)
empty vacío/-a (6)
encounter encontrarse (ue) (con)
end terminar (3); **at the ~ of** a fines de (6)
energy energía (f) (3)
engine motor (m) (8)
engineer ingeniero/-a (m/f); **engineering** ingeniería (f)
England Inglaterra (1)
English inglés/-esa (m/f) (1)
enjoy disfrutar de (7); gozar de (12); **~ oneself** divertirse (ie, i)
enter entrar (1)
entrance entrada (f) (1)
envelope sobre (m) (4)
enviable envidiable (10)
envious envidioso/-a; **to be ~** tener envidia (3)
envy: I'm green with ~! ¡Qué envidia! (4)

epoch época (f) (6)
error error (m); **in ~** equivocado/-a (3)
establish establecer (7); fundar (6)
esteem estimar (12); **esteemed ...** estimado/-a... (10)
Europe Europa (f) (12)
every todo/-a; **~ day** todos los días; **everyone** todo el mundo; **everything** todo (4)
exchange cambiar (6); **~ money** cambiar dinero (6); **~ house** casa (f) de cambio (7); **~ rate** cambio (m) (7); **in ~** a cambio de (11)
exciting emocionante
excuse perdonar (7); **Excuse me. (asking for permission)** Con permiso. (1)
exercise ejercicio (m) (P)
exhausted agotado/-a (6); medio muerto/-a (11)
exhibition exposición (f) (6)
exit salida (f) (1)
expectation anticipación (f) (12)
expensive caro/-a (4); costoso/-a
eyebrows cejas (f pl) (11)
eyelashes pestañas (f pl) (11)
eyelids párpados (m pl) (11)
eyeliner delineador (m) (11)
eyes ojos (m pl) (8)
eyeshadow sombras (f pl) (11)

F

fail fracasar (11)
faint desmayarse (9)
fair justo/-a (12)
fall: (season) otoño (m) (4); caer; **~ asleep** dormirse (ue, u); **~ down** caerse (8); **~ in love (with)** enamorarse (de) (11); **be falling apart / a wreck** estar hecho/-a pedazos (9)
family familia (f) (1)
famous / well-known; be ~ tener fama (3)
far lejos de (3)
farewell despedida (f) (1)
farmer granjero/-a (m/f) (12)
fascinating fascinante
fat gordo/-a (3)
father padre (m) (1)
fault culpa (f) (11); **at ~** culpable (11); **be at ~** tener la culpa (11)
favor: to acknowledge a ~ agradecer (10)
favorite favorito/-a
fear temer(se) (11); miedo (m)
fearful miedoso/-a (11)
February febrero (1)
feed alimentar (11)
feel sentirse (ie, i) (3); **~ like (doing something)** tener ganas de (2)

fence barrera (f) (9)
fever fiebre (f) (9)
fifteen quince (1)
fifth quinto/-a (2)
fifty cincuenta (1)
fight luchar (8); pelear (8)
file archivo (m)
filled colmado/-a (7)
finances finanzas (f pl) (12)
find encontrar (ue) (2)
finger dedo (m) (8)
fire fuego (m) (7)
firefighter bombero/-a (m/f) (12)
fireplace chimenea (f) (7)
firmness fortaleza (f) (9)
first primero/-a (2); **~ aid** primeros auxilios (m pl) (9)
fish pescado (m) (5); **~ (live)** pez (m) (7); **~ store** pescadería (f) (5)
fish pescar (7)
fishing club club (m) de pesca (7)
fit caber
five cinco (1)
five hundred quinientos/-as (1)
fix reparar
flame fogata (f) (7); llama (f)
flatter echar flores (11)
flavor sabor (m); **flavorless** soso/-a (5)
fleeting fugaz (9)
flight vuelo (m); **~ attendant** azafata (f) (4); **direct ~** vuelo directo (4); **non-stop ~** vuelo sin escalas (4)
flood inundación (f)
floor: (level, story) piso (m) (6); **(surface)** piso (m) (3); suelo (m) (7)
flour harina (f)
flower flor (f) (4); **~ shop** florería (f) (5)
flu gripe (f) (9)
focus enfocarse; **focused** enfocado/-a
follow seguir (i, i) (3); **following,** siguiente (7)
fondness cariño (m) (7)
food comida (f) (1); **junk ~** comida (f) rápida
foot pie (m) (8); **on ~** a pie (7); **"put your ~ in your mouth"** meter la pata (7)
football fútbol (m) americano (2)
for para (1); **~ the purpose of** con el motivo de (10)
forehead frente (f) (11)
foreign country extranjero (m) (4); **foreigner** extranjero/-a (m/f) (4)
forget olvidarse de
forgive perdonar (7)
fork tenedor (m) (7); **~ lift** transportadora (f) de horquilla
fort fuerte (m)

Glossary

fortunately afortunadamente (4)
forty cuarenta (1)
four cuatro (1)
four hundred cuatrocientos/-as (1)
fourteen catorce (1)
fourth cuarto/-a (2)
France Francia (1)
free: (no cost) gratis (6); **(unoccupied)** libre (6); **~ time** tiempo (m) libre (2)
freedom libertad (f) (6)
French francés/-esa (1)
frequently con frecuencia (6) ; frecuentemente
Friday viernes (m)
friend amigo/-a (m/f) (1)
friendly amable (1)
friendship amistad (f) (1)
fright, sudden susto (m) (8)
frighten asustar (8); **frightening** espantoso/-a (11)
front: in ~ of delante de (3); **~ desk (hotel)** recepción (f) (6); **~ yard** patio (m) delantero
full lleno/-a (6)
fun divertido/-a (4); **in ~** en broma (11); **make ~ of** burlarse de (11)
function (machines) funcionar (3)
funny cómico/-a (3)
furnishings trastos (m pl) (7)
furniture muebles (m pl) (7); **~ store** mueblería (f) (5)

G

game juego (m)
garbage basura (f)
garden jardín (m) (5); **~ shop** jardinería (f) (5)
garlic ajo (m) (5)
gasp for breath jadear (9)
generous generoso/-a (3)
gentleman caballero (m)
German alemán/-ana (1)
Germany Alemania (1)
gesture gesto (m)
get (obtain) conseguir (i, i) (3); **~ along (with)** llevarse (con) (8); **~ angry** enojarse (8); **~ better (health)** mejorarse (9); **~ dressed** ponerse la ropa, vestirse (i, i) (3); **~ furious** ponerse furioso/-a (8); **~ hurt** hacerse daño (8); lastimarse (9); **~ in touch/contact (with)** ponerse en contacto (con) (9); **~ lost** extraviarse (4), perderse; **~ smaller** empequenecer (12); **~ undressed** desvestirse (i, i) (3), quitarse la ropa; **~ up early** madrugar (3); **~ up**

levantarse (3); **~ used to** acostumbrarse a (7)
Ghanian ghaneano/-a (1)
gift regalo (m) (4)
girl chica (f) (1)
give dar (2); **~ a gift** regalar (4); **~ the appearance of** dar la impresión de (11)
glad alegre (2)
glass vaso (m) (2)
glove guante (m) (4)
go ir (1); **~ away** irse (1); **~ down** bajar (6); **~ on foot** ir a pie (7); **~ shopping** ir de compras (5); **~ straight ahead** ir todo derecho (6); **~ to bed** acostarse (3); **~ to sleep** dormirse (3); **~ to the movies** ir al cine (1); **~ up** subir (6); **~ with** acompañar (4)
goal meta (f)
gold oro (m) (4)
good bueno/-a (P); **Good afternoon.** Buenas tardes. (1); **Good bye.** Adiós. (1); **Good evening / Good night.** Buenas noches. (1); **Good luck!** ¡Buena suerte! (4); **Good morning.** Buenos días.
goodbye (closing of a letter) despedida (f) (10)
gossip chisme (m) (11); chismear (11)
gossipy (adj); gossipy person (n) chismoso/-a (11)
grades (academic) notas (calificaciones) (f) escolares (11)
graduate graduarse
gram gramo (m)
grandchild nieto/-a
grandfather abuelo (m) (1); **grandmother** abuela (f) (1)
grape uva (f)
gratitude agradecimiento (m) (9)
gray gris (f)
greed avaricia (f)
green verde (1)
greet saludar (10); **greeting** saludo (m) (1)
grilled a la parrilla (5)
grillwork reja (f) (5)
groom novio (m) (11)
group (musical) conjunto (m) (3)
grow crecer (11); **~ up** crecer (12)
Guaraní guaraní (m)
Guatemalan guatemalteco/-a (1)
guest: (in a home) invitado/-a (m/f) (4); **(in a hotel)** huésped(a) (m/f) (4)
guide guía (m/f) (7); **guidebook** guía (f) (7)
guideline pauta (f)
guts tripas (f pl) (9)
gym gimnasio (m)

H

habit costumbre (f) (7)
hair pelo (m) (1)
half medio/-a; mitad (f) (11); **~ time** medio tiempo (12)
hallway pasillo (m) (1)
ham jamón (m) (5)
hand mano (f) (8); **~ over, ~ in** entregar
handicapped impedido/-a, inválido/-a (10)
handsome guapo/-a (3)
hang (up) colgar (ue) (2)
Hanukkah Jánuca (f) (4)
happy contento/-a (2), feliz; **Happy Easter** Felices pascuas (4); **Happy New Year** Feliz Año Nuevo (4)
hate odiar (2); **hatred** odio (m) (7)
have tener (1); **~ a bad reputation** tener mala fama (7); **~ a good time** divertirse (ie, i) (3); **~ breakfast** desayunar (3); **~ lunch** almorzar (ue) (2); **~ the evening meal** cenar (3); **~ the pleasure of** tener el gusto de (10); **~ to do with** tener que ver con (9), tratarse de (9)
he él (1)
head cabeza (f) (8)
healer curandero/-a (m/f)
heap up colmar (7)
hear oír (2); **hearing** oído (m) (6)
heart corazón (m) (9)
heat calor (m)
heavy pesado/-a
height estatura (f) (9); **~ of the ridiculous** colmo (m) de lo ridículo (9)
hello aló; ¡bueno!; hola; buenos días (1)
help ayudar (2); **Help!** ¡Socorro! (6)
hey! ¡oye! (2)
hi hola (1)
high school liceo (m); escuela (f) secundaria
highway carretera (f)
hinder impedir (i, i) (10); estorbar (12)
hip cadera (f) (8)
Hispanic hispano/-a (1)
history historia (f) (2)
hit pegar (8)
hobby pasatiempo (m) (1)
hole agujero (m)
home hogar (m) (5); **at ~** en casa (1); **~ address** domicilio (m) (4)
homework tarea (f) (2)
Honduran (m/f) hondureño/-a (1)
hopscotch rayuela (f)
hope esperar (2); esperanza (f); **to lose ~** desesperarse (11)
host anfitrión/-ona (m/f) (4)
hot (temperature) caliente; **(spicy)** picante; **to be ~** tener calor (3); **it's ~ out** hace calor (4)

house casa (f) (1); **boarding ~** pensión (f)
how cómo; **How are you?** ¿Cómo está(s)? (1); **How many?** ¿Cuántos/-as (2); **How much?** ¿Cuánto/-a? (2); **How old are you?** ¿Cuántos años tiene(s)? (1); **How's it going?** ¿Qué tal? (1)
hubcap tapacubos (m) (8)
hug abrazar (8); abrazo (10)
hungry: to be ~ tener hambre (3)
hurry apurarse; prisa (f); **be in a ~** tener prisa (3)
hurt (feel pain) doler (ue)
hurt oneself lastimarse (9)

I

I yo (1)
I'm sorry! ¡Perdón! Lo siento. (3)
ice cream helado (m) (5)
idea idea (f)
ill-mannered mal educado/-a (7)
illness enfermedad (f) (9)
imagine imaginarse (8); **~ that!** ¡fíjate! (1)
immediately inmediatamente
impolite descortés; malcriado/-a (9)
important importante (3)
impossible imposible (2)
impressive impresionante (1)
in: ~ addition to además de; **~ back of (behind)** detrás de (3); **~ case en caso de que** (11); **~ exchange** a cambio (11); **~ front of** delante de (3); **~ fun** en broma (11); **~ order** en regla (4); **~ in spite of** a pesar de que (11)
inch pulgada (f) (8)
increase aumentar; crecer (11)
inexpensive barato/-a (4); de precio bajo (6)
infatuated encaprichado/-a (11)
inform poner al corriente (9); **~ oneself (about)** enterarse (de) (11); informarse de
information información; **~ sign** letrero (m) (5)
injection inyección (f) (9)
injure herir (ie, i) (9)
injury herida (f) (9)
ink tinta (f) (5)
inside dentro de (3)
intelligent inteligente (1)
interested: be ~ (in) tener interés (en) (3); **interesting** interesante (1)
intersection bocacalle (f) (5); cruce (m) de camino
interview entrevista (f)
intestines intestinos (m pl) (9)
intolerable insoportable (12)
introduce presentar (1)

invitation invitación (f) (2)
invite invitar (2)
iron hierro (m) (6); **to ~ (clothing)** planchar
irritate molestar
issue asunto (m) (11); cuestión (f)
Italian italiano/-a (1)
Italy Italia (1)

J

jacket chaqueta (f)
January enero (1)
Japanese japonés/-esa (1)
jealous: be ~ estar celoso/-a (4)
jealousy celos (m pl) (4)
jewelry joyas (f pl); **~ store** joyería (f) (5)
job trabajo (m) (2); puesto (m)
joke broma (f) (11); chiste (m); **(play a trick)** hacer una broma (11); **joker** bromista (m/f) (11)
journalism periodismo (m)
journalist periodista (m/f) (5)
judge juez (m/f) (11)
juice jugo (f) (2)
July julio (1)
jump saltar; **~ rope** saltar la cuerda
June junio (1)
jungle selva (f)
jury jurado (m) (11)
justice justicia (f)

K

keep guardar (4)
key llave (f)
kidneys riñones (m pl) (9)
kill matar (2)
kilogram kilogramo (m)
kilometer kilómetro (m)
kind amable (1)
kiss besar (8); beso (m) (10)
kitchen cocina (f) (2); **~ cupboard** alacena (f) (7); **~ sink** fregadero (m) (7)
knee rodilla (f) (8)
knife cuchillo (m) (7)
know (a fact) saber (2); **(be familiar or acquainted with), meet** conocer

L

label etiqueta (f) (4)
laborer obrero/-a (m/f) (12)
lace encaje (m)
lady dama (f) (1)
lake lago (m)
lamp lámpara (f) (3)

land tierra (f); **by ~** por tierra (6); aterrizar (4)
landscape, scenery paisaje (m) (7)
language idioma (m) (10); **~ laboratory** laboratorio (m) de lenguas (2)
large grande (1)
late tarde (3); **~ afternoon, dusk** atardecer (3); **at the very latest** a más tardar
lately, recently últimamente (11)
Latin American latino/-a (1); latinoamericano/-a
laugh (at) reírse (de) (i, i) (3)
law ley (f) (11)
lawn césped (m)
lawsuit pleito (m) (11)
lawyer abogado/-a (m/f) (11)
layer cake pastel (m) (5)
lazy perezoso/-a (3)
learn aprender (2)
leave salir (1); irse (1); **to ~ something behind** dejar (8)
lecture conferencia (f) (2)
left izquierdo/-a; **to the ~** a la izquierda (6)
leg pierna (f)
lemon limón (m) (2)
lend prestar (7)
less (than) menos (de) (6); **at least** por lo menos (6)
let dejar (8), permitir
letter carta (f) (1); **~ carrier** cartero (m/f) (4); **to mail a ~** mandar (enviar) una carta (4); **~ (of the alphabet)** letra (f); **capital ~** letra mayúscula; **lower-case ~** letra minúscula
lettuce lechuga (f) (5)
lever palanca (f) (12)
library biblioteca (f) (1)
license licencia (f) (4)
lid tapa (f) (8); **to put the ~ on** tapar (8)
lie mentir (ie, i) (3); mentira (f) (3); **white ~** mentira piadosa (11)
lift weights levantar pesas
ligament ligamento (m) (9)
light: (light colored) claro/-a (1); **(weight)** ligero/-a; luz (f); **street ~** farol (m) (5); **traffic ~** semáforo (m) (5)
like gustar
likewise igualmente (1)
limp cojear (9)
lip labio (m) (11)
lipstick colorete (m) (11), pintalabios (m) (11)
listen escuchar (1)
little pequeño/-a (1); poco (6); **~ bit of everything** un poco de todo (6)

Glossary

live vivir (1)
liver hígado (m) (9)
living room sala (f) (7)
living together convivencia (f) (7)
lizard lagarto (m)
load cargar (12)
loan préstamo (m) (7)
lobster langosta (f) (5)
lodging: be lodged alojarse (6)
loin (of beef or pork) lomito (m) (5)
long largo/-a (6)
look: ~ at mirar (1); **~ for** buscar (7); **~ like** parecerse a (6)
lose perder (ie) (4); **~ consciousness** perder el conocimiento (9); **~ hope** desesperarse (11)
lot: a ~ mucho/-a
love amor (m) (4); amar (12); **be in ~** estar enamorado/-a; **fall in ~** enamorarse de
low bajo/-a (6); **lower** bajar (6); rebajar; reducir
loyal leal (12)
loyalty lealtad (f) (12)
luck suerte (f); **Good ~!** ¡Buena suerte! (4); **What terrible ~!** ¡Qué desgracia! (8)
luggage equipaje (m) (4)
lunch almuerzo (m) (2); **eat ~** almorzar (ue)
lungs pulmones (m pl) (9)
luxurious de lujo (6)

M

magazine revista (f) (5)
mail correo (4); **~ a letter** mandar (enviar) una carta (4); **~ carrier** cartero (m/f) (4)
mailbox buzón (m) (4)
major (field of study) especialización (f)
make hacer (2); **~ a decision** tomar la decisión (11); **~ a social blunder, "put your foot in it"** meter la pata (7); **~ arrangements** hacer los arreglos (6); **~ fun (of), joke (about)** burlarse (de) (11); **~ purchases** hacer compras (5)
makeup maquillaje (m); **apply ~** maquillarse (11)
malicious malicioso/-a (11)
malignant maligno/-a (9)
man hombre (m) (1); **gentleman** caballero (m) (1); **~, sir** señor (m) (1)
manage: (handle) manejar (4); **(survive)** defenderse (ie) (10)
manager gerente (m/f) (5)
map mapa (m) (1)
March marzo (1)
maritime marítimo/-a

marriage matrimonio (m) (12)
marry casarse (con)
mascara pestañina (f) (11); rimel (m) (11)
mass misa (f) (3)
maternal materno/-a
math matemáticas (f pl) (2)
matter (issue) asunto (m) (11)
mature madurar (12)
May mayo (1)
maybe quizás (3)
meal comida (f) (1)
means: ~ of transportation medio (m) de transporte (4); **by no ~** de ninguna manera (4)
measles sarampión (m) (9)
meat carne (f)
medicine medicina (f) (9)
medium (cooked) término (m) medio
meet conocer (a); **~ with** reunirse con (4)
meeting reunión (f) (4)
memory recuerdo (m) (8)
merchandise mercancías (f pl) (6); mercaderías (f pl) (12)
merciful piadoso/-a (11)
Merry Christmas Feliz Navidad (4), Felices Pascuas (4)
meter metro (m)
Mexican mexicano/-a (1)
milk leche (f) (2)
million millón (m) (1)
mineral water agua (f) mineral (2)
mirror espejo (m) (3)
mischievous travieso/-a (8)
miss: (form of address) señorita (f) (1); **~ (a meeting or appointment)** faltar; **(long for)** extrañar (10); echar de menos (12)
mix mezclar (6)
mixture mezcla (f) (6)
moisten mojar (9)
Monday lunes (m) (2)
money dinero (m) (4), plata (f) (4); **to exchange ~** cambiar dinero (6)
more más (6); **~ than** más (de) (6); **~ than anyone** más que nadie (10); **~ than anything** más que nada (10); **~ than ever** más que nunca (10)
morning mañana (f) (1); **Good ~.** Buenos días. (1)
Moslem (Moor) moro/-a (m/f)
mother madre (f) (1)
motor motor (m) (8)
mouse ratón (m)
mouth boca (f) (8)
move: (change residence) mudarse (5); **~ (furniture)** mover (ue) (3)
movie: película (f); **~ star** estrella (m/f) de cine (10); **~ theater** cine (m)

multinational company multinacional (f) (2)
muscle músculo (m) (9)
museum museo (m) (6)
mushroom hongo (m) (5); champiñón (m); seta (f)
music música (f)
must deber (3)
mustard mostaza (f) (5)

N

name nombre (m); **first ~** nombre de pila; **surname** apellido (m); **My name is . . .** Me llamo... (1)
nap siesta (f); **take a ~** dormir la siesta (5)
napkin servilleta (f) (7)
narrow angosto/-a
nationality nacionalidad (f) (1)
nauseated mareado/-a (9)
near cerca de (3)
neck cuello (m) (8)
necklace collar (m)
need hacer falta (10)
neighbor vecino/-a (m/f) (5)
neighborhood barrio (m) (8); vecindad (f) (5); vecindario (m) (5)
neither tampoco (4); **~ . . . nor** ni... ni (4)
nephew sobrino (m) (1)
nervous nervioso/-a (2)
net red (f) (8)
never nunca (3); jamás (4)
nevertheless sin embargo (8)
new nuevo/-a (4); **New Year's Eve** Noche (f) vieja (4); **Happy New Year!** ¡Prospero Año Nuevo!
newlywed recién casado/-a (12)
news noticias (f pl)
newspaper periódico (m) (5)
next siguiente (7); **~ to** al lado de (3); **~ week** la semana siguiente/próxima; **the ~ day** al día siguiente
nice simpático/-a (1); amable (10); agradable (3)
niece sobrina (f) (1)
night noche (f) (1); **become ~** anochecer (8); **Good night.** Buenas noches.
nine nueve (1)
nine hundred novecientos/-as (1)
ninety noventa (1)
ninth noveno/-a (7)
nobody nadie (4)
noise ruido (m) (3); **noisy** ruidoso/-a (3)
north norte (m) (1)
North American norteamericano/-a (1)
northeast noreste (m) (1)

northwest noroeste (m) (1)
nose nariz (f) (8)
not at all de ninguna manera (4)
notebook cuaderno (m)
notes: (school) ~ apuntes (m pl);
  take ~ sacar/tomar apuntes
nothing nada (4); ~ **like that** nada por
  el estilo (8)
notice fijarse en (10)
noun sustantivo
nourish nutrir (9)
November noviembre (1)
now ahora
noxious nocivo/-a (9)
number número (m)
nurse enfermero/-a (m/f) (5)
nutrition nutrición (f)

O

obligation compromiso (m) (10)
obstruct estorbar (12)
obtain obtener; ~ **information about**
  informarse (11)
occasionally de vez en cuando (6), a
  veces (4)
ocean mar (m)
October octubre (1)
Of course! ¡Claro! (2); ¡Cómo no! (6)
offend ofender (7)
office oficina (f); **branch** ~ sucursal
  (f) (5)
often a menudo (6), frecuentemente
oil aceite (m) (5); **motor** ~ aceite (8)
old viejo/-a; **older** mayor
on: ~ **behalf of** de parte de (10);
  ~ **display** en exposición (6);
  ~ **time** a tiempo (3); ~ **top of**
  encima de (3)
once una vez (4)
one uno/-a (1)
one hundred cien, ciento (1)
one thousand mil (1)
onion cebolla (f) (5)
only solamente (1); único/-a (5)
open abierto/-a (3); abrir (1)
operate operar (5)
operation intervención (f) quirúrgica
  (9), operación (f) (5)
opinion: in my ~ en mi opinión (1)
opposite contrario (m), opuesto (m) (1)
optimistic optimista (3)
orange: (fruit) naranja (f); **(color)**
  anaranjado/-a (1); ~ **juice** jugo (m)
  de naranja (2)
orderly ordenado/-a
orientation orientación (f)
outline bosquejo (m)
outside fuera de (3)

outstanding sobresaliente (11)
overcome superar (12)
overfill colmar (7)
overseas ultramar (m) (6)
own propio/-a (11)
owner dueño/-a (m/f) (5),
  propietario/-a (m/f) (4)

P

pack empacar (12)
pain dolor (m) (9)
pain killer calmante (m) (9)
Panamanian panameño/-a (1)
pant jadear (9)
pants pantalones (m pl) (4)
paper papel (m) (P)
paradise paraíso (m) (6)
Paraguayan paraguayo/-a (1)
pardon perdonar (7)
parents padres (m pl) (1)
parish parroquia (f)
part-time jornada (f) parcial (12)
party fiesta (f); ~ **pooper ("wet
  blanket")** aguafiestas
  (m/f/s/pl) (1)
pass (entrance permit) pase (m) (7)
pass: (go in) pasar (1); ~ **(a course)**
  aprobar (ue); ~ **out** desmayarse (9);
  ~ **through/by** pasar por (6)
passionate ardiente (12)
passport pasaporte (m) (4)
pastime diversión (f) (8)
pastry shop pastelería (f) (5)
paternal paterno/-a
patient: be ~ tener paciencia (3)
pay pagar; ~ **attention** poner (prestar)
  atención (8); ~ **by installment**
  pagar a plazos (6); ~ **cash** pagar en
  efectivo
payment pago (m) (6)
peas arvejas (f pl) (5); guisantes (m pl)
pen pluma (f), bolígrafo (m)
pencil lápiz (m)
penicillin penicilina (f) (9)
pepper: (condiment) pimienta (f) (5);
  (vegetable) pimiento (m)
performance actuación (f) (3)
perhaps quizás (3)
person persona (f) (1)
personality personalidad (f) (3)
personnel personal (m)
Peruvian peruano/-a (1)
pessimistic pesimista (3)
pharmacy botica (f), farmacia (f)
philosophy filosofía (f)
photocopy machine fotocopiadora
  (f) (8)
photograph foto (f)

physics física (f)
picture: framed picture cuadro (m) (3)
pious piadoso/-a (11)
pill pastilla (f) (9)
pink rosado/-a (1)
pity: What a ~! ¡Qué lástima! (8)
place lugar (m); **(put)** poner (2),
  colocar (3); **take** ~ llevarse a cabo (10)
plan plan (m); ~ **to do something**
  pensar (+ inf.) (2)
plant planta (5)
plate plato (m) (2)
play jugar (ue) (2); ~ **sports** practicar
  los deportes (1)
plead rogar (ue) (10)
please hacer el favor de (10); por
  favor; **pleased to meet you**
  encantado/-a, mucho
  gusto (1)
plumber plomero/-a (m/f) (12)
polite cortés (1)
political science ciencias (f pl)
  políticas (2)
poll encuesta (f) (1)
pork cerdo (m) (5); ~ **chop** chuleta (f)
  de cerdo (5)
post office correos (m); ~ **box** apartado
  (m) postal (1)
poster cartel (m) (3)
poultry ave (f) (5)
pound libra (f)
powder polvos (m pl) (11)
powerful potente (8)
practical joke broma (f) pesada (11)
prawn langostina (f) (5)
prefer preferir (ie, i) (3)
prepare preparar (2)
prescribe recetar (9)
prescription receta (f) (9)
present regalo (m) (4)
pretty bonito/-a (4), lindo/-a (8)
previous previo/-a (10)
price precio (m) (6)
pride orgullo (m) (8)
principle principio (m) (12)
printer impresora (f) (8)
probably probablemente
problem problema (m) (4)
professor profesor(a) (m/f) (1)
profile perfil (m)
program programa (m) (2)
proof prueba (f)
property terreno (m)
prosecute procesar
protect proteger
proud orgulloso/-a (8)
prove probar (ue)
provided that con tal (de) que (11)
psychology psicología (f) (2)

punish castigar
purchase comprar (4); **make purchases** hacer compras (5)
purple morado/-a (1)
purpose fin (m) (1); propósito (m)
purse bolsa (f) (4)
put poner (2), colocar (3)

Q

quality calidad (f) (5)
quarter cuarto/-a
question pregunta (f); **ask a ~** preguntar
quickly rápido (2)
quiet: (place) tranquilo/-a (3); **(person)** callado/-a (3); **become ~** callarse (3)

R

racquet raqueta (f) (8)
radiation radiación (f)
rain lluvia (f) (3); llover (ue) (3)
rare (meat) poco hecho/-a
read leer
ready listo/-a (10)
realize darse cuenta (de) (8)
reason motivo (m) (10)
rebel rebelde (m/f) (8)
receipt recibo (m)
receive recibir
recent reciente
receptionist recepcionista (m/f) (9)
recommend recomendar (ie) (7), sugerir (ie, i) (11)
recreation diversión (f) (8)
recuperate recuperarse (12)
red rojo/-a (1); **~ wine** vino tinto (2)
red-headed pelirrojo/-a (1)
reduce reducir
refrigerator refrigerador (m) (7)
refuse (an invitation) rechazar (10)
regain: ~ consciousness volver en sí (9)
regarding, concerning en cuanto a (10)
region región (f) (1)
register (for a course) matricularse (11)
regret sentir (ie, i) (3)
regulation regla (f) (11)
reject rechazar (10)
related to relacionado/-a con (9)
relative pariente (m/f) (1)
relax descansar (1)
relic artefacto (m) (6)
relief alivio (m) (9); That's a ~! ¡Menos mal! (1)
relieve aliviar (9)
religious: ~ service servicio (m) (3)
remain quedarse (4)

remedy remedio (m) (9)
remember recordar (ue) (10)
remove quitar (3)
removed alejado/-a de (10)
renew renovar (ue) (4)
rent alquilar (6); alquiler (m) (6)
repair reparar; **~ shop** taller (m)
repeat repetir (i, i) (3)
reputation fama (f) (11)
request pedir (i, i) (3); petición (f)
requirement requisito (m) (4)
reserved reservado/-a (3)
residence hall residencia (f) (1)
resort balneario (m) (6)
respectfully respetuosamente (10)
rest descansar (1); **~ rooms** aseos (m pl), servicios (m pl)
rested descansado/-a (6)
result resultado (m)
retire jubilarse (5)
retired jubilado/-a (5)
return: (go back) regresar (3), volver (ue) (2); **~ (an item)** devolver
reunion reunión (f) (4)
rich rico/-a (4)
ride a horse montar a caballo (7)
right: (legal) derecho (m) (11); **be ~** tener razón (3); **to the ~** a la derecha
river río (m)
roasted asado/-a (5)
roll panecillo (m) (5)
roof techo (m) (7); **tiled ~** azotea (f)
room pieza (f) (6); **bedroom** cuarto (m) (1); **dining ~** comedor (m) (2); **living ~** sala (f) (7); **~ (with a bed), as in a hotel** habitación (f) (6)
roommate compañero/-a (m/f) de cuarto (1)
rope soga (f) (8)
rouge rubor (m) (11)
rude mal educado/-a (7)
rug alfombra (f) (7)
ruin arruinar (11)
run correr (2); **running water** agua (f) corriente (9)
rural campestre (7)

S

sad triste (11); **sadness** tristeza (f) (11)
saffron azafrán (m) (5)
salad ensalada (f) (5); **~ dressing** aliño (m) (5)
salary sueldo (m) (12)
sale rebaja (f) (4); liquidación (f) (4)
salt sal (f) (5)
Salvadoran salvadoreño/-a (1)
sample muestra; **blood ~** una muestra de sangre (9)

Saturday sábado (m) (2)
saucer platillo (m) (7); platito (m) (7)
save salvar (11)
say decir (2); **~ good-bye** despedirse (i, i) (3)
scarcely apenas (9)
schedule horario (m) (2)
school escuela (f); **elementary ~** escuela primaria; **high ~** escuela secundaria; liceo (m)
sea mar (m); **at ~ level** al nivel del mar (6)
seafood marisco (m)
seamstress modista (f) (5)
seaport puerto (m) (6)
season estación (f) (4)
seat asiento (m) (4)
second segundo/-a (2)
see ver (1)
seem parecer (6); **~ to be** aparentar (ie) (11)
seldom casi nunca (6)
selection surtido (m) (5)
sell vender
semester semestre (m) (2)
send (mail) a letter mandar (enviar) una carta (4)
sense: ~ of smell olfato (m) (6); **~ of touch** tacto (m) (6)
September septiembre (1)
serious serio/-a (3); **seriously** en serio (11)
serve servir (i, i) (3)
session sesión (f)
set a price through bargaining regatear (7)
seven siete (1)
seven hundred setecientos/-as (1)
seventy setenta (1)
shake hands darse la mano (1)
share compartir (6); **(stock)** acción (f) (12)
shave afeitarse (3)
she ella (1)
sheet of paper hoja (f) de papel (5)
shellfish mariscos (m pl) (5)
sheriff alguacil (m) (11)
shine relucir (11)
shirt camisa (f) (4)
shoe zapato (m); **~ store** zapatería (f) (5)
shop ir de compras (5); **(store)** tienda (f) (5); **~ keeper** comerciante (m/f) (12)
short bajo/-a (3); **~ (in length)** corto/-a (6); **~ period of time** rato (m) (10)
shoulder hombro (m) (8)
show enseñar, mostrar (ue); **late ~ (movies)** nocturna (f); **early ~** vespertina (f)
shower ducha (f) (6); **take a ~** ducharse (3)

Glossary

shrimp camarones (m pl) (5)
shy tímido/-a (3)
siblings hermanos (m pl) (1)
sick enfermo/-a (5)
sidewalk acera (f) (5)
sight vista (f) (6)
sign firmar (6); **(informational)** ~ letrero (m) (5); **(traffic)** ~ señal (f) (5)
signature firma (f)
signify denotar (10)
silence silencio (m) (3)
silk seda (f)
since puesto que (10)
sink: (bathroom) lavamanos (m) (6); **(kitchen)** fregadero (m) (7)
sir señor (m) (1)
sister hermana (f) (1); **sister-in-law** cuñada
sit down sentarse (ie) (3)
situated situado/-a (6)
six seis (1)
six hundred seiscientos/-as (1)
sixth sexto/-a (7)
sixty sesenta (1)
size tamaño (m)
skate patinar
ski esquiar (4); esquí (m); **cross-country skiing** esquí (m) nórdico; **downhill skiing** esquí (m) alpino; **water skiing** esquí (m) acuático
skin piel (f) (9)
skirt falda (f) (4)
sleep dormir (ue, u) (3); **be sleepy** tener sueño (3); **sleepyhead** dormilón/-ona! (3)
slender delgado/-a (3)
slip deslizarse (9)
slippers pantuflas (f pl)
slowly despacio (2)
small pequeño/-a (1); **get smaller** empequeñecer (12)
small suitcase maletín (m) (4); ~ **table; night table** mesita (f) (3)
smell olor (m) (6); **sense of** ~ olfato (m) (6)
smile sonreír (i, i) (3)
smoke fumar; humo (m) (6); **no smoking** no fumar (6); **smoking section** sección (f) de fumar (6)
snack bocadillo (m) (5)
sneeze estornudar (9); estornudo (m)
snow nevar (ie) (3); nieve (f) (3)
so that para que (11)
so-and-so, John/Jane Doe fulano/-a (m/f) (11)
soak empapar; **get soaked** empaparse (9)
soap jabón (m) (6); ~ **opera** telenovela (f)

soccer fútbol (m) (2)
social club club (m) social (7)
sociology sociología (f)
sofa sofá (m) (7)
soft drink refresco (m) (2)
sole (fish) lenguado (m) (5)
solve resolver (ue) (4)
some unos/-as; ~ **other time** en otra ocasión (3); **someone** alguien (1); **something** algo (4); **something like that** algo por el estilo (8); **sometimes** a veces (4)
sorry: be ~ sentir (ie, i) (3)
south sur (m) (1)
southeast sureste (m) (1)
southwest suroeste (m) (1)
souvenir recuerdo (m) (8)
space espacio (m) (7)
Spain España (1)
Spaniard español(a) (1)
Spanish castellano (m) (10); español (m); **Spanish-speaking** de habla española (10); **Spanish-speaking person** hispanohablante (m/f) (10)
speak hablar
spend: (time) pasar (3); ~ **money** gastar (11)
spicy picante (5)
spin (thread) hilar
spinach espinacas (f pl) (8)
spiral espiral
spit escupir
spoon cuchara (f) (7); **teaspoon** cucharita (f) (7)
sport deporte (m) (2); **sports jacket** saco (m) (4)
spring primavera (f) (4)
stain manchar; mancha (f); **stained** manchado/-a
stairway escalera (f) (7)
stamp estampilla (f) (4); sello (m) (4)
stand out destacarse (11)
star estrella (f) (10)
start comenzar (ie) (2)
state estado (m) (1)
stationery store papelería (f) (5)
stay quedarse (4); ~ **temporarily (have lodging)** alojarse (6)
steak bistec (m) (5)
steering wheel volante (m) (8)
step paso (m); ~ **by** ~ paso por paso; ~ **on** pisar (9)
stepbrother/stepsister hermanastro/-a (m/f) (1)
stepfather padrastro (m) (1); **stepmother** madrastra (f) (1)
stereo estéreo (m) (3)
sterilize esterilizar (9)
stingy tacaño/-a (3)

stitch: (sew) coser; ~ **a wound** dar puntos (9)
stock acciones (f pl) (12); **Stock Exchange** Bolsa (f) (12)
stomach estómago (m) (8)
stop parar (11); parada (f)
store guardar (4); tienda (f)
stove estufa (f) (7)
straight ahead derecho
stranger desconocido/-a (m/f)
straw: This is the last ~! ¡Esto es el colmo! (9)
strawberry fresa (f) (8)
street calle (f) (1); ~ **light** farol (m) (5)
stretcher camilla (f) (9)
string cuerda (f), cordón (m); ~ **beans** habichuelas (f pl) (8)
strong fuerte (3)
structure estructura (f) (7)
student estudiante (m/f) (1); ~ **I.D.** credencial (f) escolar (4); ~ **life** vida (f) estudiantil (1)
study estudiar (1)
subway metro (m)
succeed lograr (8); tener éxito (11)
suddenly de repente
suffer padecer (12)
sugar azúcar (m) (2); ~ **bowl** azucarero (m) (7)
suggest sugerir (ie, i) (11)
suit traje (m) (4); bathing ~ **traje de baño** (4)
suitable apropiado/-a (4)
suitcase maleta (f) (4); **small** ~ maletín (m) (4)
summary resumen (m)
summer verano (m) (4)
summit colmo (m) (7)
sun sol (m)
Sunday domingo (m) (2)
support mantener (11); apoyar; apoyo (m) (12)
surgeon cirujano/-a (m/f) (5)
surgery cirugía (f)
surname apellido (m)
surprise sorprender (11); sorpresa (f)
surroundings alrededores (m pl) (7)
survive sobrevivir (11)
suspended suspendido, reprobado (11)
swallow tragar
sweat sudar (3)
sweet dulce (m); ~ **bread** pan (m) dulce (5)
sweetheart, fiancé(e) novio/-a (m/f) (11)
swim nadar (2)
swimming pool piscina (f) (6); alberca (f) (9)
swollen hinchado/-a (9)

T

symposium congreso (m)
symptom síntoma (m) (9)
synagogue sinagoga (f) (3)

table mesa (f) (7); **small ~** mesita (f) (3)
tablecloth mantel (m) (7)
tablespoon cuchara (f) (7)
tailor sastre (m) (5)
take tomar (2); **~ a blood sample** tomar una muestra de sangre (9); **~ a nap** dormir la siesta (5); **~ a trip** hacer un viaje (4); **~ a walk** dar un paseo (7); **~ advantage of** aprovechar (8); **~ away** quitar (3); **~ charge of** encargarse de; **~ into account** tener en cuenta (10); **~ off (airplane)** despegar (4); **~ off (clothing)** desvestirse (i, i), quitarse la ropa; **~ place** llevar a cabo (10)
tall alto/-a (3)
tape recorder grabadora (f) (8)
taste probar (ue) (5)
tax impuesto (m) (4)
tea té (f) (2)
teach enseñar (2)
teacher maestro/-a (m/f); profesor(a) (m/f) (8)
team equipo (m)
tease, "pull someone's leg" tomar(le) el pelo (9)
teaspoon cucharita (f) (7)
technology tecnología (f) (8)
telephone teléfono (m); **cellular ~** teléfono celular; **~ book** guía (f) telefónica (7)
television televisión (f) (1); **~ set** televisor (m) (1)
tell decir (2); **~ the truth** decir la verdad (3)
temporary pasajero/-a (12)
ten diez (1)
tendon tendón (m) (9)
tennis tenis (m) (2)
tenth décimo/a (7)
terrific fenomenal (3)
thank you gracias (1); **thank-you letter** carta (f) de agradecimiento (10)
theater teatro (m); **movie ~** cine (m)
theme tema (m) (11)
then entonces (7)
therapy terapia (f) (11)
there is (are) hay (7)
they ellos/-as (1)
thick grueso/-a (8)
thigh muslo (m) (8)
thin delgado/-a (3); fino/-a
think pensar (ie) (1)

third tercero/-a (2)
thirsty: be ~ tener sed (3)
thirteen trece (1)
thirty treinta (1)
three tres (1)
three hundred trescientos/-as (1)
throw tirar; **~ out** echar (11)
Thursday jueves (m) (2)
ticket boleto (m) (4); **round-trip ~** boleto de ida y vuelta (4)
tie corbata (f) (4)
tiled roof azotea (f)
time: (occasion) vez (f); tiempo (m); **from ~ to ~** de vez en cuando (6); **on ~** a tiempo (3)
tire llanta (f) (8)
tired cansado/-a (6); **get ~ (of)** cansarse (de) (10)
today hoy (2)
together junto/-a (8)
toilet inodoro (m) (6); **~ paper** papel (m) higiénico
tomorrow mañana (2); **day after ~** pasado mañana
touch tocar; **sense of ~** tacto (m)
tour excursión (f) (6)
towel toalla (f) (6)
tower torre (f) (6)
traffic: ~ light semáforo (m) (5); **~ sign** señal (f) (5)
tranquilizer calmante (m) (9)
transaction trámite (m)
translate traducir
travel viajar (4); **~ agency** agencia (f) de viajes (4)
traveler viajero/-a (m/f) (4); **traveler's checks** cheques (m pl) de viajero (6)
treat tratar (8)
tree árbol (m); **Christmas ~** árbol de Navidad (4)
trick engañar (11); hacer trampa (11)
trip viaje (m) (4); **take a ~** hacer un viaje; **~ (over something)** tropezar (9)
trout trucha (f) (5)
truck camión (m); **~ driver** camionero/-a (m/f) (12)
trunk (of a car) maletero (m) (8)
truth verdad (f) (3); **tell the ~** decir la verdad (3)
try on probarse (ue) (4)
Tuesday martes (m) (2)
tumor: brain ~ tumor (m) cerebral (9)
turkey pavo (m) (5)
turn doblar (6); **~ off (lights)** apagar (8); **~ on (lights)** prender (8); **~ out badly** salir mal (11); **~ out to be** resultar (11); **~ out well** salir bien (11)

twelve doce (1)
twenty veinte (1)
twin gemelo/-a (m/f) (8)
twist torcer (ue) (9)
two dos (1)
two hundred doscientos/-as (1)
typewriter maquina (f) de escribir (8)

U

UFO OVNI (objeto volador no identificado)
ugly feo/-a (3)
uncertainty incertidumbre (f) (11)
uncle tío (m) (1)
uncomfortable incómodo/-a (10)
under debajo de (3)
uneasiness zozobra (f) (8)
unexpected inesperado/-a
unfortunately desafortunadamente (4)
unfriendly antipático/-a (3)
United States Estados Unidos (1); **person from the ~** estadounidense (1)
university universidad (f) (1)
unless a menos que (11)
unload descargar (12)
unpleasant desagreable
until hasta (2)
upside down patas arriba
up-to-date al tanto de (10)
Uruguayan uruguayo/-a (1)
useful útil
usefulness utilidad (f)
useless inútil (11)

V

vaccination certificate certificado (m) de vacuna (4)
value valor (m) (7)
variety: There's a lot of ~. Hay de todo. (6)
vegetable legumbre (f) (5)
venetian blinds persianas (f pl) (7)
Venezuelan venezolano/-a (1)
verify averiguar (11)
vibration vibración (f)
vinegar vinagre (m) (5)
visa visado (m), visa (f) (4)
vomit vomitar (9)

W

wage salario (m) (12)
waist cintura (f) (8)
wait (for) esperar (3)
waiter mesero/-a (m/f) (5); camarero/-a (m/f)
waiting room sala (f) de espera (9)
wake up despertarse (ie) (3)

walk andar (7); caminar (7); paseo (m) (7); **take a ~** dar un paseo (7)
wall: exterior ~ muralla (f) (7); **interior ~** pared (f) (3)
wallet cartera (f)
want querer (2); desear (2); **~ to, feel like (doing something)** tener ganas de (2)
war guerra (f) (6)
wardrobe armario (m) (3); ropero (m)
wash lavar; lavarse (3)
waste malgastar (11)
watch mirar; **~ television** mirar la televisión (1); **~ shop** relojería (f) (5); **wrist ~** reloj (m)
water agua (f) (2); acuatico/-a; **distilled ~** agua (f) destilada (9); **running ~** agua (f) corriente (9); **~ glass (tumbler)** vaso (m) (7); **~ skiing** esquí acuático (7)
watermelon sandía (f) (8)
wave ola (f)
we nosotros/-as (1)
weak débil (3)
wealth riqueza (f) (4); **wealthy** rico/-a (4)
weapon arma (f)
wear llevar; ponerse (10); **(for the first time)** estrenar (10)
weather tiempo (m) (3); **~ forecast** pronóstico (m) del tiempo (3)
wedding boda (f); **~ engagement** compromiso (m) de matrimonio
Wednesday miércoles (m) (2)
week semana (f) (2)
weekend fin (m) de semana (2)
weigh pesar (9); peso (m) (9); **lift weights** levantar pesas
well . . . pues (7)

well-behaved bien educado/-a (8)
well-done (meat) muy hecho/-a; bien cocido/-a
well-known conocido/-a (7)
west oeste (m) (1)
what? ¿qué? (2)
whatever it might be sea lo (el, la) que sea (10)
wheel rueda (f); **steering ~** volante (8)
wheelchair silla (f) de ruedas (9)
when? ¿cuándo? (2)
where? ¿dónde? (2)
which (one)? ¿cuál? (2)
while mientras (8)
white blanco/-a (1); **~ lie** mentira (f) piadosa (11)
who? ¿quién? (1)
why? ¿por qué? (2)
wig peluca (f)
win ganar
wind viento (m)
window ventana (f) (1); **(of vehicle)** ventanilla (f) (8)
windshield parabrisas (m) (8); **~ wiper** limpiaparabrisas (m) (8)
wine vino (m) (2); **~ glass** copa (f) (7); **red ~** vino tinto (2)
winter invierno (m) (4); invernal (7)
without sin; sin que (11)
woman mujer (f) (1); señora (f) (1)
wonderful magnífico/-a (4)
wood madera (f) (6)
word palabra (f); **key ~** palabra (f) clave
work trabajo (m) (2); trabajar (1); **(machine)** funcionar (3); **Let's get to ~** ¡Manos a la obra! (2)
workbook cuaderno (m) (P)

worn out agotado/-a (6)
worry preocupación (f) (11)
worse peor
worth: be ~ valer (1)
wound herida (f) (9); herir (ie, i) (9)
wrap envolver (ue); **wrapped up** envuelto/-a
wrestling lucha (f) libre
write escribir (P)
wrong equivocado/-a (3); **be ~** estar equivocado/-a

X

x-ray radiografía (f) (9)

Y

yard patio (m) (5); **back ~** traspatio (m); **front ~** patio (m) delantero
year año (m) (1)
yearbook anuario (m)
yellow amarillo/-a (1)
yesterday ayer (2); **day before ~** anteayer
yogurt yogur (m) (5)
you (familiar pl) vosotros/-as (1); **(familiar sing)** tú (1); **(formal sing)** usted (1); **(pl)** ustedes (1)
you're welcome de nada
young joven; **~ person** joven (m/f) (1)
younger menor

INDEX

a
   as preposition, 460
   personal, 180
   with time expressions, 66
abrir, as irregular verb, past participle, 201
acordar de, 461
Activities.   *See* Sports and activities
Address
   of apartment, 309
   of domicile, 32
   numbers with, 309
   of office, 309
   titles of, 15, 17, 494–495
Adjectives
   changing to adverbs, 154
   comparing
      mayor, 139, 542
      menor, 139, 542
      más/menos... que, 139
      tan... como, 139
      tanto... como, 140
   forming generalizations, 340–341
   gender agreement with nouns, 35–36
   past participle as, 201
   possessive, 35–36, 381
Adverbs
   changed from adjectives, 154
   comparing, 139
Advertisements, 28–30
aprender a, 460
Articles, and gender, 8–9
-ar verbs
   present participle, 260
   preterite tense, 157
   regular, 49–50
   stem-changing, present tense, 93–94
ayudar a, 460

Bathrooms, 272
Bilingualism, 76–77
Body (*see also* Physical states)
   face, 500
   parts of, 350
buscar, preterite spelling change of, 157

Calendar, Hispanic, 64
Car, parts of, 362
casarse con, 460
Chicanos, 172–173, 440
Children
   games of, 358–359

   raising, 368
-ción ending, 2
Classroom, 7
Clothing, 178–179 (*see also* Fashion)
Cognates, 2
Colloquialisms, 165
Colombia, geography of, 320
Colors, 32
comenzar, preterite spelling change of, 157
comenzar a, 460
Commands
   familiar, 351–352
      negative, 352
   formal, 337–338
Comparisons, 542, 139–140 (*see also*
   Adjectives; Adverbs; Nouns)
Comportment, 302–303, 508–509
con, as preposition, 460–461
Conditional statements.   *See* Hypothetical
   statements
Conditional tense, 447
   and *si* clause, 474–475
conducir, as irregular verb, present
   tense, 81
confiar en, 461
Connecting words, 88
conocer
   as irregular verb, present tense, 81
   meaning in preterite, 203
   versus *saber,* 244
consentir en, 461
construir, preterite spelling change of, 157
contar
   con, 461
   de, 461
   as stem-changing verb, 382
Context, reading and, 73
Cosmetics, 500
Countries, 55
   and cities, 53
   names of, 45
Court, 486
cubrir, as irregular verb, past
   participle, 201
curanderos, 386–387 (*see also* Medicine)
Customs office, 176

dar, as irregular verb
   present subjunctive, 298
   present tense, 81
   preterite tense, 184
Dates, numbers and, 46–48

Days
   Día del Santo, 457
   of the week, 64
de, as preposition, 461
decir, as irregular verb
   affirmative familiar command, 351
   conditional tense, 447
   future tense, 443
   past participle, 201
   present tense, 81
   preterite tense, 184
dejar de, 461
describir, as irregular verb, past
   participle, 201
descubrir, as irregular verb, past
   participle, 201
desear, + infinitive, 91
Diminutives, 315
Dining
   place settings, 319
   in Spain/Latin America, 212 (*see also*
      Food)
Directions
   geographical, 55
   giving, 259
Direct object, 216–217 (*see also* Pronouns)
divertirse, as stem-changing verb, present
   participle, 260
doler, use of, 408–409
dormir, as stem-changing verb, 113, 383
   present participle, 260
dormirse, 501
Drinks, 90

Education
   bilingual, 76–77
   grades, 471
   systems of, 220
   U.S. versus Latin America, 62–63
empezar a, 460
en, as preposition, 461
enchufes, 526–527
entender, as stem-changing verb, 382
entrar en, 461
-ero/-a ending, 214
-er verbs
   present participle, 260
   preterite tense, 168–169
   regular, 68
   stem-changing, present tense, 93–94
-ería ending, 214

escribir, as irregular verb, past participle, 201
esperar, + infinitive, 91
estar
  as irregular verb
    present subjunctive, 298
    present tense, 22
    preterite tense, 184
  with present and past participles, 519–520
  and present progressive, 259–260
  versus *ser*, 22–23, 36
  with weather, 110
Expressions
  of accident, 487
  affirmative, 179–180
  of anticipation, 504–505
  of chance, 487
  common classroom, 7–8, 12
  of courtesy, 8, 293, 320–321, 337–338, 406, 463–464
  of emotion, 349–350, 354–355
  of frequency, 274
  for generalizations, 340–341, 363
  of impersonal statements. *See* Expressions for generalizations
  of money, 161
  negative, 179–180
  of opinion, 532
  with *por*, 264
  of possibility, 532
  for shopping, 295
  for sneezing, 406
  su casa, 293
  with *tener*, 123
  of time, 65–66

Family relationships, 18, 55, 344, 479
Farewells, 55
Fashion, in Latin America, 188 (*see also* Clothing)
Festivals, 266
fiestas, 452
Food (*see also* Dining)
  condiments, 225
  hispanic, 223–224
Foreign language study, 89
fotonovelas, 133–134
Furniture, 135
Future tense, 442–443
  expressed with infinitive, 91
  forming, 443
  and *si* clause, 474

García Márquez, Gabriel, 347
Gender
  of adjectives, 35–36
  of nouns, 8–9
Gerund. *See* Present participle
Greetings, 14, 19, 39–40, 55
Groups
  going out in, 531

  versus individual, 472
  solidarity of, 479
gustar
  indirect object pronoun and, 226
  use of, 79, 226

haber
  forming past participle, 201
  as irregular verb
    conditional tense, 447
    future tense, 443
    present subjunctive, 299
hacer
  as irregular verb
    conditional tense, 447
    future tense, 443
    past participle, 201
    present tense, 81
    preterite tense, 184
  meaning "ago," 204
  with weather, 110
hacerse, 501
hispanohablantes estadounidenses, 440
History, preserving, 258–259
Home, U.S. versus Hispanic, 142
Hour. *See* Time
House, inside, 308
Hypothetical statements, 474–475

Imperfect tense, 246–247
  to express frequency, 274
  versus preterite, 276
Impersonal statements, 363 (*see also* Subjunctive; Expressions)
Indirect object, 228–229 (*see also* Pronouns)
Infinitives
  and direct object pronouns, 217
  as nouns, 472–473
insistir en, 461
Introductions, 39–40
invitar a, 460
ir(se), 501
  as irregular verb, affirmative familiar command, 351
ir
  + *a* + infinitive, 91, 110
  as irregular verb
    imperfect tense, 246
    present subjunctive, 299
    present tense, 23–24
    preterite tense, 184
Irregular verbs
  in imperfect, 246
  irregular *yo* forms, 80–81
  past participles of, 201
  present subjunctive, 298–299
  in preterite, 184–185
-ir verbs
  present participle, 260
  preterite tense, 168–169

  regular, 68
  stem-changing, 113–114

Latin America, map of, 47
leer, preterite spelling change of, 157
llegar, preterite spelling change of, 157
Location, indicating origin, 53
Lodgings, in Spain/Latin America, 208

Mail, 166
Map
  Colombia, 283
  Latin America, 47
  world, 153
mayor, 139, 542
Medicine
  emergency room, 407
  farmacia, 391
  medical care, 401–402
menor, 139, 542
mentir, as stem-changing verb, 383
Metric system, 122, 415
Mexico, states of, 44
Money, 160
  foreign exchange, 243
  paying the check, 242, 426
  regateo, 326
Months
  of the year, 48, 55
morir, as irregular verb, past participle, 201
más/menos... que, 139
más de, 458
más que, 458

Names
  diminutives, 315
  first, 199
  last, 83–84
Nationalities, 55
Negative constructions, 179–180
Neighborhoods, 200
Nouns
  adjective agreement with, 35–36
  -ción ending, 2
  comparison of, 139–140
  gender of, 8–9
  infinitives as, 472–473
  omission of, 394
Numbers
  and *más que/más de*, 458
  one hundred through one million, 46–48
  one through one hundred, 33
  ordinal, 309

Objects. *See* Direct object; Indirect object
ojalá, 427
olvidar de, 461
oír, as irregular verb, present tense, 81

palancas, 526–527
pan, 231–232
para
    versus *por,* 166, 262–264
Past participle, 200–202
    with *estar,* 520
    irregular, 201
pedir, as stem-changing verb, 383
pensar, + infinitive, 91
pensar en, 461
Personal relationships, 531 (*see also* Family relationships, 536)
Physical states, 392–393
poder
    as irregular verb
        conditional tense, 447
        future tense, 443
        preterite tense, 184
    meaning in preterite, 203
poner, as irregular verb
    conditional tense, 447
    future tense, 443
    past participle, 201
    present tense, 81
    preterite tense, 184
ponerse, 501
por, versus *para,* 166, 262–264
Possession, adjectives of, 35–36, 381
preferir, as stem-changing verb, 113
Prepositions, 460–461
    a, 460
    con, 460–461
    de, 461
    en, 461
    with infinitives as nouns, 473
Present participle
    and direct object pronouns, 217
    with *estar,* 519–520
    forming, 259–260
Present perfect tense. *See* Verbs
Present progressive. *See* Verbs
Preterite tense, 156–157
    -ar verbs, 157
    -er/-ir verbs, 168–169
    versus imperfect, 276
    irregular verbs in, 184–185
    use of, 156–157, 203–204
probarse, 501
Professions, 518–519
Pronouns
    direct, 216–217
    direct object
        and gerunds, 217
        with indirect object, 311–312
        and infinitives, 217
        with informal commands, 337–338
    indirect object, 228–229
        with direct object, 311–312
        gustar and, 226
        with informal commands, 337–338
    reflexive, 126–127
        with informal commands, 337–338

Proverbs. *See refranes*
Public transportation, 251–252

querer
    as irregular verb, preterite tense, 184
    meaning in preterite, 204
quinceañera, 337
quitarse, 501

radionovelas, 133–134
Reflexive verbs, 126–127, 501
    in perfect tense, 202
refranes, 541
Religion, legends of, 281–282
romper, as irregular verb, past participle, 201

saber, versus *conocer,* 244
    as irregular verb
        conditional tense, 447
        future tense, 443
        present subjunctive, 299
        present tense, 81
        preterite tense, 184
    meaning in preterite, 204
salir, as irregular verb
    affirmative familiar command, 351
    conditional tense, 447
    future tense, 443
    present tense, 81
saludos. *See* Greetings
Schedules, 105, 121
Seasons, of the year, 152
seguir, as stem-changing verb, present participle, 260
seguro de, 461
ser
    versus *estar,* 22–23, 36
    expressing generalizations with, 340–341
    as irregular verb
        imperfect tense, 246
        present subjunctive, 299
        present tense, 22–23
        preterite tense, 184
servir, as stem-changing verb, 113
Shopping, 294–295
    products and stores, 213, 214
    regateo, 326
si clauses, 474–475, 522
Soccer, 362
soñar con, 460
Spanish
    origins of, 10–11
    varieties of, 6–7
Sports and activities, 77–78, 130
    of children, 358–359

Stem-changing verbs
    e to *i, i,* 113–114
    e to *ie,* 93–94
    e to *ei, i,* 113–114
    o to *ue,* 93–94
    o to *ue, u,* 113–114
    present participle, 260
    present subjunctive, 299, 382–383
    present tense, 93–94, 113–114, 382–383
    preterite tense, 185
Subjunctive
    with conjuctions, 490–491
    with expressions of anticipation, 504–505, 522
    with expressions of denial, 365, 431, 523
    with expressions of desire, 323, 431
    with expressions of disbelief, 365, 522
    with expressions of doubt, 365, 431, 523
    with expressions of emotion, 354–355, 431, 522
    with expressions for generalizations, 341, 431, 522
    with expressions of influence, 323, 431, 522
    with expressions of uncertainty, 365
    forming commands, 337–338, 351–352
    imperfect, 397, 430–431, and *si* clause, 474–475
    with *ojalá,* 427
    outside personal experience, 297–298, 411, 430
    present tense, forming, 298–299
    review of use, 522–523
Superlatives, 542

tan... como, 139
tanto... como, 140
tardar en, 461
Technology, 335–336
telenovelas, 133–134
Telephone, 108–109, answering, 107, 117
tener
    expressions with, 123
    as irregular verb
        affirmative familiar command, 351
        conditional tense, 447
        future tense, 443
        present tense, 23
        preterite tense, 184
tiempo. *See* Weather
Time (*see also* Schedules)
    ¿A qué hora... ?, 66
    half hour, 66
    punctuality, 435
    quarter hour, 66
    range of hours
        afternoon, 27
        evening, 27
    telling, 61, 65–66
    twenty-four hour clock, 72
Titles. *See* Address, titles of

traer, as irregular verb
   present tense, 81
   preterite tense, 184
tú, versus usted, 16, 19, 97

usted, versus *tú*, 16, 19, 97
ustedes, versus *vosotros*, 97

venir, as irregular verb
   conditional tense, 447
   future tense, 443
   present tense, 81
   preterite tense, 184

ver, as irregular verb
   imperfect tense, 246
   past participle, 201
Verbs (*see also* Irregular verbs; Reflexive verbs; Stem-changing verbs; specific verbs)
   imperfect, 246–247 (*see also* Imperfect tense)
   irregular, 21–24, 80–81
   present perfect, 200–202
   present progressive, 259–260
   preterite, 156–157 (*see also* Preterite tense)
   regular *-ar*, 49–50
   regular *-er/-ir*, 68

volver, as irregular verb, past participle, 201
volverse, 501
vosotros, versus *ustedes*, 97

Water, potability of, 273, 379
Weather, 110
Women, and work, 487
World citizens, 547–548

You
   formal versus informal, 16, 19, 97
   use of *tú, usted, ustedes, vosotros*, 97

PHOTOGRAPHS

Page 1: Peter Menzel; **page 13:** Stuart Cohen/Comstock; **page 39:** Kathy Squires; **page 59:** Robert Frerck/Odyssey; **page 83:** Reuters/Bettmann; **page 99:** Peter Menzel; **page 103:** Stuart Cohen; **page 125:** Ann & Myron Sutton/FPG; **page 147:** Stuart Cohen; **page 181:** Stuart Cohen/Comstock; **page 188:** Reuters/Bettmann; **page 195:** Stuart Cohen; **page 209:** Beryl Goldberg; **page 228:** Peter Menzel; **page 237:** Stuart Cohen; **page 241:** Stuart Cohen/Comstock; **page 251:** Stuart Cohen; **page 255:** Robert Frerck/Odyssey (top, middle), Kanus/Superstock (bottom); **page 258:** Robert Frerck/Odyssey; **page 267:** Rob Crandall/Image Works; **page 273:** Robert Frerck/Odyssey; **page 281:** UPI/Bettmann; **page 289:** Stuart Cohen/Comstock; **page 331:** Dave Bartruff/FPG; **page 347:** AP/Wide World; **page 375:** Bonnie Kamin/Comstock; **page 378:** Stuart Cohen; **page 404:** L. Rorke/Image Works; **page 421:** Robert Frerck/Odyssey; **page 467:** Peter Menzel; **page 480:** David Kupferschmid; **page 513:** Stuart Cohen/Comstock.

LITERATURE AND REALIA

Page 11: Advertisement reprinted courtesy of Restaurante Duroc, Bogotá, Colombia; **page 72:** Excerpt from *TV Tele-Guida*, No. 1868, 28 mayo–3 junio 1988, p. 4, Mexico; **page 92:** Advertisement reprinted courtesy of Cafe Bustelo; **page 112:** Excerpt from movie listing reprinted from *El Pais*, 30 de junio de 1988, p. 45, Spain; **page 172:** Application reprinted courtesy of Consulate of Republica de Chile; **page 177:** "La Broca" reprinted courtesy of Federación Nacional de Cafeterios de Colombia; **pages 229 and 408:** Comic strips reprinted from *Hoy es tu día, Carlitos* by Charles Schultz, Editorial Nueva Imagen; **pages 306–307:** "San Antonio: La ciudad del Río" reprinted from *Jet Set*, Ano XV, Numero 7, pp. 12–13; **page 347:** "Los suyos" by Gabriel García Márquez reprinted from *Conversaciones con Plinio Apuleyo Mendoza: El Olor de la Guayaba*, Editorial La Oveja Negra, 1982, Colombia; **page 449:** Horoscope "En el cielo: El amor," by Daisy Trinidad, reprinted from *Más*: Envierno 1990, Vol. II, No. 2, Univision Publications. Illustrations by Andrea Arroya.